THE STOIC TRADITION
FROM ANTIQUITY
TO THE EARLY MIDDLE AGES-II

STUDIES IN THE HISTORY

OF

CHRISTIAN THOUGHT

EDITED BY

HEIKO A. OBERMAN, Tübingen

IN COOPERATION WITH

HENRY CHADWICK, Cambridge

JAROSLAV PELIKAN, New Haven, Conn.

BRIAN TIERNEY, Ithaca, N.Y.

E. DAVID WILLIS, Princeton, N.J.

VOLUME XXXV

MARCIA L. COLISH

THE STOIC TRADITION
FROM ANTIQUITY
TO THE EARLY MIDDLE AGES-II

LEIDEN

E. J. BRILL

1985

THE STOIC TRADITION
FROM ANTIQUITY
TO THE EARLY MIDDLE AGES

II. *Stoicism in Christian Latin Thought through the Sixth Century*

BY

MARCIA L. COLISH

LEIDEN

E. J. BRILL

1985

ISBN 90 04 07268 3

To Gérard Verbeke

CONTENTS

PREFACE

In bringing the second and last volume of this study to a close it is my welcome duty to acknowledge the aid of the institutions and individuals whose generosity has helped it to see the light. In the foremost place are the National Endowment for the Humanities and the National Humanities Center in Research Triangle Park, North Carolina. Fellowships from both of these organizations in 1981-82 made possible the completion of the research and writing of this volume and the Center as well provided a gracious and stimulating environment for my work during that academic year. Publishers who hold copyrights on portions of the material in the book that appeared in print previously in a somewhat different form have been most courteous and cooperative in allowing me to present it here. In particular I would like to thank the Pontifical Institute of Mediaeval Studies at the University of Toronto for permission to use the material on Augustine in my "The Stoic Theory of Verbal Signification and the Proble of Lies and False Statements from Antiquity to St. Anselm," in *Archéologie du signe,* ed. Lucie Brind'Amour and Eugene Vance, Papers in Mediaeval Studies, 3 (Toronto: Pontifical Institute of Mediaeval Studies, 1983), pp. 17–43 and the University of Pittsburgh Press for permission to use my "Cosmetic Theology: The Transformation of a Stoic Theme," in *Assays: Critical Approaches to Medieval and Renaissance Texts,* volume 1, ed. Peggy A. Knapp and Michael A. Stugrin (Pittsburgh: University of Pittsburgh Press, 1981), pp. 3–14.

My gratitude to these institutions is matched fully by the thanks I owe to individual colleagues whose encouragement and criticism and whose personal and professional assistance have been a great source of support. Various parts of this book were presented as lectures and papers before a number of scholarly audiences, at Cerisy-la-Salle, the University of Rochester, the University of Kent at Canterbury, Villanova University, Yale University, and the University of Pennsylvania, while the research was in progress. In all cases I received fresh insights and valuable correction from members of these groups too numerous to mention. In a much more specific vein I would like to express my lively thanks to William J. Courtenay, Robert E. Lerner, Francis C. Oakley, and Jaroslav J. Pelikan. Both their enthusiasm for this project and their longanimity since its inception have been remarkable and deeply appreciated. My debts to them are ongoing and have expanded over the years. Both Elizabeth A. Clark and Karl F. Morrison have read the entire typescript and their supportive criticisms have been of inestimable value.

It is an equal pleasure to record my gratitude to scholars and friends more recently met. Among those whom I had the privilege of knowing in 1981–82 thanks to the hospitality of the National Humanities Center and its neighboring universities are Christopher Gill, whose patient attention and acute questions helped to clarify many matters in the working out of the last two chapters, and Joseph S. Wittig, whose timely generosity in the loan of material vital to the writing of the last chapter was a godsend. The dedication of this volume, as well as its predecessor, to Gérard Verbeke, expresses the continuing inspiration which his work has given me throughout the entire project. The more that I have learned about the Stoic tradition in this period the more profoundly I have admired and respected his ground-breaking studies in the field. I am also deeply grateful to Heiko A. Oberman. As editor of the Studies in the History of Christian Thought his support and collaboration have been invaluable and his energy and efficiency dazzling. There is one final acknowledgment I take pleasure in recording which, although harder to specify, has been no less important to me. This is the debt I owe to the colleagueship of E. Ann Matter, given in the final stages of the completion of the work during a period not lacking its own pressures in her own life. The fact that I knew she was there lightened immeasurably some of the difficulties under which I labored as well at the time. Even as all of these people in their own individual ways assisted me in making this book as good as I could make it, it remains true that its deficiencies are all my own.

A final word on orthography and related matters. As in the first volume, I have Romanized the spelling of Greek words and I have retained the same conventions regarding the capitalization of Latin words at the beginning of sentences. The editors of medieval texts march to their own drummers in rendering "u" for "v" and "j" for "i" and I have found it simplest to follow their practices in citing titles of works they have edited and in quoting passages from them. In some cases, also, the apparently aberrant spellings that result may be of interest philologically in illustrating the ways in which early medieval Latin was beginning to develop into some of the Romance vernaculars. I have also given in translation the titles of several works, such as Augustine's *Confessions* and *City of God* and Boethius' *Consolation of Philosophy*, which are so well known by these English titles that referring to them in their Latin originals would approximate an affectation. I trust that no reader will be annoyed or misled by the inconsistencies that result from these editorial decisions.

M. L. C.
Oberlin, Ohio

LIST OF ABBREVIATIONS

ACW	Ancient Christian Writers
AL	*Aristoteles latinus*
AJP	*American Journal of Philology*
AS	*Augustinian Studies*
Budé	Collection des Universités de France, publiée sous le patronage de l'Association Guillaume Budé
CC	Corpus christianorum, series latina
CP	*Classical Philology*
CSEL	Corpus scriptorum ecclesiasticorum latinorum
FC	Fathers of the Church
JEH	*Journal of Ecclesiastical History*
JTS	*Journal of Theological Studies*
Loeb	Loeb Classical Library
MGH	*Monumenta germaniae historica*
NS	*New Scholasticism*
OSA	Oeuvres de Saint Augustin
PL	*Patrologia latina cursus completa*, ed. J. P. Migne
RA	*Recherches augustiniennes*
REA	*Revue des études anciennes*
REAug	*Revue des études augustiniennes*
RechSR	*Recherches de science religieuse*
REL	*Revue des études latines*
RSPT	*Revue des sciences philosophiques et théologiques*
RSR	*Revue des sciences religieuses*
RTAM	*Recherches de théologie ancienne et médiévale*
SC	Sources chrétiennes
TAPA	*Transactions of the American Philological Association*
VC	*Vigiliae Christianae*
ZkT	*Zeitschrift für katholische Theologie*

INTRODUCTION

The following volume is the sequel to our *The Stoic Tradition from Antiquity to the Early Middle Ages, I: Stoicism in Classical Latin Literature* and completes the project which the first volume initiated. The study of the Christian Latin writers of the apologetic and patristic age stems from the same desire to investigate the Stoic tradition in the Latin west systematically up through the sixth century, in a milieu where it has received even less sustained attention than is true for the classical Latin authors. The second volume shares with the first the same basic focus and the same methodological concerns, as a consequence of the fact that the treatment given to the Stoicism of the Christian Latin writers reflects a similar kind of scholarly myopia. As is the case with the pagans, the Christian authors influenced by Stoicism in this period have been approached most typically from the standpoints of *Ideengeschichte*, philology, or *Quellenforschung*. Scholars have largely confined themselves to the study of individual Stoic themes, to the citation of parallel texts from Christian authors and their Stoicizing forebears, and to the detection of their overt *testimonia* to Stoicism. These methods have been seen as delineating satisfactorily the outer limits and the inner structure of the influence of Stoicism on the apologists and Church Fathers. Likewise, the appeal of *Quellenforschung*, and even of single-source *Quellenforschung*, has remained surprisingly compelling despite the increasing remoteness of these authors from the original sources of Stoicism and the proliferation of the possible indirect routes by which it reached them.

Aside from sharing the limitations which these highly constricted approaches promote for the assessment of Stoicism in pagan writers, the treatment of the Christian writers has also suffered from a pervasive classical bias. Rather than being read as thinkers whose attitudes toward Stoicism and whose uses of it are subjects important in their own right, the Christian Latin authors have all too often been regarded as mere preservers or transmitters, passive channels through which the classical ideas at issue made their precarious way into the post-classical world. This perspective has the regrettable effect of reinforcing the belief that the task of interpreting the history of the Stoic tradition from antiquity to the early Middle Ages is exhausted by the isolation of texts indicating the brute survival of Stoicism. Depending on which Stoicizing classical author's *Nachleben* this exercise is designed to illustrate, it has led to an overemphasis on either the Greek or the Latin classical sources available to Latin Christians in the apologetic and patristic age and to a willingness to ignore the idea that they could also have derived some of their information on Stoicism from earlier or contemporary Greek and Latin Christian writers as well.

The classical bias, the reading of texts out of their contexts, the narrowly philological method, and the view that early medieval authors were neither selective nor independent in their handling of Stoic material which inform the interpretive outlooks just described has also been matched in some quarters with the equally circumscribed view that Neoplatonism was the major, or even the only, philosophical school with which the Christian Latin writers felt a need to come to grips as Christians. One of the conclusions that will emerge from this study is that Stoicism bulked much larger on the mental horizon of the Latin apologists and Church Fathers than has generally been acknowledged. A number of the thinkers discussed below saw the Stoa as the principal form of pagan wisdom they had to address, whether they awarded it praise or blame. Even in the case of those whose debts to Neoplatonism or Aristotelianism were far more extensive, Stoicism often conditioned their handling of those traditions, and vice versa. Stoicism was sometimes combined eclectically with Neoplatonism or Aristotelianism to form a composite in which the Stoic ingredients played a critical role. In this respect, the intellectual contexts in which the Christian thinkers' particular applications of Stoicism were made remains the paramount consideration for the historian. Our own examination of these thinkers has led in some cases to a reappraisal not only of the amount and type of Stoicism in their thought but also of its relationship to the other philosophical materials which they had at their disposal. Models for some of the new combinations that resulted were provided by the philosophical syncretism already characteristic of the late Hellenistic period. In some cases they were set forth most prototypically by the Greek Christian apologists and Church Fathers. But in other cases they resulted from the temperamental inclinations, the urge to make a personal assessment of the issues, or the theological or literary exigencies inspiring the Latin Christian writers themselves.

For these reasons it is just as important in the present volume as in its predecessor to examine the Stoic tradition neither topically nor philologically but through an analysis of the individual thinkers whose writings supply the framework in which it can best be appreciated. We shall be dealing, hence, not with ideas in the abstract but with ideas as they live and work in the minds of individual thinkers, who themselves lived and worked in their own particular time and place, with their own personal and professional agendas. All or most of the Christian thinkers we shall meet in this book received the best classical education available in their day and all of them saw Stoicism as part of the classical culture that played an integral role in their formation. Many of them were converts, especially in the earlier portions of the story. Whether as men trying to make sense out of their own intellectual experience or as spokesmen of a beleaguered Christian community in a hostile pagan environment they frequently felt the need to make explicit their attitudes toward the relationship, or lack of relationship, that they saw between Stoicism and Christianity. This imperative did not necessarily abate when the Christian Church became a legitimate corporation and, then, the official religion of the Roman state in the fourth century. The intense preoccupation not only with paganism but also with heretical and schismatic alternatives to the orthodox faith which marks that century inspired many of the Church Fathers and lesser theologians of the day to characterize their opponents as having fallen into error because of their attachment to Stoicism. At the same time, many of them could use Stoicism as a corrective to other theological positions which they sought to refute. Then, as the Roman Empire collapsed and gave way to a western Europe and north Africa ruled by a series of pagan or Arian Germanic tribes, the polemical exigencies of the earlier patristic age were yoked with the new educational and administrative responsibilities that devolved upon the leaders of the Church by default. In their own way, these duties continued to require a self-conscious attitude toward Stoicism, and toward the classical tradition more broadly, on the part of the Christian Latin writers of the late patristic period and required them to adjust their orientation to the political and social circumstances of the immediately post-Roman world. Whether as laymen or, more usually, as priests, prelates, and monastic leaders, the Christian thinkers who dominate the intellectual history of the Latin world between the third and the sixth centuries faced a host of shifting and competing demands over the course of this period, which must be taken into account in understanding what they made of Stoicism, and what they did with it. Their manifold tasks as statesmen and theologians, as scholars and controversialists, as pastors and pedagogues, no less than their own personal literary and philosophical inclinations, all helped to shape their approaches to Stoicism and help to account for the selectivity they displayed in their use of that tradition.

While the circumstances of their lives and the historical settings in which they lived grew increasingly different from those of their classical forebears and their Greek Christian predecessors and contemporaries, it must be borne in mind that the Latin Christian authors themselves were well aware of the access to Stoicism provided by these two media. The appropriation of Stoicism by the Greek Christian authors and their in-

fluence on their Latin compeers have been given able recent surveys by
Michel Spanneut and by Gérard Verbeke, who have also provided useful guides to the existing literature on these topics.[1] The first volume of
our own present study has sought to clarify the role of Stoicism in the
classical Latin mind. It would be redundant indeed to recapitulate all
of this material at the points where it is relevant in the volume at hand.
Readers are therefore urged to make use of the classical and Greek patristic backgrounds to the Latin Christian authors supplied by Spanneut, Verbeke, and by *Stoic Tradition*, I, should they need to do so.

Yet another observation must be made in considering the ways in
which our authors viewed Stoicism as a component of pagan culture in
measuring themselves as Christians. We should be on guard against attributing to them an anachronistic *optique* on the question of the relationship between Stoicism, or of the Hellenistic world of thought more
loosely, and the origins of Christianity. This topic became a subject of
lively and even of agitated discussion in modern times, inspiring a lengthy
controversy which has abated only quite recently.[2] Scholars approached
this issue from a variety of points of view, ranging from Biblical hermeneutics to the scientific study of the classics and from the internal feuds
of competing Christian confessions to the polemics for and against
Christianity itself in an age of secularism. Depending on their perspectives, some contributors to the debate stressed the radical disparities between Stoicism and the New Testament faith while others emphasized
their parallels. Among the latter group, some saw one or more of the New
Testament authors as influenced by Stoicism, whether substantively,
formally, terminologically, or all three. Still other scholars argued that
the Roman Stoics were themselves influenced by early Christianity. Interesting as these rival views may be as indicative of shifting currents of
opinion in modern thought on the nature of early Christianity in its
Mediterranean setting, they do not shed much light on how the Latin
apologists and Church Fathers viewed this question themselves.

To be sure, some of our authors saw close parallels between Stoicism
and the Bible and took this to mean that Stoicism could be regarded as
an authentic source of wisdom. A truth, for them, did not have to be

---

[1] Michel Spanneut, *Permanence du Stoïcisme de Zénon à Malraux* (Gembloux, 1973), ch.
5; *Le Stoïcisme des pères de l'Église de Clément de Rome à Clément d'Alexandrie*, 2me éd. (Paris,
1969); Gérard Verbeke, *The Presence of Stoicism in Medieval Thought* (Washington, 1983).
Verbeke takes a similarly topical approach to Stoicism in the patristic authors and treats
Spanneut's handling of them as basically adequate. At the same time, he stresses, quite
rightly, in ch. 1, the severe limits of the purely philological approach to this subject.

[2] For the historiography of this question see Marcia L. Colish, "Pauline Theology
and Stoic Philosophy: An Historical Study," *Journal of the American Academy of Religion*,
47, Supplement (March 1979), B 1–21.

unique in order to be true; and the more people who professed it, the better. A number of Latin apologists and Church Fathers thought that, whenever Stoicism coincided with Christianity, the philosophers could be accepted *tout court*, while others insisted that they had acquired their wisdom from the Bible, however implausible such a claim might be on the grounds of chronology. Wherever they stood on the origins of Stoic wisdom, those who accepted it as a true wisdom felt free to exploit its perceived concord with Christianity for apologetic purposes, in arguing for the ease of the transition from paganism to the Christian faith which it made possible. Indeed, in the case of the anonymous fourth-century forged correspondence between Seneca and St. Paul, this idea was escalated into the conclusion that the philosopher had actually been converted by the apostle.[3] On the other hand, a great many Latin Christian writers up through the sixth century saw Stoicism as fundamentally antithetical to Christian theology and ethics alike or, at best, as a set of doctrines requiring drastic criticism, modification, and supplementation before it could be given a hearing. Still another approach to Stoicism widespread in this period was to draw from it particular topics, ideas, and principles and to Christianize them or to use them as constructive tools for the formulation and defense of Christian doctrine, whether against heresy or against paganism itself. There are even cases in which Latin apologetic and patristic authors wielded one Stoic doctrine, of which they approved, against another, to which they took exception. There is clearly no single or univocal answer to the question of the relationship between Stoicism and Christianity to be found in the Latin Christian writers of this period. In fact, the diverse approaches just mentioned may occur even in the work of the same author, depending on the immediate theological or rhetorical requirements of his argument. We should, therefore, be prepared to find an extremely variegated spectrum of views toward Stoicism, both in its relations with competing schools of philosophy and in its encounter with Christianity, in the thinkers discussed in this book.

In comparing the Latin Christian writers with their classical Latin precursors we will also notice both similarities and disparities in the range of their interests in Stoicism and in the kinds of issues to which they apply it. One sharply etched difference is that the Christian writers display a knowledge of Stoicism far broader than the classical Latin writers, a phenomenon particularly striking in the case of logic and physics. The

---

[3] For references to the text of this work and the literature on it see Marcia L. Colish, *The Stoic Tradition from Antiquity to the Early Middle Ages*, I: *Stoicism in Classical Latin Literature*, Studies in the History of Christian Thought, ed. Heiko A. Oberman, 34 (Leiden, 1985), ch. 1, pp. 15–16 nn. 11, 12.

Christian thinkers are far less exclusively ethical in their focus than the classical authors, a function of the appeal which Stoic physics and logic held for them in the resolution of specifically Christian dogmatic and exegetical problems. At the same time, we will note that for the Christian no less than for the classical writers, particular clusters of Stoic ideas tend to be invoked for similar purposes across the period studied, or are associated with particular literary genres. Changing political or social circumstances will occasionally lead thinkers in both groups to make analogous reformulations of certain standard Stoic *topoi*.

Another major difference between the thinkers considered in the first and second volumes of this study, outside of the obvious need to invent new genres of Christian literature on the part of the Christians to address their new religious concerns, is the fact that a great many of the Christian authors wrote in more than one genre. The generic model of organizing the material in the first volume has thus been replaced by a more chronological organization in the second. Here, too, a concise biographical orientation is provided for each thinker in order to place him, which may be most useful in those chapters dealing with a number of figures who can be grouped thematically or generically more cogently than in a strict chronological order within their own period. No chapter presenting general conclusions has been provided, a decision that has been made quite deliberately. Despite the existence of considerable interaction and influence among the Latin apologists and Church Fathers over time, the effects of their multiple perspectives on Stoicism are not really cumulative. No figure in this period, however authoritative, produced what might be called a canonical position on Stoicism that was accepted as such by his contemporaries and successors. Each new generation of Latin Christian thinkers up through the sixth century felt the same freedom to mine its immediate predecessors as selectively as it wished in addressing the host of more or less indirect sources of Stoicism of which it made use. The result is that the Latin apologetic and patristic age produced a number of highly individualized adaptations of Stoicism, all of which could and did serve as contrasting and competing models of its appropriation by Christians for their later medieval readers.

This study begins with the Latin apologists, the earliest of the Christian Latin writers, among whom the clearly marked alternative approaches to Stoicism typical of the whole period will already be quite visible. The second chapter, on St. Ambrose and St. Jerome, will continue to show how contemporaries in the early patristic age could appraise and apply Stoicism very differently, as a function of their own intellectual temperaments and professional concerns. The less towering

Christian writers of the fourth and fifth centuries will be studied in the third chapter. These men participated in a range of endeavors from theology, both dogmatic, moral, and controversial, to poetry, to theodicy, and to monastic literature. While many of them are minor figures they none the less made important contributions to the absorption and Christian reformulation of the Stoic tradition in their own right, as well as providing a contemporary perspective on the major Church Fathers who flank them on either side. The fourth and longest chapter will be devoted to St. Augustine, as a witness to the massive role he played in the Stoic tradition on all fronts and as the most extended example of the multiplicity of attitudes toward it that could coexist in the thought of a single individual in this period. The fifth and final chapter will consider the Latin Christian writers of the sixth century, both great and small, who, in the fragmented world in which they lived, sought to salvage and to preserve the achievements of the past while simultaneously finding creative ways of applying Stoicism to the needs of their own time and to the very uncertain future which they could see ahead of them.

While this book makes no attempt to trace the fortunes of Stoicism in the western mind after the sixth century, the fact that it did indeed have a long and healthy posterity in the later Middle Ages and Renaissance is a consequence, in no small part, of the labors of the Latin Christian thinkers from the third to the sixth centuries no less than those of the classical authors studied in volume I. Precisely how significant the role of these classical and early medieval thinkers was in relation to the Stoic material found in medieval Byzantium and Islam that was translated into Latin in the twelfth and thirteenth centuries is a question that must remain in abeyance at the present time. The scholarly investigation of the Stoic tradition in Byzantium and Islam is still in its infancy. We currently possess only the sketchiest and most superficial sense of what lies beyond the wall of silence erected by the numerous sources in manuscript that await the attention of scholars with the linguistic and paleographical expertise to give them voice. At some future time, when more is known about the Byzantine and Islamic streams of post-classical Stoicism that flowed into high medieval Latin culture, it will be possible to compare them with the Latin classical, apologetic, and patristic streams and to assess their precise relationships and relative influence. Still, when one considers the breadth of the information on Stoicism made available through the Latin tradition itself, and in forms often more appealing to medieval and Renaissance readers than the scholastic literature undergirded by the Greco-Arabic translations, one may venture to state with some confidence that the contributions to the Stoic tradition made by the pagan and Christian Latin writers up through the sixth century are and remain a vital and enduring component in its ongoing history.

CHAPTER ONE

THE LATIN APOLOGISTS

Spanning the period from the early third to the early fourth century, the Latin apologists were all men highly educated in the Latin culture of their day, in several cases holding positions as professional rhetoricians and advocates. Most of them were converts to the Christian faith and were conversant with contemporary Greek Christian literature. They were fully capable of drawing on the philosophical material made available to them by both the pagan and the Christian traditions. Their urge to take a position on the relationship between Christianity and Greek philosophy sprang from the need to make sense of their own intellectual experience no less than from the need to defend the new faith and to arm their co-religionists for survival in a hostile environment. From Tertullian to Lactantius, they reveal a knowledge of Stoicism that is striking for its extent, whether they use it with sophistication or with casual familiarity. All the apologists take an independent view of Stoicism, agreeing with some of its principles and disagreeing with others, positions stemming as much from the circumstantial needs of apology as from personal conviction. Their approaches to Stoicism are quite varied, running the gamut from sharp hostility to warm approval and from incidental references to decisive reformulations of Stoic teachings in the light of Christian doctrine. More than one of these viewpoints can be found at times in the work of a single apologist. Taken as a group, the Latin apologists draw most heavily on Stoic physics and ethics, paying much less attention to logic. In those areas where they refer to Stoicism they tend, more often than not, to credit the school expressly with its teachings. There are occasional inaccuracies and omissions in their handling of Stoic ideas, reflecting in part the rhetorical demands of their apologetic strategy. But, despite the range of uses to which they put it, the Latin apologists are united in treating Stoicism as a major, or even as the major form of pagan wisdom which they regard as imperative to distinguish from Christian wisdom or to correlate with it.

I. TERTULLIAN

Tertullian (ca. 155–220) occupies a special place in the history of the Latin Stoic tradition. The first of the Latin Christian authors, he produced apologies addressed to pagans, polemical writings directed against heretics, and ethical treatises designed to discipline and console the faithful. One of his aims was to reexpress Christian doctrine in the mode of contemporary Latin culture so as to widen its appeal beyond the confines of the Jewish Christianity prevalent in his day.[1] Another equally pressing objective was to underline the distinction between Christian doctrine and those pagan ideas that he felt were false in themselves and likely to lead Christians into heresy. The fact that Tertullian took on a number of different literary assignments at the same time, no less than the oratorical training that prepared him for his pre-Christian profession as an advocate, led him to make many statements that are apparent contradictions. His observers in modern times have not always been sure whether he is saying what he really means or scoring a debater's point, whether, indeed, he is a man with consistent opinions about philosophy or a mere rhetorician. This initial difficulty is complicated by the fact that Tertullian embraced the Montanist heresy in about 206 or 207.[2] Some scholars have claimed that Montanism inspired a new rigorism in Tertullian, reflected in a growing lack of sympathy with pagan culture in general and with philosophy in particular. There is, at any rate, one point on which there is no debate: Stoicism is the classical philosophy to which Tertullian adverts most frequently. It is the favorite weapon in his philosophical arsenal. His attitude toward philosophy *per se* is manifested, above all, in his attitude toward Stoicism and in his use of it. But, by the same token, the question of Tertullian's Stoicism cannot be detached from his broader conception of philosophy, the chief aspect of pagan culture against which and in terms of which he seeks to defend and promote the Christian faith.

The glaring inconsistencies in Tertullian's approach to philosophy have not failed to inspire conflicting interpretations on the part of his commentators. The problem can be stated most concisely by juxtaposing several of Tertullian's most pungent and aphoristic lines. On the one hand, he assumes the stance of an irreconcilable opponent of philosophical reason in his *Fiunt non nascuntur Christiani*,[3] *Incredibile est, quia ineptum est*,[4] and, most dismissively of all, *Quid ergo Athenis et Hieroso-*

---

[1] Jean Daniélou, *A History of Early Christian Doctrine before the Council of Nicaea*, trans. David Smith and John Austin Baker (London, 1977), III, 136, 139–88.

[2] The chronology of Tertullian's works followed here is the one established by Jean-Claude Fredouille, *Tertullien et la conversion de la culture antique* (Paris, 1972), pp. 487–88, supported by Francine Jo Cardman, "Tertullian on the Resurrection," (Yale University Ph.D. diss., 1974), pp. vi–vii. For other schemes see Timothy David Barnes, *Tertullian: A Historical and Literary Study* (Oxford, 1971), p. 55; Robert E. Roberts, *The Theology of Tertullian* (London, 1924), p. 79.

[3] Quintus Septimus Florens Tertullian, *Apologeticum* 18.4, ed. E. Dekkers, in *Opera*, CC, 1–2 (Turnhout, 1954). This edition will be the one cited unless otherwise indicated.

[4] *De carne Christi* 5.25, ed. and trans. Jean-Pierre Mahé, SC, 216 (Paris, 1975).

lymis?[5] On the other hand, Tertullian presents himself as a sympathetic adherant of the sort of natural theology supported by philosophical reasoning in his *Seneca saepe noster,*[6] *Magistra natura, anima discipula est,"*[7] and most warmly of all in his *O testimonium animae naturaliter Christianae.*[8] Two of these antithetical asseverations, it will be noted, occur in the very same work. The polar contrasts they reflect can be documented throughout Tertullian's *oeuvre,* both in the Catholic and in the Montanist phases of his career.

The simplest way to resolve the antinomy is to subject it to reductionism. The neatness of this solution has appealed to a number of scholars, who have argued that either the pro-philosophical or the anti-philosophical stance represents Tertullian's real convictions and that any discordant notes can be ignored or explained away. One group regards Tertullian as an obscurantist, hostile to the philosophical mentality as such despite his occasional recourse to philosophical arguments as an apologetic device. Proponents of this position have usually formulated it in terms of the high medieval conception of reason and revelation and the ways that they were synthesized or separated by scholastic and post-scholastic thinkers.[9] Rivalling this group is a school of thought whose members share the same anachronistic formulation of the issue but who stress Tertullian's sincere belief in the existence of a natural, objective, rational knowledge of God, seen as a *praeambulum fidei.* For their part, they do not hesitate to write off his attacks on philosophy as a mere rhetorical flourish.[10]

---

[5] *De praescriptione haereticorum* 7.9, ed. R. F. Refoulé. A good bibliography on this issue is supplied by Fredouille, *Tertullien,* pp. 301–03.

[6] *De anima* 20.1, ed. J. H. Waszink.

[7] *De testimonio animae* 5.1, ed. R. Willems.

[8] *Apol.* 17.6. A good bibliography on this issue is provided by Norbert Brox, "Anima naturaliter non christiana," *ZkT,* 91 (1969), 70–75.

[9] Étienne Gilson, *History of Christian Philosophy in the Middle Ages* (New York, 1955), pp. 44–45; André Labhardt, "Tertullien et la philosophie ou la recherche d'une 'position pure'," *Museum Helveticum,* 7 (1950), 159–80; R. A. Markus, in A. H. Armstrong and R. A. Markus, *Christian Faith and Greek Philosophy* (London, 1960), pp. 139–40; R. A. Norris, *God and World in Early Christian Theology* (New York, 1965), pp. 104–07; E. K. Rand, *Founders of the Middle Ages* (New York, 1957), pp. 12, 41; Carlo Scaglioni, "'Sapientia mundi' e 'dei sapientia': L'Esegesi di I. Cor. 1, 18–2, 5 in Tertulliano," *Aevum,* 46 (1972), 183–96, 213–15; Ulrich Wickert, "Glauben und Denken bei Tertullian und Origenes," *Zeitschrift für Theologie und Kirche,* 62 (1965), 161–68; Bernard Williams, "Tertullian's Paradox," *New Essays in Philosophical Theology,* ed. Antony Flew and Alasdair MacIntyre (London, 1961), p. 188, who, however, misses the point by treating the paradox as a purely logical one. Gerald Lewis Bray, *Holiness and the Will of God: Perspectives on the Theology of Tertullian* (Atlanta, 1979) presents Tertullian's thought in as a-philosophical a manner as possible. He provides a useful general bibliographical orientation, pp. 8-38.

[10] Lorenz Fuetscher, "Die natürliche Gotteserkenntnis bei Tertullian," *ZkT,* 51 (1927), 217–51; Josef Lortz, *Tertullian als Apologet,* Münsterische Beiträge zur Theologie, 9–10 (Münster, 1927–28), I, 352–73, 381–93; "Vernunft und Offenbarung bei Tertullian," *Der*

The fact that so much evidence has to be suppressed if one is to regard Tertullian either as a proto-fideist or a proto-Thomist has prompted the development of a much more sophisticated range of opinions. The scholars in this category argue that Tertullian's paradoxes are deliberate, a reflection of his oratorical culture and a function of the rhetorical needs of the particular works in which he places them. According to this view, Tertullian was interested neither in supporting nor in undermining philosophy or philosophical reasoning as such. His aim, rather, was to vanquish the particular opponents with whom he crossed swords in his various apologies. Thus, it is imperative to pay attention to the contexts in which his *obiter dicta* occur. He attacked the philosophical mentality in apologies directed against heretics whose errors, he held, had resulted from a misappropriation of philosophy to the point of obscuring or falsifying Christian doctrine. He drew on the philosophical mentality in order to invoke the support that pagan thought could provide for Christian doctrine, so as to make it more accessible to the gentiles. In both cases Tertullian made use of literary *topoi* familiar to his audiences, *topoi* deriving from classical rhetoric and from the Biblical tradition alike. Both the assignment he took on, his own education, and that of the people he addressed made a rhetorical approach to philosophical argument natural for Tertullian. His thought must thus be understood in its particular historical, cultural, and existential setting. This interpretation has been advanced in two forms. One seeks merely to propose the rhetorical understanding of Tertullian as a means of overcoming the myopia of the reason vs. revelation school.[11] The second goes well beyond that point.

Katholik, Folge 4, 11 (1913), 124–40; Gotthard Rauch, *Der Einfluss der stoischen Philosophie auf die Lehrbildung Tertullians* (Halle, 1890); Gerhard Ring, *Auctoritas bei Tertullian, Cyprian und Ambrosius*, Cassiciacum, 29 (Würzburg, 1975), pp. 83–91; Roberts, *Theology of Tertullian*, pp. 63–75; C. DeLisle Shortt, *The Influence of Philosophy on the Mind of Tertullian* (London, 1933), pp. 19–21, 35, 37–47, 99–101; Bardo Weiss, "Die 'anima naturaliter christiana' in Verständnis Tertullians," *Mitteilungen und Forschungsbeiträge der Cusanus-Gesellschaft*, 13 (1978), 293–304.

  ¹¹ Barnes, *Tertullian*, pp. 205–06, 210; Johannes B. Bauer, "'Credo quia absurdum' (Tertullian, De carne Christi 5)," *Festschrift Franz Loidl zum 65. Geburtstag*, ed. Viktor Flieder (Wien, 1970), I, 9–12; R. Braun, "Tertullien et la philosophie païenne: Essai de mise au point," *Bulletin de l'Association Guillaume Budé*, 4ᵉ sér., 2 (1971), 231–57; Brox, "Anima naturaliter non christiana," *ZkT*, 91 (1969), 70–75; Daniélou, *Hist. of Early Christian Doctrine*, III, 225–31, 403; Vianney Décarie, "Le paradoxe de Tertullien," *VC*, 15 (1961), 23–31; Fritz-Peter Hager, "Zur Bedeutung der griechischen Philosophie für die christliche Wahrheit und Bildung bei Tertullian unde bei Augustin," *Antike und Abendland*, 24 (1978), 76–79; Adolf Harnack, *History of Dogma*, trans. Neil Buchanan and James Millar (London, 1910–12), II, 196–98, 226; V, 17, 21, 24; James Morgan, *The Importance of Tertullian in the Development of Christian Dogma* (London, 1928), pp. 99–107; François Refoulé, "Tertullien et la philosophie," *RSR*, 30 (1956), 42–45; George Schelowsky, *Der Apologet Tertullianus in seinem Verhältnis zu der griechisch-römischen Philosophie* (Leipzig, 1901); H. B. Timothy, *The Early Christian Apologists and Greek Philosophy Exemplified by Irenaeus, Tertullian and Clement of Alexandria* (Assen, 1973), pp. 47–49, 52, 83–84.

Its proponents emphasize that the rule of faith was Tertullian's primary criterion. Philosophy thus remained always in a subordinate position as a source of truth for him, while pastoral no less than polemical considerations governed his use of it.[12]

The most far-reaching shift in interpretation has been proposed by a number of scholars who argue that Tertullian's chief goal and accomplishment as a theologian transcend a purely utilitarian or ancillary treatment of classical philosophy and rhetoric. Rather, they claim, as a Christian thinker Tertullian did not use his classical education in a calculating or disinterested manner. His faith did not uproot him from his culture. Classicism was a true spiritual formation for Tertullian, which he drew upon without hesitation to explore and deepen his faith, and not merely to defend it. At the same time, in so doing he achieved a conversion of classical culture by grafting it onto Christianity, thereby transforming it in the light of Christian needs and concerns, a process far more organic and integral than would have been possible if his philosophizing had been nothing but an *ad hoc* polemical strategy.[13]

In documenting their varying conceptions of Tertullian the commentators have brought to light many important Stoic elements in his thought, which will assist us in our more limited task of placing him in the Stoic tradition. However, the desire to defend a thesis has occasionally led scholars to miss or to overinterpret Tertullian's Stoicism, to attribute to Stoicism ideas that were philosophical commonplaces, to confuse parallels with influences, to ignore the mistakes Tertullian sometimes makes in his treatment of Stoicism, and to bypass some of the most significant changes in Stoic doctrine that he effects as he applies it to Christian problems.

Our own investigation of Stoicism in Tertullian makes it impossible to sustain the view that he is primarily or exclusively a supporter, an enemy, or a transformer of Stoicism. He does all of these things simultaneously and to approximately the same degree. No one of these activities is any more typical of his outlook than the other two. In all three cases he draws heavily on the thought of his Greek apologetic predecessors and contemporaries. While he does achieve some independent in-

---

[12] Cardman, "Tertullian," pp. 20–21; Fredouille, *Tertullien*, pp. 303–57; Joseph Moingt, *Théologie trinitaire de Tertullien* (Paris, 1966), I, 31; Johannes Quasten, *Patrology* (Westminster, Md., 1953), II, 321; Carlo Tibiletti, "Filosofia e cristianesimo in Tertulliano," *Annali della Facoltà di lettere e filosofia, Università di Macerata*, 3–4 (1970–71), 97–133; Harry Austryn Wolfson, *The Philosophy of the Church Fathers*, 3rd rev. ed. (Cambridge, Mass., 1970), I, 102, 104–05.

[13] Fredouille, *Tertullien*, pp. 29–35, 484 and passim; Stephan Otto, *"Natura" und "Dispositio": Untersuchung zum Naturbegriff und zur Denkform Tertullians* (München, 1960), pp. 5–6, 74–96 and passim.

sights, one of his chief contributions to the Stoic tradition lies in the fact that he made these philosophical and theological issues available in Latin thought for the first time. He thus provides *topoi* and models for his Latin Christian successors, whether or not they answer particular questions in the same way. Equally important, Tertullian is unusual among the Latin apologists for the range of philosophical themes he treats. He emphasizes the metaphysical, physical, and anthropological content of Stoicism, in contrast to the almost preclusively ethical interests of many other Latin authors of his day, whether Christian or pagan. He thus serves as a major vehicle for the transmission of Stoic teachings in those fields, whether in and of themselves or in connection with Christian doctrinal issues.

The Stoic ideas that Tertullian uses are generally isolated concepts which he shows no interest in relating to the rest of the Stoic system. To the extent that he notes any connections among them he does so out of a desire to stress the theological and logical interdependence of those Christian doctrines with which he associates them. Some of the same Stoic ideas can be found in each of the three subdivisions of Tertullian's work; he may criticize them in one context, praise them in another, and Christianize them in the third. For our purposes it is these three different contexts that provide the most intelligible categories in which to analyze Tertullian's Stoicism, rather than chronological or topical groupings. Two generalizations can be made at the outset. The range of Stoic themes that Tertullian draws on and the types of works that are involved are narrowest in those contexts where he attacks Stoic philosophy. Both grow broader and more diverse in those contexts where he invokes the support of Stoic doctrine or recasts it in the light of Christianity.

The first category we will consider is the one where Tertullian wants to show that philosophy, especially Stoicism, leads to error and heresy, or that it is otherwise inadequate. Here he confines his attention almost exclusively to the nature of God and to the posthumous condition of the human soul. Epistemological and ethical concerns receive short shrift. Approximately half of the apposite references occur in works addressed to the pagans, written in his early years. The other half appear in polemics against heretics or Judaizers, some dating from his early career and others deriving from his Montanist period. Only one reference occurs in a hortatory work, the *De spectaculis*. In this context Tertullian is more likely than not to attribute Stoic doctrines expressly to the Stoa or to its individual members. When this is the case he tends to single out the early Stoics or Seneca, ignoring the middle Stoics entirely. He occasionally misrepresents Stoic doctrine, sometimes on points which he reports correctly elsewhere.

The chief topic that Tertullian takes up in this category is the nature of God and His relation to the universe. Both the pagans and the heretics who have been seduced by them, he charges, have fallen into error. Echoing a line of argument developed in Cicero's *De natura deorum*, he asserts that no philosopher can speak with authority on the nature of God because various schools of philosophy disagree on that subject, a lack of consensus which, he holds with Philo, is the more deplorable since they all raided Holy Scripture for their theology in the first place. In any event, he says, the Platonists see God as incorporeal and the Stoics see Him as corporeal, Zeno teaching that He resembles fire. The Epicureans think that God is inactive in the world; the Platonists think that He is immanent in the world; while the Stoics, according to Tertullian, think that God resides outside of the world, manipulating it externally.[14] Tertullian illustrates this striking misconception of Stoic physics with an equally striking image, which he does not hesitate to use antithetically in another connection. Zeno's separation of God from the world, he says, can be compared with the simultaneous presence of honey and wax in a honeycomb. The two entities are juxtaposed but neither permeates the other: *Ecce enim Zeno quoque materiam mundialem a deo separat, vel sic <eu>m per illam tamquam mel per favos transisse dicit.*[15] Another feature of the divine nature which Tertullian defends against Stoicism, as espoused by the heretic Marcion, this time more accurately if less expressly, is the doctrine that God cannot be described as impassive, in the sense of Stoic *apatheia*. Although He is immutable, He is loving and merciful to man.[16]

Tertullian attributes other physical errors to the Stoics as well. The followers of Chrysippus, he notes, ridicule Christians for their belief in demons.[17] Like Platonism, Stoicism has deluded the heretic Hermagoras into the belief in the eternity of matter.[18] Zeno, who says that the basic constituent of the cosmos is air or aether, can be classed with the other

---

[14] *Ad nationes* 2.2.1–2.2.20, ed. J. G. P. Borleffs; *Apol.* 47.1–7; *De praescr. haer.* 43.1. See also Timothy, *Early Christian Apologists*, p. 42; Icilio Vecchiotti, *La filosofia di Tertulliano: Un colpo di sonda nella storia del cristianesimo primitivo* (Urbino, 1970), pp. 63–64, 69–71, 77–78.

[15] *Ad nat.* 2.4.10.

[16] *Adversus Marcionem* 1.26, 2.27, ed. and trans. Ernest Evans (Oxford, 1972); *De praescr. haer.* 7.3; *De test. an.* 2. An excellent discussion of this question can be found in Ermin F. Micka, *The Problem of Divine Anger in Arnobius and Lactantius*, Catholic University Studies in Christian Antiquity, 4 (Washington, 1943), pp. 24, 27–30. See also Pierre de Labriolle, "Apatheia," *Mélanges de philologie, de littérature et d'histoire anciennes offerts à Alfred Ernout* (Paris, 1940), p. 218; E. P. Meijering, *Tertullian contra Marcion: Gotteslehre in der Polemik Adversus Marcionem I-II* (Leiden, 1977), p. 147.

[17] *De test. an.* 3.1–3.

[18] *Adversus Hermogenem* 1.1, ed. A. Kroymann. Noted by Barnes, *Tertullian*, p. 123; Quasten, *Patrology*, II, 276; J. H. Waszink, "Observations on Tertullian's Treatise against Hermogenes," *VC*, 9 (1955), 129–30.

philosophers who have animated all the heresies,[19] an idea that inspires Tertullian's critique of Marcion as a Stoicizer in his classic "What has Athens to do with Jerusalem?" outburst, stigmatizing all philosophy including Stoicism as a form of vain curiosity that deflects believers from the Gospel.[20]

There are also mistaken ideas on the human soul and its condition after death which Tertullian blames on the Stoa, although he does not always deal with Stoic doctrine very knowledgeably on this point. He disagrees with the view, which he simply calls Stoic, that the souls of the wise alone ascend to heaven to dwell in the region of the moon, a notion he rejects because he thinks it would prevent the souls of departed sages from concerning themselves with men on earth.[21] Also, and specifically against Marcion, he objects to the idea, which he attributes to Seneca sometimes alone and sometimes in the company of Epicurus, that the soul dies with the body, a position offensive to Tertullian because it negates the doctrines of the immortality of the soul and the resurrection of the body.[22] Here we see Tertullian adverting to ideas which are not necessarily unique to Stoicism or to teachings which neither Seneca nor the Stoics as a whole maintained consistently.

The smallest number of instances where Tertullian contrasts Stoicism unfavorably with Christianity concerns ethics and epistemology. He seizes on one of the most celebrated Stoic *exempla virtutis*, Cato of Utica, and stands it on its head. Cato had been praised both for his *apatheia* and his *eupatheia* in the famous incident when he divorced his wife Marcia so that she could marry a friend of his who lacked heirs. Apart from the fact that Tertullian confuses Cato of Utica with his ancestor, Cato the Censor, he cites this event as an example not of pagan virtue but of pagan vice, in which Cato the husband acts as a pander for his own wife.[23] A final instance is Tertullian's treatment of the topic of natural law, which, in his anti-Stoic stance, he views with far more coolness than he does in other contexts. By natural law he means both the order of the universe and the moral bonds that unite all men, as well as man's natural capacity to know them, a distinctively Stoic amalgam although he

---

[19] *Adv. Marc.* 1.13.3. Noted by Timothy, *Early Christian Apologists*, p. 45; Vecchiotti, *La filos. di Tertulliano*, pp. 332–33.

[20] *De praescr. haer.* 7.1–13.

[21] *De anima* 54.1–54.3, 55.4, ed. J. H. Waszink.

[22] *Adv. Marc.* 5.19.7; *De an.* 42.1–2; *De resurrectione mortuorum* 1.4, ed. J. G. P. Borleffs. Noted by Adhémar d'Alès, *La théologie de Tertullien*, 3me éd. (Paris, 1905), pp. 202–03; Cardman, "Tertullian," pp. 17–18; Meijering, *Tertullian contra Marcion*, pp. 76–77, 166; Timothy, *Early Christian Apologists*, p. 46.

[23] *Apol.* 39.12–13. This point has been misinterpreted by Stephanus Oświecimski, *De scriptorum romanorum vestigiis apud Tertullianum obviis quaestiones selectae* (Kraków, 1954), pp. 47–64.

does not name it as such. All men can know God and the good by natural law *(naturale iuri)*, he avers, but this knowledge is by no means adequate to man's needs. It does not constitute the saving knowledge of God's ethical commandments or of God's transcendent power over nature, nor does it create a personal relationship between man and God. These vital epistemological and moral conditions are met only by revelation,[24] first in the Mosaic covenant and consummately in the Gospel.[25] In this instance, Tertullian rigorously deemphasizes any harmony that can be found between pagan truth and Christian truth in the light of the superiority of revelation.

In the second category of Tertullian's thought, where he treats Stoicism as fully consonant with the Christian faith, he reverses his strategy dramatically. Here, he uses Stoicism as a weapon against pagan errors, those found among the pagans themselves or, more usually, those that have led heretics astray. Polemics against the heretics are more strongly represented than apologies addressed to pagans. The heretics Marcion and Hermagoras, whom he elsewhere chastises because of their Stoicism, are joined by Valentinian and cast as Platonists, Gnostics, or materialists whose mistaken views can be corrected by recourse to Stoicism. Tertullian also devotes some attention to the Christians within the fold in this context, drawing upon Stoic ethics as a support for Christian teachings. His most salient shift in emphasis in the pro-Stoic category of references is his concern with epistemological questions. Tertullian here relates epistemology integrally with physics and anthropology and gives it pride of place. In this second category, as in the first, Tertullian sometimes attributes the Stoic ideas he appropriates to their authors by name or by school, singling out the early Stoics and Seneca for special attention.

The largest single topic to which Tertullian adverts in this category is natural theology. He draws freely on the Stoic argument for the existence of God and His primary attributes on the evidence of the created order and on the basis of man's natural rational capacity to perceive God's connection with the creation. He appeals repeatedly to *consensus omnium*, which the Stoics traditionally associated with this line of reasoning. Tertullian occasionally uses the same strategy against polytheism or as an argument against the futility and inconclusiveness of pagan

---

[24] *De an.* 2.2; *De spectaculis* 2.4–5, ed. E. Dekkers; *De res. mort.* 42. Noted by Cardman, "Tertullian," pp. 147–48; Robert M. Grant, *Miracle and Natural Law in Graeco-Roman and Early Christian Thought* (Amsterdam, 1952), p. 24; Otto Schilling, *Naturrecht und Staat nach der Lehre der alten Kirche* (Paderborn, 1914), pp. 65–66.

[25] *Adversus Iudaeos* 2, ed. A. Kroymann, where the argument is aimed against the sufficiency of the Mosaic law. See Cardman, "Tertullian," p. 146.

theology in the manner of Cicero's *De natura deorum,* beating the pagans with their own stick. When he does so, however, he also correlates man's natural knowledge of God with revelation, observing that God provides a fuller and more authoritative knowledge of Himself and His moral law in Holy Scripture.[26] Thus, while Tertullian relates the Stoic position on the subject positively and accurately, he treats it as an ancilla to Christian truth.

On other occasions he uses the same Stoic position to assault philosophy as such, unhesitatingly linking it with a fundamentally un-Stoic epistemology. The soul's natural testimony of God's existence, he says, has greater validity than philosophical reasoning, for it is found universally, even among persons with no philosophical training. Tertullian thereby implies that philosophy is irrelevant and useless as a source of information about God.[27] But, how does man acquire this natural knowledge, so superior to the quibbles of the philosophers? According to Tertullian, it springs from ideas innate in the human mind *(congenitae et ingenitae conscientiae),* a doctrine that seriously compromises the Stoic content of his position.[28] Rather than Christianizing the *consensus omnium* argument he appears to be Platonizing it.[29]

At the same time Tertullian reports the epistemology of the Stoics accurately while applauding its foundation in sense data as a useful argument against the Platonic depreciation of the senses, on the one hand, and the Epicureans' unfettered reliance on the senses, on the other. In Tertullian's mind a sensationalistic epistemology is linked with the reality of the material world. Both doctrines serve as weapons against Marcion's denial of the reality of Christ's incarnation, an error which Ter-

---

[26] *Apol.* 17.4–6, 18.4.

[27] *De test. an.* 5.1.

[28] Ibid. 5.3. This point has been noted correctly by Giuseppe Lazzati, "Il 'De natura deorum' fonte del 'De testimonio animae' di Tertulliano?" *Atene e Roma,* ser. 3, 7 (1939), 154, 160–66. On the other hand it has been ignored or misconstrued by other commentators who trace Tertullian's natural theology argument back to Stoicism; see, for example, Barnes, *Tertullian,* p. 113; Theodor Brandt, *Tertullians Ethik: Zur Erfassung der systematischen Grundanschauung* (Gütersloh, 1928), pp. 25–26; Cardman, "Tertullian," p. 149; Daniélou, *Hist. of Early Christian Doctrine,* III, 212–14; Fredouille, *Tertullien,* pp. 243–45; Richard Heinze, "Tertullians Apologeticum," *Bericht über die Verhandlungen der königlich sächsische Gesellschaft der Wissenschaft zu Leipzig,* philologisch-historische Klasse, 62 (1910), pp. 376–77; Lortz, "Vernunft und Offenbarung," *Der Katholik,* Folge 4, 11 (1913), 139–40; Klaus Oehler, "Der Consensus omnium als Kriterium der Wahrheit in der antiken Philosophie und der Patristik," *Antike und Abendland,* 10 (1961), 118–19; Franz Seyr, "Die Seelen- und Erkenntnislehre Tertullians und die Stoa," *Commentationes Vindobonenses,* 3 (1937), 51–74; Quasten, *Patrology,* II, 264–66; Vecchiotti, *La filos. di Tertulliano,* pp. 241–45, 250–54.

[29] Cf. on the other hand Lortz, *Tertullian,* I, 213, 226–48; Otto, *"Natura" und "Dispositio",* pp. 3, 17–37 and passim; Johannes Stier, *Der specielle Gottesbegriff Tertullians* (Göttingen, 1899), pp. 8–16; *Die Gottes- und Logos-Lehre Tertullians* (Göttingen, 1899), pp. 8–16.

tullian attributes to Marcion's Platonism.[30] This particular use of Stoicism to rectify a Platonizing Christology is a special case of Tertullian's more general use of the Stoic natural theology argument against heretics whose Platonism or Gnosticism inclines them to a dualistic separation of the creator God from the physical world, denying His manifest evidences in the creation.[31]

A similar motivation informs Tertullian's applications of the Stoic doctrines of the *logos*, the corporality of all beings, and the seminal reasons. In each case, when Tertullian advocates the Stoic position he does so in order to defend a Christian view of the relation between God and man, usually against Platonism or Gnosticism. He defines God the *logos* Stoically as word and reason (*sermo, ratio*) and as artificer (*artifex*), attributing these names to Zeno and Cleanthes who, he notes, identify the divine *logos* with destiny and with the spirit pervading the universe. While he emphasizes the notion that God is spirit, Tertullian's evocation of Stoic linguistic theory, not to mention the analogy he draws between God's relation with the world and the sun's relation with its own rays, which are a portion and extension of their source, makes inescapable his wish to underline God's creative will and freedom and the intimate connection between God and the material world.[32] He wants to defend this conception of God against two equally offensive ideas, one, that the world emanates from God by necessity and the other, that God withholds Himself from any direct contact with the creation. Hermagoras, in particular, is guilty of maintaining the latter view. In criticizing this position Tertullian uses the same image, the permeation of the honeycomb by the honey, that he uses elsewhere as an argument supporting the distinction between God and the world: *Stoici enim volunt deum sic per materiam decucurrisse, quomodo mel per favos* ("The Stoics think that God permeates the world in the same way as honey in the comb.")[33] In the present context, however, what he wants to show is that God and man

---

[30] *De an.* 17.1–4, 17.14. Tertullian's advocacy of Stoic sensationalism, although not its context, has also been noted by Daniélou, *Hist. of Early Christian Doctrine*, III, 387–88; Lortz, "Vernunft und Offenbarung," *Der Katholik*, Folge 4, 11 (1913), 133; Seyr, "Die Seelen- und Erkenntnislehre," *Commentationes Vindobonenses*, 3 (1937), 51–74.

[31] *Adv. Marc.* 1.3.2–3; *Adversus Valentinianos* 3.2–5, 15.1–3, ed. A. Kroymann. Claudio Moreschini, "Tertulliano tra stoicismo e platonismo," *Kerygma und Logos: Festschrift für Carl Andresen zum 70. Geburtstag*, ed. Adolf Martin Ritter (Göttingen, 1979), pp. 367–79 makes this point well but does not situate it in the broader contexts in which Tertullian makes use of these philosophies.

[32] *Apol.* 18.11–13, 21.10–14. Noted by René Braun, *"Deus Christianorum": Recherches sur le vocabulaire doctrinal de Tertullien* (Paris, 1962), pp. 385–86. On the other hand, Lortz, *Tertullian*, I, 190–91, 198 and Vecchiotti, *La filos. di Tertulliano*, pp. 155–65 have difficulty admitting the materialist emphasis here while Norris, *God and World*, pp. 113–16 has difficulty making sense of it at all.

[33] *Adv. Herm.* 44.1.

are at home in the universe and with each other, minimizing the distance between matter and spirit.

The same concern prompts Tertullian to espouse the Stoic doctrine that everything which exists is a body: *Unam omnibus formam solius corporalitatis, quae substantiae res est* ("All things have one form of simple corporeality, which is a substantial thing.")[34] In particular, the human soul must be seen as neither too rarefied, alienating it from the body, nor too gross, as Hermagoras thinks, alienating it from God. At the same time, other heretics err in supporting the Platonic notion of a purely immaterial and preexistent soul. Tertullian seeks to annihilate all these opponents with a single blow. Enlisting the aid of Zeno, Cleanthes, and Chrysippus, he describes the human soul as a breath of God *(ex dei flatu)*.[35] This formula insists simultaneously on the material nature of the soul, on its intimate substantial relationship both with the body and with God, and on its status as a created being.

Another objectionable feature of the doctrine of the soul's preexistence, for Tertullian, is that it may lead to the Gnostic idea that men can be classified as capable of enlightenment or not on the basis of their given natures. In opposing such a fatalistic and aristocratic psychology he calls upon the principle of seminal reasons, praising Seneca *saepe noster* as its source, although this is not the only argument on which he rests his case. All of man's psychic potentialities, he states, are implanted in man's soul at birth, growing with each person as he develops and providing for his spiritual progress. At the same time, man's sanctification is not automatic. Man's moral choices depend on his own free will and on the grace of God; he is not fated to develop or act in any particular way merely on the basis of his unconscious natural endowment.[36] Here Tertullian supplements the Stoic position with Christian doctrine. In the one reference in this category where he considers a specific moral choice, he also supplements his Stoicism, but this time with an example drawn from another philosophical tradition. Tertullian judges it permissible for Chris-

---

[34] Ibid. 36.4, trans. J. H. Waszink, ACW, 24 (Westminster, Md., 1956). This point has been noted by Ernest Evans, intro. to his ed. of *Adversus Praxean* (London, 1948), p. 53; Adolfo Faggi, "Il 'somatismo' o 'corporatismo' degli Stoici," *Atti della Reale Accademia delle scienze di Torino*, classe di scienze morali, storiche e filologiche, 67 (1931–32), p. 66; Meijering, *Tertullian contra Marcion*, p. 131; and Albert Warkotsch, trans., *Antike Philosophie im Urteil der Kirchenväter: Christliche Glaube im Widerstreit der Philosophie* (München, 1973), p. 89, in addition to many of the authors cited in note 11 above.

[35] *De an.* 4.1. See note 11 and also Barnes, *Tertullian*, p. 207; Brandt, *Tertullians Ethik*, pp. 43–57; Pierre Courcelle, "Deux grands courants de pensée dans la littérature latine tardive: Stoïcisme et néo-platonisme," *REL*, 42 (1965), 122–23; Harald Hagendahl, *Latin Fathers and the Classics: A Study of the Apologists, Jerome and Other Christian Writers* (Göteborg, 1958), p. 80; Quasten, *Patrology*, II, 287–89.

[36] *De an.* 20.1, 21.4–6. See also Daniélou, *Hist. of Early Christian Doctrine*, III, 221–23.

tians to wear a *pallium*, that is, to pursue a life of learning, on the grounds that they may thereby contribute as much to the common weal as they might in an active political or military career. This is certainly an authentically Stoic rationale for *otium philosophicum*, although Tertullian cites the example of Epicurus as well as that of Zeno in advocating it.[37]

Tertullian thus at times combines or complements Stoicism with ideas deriving from other sources, whether pagan or Christian, in contexts where he makes positive use of it. This is a much more noticeable and systematic characteristic of the third category of references to Stoicism in his thought. Here Tertullian applies Stoicism to the solution of Christian problems in such a way as to alter fundamentally its directionality and meaning. On some occasions his role is that of a transmitter, making available in Latin an application of Stoicism to Christianity that had already been made by his Greek Christian predecessors. On other occasions he is much more independent. His originality at times leads him to depart either from Stoicism or from the Christian doctrines he is calling upon Stoicism to defend. Although his chief antagonists in this connection are heretics he is thus led at times to assert heterodox ideas himself. The physics and psychology of the Stoa account for most of the references in this category although Tertullian adverts to ethics more frequently here than when he presents himself either as a critic or as a supporter of the Stoa.

The most important group of Stoic teachings which Tertullian alters by associating them with Christianity are the doctrines of the *logos*, the corporeity of God and of the human soul, *krasis*, or the Stoic conception of mixture, and the *hegemonikon* or ruling principle of the soul. Several kinds and degrees of change are involved. In the first place, not all of these themes are correlatives of each other in Stoic thought but Tertullian treats them as an intimately connected complex of ideas. In some contexts he uses this complex of ideas to criticize the Platonic and Gnostic depreciation of matter insofar as it leads to heretical belief on such subjects as God's relation to the created world, man's ethical attitude toward the body, and man's posthumous survival. These topics may be thought of as legitimate issues found in Stoicism itself that have parallels in Christianity, although the Stoics did not necessarily use the ideas that Tertullian does to support their position on them. In other contexts he goes still further, drawing on these Stoic doctrines as analytical tools for treating central problems of Christian dogma, such as Trinitarian theology, the hypostatic union, man's free will, and the mode by which the

---

[37] *De pallio* 5.4–5, ed. S. Costanza (Napoli, 1968). Noted by Barnes, *Tertullian*, pp. 230–31. Johannes Geffcken, *Kynika und Verwandtes* (Heidelberg, 1909), pp. 53–138 interprets this passage as a Stoicizing satire on luxurious clothing.

sacraments operate, issues that have no real parallels in Stoic philosophy. It is, indeed, the integral connections among these theological topics that inspires his selection and association of the Stoic ideas that he
draws on to discuss and defend them. But, this procedure sometimes results in his muddying of the waters of Stoicism and Christianity alike.

Tertullian's connection of the Stoic doctrine of the *logos* with the doctrine of God's corporeal nature is an instance of his use of Stoic physics
to explain how God creates the material world and how Christ, both in
His incarnate state and as He proceeds from the Father before the incarnation, can be consubstantial with the Father and equal to Him. This
twofold concern lies behind his attack on Praxeas, whom he excoriates as
a Gnostic and a Monarchian: *Quis enim negabit deum corpus esse, etsi deus spi-*
ritus est? ("For who will deny that God is body, although God is a spirit?") [38]
This rhetorical question is more than an apologetic sally. Tertullian
seems to be firmly convinced of the Stoic principle that everything that
is, is a body. He seems genuinely incapable of conceiving of a being that
is purely spiritual. This belief in God's corporeity, at the same time, provides him with a means of stressing the intimacy between God and creation and the dignity of matter as a suitable medium through which to
manifest Himself in the salvation of mankind. The nodal link in this association of ideas is the person and work of Christ, which in turn serves
as a means of explaining the human constitution and man's ultimate redemption and resurrection. [39]

The two key Stoic concepts on which Tertullian bases his Christology
are *logos* and *krasis*. [40] *Logos*, as he is well aware, has both Biblical and
Stoic associations. He evokes both senses of the term in discussing the
nature of Christ. He wants to emphasize the consubstantiality of the Son
with the Father over against heretics who reject the principle that the

---

[38] *Adversus Praxean* 7.7–9, ed. A. Kroymann and E. Evans, trans. Evans (London, 1948),
p. 138. See also Braun, *"Deus Christianorum"*, pp. 167–97; Moingt, *Théologie trinitaire*, II,
301–04; Norris, *God and World*, pp. 112–13; Roberts, *Theology of Tertullian*, p. 127; Stier,
Der specialle Gottesbegriff, pp. 30–38; *Die Gottes- und Logos-Lehre*, pp. 30–38; G. C. Stead,
"Divine Substance in Tertullian," *JTS*, n.s. 14 (1963), 46–66. Otto, *"Natura" und "Dis-*
positio", pp. 38–43 is unconvincing in his claim that Tertullian is trying to defend God's
transcendence at this point.

[39] The connections among these doctrines have been drawn well by Daniélou, *Hist.*
of Early Christian Doctrine, III, 215–21; Gérard Verbeke, *L'Évolution de la doctrine du pneuma*
du Stoïcisme à S. Augustin (Paris, 1945), pp. 440–511.

[40] The best general study of this subject is Raniero Cantalamessa, *La cristologia di Ter-*
tulliano (Friburgo, 1962), pp. 11–13, 18–27, 52–54, 192–93 and passim. Moingt, *Théologie*
trinitaire, I, 36–48 provides a detailed analysis of the literature pertaining to the Stoic
influence on Tertullian's Trinitarian thought. An excellent guide to the different concepts of mixture in Greek philosophy, including *krasis*, and their use by Greek Christian
thinkers in dealing with the hypostatic union is given by Wolfson, *Philos. of the Church*
Fathers, I, 372–92.

fullness of divinity dwells in Christ. At the same time, by drawing upon the Stoic philosophy of language and the relation between the sun and its rays in describing the procession of the Word he identifies the divinity of Christ with a divine nature that is itself corporeal, however rarefied its substance.[41] Tertullian's belief in the corporeity of God makes it easy for him to conceive of a Christ Whose divine nature is likewise corporeal, although this is scarcely an orthodox position. The fact that he sees Christ's divine nature as corporeal also simplifies the problem of explaining how Christ's divine and human natures can be combined in a single person. Here the idea of *krasis* comes readily to hand, providing him with a rationale for a concept of mixture in which two material substances coexist in the same space at the same time without losing their own distinct natures or forming a new *tertium quid*. The two natures of Christ, Tertullian says, are not confused but yet conjoined in one person *(non confusum sed coniunctum, in una persona deum et hominem Iesum)*; the incarnate Son is man mingled with God *(homo deo mixtus)*.[42] Thus, he argues, it is impossible to reject either the divinity of Christ or His humanity, the latter point being the thrust of Tertullian's *De carne Christi*, directed against Marcion,[43] while the former point is the thrust of his apology against the Monarchianism of Praxeas and of the *Apologeticum* directed against the pagans who see the incarnation as a scandal or as a contradiction in terms.

The principle of *krasis* not only accounts for the hypostatic union of divine and human natures in Christ, understood as the mixture of two different grades of corporeal existence. It also provides the foundation for Tertullian's explanation of Christ's saving action in the flesh, from His crucifixion to His resurrection, as well as of His communication of His redemption to mankind. Human psychology, the union of a corporeal soul with a corporeal body, can be analogized to Christ's nature and mode of operation. The dignity of matter that is involved on both sides of the analogy makes plausible a Christian life that enjoins physical sacraments and ascetic sacrifices as aids to salvation. Since the divine nature itself is corporeal, its capacity to act by means of material sacra-

---

[41] *Apol.* 21.10–14. See also Anathon Aall, *Der Logos: Geschichte seiner Entwicklung in der griechischen Philosophie und der christlichen Litteratur* (Leipzig, 1896–99), II, 371–80; Braun, *"Deus Christianorum"*, pp. 256–72; Evans, intro. to his trans. of *Adv. Prax.*, pp. 32, 37; Moingt, *Théologie trinitaire*, I, ch. 2, 4; II, 358; III, 1019–24, 1026–62.

[42] *Adv. Prax.* 27.37–39; *Apol.* 21.14; *De carne Christi* 15. Noted by Braun, *"Deus Christianorum"*, pp. 313–14; Cantalamessa, *La cristologia*, pp. 135–50; Ernest Evans, intro. to his trans. of *De carne Christi* (London, 1956), pp. vii–viii.

[43] *De carne Christi* 5.25. Cantalamessa, *La cristologia*, pp. 69–70 overinterprets the Stoicism of this treatise, seeing the doctrine of seminal reasons as the rationale for the incarnation.

ments is perfectly appropriate. And, in so acting, God spiritually transforms the Christian with no suspicion of pantheism. At the same time, unless the body were good and worthy, there would be no merit in disciplining it or offering it up to God. The *krasis* of two corporeal natures in the union of man's body and soul also provides Tertullian with a basis for defending the doctrine of man's physical resurrection. He links this doctrine with the Stoic idea of the *hegemonikon*, which he calls the *principalitas*, in explaining the harmonious governance of all of man's intellectual, spiritual, and vital functions by the ruling principle, located in the heart.[44]

The corporality of the human soul thus follows logically from Tertullian's conception of the corporality of God's nature and of the nature of Christ as a *krasis* of two types of bodies. Tertullian expressly traces this doctrine to Zeno, Cleanthes, and Chrysippus.[45] He cites a number of arguments which the Stoics themselves had offered in support of this view, derived from the psychosomatic interdependence of body and soul evident in common experience,[46] and adds a number of Biblical arguments that point in the same direction, such as the existence of dreams, visions, and prophesies.[47] The soul, he urges, has the physical attributes which the Stoics saw as inherent in bodies, including external form, three-dimensional extension in space, and color.[48] Tertullian sums up his position on the soul most fully and concisely in the *De anima:*

> Definimus animam dei flatus natam, immortalem, corporalem, effigiatam, substantia simplicem, de suo sapientem, varie procedentem, liberam arbitrii, accidentis obnoxiam, per ingenia mutabilem, rationalem, dominatricem, divinitricem, ex una redundantem.[49]

---

[44] *De an.* 12.16; *De patientia* 13, ed. J. G. P. Borleffs; *De res. mort.* 7.1–8.6, 15.1–8, 17.2–9, 33.10, 53.7–10. The best study of the latter work is Cardman, "Tertullian." See also Paolo Siniscalco, *Ricerche sul "De resurrectione" di Tertulliano,* Verba Seniorum, n.s. 6 (Roma, 1966), pp. 112–36, 172–77. On the role of the flesh in general in Tertullian's view of redemption see also Otto, *"Natura" und "Dispositio",* pp. 140–53.

[45] *De an.* 5.3–4, 5.6.

[46] *De an.* 5.5, 6.5–7.

[47] *De an.* 7.1–4, 9.1, 9.3–4, 43.2–12, 46.4–11, 47.2, 49.3. On divination see Lortz, *Tertullian,* I, 264–65.

[48] *De an.* 9.1, 9.3–5.

[49] *De an.* 22.2, trans. J. H. Waszink (Amsterdam, 1947). See also *Adv. Marc.* 5.15.8. The best treatment of Tertullian on the soul is Heinrich Karpp, *Probleme altchristlicher Anthropologie: Biblische Anthropologie und philosophische Psychologie bei den Kirchenvätern des dritten Jahrhunderts* (Gütersloh, 1950), pp. 41–91. Other good studies include Alès, *La théologie de Tertullien,* pp. 62–63, 120, 137–38; Cardman, "Tertullian," pp. 1–2, 39–41; A. J. Festugière, "La composition et l'esprit du *De anima* de Tertullien," *RSPT,* 33 (1949), 129–61; Roberts, *Theology of Tertullian,* pp. 154–56; Seyr, "Die Seelen- und Erkenntnislehre," *Commentationes Vindobonenses,* 3 (1937), 51–74; Waszink, intro. to his ed. of *De anima,* pp. 8*–14*; Vecchiotti, *La filos. di Tertulliano,* pp. 394–406, 411–16, 424–29.

The soul, therefore, we declare to be born of the breath of God, immortal, corporeal, possessed of a definite form, simple in substance, conscious of itself, developing in various ways, free in its choices, liable to accidental change, variable in disposition, rational, supreme, gifted with foresight, developed out of the original soul.

Free will is one of the qualities which Tertullian joins the Stoics in attributing to the human soul. Yet, it is this very endowment of man which prompts Tertullian to reject the psychology of the Stoa on one critical point, the idea that the human *logos* is a fragment of the divine *logos,* and is hence constubstantial with God. In contrast Tertullian draws a distinction between God's spirit *(spiritus)* and His breath *(flatus, afflatus)* and insists that man is born of His breath, not His spirit. Tertullian's emphasis on this point prevents him from falling into pantheism. But this is not his reason for taking the stand he takes. Rather, it is his desire to assign to man and not to God the freedom to sin and the responsibility for human choices that inspires him to stress the substantial difference between divine and human nature.[50] While he feels free to integrate man's soul into the rest of the cosmos in citing the cyclical alternations of the seasons and the myth of the Phoenix as an argument for the resurrection of the body,[51] he draws the line, for ethical not for physical reasons, at the full Stoic identification of man and God.

Tertullian's treatment of ethical topics themselves in this final category of his thought is heavily dependent on Stoicism, while at the same time he transforms the Stoic themes he uses in the light of Christian values and concerns. Scholars have occasionally overinterpreted Tertullian's ethics in this connection, either attributing to Stoicism ideas that are ethical commonplaces,[52] or seeing him as a Stoic rigorist in his adherance to the norm of life in accordance with nature,[53] or treating him as an advocate of a view of the world so corrupted by the devil that all

---

[50] *De an.* 11.2–6; *Adv. Marc.* 2.9. Meijering, *Tertullian contra Marcion,* pp. 113–14 and Roberts, *Theology of Tertullian,* p. 154 have commented on but have missed this point.

[51] *De res. mort.* 12.1–9. See Cardman, "Tertullian," pp. 44–45.

[52] Fredouille, *Tertullien,* pp. 14, 162–63, 165, 170, 438 does this for the *De exhortatione castitatis,* the *De ira,* and the *De pudicitia;* Daniélou, *Hist. of Early Christian Doctrine,* III, 324 and Michel Spanneut, *Tertullien et les premiers moralistes africains* (Gembloux, 1969), p. 40 do it for the *De patientia;* and Carlo Tibiletti, "Stoicismo nell'Ad martyras di Tertulliano," *Augustinianum,* 15 (1975), 309–23 does it for the *Ad martyras.*

[53] This point has been made in general by Stephan Otto "Der Mensch als Bild Gottes bei Tertullian," *Münchener theologische Zeitschrift,* 10 (1959), 278–82; *"Natura" und "Dispositio",* pp. 44–73; and, with specific reference to Tertullian's lost work on marriage, reconstructed from St. Jerome, by Carlo Tibiletti, "Un opuscolo perduto di Tertulliano: Ad amicum philosophum," *Atti dell'Accademia delle scienze di Torino,* classe di scienze morali, storiche e fililogiche, 95 (1960–61), pp. 122–66. On the reconstruction of this text see also Paolo Frassinetti, "Gli scritti matrimoniali di Seneca e Tertulliano," *Rendiconti del Istituto lombardo di scienze e lettere,* classe di lettere e scienze morali e storiche, 88 (1955), pp. 151–88.

appeals to natural ethics have to be rejected.[54] Tertullian's handling of
Stoic ethics cannot really be described in any of these ways. It is true
that he often counsels asceticism; but this position stems from his conception of the flesh as good and as hence a worthy sacrifice to offer to
God, not from the Stoic definition of reason as good and the a-rational
as either evil or indifferent. He sometimes presents Stoicism as consonant with Christian ethics, but only to a limited degree. For Tertullian,
virtue is never an end in itself. The Christian rationale for ethical choices
is the only decisive one. Also, he sometimes abandons the Stoic norm of
virtue as life in accordance with nature, urging that Christian duty transcends natural goods and obligations.

The best example of a work in which Tertullian presents Stoicism as
ancillary to Christian virtue and then proceeds to assimilate Stoicism to
Christianity to the point where it retains none of its own integrity is his
De patientia. Tertullian begins by observing that all the philosophical
schools have praised patience as a virtue, despite their other differences.[55] But the model for Christian patience is to be found in the patience of God and the long-suffering of Christ, not in the teachings of the
schools.[56] Furthermore, he adds, as a virtue patience does not spring from
man himself, although he must manifest it in both mind and body.
Rather, it can be understood as a function of the virtue of charity, which
is a gift of the Holy Spirit,[57] Who endows man with equanimity in order
to frustrate the devil, the source of impatience.[58] Here we see Tertullian
emptying the virtue of patience of its autarchic Stoic meaning as a correct and rational judgment enforced by the will and substituting for it a
heteronomous supernatural explanation of its motivation and dynamics.

Tertullian's De corona is another example of his complete inversion of
the Stoic structure of values. The issue he addresses in this work is
whether Christians should serve in the army and wear the crowns or
chaplets of flowers awarded by victorious generals. Tertullian says no,
on two grounds. His first argument, an instance of Montanist extremism, asserts that all things are forbidden to Christians that are not expressly permitted by Scripture.[59] The second is a natural law argument,
a Stoic strategy for which he cites the authority of St. Paul[60] but which

---

[54] Otto, "Natura" und "Dispositio", pp. 96–135; Roberts, Theology of Tertullian, p. 220.
[55] De pat. 1. A good analysis of this work is provided by Fredouille, Tertullien, pp.
363–402. C. Rambaux, "La composition du De patientia de Tertullien," Revue de philologie,
53 (1979), 80–91 sees no Stoic ingredients in this treatise.
[56] De pat. 3.
[57] De pat. 12–13.
[58] De pat. 11.
[59] De corona 2.4, ed. A. Kroymann.
[60] De cor. 6.1–3.

he turns upside down. The natural function of the flowers out of which the crowns are fashioned, he notes, is to please the senses of sight and smell. Now a man cannot see or smell flowers if they are on his head. Thus, he concludes, the wearing of floral crowns is contrary to nature and immoral.[61] Here we see Tertullian invoking the Stoic *secundum naturam vivere* criterion to defend a concept of duty in which a Christian's moral obligations, understood in the narrowest of Scriptural terms, militate against the civic responsibilities which the Stoics held were incumbent on all men by nature.

A final example, and one of Tertullian's most interesting ethical treatises, is his *De cultu feminarum*. Here too we find him borrowing the Stoic ethical criterion of virtue as life in accordance with nature and transforming it. In so doing Tertullian invents a new genre of Christian hortatory literature, cosmetic theology as addressed to women. The Stoic idea to which he harks back is the principle that it is immoral to improve on one's natural appearance. While in theory the Stoics had aimed this message at men and women alike, in practice they had directed it primarily to men. The sage, they taught, leaves his hair uncut and his beard unshaven. Outside of the fact that he proclaims his commitment to wisdom and virtue by leaving his natural appearance alone, the chief importance that the Stoics attached to the sage's grooming lay in his impact on other men. For the rigorists among the Stoics, the shaggy, bearded sage proclaimed his detachment from the ruling tonsorial fashions as *adiaphora*. For the moderates, conformity to the ruling fashions was preferred as a public relations gesture. Messiness could be just as much an affectation as a too *soigné* look, while a conventional appearance would enable the sage to avoid losing his audience. Although they also criticized the female propensity for cosmetics, dyed hair, and elaborate clothing on grounds of modesty and moderation, the Stoics, whether rigorists or not, focused their attention on men and on the ethical and pedagogical impression that their presentation of self would make on other men.

Tertullian's *De cultu feminarum* at first seems to proclaim his allegiance to the Stoic criterion of nature. Clothing dyed with precious colors is unnatural and hence immoral, he asserts; if God wanted wool to be blue or purple He would have created sheep with fleeces in those colors.[62] Similarly, warming to his subject, he charges that the use of cosmetics and hair dye by women is unnatural and impious as well as injurious to the health and an unsuccessful way of trying to mask one's age.[63] But

---

[61] *De cor.* 5.1–4, 7.1–2.
[62] *De cultu feminarum* 1.8.2, ed. A. Kroymann.
[63] *De cultu fem.* 2.5.2–4, 2.6.1–4.

Tertullian is not content to chastise women for the vanity or folly that inspires them to try to improve on nature. His main argument rests on the point that feminine beauty provokes masculine lust.[64] From a Stoic standpoint, if a woman is beautiful by nature, her beauty is admissible and good. For Tertullian, on the other hand, women ought to be ashamed of their beauty. In trying to explain why he refers to a Jewish apocryphal tradition according to which the fallen angels, attracted by the charms of the daughters of men, copulated with them and taught them the arts of coquetry.[65] Women are morally at fault for having sinned with the fallen angels and they ought to do penance for the attractions with which nature endows them. A modest appearance, without improvements superadded to nature, does not suffice for them. Rather, Tertullian says, women should take pains to conceal their natural attractions.[66] For women, it is not merely improving on nature that is immoral; in their case, nature as such is unacceptable as a moral criterion. More or less as an afterthought Tertullian also condemns men who enhance their natural appearance in order to appeal to women.[67] But he does not exhort men to a penitential cloaking of their masculine charms. For men, the norm of nature may be followed without hesitation but for women this is not allowed.

For all its ostensible debts to Stoicism, Tertullian's argument in the *De cultu feminarum* thus ends by turning Stoic ethics inside out. He rejects a number of its central premises, such as the moral equality of men and women and the assessment of moral acts in terms of the agent's inner intentionality. Aiming his attack chiefly against women, he sees them as passive beings who can be defined in purely sexual terms. Their natural attributes are not important in their own right but only insofar as they cause men to act. Tertullian sees the natural condition of women as intrinsically flawed, not on account of any conscious choices they may have made but because of the inadvertant erotic effect that they have on the opposite sex. Men may sin when they improve on nature but women sin whether they improve on nature or adhere to it. Tertullian's cosmetic theology is a substantive departure from Stoic ethics. His *De cultu femi-*

---

[64] *De cultu fem.* 2.21. One might contrast Tertullian here with the "beauty unadorned" theme found in classical love poems, in which the lady is enjoined by the speaker not to improve on nature because her natural attractions are sufficient or because she is more attractive *au naturel*, advice that is designed to emphasize her erotic appeal, not to minimize it. On this tradition see Archibald A. Day, *The Origins of Latin Love-Elegy* (Oxford, 1938), pp. 39–47.

[65] *De cultu fem.* 1.1.1–2. On this apocryphal tradition see Daniélou, *Hist. of Early Christian Doctrine*, III, 164, 167.

[66] *De cultu fem.* 2.2.5, 2.4.1.

[67] *De cultu fem.* 2.8.1–3.

narum may reflect the influence of the anti-feminist tradition in classical literature but its chief inspiration is an anti-feminist attitude that goes back to a Biblical, if apocryphal source, an attitude destined to have a long future ahead of it in Christian ascetic and hortatory literature.

Several conclusions emerge from our consideration of Stoicism in Tertullian's thought. The areas of Stoic philosophy which interest him the most are physics and anthropology. He shows an accurate knowledge of the principle of the corporeity of all beings, including God and the human soul, the *logos, krasis,* and the *hegemonikon,* and a general agreement with these teachings except for the Stoic identification of the divine and human *logoi.* He usually treats these themes positively, whether as an extrinsic support for the Christian faith or as a means of formulating and explicating central Christian doctrines. His adherance to some of these ideas, indeed, inclines him to depart from Christian orthodoxy at some points despite his own zealous attacks on heresy. Tertullian's use of Stoic epistemology and ethics is much more limited. He does not seem to have grasped the inner logic of these branches of the Stoic system and he is quite likely to report the ideas in question inaccurately or to alter them significantly. Good examples of this procedure are his association of Stoic empiricism with the non-Stoic doctrine of innate ideas, an association that, in turn, restricts the Stoic dimensions of his natural theology. Another case is the freedom with which he uses the Stoic criterion of virtue as life in accordance with nature.

The particular uses to which Tertullian puts his Stoicism are dictated by the exigencies of the contexts in which they occur. Since he is not interested in developing a systematic theology or a systematic position on Stoicism, he should not be read as if he were working toward either of these goals. He is just as likely to criticize Stoicism as a source of heresy and to use it in a positive if ancillary manner or to combine it with Christian doctrine in such a way as to alter its essential meaning. No one of these orientations is predominant. Tertullian's works thus made available in Latin Christian thought not only a vocabulary of Stoic concepts but also a range of ways in which a theologian might use them. His Latin Christian contemporaries and successors had his own example to draw upon as well as the pagan Latin authors and the Greek Christian sources on which Tertullian himself based his thought. It remains to be seen just how formative Tertullian's approaches to Stoicism actually proved to be.

II. MINUCIUS FELIX

There is no doubt whatever that Minucius Felix (ca. 200–45) was profoundly influenced by Stoicism.[68] In his only known work, the dialogue *Octavius*, the Christian interlocutor by that name draws heavily on Stoicism to support the claim that Christianity is a reasonable faith, over against the position of Caecilius, cast as an Academic skeptic, who offers a conventional defense of polytheism. The differences between Minucius and Tertullian in tone and technique are striking.[69] In choosing to portray the pagan opposition in terms of skepticism and conventional piety rather than in terms of the weightier objections that positive philosophy could level against the Christian faith, Minucius simplifies considerably the task of disarming that opposition, while at the same time making it possible for himself to present his apology in a graceful and elegant style. This rhetorical decision makes it unnecessary for him to address the serious philosophical questions raised by a revealed theology as such or by the paradoxes of the central dogmas of Christianity. Since he chooses

---

[68] There is marked scholarly consensus on this point, although there is some debate as to whether Cicero or Seneca served as Minucius' chief source. See, in general, Aall, *Der Logos*, II, 324–34; Gaston Boissier, *La fin du paganisme: Étude sur les dernières luttes religieuses en occident au quatrième siècle*, 4me éd. (Paris, 1903), I, 288–89; Daniélou, *Hist. of Early Christian Doctrine*, III, 189–207 who, however, tends to overinterpret the Stoic content in Minucius; Grant, *Miracle and Natural Law*, pp. 24–25; G. Quispel, "Anima naturaliter christiana," *Latomus*, 10 (1951), 163–69; Roberts, *Theology of Tertullian*, pp. 56–57; Schilling, *Naturrecht*, pp. 64–65; Spanneut, *Tertullien*, p. 57. Scholars emphasizing Cicero as Minucius' main source include Carl Becker, "Der 'Octavius' des Minucius Felix: Heidnische Philosophie und frühchristliche Apologetik," *Sitzungsberichte der bayerische Akademie der Wissenschaften*, philosophisch-historische Klasse, 2 (München, 1967), pp. 12–19; Ernst Behr, *Der Octavius des M. Minucius Felix in seinem Verhältnisse zu Cicero's Büchern de natura deorum* (Gera, 1870); G. W. Clarke, intro. to his trans. of *Octavius*, ACW, 39 (New York, 1974), pp. 26–29, 136 n. 18; Sisto Colombo, "Osservazioni sulla composizione letteraria e sulle fonti di M. Minucio Felice," *Didaskaleion*, 3 (1914), 79–121; Ferdinand Kotek, "Anklänge an Ciceros 'De natura deorum' bei Minucius Felix und Tertullian," *Jahres-Bericht des kais. kön. Ober-Gymnasiums zu den Schotten in Wien*, 1900–01 (Wien, 1901), pp. 3–49; Icilio Vecchiotti, *La filosofia politica di Minucio Felice: Un altro colpa di sonda nella storia del cristianesimo primitivo* (Urbino, 1973), pp. 36, 124–27, 195, 220. Scholars emphasizing Seneca as his main source include Franz Xaver Burger, *Minucius Felix und Seneca* (München, 1904); Courcelle, "Deux grands courants," *REL*, 42 (1965), 129–30; "Virgile et l'immanence divine chez Minucius Felix," *Mullus: Festschrift Theodor Klauser*, *Jahrbuch für Antike und Christentum*, Ergänzungsband, 1 (Münster-Westfalen, 1964), pp. 34–42, where he also sees Vergil as a possible intermediary; Paul Faider, *Études sur Sénèque* (Gand, 1921), pp. 84–85. Those who grant equal honors to Cicero and Seneca include Harry James Baylis, *Minucius Felix and His Place among the Early Fathers of the Latin Church* (London, 1928), pp. 108, 124–43; Jean Beaujeu, intro. to his ed. and trans. of *Octavius*, Budé (Paris, 1964), pp. xxxii–xxxvii; Rudolf Beutler, *Philosophie und Apologie bei Minucius Felix* (Weida i. Thür., 1936); Quasten, *Patrology*, II, 158–59; Gerald H. Rendall, "Minucius Felix," *Church Quarterly Review*, 128 (1939), 128.

[69] There has been some debate on the question of whether Minucius' *Octavius* antedates Tertullian's *Apology* and whether Minucius used Tertullian as a source. For a review of the literature see Beaujeu, intro. to his ed. and trans. of *Octavius*, pp. xxxviii, xliv–lxvii; Becker, "Der 'Octavius' des Minucius Felix," pp. 74–97; Clarke, intro. to his trans. of *Octavius*, pp. 9–10.

deliberately to write in the genre of a *Protrepticus,* he can present Stoicism quite simply as a doctrine that harmonizes with Christianity, selecting those aspects of it that point the pagan toward the Gospel, while avoiding any consideration of the precise nature and limits of Stoicism as an *ancilla fidei.*[70] Finally, since he does not discuss dogmatic specifics, Minucius has no need to essay a reformulation or defense of Christian doctrine in philosophical terms.[71] His use of Stoicism is therefore narrower and at the same time more general than Tertullian's. Tertullian sometimes asserts that Stoicism is consonant with Christianity and that it can serve to correct pagan errors, but this is only one of a number of positions that he takes toward the Stoa. For Minucius this stance is the sum total of his apology. Despite these differences in range and emphasis the two apologists have a number of things in common. Skillful debaters, neither relies exclusively on Stoicism to make his case. Both draw primarily on Stoic physics and natural theology. And, for Minucius even more than for Tertullian, Stoicism is capable of performing the tasks he assigns to it because it signifies, both to the author and to his audience, an accepted body of wisdom about man and the universe.

The speech that Minucius gives to his Christian interlocutor Octavius can be subdivided into two parts. In the first he defends monotheism, appealing initially to reason, then to authority, and finally to a negative argument against polytheism. The position that Minucius advances in this section of his apology supports Christianity, to be sure, but it would also support any other version of monotheism. He draws upon Stoicism in all three subsections of this part of Octavius' speech, diverging from it only at one point. In the second part of his speech Octavius justifies a number of beliefs and practices peculiar to Christianity and exculpates Christians from erroneous or irrelevant charges that the pagans have leveled against them. Here, he relies somewhat less exclusively on Stoic arguments.

The Stoic doctrines of *consensus omnium,* divine providence, theodicy, and allegorical theology arm Minucius for his first sally. All men, he notes, possess reason and are capable of attaining wisdom and arriving at a natural knowledge of God through a consideration of the beauty, order, and harmonious coordination of the universe, which testify to the existence of an intelligent, benevolent, and provident creator.[72] This cre-

---

[70] This point has been well made by Baylis, *Minucius Felix,* ch. 5 and Beaujeu, intro. to his ed. and trans. of *Octavius,* pp. xiv–xix, lxxix–xciv.

[71] Cf. the overenthusiastic efforts to depict Minucius as an exponent of revealed theology by Becker, "Der 'Octavius'," pp. 65–74 and V. Carlier, "Minucius Félix et Sénèque," *Le Musée Belge,* 1 (1897), 258–93.

[72] Marcus Minucius Felix, *Octavius* 16.5–6, 17.3–11, 18.1–7, ed. Beaujeu.

ator, he adds, concerns Himself with His creation, although He is invisible, intangible, and infinite, transcending the capacity of the human mind to fathom,[73] a conception of God that takes Minucius away from the Stoic identification of God with the material universe and the human *logos*. Nonetheless, he proceeds to buttress this natural theology argument with an appeal to authority. He relies heavily on the Stoics among the poets and philosopher he cites, although they are not his only witnesses. He observes that Zeno, Chrysippus, and Cleanthes held that God is a reasonable and providential being, the soul of the natural world, composed of aether, equivalent with fate or necessity, Who can also be regarded as the natural law that serves as the first principle of all things. He adds that Zeno showed that the gods of the popular pantheon were merely personifications of the one God.[74] This point serves as Minucius' logical transition to the negative side of his argument, where he advances the Stoic position that the gods are allegorizations of natural forces,[75] urging at the same time that Rome owed her success not to the gods but to the audacious and even unscrupulous actions of men.[76]

In moving to the second part of Octavius' speech, where he defends beliefs and practices specific to Christianity as such, Minucius calls upon the Stoic doctrines of God's presence in the world, the cycle of *ekpyrosis* and *diakosmesis*, the moral equality of all men, and the idea of virtue as true liberty. He attributes these ideas to the Stoa on only one occasion. Minucius' recourse to other kinds of arguments in this part of the dialogue can be seen most clearly in his ruling that Caecilius' charge of immorality against the Christians is inadmissible because it is based on heresay evidence, a lawyer's point.[77] The fact that the Christians do not use temples or shrines, he notes, can be justified in the light of the principle that God dwells within the world and man, thus obviating the need for special buildings set aside for ritual purposes.[78] Minucius uses the Stoic theory of the cyclical conflagration of the cosmos to rationalize the Christian belief in the eventual end of the *saeculum* and the resurrection of each individual Christian,[79] although he agrees with Tertullian that the Stoics originally borrowed this idea from the Old Testament. His only nod in the direction of Stoic ethics occurs in the context of his argument

---

[73] *Oct.* 18.8.

[74] *Oct.* 19.1–20.2. On God as the bond of the universe in Minucius see Michael Lapidge, "A Stoic Metaphor in Late Latin Poetry: The Binding of the Universe," *Latomus*, 39 (1980), 823.

[75] *Oct.* 20.3–24.8.

[76] *Oct.* 25.1–2, 26.1–27.8.

[77] *Oct.* 28.1–31.4.

[78] *Oct.* 31.7–9, 32.1–6.

[79] *Oct.* 34.1–12, 35.1–36.2. This point is disputed by Becker, "Der 'Octavius'," pp. 51–52.

that Christians are credible exponents of truth and goodness despite their lack of wealth and social position. Here, he states that all men are morally equal and that virtue alone confers true nobility. In particular, the Christians' detachment from wealth can be seen as an expression of the autarchy of the sage and his consequent freedom from the vicissitudes of fortune.[80] However, Minucius does take pains at this juncture to distinguish his own ethical position from that of the Stoa by observing that the Christian does not regard virtue as an end in itself but as a means to happiness in the next life.[81]

There are, then, a few departures from Stoicism in Minucius' apology, but they are relatively minor. The rhetorical strategy which he adopts leads him to emphasize the parallels between Stoicism and Christianity, parallels that he makes as overt as possible while ignoring the differences between those two bodies of thought. This same rhetorical strategy also informs his selection of Stoic doctrines and the relatively superficial manner in which he treats them. His apology resonates with arguments familiar to readers of the pagan Latin authors of a Stoicizing bent. These literary and substantive reminiscences of classical writers such as Cicero and Seneca are a deliberate attempt on Minucius' part to insert Christianity into the mainstream of the culture possessed by the educated Romans he chose to address. The fact that this kind of apologetic stance was plausible to Minucius is eloquent testimony to the place that Stoicism enjoyed in his own day as a recognized body of philosophical wisdom.

III. St. Cyprian

Cyprian, who served as bishop of Carthage from 249 to 258, is the first Latin Christian author in our story who held office in the ecclesiastical hierarchy. During his episcopacy the Church suffered imperial persecution and a schism under the leadership of Novatian. The same years witnessed an outbreak of plague in Cyprian's own diocese. He thus felt called upon to consider administrative problems and to produce works of consolation and exhortation for his flock. Cyprian's debt to Stoicism has been rather exaggerated. A number of scholars have seen Stoic influence in his treatise on patience,[82] his ecclesiology,[83] his views on the

---

[80] *Oct.* 36.3–38.7.

[81] *Oct.* 38.4.

[82] See Edward White Benson, *Cyprian: His Life, His Times, His Work* (New York, 1897), pp. 440–48; Courcelle, "Deux grands courants," *REL*, 42 (1965), 123; Joseph H. Fichter, *Saint Cecil Cyprian: Early Defender of the Faith* (St. Louis, 1942), p. 182; Quasten, *Patrology*, II, 359; Spanneut, *Tertullien*, pp. 95–96, 98; Carl Ziwsa, "Entstehung und Zweck der Schrift Cyprians 'de bono patientia'," *Festschrift Johannes Vahlen zum siebenzigsten Geburtstag gewidmet von seinen Schülern* (Berlin, 1900), pp. 543–49.

[83] Daniélou, *Hist. of Early Christian Doctrine*, III, 436; Oehler, "Der Consensus omnium," *Antike und Abendland*, 10 (1961), 120–23.

coming apocalypse,[84] and, in an extremely uncritical fashion, in virtually everything he wrote.[85] The ideas to which these assessments refer are commonplaces with no special Stoic coloration. There are actually only three works of Cyprian where authentic Stoic material may be found, his *De habitu virginum*, his *De mortalitate*, and one of his letters. He draws exclusively on Stoic ethics in these works, agreeing with Stoicism in two of them and disagreeing sharply with it in the third. Cyprian's dependence on the Stoic ideas he cites is as superficial as it is limited. He invariably inserts his Stoic references into a basically Scriptural argument, in no sense relying on them to make his point.

In its genre Cyprian's *De habitu virginum* is cousin to Tertullian's *De cultu feminarum*. It is likewise derived ultimately from the Stoics' cosmetic theology. Cyprian's treatise on female adornment is much more narrowly Christian than Tertullian's, since it was written not for women in general but for women living as consecrated virgins. At the same time, Cyprian expresses a much more genuinely Stoic respect for the idea of nature as an ethical criterion. Most of his case is based on Scriptural injunctions to womanly modesty, which he applies to the specific vocational commitment of the women he addresses, personal ornamentation being particularly unseemly for women vowed to celibacy. He does, however, offer one argument based on the norm of nature. Cosmetics and hair dye, he notes, are immoral because they seek to improve on nature, which is an offense at once against the God Who created nature and against the truth.[86]

The *De mortalitate* was addressed to a much wider audience, the entire Christian community of Carthage, to console them during a plague. Cyprian adverts to two Stoic ethical principles in this treatise, the tranquillity resulting from the conceptualization of passing woes such as plagues as *adiaphora* and the *magnitudo animi* that enables the wise man to confront and to overcome tests of virtue of this type. He embeds both principles in an argument that is thoroughly Christian, both in terms of the Biblical citations with which it is replete and in terms of his subordination of the Stoic virtues he enjoins to a prayerful Christian faith and hope in the life to come and to an understanding of Christian suffering as a redemptive participation in the cross of Christ. Thus, Cyprian goes well beyond the Stoic conception of natural virtue as its own definition, source, and reward.[87]

---

[84] Daniélou, *Hist. of Early Christian Doctrine*, III, 246, 255–56.

[85] Hugo Koch, *Cyprianische Untersuchungen* (Bonn, 1926), pp. 286–313.

[86] St. Cyprian, *De habitu virginum* 15.16, ed. G. Hartel in *Opera omnia*, CSEL, 3:1–3 (Vienna, 1868–71).

[87] *De mortalitate* 14.225–229, ed. M. Simonetti, CC, 3A (Turnhout, 1976). Noted by Giorgio Barbero, "Seneca e la conversione di San Cipriano," *Rivista di studi classici*, 10

In the foregoing cases Cyprian selects Stoic teachings that accord at least in part with Christian values. In the final example he takes issue with a Stoic ethical principle, the idea that all vices are equal. The context is a letter he wrote to Antonian, bishop of Numidia, in 251 or 252, concerned with the policy of the Church toward Christians who had supported the Novatian schism but who later repented and sought to be restored to communion. While he advocates forgiveness, Cyprian also observes that the lapsed had embroiled themselves in the schism to varying degrees and urges that they should not be treated with equal severity when they are readmitted to the fold. He contrasts his position with the Stoic notion that all sins are equal, warning that there is a large discrepancy between Scripture and the teachings of the philosophers on this point.[88]

Cyprian's appeals to Stoic ethics are less a deliberate effort to typify pagan wisdom by identifying it with the Stoa, in the manner of Tertullian or Minucius, and more an allusion to familiar concepts taken individually for whatever they are worth in his estimation. Writing exclusively for Christian readers, he does not call upon the Stoics to demonstrate the plausibility of Christian teachings but rather, and merely, to amplify Christian arguments in an idiom whose general significance he does not feel called upon to assess.

IV. NOVATIAN

Novatian (ca. 200–58), Cyprian's schismatic *bête noire*, was a contemporary whose critics described him as well educated in Stoicism.[89] This fact seems to have led some modern scholars to exaggerate his dependence on the Stoa even more extensively than is the case with Cyprian.[90]

(1962), 16–23; Paul Monceaux, *Histoire littéraire de l'Afrique chrétienne depuis les origines jusqu'à l'invasione arabe* (Paris, 1902), II, 307–09; Quasten, *Patrology*, II, 357.

[88] *Ep.* 55.16, ed. Le Chanoine L. Bayard, 2ᵐᵉ éd., Budé (Paris, 1945–61). Noted by Koch, *Cyprianische Untersuchungen*, pp. 272–75; "Zum Novatianischen Schrifttum," *Zeitschrift für Kirchengeschichte*, 38 (1920), 88; Spanneut, *Tertullien*, p. 79; Giuseppina Stramondo, "Echi e riflessi classici nel *De mortalitate* di Cipriano," *Orpheus*, 10 (1963), 164, 169–70, who, however, locates the point in the wrong work.

[89] Cyprian, *Ep.* 55.24. Noted by Quasten, *Patrology*, II, 216. For a good biography and an up-to-date bibliography on Novatian see G. F. Diercks, intro. to his ed. of Novatian, *Opera*, CC, 4 (Turnhout, 1972), pp. viii-xiii, xxix-xl; Russell J. DeSimone, comment on his trans. of Novatian, *The Trinity*, FC, 67 (Washington, 1972), ch. 1, pp. 22 n. 6, 39.

[90] The most wholesale overinterpretation is by Hermann Josef Vogt, *Coetus sanctorum: Der Kirchenbegriff des Novatian und die Geschichte seiner Sonderkirche* (Bonn, 1968), pp. 20, 136–38. Rather tenuous attributions of Stoic anthropology and logic have been made to Novatian, respectively, by Jean Daniélou, "Novatien et le *De mundo* d'Apulée," *Romanitas et Christianitas: Studia Iano Henrico Waszink*, ed. W. den Boer et al. (Amsterdam,

Here too the ideas in question are commonplaces whose Stoic derivation is tenuous. There are two works of Novatian where some evidence of Stoicism can be found. Novatian's *De bono pudicitiae* is based on Tertullian's *De cultu feminarum*. Addressed to women in general and to them alone, it argues that cosmetics, hair dye, and elaborate clothing sin against the modesty that guards chastity, adding that they are unnatural, an impious criticism of God's handiwork. However, Novatian departs both from Tertullian's penitential asceticism and from the Stoic norm of life in accordance with nature in adhering to the norm of moderation instead. Modesty, he states, can be defined as the avoidance of any form of extravagance, a decidedly Aristotelian criterion. Thus, he concludes, a moderate amount of self-enhancement is permissible.[91]

The second context in which Novation adverts to Stoicism is in his doctrine of God. He describes God as fiery and as pervading all things, endowing them with life and binding the universe together in a harmonious whole,[92] an idea evoking the Stoic conception of *pneuma*. Like Tertullian, he also alludes to the Stoic doctrine of *krasis* in describing the hypostatic union, stating that Christ's divinity was "permixed" *(permixtio)* with His humanity.[93] However, in neither of these two applications of Stoic physics is it clear whether Novatian subscribes to Tertullian's materialistic conception of the divine nature.

V. Arnobius

Arnobius of Sicca (d. 327) is another Latin apologist who, like Novatian and Tertullian, makes use of the idea of *krasis* and a number of other physical teachings of the Stoa to combat antagonistic theological views. A convert and a professional rhetorician of some note, he wrote one chief work, the *Adversus nationes,* directed against the pagans. He is unique among the Latin Christian writers of his age for his rejection of all but one of the Stoic doctrines to which he refers. Following Tertul-

---

1973), pp. 75–79; *Hist. of Early Christian Doctrine,* III, 245–50 and Quasten, *Patrology,* II, 226; while equally tenuous applications of Stoic ethics are seen by Courcelle, "Deux grands courants," *REL,* 42 (1965), 123; C. B. Daly, "Novatian and Tertullian: A Chapter in the History of Puritanism," *Irish Theological Quarterly,* 19 (1952), 33–43; and Quasten, *Patrology,* II, 223–24.

[91] Novatian, *De bono pudicitiae* 12.2–4, ed. Diercks. This ed. will be used for all citations to Novatian.

[92] *De trinitate* 2.1, 8.9. Noted by A. d'Alès, *Novatien: Étude sur la théologie romaine au milieu du III* siècle* (Paris, 1924), p. 97; Daniélou, *Hist. of Early Christian Doctrine,* III, 233–38, 239–44; DeSimone, comment on his trans. of *The Trinity,* pp. 26 n. 3, 41 n. 28; Lapidge, "A Stoic Metaphor," *Latomus,* 39 (1980), 823.

[93] *De trin.* 11.1, 24.8–11, 25.3, 25.5. Noted by DeSimone, intro. to his trans., p. 16. Cf. Wolfson, *Philos. of the Church Fathers,* I, 127–37.

lian, he adverts to the principle of *krasis* as an explanation of how the human body and soul are joined without resulting in a *tertium quid*. However, he disagrees with this explanation, which he interprets to mean that the soul is not affected by its union with the body, refuting it with the counter-claim that the soul is indeed conditioned by the actions, sufferings, and sins of the flesh.[94] Arnobius thus completely inverts the argument in Tertullian's *De anima*, where *krasis* is used, along Stoic lines, to support a psychosomatic conception of the human constitution. On another point, this time relating to the divine nature, Arnobius also inverts Tertullian's argument, supporting the Stoic idea of *apatheia* as an adequate description of the true God. For Arnobius God's impassibility is a function of His transcendence and an index of His superiority to the emotional, capricious, and anthropomorphically conceived gods of the pagans.[95] Moving from theology proper to cosmology in general, he returns to his criticism of the Stoics in describing as absurd the theory of cosmic conflagration taught by Zeno, Chrysippus, and Panaetius.[96] Although his attribution of this doctrine to Panaetius is incorrect and although his references to Stoicism are limited to the three passages just mentioned, Arnobius clearly stands in the tradition of Christian apologists seeking to combat the pagans either by means of a frontal attack on Stoicism, equated with pagan error, or by using Stoicism to beat the pagans with their own stick.

VI. Lactantius

Lactantius (ca. 250–326) is the last of the Latin apologists and the first Latin Christian author to write in the age of Constantine, when the victory of Christianity over paganism seemed assured. He was a pupil of Arnobius and, like him, a convert, forced to resign from his chair of rhetoric at Nicomedia following an imperial edict of 303 excluding Chris-

---

[94] Arnobius Afer, *Adversus nationes libri VII* 2.7, 2.26, 2.30, ed. C. Marchesi, 2ª ed. (Torino, 1953). This point has been noted by Ernest L. Fortin, "The *Viri Novi* of Arnobius and the Conflict between Faith and Reason in the Early Christian Centuries," *The Heritage of the Early Church: Essays in Honor of the Very Reverend Georges Vasilievich Florovsky*, ed. David Neiman and Margaret Schatkin, Orientalia Christiana Analecta, 195 (Roma, 1973), pp. 211–14; Micka, *The Problem of Divine Anger*, p. 49.

[95] *Adv. nat.* 7.4–8, 7.36. The best treatment of this point is by Micka, *Divine Anger*, pp. 2, 39–46, 61–77. See also George McCracken, intro. to his trans. of *Adversus nationes*, ACW, 7–8 (Westminster, Md., 1949), I, 28–29; H. D. McDonald, "The Doctrine of God in Arnobius, *Adversus Gentes*," *Studia Patristica*, 9, part 3, ed. F. L. Cross, Texte und Untersuchungen zur Geschichte der altchristlichen Literatur, 94 (Berlin, 1966), pp. 77–78; Henri LeBonniec, "Tradition de la culture classique: Arnobe, témoin et juge des cultes païens," *Bulletin de l'Association Guillaume Budé*, 4ᵐᵉ sér., 2 (1974), 212–13.

[96] *Adv. nat.* 2.9.

tians from public posts. Lactantius experienced exile and persecution for more than a decade but in 317 he acquired the patronage of Constantine, which he retained for the rest of his life. For Lactantius Constantine was a personal hero as well as a turning point in Christian history as a whole. With the exception of his *De opificio dei* (303–04) all his apologies were written under Constantine's aegis. Most of Lactantius' works are polemics against paganism, especially Epicureanism. However, apology of this type was not his only concern. His *De ave Phoenice*, for example, is a straightforward retelling of the classical myth of the Phoenix. He makes no effort to Christianize the myth and his presentation of it is devoid of any Stoic or Herculean associations.[97] One of Lactantius' apologies, the *De mortibus persecutorum*, is completely unphilosophical in its approach. Instead, he argues historically, trying to prove that the persecuting emperors of the age just past were also bad rulers and that they all met horrible deaths, in contrast to the emperors who tolerated Christianity, who were all model rulers. This quest for a relevant past, while it clearly involves a selective distortion of the historical record, does not depend on philosophical reasoning. Lactantius' three remaining apologies, the *De opificio dei*, *De ira*, and *Institutiones divinae*, are, however, philosophically argued. They all reveal a heavy dependence on Stoicism, which Lactantius derives from a number of sources[98] and which he uses quite freely.

[97] Lucius Caecilius Firmianus Lactantius, *De ave Phoenice* 170 in *Opera omnia*, ed. Samuel Brandt and George Laubmann, CSEL, 19, 27 (Vienna, 1890–97). All references to Lactantius will be drawn from this edition. A good analysis of the poem is provided by Brian Stock, "Cosmology and Rhetoric in *The Phoenix* of Lactantius," *Classica et mediaevalia*, 26 (1965), 246–57. The best review of the question of Christian authorship and interpretation of the poem is provided by Marialuisa Walla, "Der Vogel Phönix in der antiken Literatur und die Dichtung des Laktanz," (Universität Wien, Ph.D. diss., 1965), pp. 119–31, 186–93. The most recent argument for the thesis that Lactantius Christianizes the theme is Carl Martin Edsman, *Ignis Divinus: Le feu comme moyen de rajeunissement et d'immortalité. Contes, légendes, mythes et rites* (Lund, 1949), pp. 127–203. Salvatore Gennaro, "Il classicismo di Lattanzio nel 'de ave phoenice'," *Miscellanea di studi di letteratura cristiana antica*, 9 (1954), 1–18 interprets the poem as Christianized Epicureanism.

[98] Cf. the efforts to analyze Lactantius in terms of single-source *Quellenforschung*. Cicero has been seen as his chief source by Luigi Alfonsi, "Cultura classica e cristianesimo: L'impostazione del problema nel proemio delle *Divinae institutiones* di Lattanzio e nell'*Ep*. XVI di Paolino da Nola," *Le Parole e le Idee*, 8 (1966), 163–73; Bernhard Barthel, *Über die Benutzung der philosophischen Schriften Ciceros durch Laktanz*, I, Beilage zum Programm des königl. Gymnasiums in Strehlen, 244, (Strehlen, 1903); Franz Fessler, *Benutzung der philosophischen Schriften Ciceros durch Laktanz: Ein Beitrag zur klassischen Philologie* (Leipzig, 1913). Seneca's influence has been emphasized by Ursicino Domínguez del Val, "El senequismo de Lactancio," *Helmantica*, 23 (1972), 300–23; Hubertus Jagielski, *De Firmiani Lactantii fontibus quaestiones selectae* (Königsberg, 1912), pp. 54–77; Winfried Trillitzsch, *Seneca im literarischen Urteil der Antike: Darstellung und Sammlung der Zeugnisse* (Amsterdam, 1971), I, 130–43; II, 363–69. Varro has been seen as Lactantius' chief source by Samuel Brandt, "Über die Quelle von Laktanz' Schrift De opificio dei," *Wiener Studien*, 13 (1891), 255–92.

There are some obvious parallels between Lactantius' philosophical apologies and those of previous Latin apologists as well as some salient differences. Lactantius can be compared most readily with Minucius Felix. Both authors write in a flowing, polished, and lucid Latin style. Both aim their apologies at pagans and neither has recourse to Scriptural arguments. Both emphasize the doctrine of providence as the chief connection between Stoicism and Christianity and neither deals with the speculative dogmas of the Christian faith. However, unlike Minucius, Lactantius is not trying to underline the affinities between Christianity and pagan philosophy, as typified by Stoicism, in order to suggest how easy the transition from paganism to Christianity would be.[99] Nor does he share Tertullian's interest in using Stoicism as a means of formulating Christian doctrines or of validating them externally against pagans and heretics.[100] Rather, he writes with one aim only, to show that Christianity is superior to pagan philosophy. But, unlike Cyprian, he does so without invoking the authority of Scripture. He emphasizes the limits of philosophy as a source of truth, particularly in the field of ethics. He acknowledges that philosophers may have hit upon the truth accidentally. When this is the case the Christian may borrow the philosophers' ideas.[101] But the purpose of such borrowings is essentially a matter of tactics. As a debater Lactantius subscribes to the principle that it is pointless to argue from authority unless the authorities involved are recognized as such by one's opponent. Since he addresses himself exclusively to pagans, he confines himself to pagan sources. While he sometimes calls upon other

---

[99] See on the contrary Mary Francis McDonald, intro. to her trans. of *The Divine Institutes*, FC, 49 (Washington, 1964), p. 4; Leonhard Thomas, *Die Sapientia als Schlüsselbegriff zu den Divinae Institutiones des Laktanz mit besondere Berücksichtigung seiner Ethik* (Freiburg, 1959).

[100] See on the contrary Vincenzo Loi, "Il concetto di 'iustitia' e i fattori culturali dell'etica di Lattanzio," *Salesianum*, 28 (1966), 605, 618–20; "Problema del male e dualismo negli scritti di Lattanzio," *Annali della Facoltà di .ettere, filosofia e magistero dell'Università di Cagliari*, 29 (1961–65), 37–39, 52–53, 83–89; Julia Siegert, *Die Theologie des Apologeten Lactantius in ihrem Verhältnis zur Stoa* (Bonn, 1921), pp. 6–7.

[101] Noted by Faider, *Études sur Sénèque*, pp. 87–89; Joseph-Rhéal Laurin, *Orientations maîtresses des apologistes chrétiens de 270 à 361*, Analecta Gregoriana, 61, Series facultatis historiae ecclesiasticae, B–10 (Roma, 1954), pp. 226–28; Marion Lausberg, "Christliche Nächstenliebe und heidnische Ethik bei Laktanz," *Studia Patristica*, 13, part 2, ed. Elizabeth A. Livingstone, Texte und Untersuchungen zur Geschichte der altchristlichen Literatur, 116 (Berlin, 1975), pp. 29–34; René Pichon, *Lactance: Étude sur le mouvement philosophique et religieux sous le règne de Constantin* (Paris, 1901), pp. 93–94, 96–98, 101, 105, 107–10; Antonie Wlosok, *Laktanz und die philosophische Gnosis: Untersuchungen zu Geschichte und Terminologie der gnostischen Erlösungsvorstellung*, Abhandlungen der Heidelberger Akademie der Wissenschaften, philosophisch-historische Klasse, 1960, no. 2 (Heidelberg, 1960), pp. 180–81. Olof Gigon, "Lactantius und die Philosophie," *Kerygma und Logos*, ed. Adolf Martin Ritter, pp. 196–203 sees Lactantius' view of philosophy as completely negative and as making no differentiation among its schools.

philosophical schools, he appeals most consistently to Stoicism in constructing the case that he makes against all the pagan views he attacks, including several Stoic positions to which he takes vigorous exception.

Lactantius has frequently been described as an intellectual bantamweight, lacking a profound or speculative mind. He is typically treated as an eclectic whose understanding of philosophy was shallow and whose use of it was strictly *ad hoc*.[102] It is certainly true that he is not interested either in plumbing the depths or scaling the heights of Christian theology or of Greek philosophy. Nor does he seek to produce any sustained or systematic synthesis between them. At the same time, his knowledge of Stoicism is far from superficial and his use of it is far from incidental. He conveys a considerable amount of information about the ethics and psychology of the Stoa and his treatment of the Stoic doctrine of providence and theodicy is the most sustained of any of the Latin apologists. What is still more noteworthy is Lactantius' grasp of the organic connections joining Stoic ethics, anthropology, epistemology, and physics. In this sense, despite his occasional errors or omissions, he displays an understanding of the Stoic system far more integral than that of the other Latin apologists before his time.

Lactantius refers to four main themes in Stoic physics, three in passing and the fourth in great detail. Taken together they illustrate the range of his attitudes toward philosophy in general and toward Stoicism in particular. The nature of God is the central issue in each case. Lactantius agrees with the Stoic idea that God has a material nature. He states that heat and moisture are the two most important elements because God's virtue resides in them.[103] This position distorts the Stoics' teaching, in which air and fire are seen as the material components of the divine aether. Lactantius refers to this point incidentally without mentioning the Stoa expressly and without considering the manner in which God's power may be said to inhere in matter. Turning to a more specifically Christian doctrine, the generation of the Word, he says that the Stoic term *logos*, meaning the word spoken, can be applied with propriety to the second Person of the Trinity, as an instance of a pagan philosophical concept that may be assimilated into Christian usage when the

---

[102] See R. M. Ogilvie, *The Library of Lactantius* (Oxford, 1978), pp. 82–83; J. Stevenson, "Aspects of the Relations between Lactantius and the Classics," *Studia Patristica*, 4, part 2, ed. F. L. Cross, Texte und Untersuchungen zur Geschichte der altchristlichen Literatur, 79 (Berlin, 1961), pp. 500–02, as well as the authors cited in note 101.

[103] *Institutiones divinae* 2.9.16. The traces of Stoic materialism in Lactantius' idea of God are noted and discussed sensitively by Verbeke, *L'Évolution*, pp. 469–82. Cf. on the other hand Vincenzo Loi, *Lattanzio nella storia del linguaggio e del pensiero teologico pre-niceno* (Zürich, 1970), pp. xv-xvi, 34–38, 155–67, 274–76, who has difficulty with this view and who argues unconvincingly that Lactantius' conception of God's nature is Platonic.

idea it stands for is congruent with Christian truth.[104] In the first of these two examples Lactantius' allusion to Stoic physics is vague and casual and not particularly accurate. In the second case his reference to Stoicism is far more precise, express, and considered. In neither case, however, does Lactantius concern himself with the plausibility of transferring a materialistic Stoic conception to the Christian God. His third Stoic theme is the allegorization of the pagan gods. Lactantius is sharply critical of this theological strategy and places stringent limits on the extent to which it can be appropriated by Christians. He notes that the Stoics, and after them Cicero, allegorized the pagan gods as manifestations of the forces of nature. This view, he says, is acceptable so far as it goes, since it recognizes that these gods are not truly divine. On the other hand, it does not convey what the true God really is. The Stoic demythologizing of the gods might well lead to the false notion that the forces of nature are divine and worthy of man's worship, an idolatry whose dangers have already been documented in Lucilius' speech from Cicero's *De natura deorum*. Neither can the universe as a whole be a god, as the Stoics maintain. If its individual parts are not divine, neither is the whole.[105] Here we see Lactantius using Stoic allegoresis as a weapon against popular polytheism while at the same time strenuously objecting to the pantheistic or monistic theology that the Stoa substituted for it.

The feature of Stoic theology that Lactantius explores in the most detail and the one that he sees as the nodal principle linking ethics, psychology, epistemology, and physics is the doctrine of providence and theodicy. He devotes an entire treatise to this theme, the *De opificio dei*, and he returns to it repeatedly and at great length in his *De ira dei* and *Institutiones* in his efforts to refute the Epicurean conception of God and His relation to the universe. Lactantius expressly credits Zeno and Chrysippus with this constellation of ideas, noting its later support by Cicero and Seneca as well. Following the classic Stoic line of reasoning, he argues that the creation, including human nature, testifies to the intelligence and beneficence of the creator in its beauty, harmony, and order, and in the adaptation of all its parts to their respective ends, with man himself being the end for which the rest of the universe exists.[106]

---

[104] *Inst.* 4.9.1–4. See Loi, *Lattanzio*, pp. 167–71, 194–99, who interprets this passage in an immaterial, Platonic sense.

[105] *Inst.* 1.17.1–5, 2.5.1–42. He notes, further, *Inst.* 7.3.1–27, that the identification of God with nature in this manner conflicts with God's transcendence and is an example of the errors of the philosophers.

[106] *De ira dei* 9.1–13.25; *De opificio dei* 2.1–8.1, 10.1–14.9; *Inst.* 1.2.2–6, 1.5.19–21, 1.5.26–28, 2.10.14–16, 7.3.12–7.4.19, 7.7.9. This point has been widely noted. See Hagendahl, *Latin Fathers*, pp. 64–66; Endre von Ivánka, "Die stoische Anthropologie in der lateinischen Literatur," *Anzeiger der österreichische Akademie der Wissenschaften*, philosoph-

Yet, the same Stoic conception of God as rational and benevolent provides Lactantius with the ammunition he uses against another Stoic position, the principle of *apatheia* as applied to God. Lactantius ranges
himself among those apologists who object to the idea of an impassible
deity, although he attaches this belief to Epicureanism and not to some
heretical byproduct of it. The providence of God, for Lactantius, cannot
be divorced from His justice. Thus, he argues, it is inconsistent to claim
that God cares for the world unless one accepts the idea of a God Who
feels compassion for the afflicted, love for the pious, and anger at man's
sin. Certain forms of affection and anger, he notes, are reasonable. God
would be neither just nor reasonable unless He possessed these feelings.
Hence, he concludes, the Stoic argument for providence and theodicy
refutes the Stoic doctrine of *apatheia* as virtuous in general or as a positive attribute of the deity in particular.[107] While this analysis applies one
Stoic idea against another for the purpose of disproving Epicureanism,
it also involves the strategic omission of the Stoic principle of *eupatheia*,
which Lactantius could have used to resolve the inconsistency that he
posits initially. His stress on justice as God's prime attribute also enables him to invoke the norm of *suum cuique* and to associate Aristotelianism with the Stoicism in his critique of divine *apatheia*.

The Stoic notion of an intelligent creator manifesting himself in an intelligible creation provides Lactantius with the connection between the
doctrine of providence and certain epistemological ideas that he derives
from the Stoa. Unlike all other creatures, he notes, man possesses the
faculty of reason, which enables him to know that God is a rational being
and to grasp the evidence of His nature in the beauty and order of the
cosmos.[108] The Stoics' particular form of rationalism further serves Lactantius in his attack on idle speculation that yields no prudential results[109]
and on skepticism. Regarding the latter, he applies the Stoic conviction
of the possibility of certain knowledge against the skeptic Arcesilas,
showing that Arcesilas' position is a *reductio ad absurdum*, since he claims
that nothing can be known with certitude while at the same time pos-

---

isch-historische Klasse, 87 (1950), pp. 178–92; Laurin, *Orientations maîtresses*, pp. 206–07;
Loi, *Lattanzio*, pp. 54–61, 67–69, 104–06, 113–14, 118–21, 134, 142–44; Arthur Stanley
Pease, "Caeli enarrant," *Harvard Theological Review*, 34 (1941), 193; Dionysius Pietrusiń-
sky, "Quid Lactantius de ethnicorum philosophia, litteris, eloquentia iudicaverit et
quomodo iis usus sit," *Latinitas*, 12 (1964), 274.
[107] *De ira dei* 1.1–2.10, 5.1–17, 7.13–8.10, 9.1–13.25, 17.1–18.14, 22.5–23.14. Good
discussions are provided by Laurin, *Orientations maîtresses*, pp. 292–96, 302; Loi, *Lattanzio*,
pp. 44–48, 88–97; Micka, *Divine Anger*, pp. 2, 90–142; Pichon, *Lactance*, pp. 158–71;
Quasten, *Patrology*, II, 399. Hagendahl, *Latin Fathers*, pp. 70–71 is unconvincing in the
claim that Lactantius is ignorant of Christian discussions of this question.
[108] *De opif. dei* 2.1–8, 10.1–14.9.
[109] *Inst.* 3.4.1–2.

iting this claim as a certain truth.[110] If Lactantius agrees with the Stoic position on reason in these respects he remains somewhat vague and un-Stoic in describing the reception of sense data and their formation into concepts by the mind. He agrees with the Stoa that the mind of the knower goes out to the sensed object through the sense organs. However, he does not combine this aspect of the process of sensation with a concurrent flow of *pneuma* from the object to the sense organ, as the Stoics taught.[111]

The idea that man possesses a central *hegemonikon* which directs his senses and his other vital and intellectual functions is the chief bond between Lactantius' theology and his psychology. Indeed, most of what he has to say about the nature and destiny of the soul he treats in the context of his defense of his doctrine of God. Lactantius gives an extremely clear and detailed description of the human mind understood in terms of the Stoic *hegemonikon*. One single mind, he notes, governs the many and variegated functions of the human body and its diverse sense organs. From this single directive mind also spring the various passions which move men to anger, desire, joy, fear, and sorrow *(iram, cupiditatem, laetitiam, metum, miserationem)*.[112] And, just as one single mind controls all of man's operations and is the seat of the passions, so there is one governing intelligence in the cosmos.[113] Despite his fidelity to Stoicism on this point, however, Lactantius feels free to reject Stoic psychology in several other respects. Even as God extends throughout the universe, he argues, so the human mind has no fixed location in the body,[114] a view departing from the Stoic location of the *hegemonikon* either in the brain or the heart. Lactantius is also rather vague about the composition of the soul. He agrees with the Stoa in giving the soul a material nature but says it is a combination of blood, fire, and air, rather than the Stoic fire and air; and he criticizes the Stoic idea that the soul is transmitted physiologically from parent to child.[115] The final topic relating to the soul that

---

[110] *Inst.* 3.6.7–20.

[111] *De opif. dei* 8.9–12.

[112] *Inst.* 1.3.20.

[113] *Inst.* 1.3.20–22. On the *hegimonikon* idea see Karpp, *Probleme altchristlicher Anthropologie*, p. 135. On monotheism see Fritz Wehrli, "L. Caelius Firmianus Lactantius über die Geschichte des wahren Gottesglaubens," *Philomathes: Studies and Essays in the Humanities in Memory of Philip Merlan*, ed. Robert B. Palmer and Robert Hamerton-Kelly (The Hague, 1971), pp. 251–57. On the other hand, McDonald, intro. to her trans. of *Institutes*, p. xxii and Quasten, *Patrology*, II, 406–07 unaccountably see Lactantius as a dualist.

[114] *De opif. dei* 16.10–12.

[115] *De opif. dei* 17.1–19.10. Cf. Karpp, *Probleme altchristlicher Anthropologie*, p. 133, who sees Lactantius' view of the soul's composition as Stoic, and Loi, *Lattanzio*, pp. 183–89, who sees it as self-contradictory.

Lactantius addresses is its fate after death. He cites with approval those Stoics who teach that the soul is immortal and that it receives posthumous rewards and punishments. He sees this position as a logical corollary of the doctrine of a just God. However, he confuses it with the transmigration of souls, a view which he attributes erroneously to the Stoa. He also ignores the school's lack of unanimity on eschatology; he claims that the Stoics stumbled on whatever truths they possess in this area by accident; and he seeks to undermine their credibility by arguing that they failed to convince their opponents.[116] As in the case of his epistemology, Lactantius tends to use Stoic psychology to support theological themes that are of central importance to him. Other aspects of the doctrines involved he reports in a sketchy and semi-accurate manner.

The area in which Lactantius is the most critical of the Stoa and the most inclined to cite Stoicism as an index of the errors of the philosophers is ethics. The few precepts of Stoic ethics that he accepts, such as Cicero's definition of natural law as right reason,[117] he admits grudgingly, either as unwitting testimonies to the truth or as principles that require rigorous qualification. It is in the section of his *Institutiones* devoted to ethics that Lactantius develops most fully his argument against the authority of the pagan philosophers. Their claims are inadmissible, he says, because the schools disagree,[118] because the philosophers themselves were not always virtuous men,[119] because philosophy is impractical since so few people have the leisure to study it,[120] and because, even in those cases where the philosophers approach the truth, they are naive in believing that a secular rationale for ethical action suffices. Their teaching lacks the weight of divine authority and their psychology of virtue makes virtue impossible to sustain without the assurance of a future reward.[121]

Apart from these generalized and not very rigorous assaults on philosophical ethics, in which Lactantius often singles out the Stoa or individual Stoics to illustrate his argument, he concentrates his attack on two points: the Stoics' definition of virtue and their analysis of the pas-

---

[116] *Inst.* 3.18.1–6, 7.7.9–14. Jean Doignon, "Le *Placitum* eschatologique attribué aux Stoïciens par Lactance *(Institutions divines* VII 20): Un exemple de contamination de modèles littéraires," *Revue de philologie,* 51 (1977), 43–55 is unduly skeptical concerning the attribution of at least some of this eschatology to some of the Stoics.

[117] *Inst.* 3.22.33, 6.8.6–10. Noted by Schilling, *Naturrecht,* pp. 70–72, Spanneut, *Tertullien,* p. 148.

[118] *Inst.* 3.7.8–10, 5.3.1–2.

[119] *Inst.* 3.15.1–3.17.43.

[120] *Inst.* 3.25.5–13.

[121] *Inst.* 3.27.1–11.

sions. Lactantius disagrees with the idea of virtue as the *summum bonum*, virtue as an end in itself, and virtue as life in accordance with nature. The highest good, he states, cannot make us happy unless it has always been in our power. Thus, virtue cannot be the highest good because it is acquired at some point and has not always been in our possession.[122] Here Lactantius invokes the Stoic principle that the only things that are ethically relevant are the things that are in our power, while employing it as a weapon against the Stoic definition of virtue itself. In a similar vein, he uses the Stoic definition of the happy life as a state that nothing can vex or diminish to attack the notion that such happiness can be found on earth. The permanent possession of beatitude that would match this definition, he argues, is available only in the next life.[123] Thus, he concludes, virtue is not the highest good nor an end in itself but a means to that end.[124] In the foregoing cases Lactantius' technique is to hurl one Stoic principle against another. In other cases his strategy involves the omission or misconstruction of relevant Stoic principles. Thus, in opposing the idea that knowledge is a virtue on the grounds that one can know what is right and choose not to follow it,[125] he ignores the critical role played by the will in the Stoic analysis of moral judgment and action. And, in rejecting Zeno's ethical criterion of life in accordance with nature because it would admit instinctual behavior as virtuous,[126] he ignores the role of the *hegemonikon* which he cites with approval elsewhere as well as the essentially intellectualistic conception of nature which the Stoics held.

In his extended critique of the Stoic theory of the passions Lactantius does not rely exclusively on Stoic precepts, whether applied dialectically or omitted strategically. While he does ignore the doctrine of *eupatheia*, he appeals mainly to an alternative philosophical outlook, Aristotelianism, as a source of arguments against the Stoa. He objects forcibly to the Stoic definition of the passions, which he identifies correctly as pleasure, sadness, fear, and desire *(laetitia, maestitia, metus, cupiditas)*, asserting that they are neither vices nor diseases of the soul. While he retains the Stoic idea that the passions spring from the soul and not from the body, he argues that some passions, such as brotherly love, are good. The criterion for judging the passions is their inspiration and their end. They are good if they flow from and are referred back to the love of God

---

[122] *Inst.* 3.8.3–19.
[123] *Inst.* 3.12.1–20.
[124] *Inst.* 3.8.24–26, 3.8.35–42. This point has been noted by Paul Gotthold Frotscher, *Des Apologeten Lactantius Verhältniss zur griechischen Philosophie* (Leipzig, 1895), p. 75; Spanneut, *Tertullien*, pp. 128, 145.
[125] *Inst.* 6.5.4–11.
[126] *Inst.* 3.8.20–24.

and one's fellow man. The passions are good, also, if they are neither
excessive nor defective in action. The Peripatetics, who advance this
golden mean and who teach that the passions are natural and capable
of being oriented toward virtue, are thus more correct than the Stoics,
who would extirpate the passions and replace them with *apatheia*. Yet,
Lactantius faults the Peripatetics as well because their conception of virtue is referred to this world and not to God.[127] Apart from his omission
of the idea of *eupatheia*, an omission which distorts the Stoic theory of the
passions, Lactantius gives a more substantial and detailed presentation
of Stoic ethics than any of the other Latin apologists. His rejection of
apatheia as an acceptable moral state for man is closely related to his rejection of *apatheia* as an adequate description of God. The theological
concern that unites these physical and ethical themes serves, even at the
point of Lactantius' most vehement criticism of the Stoa, to underscore
his appreciation of the intimate bond between the divine and human *logoi*
that is such a central feature of the Stoic system.

Symptomatic of Lactantius' use of Stoicism to criticize those Stoic ideas
that offend him is his treatment of Hercules.[128] In the section of the *Institutiones* where he stigmatizes the pagan gods for their immorality, he
turns the tables on Stoic ethics and theology alike by presenting his own
version of Hercules as an example of vice, not as an example of virtue
more Stoicorum. According to Lactantius, Hercules represents lust and
adultery. His physical strength in no sense signifies moral strength and
his death bespeaks vanity, not self-sacrifice. Hercules' death by fire and
subsequent apotheosis, for Lactantius, has no reference whatever to resurrection, whether pagan or Christian. Lactantius' dismissal of any possible consonance between the Stoic Hercules and Christian virtue, which
he achieves by applying the Stoics' own demythologizing allegoresis of
the pagan gods to Hercules himself, suggests the limits that he places on
any real concord between the Stoa and the Gospel, beyond what may be
useful for the purposes of rhetorical apologetics. In assessing Lactantius'
treatment of Stoicism as a whole, this evidence must be recognized alongside of his extensive and often accurate reporting of important Stoic ideas,
whether he agrees with them or not, and his indisputable grasp of the
interrelations among the branches of Stoic philosophy.

---

[127] *Inst.* 3.23.8–11, 6.14.1–6.16.11, 6.17.1–29, 6.19.1–11. Noted by Courcelle, "Deux
grands courants," *REL*, 42 (1965), 123; "Points de vue patristique sur le Stoïcisme romain," *Actes du VII* congrès de l'Association Guillaume Budé*, Aix-en-Provence, 1–6 avril 1963
(Paris, 1964), pp. 256–57; Hagendahl, *Latin Classics*, pp. 338–41; Labriolle, "Apatheia,"
Mélanges Ernout, p. 220; Max Pohlenz, *Vom Zorne Gottes: Eine Studie über den Einfluss der
griechischen Philosophie auf das alte Christentum* (Göttingen, 1909), p. 54; Spanneut, *Tertullien*, pp. 150–51, 154–58, 177–78.
[128] *Inst.* 1.18.3–10, 1.18.13–17, 1.9.1–11.

Lactantius' hostility to Hercules points to another consideration as well, the need to appreciate his apology in its own personal and historical setting. In his attacks on the pagan gods he concentrates on deities such as Hercules, one of the most popular gods of pagan Rome and a god venerated especially by Maximian and Diocletian, emperors whose policy of persecution had just given way to the glorious new age of Constantinian toleration.[129] Lactantius' attachment and gratitude to his patron may well have influenced his handling of this theme. It is also noteworthy that he singles out Epicureanism as the single most dangerous enemy of the Christian faith. This attitude is curious in an age when Neoplatonism had replaced other philosophies both as an alternative to Christianity and as its most virulent antagonist, in the person of Porphyry. It has been suggested that Lactantius focused his apology against Epicureanism as an attack on an important official of state who was an adherant of that school and a personal enemy. Alternatively, it has been argued that Lactantius' concern with Epicureanism reflects an ignorance of contemporary intellectual movements and an uncritical dependence on Cicero as an index of the problems he needed to address.[130] Whether Lactantius' anti-Epicureanism sprang from a sense of personal threat or from a reverence for Cicero so great that it blinded him to the philosophical developments of the previous four centuries, it does mark the end of an era in many ways. As is true for the other Latin apologists, Lactantius' use of Stoicism, whether positive or negative, attests to its popularity as an accepted source of wisdom. Yet, at the same time, the pride of place that Stoicism had occupied in the Roman mind was rapidly giving way in the fourth century to the very Neoplatonism that Lactantius ignored. The Latin Christian thinkers who came after him would find themselves incapable of neglecting it.

---

[129] Stevenson, "Aspects of the Relations between Lactantius and the Classics," *Studia Patristica*, 4, part 2, p. 503. In more general terms see also François Heim, "L'influence exercée par Constantin sur Lactance: Sa théologie de la victoire," *Lactance et son temps: Recherches actuelles*, Actes du IVᵉ colloque d'Études historiques et patristiques, Chantilly, 21–23 septembre 1976, ed. J. Fontaine and M. Perrin (Paris, 1978), pp. 55–70.

[130] Stevenson, "Aspects," pp. 497–98, 500–02.

CHAPTER TWO

ST. AMBROSE AND ST. JEROME

During the generation between the last of the Latin apologists and the first of the Latin Church Fathers, Christian thought confronted new dilemmas of major and unprecedented proportions. The legitimization of the Church had ended, for a time, the persecution of Christians. But the new public status of the Church coincided with a wave of theological controversy concerning the Trinity and the nature of Christ which churchmen were now in a position to debate openly and to legislate upon in the forum of the ecumenical council. Violent disagreements on these critical doctrines of the Christian faith flowed both into and out of the Council of Nicaea of 325. The defense of the Nicene Creed against the Arians and a host of other heretics became an urgent priority for the Christian writers of the fourth century. To be sure, the Trinity and the nature of Christ were subjects amenable to conceptualization in philosophical terms and they certainly drew many Greek patristic theologians to Stoicism as a means of explicating the orthodox position. In the west, however, the chief controversialists to enter the fray dissociated themselves from this strategy. There is only one exception in the fourth century, Marius Victorinus, who will be discussed in the next chapter; but he is an exception who proves the rule. It is true that Tertullian had earlier applied Stoicism to his own Christology and Trinitarian theology. His Latin successors in the next century did not follow his lead. Possibly because they wished to detach themselves from the materialistic connotations of Tertullian's doctrine or because his lapse into Montanism had tarnished his reputation, they chose to argue primarily on Scriptural rather than on philosophical grounds. The two earliest Latin Church Fathers, St. Ambrose and St. Jerome, were both deeply embroiled in controversies with opponents of the Nicene faith. Like the other Latin Christian writers of their century, they bypassed Stoicism in that connection. Instead, they used it to address a range of other problems, reflecting both their own personal interests and the equally pressing moral and pastoral concerns of the post-Constantinian Church.

I. St. Ambrose

In moving from the apologists to St. Ambrose (339-97) we move to a new historical situation that brought with it possibilities for a new theological and pastoral emphasis and new uses of Stoicism on the part of

Christian thinkers. Elected bishop of Milan in 374 during a period
fraught with the Arian heresy, which received periodic support from the
imperial court, Ambrose was no stranger to controversy. He devoted
several treatises to the defense of orthodox Trinitarian and Christological doctrine. His famous innovations in Christian hymnography reflect
much the same anti-heretical concerns. His defense of Christianity
against the late fourth-century pagan reaction in the Altar of Victory incident is equally well known. At the same time, Ambrose's works are far
broader in scope than those of any of the apologists, granting the fact
that there were some apologists whose interests were not confined to
controversy. Biblical exegesis, applied primarily to the Old Testament,
makes up the largest single segment of Ambrose's *oeuvre*. His most signal
contribution to Biblical scholarship was his Latinization of the pol-
ysemous interpretation of the text pioneered by Philo and first applied
to Christian exegesis by Origen. Apart from his exegetical and controversial writings Ambrose also produced works of straightforward theological exposition. While it can also be read as an attack on Manicheism, his *Hexameron*, a Latinization of the genre first used as a schema for
discussing the creation by St. Basil, is the most signal case. Ambrose also
wrote a number of treatises on specific ethical topics, both individual and
social. Ethics is also the chief concern he reflects in his commentaries on
the Old Testament patriarchs and it is expounded most exhaustively in
his *De officiis ministrorum*. Written for the edification of the diocesan clergy
of Milan, this is his longest, his best known, and his most influential work.
It is also his most important work from the standpoint of the Stoic tradition, a fact visible in the scholarly attention it has received. Four funeral orations and a group of letters, mostly dealing with political and
administrative problems, complete the Ambrosian canon.

One of the most striking features of Ambrose's *oeuvre* as a whole is the
relatively small number of works in which material pertinent to the Stoic
tradition is to be found. For the most part this material occurs in his exegetical and pastoral writings. Even in those treatises where the Stoic
content is the richest Ambrose approaches the subject matter from a
Biblical point of view. His method is that of a Scripture scholar and his
illustrative examples are typically drawn from the Bible. He repeatedly
attributes the Stoic and other philosophical ideas that he approves of expressly to the Bible, claiming that the Greeks borrowed them from that
source. Ambrose's appeal to philosophy is confined almost exclusively
to ethics. To the extent that he raises physical questions in the *Hexameron*
he bypasses Stoicism in favor of Neoplatonism or Aristotelianism.[1] His

---

[1] The best treatment of the philosophical content of this work is Jean Pépin, *Théologie*

anthropology is also derived from these two schools.[2] In his ethics he
freely combines Platonic, Neoplatonic, and Aristotelian ideas with Stoicism in a manner that is not always commensurate with the practice
either of the middle Stoics or of Cicero, his chief mentor. He is massively
inconsistent in his treatment of one of the major Stoic themes of which
he was a transmitter, the doctrine of natural law.

Ambrose's attitude toward philosophy in general and toward Stoicism in particular has received varying appraisals. He has been seen as
a fundamentally unspeculative Roman,[3] as a thinker whose strongest ties
were to Neoplatonism,[4] as a mind that changed over time, being more
Stoic and Neoplatonic in his early work and more Biblical in his later
work,[5] and as a theologian whose aim was the systematic depreciation
of philosophy, using it only in the strictest subordination to Christian
truth.[6] Many of these views are undercut by the tendency of the commentators to limit their analyses to Ambrose's express references to philosophy or by their failure, in some cases, to differentiate one school from
another. Some scholars have cast their nets too narrowly, a fact reflected
by the preemptive focus of the commentary on the *De officiis ministrorum.*
When all of Ambrose's works are considered and when his use of Stoicism is put in context, what emerges is an Ambrose who is trying neither
to prove the inferiority of philosophy to the Gospel nor to synthesize it
systematically with the Gospel. Ambrose does not labor under the uncritical delusion that Stoicism is isomorphic with Christianity. Nor does
he reveal the slightest need to agonize or to fulminate over the relations
between Athens and Jerusalem. He makes the discriminations, choices,
and adjustments that he wishes to make, whether early or late, with an
independent spirit and in a calm and businesslike manner. There is no

---

cosmique et théologie chrétienne (Ambroise Exam. I.1.1–4) (Paris, 1964), passim and esp. parts
1–3, pp. 113–17, 125, 356–66, 513–25. This study refutes the claims for Stoic influence
made by Guilelmus Gossel, *Quibus ex fontibus Ambrosius in describendo corpore humano hauserit
(Ambros. Exaem. VI 54–74)* (Leipzig, 1908), pp. 50–67.

   [2] This point has sometimes been confused by authors insufficiently circumspect concerning the sources of middle Stoic psychology and anthropology. See, for example, Robert
T. Otten, *"Amor, caritas* and *dilectio:* Some Observations on the Vocabulary of Love in
the Exegetical Works of St. Ambrose," *Mélanges offerts à Mlle. Christine Mohrmann* (Utrecht,
1963), p. 75; Wolfgang Seibel, *Fleisch und Geist beim heiligen Ambrosius* (München, 1958),
passim and esp. pp. 7–9, 16–69.

   [3] F. Homes Dudden, *The Life and Times of St. Ambrose* (Oxford, 1935), I, 14–16.

   [4] Pierre Courcelle, "L'humanisme chrétien de Saint Ambroise," *Orpheus*, 9 (1962),
21–34; Goulven Madec, *Saint Ambroise et la philosophie* (Paris, 1974), pp. 12–19. Madec
supplies a useful and up-to-date review of the literature, pp. 13–17.

   [5] Ernst Dassmann, *Die Frömmigkeit des Kirchenvaters Ambrosius von Mailand: Quellen und
Entfaltung* (Münster, 1965), pp. 11, 32–38, 40–74, 154–55, 183, 218, 234–301.

   [6] Sofia Vanni Rovighi, "Le idee filosofiche di Sant'Ambrogio," *Sant'Ambrogio nel XVI
centenario della nascita*, Pubblicazioni dell' Università cattolica del S. Cuore, serie 5ª: Scienze
storiche, 18 (Milano, 1940), pp. 237–58.

indication that he views this process as a means of resolving any pressing personal problems.

In the field of ethics, his primary interest, Ambrose draws freely and extensively on the Stoics. He borrows both specific ideas and formulae and ways of posing and arguing the issues. He combines Stoic with Platonic and Aristotelian doctrine, largely in the field of anthropology. These conjuctions are strongly reminiscent of Ciceronian ethics; but Ambrose is by no means a slavish imitator of his revered model. Sometimes his philosophical amalgam is different from Cicero's. Even when it is the same, Ambrose uses it for fundamentally different purposes, with a shift in tone and directionality that drastically alters its emphasis. Stylistically Ambrose substitutes an exegetical method and a barrage of Scriptural examples for Cicero's mode of argument. This stylistic change is a reflection of Ambrose's replacement of Cicero's this-wordly ethic with a Christian ethic, which revalues the Stoic themes that Ambrose uses by situating them in a framework of divine grace and human redemption, viewed from the perspective of the life to come.

Ambrose sometimes defeats the reader's initial expectations by treating Stoicism in a merely incidental manner in contexts where one would think him more inclined to advert to it *in extenso*. His protracted discussion of creation in the *Hexameron*, for example, does not inspire him either to support or to refute Stoic physics and metaphysics. The two issues most evocative of Stoicism that he raises in this work he handles in neither a physical nor a Stoic way. Ambrose makes his own contribution to the topic of cosmetic theology, which derives originally from the Stoics and which was Christianized by the apologists, starting with Tertullian. Ambrose agrees that people should not alter or improve upon the image of God in themselves, a practice that would sin against truth while at the same time insulting the Creator and deceiving their fellow men. Like Tertullian and others he addresses this exhortation primarily to women and their use of cosmetics, but not exclusively, although he does not specify what the analogous masculine failings might be. Ambrose's chief innovation in the handling of this topic lies in the fact that he does not approach it from the standpoint either of sexual ethics, the monastic vocation, or asceticism. Rather, he sees it as one among a larger group of moral problems which all involve deception, cruelty, or dishonesty in one way or another. Another new wrinkle in Ambrose's treatment of cosmetic theology is that he does not invoke the norm of nature in this connection, even though he raises the question in a treatise on the creation of the universe.[7]

---

[7] St. Ambrose, *Exameron* 6.8.47, ed. Carolus Schenkl in *Opera*, CSEL, 32:1 (Vienna,

Ambrose does appeal to nature, however, in his reference to a second Stoic-type theme in the *Hexameron*, the myth of the Phoenix. He retells the ancient tale quite fully and explains that God has created the Phoenix as a natural proof of the Christian doctrine of the resurrection. While this position indicates Ambrose's willingness to resort to a natural theology argument, two features of his handling of the Phoenix limit its Stoicism. First, he empties the myth of its cyclical content and ignores the idea of resurrection through struggle and suffering. Second, he treats the Phoenix as a sign created by God for man's instruction, shadowing forth His care for man, as part of the generally allegorical understanding of creation that typifies the entire treatise.[8]

The Phoenix also recurs as a token of man's resurrection in one of Ambrose's funeral orations on the death of his brother Satyrus. Satyrus' virtues are given a vaguely Stoic coloration in this work and Ambrose certainly depends upon the Cynic-Stoic *consolatio* tradition formally and stylistically. At the same time, he gives a distinctly Biblical tonality to the Stoic formulae he invokes, noting that conformity with nature as a moral criterion requires the honor and worship of the Christian God. He also includes a number of other arguments for the resurrection drawn from the Bible, alongside of the myth of the Phoenix.[9]

The assimilation of nature and natural law to the law of God is a theme that occurs repeatedly in Ambrose's exegetical and ethical works. He handles it very inconsistently in works large and small throughout his *oeuvre*. Sometimes he Biblicizes the idea of natural law, subordinating it radically to God's transcendent order and creative will. At other times he treats nature as a norm, accessible to man by reason, that counsels the equality of all men, the common sharing of property, the priority of the common good, and other Stoic desiderata.[10] He develops both sides

---

1897–1968). All references to Ambrose's works, except as indicated, will be taken from this ed.

[8] Ibid. 5.23.79.

[9] *De excessu fratris* 2.59, ed. Otto Faller, CSEL, 73. On this work see also Courcelle, "L'humanisme chrétien," *Orpheus*, 9 (1962), 30; *Recherches sur Saint Ambroise: "Vies" anciennes, culture, iconographie* (Paris, 1973), pp. 24-33; Charles Favez, "L'Inspiration chrétienne dans les *consolations* de saint Ambroise," *REL*, 8 (1930), 82–91; Madec, *Saint Ambroise*, p. 29; Maria Luisa Ricci, "Definizione della *prudentia* in Sant'Ambrogio (a proposito di *De Excessu fratris* 44–48)," *Studi italiani di filologia classica*, 41 (1969), 247–62.

[10] The best treatment of this entire topic, which preserves a lively and nuanced sense of the ambiguities of Ambrose on natural law, is Baziel Maes, *La loi naturelle selon Ambroise de Milan* (Roma, 1967), esp. pp. 6–8, 19, 26–28, 33–37, 47, 50–64, 123–38, 146–47, 151–62. Some authors have oversimplified the question, treating Ambrose's view as an untinctured transmission of Stoic natural law theory. See, for instance, Thomas Gerhard Ring, *Auctoritas bei Tertullian, Cyprian und Ambrosius* (Würzburg, 1975), pp. 130–33; Otto Schilling, *Naturrecht und Staat nach der Lehre der alten Kirche* (Paderborn, 1914), pp. 139–45; Michel Spanneut, *Le Stoïcisme des pères de l'église de Clément de Rome à Clément d'Alexandrie*

of this doctrine most fully in the *De officiis ministrorum*, where he neither attempts or achieves a resolution of the discrepancies just indicated. Indeed, he does not manifest any awareness that the discrepancies are there at all. The same kind of treatment of natural law can be found in a number of Ambrose's briefer writings as well. Thus, in *De fuga saeculi* he argues that there is a natural and a written law, the natural law inscribed in the human heart and the written law carved upon the tablets of the Ten Commandments. Although each man possesses the natural law within himself, Ambrose continues, this does not warrant antinomianism with respect to God's law. Rather, man fulfills the natural law when he obeys God's commandments voluntarily, internalizing them and then manifesting them as the law of his own being. This analysis shows a structural parallel with the Stoic conception of law and the Stoic program of internalizing the cosmic *logos* as the governing principle in ethics. But Ambrose Christianizes the content. God's law, for him, is not the rational order of the cosmos but an ordinance given in love to lead men to acknowledge their own sinfulness, the inability of the Mosaic law to effect the change of heart required for redemption, and the consequent necessity of the grace of Christ.[11] Similarly, in the *De Nabuthae*, in treating the idea that all men have a common right to the goods of the earth as a corollary of their common nature, Ambrose redefines this connaturality, viewing it as a consequence of God's redemption.[12]

In some contexts, however, Ambrose uses Biblical material to illustrate a Stoic conception of nature and to reinforce its ethical claims, even when he is considering apostolic injunctions. In *De Noe*, for instance, he interprets the three sons of Noah as modes of classifying ethical acts as good, bad, and *adiaphora*. Each son possesses a good by nature but not all of them exercise it rightly, according to the traditional Stoic definition of the good as conformity with nature.[13] In still another area connected with the Stoic theme of *naturam sequere*, Ambrose's treatises and

---

(Paris, 1957), pp. 256–57. Others have oversimplified Ambrose in the other direction, completely Biblicizing his position. See, for instance, Dudden, *Life and Times*, II, 520–21; Dominicus Löpfe, *Die Tugendlehre des heiligen Ambrosius* (Sarnen, 1951), pp. 33–38, 42, 72–77, 99; Carlo Alberto Maschi, "Un problema generale del diritto in Sant'Ambrogio e nelle fonti romano-classico," *Sant'Ambrogio* (Milano, 1940), pp. 423–30, although in this case the author's inspiration is the plausible wish to distinguish between Ambrose's views and the Roman jurisprudential concept of *ius naturale*; Michel Poirer, "'Consors naturae' chez Saint Ambroise: Copropriété de la nature ou communauté de nature," *Ambrosius Episcopus*: Atti del Congresso internazionale di studi ambrosiani nel XVI centenario della elevazione di sant'Ambrogio alla catedra episcopale, Milano, 2–7 dicembre 1974, ed. Giuseppe Lazzati (Milano, 1976), II, 331–32.

[11] *De fuga saeculi* 3.15, ed. Carolus Schenkl, CSEL, 32:2.

[12] *De Nabuthae* 1.2–3, ed. Carolus Schenkl, CSEL, 32:2. Noted by Poirer, "'Consors naturae'," pp. 331–32.

[13] Maes, *La loi naturelle selon Ambroise*, pp. 92–94.

letters on marriage, widowhood, and virginity, he sometimes underscores the Stoic teaching on the equality of spouses and on marriage as
a natural and virtuous state, amplifying the Stoic praise of family life as
a school for virtue by attaching to it the notion of the family as the cel-
lular unit of the Church. Even in those writings where he promotes consecrated virginity as a Christian calling and urges widowed persons not
to remarry he notes that this advice cannot be followed unless the individual transcends nature. Such vocations require a special God-given
grace. They are a response to divine counsels and are not precepts incumbent on all in terms of which other callings are to be judged.[14] In
these works, then, Ambrose acknowledges the normative value of nature
for most people even while praising the supernatural gifts that enable a
few people to go beyond them.

Apart from the *De officiis ministrorum* there are two other works in which
Ambrose forges the same sorts of structural and doctrinal relationships
between Stoicism and Christianity that appear in his *magnum opus*. The
first is a series of letters addressed in ca. 386 to Simplicianus, a member
of the Milanese Christian community.[15] Ambrose's starting point is exegetical, his remarks in these letters being an effort to elucidate I Corinthians 7:23: "You were bought with a price; do not become slaves to
sin." He does this by sketching a picture of a Christian wise man who
bears a striking resemblance to the Stoic sage. The chief characteristic
of the wise man, says Ambrose, is equanimity. Unaffected either by good
or bad fortune, he possesses tranquillity of mind, the only true riches.
The peace he enjoys is the peace that passes understanding; his riches
are the heavenly rewards that are the Christian's true inheritance. His
untroubled soul is rooted in faith, grounded in charity, and perfected in
Christ. Faith, indeed, is the wisdom that makes the wise man free. Such
a man is liberated by the law of nature. Since he has made the law of
Christ connatural to himself he is not moved by any external considerations. He calmly chooses the good and is without fear. His *apatheia* is
the redemption from sin purchased by the blood of Christ. In the brief
compass of these two letters, Ambrose preserves very clearly the structural configuration of the Stoic sage and the psychological correlatives
between his inner nature and the external law of nature which he makes

---

[14] See, for instance, *Epistola* 63, to the church at Vercelli, 396, *PL*, 16, cols. 1157–1158,
1247, 1251. On this point see Ernst Bickel, *Das asketische Ideal bei Ambrosius, Hieronymus
und Augustin: Eine Kulturgeschichtliche Studie* (Leipzig, 1916), pp. 21–23, 27, 37; William
Joseph Dooley, *Marriage according to St. Ambrose* (Washington, 1948), pp. 37, 77.

[15] *Ep.* 37–38, *PL*, 16, cols. 1130–1145. A similar association of ideas in connection
with Ambrose's frequent citation of Proverbs 17:6b has been brought out by Vincent R.
Vasey, "Proverbs 17.6b (*LXX*) and St. Ambrose's Man of Faith," *Augustinianum*, 14 (1974),
259–76.

the law of his own being. At the same time, Ambrose radically Christianizes the ethical content of this ideal and the dynamics that sustain it. Divine grace makes the sage possible, not his own intellectual and moral autonomy. Ambrose parallels the Christian substance of his image of the sage with a Christian style of argument, since he decorates it throughout with Old Testament examples.

Even more Scriptural in emphasis and argument is Ambrose's treatment of the sage in his exegetical work *De Iacob et beata vita*. This treatise was written as a companion piece to his commentaries on Abraham, Isaac, and Joseph, each patriarch representing a particular moral type. Abraham stands for faith; Isaac stands for sincerity of heart; Joseph stands for purity. Jacob's preeminent virtue is fortitude in the midst of struggle. He stands for the soul's endurance of toils;[16] he is a kind of Christian Hercules. Ambrose applies the attributes of the Stoic sage to him by way of a moral and typological exegesis of those parts of the book of Genesis where his story is told. The same kind of Christianizing of the moral dynamics of the Stoic sage that he sketches in brief in *Epistolae* 37 and 38 he presents here in a more sustained and extended form. At the same time Ambrose strikes another note in the *De Iacob* which he develops more fully in the *De officiis ministrorum*. He not only Christianizes the Stoic sage, he also tinctures Stoic ethics at some points with insights derived from other philosophical schools. What he borrows, Christianizes, and transmits, therefore, is not a pure and unadulterated Stoicism but Stoicism as he himself appropriates it.

This point is visible at the very outset of the treatise in Ambrose's definitions of some of his key terms relating to the virtues and the passions. Prudence or right reason, he begins, in the virtue that curbs man's natural impulses and that counsels those choices that are to man's advantage, as well as enforcing God's law upon man's conscience. While Ambrose gives a traditional Stoic description of prudence as the knowledge of things divine and human and while he preserves the typical Stoic emphasis on practical rather than speculative wisdom, he modifies Stoic prudence in two ways. First, he sees the passions, which it is reason's task to subjugate, as natural, a notion deriving from Platonic and Aristotelian anthropology. On the other hand, he offers no suggestions as to how the passions actually can contribute to virtue under reason's guidance, an approach that indicates his affinities with the Neoplatonic view of the body as a prison in which the soul is incarcerated and from which it must be freed by reason. Second, Ambrose maintains that reason is not autonomous in man and that it must be informed by the

---

[16] *De Ioseph* 1.2, ed. Carolus Schenkl, CSEL, 32:2.

divine law in order to know why and how to check the passions.[17]

Neither Ambrose's view of the passions as natural albeit infrarational nor his analysis of them is strictly Stoic although he preserves the standard quartet of pleasure, pain, desire, and fear. Elsewhere, in addressing the question of how repentant Arians should be readmitted to the Christian fold, he criticizes those who, *Stoicorum quodam more* ("in a Stoic sort of way") think all sins are equal, arguing instead that penalties should be adjusted according to the severity of the sins.[18] In the *De Iacob*, in an analogous manner, he hierarchizes the passions and, by implication, the sins flowing from them. Some passions he sees as general, feeding all the vices and affecting both the body and the soul. Other passions are specific either to the soul or the body. The Stoic quartet of pleasure, pain, fear, and desire are in the first group. However, unlike the early Stoics, who associate pleasure with pain as false judgments concerning present goods and fear with desire as false judgments concerning future goods, Ambrose omits entirely the category of judgment as the origin of the passions. With the Platonists and Aristotelians, with the middle Stoics and Cicero, he roots them in man's subrational nature. He also subdivides and coordinates them in his own way. Ambrose sees pain and pleasure as the most basic of the passions. Desire, and its companion joy, are related to pleasure, coming before and after it. Fear, and its companion sadness, are related to pain, coming before and after that passion. This discussion is a sequential report of the feelings man experiences under the circumstances indicated, not an analysis of the genesis of the passions. Ambrose goes on to list pride, avarice, ambition, envy, and strife as the passions pertaining to the soul. Luxury and gluttony are the chief passions pertaining to the body. This distinction, once more, shows his rejection of the monistic psychology of the Stoa and his preference for a more hierarchical view of the human constitution.

Taking a stance independent of all the philosophical schools, Ambrose chooses temperance as the leading virtue, rejecting both the Aristotelian-Ciceronian emphasis on justice and the Stoic emphasis on prudence. He sees temperance as the primary virtue not only because it is the first virtue learned by man, who can acquire it even before the age of reason, but also because it is the virtue that enables man to tame the passions. Temperance is thus the mistress of all moral education.[19] This consideration of temperance is interesting for the light it sheds on Am-

---

[17] *De Iacob et beata vita* 1.1.2–1.1.4, ed. Carolus Schenkl, CSEL, 32:2.

[18] *De poenitentia* 1.2.5, ed. Otto Faller, CSEL, 73. The parallels between Ambrose and Cyprian on this point in analogous contexts have been noted by Roger Gryson in his trans. of this work, SC, 179 (Paris, 1971), pp. 56–57 n. 1.

[19] *De Iacob* 1.2.5.

brose as a psychologist. In contrast to the philosophical positions he inherited, which analyze the virtues and their interrelations either in terms of their normative functions or their formal ends, he approaches the question from a developmental point of view, noting that human beings can acquire the self-discipline enabling them to control their impulses before they come to an understanding of why these impulses are wrong. Self-control precedes enlightenment; and the discipline enforced by temperance assists the individual in his eventual understanding and internalizing of moral values.

However, temperance and the other cardinal virtues, important as they are in this connection, are not, for Ambrose, sufficient. Man, he observes, did indeed have the natural law written on the fleshy tablets of his heart, but he failed to abide by it, falling into sin. God then handed down the Mosaic law. But the covenant of the old law did not justify man either; it merely added to his burdens. God therefore provided the law of Christ, which offers man release from sin and which substitutes for the natural law and the Old Testament law the principle of grace.[20] The new man who emerges from this new principle owes much to the Stoic sage, to be sure, but his motivating spirit is Christian and he is depicted in terms of Biblical examples, in this case the example of Jacob.

Jacob, as Ambrose's model of virtue, has been perfected by the exercise of reason.[21] His good is the good within and he is indifferent to externals. The *summum bonum* he recognizes is the love of virtue as an end in itself, a love which harmonizes his inner and outer being and which unites both to God.[22] He is thus unaffected by adversity, loss, and misfortune, and here Ambrose lists the standard Stoic *adiaphora*. Such concerns are accidental to virtue and they cannot perturb the wise man, although for Ambrose Jacob's equanimity derives from faith in God and is sustained by his joy in God's nearness.[23] Like the Stoic sage, Jacob possesses all things—power, wealth, nobility, vigor, and industry. He is invulnerable to the vicissitudes of life, maintaining his *apatheia* under all circumstances. His tranquillity of mind, however, is not grounded in his own autarchy but is nourished by his meditation on God's Word and by the grace of God's presence.[24] In his inner assurance and his energetic, unruffled undertaking of the labors that confront him, Ambrose's Jacob actually bears a closer resemblance to Ambrose himself than he does either to the Stoic Hercules, tested by trials, plunged into madness, and

---

[20] Ibid. 1.6.20–21.
[21] Ibid. 1.7.29.
[22] Ibid. 1.7.30.
[23] Ibid. 1.7.31–1.8.38.
[24] Ibid. 1.8.39.

apotheosized through his own immolation or to the Biblical Jacob, the visionary who wrestled with the angel.

The simultaneous reliance upon and independence from his sources that Ambrose reveals in the *De Iacob* is displayed in its most elaborate and impressive form in his *De officiis ministrorum*. This single work has received most of the attention that scholars concerned with Ambrose's Stoicism have lavished upon him. In the work itself he expressly acknowledges his dependence on Cicero's *De officiis* and on Panaetius, although he also notes that Biblical authors, no less than philosophers, have discussed the topic of duty.[25] The first part of this acknowledgement has received a virtually preclusive emphasis from many commentators, who see Ambrose as the transmitter of an uncontaminated Stoicism in this work. Typical of this position are the remarks of Harald Hagendahl: "Ambrose's exposition proves to be a mosaic composed of nothing but Ciceronian pieces;" and "it is remarkable how much of the Stoic doctrinal system has been left untouched."[26] A more flamboyant version of this same appraisal is Raymond Thamin's description of the treatise as "un vrai coup d'état intellectuel."[27] A major feature of this school of thought, outside of its tendency to underrate any non-Stoic elements in the ethics of the *De officiis ministrorum* whether derived from Christianity, other philosophical positions, or Ambrose himself, is to treat his model, Cicero, as an orthodox exponent of Stoic ethics. As we have shown elsewhere, this view of Cicero is not tenable.[28]

There is a second group of scholars, standing much closer to the middle of the interpretive spectrum, who see Ambrose as drawing heavily on Stoic ethics and combining it freely and even uncritically with Christian ethics, showing no sensitivity to the possible discrepancies between

---

[25] *De officiis ministrorum* 1.7.24, 1.8.25, *PL*, 16, cols. 30, 31.

[26] Hagendahl, *Latin Fathers*, pp. 366, 371–72 for the quotations cited and, in general, on Ambrose, pp. 347–72.

[27] Raymond Thamin, *Saint Ambroise et la morale chrétienne au IV* siècle: Étude comparée des traités "Des devoirs" de Cicéron et de Saint Ambroise* (Paris, 1895), p. 1 and, in general, pp. 201–309. Thamin is very closely followed by Rand, *Founders of the Middle Ages*, pp. 79–83. Other leading members of this school include Pierre Courcelle, "Deux grands courants," *REL*, 42 (1965), 123–24; M. B. Emeneau, "Ambrose and Cicero," *Classical Weekly*, 24 (1930), 49–53; Paul Ewald, *Der Einfluss der stoisch-ciceronianischen Moral auf die Darstellung der Ethik bei Ambrosius* (Leipzig, 1881); Otto Hiltbrunner, "Die Schrift 'De officiis ministrorum' des hl. Ambrosius und ihr ciceronianisches Vorbild," *Gymnasium*, 71 (1964), 174–89, who also supplies a review of the literature pp. 174–75; R. A. Markus, in Armstrong and Markus, *Christian Faith and Greek Philosophy*, p. 102; Maurice Testard, "Étude sur la composition dans le *De officiis ministrorum* de Saint Ambroise," *Ambroise de Milan: XVI* centenaire de son élection épiscopale*, ed. Yves-Marie Duval (Paris, 1974), pp. 182–83; "Observations sur le thème de la *conscientia* dans le *De officiis ministrorum* de saint Ambroise," *REL*, 51 (1973), 226–27, 238–39, 252–53.

[28] Marcia L. Colish, *The Stoic Tradition from Antiquity to the Early Middle Ages*, I: *Stoicism in Classical Latin Literature*, ch. 2, part 7. On the *De officiis* in particular see pp. 143–520.

these two bodies of thought.[29] A third major school of commentators, on the other hand, stresses that Ambrose was well aware of the differences between Stoicism and Christianity and that he accented them, whether in order to argue for the superiority of Christian revelation or to employ pagan philosophy in its service.[30] Many members of this third group share with their confrères in the first a belief in the purity of Cicero's Stoicism that cannot be sustained. The most balanced view of the *De officiis ministrorum* that has been put forth to date is that of Goulven Madec.[31] Madec recognizes that Ambrose was fully capable of quoting Cicero while giving a very different sense to his terminology, a sense that may be Ambrosian and not merely Christian. He is correct in noting that Ambrose sought neither to synthesize Christianity with Stoicism nor to contrast them systematically in a tendentious manner. His real goal, rather, was to use whatever authentic wisdom was available for the pedagogical purposes at hand in the *De officiis ministrorum*.

One must agree with Madec thus far; still, more is going on in the *De officiis ministrorum* than even he has noticed. Ambrose is not only using the ideas he has received for his immediate practical ends. He is both more speculative and more creative than he has been judged to be. Ambrose redefines the cardinal virtues not only in terms of Christian faith

---

[29] See, for instance, J. T. Muckle, "The De Officiis Ministrorum of Saint Ambrose," *Mediaeval Studies*, 1 (1939), 63–80; Maria Luisa Ricci, "Fortuna di una formula ciceroniana presso Sant'Ambrogio (a proposito di *iustitia*)," *Studi italiani di filologia classica*, n.s. 43 (1971), 222–45; Theodor Schmidt, *Ambrosius, sein Werk de officiis libri III und die Stoa* (Augsburg, 1897).

[30] See, for instance, Alcuin F. Coyle, "Cicero's De officiis and the De officiis ministrorum of St. Ambrose," *Franciscan Studies*, 15 (1955), 224–56; Th. Deman, "Le 'De officiis' de saint Ambroise dans l'histoire de la théologie morale," *RSPT*, 37 (1953), 409–22; Joannes Draeseke, "M. Tulli Ciceronis et Ambrosii episcopi Mediolanensis de officiis libri tres inter se comparantur," *Rivista di filologia e di istruzione classica*, 14 (1876), 121–64; Dudden, *Life and Times*, II, 502, 505, 508–10, 516–19, 521–36, 544–45, 551–54; F. Hasler, *Ueber das Verhältnis der heidnischen und christlichen Ethik auf Grund einer Vergleichung des ciceronianischen Buches "De officiis" mit dem gleichnamigen des heiligen Ambrosius* (München, 1866), pp. 18–48; Pierre de Labriolle, "Le 'De Officiis ministrorum' de saint Ambroise et le 'De Officiis' de Cicéron," *Revue des cours et conférences*, 16:2 (1907–08), 177–86; *The Life and Times of St. Ambrose*, trans. Herbert Wilson (St. Louis, 1928), pp. 186–204; Angelo Paredi, *Saint Ambrose: His Life and Times*, trans. M. Joseph Costelloe (Notre Dame, 1964), pp. 317–21; Jakob Reeb, *Ueber die Grundlagen des Sittlichen nach Cicero und Ambrosius: Vergleich ihrer Schriften de officiis*, Programm der kgl. Studien-Anhalt Zweibrücken zum Schlusse des Studienjahres 1875/76 (Zweibrücken, 1876). Peter Circis, *Ennoblement of the Pagan Virtues: A Comparative Treatise on Virtues in Cicero's Book De officiis and in St. Ambrose's Book De officiis ministrorum* (Rome, 1955) is an effort to demonstrate the superiority of Christian to pagan ethics in the guise of a scholarly work. Hans von Campenhausen, *The Fathers of the Latin Church*, trans. Manfred Hoffmann (London, 1964), p. 124, sees many of the same departures from orthodox Stoicism in Ambrose as are noted by other scholars above but interprets them as indications of his preference for other philosophical positions.

[31] Madec, *S. Ambroise*, pp. 82–85, 90–97, 133, 139–41, 162–66, 180–82, 342, 344–45.

and grace as preconditions for eternal life but also in terms of Platonism and Aristotelianism and in the light of his own ethical and psychological predilections. His redefinitions have the effect of deStoicizing the virtues in some respects and treating them, in other respects, in a more integrally Stoic manner than Cicero does. Cicero himself had modified a number of key Stoic ethical categories. Ambrose's alterations of the same categories are not always consistent with Cicero's. Even when they are the same, his reasons for making them are quite different. Ambrose's own perspective and concerns thus lead him to depart decisively from Cicero, however close his formal adherance to the *De officiis* may be. Although he structures the *De officiis ministrorum* in terms of Cicero's distinction between the *honestum* and the *utile*, his strategy for reconciling the apparent conflict between them is the obverse of Cicero's. Finally, Ambrose does not come to grips consistently with one of Cicero's major contributions to the Stoic tradition, the doctrine of natural law. A fully nuanced appreciation of Ambrose's achievement in this treatise, and of his own place in the Stoic tradition, must take all of these considerations into account.

Following Cicero's organizational scheme, Ambrose divides the *De officiis ministrorum* into three books, the first defining the key terms of *honestum* and *utile* and analyzing the *honestum* under the heading of the four cardinal virtues, the second treating the *utile*, and the third discussing the reconciliation of the *honestum* and the *utile*. As with Cicero, his initial definitions are not entirely Stoic. The *honestum*, he states, deals with moral dignity and integrity (*ad decus honestatemque vitae*) while the *utile* deals with the conveniences of life (*ad vitae commoda*). Both the *honestum* and the *utile* admit of gradations, for Ambrose; hence the inquiry will involve a comparison of the merits of different values within each category.[32] Three points are immediately noticeable about Ambrose's handling of these terms. First, following Cicero, he sees gradations in the *honestum*, reflecting an Aristotelian preference for a hierarchy of goods over the unitary Stoic *summum bonum*. Second, he does not equate the *honestum* with the Stoic *summum bonum* as such. Neither had Cicero, but Ambrose's reasons are quite different. Cicero had criticized the Stoic *summum bonum* because it did not include bodily goods; his own definition of the *honestum* consequently identifies it with the *media officia* as the norm and he places the *honestum* so defined under the judgment of the *utile*. Ambrose also treats the *honestum* not as a norm but as a means to an end. But the end toward which the *honestum*, no less than the *utile*, is directed is the blessed life to come:

---

[32] *De officiis ministrorum* 1.9.27, *PL*, 16, col. 31-32.

Nos autem nihil omnius nisi quod deceat et honestum sit, futurorum magis quam praesentium metimur formula: nihilque utile quod ad vitae illius aeternae prosit gratiam definimus, non quod ad delectionem praesentis.[33]

We posit the rule that nothing is fitting or right unless it is oriented toward future goods more than to present ones; and we state that nothing is useful unless it directs us to the grace of that life eternal, and not to the enjoyment of the present.

Third, while Cicero departs from the Stoa in treating the advantages of this life as goods, Ambrose departs from the Stoa in treating them as evils.[34]

Prefacing his next move with the idea, found frequently in Ambrose as well as in the apologists, that the philosophers derived their wisdom from the Bible,[35] he proceeds to endow the duties, whether perfect (*perfectum*) or ordinary (*medium*), with a Christian content, both in the way he describes them and by his illustration of them with Scriptural examples. The ordinary duties, he says, involve the fulfillment of the Ten Commandments, an obedience which, while necessary, is not sufficient. The perfect duties include the apostolic counsels as well.[36] In order for the system in which these duties are situated to work, Ambrose observes, one must hold that God takes cognizance of human actions, rewarding virtue and punishing vice, a point missed by Epicurus and Aristotle. But, in arguing for God's care for man, Ambrose parts company with Minucius Felix and Lactantius and ignores the Stoic arguments for theodicy. Instead, his support for God's providence, benevolence, and justice is purely Biblical, resting on God's revealed promises to man.[37]

In moving to the definition of the cardinal virtues which govern the duties, Ambrose nods in the direction of Panaetian casuistry, agreeing that the individual's age, condition, and ability affect the application of the duties to him. Like Cicero he omits sex as a factor in this list, a circumstance that, in his case, can be explained by the exclusively masculine occupational group to which he addresses the *De officiis ministrorum*. This preface to the cardinal virtues also gives Ambrose the occasion to yoke Stoic doctrine to insights derived from other philosophical traditions. In commenting on the point that the chief duty of youth is modesty, which counsels decorum,[38] he urges, à propos of decorum: *Naturam*

---

[33] Ibid. 1.9.28, *PL*, 16, col. 32.
[34] Ibid. 1.9.29.
[35] Ibid. 1.11.36.
[36] Ibid. 1.11.36–39.
[37] Ibid. 1.13.47–50, 1.14.51–1.16.64.
[38] Ibid. 1.17.65–1.24.105.

imitemur: ejus effigies, formula disciplina, forma honestatis est ("Let us follow nature. Her imitation is a principle of education and a model of virtue.")[39] This sounds completely Stoic. But Ambrose goes on to advocate the Aristotelian golden mean (*modum tenere in omnibus*)[40] and to describe virtue as a *habitus* that operates by curbing nature. The passions are implanted in man's nature, he states, and cannot be uprooted. Yet, by continual practice and determination they may be ruled by reason, so that inner tranquillity becomes a connatural condition. Like Cicero, Ambrose accepts the Platonic and Aristotelian adaptations of Stoic anthropology admitted by Panaetius but he goes much farther than Cicero in limiting the ethical relevance of bodily goods related to the passions.

Ambrose's definitions of the cardinal virtues themselves, which take up most of Book 1, show a similar independence in his handling of his sources. He defines prudence as the search for truth, the desire for full knowledge, not as the possession of wisdom, either in a speculative Platonic and Aristotelian sense or in a practical Stoic sense. This definition is Ambrose's own. He has recourse to the traditional Platonic and Aristotelian definition of justice as Romanized by Cicero. Justice *suum cuique tribuit, alienum non vindicat, utilitatem propriam negligit, ut communum aequitatem custodiat* ("gives to each his own, does not harm others, ignores its own interest in order to care for the common weal,") although the element of self-abnegation is more pronounced in Ambrose's formula than in Cicero's. Ambrosian fortitude strikes the characteristic Stoic note of *magnitudo animi* that underlies this virtue in both military and civic pursuits. Temperance, for Ambrose, is the preservation of right order and method in everything we say or do, a definition reflecting the Panaetian and Ciceronian norm of decorum in both its ethical and rhetorical dimensions.[41] It is also a definition that suggests the ethical priorities indicated by Ambrose in the *De Iacob*. Unlike the Stoics, who saw prudence as the chief virtue since all ethical choices require correct intellectual judgments and must be conformable with reason, and unlike Aristotle and Cicero, who evaluated all ethical acts in the light of justice because the end of justice is the common good, Ambrose makes temperance the key virtue. In *De Iacob* he does so because self-discipline precedes enlightenment. Here he accents temperance by making decorum the rule governing the exercise of all the other virtues.

There is a still more radical shift afoot in Ambrose's handling of the virtues. Although he does not necessarily adhere to Stoic definitions of the virtues in all respects, he restores to this topic a central Stoic prem-

---

[39] Ibid. 1.19.84, *PL*, 16, col. 48.
[40] Ibid. 1.20.89, *PL*, 16, col. 50.
[41] Ibid. 1.24.115, *PL*, 16, col. 57.

ise, the unity of the virtues as manifestations of a fixed ethical orientation toward the good on the part of the moral subject. He does this in
two ways, by showing that the virtues mutually imply each other and
by choosing as his fixed ethical intention a Christian motivation in place
of the rational autarchy of the Stoa. For Ambrose, faith and charity are
the conditions that make possible all the virtues in turn. In the case of
prudence, the knowledge involved in this virtue is faith. This notion explains Ambrose's definition of prudence as a state of longing for a
knowledge that is, as yet, unconsummated. It also explains his choice of
Abraham as the Biblical worthy who best exemplifies prudence. The faith
which Ambrose equates with prudence entails the acceptance of nature,
in the sense of recognizing man's status as the creation of a God Whose
ways govern the world even at the expense of human expectations. In
the same way, nature here means man's acknowledgement that his own
desire for truth is infused in him by God. Prudence necessarily involves
duties because it inspires man to accord to the Creator the honor and
obedience that is due Him. Prudence is thus inseparable from justice,
since it renders to God what is appropriate to Him. In the same way, it
is inseparable from all the other virtues since each likewise requires man's
recognition of God's gifts and rights.[42]   In the case of justice, what is
involved are one's obligations to oneself, one's family, the community,
and God, in ascending order of importance. Justice, too, implies the other
virtues, since it requires the knowledge of what is fitting, the courage to
act rightly, and decorum in translating intention into action. In determining how best to apply the traditional *suum cuique* formula, Ambrose
states that charity is the norm of justice.[43] On this basis he overrides
Cicero's principle that private property rights have any claims at all in
relation to the common good. Although in dismissing Cicero's idea of
justice as coordinating private and public rights Ambrose lumps it together with the "philosophers'" position as such, the express warrant he
invokes for so doing is Stoicism. The Stoics, he acknowledges, supported
the doctrine of common ownership on the grounds of its consistency with
nature, a position he applauds even though he thinks the Stoics derived
it from the Old Testament.[44] In essence Ambrose is more Stoic on this
point than Cicero is. At the same time he alters profoundly the institutional expression of justice:

---

[42] Ibid. 1.25.117–1.27.126.
[43] Ibid. 1.27.127–1.28.131.
[44] Ibid. 1.28.132–133. On Ambrose's position on private property in the *De off. min.*
see Louis J. Swift, "*Iustitia* and *ius privatum*: Ambrose on Private Property," *AJP*, 100
(1979), 176–87.

Fundamentum ergo est justitiae fides; justorum enim corda meditantur fidem; et qui se justus accusat, justitiam supra fidem collocat; nam tunc justitia ejus apparet, si vera fateatur, . . . id est, Christum in fundamenta Ecclesiae. Fides enim omnium, Christus; Ecclesia autem quaedam forma justitiae est. Commune jus omnium in commune orat, in commune operatur, in commune tentatur.[45]

The foundation of justice is therefore faith, for the hearts of the just meditate on faith. The man who charges himself as just sets justice upon faith, for his justice is manifest when he confesses the truth, . . . that is, Christ as the foundation of the Church. For Christ is the faith for all men. But the Church is, as it were, the outward form of justice. She is a common law for all; in common she prays; in common she works; in common she is tempted.

For Cicero, the institutional correlative of justice is the good society which he identifies with the Roman Republic. Ambrose substitutes the Christian church as a visible community grounded in faith both for Cicero's ideal republic and for the Stoic cosmopolis ruled by natural law.

The duties that Ambrose derives from justice likewise supersede the obligations of nature. This is certainly the case for the major aspect of justice he discusses, kindness (*beneficentia*) or good will (*benevolentia*). A person adorned with this virtue freely and sincerely wills the good of others, with no thought of his own reputation and advantage. He returns benefits to those from whom he has received them. But, for Ambrose, in contrast with Cicero, the facts of the case and the needs of the others are the only worthy considerations to bear in mind. One's personal feelings and affections must be disregarded, although one must proceed with decorum.[46] In Ambrose's view the good will basic to beneficence springs not merely from the fact that all men share a common nature but mainly from the fellowship of faith, the bond of baptism, the kinship created by grace, and the communion of the sacraments: *Tantum valet benevolentia, ut plerumque pignora vincat naturae* ("And so important is good will that it often triumphs over the pledges of nature.")[47]

In the case of fortitude Ambrose confines himself to its civic manifestations, considering the clerical audience for whom he is writing. He follows the Stoics in asserting that fortitude is the force of intellect and will and not mere physical strength, and that it entails the prevention of harm as well as its correction. Here he agrees with Aristotle, Panaetius, and Cicero and, as is often the case when he supports philosophical ideas overtly, he says that they appropriated this notion from the Bible.[48] For-

---

[45] *De off. min.* 1.29.142, *PL*, 16, col. 64-65.
[46] Ibid. 1.30.143–1.32.169.
[47] Ibid. 1.34.174, *PL*, 16, col. 74.
[48] Ibid. 1.36.179–180.

titude is closely associated with the other virtues. It depends on the ability to rule oneself and to maintain equanimity. Thus, it entails temperance. It counts externals as unimportant and strives only for the highest good. While it does not shrink from danger it does not attempt the impossible or take unreasonable risks, thus showing its connection with prudence. At the same time, for Ambrose, the source of fortitude is Christ. It is He Who grants to the brave the strength and endurance which they manifest in this virtue.[49]

The fourth and last virtue, temperance, has as its basic condition and chief characteristic tranquillity of mind. Ambrosian temperance is most clearly linked to the virtue of prudence, for it involves self-knowledge in performing the duties appropriate to the individual's talents, obligations, and circumstances. Temperance also supplies the decorum that governs the practice of all the other virtues. Decorum, indeed, is the main rubric under which Ambrose analyzes temperance. What interests him particularly about decorum is its role in guiding the exercise of virtue, rather than the conditions of self-knowledge and self-rule that make it possible. He is much less interested in contemplating autarchy in itself as a psychological state than with examining its consequences in action.

The principal features of decorum, for Ambrose, are its internal consistency and harmony and its correspondence with nature; *decorum est secundum naturam vivere, . . . et turpe est quod sit contra naturam* ("for decorum is life in accordance with nature, . . . and vice is what is contrary to nature.")[50] This observation brings Ambrose face to face with the topic where his own most salient inconsistency resides. From virtue as life in accordance with nature he moves to a discussion of the passions, which blurs the Stoicism, not to mention the intrinsic clarity, of his idea of nature itself. The passions, Ambrose states, are natural. They must be controlled by reason.[51] Although natural, the passions conflict with virtue, which Ambrose defines as *naturalis quaedam censura et gravitasque morum* ("a sort of natural judgment and seriousness of manner.")[52] Here Ambrose wavers between the early Stoic identification of reason and virtue with nature, with its correlative view of the passions as contrary to nature, and the Platonic, Aristotelian, middle Stoic, and Ciceronian conception of the passions as natural but as subject to the rule of reason if they are to lead to virtue. He does not see the problem involved in using nature simultaneously in both senses, although this enables him to

---

[49] Ibid. 1.36.181–1.38.201.
[50] Ibid. 1.46.222, *PL*, 16, col. 89-90. For the whole discussion of temperance see 1.43.219–1.46.222.
[51] Ibid. 1.47.227–229.
[52] Ibid. 1.47.229, *PL*, 16, col. 91.

invoke nature as an ethical norm while at the same time instructing one natural faculty to repress another. Completely absent from Ambrose's analysis is the Stoic idea of *eupatheia*, which might have provided at least a partial solution to the dilemma. The only passions he addresses are such impulses as anger, anxiety, lust, and luxury. His inconsistency on what nature is and whether virtue means following nature or overcoming it is paralleled by his inconsistency in treating the theme of natural law as a moral norm. At the conclusion of his analysis of temperance, which ends his consideration of the cardinal virtues in Book 1, he reiterates the point that Christ is the foundation on which all the virtues rest.[53] Yet the ambiguity remains as to whether he means a Stoicized Christ understood as the *logos* of the natural world or a Biblical Christ Whose liberating grace transcends nature.

If Ambrose's *honesta* are not Stoic ends in themselves but means to the end of eternal life this is even more true of his *utilia*, the subject of Book 2 of the *De officiis ministrorum*. Ambrose begins this section of the work by criticizing the various philosophical definitions of the *summum bonum* as consisting in knowledge, pleasure, freedom from pain, the combination of pleasure and freedom from pain, virtue *per se*, a position he attributes correctly to Zeno, or a combination of virtue and bodily advantage, as the Peripatetics teach. In contrast to all of these views he argues that the happy life involves the combination of faith and good works which Scripture prescribes as the means to eternal joy. Properly speaking, then, eternal life is the *summum bonum*. Faith and works alone can empower man to withstand the adversities and vicissitudes of life. None of the philosophical schools can offer a source of strength that is remotely comparable with the divine grace that engenders faith and works. Here Ambrose preserves the psychological rationale that persuades the Stoics to posit virtue as the only good. But, finding autarchy inadequate to bear the psychic weight that the Stoics ask it to carry, he substitutes God as a support whose strength is infinite. This Christian reformulation of Stoic *apatheia* brings other alterations in its suite. It leads Ambrose to revalue both suffering and wordly goods. Far from being an *adiaphoron* or an adversity that man should learn to master, suffering, he holds, can have a positive redemptive function. By the same token, the things of this world regarded as goods or as preferables by the philosophers may actually be impediments to virtue. To the extent that Ambrose credits any of the philosophical schools with approximating his definition of the *summum bonum*, he repeats that they have borrowed it from the Bible.[54] But the

---

[53] Ibid. 1.50.251.
[54] Ibid. 2.1.3–2.5.21.

main thrust of his consideration of the *summum bonum* is to relativize the *honestum* which he had treated under the heading of the four cardinal virtues.

Ambrose reinterprets the *utile* even more extensively. He analyzes it under the rubric of what is conducive to the virtues of faith and works that in turn lead to eternal life, not in terms of worldly advantage. Ambrose's *honestum* and *utile* actually coincide, since he sees both as means to the same end. Both are directed toward the imitation and service of Christ.[55] Still, he borrows the strategy of Book 2 of Cicero's *De officiis* in arguing that virtue is useful. Nothing, after all, could be more to man's advantage than the love of God. And nothing could be more effective in winning people's good opinion and inspiring them to seek this love than the possession of it oneself, a moral state that cannot be faked.[56] As with Cicero, Ambrose recapitulates the virtues he has already discussed in Book 1 in order to illustrate this point in the case of each of them, citing some *exempla utilitatis* from recent Christian history as well. None the less, what he actually does in his own second book is to turn Cicero inside out. This he accomplishes not merely by redefining the *summum bonum* in Christian terms but by altering the relationship that Cicero had posited between the *honestum* and the *utile*. In a sense both authors redefine the *honestum* as the *utile*, Cicero by obliterating the idea of virtue as an end in itself and Ambrose by presenting the *honestum*, like the *utile*, as a means to eternal life. But at the same time Ambrose reclassifies the *utile* as a species of the *honestum* by taking it out of the sphere of worldly advantage altogether and by associating it, along with the *honestum*, with man's redemption.

With this foundation laid, Ambrose makes short work of reconciling the *honestum* and the *utile*, the task of Book 3. In essence, he notes, this is a false problem. It is true that the Stoics themselves, in contrast to Cicero, would have viewed the assignment as a false problem as well, although for quite different reasons. For the Stoics, the *utilia* are *adiaphora*, preferables that may be graded but that are morally neutral as a group, distinct in kind from the *summum bonum*. For Ambrose, on the other hand, there is no real difference between the *honestum* and the *utile* since both are understood only with reference to the love of God and the pastoral responsibility of drawing men to it.[57] In handling the question of how to choose among alternative courses of action the issue for Ambrose is therefore not the grading of either the *utile* or the *honestum* as such but rather the appeal to a completely different standard: which course of ac-

---

[55] Ibid. 2.6.22–2.7.29.
[56] Ibid. 2.8.40–2.29.151.
[57] Ibid. 3.2.8–9, 3.2.12.

tion is the most edifying, the most helpful to the most people, the most Christlike?[58] This criterion, Ambrose observes, is good not only because it is Christian but also because it is in conformity with nature, since men are bound by the law of nature to work for the common weal, which in this case means the redemption of one's fellow man. The virtuous life is in accordance with nature, he concludes, because God made all things very good,[59] a formulation of this issue which continues to leave open the question of whether the goodness of nature is intrinsic to it or whether its goodness derives from the redemption of nature by grace.

Most of Book 3 of the *De officiis ministrorum* is composed of examples, generally drawn from the Old Testament but with a few from classical sources, illustrating the point that vice has no utility and that honest ends cannot be attained by dishonest means, following the schema of the last book of Cicero's *De officiis*. Ambrose also adverts to a specifically Stoic and Ciceronian theme in this connection, friendship. His handling of this topic, as is the case with several others in the *De officiis ministrorum*, is both more and less Stoic than Cicero's. Ambrose dismisses worldly advantage as an aspect of friendship, agreeing with the Stoics that friends are freely chosen because of the moral excellence they recognize in each other. At the same time, the virtue that binds them together is charity. While they possess this virtue, they are also Christians *in via*, not fully perfected Stoic sages. Thus they have a right and a duty to correct each other's faults. Ambrose agrees with Cicero that one may never do evil to please a friend, a consideration that would never arise in a strictly Stoic context. *A fortiori*, he adds, the faith may never be set aside for a friend.[60] The pattern of Christ, here as elsewhere, is the one that Ambrose enjoins his readers to follow. His inclusion of the topic of friendship is a good reflection of his rhetorical concern with fitting the argument to the audience, coupled with his pastoral interest in addressing their situational needs. As clergymen many of his readers will live detached from the usual social and affective networks. Ambrose's Christianization of the Stoic-Ciceronian theme of friendship, with which he closes the *De officiis ministrorum*, is an excellent index of his broader approach to the Stoic tradition and to his other acknowledged sources. For, in this instance we can see him exercising his own judgment, investing the concepts, arguments, and structures that he borrows with his own meanings, even at the points where he appears to be at his most imitative, so as to unite the interest they inspire in him as a psychologist and an ethicist with his practical responsibilities as a pastor and teacher.

---

[58] Ibid. 3.2.13–3.3.15.
[59] Ibid. 3.3.22–3.4.28.
[60] Ibid. 3.22.126–138.

In comparing Ambrose's use of Stoic ethics with Cicero's more generally a number of conclusions can now be drawn. Ambrose certainly appropriates much of Cicero's format, terminology, strategy, and schema although he often invests them with a very different content and meaning. He makes some of the same substantive modifications of Stoic doctrine as Cicero does, notably in his admission of Platonic and Aristotelian anthropology. However, Cicero and Ambrose make these changes for contrasting reasons. Cicero's aim is to soften the rigor and the austere rationalism of the Stoic *summum bonum*. He accepts the infrarational faculties in man as ethically relevant in order to support the positive value of bodily goods. Ambrose's aim in rejecting the monistic psychology of the early Stoa is to underscore the distinction between the body and the soul, as a means of elevating the soul over the body in the light of the soul's eternal destiny. In effect he uses a Platonic and Neoplatonic anthropology against the Stoa in the service of Christian ends. Cicero, while he attacks the Stoic conception of the sage as an unattainable ideal, still adheres to the autarchic psychology of the Stoa as the strongest bulwark against the vicissitudes of fortune and as the surest means of self-consolation. Ambrose retains the idealism of the Stoic sage in all its rigor but energizes him with the liberating power of divine grace.

Ambrose restores an authentically Stoic emphasis to the idea that all the virtues imply each other, even though he rejects the correlative principle that all the sins are equal. However, the unity which he sees underlying the virtues is a corollary not only of their functional interrelationships but also of their common foundation in faith and charity. He supplements these Christian virtues with Peripatetic *habitus* and counsels the golden mean, not ascetic extremism, in their exercise. To the extent that Ambrose elevates one virtue above the others his choice rests on temperance rather than on Stoic prudence or Aristotelian-Ciceronian justice. This preference reflects the fact that his approach to the virtues is not primarily a formal or teleological one; rather, he assesses them from a developmental and functional standpoint. Self-discipline precedes understanding in the acquisition of virtue and decorum governs the practice of virtue. Ambrose follows Cicero in redefining the *honestum* and in rejecting its identification with the Stoic *summum bonum*. Like Cicero he coordinates the *honestum* with the *utile* by treating them both as useful. However, his definition of the *utile* orders it, like the *honestum*, to eternal life while Cicero's definition of the *honestum* has the effect of lowering the ceiling of the *summum bonum* to the level of goods that can serve man's worldly advantage. The result of Cicero's reformulation of the *honestum* and the *utile* is to assimilate the *honestum* to the *utile*; the result of Ambrose's handling of the same topic is exactly the reverse. Instead of bringing the Stoic sage down to earth, where his inner autonomy can be retained while its demands are moderated, Ambrose seeks to bring the Stoic sage into the fullness of being through Christian redemption, a process neither purely autonomous nor purely heteronomous, working as it does both above him, in him, and through him and drawing him and his fellow man to God in the Christian community, both in this life and the next.

The major and irreducible ambiguity that remains in Ambrose's treatment of Stoic themes lies in his conflicting conceptions of nature and natural law. He sometimes identifies nature with reason, sometimes with the infrarational faculties in man that give rise to the passions, and sometimes with a world created and redeemed by a revealed God, radically conditioned by man's sin and Christ's salvation and, as such, knowable by faith. The common nature shared by men in Ambrose's thought partakes of nature in all of these senses, notwithstanding the inconsistencies that result. In spite of this unresolved difficulty, Ambrose occupies an important place in the history of the Stoic tradition. His ethical theology Christianizes that tradition in a creative and judicious way. Sometimes selectively, sometimes integrally, and sometimes by filling old bottles with new wine, Ambrose reexpresses the Stoic doctrine of the sage and the Stoic vision of the good life in his own portrayal of the Christian sage and by his relocation of the Stoic cosmopolis in the Christian Church.

II. St. Jerome

St. Jerome (ca. 347–420) is generally reputed to be the greatest humanist among the Church Fathers. His literary and editorial achievements certainly entitle him to that claim. He is, however, much less important than Ambrose in the history of the Stoic tradition. Jerome's knowledge of philosophy is that of a well-rounded amateur.[61] His interest in the subject is superficial. He rarely formulates the concerns that he sees as most pressing in philosophical terms. To the extent that the pagan classics represented a problem to Jerome he poses and solves that problem in terms of literature. The famous dream he reports, in which he was judged by God and cast into outer darkness for being a Ciceronian, the rhetorical question he subsequently poses, *Quid facit cum*

---

[61] J. N. D. Kelly, *Jerome, His Life, Writings, and Controversies* (London, 1975), pp. 16–17. Kelly provides a sound and balanced assessment. The most exhaustive bibliography on Jerome's relation to the classics can be found in the preface of his *Opera exegetica*, ed. Paul de Lagarde, Germanus Morin, and Marc Andriaen, CC, 72 (Turnhout, 1959), pp. ix-lix.

psalterio Horatius? cum evangelis Maro? cum apostolo Cicero? ("What has Horace to do with the Psalter, Vergil with the Gospels, Cicero with Paul?")[62] and the resolution he proposes in his equally famous comparison between the classics and the pagan woman of Deuteronomy whom the Israelite may marry after she has been purified,[63] are all equally telling. As has often been noted, Jerome's stated anxieties did not really interfere with his attachment to the classics.[64] There is a distinctly rhetorical cast to the way he presents the issue to Eustochium, the addressee of the letter in which he describes his Ciceronian dream. She was not only a member of his circle of high-born ascetic lady friends but also a descendant of Scipio. For her benefit he evokes the *Somnium Scipionis* and other literary models of dreams of judgment, both pagan and Christian.[65] The Biblical passage that he uses to lay the problem to rest is also important as an index of Jerome's mentality. He chooses an erotic image—the foreign woman, beautiful, tempting, intrinsically desirable, a prize of war who is in the Israelite's power but who is forbidden to him by the law of God. Yet, after she is purified, he may espouse her. The nuptials, however, do not make her his equal. She may be loved and enjoyed but, for Jerome, she is and remains the subordinate of her husband.

Both secular learning and pagan error are categories that Jerome views from a literary perspective, whether he is commenting on their appeal, their danger, or their utility. It is the aesthetic attraction of the authors and not the wisdom of the philosophers that is the lure. Jerome's recourse to philosophy is thus as inconsequential as it is indiscriminate. He does not single out the Stoics for special attention. Nor is he more or less likely to typify them as repositories of truth or as wellsprings of error than is the case with the other schools.[66] He occasionally stumbles over Stoic doctrines, either misunderstanding their content or applying them inappositely. His use of Stoicism is rarely integral, either in his grasp of

---

[62] *Epistula* 22.29.7; for the story of the dream 22.30.1–5, to Eustochium, ca. 384, ed. Isidorus Hilberg, CSEL, 54–56 (Vienna, 1910–18); trans. Charles Christopher Mierow, ACW, 33 (Westminster, Md., 1963).

[63] *Ep.* 21.13.1–9, to Pope Damasus, 383; *Ep.* 70.2–5, to Magnus, 397.

[64] For excellent recent treatments and references to the literature on this point see Kelly, *Jerome*, pp. 41–44; Edwin A. Quain, "St. Jerome as a Humanist," *A Monument to Saint Jerome: Essays on Some Aspects of His Life, Works and Influence*, ed. Francis X. Murphy (New York, 1952), pp. 220–23.

[65] This point has been brought out very clearly by Paul Antin, "Autour du songe de S. Jérôme," *Recueil sur saint Jérôme* (Bruxelles, 1968), pp. 71–100, who also provides the most detailed bibliographical review of the Ciceronian dream.

[66] See, on the other hand, Rudolf Eiswirth, *Hieronymus' Stellung zur Literatur und Kunst* (Wiesbaden, 1955), p. 44; Arthur Stanley Pease, "The Attitude of Jerome towards Pagan Literature," *TAPA*, 50 (1919), 161–65, who do not make the necessary distinctions concerning genre and context.

the ideas involved or in the way he incorporates them into his thought. Jerome treats Stoicism in an essentially decorative manner. The Stoa occasionally provides illustrations for his arguments but it practically never contributes to their substance. While he is interested primarily in Stoic ethics he also refers to a number of physical and anthropological themes. His judgment on Stoicism is neither wholly negative nor wholly positive, whether he expresses his attitude overtly or not.

For Jerome, unlike Ambrose, the genre of the works in which his references to Stoicism occur and the particular contexts in which they appear are likely to affect the position he takes. Another factor that conditions Jerome's approach to the Stoa is his personality. In moving from Ambrose to Jerome we move away from the confident, judicious administrator whose achievement of a new and balanced integration of his sources bespeaks his inner serenity, his intellectual penetration, and his awareness of his pastoral responsibilities. Instead, we move to a man who is brilliant but embittered, whose richly merited renown as a Scripture scholar did not give him inner peace, a man driven to ascetic extremism by his inability to deal with the body, a man incapable of human relationships that he could not dominate, who had a flair for antagonizing people and turning friends into enemies and who could, at the same time, be genuinely surprised and hurt by the hostility that his behavior provoked in others.[67]

Jerome manifests this temperament in the various kinds of works that he wrote. Each genre also reveals a different kind of response to Stoicism. The largest single subdivision of his *œuvre* comprises his exegetical works, produced as an adjunct to his greatest scholarly accomplishment, his translation of the Vulgate Bible. As an exegete Jerome is at his most professional and confident. He generally sees philosophy as irrelevant to the elucidation of the Biblical text. His references to Stoicism in this context are thus sparse and incidental and they are more likely to be negative and incorrect here than anywhere else. A second major group of Jerome's writings are the polemics he addressed to heretics or others he disagreed with. Jerome chose his controversies because of their personal dimensions for him. He never engaged in any debate unless he could recast it in *ad hominem* terms. He selected his antagonists and arrayed his weapons both out of personal animus and out of the desire for self-protection. His role in the Origenist controversy is a signal case in point. In his early years Jerome had translated a number of Origen's

---

[67] A convincing assessment of Jerome's personality making judicious use of Freudian categories has been contributed by Charles-Henri Nodet, "Position de Saint Jérôme en face des problèmes sexuels," *Mystique et continence*, Travaux scientifiques du VIIᵉ congrès international d'Avon (Paris, 1952), pp. 308–56.

Biblical commentaries into Latin and had praised him warmly as an exegete. When he entered the lists against Origen's views in other areas in the latter part of his career he found a need to tar several contemporaries with the Origenist brush as a means of asserting his own orthodoxy. For this purpose Jerome did not hesitate to stab former friends in the back or to resort to oratorical overkill. Given Jerome's propensities as a controversialist is it not surprising to find him adopting a Tertullianesque stance and style in these works. He follows the line that the philosophers, including the Stoics, have led Christians into error. In the light of what he sometimes says elsewhere about the same or related doctrines, this argument has to be understood as a rhetorical ploy. The third group of Jerome's writings include his *De viris illustribus* and letters. Stoic references are the densest here and are related the most preclusively to ethics. Although these works are by no means free from polemic or self-advertisement, Jerome's attitude toward Stoicism is, on the whole, more positive than in his controversial and exegetical treatises. Here too, however, he tends to apply the Stoic themes he uses for the purpose of coloristic illustration or amplification; and the Hieronymian temperament is visible at every turn.

One topic that cuts across all the genres of Jerome's writing and that reflects his literary bent is his interest in the Stoics as stylists. Jerome is the first Latin Christian author to pay any attention to this subject although it occurs repeatedly in classical Latin literature. Jerome freely mixes praise and blame. He is familiar with Chrysippus' reputation for logical rigor matched by verbal precision. In a controversial work dedicated to Pammachius, son-in-law of his chief dévotée Paula and a supporter of Jerome in the anti-Origenist campaign, he compliments Pammachius for his learning, saying that he is more fluent than Demosthenes, acuter than Chrysippus, and wiser than Plato.[68] Jerome applies the same description to an antagonist, Vigilantius, who had accused Jerome himself of succumbing to the Origenist heresy. Jerome attacks Vigilantius in turn for boasting that he, Jerome, had hesitated to rebut him because he feared the sting of Vigilantius' satire, as sharp as that of Chrysippus,[69] and sets about the refute him. The same Chrysippian trait is mentioned in another polemical work dealing with Origenism, an apology directed against Rufinus, a former friend whom Jerome criticized for his objections to his own exegetical style. Rufinus, he says, claims that Jerome's exegesis is both Origenist and inconsistent. Seeking to confute the first charge by demolishing the second, Jerome responds that stylistic

---

[68] *Contra Joannem Hierosolymitanum ad Pammachium* 4, *PL*, 23, col. 374C.
[69] *Ep.* 61.3.1.

variety is perfectly acceptable, citing a number of classical authors whose
styles differed, including Chrysippus, whose writing, he notes, was in-
tricate and thorny.[70] On the other hand, in a letter to Pammachius discussing Biblical translation, he urges a plain and simple style, arguing
that the apostles, who spoke in this manner, overcame thereby both the
syllogisms of Aristotle and the contorted ingenuities of Chrysippus.[71]
Apart from his repeated acknowledgment of Chrysippus' style, which he
approves or disapproves depending on the context, Jerome is also aware
of the Stoic contribution to the *consolatio* as a literary-philosophical genre.
In a letter written to Heliodorus to comfort him on the death of his
nephew, a man whom Jerome also numbered among his correspondents, he notes that he has consulted a number of consolatory writers,
including Posidonius, as sources for material that may help him assuage
Heliodorus' grief.[72]

Jerome's approach to other Stoic themes is much more likely to be
conditioned by the type of work in which they appear. In his Scriptural
commentaries he runs the gamut from offhand references to undiffer-
entiated rejections of the Stoa along with all other schools to erroneous
reports on the Stoics' teachings to disagreement or agreement with their
views, correctly stated, whether expressly attributed to them or not. He
mentions Zeno as the founder of the Stoa in passing, by way of identifying Cyprus, his birthplace; he compares St. Paul's advice on the pur-
gation of man's sins with the sweats and hellebore prescribed by Chrysippus,[73] a cure that Jerome seems to be unique in attributing to him.
He levels several broadsides against philosophy as such, castigating Platonists, Aristotelians, Stoics, and Academics without distinguishing their
doctrines, as wolves among the flock leading Christians into heresy,[74] as
idolaters,[75] and as fools because of their ignorance of the true God.[76]
When it comes to Stoic theology more specifically, however, he ascribes
to Zeno and the Stoics, as well as to Vergil, the belief in one God who
is spirit and who binds the universe together,[77] ignoring the material nature of the Stoic God and his consubstantiality with the natural world.

---

[70] *Apologia adversus Rufini libri duo* 1.16, PL, 23, cols. 428A–429A.

[71] *Ep.* 57.12.

[72] *Ep.* 60.5.2.

[73] *In Hieremiam libri VI* 1.21.2, ed. Siegfried Reiter, CC, 74 (Turnhout, 1960); *Commentarium in Epistolam S. Pauli ad Galatas* 1.1, PL, 26, col. 350C.

[74] *Commentarium in Epistolam S. Pauli ad Titum* 3, PL, 26, col. 663A.

[75] *Commentariorum in Danielem* 1.1.26, ed. Franciscus Glorie, CC, 75A (Turnhout, 1964).

[76] *Commentarius in Ecclesiasten* 10.15, ed. Paul de Lagarde, Germanus Morin, and Marc
Adriaen, CC, 72 (Turnhout, 1959).

[77] *Commentariorum in Esaiam* 16.57.16, ed. Marc Andriaen, CC, 73A (Turnhout, 1963);
Commentariorum in Epistolam S. Pauli ad Ephesios 2.4, PL, 26, col. 529A. The latter passage
has been noted by Hagendahl, *Latin Fathers*, p. 124.

The majority of Jerome's citations of Stoicism in his exegetical works are ethical in focus. In this connection his treatment of the Stoa ranges from misunderstanding to disagreement to agreement. He attributes to the Stoa the distinction between wisdom (*sapientia*) and prudence (*prudentia*) that he posits, wisdom encompassing the knowledge of things divine and human and prudence applying to transient goods.[78] This conception smacks more of Platonism than of Stoicism, since the Stoics defined wisdom as prudence, combining in this virtue both the knowledge of things divine and human and the application of that knowledge in practice. There are two points at which Jerome stands in sharp opposition to Stoic ethics, one acknowledged and the other not. In commenting on St. Mark's report of the transfiguration of Christ, he contrasts the Christian transformation which it signifies with the moral transformation which the philosophers claim for their own systems. Referring here to Zeno as well as to Plato, Aristotle, and Epicurus, he attacks the lot as whited sepulchers who veiled their earth-bound teachings with dazzling words,[79] a criticism interesting not only on theological grounds but also for its Hieronymian sensitivity to the temptations hidden behind literary art. The second instance, which is also suggestive in the light of Jerome's aversion from sexuality, is his remark that, whenever the Scriptural text mentions the female or weaker sex, the reader should understand the passage as a reference to material things, since women are more enmeshed in matter than men are. This anti-feminist value judgment arises from his exegesis of Pharaoh's order that the sons of the enslaved Israelites be slain, but not the daughters. Holy Scripture, says Jerome, never mentions females when the author is speaking metaphorically about things pertaining to the redemption of the spirit.[80] This idea is a flat rejection of the Stoic position on the moral equality of the sexes, a principle that Jerome himself supports in detail elsewhere in his writings.

There are also a number of points in Jerome's Biblical commentaries where he agrees overtly with Stoic ethical teachings and reports them quite accurately. This is particularly true of his discussion of virtue and the passions. His most generous remarks on Stoic ethics in his exegetical works occur in his commentary on Isaiah, where he recapitulates with fidelity and approval the Stoic definitions of virtue, vice, and the *adiaphora*:

---

[78] *In Esaiam* 2.5.21, CC, 73; *Ad Ephesios* 1.1, *PL*, 26, col. 482A.

[79] *Tractatus in Marci Evangelium* 6.140–155, new ed., ed. Germanus Morin, CC, 78 (Turnhout, 1958).

[80] *In Ecclesiasten* 2.8, CC, 72. Jerome may also have derived this idea from Marius Victorinus. See below, ch. 3, p. 132.

Divitiae autem et sanitas corporis et rerum omnium abundantia, et his contraria, paupertas, infirmitas et inopia, etiam apud philosophos saeculi nec inter bona reputantur nec inter mala, sed appellantur indifferentia. Unde et Stoici, qui nostro dogmati in plerisque concordant, nihil appellant bonum, nisi solam honestatem atque virtutem; nihil malum, nisi turpitudinem.[81]

For wealth and bodily health and the abundance of all things, and their opposites poverty, sickness, and want, are likewise classified by the worldly philosophers as neither among the goods nor the evils, but are called things indifferent. And hence the Stoics, who agree with our teachings in many respects, call nothing good except uprightness and virtue alone and nothing evil except vice.

This passage, it might be noted, is not lacking in a polemical thrust, since it is an attack on the Judaizers in the Church who wish to equate Christian virtue with the prescriptions of the Mosaic law.

Jerome also provides a fairly extended treatment of the passions in his exegetical works, in which he likewise uses Stoic doctrine to support his interpretation of the Bible and its ethical imperatives. To begin with, he posits a distinction between passion (*passio*) and temptation (*propassio*) in his analysis of the passage where St. Matthew reports Christ's statement that any man who looks lustfully upon a woman has already committed adultery with her in his heart. According to Jerome, a temptation is not in itself a sin. The sin consists in capitulating to the temptation by consenting intellectually to the passion toward which it draws one.[82] This discussion reflects a Stoic understanding of moral choice as intellectual assent, in this case assent to a erroneous judgment concerning a false good. Jerome also shares with the Stoics the conception of *eupatheia*, being one of the first Latin Christian authors to devote attention to this topic. In distinguishing pleasure (*laetitia*) from joy (*gaudium*) as a gift of the Holy Spirit he observes that the Stoics also differentiate them. *Laetitia* is unrestrained; it can include physical as well as mental pleasures; it may be a response to vicious as well as virtuous objects of delight. But *gaudium* is the spiritual elation at those spiritual goods that merit exultation[83] It is true that, in this context, Jerome is using the terms to contrast the heavenly joys granted by God with earthly pleasures. Still,

---

[81] *In Esaiam* 4.11.6–9, CC, 73, p. 151. This point has been noted by Paul Antin, "Les idées morales de S. Jérôme," *Recueil sur saint Jérôme*, pp. 329, 336; Hagendahl, *Latin Fathers*, pp. 233–34.

[82] *Commentariorum in Matheum* 1.5.28, ed. D. Hurst and M. Andriaen, CC, 77 (Turnhout, 1959). Antin, "Les idées morales," p. 334 notes that, in his commentary on the book of Wisdom, Jerome also uses the term *conscientia* in a Stoic sense to mean the intellectual apperception of moral phenomena.

[83] *In Epistolam S. Pauli ad Galatas* 3.5, *PL*, 26, col. 447B–C.

he preserves the idea that some passions are good, if they are in accordance with the *summum bonum*. Another gift of the Spirit, along with *gaudium*, is *pax*, the peace of Christ that passes understanding, which Christians alone possess as their inheritance. Although here, too, Jerome is speaking about a gift of grace, he describes and illustrates it in Stoic terms. The peace of Christ is marked by *tranquilla mens nullis passionibus perturbetur* ("a tranquil mind undisturbed by any of the passions") and by a benignity of temper in which all the goods coincide and which Zeno and the Stoics defined as a feeling (*affectus*) good in itself and conducive to virtue.[84]

At the same time, Jerome is quick to agree that not all the passions are *eupatheia* and that virtue must be exercised to overcome the *perturbationes* that lead to vice. Quoting Vergil, he names the four standard Stoic passions: pleasure (*laetitia, gaudium*), pain (*dolor, aegritudo*), fear (*timor, metus*), and desire (*desiderium, cupiditas, spes*). While he uses the term *gaudium* inconsistently here, he preserves the Stoic grouping of the first two passions as associated with the present and the second two as associated with the future. However, he attributes this doctrine to all the schools of philosophy with no differentiation.[85] Man's goal, he none the less agrees, is freedom from these passions, a state of *apatheia* which he sees as appropriate to a bishop or priest along with marriage to one wife at the most.[86] Jerome's overall position on the passions in his exegetical works is consistent with Stoicism, sometimes to a remarkable degree, although even when he is at his most supportive of Stoic ethics in these writings he treats it not as constitutive but as illustrative of whatever point he is making at the time.

In his polemics Jerome is fully capable of turning around the same Stoic teaching on the passions which he cites with such approval in his exegetical works, attacking it instead as an error that has led Christians into heresy. In his dialogue against the Pelagians, for instance, he restates clearly and in detail the four Stoic passions as pleasure and pain, pertaining to the present, and fear and desire, as pertaining to the future. Zeno and Chrysippus, he notes, taught that these passions could be extirpated completely while the Peripatetics argued that they could not be uprooted but that reason could rule and moderate them. He mentions Cicero, Origen, and Josephus as sources for these views. Jerome

---

[84] Ibid., col. 448A. For the whole passage see 448A–C.

[85] Ibid., col. 449C; *Commentariorum in Ioelem prophetam* 1.4, ed. M. Andriaen, CC, 76 (Turnhout, 1969). Noted by Hagendahl, *Latin Fathers*, pp. 331–38, who also cites references to this theme that will be discussed below. Silvia Jannaccone, "Sull'uso degli scritti filosofici di Cicerone da parte di S. Girolamo," *Giornale italiano di filologia*, 17 (1964), 339 is shortsighted in seeing Cicero as Jerome's only or most likely source for this idea.

[86] *In Epistolam S. Pauli ad Titum* 1, *PL*, 26, col. 604A.

vigorously rejects the Stoic position on the grounds that it promotes a
false confidence in man's power to perfect himself morally unaided by
God's grace, a belief of the Pelagians and other heretics.[87]

This identification of Stoic *apatheia* with the possibility of human sinlessness which Jerome ascribes to the Pelagians is not entirely accurate.
On one level, he equates the ability to work out one's own salvation by
oneself with a perfect freedom from sin. On another level he connects
the latter moral state with the intellectualistic psychology of the Stoa. It
is not clear that the Pelagians advocated either position. Still, in his effort to yoke these doctrines to each other, Jerome calls on the assistance
of the Stoic idea of fate. The capacity never to sin, he notes, applies only
to God; it cannot be attributed to man. In exploring this point he refers
to the distinctions between possibility and impossibility made by Diodorus and Chrysippus. Diodorus, he observes, said that the possible includes only what is true now and what will truly occur in the future.
Anything that can happen is thus possible and anything that cannot
happen is impossible. Chrysippus refined this view by noting that there
are some possibilities that will not occur even though they might occur.
It is possible, for example, for a pearl to break even if a particular pearl
is not going to break. In the mouth of Atticus, the orthodox speaker in
the dialogue, Jerome supports Chrysippus' position because its admission of future contingencies enables him to argue that a man who is not
sinning currently still retains the capacity to fall into sin at a later time.
Hence, he concludes, man always retains the *posse peccare* in this life.[88]

A striking feature of Jerome's analysis of the Stoic doctrine of possibility and impossibility is that he does not make use of the apposite Stoic
formula for describing God's inability to do evil. This omission is particularly noticeable in the light of the extended discussions of God's anger conducted by the apologists. The contrast that Jerome draws with
the human condition of *posse peccare* is God's *posse non peccare*. A more precise and accurate term to use in this connection would have been God's
non posse peccare, applying the Stoic logical technique of negating the entire proposition rather than the verb alone to denote a being who has

---

[87] *Dialogus adversus Pelagianos*, praefatio 1, 2.6, *PL*, 23, cols. 517A–519B, 566C–567B.
This point, as well as Jerome's misinterpretation of the doctrines involved, has been noted
by Kelly, *Jerome*, p. 315. See also Hagendahl, *Latin Fathers*, pp. 260–63; Pierre de Labriolle, "Apatheia," *Mélanges Ernout*, p. 220; Ilona Opelt, *Hieronymus' Streitschriften* (Heidelberg, 1973), pp. 128, 137; Maurice Testard, *Saint Jérôme: L'Apôtre savant et pauvre du
patriciat romain* (Paris, 1969), p. 76. Georges de Plinval, *Pélage: Ses écrits, sa vie et sa réforme*
(Paris, 1943), pp. 202–06 has established that the Pelagians' reputation for Stoicism is
unfounded.

[88] *Adversus Pelagianos* 1.9, *PL*, 23, cols. 524D–525D. On this point see Hagendahl, *Latin
Fathers*, p. 118; Opelt, *Hieronymus' Streitschriften*, pp. 130–31.

always transcended both the *posse peccare* and the *posse non peccare*. Both of these states, after all, reflect contingencies that have never applied to God. The term Jerome uses to describe God's sinlessness is one that also applies to human beings when they in fact choose not to sin. This is a choice that a man could make whether he believes that he is making it with God's help or, as the Pelagians hold, by himself.

The perverse moral independence which the Pelagians display, in Jerome's estimation, is reflected not only by their alleged adherence to the Stoic theory of *apatheia* but also in another respect. The Pelagians, he charges, refuse to be instructed by Scripture and ecclesiastical tradition. Instead, they insist on figuring things out for themselves, however long it takes, invoking Zeno as an example of patience and persistence in the quest for wisdom. Far from manifesting these virtues, Jerome argues, they are appealing to Zeno to support their own arrogance and willful ignorance.[89] Even in just this one polemical dialogue against the Pelagians, then, we can get an excellent sense of Jerome's casualness, his lack of interest in the implications of the ideas he borrows, his inconsistency, his use of *ad hominem* arguments, and, in short, the essentially rhetorical manner in which he resorts to Stoic ethics as a controversialist.

If this is true for the anti-Pelagian Jerome he reserves his most elaborate oratorical onslaughts for his *Contra Jovinianum*. In addition to being a former friend, whose differences of opinion Jerome viewed as a personal betrayal, Jovinian had the temerity to disagree with him on sexual ethics, a topic that Jerome was constitutionally incapable of discussing in a temperate manner. Jovinian had at first been attracted to the monastic life. But, finding that monasticism was not his true vocation he changed his mode of life and wrote in support of the virtues of marriage as equal in holiness to celibacy and virginity. Jerome's use of Stoicism against Jovinian is at the same time vague, inconsistent, and inapposite. He is aware of the general Stoic position that the wise man should marry, attributing it correctly to Chrysippus. He simultaneously tries to dismiss it by arguing that since Chrysippus described bachelorhood as an offense against Jupiter and since Jupiter does not exist, the major premise falls.[90] Despite his recognition of the Stoics' view of marriage he tries to marshal support from among their ranks for his own brief for celibacy. He does not always seize the sharpest weapons in the Stoic armory for this purpose. Jerome uses the well-worn device of citing *exempla virtutis*, mentioning a number of Roman women who remained virgins or who at least refused to remarry after they were widowed. In this context

---

[89] *Adversus Pelagianos* 1.29, *PL*, 23, cols. 547A–548A.
[90] *Contra Jovinianum* 1.48, *PL*, 23, col. 293A.

he refers to Marcia, the wife of Cato of Utica, whom he divorced so that she could marry and bear children to his childless friend Hortensius and whom he remarried, in a celibate union, after Hortensius' death.[91] As stated this tale scarcely supports Jerome's case against the marriage of virgins and the remarriage of widows.

Jerome further observes that Aristotle, Plutarch, Tertullian, and "our Seneca" have written on marriage and that he will quote some extracts from their work as ballast for his argument. A quotation follows, but the text does not clarify which of these authorities he is citing. Further, the substance of the quotation, which treats the governance of the passions by reason, is not entirely to the point. Even if the source is indeed Seneca, which cannot be demonstrated since the Senecan treatise in question is not extant and no independent comparison can be made between it and the *Contra Jovinianum*, the author quoted is criticizing besotted and overly uxorious husbands as foolish. He is not criticizing marriage as such.[92] Jerome takes the position that sexual intercourse between spouses can be condoned only for the purpose of procreation.[93] He might well have supported this view by referring to Musonius Rufus, the one Stoic rigorist who departed from the school's consensus on the subject, or to Lucan, who characterizes Cato as a Musonian husband and father in the *Pharsalia*. But Jerome makes no appeal to the only Stoic authors who could have come to his assistance. In any case, his whole approach to the question of sexuality in marriage is remote from that of the Stoics. The self-discipline preached by the Musonian tradition orders procreation to the common weal and views family life as a school for virtue. On the other hand, Jerome seeks to elevate asexuality over sexuality as such. He does not take this line out of a Pauline sense of the imminent passing

---

[91] Ibid. 1.46, *PL*, 23, col. 288B–C.

[92] Ibid. 1.49, *PL*, 23, cols. 293A–294B. The problems in ascertaining Jerome's real dependence on Seneca here have been brought out well by H. Hagendahl, "Jerome and the Latin Classics," *VC*, 28 (1974), 223–25 and F. Schultzen, "Die Benutzung der Schrift Tertullians 'de monogomia' und 'de ieiunio' bei Hieronymus adv. Iovinianum," *Neue Jahrbücher für deutsche Theologie*, 3 (1894), 486–93. See also Paul Antin, "Touches classiques et chrétiennes juxtaposées chez saint Jérôme," *Recueil sur Saint Jérôme*, p. 52; Philippe Delhaye, "Le dossier anti-matrimoniale de l'*Adversus Jovinianum* et son influence sur quelques écrits latins du XIIᵉ siècle," *Mediaeval Studies*, 13 (1951), 66–70; Nodet, "Position de S. Jérôme," *Mystique et continence*, pp. 308–56. On the other hand, some scholars fail to perceive the problems involved in assessing Jerome's use of Seneca here. See, for instance, Eiswirth, *Hieronymus' Stellung*, p. 44; Silvia Jannaccone, "S. Girolamo e Seneca," *Giornale italiano di filologia*, 16 (1963), 326–38; Carlo Tibiletti, "Cultura classica e cristiana in S. Girolamo," *Salesianum*, 11 (1949), 116; Winfried Trillitzsch, "Hieronymus und Seneca," *Mittellateinisches Jahrbuch*, 2 (1965), 42–54. Some of the same problems apply to Jerome's use of Tertullian and are not noted sufficiently by Claudio Micaeli, "L'influsso di Tertulliano su Girolamo: Le opere sul matrimonio e le seconde nozze," *Augustianum*, 19 (1979), 415–29.

[93] *Contra Jovinianum* 1.20, *PL*, 23, col. 249B–C.

of the age or out of a preference for an alternative philosophical position, such as Platonism or Neoplatonism, that would devalue the body. Rather, Jerome's whole approach to this topic reflects his own temperamental aversion from sexuality as unclean, repulsive, and threatening. The repulsion, however, is the obverse of an attraction that can be controlled only if it is denied. Life, for Jerome, is full of temptation and the choice of celibacy is a means of minimizing risks by limiting drastically the number of one's options. It is a strategy of containment, not of catharsis. Jerome takes some comfort in the comparison with philosophers like the Platonists and Stoics, who frequented groves and temple porticoes as part of their ethical discipline, so that the sanctity of these precincts would incline their minds to virtue.[94] He seems to see an analogy between this practice and the monk's flight to the desert. Still, the main thrust of Jerome's use of the Stoics in his attack on Jovinian is to depict them, and other philosophers, as tokens of the misguided pagan ingenuity that has poisoned Jovinian's mind, a rhetorical gambit for which he is prepared to reject Stoic principles that he defends elsewhere in an argument which twists much of the Stoicism he cites while ignoring the positions of the school that would have been the most useful to his case. The points that he does try to make are basically debater's points. Of Jovinian he says, in a passage redolent of both Tertullian and Horace:

> Hierosolymam Citio, Judaeum Cypro, Christum Zenone commutat. Si non licet a virtutibus paululum declinare, et omnia peccata sunt paria, ejusdemque criminis reus, qui panem esuriens surripuerit, et qui hominem occiderit: tu quoque maximorum scelerum reus teneris.[95]

> He exchanges Jerusalem for Citium, Judaea for Cyprus, Christ for Zeno. If we may not depart a hair's breadth from virtue, and all sins are equal, and a man who in a fit of hunger steals a piece of bread is no less guilty than he who slays a man: you must, in your turn, be held guilty of the greatest crimes.

And so, congratulating himself on having *veterumque Zenonis sententiam, tam communi sensu, quam divina lectione contrivamus* ("pulverized Zeno's old opinion no less with common sense than with the words of inspiration,")[96] Jerome lays to rest his case against Jovinian, "our Zeno."[97] It

---

[94] Ibid. 2.9, *PL*, 23, col. 311C.

[95] Ibid. 2.21, *PL*, 23, col. 329A–B, trans. W. H. Freemantle, St. Jerome, *Letters and Select Works* in *A Select Library of Nicene and Post-Nicene Fathers of the Church*, 2nd ser., ed. Philip Schaff and Henry Wace (New York, 1893), vol. 6.

[96] Ibid. 2.35, *PL*, 23, cols. 348B–349A, trans. Freemantle.

[97] Ibid. 2.33, *PL*, 23, col. 345A.

cannot be said that he has done much more than to rifle his sources has-
tily and uncritically. The most telling example is Jerome's rejection of
the principle that all sins, and hence all virtues, are equal, by means of
which he seeks to undermine Jovinian's claim that all vocations in the
Church are equally Christian. Jerome states that this equality of vocations cannot be maintained since the graces that people receive are different.[98] In making this very assertion he invests St. Paul with as much
plasticity as the Stoa. For, as the apostle would have it, the diversity of
gifts manifests the same spirit, a principle that complements the Stoic
equalization of the virtues as stemming from a single fixed intentionality
and one that supports Jovinian's position on marriage more strongly than
it supports the opposite position which Jerome is trying to defend.

While ethics holds pride of place in Jerome's controversial works there
is one final instance, connected with his attack on Origenism, in which
he refers to a physical doctrine of the Stoa, although not expressly. He
adverts rather vaguely to the idea of *logos spermatikos* in criticizing Origen's teaching on the resurrection. Origen, he says, explains man's capacity to be transformed from flesh to spirit in the next life as a seed implanted in his nature by God, Who brings it to posthumous fruition.
Jerome rejects Origen's eschatology on Scriptural grounds, noting that
what the Bible promises is a resurrected body different from man's
earthly body but none the less flesh and not pure spirit.[99] In this passage
he seems to be confusing two disparate issues, Origen's conception of
man's nature and destiny and the *logos spermatikos* as a way describing
man's potentialities, whatever they may be believed to be. In any event,
he attributes the idea of *logos spermatikos* to the Greeks in general, not to
any one philosophical school. While this passage is a digression from
Jerome's more typical concern with Stoic ethics in his stance as a polem-
icist, his discussion of the resurrection still falls into one of the two categories of arguments involving Stoicism that he is most likely to advance
in this genre—Stoicism as a form of error that has seduced Christians
from the truths of the faith, the other being Stoicism as an extrinsic support for causes that he advocates for other reasons. In either case, the
test for his inclusion of Stoic ideas is less their real conceptual applicability to his case than their perceived rhetorical utility.

Rhetoric is by no means absent from the third and last subdivision of
Jerome's works, his biographies and letters. In these writings he is concerned above all with ethics, producing Christian *exempla virtutis* that can
be substituted for their pagan rivals and offering advice and moral com-

---

[98] Ibid. 2.22–35, *PL*, 23, cols. 329A–349A.
[99] *Contra Joannem* 26, *PL*, 23, cols. 393B–396C.

ment to his correspondents. His letters reflect the formal influence of both the Senecan epistle as a moral treatise and the Horatian epistle as a medium for satire. His biographies and letters give Jerome the opportunity to belabor his favorite themes, to underscore points he makes in his controversial works, to reimburse creditors, and to inflate his own importance. While his handling of Stoicism in these works is sometimes inaccurate and while it is striking by its complete absence from his saints' lives, most of his references of Stoicism in his *De viris illustribus* and letters are correct and to the point. Jerome is much more likely to approve of Stoic doctrine and to take it seriously in this segment of his *œuvre* than in any of the other genres in which he writes.

Jerome is interested in Stoicism in his biographies and letters chiefly as a source of ideas for delineating the Christian sage. To this end he feels free to use unorthodox models, both in the sense of examples of virtue who are not Christian and in the sense of pagan concepts that reinforce his own moral views. Numbered among the 135 *vitae* in the *De viris illustribus* are several personages who were heterodox or even non-Christian, including Philo Judaeus, five pagan philosophers among whom he lists three Stoics, and seven heretics or schismatics. To confuse matters still further, one of the people whom Jerome treats as a pagan philosopher is actually Justin, a Christian martyr. Jerome's principle of selection in the *De viris illustribus* is the contribution that a figure has made to Christian thought, not who he was or what he was like as a moral personality. This canon enables him to begin with St. Peter and to end with himself. The self-promoting aspect of the work also explains his inclusion of Pope Damasus, whose service to Church history is limited strictly to his patronage of Jerome during a pontificate that was otherwise as brief as it was forgettable. Many of the *vitae* are potted biographies, sketchy and pedestrian, whose literary merit is negligible and whose descriptions of their subjects are too perfunctory to make them particularly useful as models of virtue. Another idiosyncratic feature of the *De viris illustribus* is Jerome's deemphasis of Greeks and his overemphasis of Latin Christians, a tendentious feature of the work that leads him to include several personages of decidedly limited importance.

Jerome relates the lives of philosophers in the *De viris illustribus* and elsewhere[100] in order to make the point that leading pagan intellectuals recognized the truth of the Christian faith and defended it expressly in word and deed. In order to support this thesis for the particular philos-

---

[100] *Ep.* 70.4–5, to Magnus, 397. The dimensions and extent of Jerome's sympathy with these philosophers are treated far too vaguely by Francis E. Tourscher, "Studies in St. Jerome and St. Augustine: The Classics and Christian Culture," *American Ecclesiastical Review*, 61 (1919), 648–63.

ophers he includes Jerome has to manipulate the historical record, or to approach it with an unsettling credulity. He attributes writings and activities to his chosen philosophers for which there is little or no solid evidence. The three Stoics in question are Aristides, Pantaenus, and Seneca. Aristides was a Christian convert who wrote an apology for the faith which he dedicated to the emperor Hadrian.[101] While he was an Athenian philosopher, there is no evidence to show that he was a Stoic. His actual dates would make the emperor Antoninus Pius a more plausible dedicatee. Pantaenus is another convert who was possibly a Stoic. As Jerome tells the tale, he was sent to India on a fact-finding mission by the bishop of Alexandria. There he discovered a Christian community that had been founded by the apostle Bartholomew, whose preaching had been preserved in a Hebrew codex which Pantaenus brought back with him to Alexandria. Pantaenus served as the teacher of Clement of Alexandria as well as being a philosopher, a commentator on Scripture, and an episcopal legate.[102] Many of the elements of this story are shaky. Eusebius, Jerome's source, reports Pantaenus' biography as legend, which Jerome does not hesitate to convert into fact. Less replete with circumstantial detail but more important for its promotion of a major historical misunderstanding is Jerome's presentation of Seneca. He describes Seneca correctly as a Cordovan, a disciple of the Stoic Sotion, the uncle of Lucan, the tutor of Nero, and a leading politician of his day, all of which information was available in the Roman historians. For Jerome, Seneca was a virtuous man, his chief moral trait being his continent life (*continentissimae vitae fuit*), an excellence that passes over in silence Seneca's two marriages. Jerome classifies Seneca as a saint primarily because of the forged correspondence he was believed to have exchanged with St. Paul, which Jerome takes to be authentic. He makes no attempt to apply his formidable skills as a textual critic to this document,[103] although the discrepancies between the fourth-century Latin in which it is written and the Latin of the first century from which it purports to date might well have struck the eye of a philologist with Jerome's expertise. Fact and fancy thus mingle indiscriminately in the lives of his three Stoic philosophors. The accent in these biographies, as in those of the Christian worthies in the *De viris illustribus*, is less on displaying the sanctity of their subjects than on praising their scholarship.

The pagan models that Jerome incorporates in his letters involve both Stoic ethical formulae and the stylistic example of the Latin satirists,

---

[101] *De viris inlustribus* 20, ed. Carl Albrecht Bernouilli (Frankfurt, 1968 [Repr. of Freiburg i. B., 1895 ed.]).

[102] Ibid. 36, 38.

[103] Ibid. 12.

some of whom had also drawn upon Stoic ethics.[104] At the same time, the Roman satirists had often exposed Stoicism to ridicule. Jerome does not always follow the Stoic line in his letters. However, he shows somewhat more interest in the doctrinal content of Stoicism in the letters than he does in his biographies. In those areas where Jerome takes issue with the Stoa he assumes the stance that he takes in his polemical works, arguing that Stoic ideas lead to heresy or error. Thus, in response to Marcellinus and Anapsychia, a married couple who had written to ask Jerome's opinion on the origin of the soul, he reviews the positions of the major schools, mentioning the Stoic idea that the human soul is consubstantial with the divine essence, a point that leads him to yoke Stoic anthropology with Manicheism and Priscillianism.[105] Similarly, in a letter to Ctesiphon, who had solicited Jerome's views on the Pelagian heresy, he associates the overconfident ethics of that sect with the Stoic theory of the passions. Here as elsewhere he names the four Stoic passions correctly, relating pleasure and pain to the present and fear and desire to the future, as well as attacking the notion that reason alone can uproot them from man's nature.[106]

Not all of Jerome's criticisms of Stoic ethics in his letters are framed in polemical terms. Sometimes they are found in letters written in a more personal vein, as is the case with his discussion of suicide in an epistle to Paula. The occasion for this communication was the death of Blesilla, a daughter of Paula, whom she was mourning by fasting with the wrong inner intention, as Jerome sees it. Paula's fasts, he says, are a form of self-indulgence through which she is nursing and reinforcing her grief. He contrasts her behavior with the true fasting that is a response to God's will. If fasting is not undertaken for the right reasons, he concludes, it is no more meritorious in God's sight than the anorexic self-destruction of such pagans as Zeno and Cato.[107] This analysis, despite its predictable Christian rejection of suicide as such, is interesting for its combination with an authentically Stoic principle, the idea that the essence of a moral act lies in the internal motivation of the subject.

On the whole Jerome is more inclined to reflect a positive than a neg-

---

[104] David Wiesen, *St. Jerome as a Satirist: A Study in Christian Latin Thought and Letters* (Ithaca, 1964) provides an outstanding analysis of the literary parallels between Jerome and the Roman satirists but his treatment of the philosophical content of these authors is not reliable.

[105] *Ep.* 126.1, to Marcellinus and Anapsychia, 410–12. Henry Chadwick, *Priscillian* (Oxford, 1976), p. 205 has commented on this passage and has noted that there is no evidence that the Priscillianists held this view of the soul.

[106] *Ep.* 133.1, to Ctesiphon, 415.

[107] *Ep.* 39.3.5–6, to Paula, 389. Noted by Mary Louise Carlson, "Pagan Examples of Fortitude in the Latin Christian Apologists," *CP*, 43 (1948), 101.

ative attitude toward Stoic ethics in his letters. But, even when he approves of the ideas in question he gives them his own personal emphasis or adjusts them to the situational concerns of his correspondents, taking his own relationships with those correspondents into account. In a more or less straightforward vein he addresses a consolatory epistle to Julian, who had recently lost his wife and two children. Urging him to take heart, Jerome observes that these afflictions are what the philosophers call *adiaphora*, which cannot affect the internal goods that lie within each man's control.[108] In a manner equally apposite, but one that Christianizes the Stoic doctrine involved, he advises Paulinus of Nola that his proposed pilgrimage to the Holy Land is neither necessary nor especially meritorious. Since Paulinus has renounced the world and stands firm in the faith, he can pursue his vocation just as well at home.[109] The Stoic *topos* here is the idea that the sage, since he possesses all things, is happy wherever he is.

Another theme, which undergoes even more specific modification in Jerome's hands, is cosmetic theology. Jerome makes his own particular contribution to this topic by situating it in two contexts where it had not been located before by Latin Christian writers, the vocation of widowhood and the attack on heretics. The first of these concerns was dear to Jerome's heart. It can be seen as an extension of Cyprian's application of cosmetic theology to the vocation of the consecrated virgin. In letters about widows or addressed to them Jerome criticizes widows who wear elaborate clothing, cosmetics, and fashionable hairstyles. Apart from doing violence to nature, such practices, he says, are a sign of vanity and even the mark of Antichrist. Since widows should not remarry, they should not seek to attract the admiration of men.[110] On another level Jerome's association of hair dye, cosmetics, and becoming clothes with Antichrist enables him to direct cosmetic theology against the Montanists. Since Montanus' female associates accoutered themselves à la mode, he charges, they cannot have been true prophets.[111] While Jerome resorts here to an *ad feminam* argument whereby he challenges the truth claims of Montanism by casting aspersions on the modesty and chastity of Montanist women, his position also effects a reconstitution of the original rationale for cosmetic theology that the Stoics had developed and that Jerome's Christian predecessors had ignored as a function of their feminizing of this tradition. The Stoics judged the sage's presentation of self, whether conventional or unconventional, not only in terms of its

---

[108] *Ep.* 118.3.3, to Julian, 406.
[109] *Ep.* 58.1–4, to Paulinus of Nola, 395.
[110] *Ep.* 38.3.2, to Marcella, 385; *Ep.* 54.7.1–3, to Furia, 394.
[111] *De viris inl.* 40.

consonance with nature. They also considered its effect on his credibility as a proponent of wisdom to the society around him. Although Jerome adheres to the feminization of cosmetic theology that had characterized the *topos*, in Christian hands, since Tertullian, his treatment of the Montanist women is noteworthy in that he views them not only as sexual beings but also in their public role as preachers and missionaries.

While Jerome invokes nature as a norm in the case of cosmetic theology, nature is an ethical criterion that has an extremely limited and purely circumstantial appeal for him. Jerome calls upon natural law only when he must do so in order to avoid offending a correspondent, particularly one who is a friend and supporter and whose good will he has a stake in retaining. An excellent case in point is Pammachius, Jerome's ally in several controversial encounters and a relative by marriage to the family of devout and wealthy women who were his closest associates and patrons. In one letter to Pammachius, reiterating his argument against Jovinian, Jerome notes that marriage is permissible, *ne videar damnare naturam* ("lest nature be condemned.")[112] However, he approaches the question in terms of the gifts God grants to each person, not on the level of natural ethics. If Jerome wants to avoid condemning nature in this passage, considering the fact that Pammachius was a married man, he has no wish to uphold nature as a criterion. Virginity, he argues in the same letter, is the higher way, even though it is made possible by a special calling that transcends nature. On the other hand, in letters where he is free from the rhetorical necessities at work in his correspondence with Pammachius, he speaks quite differently on the same subject. In counseling a widow who shuns remarriage, he praises her choice. While the sexual instinct has been given by God for the procreation of children, he says, it is a drive that always threatens to shatter those constraints, leading men to vice. Continence, although it entails breaking the law of nature, is preferable.[113] The law of nature is a topic that Jerome discusses largely in the context of sexual ethics. In this connection he feels impelled to honor it only as a *captatio benevolentiae* and only when the circumstances so require.

Jerome's most integral and generous use of Stoic ethics in his *oeuvre* as a whole is found in his treatment of virtue and Christian vocation in his letters to and about persons presented as worthy of emulation and in the epistles instructing parents how to rear their children. Jerome always remains sensitive to the need to flatter and encourage his correspondents.

---

[112] *Ep.* 49.4, to Pammachius, 393.

[113] *Ep.* 54.9.1–5, to Furia, 394. Giacomo Violardo, *Il pensiero giuridico di San Girolamo* (Milano, 1937), pp. 34–40 has collected a number of locations where Jerome refers to natural law but makes no effort to show how and in what contexts he uses the concept.

At the same time, he imparts an authentic Stoic sense to the themes he discusses in these contexts, approaching them quite differently here than in his other writings. Against Jovinian and elsewhere, for instance, Jerome argues that neither the virtues nor the vices are equal. But in a letter to Pammachius he asserts the exact opposite, by way of praising Pammachius and his relatives. Jerome observes that *quattuor virtutes describunt Stoici ita sibi invicem nexas et mutuo cohaerentes, ut qui unam non habuerit, omnibus careat* ("according to the Stoics there are four cardinal virtues that are so closely related and mutually coherent that he who lacks one lacks all.")[114] Pammachius, his late wife Paulina, his sister-in-law Eustochium, and his mother-in-law Paula each possess all four virtues, he goes on; yet each manifests one of the virtues in a preeminent way. Pammachius, a senator who abandoned the world to follow Christ and who embraced the monastic life after the death of his wife, exemplifies prudence. Paula is an example of justice in her detachment from riches and her division of her property among her children. Eustochium illustrates courage in her unswerving dedication to her calling as a consecrated virgin. Paulina's temperance is revealed in her honest assessment of her own capacities and her choice of marriage rather than a heroic vocation like her sister's, which she would not have been able to fulfill. Instead, she accepted the humbler condition of honorable wedlock for the sake of offspring and Christian companionship that she could enjoy with Pammachius, her like-minded husband.[115] While Jerome's presentation of the virtues in this letter is clearly tinctured by the wish to compliment Pammachius and his family, from whom he received a great deal of income both psychic and economic, and while his definitions are geared to the personalities of the individuals involved, he none the less preserves the Stoic principle that the virtues mutually imply each other.

In his letters Jerome also revives the authentic Stoic doctrine of the moral equality of the sexes. By precept and example he sets forth the idea that women are just as capable as men of acquiring and exercising virtue. For Jerome this is particularly true in the case of women who deny their sexuality and live as consecrated virgins and widows. While he is distinctly uncomfortable with the biological dimensions of their existence he has no difficulty in appreciating women as minds or souls. In no

---

[114] *Ep.* 66.1, to Pammachius, 397.

[115] Ibid. 66.1–3. This letter has been analyzed well by Antin, "Les idées morales de S. Jérôme," *Recueil sur saint Jérôme*, p. 329 and Charles Favez, *La consolation latine chrétienne* (Paris, 1937), p. 109. On the other hand, Jean Préaux, "Les quatre vertus païennes et chrétiennes: Apothéose et ascension," *Hommages à Marcel Renard*, ed. Jacqueline Bibauw (Bruxelles, 1969), I, 639–43 misses the point about the interconnections of the virtues and sees the question purely as a Christianizing of Platonic or Neoplatonic, not of Stoic, ethics.

sense does he lower his standards, either intellectual or moral, in advising them or in commenting on their mode of life. This fact emerges very clearly in the two letters Jerome addresses to parents seeking his counsel on the education of daughters whom they intended to prepare for a life as consecrated virgins.[116] Jerome's pedagogical program stresses the intellect as well as the soul. Girls, he urges, should receive rigorous intellectual training from infancy, their toy blocks marked with the letters of the alphabet so that even their childish play will be instructive. Formal learning should begin with grammar, with teachers and nurses chosen for their purity of diction as well as for their upright character. Once the pupil has attained a sufficient mastery of language she should concentrate her studies on the Bible, beginning with the Psalms and then proceeding to the Proverbs, the Gospels, the Acts of the Apostles, the Prophets, and the rest of the Old and New Testaments, supplemented with various Latin Christian writers. This sequence of readings reflects Jerome's awareness of child psychology. It is designed to move the student progressively from easier to more difficult material. The Psalms come first because they can be sung as well as read, an activity that will capture the student's interest. Likewise, she should be given incentives with small rewards for good work, praise for achievement, and fellow students for stimulation. Jerome rules out music, except for psalm singing, and includes the traditional feminine crafts of spinning and needlework. His reasons for these curricular choices are not specified, but they may be as much moral as intellectual. Ethical instruction and discipline are provided primarily by segregating the pupil from men and from frivolous women, by her association with parents, tutors, and servants who offer edifying examples, by sobriety and moderation in food and clothing, and by the avoidance of public gatherings except attendance at church and at social functions where the girl is chaperoned by her parents.

Most of the ideas reflected in Jerome's pedagogical letters are derived directly from Quintilian and indirectly from Chrysippus, both in the choice of a teacher who is a sage, a *vir bonus dicendi peritus* and not merely a man proficient in his subject, and in the sphere of educational psychology.[117] It has been argued that Jerome's prescriptions disregard the

---

[116] *Ep.* 107.4–13, to Laeta, 403; *Ep.* 128.1–3, to Gaudentius, 413.

[117] This point has been brought out well by Charles Favez, "Saint Jérôme pédagogue," *Mélanges de philologie, de littérature et d'histoire anciennes offerts à J. Marouzeau* (Paris, 1948), pp. 173–81; Kelly, *Jerome*, pp. 273–75. Johannes N. Brunner, *Der hl. Hieronymus und die Mädchenerziehung auf Grund seiner Briefe an Laeta und Gaudentius: Eine patristisch-pädagogische Studie* (München, 1910) gives an excellent summary of the contents of these letters but does not correlate them with associated topics found elsewhere in Jerome's writings.

needs of normal children and that he followed a different model for the
education of boys at his own monastery in Bethlehem.[118] Yet, the very
stringency of the program he lays down for girls bespeaks his respect for
their intellectual capacities. These are girls, furthermore, who need to
be prepared for an ascetic life lacking the advantages of group reinforce-
ment provided by a monastic community. The fact that Jerome is offering guidance by long distance for the education of children whom he does
not know personally and who will not be trained under his own super-
vision may be another condition affecting his advice. His pedagogical
letters certainly make it clear that he regards women as fully capable of
theological scholarship no less than of the moral rigors of the ascetic life.
Both of these achievements also win his praise in the comments he makes
to and about exemplary women, from Demetrias who took the veil on
the eve of her wedding[119] to Marcella, who combined learning, generosity, moderation, and chastity with the courage to be the first Roman
woman to live as a nun. For, as Jerome says, *virtutes non sexu sed animo
iudicamus* ("we judge people's virtues not by their sex but by their character.")[120] Thus, despite his occasional recourse to the anti-feminist tradition in other contexts and his uncritical acceptance of the status that
law and convention accorded to woman in his day, Jerome makes a significant contribution to the resuscitation of the Stoic doctrine of sexual
equality and to the development of Christian feminism.

There are, then, a few areas in which Jerome reflects an integral grasp
of Stoic ethics and where he coordinates it appositely with Christian
problems and concerns. On balance, however, the Stoic gleanings from
his works are few, his uses of them are tendentious and superficial, and
he is not interested in their implications or interconnections. The rhetorical exigencies of the particular genres in which he wrote or of particular works themselves and his lack of a professional need or inclination to write a systematic treatise on any subject account for the
inconsistencies and contradictions in his borrowings from Stoicism. Jerome rarely relies on Stoicism for the substance of his arguments. More
typically he incorporates Stoic ideas into those arguments as a quick and
often imprecise way of characterizing individuals and positions that he
disagrees with, or as a learned illustration or coloristic dilation of a view
he maintains for other reasons. The currency he gives to the myth of

---

[118] Kelly, *Jerome*, p. 275.

[119] *Ep.* 130, to Demetrias, 414; Noted by Hagendahl, *Latin Fathers*, p. 257.

[120] *Ep.* 127.5.3, to Principia, 412. This point has been developed well by M. Turcan,
"Saint Jérôme et les femmes," *Bulletin de l'Association Guillaume Budé*, 1968, pp. 259–72.
On the other hand Wiesen, *St. Jerome as a Satirist*, ch. 4 and p. 114, notes only the anti-
feminist aspects of Jerome's treatment of women.

Seneca's correspondence with St. Paul may have provided some back-handed assistance to the later medieval popularity of Seneca as a Stoic sage and philosopher. Jerome's own approach to Stoicism is less philosophical than literary. Philology is his vocation and belles lettres his avocation and delight. He is far more exclusively rhetorical in his handling of Stoicism than Tertullian, the coiner of the concept of *Seneca noster*. Both Tertullian and Lactantius, who has also been depicted as a mere rhetorican and transmitter, are more interested in the doctrinal content of Stoicism than Jerome and make more creative use of it than he does. Jerome's place in the Stoic tradition is less impressive than that of the major Latin apologists and still less significant than Ambrose's. Yet, Jerome's authority as a Biblical scholar earned for his writings a place that transcended the controversies and personalities of his day and that kept in circulation the information he provides and the applications he makes of the Stoic doctrine of the passions, the virtues, and sexual equality.

CHAPTER THREE

LESSER CHRISTIAN WRITERS OF THE
FOURTH AND FIFTH CENTURIES

The authors treated in this chapter span the period covered by the careers of the major Latin Church Fathers. Writing in the genres of poetry, history, and theology both pastoral, monastic, moral, and dogmatic, they provide a useful contemporary perspective, from the valleys and foothills of the age, from which to view the peaks represented by Jerome and Ambrose on the one side and Augustine on the other. Apart from bringing into clearer focus the achievements of the Church Fathers as reformulators of Stoicism in the early Middle Ages, these authors are instructive in their own right for the range of issues bearing on the Stoic tradition which they themselves consider. While some of them appropriate Stoicism in an essentially peripheral or decorative manner or apply it to moral concerns at the margins of Christian thought, others reflect an integral and sometimes fully conscious grasp of Stoicism and use it to address the most pressing of contemporary theological questions. As is the case with their better known confrères, some of these lesser writers have suffered from an overinterpretation or misinterpretation of their relation to the Stoic tradition. More typically, however, they have suffered from scholarly disinterest, the fate of figures whose evident lack of glamor has deflected commentators away from them despite their interest as representatives of their time. For all their acknowledged status as comparatively minor authors, however, they are important and sometimes influential links in the chain of *auctoritates* who brought Stoicism into the purview of the Latin Middle Ages. In addition, taken as a group, they show that their age had a less superficial and less preclusively ethical interest in Stoicism than the writings of Jerome and Ambrose alone might lead one to suspect.

I. Latin Christian Poets

Collectively, the Latin Christian poets of the fourth and fifth centuries present the greatest diversity of attitudes toward Stoicism of any group of authors in this period. Working on a small scale, with an admitted lack of literary panache in many cases, they run the gamut from the artificial to the profound, from the frankly imitative to the original in the application of Stoicism to the themes they address. As men of letters educated in the classics, these poets naturally looked to the ancients for formal and stylistic models. Despite this fact, their appropriations of Stoicism cannot always be explained as borrowings from pagan Latin poets of a Stoicizing bent. The Stoic sage, who occupies much of the attention of the classical Latin poets, for better or for worse, is striking for his absence among their Christian Latin successors. The ethical doctrines of the Stoa that bulk the largest in these Christian authors are doctrines less central to the Stoics' own teaching. The most prominent moral theme they treat is cosmetic theology, which the poets absorbed largely from previous Christian hortatory writers but which they alter strikingly both in focus and application. In several cases the Christian Latin poets are also concerned with the broad cosmological and moral issue of providence and free will, exploring this topic in the form of Stoic theodicy. Here they draw not so much on the classical poets as on sources such as Cicero, whether mediated or not through the Latin apologists. There are also some poets in this group who reflect the rhetorical tradition as much if not more than the poetic, writing versified versions of epeidectic oratory. These writers use the Stoic themes they adduce purely as coloristic devices designed to display their own erudition and to compliment the addressees of their poems. The traits just noted run through the corpus of pertinent Christian Latin poetry without regard to time or place and without respect to the literary quality of the poems involved. Thus, the authors can be subdivided most cogently into a first group, whose references to Stoicism are erroneous, commonplace, or trivial, and a second group, who handle their Stoic material in a more serious and original manner.

A) Marius Victor

There are three authors who need to be discussed, even if briefly, for their erroneous or commonplace use of Stoicism or for the misinterpretation of their real attitudes toward it. They are Marius Victor, Arator, and the author of the *Querolus*, all dating to the fifth century. Marius Victor (fl. 425–50) was a professional rhetorician from Marseilles who wrote several poems. One, the *Alethia*, is of a type common in this period, the retread of a book of the Bible in Latin epic prosody. The *Alethia* is a hexameter version of Genesis in which the author refers repeatedly to *semina*, *germina*, or *semina rerum* in discussing the creation of the universe.[1] While the terminology is of Stoic derivation, Marius uses it with-

---

[1] Claudius Marius Victor, *Alethia* 1.2, 1.23, 1.54, 1.92, 1.95, 1.116, 1.221, 1.264, ed. P. F. Hovingh, CC, 128 (Turnhout, 1960). This poem has been read in an overly Stoicizing manner by Michael Lapidge, "A Stoic Metaphor in Late Latin Poetry: The Binding of the Universe," *Latomus*, 39 (1980), 827–28.

out the specific attributes attached to the Stoic *logos spermatikos*. In his hands these terms are synonymous with creation in general without any notion of creatures emerging at a later date on the basis of their earlier implanted seminal qualities.

B) Arator

Arator, whose *floruit* is the mid-fifth century, was a native of Milan and a cleric and statesman who lived during the Ostrogothic conquest of Italy. Sent as an ambassador to Theodoric by the Dalmatians, he later became private secretary and finance minister to his successor Athalaric. Arator's poem *De actibus apostolorum* was dedicated to Pope Vigilius and is parallel in style and genre to Marius' *Alethia*, recasting a book of the Bible, in this case the Acts of the Apostles, in Vergilian hexameters. The one passage of Arator pertinent in our inquiry is his description of St. Paul preaching to the Athenians. Arator's treatment of this scene raises some questions about his grasp of Stoicism and the theology of Acts alike. Arator comments on how Paul has triumphed over the sects and dogmas of paganism, listing Epicureanism and Stoicism as examples. He does not appear to notice that the Paul of Acts stresses the harmony between pagan and Christian monotheism. Instead, he presents the Stoics, like the Epicureans, as atheists and as totally inimical to Christian doctrine. Outside of emptying Paul's speech of its real content, Arator also reverses Paul's rhetorical strategy, depicting him as a dogmatic and haughty sermonizer rather than as an adroit and tactful speaker stressing the common humanity that unites him with his pagan audience.[2]

C) The Querolus

Our third example, the *Querolus*, is a case not of misconceived Stoicism on the part of the author but of misinterpretation on the part of some commentators. Also given the title *Aulularia*, this work is a comedy modeled on Plautus. The author is unknown although his Latin and his dedication of the work to one Rutilius, perhaps Rutilius Namatianus, have suggested that the *Querolus* was written in Gaul in the early fifth century.[3] Despite his debt to Plautus, the author does something that no

---

[2] Arator, *De actibus apostolorum* 2.489–490, ed. Arthur Patch McKinlay, CSEL, 72 (Vienna, 1951). There is a good discussion of Arator in Charles Witke, *Numen litterarum: The Old and the New in Latin Poetry from Constantine to Gregory the Great* (Leiden, 1971), pp. 223–27.

[3] This date is the one accepted by most commentators although Francesco Corsaro, *Querolus: Studio introduttivo e commentario* (Bologna, 1965), pp. 7–12 reviews the literature on this question and dates the work to the period 383–410. The most recent treatment

classical comedian would ever have done—he states the moral of the play first and lets the action illustrate it, as well as giving a plot summary in his dedicatory prologue. According to the author, the theme of the play is the power of fate; the story concerns a man saved from loss by destiny and a trickster foiled by his own strategems. Lest the point escape the reader, it is restated by the character Lar Familiaris in the speech opening the play.[4] This heavy-handed introduction has inclined a number of scholars to assert that the *Querolus* is an expression of the Stoic doctrine of fate and destiny, in which popular opinions to the contrary are disproved,[5] or at least that it reflects a position of philosophical eclecticism in which Stoicism holds pride of place.[6] To what extent does the play bear out these assessments?

The main character, Querolus, is a selfish, dissatisfied, and not overly intelligent young man, the son of a deceased miser, Euclio. Rather than entrusting his son's inheritance to him outright, Euclio before he dies buries his gold under some ashes in a funerary urn whose inscription identifies its contents as the remains of someone else. The trickster Mandrogerus and his accomplices Sycophanta and Sardanappalus break into Querolus' house, steal the urn, and then throw it away, thinking that ashes are all it contains. Querolus regains the urn and recovers his inheritance. Interlarding the scenes in which this action takes place are lengthy dialogic passages involving Lar both with Querolus and with Mandrogerus. The dialogue between Querolus and Lar, ostensibly designed to treat the question of why the wicked flourish and the righteous suffer, is actually a means of displaying Querolus' laziness, impatience, dishonesty, and self-indulgence. Querolus considers himself virtuous but instead reveals himself to be undeserving of good fortune.[7] The dialogue between Lar and Mandrogerus is set up to enable Lar to refute the claims of witchcraft, magic, astrology, and other pseudo-sciences as accurate ways of predicting or controlling events.[8] After the dénouement, Lar asserts that the outcome shows that man neither gains nor loses anything except through the will of an all-powerful God, a point reinforced by a

---

places the work between 410 and 417. See Jochen Küppers, "Zum Querolus (p. 17.7–22R*) und seiner Datierung," *Philologus*, 123 (1979), 303–23.

[4] *Querolus sive Aulularia*, praefatio; 1.1, ed. Gunnar Randstrand, Göteborgs Högskolar Årsskrift, 57:1 (Göteborg, 1951).

[5] Nora K. Chadwick, *Poetry and Letters in Early Christian Gaul* (London, 1955), pp. 134–41; René Pichon, *Les derniers écrivains profanes* (Paris, 1906), pp. 236–40.

[6] Francesco Corsaro, "Garbata polemica anticristiana nella anonima commedia tardo-imperiale *Querolus sive Aulularia*," *Miscellanea di studi di letteratura cristiana antica*, 13 (1963), 11–21; *Querolus*, pp. 42–49. Corsaro's view of the author as anti-Christian has not won wide support.

[7] *Querolus* 2.2.

[8] Ibid. 2.3.

minor character in the next scene who agrees that the benefits Querolus has received are a gift of God, not the result of his father's diversionary arrangements before the fact.[9]

A close look at the play, however, belies these kinds of philosophical claims. As the unravelling of the plot shows, Querolus is not a man who attracts good fortune either because of his virtues or because of the will of God. He is deserving of his inheritance not because he merits it but because he is his father's sole legitimate heir. It is not fate or destiny that accounts for his recovery of the treasure but his father's craft and foresight. Knowing that his son is stupid enough to be swindled, Euclio organizes matters to avert such an outcome. To the extent that the *Querolus* raises any real philosophical questions, they are not questions about fate but about deception and truth-telling. In his initial exchange with Querolus, Lar points out that perjury is an evil and that one can lie by remaining silent. Querolus in turn admits to having borne false witness and to having broken oaths, but seeks to exculpate himself. For his part, Mandrogerus is a self-professed confidence man. As for Euclio, in his effort to protect his son's inheritance he places his gold in an urn with a deliberately misleading inscription. All three characters thus misrepresent the truth although in Euclio's case one might well ask whether the ends justify the means.

More to the point, however, is the fact that, whatever its literary demerits, the *Querolus* is and is meant to be a comedy. Loose ends and inconsistencies abound in the speeches of Lar, the acknowledged sage, as well as in the protestations of the other characters. The obvious lack of congruency between the author's ostensible theme and what actually happens in the play is itself another source of amusement. All the positions advanced by all the speakers, including the author in the prologue, are commonplaces, understood as such by author and audience alike; they are all being taken off, without exception. The author's goal is not to advance any particular philosophy, Stoic or otherwise, but to juxtapose ideas and action in a manner calculated to induce laughter.[10]

D) Ausonius

Scholars who have difficulty with the idea that fifth-century Gallic Christians like the author of the *Querolus* and his audience might have appreciated some comic relief from the grim political realities of the age

---

[9] Ibid. 5.1–2.
[10] This perspective has been brought out refreshingly by Wilhelm Süss, "Über das Drama 'Querolus sive Aulularia'," *Rheinisches Museum für Philologie*, n.F. 91 (1942), 59–122, whose article is also the best general commentary on the play.

may do well to contemplate the attitudes of our next two poets, Ausonius and Sidonius Apollinaris. Aside from occupying important positions in the educational, civic, and, in Sidonius' case, the ecclesiastical establishments of fourth and fifth-century Gaul these men were also recognized as leading littérateurs of their day. At the same time, and indeed, in virtue of their adherance to the canons of contemporary rhetorical poetry at its most elaborate and conventional, both Ausonius and Sidonius take an attitude toward Stoicism and toward ideas as such that is devoid of doctrinal content, purely illustrative and decorative.

In the case of Ausonius (310–393/94) this taste stems from a wholehearted commitment to the linguistic arts. Born in Bordeaux and educated there and in Toulouse, he held chairs of grammar and rhetoric in his native city and was appointed tutor to the young emperor Gratian in ca. 364. His pupil's accession to the throne in 375 brought with it high office for Ausonius, who was made prefect of Gaul in 378 and consul in 379. In the latter year he retired to Bordeaux. Ausonius wrote a large number of poems of various kinds, as well as letters. The poems in which he refers, expressly or not, to Stoic themes, are not the ones that critics have singled out as Ausonius' best efforts. With one exeception these references to Stoicism are positive but in all cases they are essentially superficial. Ausonius' disinterest in the technicalities of philosophy is reflected in one of his eclogues where, in a list of kinds of fractious behavior that disrupt the smooth flow of human relations, he includes the meaningless logic-chopping debates of the philosophers, illustrating the point with the first of the Stoic hypothetical syllogisms, "If it is light, it is day."[11]

Although hostile to the Stoics in the above passage, Ausonius indicates elsewhere that he has no particular philosophical preference of his own. In a poem written to advertise the merits of his own works, he observes that they contain something for everyone. Venus smiles on one page, Minerva on another; Stoicus has partes, has Epicurus amat ("the Stoic likes these parts, the Epicurean those.")[12] What "the Stoic" actually professes, however, is a matter on which Ausonius remains rather vague. In a poem complimenting the pedagogues of Bordeaux, he praises the grammarian and rhetorician Nepotianus for his fluency and acuteness in argument, noting that he is equal to Cleanthes the Stoic.[13] The

---

[11] Ausonius, Eclogarum liber 3.18, ed. Sextus Prete in Opuscula (Leipzig, 1978); trans. Hugh G. Evelyn White, Loeb (London, 1919–21), I, 170–72. Prete's ed. will be used for all citations.

[12] Epigrammata de diversis rebus 25.6, trans. White, II, 168.

[13] Commentatio professorum burdigalensium 15.11. The claim that Ausonius here is endowing Nepotianus with Stoic ascetic virtue, made by Jacqueline Hatinguais, "Vertus universitaires selon Ausone," REA, 55 (1953), 379–87, far exceeds the textual evidence.

one text in Ausonius' poems that does have some substantive Stoic content is a passage, echoing Horace's *Satire* 2.7.8, where he describes the wise man:

> Quid proceres vanique levis quid opinio volgi ...
> Securus, mundi instar habens, teres atque rotundus,
> Externae ne quid labis per levia sidat.[14]

> What the great think, or what the fickle opinion of the empty-headed mob,
> . . . he cares not, but, after the fashion of the globe, keeps himself rounded
> and compact, too smooth for any blemish from without to settle upon him.

The disinvolvement from external opinion and the motif of the globe attached to the sage are authentically Stoic. However, in the words preceding the passage quoted, Ausonius attributes these traits to the Pythagoreans.

E) Sidonius Apollinaris

Much in the same vein is Sidonius Appolinaris, whose references to Stoicism are as purely coloristic and lacking in philosophical content. Sidonius (ca. 430–479/80), scion of a distinguished family from Lyon, received an excellent education there and married the daughter of the emperor Avitus. This connection with the imperial court was as much a liability as an asset given the turbulent political history of the time, but Sidonius was a man with the capacity to land on his feet. He delivered the panegyric celebrating his father-in-law's assumption of the consulship in 456 and shared his disgrace when Avitus fell from power shortly thereafter. Winning the pardon of the next emperor, Majorian, Sidonius was appointed to important civic posts and sent on embassies. His career in the civil administration culminated in the office of prefect of Rome in 468. In 469 or 470 Sidonius switched to ecclesiastical office with his consecration as bishop of Clermont. He was chosen not for his attainments as a theologian, which were negligible, but for his social status, connections, and administrative ability, qualities prized in bishops during these troubled times. Sidonius wrote both poems and letters in which references to Stoicism can be found. These references are shaky on doctrine and even more preclusively rhetorical than is the case with Ausonius. Indeed, Sidonius' writings of whatever genre can be under-

---

[14] *Eclog.* 2.4–7, trans. White, I, 169. The ellipsis denotes a lacuna in the original text. The Stoic and Horatian reference has been noted by White, ibid., n. 1 and by Severin Koster, "Vir bonus et sapiens: (Ausonius 363 p. 90 P.)," *Hermes*, 102 (1974), 599–619.

stood primarily as examples of set-piece oratory of one kind or another.

Typical of Sidonius' epeidectic rhetoric in verse and prose are his panegyrics and epithalamia, his letters of condolence and his thank-you notes, his florid compliments to friends and to authors he admires. His usual strategy is to compare the dedicatees to Stoics and other classical philosophers by way of praising their learning and virtue and, not incidentally, displaying his own erudition. The traits he associates with the Stoics he names for these purposes serve as conventional labels identifying them swiftly. In a panegyric on the emperor Anthemius, Sidonius depicts his addressee as a scholar no less than a statesman, listing various schools of philosophy with which the emperor is conversant. Among a host of other figures, Sidonius mentions Cleanthes, a sage who, he says, learned what he knew with much biting of his fingernails (*arroso quiquid sapit ungue Cleanthes*).[15] No reference is made to the content of that hard-won knowledge. Sidonius also includes Zeno and Chrysippus in passing,[16] with a similar absence of information about their teachings although with no remarks about their personal habits, attractive or otherwise.

Sidonius is the only known source of the nail-biting of Cleanthes and it is a mystery where he derived it. The one personal trait that spelled "Stoic" to antiquity was tonsorial style, the bearded philosopher who refrained from altering his natural appearance being a motif embroidered both by Stoics themselves and by their Roman supporters and detractors. Given Sidonius' quest for visible recognition signs on which to hang the philosophers he cites, it is not surprising that he seizes on this one. However, he attributes the Stoic position on hair to the Platonists. In a poem dedicated to Felix, praetorian prefect of Gaul and an old friend, Sidonius refers obliquely and in passing to Seneca, as a philosopher, a native of Córdoba, the tutor of Nero, and the dévoté of the unkempt and unshaven Plato.[17] The same faulty connection between Stoic cosmetic theology and Plato occurs in a letter of condolence addressed to Petreius on the death of his great-uncle, Claudianus Mamertus, about whom we will hear more below. Sidonius praises Claudianus as a man dedicated to philosophy, although not at the expense of theology and without the affectations of the philosophers, including a beard and long hair, noting

---

[15] Sidonius Apollinaris, *Carmina* 2.170, ed. and trans. W. B. Anderson, Loeb (Cambridge, Mass., 1936–65), I.

[16] Ibid. 2.175–176.

[17] Ibid. 9.323. This passing reference is not substantial enough to bear out the claim, made by Pierre Courcelle, "Deux grands courants de pensée dans la littérature latine tardive: Stoïcisme et néo-platonisme," *REL*, 42 (1965), 126, that Sidonius singles out Seneca for special praise.

that it was only in his grooming and his faith that he parted company with the Platonists.[18]

If Sidonius confuses the relations between the Stoics and the Platonists, he also confuses the relations between the Stoics and the Academics. In an epithalamium dedicated to Polemius praising the bridegroom's scholarship with the same kind of one-line references to philosophers found in his emperor panegyric, Sidonius, having mentioned the Academics, turns next to Chrysippus and Zeno, saying merely that they were Stoics and that their teachings were in accord with the Academics'.[19] The author reminds Polemius that, despite his learning, he is also a bridegroom and that he should now set aside the Stoical frown,[20] suggesting the school's reputation for ascetic rigor. This is not particularly substantial but it is as close as Sidonius comes to attributing any specific content to the Stoics' doctrine.

In other references of this type he confines himself to traits delineating the Stoics' methodology as he understands it. A thank-you note to Consentius of Narbonne, expressing gratitude for his hospitality, praises the oratorical skill of his host's father who, Sidonius says, is so fluent that not even Chrysippus could cut him short, as he did in treating the *sorites*.[21] Crabbed dialectic and lack of eloquence were faults that many ancient critics charged to the Stoics' account. Much more peculiar are Sidonius' references to them as mathematicians, which occur in letters written to Claudianus Mamertus and Faustus of Riez. Claudianus, mentioned above, was a friend and possibly the teacher of Sidonius, dedicating to him the treatise *De statu animi* which he wrote against Faustus of Riez' doctrine of the corporality of the soul. This controversy itself will be discussed in more detail below. Sidonius wrote letters replete with fulsome compliments to both authors, which display not the slightest comprehension of the substance of their controversy. He freely compares both authors with Stoics, although without mentioning Stoic anthropology, the point of the debate, in any way. Sidonius praises Claudianus for the breadth of his learning, comparing him with assorted ancient savants including Chrysippus the mathematician (*cum Chrysippo numeros*).[22] He displays just as much enthusiasm for Faustus, who, he says, evoking Jerome, Christianized pagan philosophy like the Israelite of

---

[18] *Epistolae* 4.11.1, ed. and trans. Anderson, II. M. Roger, *L'Enseignement des lettres classiques d'Ausone à Alcuin: Introduction à l'histoire des écoles carolingiennes* (Paris, 1905), p. 75 is correct in noting that the bearded sage motif in Sidonius goes back to Stoicism but misses the point that Sidonius attributes it to Platonism.

[19] *Carm.* 15.122–123.

[20] Ibid. 15.189–190.

[21] Ibid. 23.116–118.

[22] *Ep.* 4.3.5.

Deuteronomy who purified and espoused the pagan woman. Among the philosophers to whom Faustus is equal, he says, are Zeno with the frown (*Zenone fronte contracta*), Chrysippus with fingers bent to indicate counting (*Chrysippus digitis propter numerorum indicia constrictis*), and Cleanthes, once more biting his nails, numbering like Chrysippus and measuring like Euclid.[23] Left to their own devices, Sidonius adds, these Stoics, along with their Cynic and Peripatetic associates, would plunge the Christian headlong into error and heresy.[24] So much the more is Faustus to be credited for rescuing their ideas and integrating them with Christian truth. Although his intellectual gifts equal those of the pagan philosophers, Faustus is too modest to let his hair grow long or to affect the philosophers' traditional garb.[25]

The stern warnings about the dangers and limitations of Stoicism and other philosophies and the distinctly secondary place which Sidonius accords to them in this letter to Faustus, coupled with his citation of the same figures as exemplars of wisdom elsewhere, should not raise any questions about the author's real attitude. In all cases, what Sidonius has to say about Stoicism is extremely superficial and *ad hoc*, dictated by the stylistic exigencies of epeidectic rhetoric whether in prose or verse. Sidonius carries this purely decorative treatment of Stoicism farther than any of the Latin poets of his age. His most interesting and puzzling contribution to the Stoic tradition is his characterization of the early Stoics as mathematical in method and of Cleanthes as addicted to nail-biting. These attributes must have been well-known in Sidonius' time or else they would not have been able to serve the instant recognition function which they are manifestly designed to serve in his letters and poems. One may perhaps conjecture that Sidonius and his contemporaries were better versed in ancient sources that have not come down to us than our standard conception of classical culture in fifth-century Gaul might warrant.

F) Commodianus

The theme of cosmetic theology that Sidonius touches on was orchestrated in a far less peripheral manner in the second group of Christian Latin poets to whom we now turn. In contrast to the writers just examined, the next four poets all treat major issues in Christian ethics or metaphysics, or both. They bring Stoic philosophy to bear on such questions as Christian vocations and what is appropriate to them, free will

---

[23] *Ep.* 9.9.14.
[24] *Ep.* 9.9.15.
[25] *Ep.* 9.9.14.

and providence, and theodicy, writing out of a communal and sometimes personal need to find the answers. Two of these poets, Paulinus of
Nola and Prudentius, are outstanding exponents of the Christian Latin
literature of their age; the other two, Commodianus and Dracontius, have
earned less critical esteem. But here again, literary merit proves to be
no automatic index of the poet's importance as a source for intellectual
history or as a contributor to the Christian reformulations of Stoicism in
this period.

The foregoing observation certainly holds true for Commodianus, one
of the most obscure of the Latin Christian poets. Neither his place of origin nor his career nor his exact dates are known, although he probably
lived in the mid-third century and may have ended his life as a bishop.
Commodianus wrote before the legitimization of the Church, a circumstance reflected in his composition of a poetic defense of Christianity directed against the Jews and pagans. His only other poem, and the one
that concerns us here, is the *Instructionum*, a moral handbook in verse
written to instruct and console the faithful as well as to attack the pagans. In one passage of this poem Commodianus develops a new approach to the theme of cosmetic theology. It has been noted that there
are textual parallels between the *Instructionum* and both Tertullian's *De
cultu feminarum* and Cyprian's *De habitu virginum*,[26] but Commodianus does
not necessarily take the same point of view as either of these predecessors. Like both of them, he aims his remarks at women exclusively. Like
Cyprian, he is concerned with a special female vocation in the Church.
However, unlike the bishop of Carthage, he is interested not in the ascetic calling of the consecrated virgin but in the privileges and responsibilities of the Christian wife. One of the most original features of Commodianus' treatment of his theme is his conception of marriage as a first-
class Christian vocation, to be understood in a wholly positive manner.
It is true that Tertullian had not confined himself to celibate women,
although he had counseled women in general to comport themselves, in
effect, like ascetics. Completely absent from Commodianus is the penitential framework in which Tertullian places his rules for female conduct, as is the law of nature as a norm for moral behavior, which Tertullian applies inconsistently for men and for women. Commodianus
substitutes the law of God for the law of nature without making any effort to assimilate the latter to the former. The negative norm against
which he is reacting is not unnatural behavior but paganism.

---

[26] Joseph Martin, commentary on his ed. of Commodianus, *Instructionum*, CC, 128
(Turnhout, 1960), pp. 52–55; Antonio Salvatore, commentary on his ed. of *Instr.* (Napoli, 1968), pp. 151–59.

Christian matrons, he argues, do have a positive right and duty to be pleasing to their husbands. However, they should seek to be appealing by their virtuous conduct, their piety, and their moral uprightness, rather than by being fashion plates. The standard embellishments of dress, cosmetics, and hairstyle which Commodianus mentions are to be set aside not merely because they signify vanity, unchastity and wordliness but because they are the tokens of the pagan culture within which Christian wives must function as counter-examples of virtue. Further, he adds, the money that wives save by avoiding these costly luxuries can be contributed instead to works of charity. The criterion that Commodianus posits in deciding what is appropriate in the matter of personal appearance is modesty, which counsels conformity to the law of God, inner morality and not external adornment:

> Lex Dei testatur tales abscedere leges,
> Ex corde quae credit femina marito probata
> Sufficiat esse non cultibus sed bona mente.[27]

> The law of God calls her to witness abstention from such laws;
> A wife is approved by her husband for her believing heart,
> And it suffices that she be not elegant but of good character.

While Commodianus clearly sets his version of cosmetic theology in an apologetic context, while he shows no interest in nature as a moral norm, and while he addresses himself to women alone, he actually comes closer in spirit to the Stoic conception of this theme than do some Christian writers whose debts to the Stoa may be more overt. Commodianus views marriage as a perfectly dignified and acceptable calling. He sees married women as moral beings in their own right who play a positive role in society at large as well as in the family. Their behavior is important to him primarily because of its relationship to their own inner ethical intentionalities and capacities, not because of its inadvertant erotic effect on men. Commodianus' concerns as a Christian apologist thus fuse with a conception of women and of marriage that is quite Stoic in flavor and that revalues them strikingly in comparison with Tertullian and Cyprian, in both human and theological terms.

G) Paulinus of Nola

An even more elaborate development of the theme of cosmetic theology is found in Paulinus of Nola (353/54–431), a poet far more re-

---

[27] *Instr.* 2.14–15, ed. Martin. The quotation is at 2.14.12–14. Salvatore gives a slightly different reading, p. 50.

nowned than Commodianus. A patrician and a pupil of Ausonius, Prudentius married and entered public life, serving as a senator and consul. Following his wife's death he became a monk, founding several churches and a monastery for himself and his associates. He was made the bishop of Nola in ca. 409, a position he retained for the rest of his life. Paulinus wrote several dozen poems and letters, as well as a panegyric on Theodoric the Ostrogoth. He treats the subject of cosmetic theology in one of his poems and two of his letters, in each case adding a new variation on the theme and reflecting throughout an even-handed approval of marriage and monasticism as worthy Christian callings.

In a vein reminiscent of Commodianus, Paulinus composed a poem to celebrate the marriage of a young couple, Julianus and Titia, in ca. 400/05. This is the first Latin Christian epithalamium in which the appearance and conduct suitable to both spouses is given consideration. Julianus and Titia were both the children of bishops and the bridegroom was a clergyman, who later became bishop of Eclanum and ran afoul of the Augustinian party in the anti-Pelagian debates of the mid-fifth century. The issue in Paulinus' poem is not merely how Christian spouses should comport themselves but how a cleric and his wife should behave, recognizing that their conduct is important not only before God and in their own private relationship but as an example to the Christian community which they lead. In the portion of the poem addressed to the bride, Paulinus counsels abstention from luxurious clothes, jewelry, cosmetics, and hairstyles for the same reasons as Commodianus, although he also invokes the norm of nature. He adds some thoughts on how the wedding ceremony itself should be celebrated. The specific nuptial ceremonies and adornments which he attacks are those associated with pagan weddings, for which Christians in general and clerics in particular must find substitutes. The bride should replace wordly fashions with nature, setting aside external embellishments and offering instead her own inner virtues and intellectual attainments. Like Commodianus, Paulinus sees the decoration of the body as the index of an empty mind and not merely as a sign of unchastity in women. He agrees that a married woman has the right and duty to please her husband and that she should do so in terms of her character and intelligence. Paulinus' advice to Titia can thus be seen as a decisive remodelling of the "beauty unadorned" theme of the classical love poets into the "virtue unadorned" conception of the Christian wife.[28] But he does not stop there. Paulinus also devotes

---

[28] Paulinus of Nola, *Carmina* 25.27–90, ed. Guilelmus de Hartel, CSEL, 30 (Vienna, 1894). P. G. Walsh, in the intro. to his trans. of Paulinus' poems, ACW, 40 (New York, 1975), pp. 13–14, has brought out clearly the anti-pagan dimension. Witke, *Numen litterarium*, p. 95, sees this poem as evocative of Tertullian but is unconvincing.

a section of the poem to Julianus' deportment. Here he gives exactly the same kind of advice to the bridegroom as he has given to the bride. A Christian husband, *a fortiori* a married cleric, should shun jewelry and costly raiment and should adorn himself with his virtues as a means of better pleasing his wife, a wife whose own moral and intellectual character will incline her to esteem him the more highly for his intelligence and virtue than for his sartorial elegance.[29] Thus, Paulinus treats the husband and wife as moral equals, both in principle and in practice. In neither case is he preoccupied with physical attractiveness as a stimulus to lust and in each case he treats his dedicatees as three-dimensional human beings whose primary appeal for each other lies in the sphere of mind and character.

If Paulinus makes a significant contribution to the topic of cosmetic theology in connection with marriage in the poem just discussed, he also adds to it in the context of the monastic calling, mainly by re-masculinizing it. Earlier Christian writers, to be sure, had applied cosmetic theology to ascetic and celibate vocations. But, in the case of Cyprian and Jerome, the exhortation and advice were aimed at consecrated virgins and widows. Paulinus is the first Latin Christian writer to develop a cosmetic theology for men vowed to the monastic life. While the spirit of the two letters in which he does so is similar to that of his Christian epithalamium, closer, indeed to it than to Cyprian and Jerome, the specific recommendations, of course, are different. Here, although he makes a point of overriding the norm of nature in his prescriptions for monks, he also restores an authentically Stoic sense to the topic. He does this not only by interiorizing the meaning of the individual's outward appearance but also by considering the impact of the monk on his society, as an exponent of a particular form of wisdom. Paulinus' letters on monastic comportment are thus of additional interest for the evidence they give about monks as public figures. Also, given the prevailing masculine hairstyles in his day, he faces some difficulties in combining the monastic tonsure with the standard *topos* of the bearded philosopher with uncut hair.

Monks, Paulinus urges, must avoid fine clothes. They should gird their cloaks with a piece of rope, shunning the belt that is the sign of military or civic office in contemporary society. This sartorial choice will reflect the commitment to poverty and the abandonment of wordly ambition that mark the monk's calling. Monks, he adds, should even adopt a messy and disreputable presentation of self, hiding their natural physical attractions for the sake of detachment and chastity. Similarly, they should

---

[29] *Carm.* 25.91–102.

not let their hair grow long. Nor should they trim it artfully, avoiding the fashions of Germanic conquerers and late Roman elegants alike. They should keep their hair closely but irregularly cut, except for the tonsure shaved off at the brow. These strictures concerning dress, grooming, and tonsure, aside from testifying to the monk's forswearing of wealth, power, and sexual pleasure, are also indices of his corresponding concern for his inner moral beautification.[30] The matter of tonsure, however, does give Paulinus pause. In a manner analogous to Juvenal, who had to regroup in confronting the fashion for beards set by the emperors in the second century, Paulinus has to revamp the idea of tonsorial unconventionality that was part of the traditional *topos*. He emerges with a creative and influential solution. The shaving of the monk's brow, he says, is not the same as shaving the beard in conformity with the mode. Rather, it is an outward sign of the purification of the monk's soul: *novacula nobis Christus deus est* ("Christ the Lord is our razor.")[31] More broadly, and despite this necessary modification, Paulinus preserves the Stoic flavor of the *topos* by insisting on the importance of outward appearance as the manifestation of inner moral intentions and as a form of public witness. Paulinus' particular Christianizations of the theme of Stoic cosmetic theology, both for monks and for married people of both sexes, is his chief contribution to the history of the Stoic tradition and a testament to the balanced and positive way in which he fuses it with the theology of Christian vocation in each case.

H) Prudentius

Prudentius (ca. 348–ca. 405) is unquestionably the most prodigious of the Christian Latin poets of the fourth and fifth centuries. A Spaniard, an advocate, and a civil servant, he held a number of important public posts. In his old age he gave up his political career and devoted himself to Christian poetry, producing a substantial *œuvre* of high literary quality. His works include the *Cathemerinon*, a collection of hymns; the *Contra orationem Symmachi*, a defense, like that of Ambrose, of the Christian position in the Altar of Victory incident; the *Dittochaeon*, on the Bible; the *Peristephanon*, on the martyrs; the *Apotheosis*, on the divine nature; the *Psychomachia*, on the battle of the vices and virtues; and the *Hamartigena*, on the origins of sin. For our purposes the last two poems are the most important. Prudentius expressly criticizes philosophers in general, the followers of Hercules,[32] and the bearded philosophers (*sophistas barbatos*)

---

[30] *Epistula* 22.2, ed. Guilelmus de Hartel, CSEL, 29 (Vienna, 1894).

[31] *Ep.* 23.10, p. 168.

[32] Prudentius, *Hamartigena* 402–404, in *Carmina*, ed. Mauricius P. Cunningham, CC, 126 (Turnhout, 1966). All references to Prudentius will be made to this edition.

in particular[33] as exponents of paganism and wordly vanity. He also treats the topic of cosmetic theology, applying it both to men and women, although without the egalitarianism of Paulinus. But his chief interest here, in comparison with Commodianus and Paulinus, is that he raises the question of personal appearance in a much broader philosophical context, that of providence and free will and the genesis of vice and virtue. Prudentius does draw on Stoic theodicy and psychology in this connection, but he is not always consistent in handling the moral and anthropological implications of that position.

The most clearly Stoicizing of Prudentius' works is the *Hamartigena*, a poem written to refute the doctrine of metaphysical dualism and, within a monotheistic system, the consequent charge that the Creator must be responsible for evil. As with many other proponents of Stoicizing theodicy, whether pagan or Christian, he argues that the sufferings of men are the result of their own free choices and attitudes. As an example of misdirected free will, he cites the decision to embellish one's appearance with elaborate clothing, toiletries, and jewels, as if one's God-given nature were not sufficient. Both men and women are guilty of the falsification, the *luxuria*, and the denial of nature and God which this practice entails, although Prudentius also thinks that it is a particular indication of mental feebleness in the case of women.[34] This sexual inequity aside, the main point Prudentius wants to make in the *Hamartigena* is consistent with Stoic psychology. The human mind and will, he says, are the sources of vice, not the body. If the mind voluntarily consents to an evil temptation, then sin occurs and men bring suffering on themselves and others. But temptation, personified as the devil, has no automatic power over man.[35] While Prudentius inserts an external spiritual force here, the devil, he does so in order to reinforce the idea that the source of evil is not matter or the body. Even though he departs from the autarchy of Stoic psychology in this respect, he retains an explanation of the genesis of vice and virtue rooted in an intellectualistic anthropology in which free will plays a critical role.

On the other hand, in Prudentius' must famous poem, the *Psychomachia*, his fidelity to these Stoic principles is shaky. Here, in treating the same topic of the dynamics of vice and virtue, he states that vice is a function of man's bodily nature while virtue is the action of the soul rebelling against its corporeal prison. While he continues to emphasize free

---

[33] *Contra orationem Symmachi* 2.890–891, p. 242.

[34] *Hamart.* 264–297.

[35] Ibid. 553–561. This point, and its Stoic derivation, have been brought out well by Gaston Boissier, *La fin du paganisme: Étude sur les dernières luttes religieuses en occident au quatrième siècle*, 4ᵉ éd. (Paris, 1903), II, 131.

will in the analysis of ethical choice in the *Psychomania*, his whole handling of the question has a decidedly Neoplatonic coloration.[36] Further,
when Prudentius moves to the actual strategies he proposes for the battle of virtue against vice, he prescribes neither a Stoic nor a Neoplatonic
tactic but a Christianized Aristotelianism. In her struggle with Avarice,
Frugality posits as the norm in food and dress man's natural needs, which
she measures in terms of the Peripatetic golden mean. Prudentius adds
that men should look to God to provide the things that this criterion entails.[37] Thus, on a practical level, Prudentius offers eclectic analyses and
solutions to the problems that he poses in Stoicizing terms on the wider
metaphysical canvas of the *Hamartigena*.

I) Dracontius

Theodicy, a major interest of Prudentius, is the central theme of the
De laudibus dei of Dracontius (fl. 480–490), the last in our group of poets.
An attorney and civil servant from north Africa, Dracontius held the post
of proconsul of Carthage under Vandal rule. Some of his poems, such as
the *Romulea* and *Orestes tragoedia*, are straightforward recapitulations of
classical works and subjects. Dracontius wrote a poem complimenting
another ruler, probably the Byzantine emperor, which unleashed the
wrath of the Vandal king Guthamund, who imprisoned him on that account. Dracontius' *Satisfactio* and *De laudibus dei* were written in prison.
The first is an apology dedicated to Gunthamund in the hope of winning
the author's release, to which the king was not responsive. The *De laudibus dei*, Dracontius' Christian-Stoic theodicy, may have led to his re-
prieve. His ultimate fate is unknown. In any event, the philosophical and
theological issues that he raises in the *De laudibus dei* do not interest him
for the apologetic reasons that had inspired previous authors of Stoicizing Christian theodicies from Minucius Felix to Prudentius. Rather, the
poem springs from his existential needs as a prisoner quite possibly faced
with the summary rage of the Vandal. As such this work is interesting
not only for the blend of Stoicism and Christianity that Dracontius con-
cocts but also as a precursor of Boethius' more celebrated contribution
to this genre of prison literature in the following generation.

The *De laudibus dei* is presented in three books, of which the first is the
most important for our purposes. Dracontius combines the standard
Stoicizing arguments for a rational and benevolent deity on the basis of
the order, beauty, and harmony of the creation with a discussion of the

---

[36] *Psychomachia* 890–915.
[37] Ibid. 611–628.

natural world organized along the lines of a hexameron. In describing the created order Dracontius follows the Stoa in seeing fire as the primordial element out of which the other elements are formed, although he treats this topic in the context of creation *ex nihilo*.[38] To this he attaches the proofs of God's care for man by His gift of the world to man, the law and the grace He supplies to errant humanity, and the guidance He provides in dreams, portents, and prophesies.[39] A final instance of God's beneficence is the example of the Phoenix, whose cyclical immolation and rebirth is a natural token of the renewal of the seasons, the rising and setting of the sun, the waxing and waning of the moon, the ebb and flow of the tides, no less than of the resurrection of the dead in the life to come.[40] This argument recalls more than a few apologists on the same subject. Similarly, Dracontius views these forms of natural regeneration as occurring within the *saeculum*, not as a cyclical conflagration and reconstitution of the entire cosmos in the Stoic sense. Book I of the *De laudibus dei* thus combines natural with supernatural *indiciae* of God's loving care for man, dovetailing the primarily Stoic material involved in the first instance effectively with the Christian data. The second and third books are confined to the evidence from the order of grace. As a Christian-Stoic theodicy the poem is a success. As an exercise in self-consolation, we may hope that it was either efficacious or unnecessary.

II. SALVIAN AND THE CHRISTIAN INTERPRETATION OF HISTORY

For Dracontius, as for the other Christian authors of Stoicizing theodicies we have already examined, theodicy is conceived in cosmological terms, whether for apologetic, for pastoral, or for personal reasons. The fifth-century theodicy of Salvian, monk and priest of Lérins and author also of a *De ecclesia* and several letters, is more thoroughly informed by Stoicism than any other of his time. Among previous and contemporary theodicies, Salvian's *De gubernatione dei* is distinctive for a historical rather than a cosmological focus. It is not the evil in the universe or the perennial failings of men that he seeks to rationalize but the sufferings and injustices brought about by the contemporary historical situation in fifth-

---

[38] Dracontius, *De laudibus dei* 1.23–26, ed. and trans. James F. Irwin (Philadelphia, 1942). The point about creation *ex nihilo* is made at 2.201. Lapidge, "A Stoic Metaphor," *Latomus*, 39 (1980), 831–33 gives a good account of the strengths, but not the limits, of Dracontius' Stoic borrowings.

[39] Ibid. bk. 1 in general and on prophesy and portents in particular 1.40–109, 1.525–527.

[40] Ibid. 1.653–666, 1.683–684.

century Gaul, whose structural and functional deficiencies were the consequence of political turmoil and a corrupt, unwieldy governmental system that was all too obviously not working. Thus, in Salvian's hands,
theodicy is transformed from an account of the cosmos and an explanation of human nature into an interpretation of history.

This being the case, Christian historiography is another genre of contemporary Latin literature within which Salvian's work can be situated.
Here too his *De gubernatione dei* marks an important departure by virtue
of its strongly Stoicizing elements. Despite the fact that the Christian
historians of the apologetic and patristic age had before them the models
for incorporating Stoicism into the interpretation of human character and
historical events provided by the Roman historians and epic poets, their
writings are marked by a pervasive disinterest in a philosophical approach. This trait is equally visible in the two most prevalent subgenres
of Christian historiography that characterize this period, hagiography
and universal history. Hagiography itself undergoes a significant development from the earliest martyrologies to the lives of major monastic reformers and bishops. But, whether the saints manifest heroism in the
Colosseum, asceticism in the Egyptian desert, or miraculous wonder-
working powers in Gaul, the hagiographers tend to view them from the
skin out. The saints are presented as made men or women; their holiness
is a function of the power and grace of God which they have already received and the hagiographer pays no attention to their inner life or personal development. Thus, hagiographical writers bypass the Stoic sage
as a model for the Christian saint, despite his demonstrated utility for
that purpose in the hands of contemporary moral theologians. For their
part, the writers of universal history are preoccupied with chronology,
the ages of the world, the relationship between Biblical events and the
rise and fall of secular empires, and, more broadly, the intersection between *Heilsgeschichte* and history *tout court*. They see no pressing need to
conceptualize God as the lord of history in terms of the Stoic *logos*. In
drawing on Stoic theodicy as a framework for a Christian interpretation
of history, Salvian thus displays a far more philosophical attitude than
most of his confrères working in this medium. Indeed, the only contemporary with whom he can truly be compared in this connection is Augustine, whose *City of God* also seeks to explain a condition of acute political crisis while at the same time attaching that explanation to universal
history. While Salvian's historical theodicy is not as sweeping or ambi-
tious as Augustine's, it is certainly far more specifically Stoic.

The seriousness with which Salvian draws on Stoic arguments has
sometimes been called into question. Salvian has been dismissed as a
writer who thought that Christianity and philosophy were fundamen-

tally incompatible[41] or as a man lacking a profound interest in philosophy as such, his distaste for the subject being particularly discernible in a passage of the *De gubernatione dei* where he condemns Socrates for his doctrine of the community of wives and Cato as a procurer for his own wife Marcia.[42] This latter passage has been identified correctly as an echo of Tertullian and Lactantius,[43] whose own interest in philosophy is more substantial than some critics have believed. In Salvian's case, this text is perhaps more interesting as an index of the power of literary authority over life, for he was a married man who decided, with his wife, to dissolve the marriage bond in favor of a monastic existence. Thenceforth they lived as brother and sister, and he might well have seen in the celibate remarriage of Cato and Marcia an existential parallel with his own situation. However, this one instance where he rejects a Stoic *exemplum virtutis* in no sense represents his general attitude toward Stoicism as a whole.

Writing his theodicy both *ad* and *adversus Christianos* rather than *adversus paganos*,[44] Salvian's concerns are twofold. He seeks to encourage his co-religionists living in a strife-torn Gaul whose Roman governers had proved unable to stave off barbarian invaders. At the same time, he criticizes his fellow Christians for their lukewarm faith and moral lethargy. Since they themselves are not living an upright life, he charges, some of the evils of the age are their own fault and cannot be attributed exclusively to the uncivilized Germanic conquerers and the inept Roman bureaucrats. Salvian's basic strategy of argument is also twofold. First, he aims to show that the sufferings of the just do not disprove the governance of the world by God according to a rational and benevolent plan. Second, he tries to make this case by arguments based on reason, example, and authority.[45] Most of the arguments from example and all of the arguments from authority are drawn from the Bible.[46] In the sphere of arguments from reason, however, he relies heavily on the tradition of Stoic theodicy, mediated no doubt by previous apologists among whom Lactantius holds pride of place. The very notion that God's universal governance and providence are rationally demonstrable is a Stoic idea which Salvian acknowledges as such. He also derives his major figure of

---

[41] Eva M. Sanford, intro. to her trans. of Salvian, *On the Government of God* (New York, 1930), p. 24.

[42] Michele Pellegrino, *Salviano di Marsiglia* (Roma, 1940), pp. 129–31. The reference to Cato is found in Salvian, *De gubernatione dei* 7.23.103, ed. and trans. Georges Lagarrigues, SC, 220 (Paris, 1975), II.

[43] Pellegrino, *Salviano*, pp. 131, 202.

[44] Lagarrigues, intro. to his ed. of *De gub. dei*, II, 25–26.

[45] This general strategy is sketched out in *De gub. dei* 1.4.17–1.5.26.

[46] Ibid. 1.6.27–1.12.60, 2.1.1–2.6.29.

speech for describing God's action in the world from the Stoic tradition.[47] His treatment of the sufferings of the just is similarly grounded in
the Stoic doctrine of the equanimity of the sage and the identification of
the sage's inner *logos* with the *logos* of the universe.[48] Finally, Salvian's
self-imposed role of spiritual physician, ministering to the troubled souls
of others through the medicine of reason, reflects a strong Stoic influence.[49]

Salvian begins his attack on the idea that God is indifferent to man
and that He does not concern Himself with human history by observing
that the faculty of reason and the arguments of the learned philosophers
provide solid support for his case, no less than Holy Scripture. Observing that, in antiquity, the Epicureans had asserted the thesis of divine
indifference, he notes that antiquity itself had refuted their position, citing the views of a number of pagan thinkers in this connection including
Plato, Pythagoras, Vergil, and Cicero. The weightiest pagan testimony
for God's continuing care for the world is the Stoics', whose metaphor
of God the helmsman Salvian expressly repeats:

> Stoici enim gubernatoris vice intra id quod regat semper manere testantur.
> Quid potuerunt de affectu ac diligentia dei rectius religiosiusque sentire
> quam ut eum gubernatori similem esse dicerent? Hoc utique intelligentes
> quod sicut navigans gubernator numquam manum suam a gubernaculo,
> sic numquam penitus curam suam deus tollit a mundo; ac sicut ille et au-
> ras captans et saxa vitans et astra suspiciens totus sit simul tam corporis
> quam cordis officio operi sui deditus, ita scilicet deum nostrum ab uni-
> versitate omnium rerum nec munus dignantissimae visionis avertere nec
> regimen providentiae suae tollere indulgentiam benignissimae pietatis au-
> ferre.[50]

The Stoics bear witness that He remains, taking the place of the helmsman, within that which He directs. What could they have felt more proper
and more reverent regarding the concern and watchfulness of God than to
have likened Him to a helmsman? By this they understood that as the
helmsman in charge of a ship never lifts his hand from the tiller, so never
does God remove His inmost attention from the world. Just as the helmsman steers, completely dedicated in mind and body to his task, taking ad-

---

[47] Pellegrino, *Salviano*, pp. 55–56, 72–73, 204–05.

[48] The best assessment of this point is by Wilhelm Blum, "Das Wesen Gottes und das
Wesen des Menschen nach Salvian von Marseille," *Münchener theologische Zeitschrift*, 21
(1970), 333–34; see also Sanford, intro. to her trans. of *De gub. dei*, p. 44 n. 13; Wilhelm
Zschimmer, *Salvianus, der Presbyter von Massilia, und seine Schriften: Ein Beitrag zur Geschichte
der christlich-lateinischen Literatur des fünften Jahrhunderts* (Halle, 1875), p. 46.

[49] Joachim Gruber, "Salvianus 'De gubernatione dei'," *Der altsprachliche Unterricht*, 21
(1978), 62.

[50] *De gub. dei* 1.1.3, trans. Jeremiah O'Sullivan, FC, 3 (New York, 1947), pp. 27–28.
The entire argument in which this passage is located is at 1.1.1–1.1.5.

vantage of the wind, avoiding the rocks and watching the stars, in like manner our God never puts aside the functions of His most loving watch over the universe. Neither does He take away the guidance of His providence, nor does He remove the tenderness of His benign love.

Salvian certainly Christianizes this simile, adding love to reason as an attribute of God. The rest of his argument is also based on a combination of Christian personalism and the inductive logic used by the Stoics, to show that the beauty, order, and harmony of the universe demonstrate the intelligence and good will of the Creator. At the same time, he notes, since God governs the world and controls the future, He also graciously hears man's pleas in the present.[51]

Moving from God to man, Salvian next tackles the second major problem in the *De gubernatione dei*, the sufferings of the just. The travails of the righteous, he asserts, do not refute the claim that God cares for the world and man. His technique for demonstrating this point is to define the sufferings of the just in Stoic terms. The true holy man, he states, does not really suffer even if he is beset by sickness, poverty, ridicule, and other hardships. Holy men are truly happy because they possess what they value most highly—wisdom and virtue, the goods that can never be lost. The wise man's inner attitude, his judgment and evaluation of things, determine his happiness. Salvian cites several classical examples of the sage, including the Fabii, the Fabricii, and a favorite Stoic case, Cincinnatus. All these men possessed equanimity. They enjoyed serenity; living a simple life, they scorned wealth and power even while accepting public office as a duty undertaken for the common good. Such sages may be thinkers no less than statesmen, and Salvian mentions certain philosophers among the Greeks who gave up wealth and even life itself for the common good,

> dicentes scilicet etiam in catenis atque suppliciis beatum esse sapientem: tantum virtutis vim esse voluerunt, ut non possit esse umquam vir bonus non beatus.[52]

> saying that the wise man is happy even though shackled with chains and subject to punishment. They deemed the power of virtue to be so great that a good man could never be an unhappy man.

If this detachment, this appraisal of virtue as the only good, and this measuring of moral choice against the criterion of the common weal is true for the pagan sages of unmistakable Stoic provenance whom Sal-

---

[51] Ibid. 1.4.17–1.5.26.
[52] Ibid. 1.2.10, trans. O'Sullivan, p. 32. The whole argument is at 1.2.6–1.2.12.

vian praises so warmly, so much more may it be true for the Christian, who also has the reward of eternal beatitude to motivate him. Salvian gives high marks to the Stoic view of divine providence and to the Stoic conception of the sage. He does not seek to impose limits on them in the light of Christian revelation or to treat them as merely ancillary to Christian truth. Rather, in his *De gubernatione dei*, he uses these Stoic ideas, side by side with the evidence of Scripture, to hearten and to reprove. In so doing, and despite the fact that his access to Stoic theodicy may well have been mediated by apologists who had it on their agenda for rather different reasons, Salvian manages to appropriate and to use these doctrines in a way that is simultaneously faithful to Stoicism in matter and spirit and consistent with Christianity.

III. MONASTIC LITERATURE: JOHN CASSIAN

One of the major developments in Church history during the period covered by this chapter was the rise of Christian monasticism. The monastic vocation, whether on an individual basis or in a community form, has already been mentioned as a context within which Latin Christian writers applied Stoic ideas to the solution of Christian problems, thus far largely in connection with cosmetic theology. Still more important and influential was the emergence of monastic rules and monastic theology that offered counsel on a broader range of moral and institutional questions. During this same period, the highly individualized and ascetic monasticism of the desert fathers gave way to regularized monastic communities. As is well known, the reformers who produced the most enduring rules were St. Basil and St. Benedict of Nursia (480–547). The latter composed the rule that served as the basis of western monasticism. Yet, from the perspective of the history of the Stoic tradition, it was not Benedict but John Cassian who made the most important contribution to Latin monastic literature in the patristic period. While Benedict does stress the virtues of prudence and discretion among the qualities that monks should seek in electing an abbot,[53] character traits that are not incompatible with Stoicism, his emphasis may be better understood as an expression of the Roman administrative mind at work that built practicality and adaptability into his *Rule* on every page. The greatest assistance that Benedict gave to the fortunes of Stoicism in the medieval monastery was the injunction that Benedictines read and study assiduously the *Collationes* of John Cassian.[54] For it was Cassian more

---

[53] St. Benedict, *Regula*, cap. 64, ed. Jean Neufville, trans. Adalbert de Vogüé, SC, 181–182 (Paris, 1972).

[54] Ibid. cap. 73.5.

than any other single figure who monasticized Stoicism in the west and who produced one of its most original and durable reformulations in this period.

John Cassian (ca. 360–ca. 435)[55] lived a life that well prepared him for the role he was to play, not only in the history of the Stoic tradition but also in the transition of Christian monasticism from its eremitic to its coenobitic form. His birthplace is unknown. As a young man he was attracted to the monasticism of the desert, moving to Bethlehem and to Egypt in about 380, where he met the famous desert fathers themselves. Some twenty years later he went to Constantinople, where he was ordained to the priesthood. This eastern chapter of Cassian's career is reflected in his thorough knowledge of the Greek Christian literature pertinent to his interests, particularly the writings of the Alexandrian Fathers and Evagrius Ponticus. Cassian left Constantinople for Rome in 405, possibly because of an involvement in the Origenist controversy or because of his personal association with the patriarch, St. John Chrysostom, who was currently under fire. After about a decade in Rome Cassian removed to Marseilles, where he founded the monastery of St. Victor, remaining there for the rest of his life. One of Cassian's works, the *De incarnatione*, was written to refute the Nestorian heresy. His other two literary productions, the *Institutiones* and the *Collationes*, were composed for the edification of his monks. The first is a handbook of instruction in Christian virtue. The second has the same moral objective but is cast in the form of twenty-four dialogues between young monks and the desert fathers, whose counsel they seek. Cassian's travels, his familiarity with eastern as well as western sources, and his varied experiences amply qualified him for his life's work. The monasticization of Stoic ethics had already taken a particular shape in the hands of eastern Christian authors, in the most stringent ascetic form. Cassian's contribution was far more than a mere transmission of this doctrine from Greek to Latin. Rather, it was an adaptation of Stoicism that was Cassian's own and that achieved a sensitive combination of it with Christianity.

As an ethicist Cassian preserves a lively concern for the connections between ethics and anthropology that mark the original Stoic position. He is interested in the genesis and dynamics of the vices, the virtues, and the passions as well as in practical guidelines for applying ethical principles in daily life. Cassian has learned much from Stoic psychology and casuistry alike. At the same time, he eschews the psychic autarchy that

---

[55] For Cassian's dates and the chronology of his life, about which there are some uncertainties, see Owen Chadwick, *John Cassian: A Study in Primitive Monasticism* (Cambridge, 1950), p. 189; Paul Christophe, *Cassien et Césaire: Prédicateurs de la morale monastique* (Gembloux, 1969), pp. 1–4.

is the main thrust of Stoic ethics. Man's judgment and free will are fundamental ethical categories for Cassian. But, the correct inner intention required for all virtuous acts stems not from man alone but also from Christ, dwelling in the inner man through faith. God's grace and human effort most collaborate. The emphasis that Cassian places on the human initiatives and responsibilities in this process should not obscure the fact that he sees man's moral perfection as a theandric phenomenon. In his own time he was castigated as a semi-Pelagian by supporters of Augustine's doctrine of grace, a verdict that does him an injustice. What Cassian proposes is the synergistic interaction between God and man typical of the Byzantine Church Fathers and the eastern orthodox tradition as a whole. Stoicism provides him with a way of conceptualizing the human contribution to this ethical enterprise. But it would be incorrect to suppose that he sees man as ethically autonomous either in a strictly Stoic or in a Pelagian sense.

In Cassian's understanding of that human contribution, the starting point is his analysis of the origins of vice and virtue. His consistency with the Stoa on this point, and the ethical corollaries he draws from it, are extensive if not total. All vices and all virtues, he holds, spring from one central source of vice or virtue, man's inner attitude and judgment. Hence, all virtues are one and so are all vices, reflecting as they do the fixed intentionality of the moral subject:

> Cunctarum namque virtutum una natura est, licet in multas dividi species et vocabula videatur. . . . Itaque nullam perfecte possidere probabitur, quisque elisus in earum parte dinoscitur.[56]

> For of all virtues the nature is but one and the same, although they appear to be divided into many kinds and names. . . . And so he is proved to possess no virtue perfectly, who is known to have broken down in some part of them.

The same hold true for the vices, especially pride, which poisons the entire moral personality of the person afflicted with it. While Cassian states in one place that one vice implies or leads to another, he asserts elsewhere that this is not invariably true and that a person vicious in one respect can also manifest virtue in another.[57] Still, he agrees with the Stoics in stressing that vice and virtue arise in the mind, not the body,

---

[56] John Cassian, *Institutiones* 5.11.1, ed. and trans. Jean-Claude Guy, SC, 109 (Paris, 1965); trans. Edgar C. S. Gibson, *The Works of John Cassian*, in *A Select Library of Nicene and Post-Nicene Fathers of the Christian Church*, 2nd ser., ed. Philip Schaff and Henry Wace (Grand Rapids, 1955), IX, 237.

[57] *Inst.* 12.3.

a point he makes both in general[58] and in his analysis of particular moral shortcomings such as covetousness[59] and dejection, which, he says, stems from an *inrationabile mentis confusione* ("irrational confusion of mind.")[60]

By the same token, and as a logical and psychological consequence of this position, Cassian sees the way to correct vices as a change in one's inner mental attitude, recognizing that the things that matter ethically are the things within man's own control.[61] Lacking the correct intellectual intentionality, a person will not be able to pursue the good life, whatever forms of ostensibly praiseworthy behavior he practices. Cassian's way of illustrating this essentially Stoic point has direct relevance to monastic institutions and the changes they were undergoing in his own lifetime. It would be a mistake, he says, to flee the monastic community and to seek solitude in the desert as a means of correcting a vicious soul, for *quaecumque enim vitia incurata in heremum detulerimus, operta in nobis, non abolita sentientur* ("whatever faults we bring with us uncured into the desert, we shall find to remain concealed in us and not to be got rid of,")[62] a passage that is a striking monasticization of Horace's *caelum non animum mutant/qui trans mare currunt.*

Another way of putting the same idea that the things which are ethically relevant are the things within our own control is in terms of the classic Stoic distinction among the good, the evil, and the *adiaphora*, coupled with the notion that virtue is the only good and vice the only evil. Cassian follows this line of reasoning very closely, although without always positing nature or reason as the norm for judging the good and the evil. He agrees that there are three basic ethical categories, good, evil, and indifferent (*bonum, malum, medium*), his term for the *adiaphora* reflecting direct or indirect Ciceronian influence. The good he defines as *virtus animi sola, quae fide sincera nos ad divina perducens* ("virtue of the soul alone, which leads us with a faith unfeigned to the things divine.") Its opposite, evil, is *peccatum solum, quod a bono deo nos separans* ("sin alone, which separates us from the good God.") The things indifferent, which include the standard Stoic *adiaphora*, may be conducive to the one end or the other according to the will and desire of the individual.[63] While he certainly retains the Stoic assessment of moral values as spiritual only, Cassian,

---

[58] Ibid. 5.21.1–5.
[59] Ibid. 7.1.
[60] Ibid. 9.13; see also 9.5.
[61] Ibid. 8.17.
[62] Ibid. 8.18.1, trans. Gibson, p. 262.
[63] *Collationes* 6.3, ed. and trans. E. Pichery, SC, 42, 54, 64 (Paris, 1955–59), trans. Gibson, p. 353. See also similar statements at *Coll.* 3.9–10, 6.4, 6.6, 6.8–11. Also noting Cassian's use of this Stoic concept of the *adiaphora* is Carlo Tibiletti, "Giovanni Cassiano: Formazione e dottrina," *Augustinianum*, 17 (1977), 359–60.

with equal clarity, treats the spirit as directed to supernatural as well as natural ends. The same hold true for the passions. In agreement with the Stoics, he thinks that the passions spring from the soul, not the body, in this case following the middle Stoic psychology which admits the Platonic and Aristotelian subdivisions of the soul into irascible and concupiscible as well as rational faculties and which regards passions arising from the two former functions as capable of being *eupatheia* if directed to worthy moral ends.[64]

These principles provide the foundation on which Cassian bases his practical moral advice. A faithful follower of Stoic casuistry, his chief concern is that the particular moral choices made by his monks flow from a proper inner intention and that they take the outward form most suitable in terms of times, places, persons, and circumstances, understanding that what is appropriate for one person to undertake in the quest for moral perfection may be unsuitable for someone else. This point is one he makes repeatedly, both in general[65] and with respect to particular practices such as fasting[66] or the uprooting of individual vices, such as covetousness.[67] In all cases, regardless of the specific way he manifests his fixed orientation toward the good, the upright man will possess constancy, firmness of mind, and equanimity in the face of tribulation, since he knows that things external are matters of indifference. This theme is orchestrated repeatedly in Cassian's *Institutiones* and *Collationes*. The image in which he sums it up, no less than its substance, is fully Stoic. The wise man, he says, is like a stamp made of steel that impresses its own form on events while retaining its own shape inviolate, rather than like the wax that is molded by things external to itself, assuming the shape that they impress upon it. The fixed purpose of mind which characterizes the sage and which undergirds all his virtuous intentions and actions is not, Cassian stresses, innate. It can be acquired, or lost, by correct or incorrect judgments and by the exercise of a good or bad will. Constant vigilance and effort are demanded both to acquire this praiseworthy state and to retain it.[68]

The central trait of Cassian's sage, his tranquillity of mind, his combination of *apatheia* and *eupatheia*, has occasioned more comment than any other single aspect of his ethical thought. This is rather surprising, for the doctrine itself is stated quite plainly by Cassian. Yet, questions have been raised about his meaning and his sources. One prominent theory,

---

[64] *Coll.* 24.15–16; on *eupatheia* see 7.3–4, 8.7–9.
[65] Ibid. 24.8.
[66] *Inst.* 5.5.1, 5.7, 5.9; *Coll.* 21.13–16.
[67] *Inst.* 7.21.
[68] *Coll.* 6.12, 6.16.

put forth by Owen Chadwick in the first edition of his study of Cassian, traces his teaching back to dualistic pagan philosophies, such as Manicheism, as well as to the world-denying aspects of the New Testament. From this standpoint, the moral battle is one of spirit against flesh; the passions spring from matter and the *apatheia* of the sage is equated with *anaesthesia*, a complete absence of feeling which, once attained, becomes a permanent state of sinlessness.[69] This interpretation errs in associating Stoicism with dualism as well as in misreading Cassian's teaching on the origin or the passions, which, he holds, arise in the mind and will, not the body. A second major approach sees the Egyptian monks, the Alexandrian Fathers, and especially Evagrius as Cassian's main sources, his chief accomplishment being the Latinization of the essentially Neoplatonized Stoicism which these authors had attached to Christianity. The major exponent of this view is Salvatore Marsili,[70] who has had a number of followers including Chadwick in the second edition of his book on Cassian.[71] According to this position, Cassian is still a dualist who advocates a complete suppression of the passions, deemed to spring from the flesh. Tranquillity of mind in Cassian is equated with the tradition of spiritual purification understood as detachment from matter. Once attained, this state is permanent. The main difference between Marsili and his followers and the original Chadwick interpretation is that the former attribute these ideas to Christian Neoplatonism, as filtered through an extremely ascetic Greek theological tradition, to which Stoic terminology has been attached but which does not really reflect a Stoic point of view.

There is also a third interpretation, put forth by M. Olphe-Galliard, which corrects the misconceptions of the preceding two.[72] Olphe-Galliard quite rightly notes that Cassian is not a dualist, that he does not

---

[69] Chadwick, *John Cassian*, pp. 14–15, 56, 80, 88–93.

[70] Salvatore Marsili, *Giovanni Cassiano ed Evagrio Pontico: Dottrina sulla carità e contemplazione*, Studia Anselmiana, 5 (Roma, 1936), pp. 12–19, 24, 87–103, 114–21.

[71] Owen Chadwick, *John Cassian*, 2nd ed. (Cambridge, 1968), pp. 82–96, 102–04; Christophe, *Cassien et Césaire*, pp. 20–21; Victor Codina, *El aspecto cristológico en la espiritualidad de Juan Casiano*, Orientalia Christiana Analecta, 175 (Roma, 1966), p. 12; Peter Munz, "John Cassian," *JEH*, 11 (1960), 6–8; E. Pichery, intro. to his ed. of *Coll.*, SC, 42, pp. 45–49; "Les idées morales de Jean Cassien," *Mélanges de science religieuse*, 14 (1957), 13; Tibiletti, "Giovanni Cassiano," *Augustinianum*, 17 (1977), 355–80; Ludwig Wrzoł, "Die Psychologie des Johannes Cassianus," *Divus Thomas*, ser. 2., 5 (1918), 182–83; 9 (1922), 269–70, 275–86.

[72] M. Olphe-Galliard, "La pureté de cœur d'après Cassien," *Revue d'ascetique et de mystique*, 17 (1936), 41, 47, 55–56. Other authors who interpret Cassian similarly are H.-I. Marrou, "Le fondateur de Saint-Victoire de Marseille: Jean Cassien," *Provence Historique*, 16 (1966), 302; Gregorio Penco, "La vita ascetica come 'filosofia' nell'antica tradizione monastica," *Studia Monastica*, 2 (1960), 80–81; Philip Rousseau, "Cassian, Contemplation and the Coenobitic Life," *JEH*, 26 (1975), 117.

regard the passions as arising from matter or as intrinsically evil, that he sees vices, virtues, and passions alike as originating in the mind and will, and that his doctrine of *tranquillitas animi* entails neither a complete extirpation of feeling nor the attainment of an immutable psychic state. Cassian, he notes, however dependent he may have been on Evagrius, is actually more Stoic than his source. At the same time, Cassian's Stoicism has been Christianized independently, so that it can be integrated into an ethic in which man is not spiritually autonomous and in which he continually experiences moral conversion and backsliding. This assessment is one that we share. It is amply reinforced by Cassian himself. It is also an interpretation willing to give him credit for his own achievements rather than approaching him primarily from the standpoint of philosophical and theological transmission.

The scholarly preoccupation with Cassian on tranquillity of mind and related subjects has tended to deflect attention away from another, equally important area of his thought, an area in which he is more dependent on Latin sources and in which he made his most creative adaptation of Stoicism to monastic ethics—his doctrine of friendship. Cassian invokes the classic Stoic conception of friendship between sages, freely chosen on the basis of their admiration of each other's moral excellence without regard for obligation or personal interest. Like Ambrose, his Latin predecessor in this field, he reformulates the idea in Christian terms. But in Cassian's case, the terms are specifically monastic. The monks to whom he directs his teaching will be bound together, he says, not only by their virtues and their intellectual affinities but also by their common faith and vocational commitment. True Christian friends, he states, are united

> quod nec conmendationis gratia nec officii vel munerum magnitudo contractusue cuiusquam ratio vel natura necessitas iungit, sed sola similitudo virtutem.[73]

> where the union is owing not to the favour of a recommendation, or to some great kindness or gifts, or the reason of some bargain, or the necessities of nature, but simply to similarity of virtue.

For monks this friendship also involves a spiritual union of wills in Christ. It inclines them to join together in a common life and a common habitation whether they are natives of the same place or not.[74] In answer to the question of what would happen if friends should have different goals

---

[73] *Coll.* 16.3, trans. Gibson, pp. 450–51.
[74] Ibid.

or perspectives, Cassian answers, *more Stoicorum*, that this is a false problem; friends, as he has defined them, will suffer no such disagreements.[75] This argument, acknowledged for its formal if not its substantive dependence on Cicero although its equally noteworthy Ambrosian resonance tends to be ignored, has been called the only truly Christian *De amicitia* of the period. It has been recognized as the inspiration for the twelfth-century Cistercian treatments of the theme, especially on the part of Aelred of Rievaulx.[76] It is certainly a creative transformation of Stoic ethics in Cassian's hands and, not incidentally, it may also be seen as a defense of the coenobitic life.

There are two others topics in Cassian's thought that require comment because of their Stoic content, topics less easy to integrate into an orthodox Christian context than his doctrine of friendship. Both occasioned controversy before Cassian's time and were to provoke further debate afterward. The subjects at issue are the impassiblity of God and the corporality of created spiritual beings, including the human soul. In both cases the position that Cassian takes can be explained by his wish to make a clear distinction between God and creatures, certainly a non-Stoic objective. At the same time, he falls back on Stoicism in order to bolster the Christian position on divine transcendence. While God is totally beyond man, Cassian observes, men must perforce speak of Him in metaphorical terms derived from human experience. Thus, when the Bible refers to the wrath of God, this wrath should not be understood anthropomorphically as a human passion, which, as he has explained elsewhere, results from incorrect judgment and a wrongly directed will, phenomena inconceivable in the case of God. Rather, says Cassian, we should attribute anger to God *digne Deo, qui omni perturbatione alienus est* ("in a sense worthy of God, Who is free from all passion.")[77] In interpreting this passage two important points need to be made. First, Cassian's central concern here is less the nature of God than the problem of theological language, which, he stresses, must not be taken literally. Second, he takes a middle position in the debate on God's impassibility which had agitated Christian thinkers in the apologetic age. For Cassian the reason why God suffers no *perturbationes* is not because He is pure spirit, since the passions that men experience are *perturbationes animi*. The issue is not matter versus spirit but God's inerrancy as a function of His

---

[75] Ibid. 16.5.
[76] The best and most recent treatment of this topic is Karl August Neuhausen, "Zu Cassians Traktat De amicitia (Coll. 16)," *Studien zur Literatur der Spätantike*, ed. Christian Gnilka and Willy Schetter, Antiquitas 1:26 (Bonn, 1975), pp. 181–218. See also Marsili, *Giovanni Cassiano*, pp. 5–6; Munz, "John Cassian," *JEH*, 11 (1960), 17–18.
[77] *Inst.* 8.4.3.

omniscience. Thus, His anger is reasonable and righteous, transcending even the *eupatheia* of men but in a sense analogous to them. The focus of Cassian's analysis is not the substantial difference between God and man but the functional difference between the divine mind and the human mind that makes false judgments impossible to God and metaphorical ways of speaking about Him necessary for man.

On the other hand, Cassian's inspiration for declaring that created spiritual beings, such as angels and human souls, are corporeal is precisely the wish to distinguish between the substance of the Creator and that of the creation.[78] God, Cassian states, is the only truly incorporeal being. Thus, other spiritual beings must have a corporeal nature, even if it is a very rarefied one: *Habent enim secundum se corpus quo subsistunt, licet multo tenuius quam nostra sunt corpora* ("For they have in their own fashion a body in which they exist, though it is much finer than our bodies are.")[78a] Cassian is grappling here with a genuine metaphysical problem that was to plague many medieval thinkers regardless of their philosophical allegiance. His chief model among his Christian predecessors is Tertullian. Compared with Tertullian, Cassian's solution goes only half the distance toward Stoicism. For Tertullian, as for the Stoics, all real beings are bodies, including God as well as the human soul. While Tertullian is not interested in defending the Stoic conception of a universal monism of substance, he is quick to adopt the corporality of God and the soul as a way of explaining the filiation of the Son, the hypostatic union, and the doctrine of the resurrection in the life to come. Cassian's reasons for viewing created spiritual beings as corporeal differ both from Tertullian's and from the Stoics'. First, Cassian regards the "flesh" that such beings possess in a Pauline sense, as a directionality of the will that accounts for their turning away from the good. Second, apparently unaware of any other philosophical way to distinguish created spiritual beings from God, Cassian falls back on the corporality of angels and human souls as a way of reinforcing the Christian doctrine of God's otherness. The only Latin Christian author in this period to produce a satisfactory way of differentiating philosophically between God and other spiritual beings was Augustine. The argument that Cassian develops for distinguishing God's anger from human passion adumbrates Augustine's solution, even though Cassian did not make the connection himself.

---

[78] The best study of the history of this idea in Latin Christian thought from Tertullian to the sixth century is José Madoz, "Un caso de materialismo in España en el siglo VI," *Revista española de teología*, 8 (1948), 203–30. On Cassian, see p. 205. Other scholars who have discussed this point are Marsili, *Giovanni Cassiano*, pp. 12–13, Tibiletti, "Giovanni Cassiano," *Augustinianum*, 17 (1977), 363; Wrzoł, "Die Psychologie des Johannes Cassianus," *Divus Thomas*, ser. 2, 5 (1918), 186.

[78a] *Coll.* 7.13, trans. Gibson, p. 367.

IV. Hilary of Poitiers

In his own time Hilary of Poitiers (ca. 310–68) was seen as a much more reliable exponent of Christian orthodoxy than Cassian and he was certainly a weightier authority among the Latins than the theologians whom we will consider after him in this chapter. A convert from paganism, Hilary was made bishop of Poitiers in ca. 353. The chief goal of his career was the defense of the Nicene Creed against the Arians, a hazardous activity given the Arian sympathies of the emperor Constantius, who banished Hilary from his see between 356 and 362 on this account. Hilary fought the battle for orthodoxy in treatises urging toleration dedicated to the emperor, in works of exhortation written to other Gallic bishops, and in his theological chef d'œuvre, the *De trinitate*. It was by no means unusual for theologians both before, during, and after Hilary's time to draw on Stoicism in order to explicate the doctrine of the Trinity. However, and despite the fact that it is his chief theological concern, this is not a field in which Hilary makes any application of Stoicism to Christianity. His appeals to Stoicism are confined to topics that were of far less importance to him: the corporality of the soul, the impassibility of God, and natural law. These are interests he shares with a number of predecessors, contemporaries, and successors. They are all found in works that are exegetical or homiletic in nature. In one case Hilary's use of Stoicism reflects a faintly unorthodox coloration. In all cases, he refers to the points at issue merely in passing and is quite unreflective about their philosophical or theological implications. He simply does not see these questions as having any bearing on his work as a dogmatic theologian, whether in a positive or a polemical sense.[79]

In common with many contemporary theologians, Hilary feels a need to distinguish the Christian conception of God from various pagan views, rejecting, among others, the idea that God is a material being composed of fire.[80] However, he reverts to a Stoic idea in treating the debated topic of the impassibility of God. Hilary shifts the focus here to the sufferings

---

[79] Hilary's Stoicism has been consistently overinterpreted by Jean Doignon, *Hilaire de Poitiers avant l'exil: Recherches sur la naissance, l'enseignement et l'épreuve d'une foi épiscopale en Gaule au milieu du IVe siècle* (Paris, 1971), passim and p. 131; intro. to his ed. and trans. of *In Mattheum*, SC, 254, 258 (Paris, 1978–79), I, 33, 41–43, 210 n. 7, 211–13, 301 n. 11; II, 145 n. 10; G. M. Newlands, *Hilary of Poitiers: A Study in Theological Method* (Bern, 1978), passim and esp. pp. 83, 89.

[80] Hilary of Poitiers, *Tractatus super Psalmos* 64.4, 65.7, ed. Antonius Zingerle, CSEL, 22 (Vienna, 1891). Noted by H. D. Saffrey, "Saint Hilaire et la philosophie," *Hilaire et son temps*, Actes du colloque de Poitiers, 2 septembre–3 octobre 1968 à l'occasion du XVI centenaire de la mort de saint Hilaire (Paris, 1969), pp. 257, 260.

of the incarnate Christ, a problem considerably more complicated than the question of whether God feels anger and compassion. On the one hand, Hilary is insistent on the point that Christ possessed a human body. On the other hand, in his effort to combat heresies of a docetic type, he argues that Christ possessed a nature that was incapable of feeling pain. This Christology, which is unique to Hilary and whose orthodoxy is questionable, has been interpreted in terms of Stoic *apatheia* as applied to Christ, but it cannot be described accurately in this way. What is involved here, for Hilary, is not the rational mastery over the passions that deflect an individual from the good but *anaesthesia*, a complete absence of feeling on Christ's part.[81]

More straightforwardly Stoic, if equally debatable from the standpoint of orthodoxy, is Hilary's position on the corporality of the human soul. Other Latin theologians of the apologetic and patristic age had used this idea as a means of distinguishing God from creatures, or as the basis for the explication of the relations among the Persons of the Trinity by analogy with created beings. Hilary, however, addresses it in a context that has nothing to do with dogmatic theology and which is, at best, tangential to his main line of argument. In his commentary on the Gospel of St. Matthew, he discusses the idea that one should not be overly concerned with externals, because the soul is more important than the body and the body is more important than the garments which clothe it. In this connection he observes:

> Nihil est quod non in substantia sua et creatione corporeum sit et omnium sive in caelo sive in terra sive visibilium sive invisibilium elementa formata sunt. Nam et animarum species sive obtinentium corpora sive corporibus exsulantium corpoream tamen naturae suae substantium sortiuntur, quia omne quod creatum est in aliquo sit necesse est.[82]

> There is nothing which is not corporeal in its substance and creation; and all things whether in heaven and earth, whether visible or invisible, are made of material elements. Even the species of souls, whether they possess bodies or issue from bodies, receive a corporeal substance in any case, according to their own natures, which is necessary for everything that is created.

---

[81] *In Mattheum* 31.7, ed. Doignon. Hilary's position has been brought out well by C. F. A. Borchard, *Hilary of Poitier's Role in the Arian Struggle* (The Hague, 1966), pp. 117–30; Max Pohlenz, *Vom Zorne Gottes: Eine Studie über den Einfluss der griechischen Philosophie auf das alte Christentum* (Göttingen, 1909), pp. 93–96. The point has been misinterpreted by Doignon, *Hilaire*, p. 376 n. 1; intro. to his ed., I, 44.

[82] *In Matt.* 5.8. The Stoic derivation of this idea has been noted by Doignon, intro. to his ed., I, 159 n. 9.

While this notion is certainly Stoic, it is less clear how it is related to the passage in Matthew that Hilary is using it to explicate.

Also in an exegetical setting is Hilary's final reference to Stoic doctrine, the idea of natural law. The context here is his interpretation of Psalms 118:119–20, "All the wicked of the earth thou dost count as dross;/ Therefore I love Thy testimonies." In commenting on the justice of God, Hilary argues that it binds all men, even non-believers, since the same basic moral principles that govern the behavior of Christians also rule the pagans under the heading of the natural law. The law of nature, Hilary says, teaches men not to injure others, not to steal, not to commit fraud, perjury, homicide, or adultery.[83] His stress here is on the point that people who disobey these principles sin against nature even if they are ignorant of the law of God. However, Hilary neither assimilates the law of nature to the law of God overtly, nor does he refer to the faculty of reason as the capacity enabling men to grasp the law of nature. This passage, like the others in Hilary just discussed, suggests the essentially superficial approach that he takes toward Stoic philosophy. It also suggests that contemporary eminence as a theologian is not necessarily an index of the contribution to the history of the Stoic tradition which a Latin Christian writer in this period was able to make.

V. Minor Theologians of the Fourth and Fifth Centuries

We now come to a group of six thinkers who merit our brief attention, although they did not attain the stature of Hilary and although they are less important than Cassian as exponents of the Stoicizing of Christianity. The Stoic topics treated by the first three, Julius Firmicus Maternus, Filastrius of Brescia, and Gaudentius of Brescia, are strictly miscellaneous. The theme addressed by the latter three, Faustus of Riez, Claudianus Mamertus, and Gennadius of Marseilles, is the corporality of angels and the human soul, which links them to both Hilary and Cassian. While none of these six figures is particularly weighty, all are illustrative of the aspects of Stoic thought of interest to the lesser theological lights of the day and of the particular theological problems to which they applied it, as well as of the relative accuracy with which they appropriated it.

A) Julius Firmicus Maternus

Firmicus Maternus, who lived in the fourth century, was a high-ranking scholar and statesman. His only known work, *De errore profanorum re-*

---

[83] *Tract. super Ps.* 118.11.

ligionum (343/50), dedicated to the emperor Constans, is, as the title indicates, an apology attacking pagan religions. There is one passage in this work, clearly dependent on Cicero's *De natura deorum*, where he castigates the pagans for divinizing the forces of nature, in this case representing the element air as the goddess Juno.[84] While Firmicus borrows Cicero's attack on the Stoic allegoresis of the gods, his handling of this argument is much less perspicacious than that of his source. Rather than criticizing the Stoic effort to demythologize the gods or urging that their theological allegories are a dishonest strategy for salvaging superstition, he interprets the text of Cicero literally to mean that the pagans are fools for trying to convert a natural element into a person, which is not the real issue at stake.

B) Filastrius of Brescia

Filastrius, bishop of Brescia in the 380s and 390s, was also a controversialist, who took on heretics rather than pagans in his unique work, *Diversarium hereseon liber*. He makes one express reference to the Stoics which is even farther away from their meaning than is Firmicus' interpretation of Cicero. Among the heresies he catalogues Filastrius mentions one, whose name he does not give, which teaches that birds, animals, and reptiles possess the faculty of reason, like human beings. This error, he says, springs from the falsehoods of the poets and Stoic philosophers (*poetis et filosofis Stoicis*).[85] Filastrius' attribution of this idea to the Stoics is mystifying since it is diametrically opposed to their actual position on this subject. He may have derived it from an almost equally garbled *testimonium* found in Servius.

C) Gaudentius of Brescia

Gaudentius (fl. 390s–406) succeeded Filastrius to the see of Brescia and is altogether a figure of greater substance. An active ecclesiastical statesman, he maintained close ties with many of the leading church-

---

[84] Julius Firmicus Maternus, *De errore profanorum religionum* 4.1, 2nd. ed., ed. Agostino Pastorino (Firenze, 1969). The Ciceronian parallel has been noted by Pastorino, pp. 51–52 and by Clarence A. Forbes in his trans. of this text, ACW, 37 (New York, 1970), p. 50. Our Firmicus Maternus should not be confused with the other fourth-century author of the same name who wrote the *Matheseos*, a work on astrology. Firmicus has been treated as an Arian by Jean-Marie Vermander, "Un arien méconnu: Firmicus Maternus," *Bulletin de littérature théologique*, 81 (1980), 3–16, and, while that designation is arguable, this paper assembles the most recent information on his life.

[85] Filastrius of Brescia, *Diversarum hereseon liber* 100.1, ed. F. Heylen, CC, 9 (Turnhout, 1957).

men of the day and was sent as a legate to Constantinople in 406 during the troubles connected with the exile of the patriarch, St. John Chrysostom. Gaudentius' major writings are twenty-one sermons, some topical and some exegetical in nature. In the latter vein is his tenth sermon, a commentary on Exodus. Gaudentius applies the four-fold method of Biblical interpretation to the text, focusing on the typological and moral comparison between liberation from the law of Pharoah in the Old Testament and liberation from the law of sin in the New Testament. The theme of law inspires him to consider more broadly the relationship between the *lex naturalis*, the *lex mandati*, and the *lex litterae*, the *lex mandati* being the injunctions God laid down in Scripture prior to the Mosaic covenant while the *lex litterae* is the law He gave in the Ten Commandments. The theme that Gaudentius develops is the idea of progressive revelation. Correlative to it, the form of law that applies to a particular people depends on the age in which they live and the truth to which they have access. Thus, the new law of Christ binds Christians even while it frees them from the old covenant.

It is the first kind of law which Gaudentius discusses in this passage, natural law, that is our chief concern. Although he does not give a source for his definition, it is a clear and accurate restatement of the Stoic position. Beginning with the remark that there is no sin where there is no law and that people are bound by the law instituted for and known to them, he proceeds immediately to the point:

Naturalis lex est illa, qua gentes legem litterae non habentes naturaliter ea, quae legis sunt, faciunt; quia rationabilis animae humanae natura, ut creatorem suum sentiat, ut proximum non laedat, ut non faciat, quod pati non vult, naturali quaedam lege intellegit; unde inexcusabilis est omnis homo, qui vel auctorem suum negat vel facit malum, quod per legem naturae non ignorat esse malum.[86]

The natural law is that by which the Gentiles, not having the law of the letter, naturally do those things which are of the law. For the nature of the rational human soul understands, by a certain natural law, that it may know its Creator, that it may not harm its neighbor, and that it may not do what it does not will to endure. Thus, every man is inexcusable who either denies his Author or who does evil which he knows to be evil through the natural law.

The notion that man can come to a knowledge of his moral obligations

---

[86] Gaudentius of Brescia, *Tractatus* 10.18, ed. Ambrosius Glueck, CSEL, 68 (Vienna, 1936); trans. Stephen L. Boehrer in *Gaudentius of Brescia: Sermons and Letters*, Catholic University of America Studies in Sacred Theology, 2nd ser., 165 (Washington, 1965). The whole passage is at *Tract.* 10.17–21.

through the use of reason is certainly Stoic. The most interesting feature of Gaudentius' definition of natural law is that he gives as much weight to the theological as to the ethical perceptiveness and responsibility of reason and that he delineates the duties flowing from the exercise of reason in primarily negative terms.

D) Faustus of Riez

With Faustus of Riez (ca. 400–92) we return to the debate on the Stoic doctrine of the corporality of the human soul, taken up earlier by Tertullian, Hilary, and Cassian.[87] Faustus, who became abbot of Lérins in 433 and bishop of Riez in ca. 462, was no stranger to controversy. Aside from sermons and letters he wrote a De gratia on the subject of grace and free will that led him, like Cassian, to be castigated as a semi-Pelagian. He directed his De spiritu sancto and De ratione fidei against the Arians, a risky enterprise given the Arianism of the Gothic conquerers of Gaul during his time, which resulted in his expulsion from his see between 381 and 383. The critique of Arianism is one of the settings in which Faustus wrote the two letters where he asserts that the soul is corporeal. The other theological context in which he discusses this doctrine is the human condition in the next life. Faustus expressly names Cassian as his source for the idea that the soul is corporeal;[88] but he applies it much more to the problems which Tertullian had used it to address.

Faustus' Epistula 3 was written in 468 to an unnamed priest who had requested his views on the Arian and Macedonian heresies. In response, Faustus points out that the filiation of the Son from the Father is not analogous to the parent-child relationship in creatures. Claiming the authority of the most learned fathers (eruditissimi patrum), he states that all created beings are material and corporeal. This condition applies also to angels and human souls, which have spatial extension even if they cannot always be localized in any one place. As for the material composition of these beings, Faustus says that they are made up of air and fire. God alone is incorporeal, for He alone is unbounded and diffused everywhere; the same conditions apply to Christ the Son.[89] He concludes, therefore, that the heretics have erred in applying an anthropo-

---

[87] The best study of the fifth-century chapter of this story, both for Faustus and his antagonist and Gennadius, is Madoz, "Un caso de materialismo," Revista española de teología, 8 (1948), 206–10. See also Samuel Dill, Roman Society in the Last Century of the Western Empire, 2nd rev. ed. (London, 1921), p. 414; E. L. Fortin, Christianisme et culture philosophique au cinquième siècle: La querelle de l'âme humaine en Occident (Paris, 1959), pp. 46–53.

[88] Faustus of Riez, Epistula 3, in Opera, ed. Augustus Engelbrecht, CSEL, 21 (Vienna, 1891), p. 154.

[89] Ibid., pp. 173–75, 180–81.

morphic conception of filiation to the generation of the Son, a conception which is a metaphysical dis-analogy. Faustus' *Epistula* 5 is also a
response to a question posed by one of his correspondents in 468, one
Paulinus of Bordeaux, in this case on moral rewards and punishments
after death. Unlike Tertullian, Faustus does not deal with the question
of posthumous resurrection itself. However, he states that, in contrast to
God, the souls of men and angels are corporeal as well as immortal. Both
of these attributes are necessary if the soul is to experience the full posthumous effects of its choices on earth, which, in the case of Hell, are
physical torments,[90] a conclusion which reflects a rather literal conception of the next life on Faustus' part.

E) Claudianus Mamertus

Claudianus Mamertus (ca. 400–ca. 472), priest at Vienne, plays a role
in our story thanks to his *De statu animi*, written in ca. 470 for the express
purpose of refuting Faustus' position on the soul. In this enterprise
Claudianus is a controversialist who takes his arguments where he finds
them. In a letter to a rhetorician named Sapaudus, praising learning and
the liberal arts as well as the addressee's contributions to them, he decorates his theme in the manner of Sidonius, citing many outstanding
representatives of the disciplines, including Chrysippus the logician.[91]
At the same time, Claudianus is well aware of the fact that Faustus' doctrine on the soul goes back to Stoicism. Thus, the strategy he adopts in
the *De statu animi* is to beat the Greeks with their own stick, countering
with the incorporeality of the soul as taught by the Pythagoreans, Platonists, and Neoplatonists.[92] This philosophical counter-attack is by no
means Claudianus' only line of argument; indeed, most of his treatise is
devoted to the testimony of the Bible and Christian writers. Along with
his technique of citing counter-authorities, he tries to persuade Faustus
that the orthodox position on the generation of the Son can be defended
without recourse to the notion that the soul is corporeal, providing several alternative proofs.[93] On the other hand, Claudianus ignores the
posthumous condition of the soul, the second issue that Faustus had interpreted in terms of the soul's corporality. The emphasis in the *De statu*

---

[90] *Ep.* 5, pp. 188–95.

[91] Claudianus Mamertus, *Epistula* 2, in *Opera*, ed. Augustus Engelbrecht, CSEL, 11
(Vienna, 1885), p. 206.

[92] *De statu animi* 1.23–25, 2.7. This technique of argument has been brought out well
by Fortin, *Christianisme et culture philosophique*, pp. 62–74, ch. 2–3. See also Martin Schultze,
*Die Schrift des Claudianus Mamertus, Presbyters zu Vienne, über das Wesen der Seele (De statu an-
imi)* (Dresden, 1883), pp. 56–57.

[93] *De stat. an.*1.2–3.

animi thus suggests that, in Claudianus' eyes, the most pressing theological concern of the moment was not man's condition after death but the nature of the Trinity.

F) Gennadius of Marseilles

Gennadius, the fifth-century priest of Marseilles, is best known for his *De viris illustribus*, a continuation of Jerome's work by the same title. He also compiled a *Liber ecclesiasticorum dogmatum*, although some scholars attribute it to other authors. This book, like Claudianus' *De statu animi* and Faustus' *Epistula* 3, was written with a polemical intent, to refute heresy and to defend the orthodox faith. Gennadius lists fifty-four major points of doctrine, in each case stating first the orthodox position and then cataloguing the various heterodox departures from it. He adverts to the Stoic doctrine of the soul under the heading of three heretical ideas. As with his two immediate predecessors, Gennadius assumes the stance of a heresy-hunter. But the chief heresy he attacks in the passages where he discusses the nature of the soul is not Arianism but Origenism. Gennadius criticizes the idea that men and angels were first created as pure spirits, receiving bodies as a consequence of sin. He regards this Origenist heresy as an offense against the truth both because it makes it difficult to draw a sufficiently clear distinction between God's substance and that of prelapsarian angels and men and also because it treats the body as evil and not as part of the original nature of man which God created and approved. It is this anti-Origenist agenda that leads Gennadius to argue for the corporality of angels and human souls, placing the topic in the section of his book devoted to errors concerning the creation. God, he stresses, is the only being that is incorporeal, invisible, and unconstrained by space.[94] On the other hand,

> Creatura omnis corporea: angeli et omnes caelestes virtutes corpore, licet non carne, subsistunt. Ex eo autem corporeas esse credimus, intellectuales naturas, quod localitate circumscribuntur, sicut et anima humana quae carne clauditur, et demones qui per substantiam angelicae naturae sunt.[95]

> Created beings are all corporeal: the angels and all the celestial virtues subsist in the body, even if not in the flesh. Indeed, it is on this account that we believe intellectual beings to be corporeal, that they are circumscribed by location, as is true for the human soul, which is enclosed in flesh, and demons who are of the angelic nature in their substance.

---

[94] Gennadius, *Liber ecclesiasticorum dogmatum* 11, ed. C. H. Turner in *JTS*, 7 (1906–07), 91.

[95] Ibid. 12, p. 92.

Gennadius' prime concern here is to clarify the nature of creatures in comparison with God as a metaphysical question important in its own right, not to discredit analogies drawn from creation that are applied incorrectly to God or the Trinity. He is not equally interested in the implications of Origen's anthropology for soteriology or eschatology. The chief enemies of the faith whom he attacks on the subject of the life to come are those who reject the doctrine of the immortality of the soul, whether they believe that the soul dies with the body or *post modicum intervallum, sicut Zeno* ("after a short interim, as Zeno says.")[96] This is Gennadius' only express Stoic attribution and it involves a principle that is not unique to the Stoics and one on which they held no consensus. At the same time, he cites no source, direct or indirect, for the distinctively Stoic notion of the corporality of the soul.

VI. Marius Victorinus

Although he is one of the earliest authors treated in this chapter, Marius Victorinus (281/91–ca. 361) is certainly one of the most important, not only for his profundity as a speculative theologian but also for the range and depth of his creative adaptations of Stoic thought. A distinguished rhetorician in Rome during the reign of the emperor Constantius, he converted to Christianity at some point during the 350s, when he was already advanced in age. Victorinus' scope as a teacher and writer during the pagan phase of his career went well beyond the discipline of rhetoric. Aside from producing commentaries on Cicero's rhetoric, only one of which has survived, he composed treatises on grammar and dialectic and commentaries on the *Isagoge* of Porphyry and the *Categories* and *Perihermeneias* of Aristotle. Apart from his *De definitionibus* and the famous translation of Plotinus which made this major Neoplatonist accessible to Latin readers, none of the works that the pagan Victorinus wrote in philosophy and in fields outside of rhetoric survived in remotely complete form after the patristic period. However, from the extant evidence and the *testimonia* that permit us to reconstruct his contributions to the *disciplinae*, it is clear that he was a major transmitter of Stoicism as well as of other philosophical schools, his importance in connection with Stoic logic having been noted earlier.[97] Following his conversion and the loss of his chair of rhetoric, Victorinus threw himself wholeheartedly into theological writing, producing hymns and commentaries on three

---

[96] Ibid. 16, p. 92.

[97] The major study is by Pierre Hadot, *Marius Victorinus: Recherches sur sa vie et ses œuvres* (Paris, 1971). On the hypothetical syllogisms, see M. L. Colish, *The Stoic Tradition*, I, 333.

of the Pauline epistles. Even more substantial was his work as a Trinitarian controversialist. Victorinus wrote a lengthy four-part treatise supporting Nicene orthodoxy as well as two other Trinitarian works ca. 357–61, in the thick of the debates over Arianism and other Christological polemics, debates that occasioned personal and political no less than theological clashes.[98] The Arian party itself had not hesitated to draw upon Stoicism and Neoplatonism to defend its own particular position[99] and Victorinus was well aware of the fact that he would have to meet his opponents on their own ground. In his writings, both as a professor of rhetoric and as a Trinitarian theologian, he demonstrates a solid and broad-gauged grasp of Stoicism, side by side with Aristotelianism and the Neoplatonism with which he is primarily associated. He uses all of these sources in an apposite and well-informed manner that is anything but slavish.

Victorinus certainly considers himself free to invest Stoic terminology with his own meanings or to reject the ideas that the terms were originally designed to express. He does this in theological and non-theological works alike and in a number of different areas. In commenting on Cicero's treatment of the Stoic distinction between corporeals, which have being (*esse*) and incorporeals, which do not (*non esse*), Victorinus disagrees with the distinction, arguing that things can exist and have their proper being whether they are corporeal or not. He uses this idea to support the Aristotelian notion that the category of quality can be attributed both to concrete and to abstract entities.[100] He also discusses common notions (*notionem communi*), viewing them as generalizations that do not refer substantially to what they signify, here using a Stoic term in an Aristotelian sense although without any consideration of whether common notions are self-evident, innate, or derived from sense experience.[101] Another implicit departure from a Stoic principle, that of the moral equality of men and women, occurs in a passage of Victorinus' commentary on Galatians that predates Jerome's position on the same topic. When there is a hidden sense in Scripture pointing to sacred things, he notes, the masculine gender is used by the Biblical author; the feminine gender is used with reference to things imperfect. Thus, the fact

---

[98] Pierre Hadot, intro. to his trans. of Paul Henry's ed. of Marius Victorinus, *Traités théologiques sur la Trinité*, SC, 68–69 (Paris, 1960), I, 18–60, gives a detailed explanation of the contemporary theological situation and locates Victorinus clearly in this context.

[99] Michel Meslin, *Les Ariens d'occident, 335–430* (Paris, 1967), pp. 356–64.

[100] Marius Victorinus, *De definitionibus*, ed. T. Stangl as *Tullia et Mario-Victoriana* (München, 1888) and reprinted by Hadot, *Marius Victorinus*, appendix 3, p. 342. The pagination in Hadot will be cited in references to this work.

[101] *De def.*, p. 347. Hadot, *Marius Victorinus*, pp. 171–74, mistakenly attributes both the substance and the term to Stoicism.

that Christ was born of a woman means that God comes to the aid of imperfect humanity in its state of imperfection, so as to redeem it and set it on the path toward perfection.[102] Indeed, throughout his exegesis of the Pauline epistles, Victorinus understands the human imperfections at issue as the physical desires and fallacies of the senses that distract man from pure spiritual pursuits, taking a decidedly Neoplatonic approach to the Pauline message.

At the same time, Victorinus is just as likely to appropriate Stoic doctrines expressly and accurately and to use them as a way of reformulating principles derived from other philosophical schools. This tendency is visible more than once in the field of logic, where he is inclined to substitute Stoicism for Aristotelianism even when his immediate source is scarcely of the same mind. In his commentary on Cicero's rhetoric, Victorinus follows his model generally by treating logic in a rhetorical context. But he does not share Cicero's sharp criticism of the Stoics in that connection. Discussing the Aristotelian distinction between substance and accident, Victorinus substitutes qualities for accidents, qualities that are concrete and relational specifications of an object's constitution, in a manner showing more of an affinity to the Stoic than to the Aristotelian concept of the categories.[103] Elsewhere in the same work, in commenting on Aristotle's doctrine of opposites, Victorinus notes, correctly, that they can be distinguished as contrary (*contrarium*), disparate (*disparatum*), and relative (*ad aliquid*). He then goes on to interpret this distinction in a Stoic rather than an Aristotelian manner, observing that opposites are species of one and the same genus, being (*esse*).[104] This point is followed by an explanation of being as the supreme genus of all things in terms of the Neoplatonic chain of being: "being," as a hypostasis of the divine essence, is a homynym of "being" as it applies to creatures, but the terms are not also synonymous. In this context, then, Victorinus redefines an Aristotelian distinction in Stoic terms and uses it to interpret a Neoplatonic metaphysical doctrine, a technique we will see him returning to repeatedly in his Trinitarian works.

Equally Stoic and equally independent are other passages in the same treatise where Victorinus turns to the school's ethical and theological teachings. Here, too, he does not hesitate to take issue with Cicero, as in his definition of the good. The Stoics, he notes, say that virtue is the only good (*Stoici dicunt honestatem solam bonum esse*), in contrast to Cicero,

---

[102] *In Epistulam Pauli ad Galatas* 2.1176C–1177B, ed. Albrecht Locher (Leipzig, 1972).

[103] *Explanationum in Rhetoricam M. Tullii Ciceronis*, ed. Carolus Halm, *Rhetores latini minores* (Leipzig, 1863), p. 232. Noted by Hadot, *Marius Victorinus*, pp. 93–94.

[104] Ibid., p. 228; noted by Hadot, *Marius Victorinus*, pp. 96–98.

who includes the *utile* as good along with the *honestum*.[105] While he himself departs from Cicero by urging that virtue is an end in itself and while he includes the principle of habit in ethics in the Stoic sense of *tonos* or *hexis* rather than in the Aristotelian sense of *habitus*, an idea that will also recur in his Trinitarian theology, Victorinus ignores the exclusively didactic function which the Stoics assigned to rhetoric. He also mediates between Stoicism and Neoplatonism in another passage of his commentary on Cicero where he reviews the various definitions of nature and its relationship to God put forth by different philosophical schools. He does not mention the Stoics expressly here but the position he states is certainly in accordance with their view:

> Natura est enim ignis artifex quadam via vadens in res sensibilis procreandas; etenim manifestum est omnia principe igne generari.

> Nature is a creative fire which tends, in a determined way, to generate sensible things. It is evident that all things are engendered in the beginning by fire.

As to how nature, so defined, is related to God, Victorinus states that one can draw a distinction between God and God's will. God is beyond the natural world but *voluntatem autem dei, qua mundus est, eandem esse naturam* ("God's will, by which the world exists, is identical with nature.")[106] On the one hand, Victorinus wishes to place God above the world, a view that suggests his affinities to Neoplatonism. On the other hand, his identification of nature as the creative fire with God's will shows his attachment to Stoicism. The more extensive coordination of these two positions was a problem that Victorinus did not have to confront systematically until he became a Christian and entered the lists as a leading Trinitarian theologian of his time.

Victorinus was certainly not the first Trinitarian theologian to draw on Stoic doctrine. Tertullian had applied the Stoic notion of *krasis* to the hypostatic union, an approach plausible to him in the light of his Stoic belief in the corporality of all beings, including God. This same idea enabled him to conceive of the filiation of the Son and the procession of the Holy Spirit in material terms, analogizing them to a stream of light flowing from a source of light with which it is consubstantial. The Greek

---

[105] Ibid., p. 176. Discussed by Hadot, *Marius Victorinus*, pp. 80, 87, 100, who does not note all the relevant issues.

[106] Ibid., p. 215. Hadot, *Marius Victorinus*, pp. 88–91 and Ernst Benz, *Marius Victorinus und die Entwicklung der abendländischen Willensmetaphysik* (Stuttgart, 1932), pp. 350–53 have both commented on this passage but have made no connection between it and Victorinus' Christian theology.

Christian theologians from the third century onward had repudiated this materialistic analysis of the divine nature and had chosen another Stoic principle as a means of defending the orthodox understanding of the filiation of the Son and His consubstantiality with the Father. The members of the Alexandrian and Cappadocian schools alike had used the Stoic distinction between thought and speech for this purpose, describing the unmanifested Christ as an inner thought in the mind of God, the *logos endiathetos*, while the incarnate Christ was God's outward speech, the *logos prophorikos*. This Stoic distinction enabled them to argue simultaneously for the consubstantiality of the Father and Son and the identity of the Christ manifested to men with Christ as an eternal member of the Trinitarian family.[107]

Victorinus departs from the prevailing patristic strategy of his time, for a number of reasons, not the least of which is the character of the heterodox attack that he was trying to crush. Victorinus' chief contribution to Trinitarian theology was his adoption of a different Stoic model for thinking about God, one that enables him to equate the divine nature with dynamic action and to explore that action in its reciprocal manifestations as being, life, and thought. This approach makes it possible for him to compare the interrelations among the Persons of the Trinity with the interrelationships among the functions of analogous created beings without succumbing either to anthropomorphism or Tertullianesque materialism. In addition, Victorinius' doctrine of God can be seen as a major advance over other efforts to recast this all-important Christian topic in philosophical terms. He abandons the idea of God as the form of forms, the unmoved mover, or the One beyond being. Rejecting the idea that activity or motion signify imperfection, a view shared by both the Platonic and Aristotelian schools, he draws on the Stoic conception of God as dynamic energy, associating action and motion with divine perfection and using this constellation of ideas to describe God's self-creation and plenitude of being. The triadic structure that Victorinus invokes to explore the Trinitarian relations, along with a number of other specific details in his theology, reveal his close dependence on Neoplatonism as well, whether his immediate source was Plotinus, Porphyry, or both.[108] While he probably derived a certain amount of his

---

[107] Excellent treatments of this argument in Greek patristic literature are found in Alfred Schindler, *Wort und Analogie in Augustins Trinitätslehre* (Tübingen, 1965), pp. 104–18; Michal Schmaus, *Die psychologische Trinitätslehre des hl. Augustinus* (Münster, 1927), pp. 40–48, 51–52, 54–67; and Anton Ziegenaus, *Die trinitärische Ausprägung der göttlichen Seinsfülle nach Marius Victorinus* (München, 1972), pp. 27, 35, 42, 201.

[108] There is a good deal of unanimity about the character of Victorinus' Trinitarian theology and about its ultimate dependence on Stoic thought, but considerable scholarly debate about whether his immediate source was Plotinus or Porphyry. Since many of

Stoicism through Neoplatonic intermediaries, Victorinus' departures from Neoplatonic theology are fundamental. These departures stem primarily from his application of Stoicism to Christian theology in the effort to refute Arianism. The Trinitarian position that results makes him a vital link between his Greek patristic predecessors and contemporaries and his major Latin successor, Augustine.

Victorinus' particular focus is strongly conditioned by the argument of Candidus, the Arian antagonist whose work served as the point of departure for his defense of the Nicene Creed. While there is some scholarly disagreement on whether Candidus was a real person or a pseudonymous construct created by Victorinus himself as a means of airing the views he wanted to discuss,[109] it is safe to assume that the position ascribed to Candidus was, or would have been recognized to be, an authentic statement of current Arian thought. Candidus reveals himself to be no mean opponent. The thesis of his work is that, since God is unbegotten, He must be unbegetting. Immutability is a prime and unique aspect of God; any being that begets, or is begotten, undergoes change. Thus, everything in being that is begotten, including Christ, is not-God.[110] It is Candidus, also, who takes the first step in applying both Stoic dynamism and the Neoplatonic triadic structure to the Christian God. In supporting his central thesis, Candidus states that God, as the cause of His own existence, as being itself, is at the same time being, life, and thought (*Et vero ipsum esse, ipsum est vivere et intelligere.*) These three divine characteristics, he says, exist and function in and through each other. Thus, God *in se* is three and one.[111] As a consequence, Candidus concludes, God can neither beget nor be begotten, since the triune simplicity of His nature bespeaks infinity, eternity, and immutability, while

---

the ideas in question were shared by these two Neoplatonists, the utility of single-source *Quellenforschung* is at best arguable. For a general reprise of the earlier literature see Pierre Hadot, *Porphyre et Victorinus* (Paris, 1968), I, 11–31. Recent scholars opting for Plotinus include Mary T. Clark, "The Earliest Philosophy of the Living God: Marius Victorinus," *Proceedings of the American Catholic Philosophical Association*, 41 (1967), 87–93, also the best short description of Victorinus' Trinitarian theology; and Paul Henry, "The *Adversus Arium* of Marius Victorinus, the First Systematic Exposition of the Doctrine of the Trinity," *JTS*, n.s. 12 (1950), 42–55. The leading proponent of Porphyry is Hadot, *Porphyre et Victorinus*. More recently Mary T. Clark, in the intro. to her trans. of Victorinus, *Theological Treatises on the Trinity*, FC, 69 (Washington, 1981), pp. 10–40 has come to support Hadot's position. Ziegenaus, *Die trinitärische Ausprägung*, pp. 13, 16–17, 19, 86–88, 175, 178, 357, 363, 365 treats Victorinus as more eclectic in his sources.

[109] Hadot, *Marius Victorinus*, pp. 272–75 thinks Candidus is a fiction; Ziegenaus, *Die trinitärische Ausprägung*, pp. 54–55 thinks he was a real person and also provides the most recent review of the literature on this point, pp. 74–76.

[110] *Candidi Arriani ad Marium Victorinum rhetorem de generatione divina* 1.1, ed. A. Locher in Marius Victorinus, *Opera theologica* (Leipzig, 1976).

[111] Ibid. 1.2, p. 3.

engendering and being engendered involve change and temporal sequence.[112]

Taking another tack, this one implicitly directed against the Stoic physics used by Tertullian to explain the filiation of the Son, Candidus notes that there can be an extension of being without generation. Here he cites the example of the ray of light that is consubstantial with its source. But, he asserts, since the light projected is the same as its source, the relation between them cannot be that of begetter and begotten, since inequality between parent and child is an unavoidable feature of generation as such.[113] Nor, he adds, can generation be understood under the heading of *typus*, a medical term describing the rhythmic flow of physiological processes that goes back in turn to the Stoic conception of growth and diminution, contraction and dilation, tension and relaxation as controlled by *tonos* or *pneuma*. As a self-contained tidal flow backwards and forwards within the same physical continuum, Candidus argues, *typus* cannot be a description of generation, since it does not produce a being distinct from the internal divine continuum of being. The application of *typus* to the filiation of the Son had indeed been made by contemporary Monarchian heretics and Candidus' strategy here is to attach it by implication to the Nicene theology as well.[114] Candidus adds the points that the distinctions between prototype and image and between will and act are similarly unacceptable models for the Father-Son relation, the first lacking equality and the second lacking simultaneity. He concludes that Jesus is not consubstantial with God. Jesus is an effect of God, related to Him not by generation but by operation.[115] However, the arguments mentioned earlier, which both employ and attack Stoic doctrines as armor in defense of the Arian position, are the principal arguments that Victorinus has to address, and he addresses them on the same ground as this formidable opponent.

The central point that Victorinus develops, with growing economy and sureness of touch in the elaboration of his position across his *Ad Candidum Arrianum* and his four-part *Adversus Arrium*, is that the triadic description of God in terms of the reciprocal interrelations among His activities can be reconceived as a description of the Trinity. Each form of divine activity indicated by the terms of Candidus' triad can be equated

---

[112] Ibid. 1.3–9.

[113] Ibid. 1.5.

[114] Ibid. 1.8. On this point see the excellent study by Pierre Hadot, "Typus: Stoïcisme et monarchianisme au IVᵉ siècle d'après Candide l'Arien et Marius Victorinus," *RTAM*, 18 (1951), 177–87; also Ziegenaus, *Die trinitärische Ausprägung*, pp. 58–59. On the Monarchians and their use of *typus* see also A. H. Armstrong in A. H. Armstrong and R. A. Markus, *Christian Faith and Greek Philosophy* (London, 1960), pp. 21–22.

[115] *Candidi Arriani ad Marium Victorinum* 1.6, 1.8, 1.10.

with one of the Trinitarian Persons. Once this step has been taken, it becomes possible to show that generation does not necessarily entail change or imperfection in God or inequality and difference in substance among the members of the Trinity. Victorinus makes a somewhat uncertain start in the *Ad Candidum*, advancing a number of arguments which, however interesting they may be, are not responsive to Candidus' claims. It is not until he gets to the last four chapters of the work that he really comes to grips with Candidus' version of the triadic argument. The first important note Victorinus strikes is to redefine the terms of the triad themselves. Where, in Candidus' account, the three terms are being, life, and thought, in Victorinus' account, being as such is the fundamental ground of the Godhead while moving, thinking, and acting are its manifestations in the Persons of the Trinity. As the second Person of the Trinity, the Son is simply being in act:

> Ergo et movere et intelligere et agere ab eo est, quod est esse.
> Et autem secundum quod est in actu esse, hoc est filium esse.[116]
>
> For to move and to think and to act are from Him, Who is "to be."
> And "to be" as it exists in action is to be the Son.

This passage speaks to the equality between the Father and the Son but not to the issue of how the Son can be begotten. As Victorinus now continues, act is engendered by being because being is the cause of act.[117] Having said this, he must explain next how such a cause-effect relationship differs from the cause-effect relationships in nature, marked as they are by temporal priority and posteriority. Here, Victorinus invokes the analogy of the mind's self-inherence in the process of interior thought where the product and producer are identical and simultaneous: being is turned in on itself, moving and thinking and acting within itself, without violating its state of internal repose. When being translates this inner generation of itself outward, the process is exterior and interior at the same time; it involves no change or loss; and it has no reference to temporal sequence. Thus, he concludes, since God's will and intellect, His life and act, are all one and identical with His being, they are all mutually involved in a movement in which God generates Himself, both initially and eternally, in relation to His own being. As an aspect of that self-generation, Christ is therefore not a creature. He is God's own action and being and is generated by as well as consubstantial with the Father.[118]

---

[116] *Ad Candidum Arrianum* 1.19, ed. Locher, p. 22.
[117] Ibid. 1.20.
[118] Ibid. 1.21–23.

The essential point that Victorinus holds in common with Candidus is the idea that being can be understood as action. For both thinkers, the supreme state of being is not a state of perfect immobility, with motion signifying imperfection. It is this basic position that Victorinus uses to argue that action and motion, as attributes of God, can account for the filiation of the Son and the procession of the Holy Spirit, as distinct yet equal Persons, without entailing change, priority and posteriority, or hierarchies in the divine being. Victorinus' seizure of Candidus' initiative and his decisive alteration of it in this way forge a powerful weapon against his Arian antagonist. Exactly the same strategy is developed, if more lucidly and elaborately, in Victorinus' *Adversus Arrium*.

In the first section of this treatise Victorinus gives a forthright statement of his thesis. God the Father is being, while God the Son is action. In the first instance, he says, *habet quidem ipsum quod est esse intus insitam operationem* ("that which is possesses inwardly an innate activity.")[119] For without action, being could have no life or intelligence. In the second place, action can be regarded as the external manifestation of being. In this connection, also, action is the same as being:

> Apparente enim operatione et est et nominatur operatio et ut generatio sui ipsius et aestimatur et est. . . . Hoc autem, quod est in motu esse, declaratio est eius, quod est esse, secundum actionem.[120]

> For when activity appears it both is and is called activity and it both is and is understood to be its own self-generation. . . . Thus, the "to be" that is in motion can be defined as the "to be" that exists according to action.

With this foundation laid, Victorinus proceeds to build upon it with a series of Scriptural proofs, interpreting them in the sense of the passage just quoted. He also uses the same conception of God to attack Candidus' rejection of the equality of the Father and Son if the latter is seen as the image of the former. Since Christ in His incarnation manifests the divine attributes of movement, life, and intelligence to man, St. Paul's language in II Corinthians cannot be understood in terms of earthly conceptions of image and prototype and is consistent with the claim that the fullness of divinity dwells in Christ.[121] Victorinus adds that motion, in God's case, is not to be confused with local motion on earth or with passion, corruption, growth, diminution, or other features of motion that might be attributed to natural phenomena, *more Aristotelico*. In God's case, motion is the self-movement of being itself, which is simple, simultaneous, and one. And so, he concludes, God's self-moving life is His very

---

[119] *Adversus Arium* 1.4, ed. Locher, p. 35.
[120] Ibid., pp. 35–36.
[121] Ibid. 1.19.

substance; it is not an accident. God's act of begetting does not entail change; and the outward manifestation of that act in the filiation of the Son and procession of the Holy Spirit in no sense produces beings different in substance from God the Father or inferior in nature to Him.[122]

In the subsequent sections of the *Adversus Arrium* Victorinus repeats and refines these same arguments and also addresses other objections raised by Candidus in his initial sally. Here, too, he accepts some of the Arian's premises while altering their content or directionality decisively. Candidus had used the example of the ray of light flowing from its source, understood in Stoic material terms along Tertullianesque lines, in order to show that the substantive self-extension involved in this analogy precludes generation or the manifestation of a being distinct from its source. Victorinus now attaches to this analogy the argument concerning image and prototype which he had developed in the first part of the treatise, while at the same time purging it of its materialistic connotations. Thus, he asserts, the flow of light from its source can be regarded as a proper analogy of the filiation of the Son or the procession of the Holy Spirit since motion, action, and intellection flow from being and are consubstantial with being while each is a distinct manifestation of being. Each of these attributes, he says, can be understood as a *habitus* of being, in the Stoic sense of expressing a particular manner of being.[123] A still better example, in Victorinus' estimation, is the analogy between God's Trinitarian inner life and the inner life of intelligent created beings. In both cases, intelligence, life, and motion can be distinguished by their particular forms of activity. Yet, in all cases, the particular form of activity, while it is given its name in terms of the aspect of action predominant in it, is an activity of one central being. At the same time, each aspect contains the other two. All are mutually inherent in the others both in terms of substance and in terms of operation. God, Victorinus concludes, is thus *tridynamos*;[124] vitality and energy are His prime attributes.

What Victorinus has achieved in his Trinitarian theology is a truly remarkable accomplishment, both as an act of Christian speculation and as a reinterpretation of the Stoic tradition. His is the first attempt to formulate a philosophy of the living God that avoids both Candidus' Arianism and Tertullian's materialism. Mediated through the triadic struc-

---

[122] Ibid. 1.43, 1.52–53. The same points are repeated in *De homoousio* 3, ed. Locher. Victorinus adds, in commenting on passion in this connection, that God does not suffer but that Christ does suffer in His passion as a function of His human nature, *Adv. Ar.* 1.44.

[123] *Adv. Ar.* 3.1–2, 4.8.32, 4.13, 4.15. This Stoic sense attached to the term *habitus* has been noted here by Ziegenaus, *Die trinitärische Ausprägung*, p. 123.

[124] *Adv. Ar.* 3.4, 3.7–11, 3.17, 4.13–15, 4.21–22. The term *tridynamos* occurs at 4.21.

ture he absorbed from Neoplatonism, his Stoic conception of God as the dynamic *logos* is purged of all material content and endowed with a purely spiritual energy and vitality. With this conception of God at his disposal Victorinus can treat intelligent created beings as a means of grasping the unities and distinctions in the Trinity, without having to fall back on analogies drawn from infrarational beings or processes. Victorinus thus emerges with an analogy between God and created beings that shifts the focus away from their substantial similarity. Instead, he directs attention to the parallels between the self-inherence and internal reciprocities that each of the analogates possesses, both in its substance and in its activities. He maintains the intellectualism implicit in the Greek patristic use of the Stoic notions of *logos endiathetos* and *logos prophorikos* while he expands the functions of spiritual beings to include not only speech and intellection but also action, energy, and motion. Victorinus' creative adaption of Stoic physics in this connection thus has important implications for human psychology as well as for Trinitarian theology.[126] His achievement was inspired and, to a significant degree, conditioned, by the dimensions of the Arian attack on Nicene orthodoxy to which he responded. It should be credited no less to his perceptiveness and originality as a speculative thinker.

While the preclusively anti-Arian tenor of Victorinus' Trinitarian theology did place some limits on its long term durability, his contribution is by no means confined to his own time. Victorinus is probably best known in the history of Christian thought for his influence on Augustine. He was the translator of the "books of the Platonists" read by Augustine with such great consequence. He also served as the role model of the famous rhetorician who gave up the podium for the sake of Christ and then devoted his learning to the defense of Christian truth, a model constantly before Augustine's eyes both during and after his conversion. While he is most famous as a transmitter of Neoplatonism, Victorinus is also introduced in Augustine's *Confessions* as an adherent of the Stoic idea that God dwells in the human soul and that He may be found and worshipped there, and not in particular sanctuaries.[127] This Augustinian testimony is as graceful as it is apposite. For the most enduring heritage of Victorinus' reformulation of Stoicism was the contribution that it made to Augustine's doctrine of the human soul as the supreme analogy of the Trinity in his own *De trinitate*.

---

[125] Ibid. 4.2–10, 4.22.

[126] Mary T. Clark, "The Psychology of Marius Victorinus," *AS*, 5 (1974), 149–66.

[127] St. Augustine, *Confessionum*, 8.2.4, ed. Lucas Verheijen, CC, 27 (Turnhout, 1981). This theme has received sensitive treatment by Pierre Courcelle, "Parietes faciunt christianos?" *Mélanges d'archéologie, d'épigraphie et d'histoire offerts à Jérôme Carcopino* (Paris, 1966), pp. 241–48; and Hadot, *Marius Victorinus*, pp. 246–51.

CHAPTER FOUR

ST. AUGUSTINE

INTRODUCTION

Augustine of Hippo (354-430), the greatest of the Latin Church Fathers, is also the single most important figure in the history of the Stoic tradition in the Latin west between the third and the sixth centuries. Among his Latin predecessors, contemporaries, and successors Augustine is unparalleled for the range of Stoic doctrines with which he was conversant and for the multiplicity of the applications that he makes of them. To a certain extent this achievement is a function of the breadth and profundity of Augustine's *œuvre* itself, whose immense scope and volume enabled him to orchestrate the Stoic themes he used on a far wider scale than was possible for any of his apologetic or patristic compeers. To some degree it is a consequence of his career as an ecclesiastical statesman and controversialist whose opinions were under constant pressure, both external and internal, owing to the relentless challenge of heresy and schism and, no less, to his own personal need to affirm his hard-won gains as a Christian thinker and to modify, consolidate, and universalize his inner understanding of the Christian life. And, by no means least in importance, Augustine's deep knowledge and discriminating use of Stoicism, both in ethics, logic, and physics, is a clear reflection of his speculative mentality, his yearning to grasp and to express the truth, his ardent love of ideas, a taste which is an authentic note of Augustine's intellectual temperament and which frequently outruns his need to solve immediate pastoral, exegetical, dogmatic, or moral problems. Toward the end of his *City of God*, and notwithstanding the elaborate polemical agenda he sets for himself in that work, Augustine states an *idée maîtresse* in this connection: *Nulla est homini causa philosophandi, nisi ut beatus sit* ("No man would philosophize, except to be happy.")[1] And, in the *Confessions*, his most personal work, he defines the happy life as *gaudium de veritate* ("joy in the truth.")[2] The good life and the truth are neither alternating poles around which Augustine's inner life revolved; nor are they successive stages in its development. Rather, they are simultaneous and correlative goals, whose interdependence Augustine

---

[1] St. Augustine, *De Civitate dei* 19.1, ed. Bernardus Dombart and Alphonsus Kalb, CC, 47–48 (Turnhout, 1965), 47, p. 659.
[2] *Confessionum* 10.23.33, ed. Lucas Verheijen, CC, 27 (Turnhout, 1981), p.173.

never loses sight of however much the ecclesiastical tasks before him may impose their own demands. It is within this framework, with both its centripetal imperatives and the frequent campaigns on its peripheries that Augustine's life work required him to mount, that he situates his borrowings from and uses of the Stoic tradition.

Augustine is equally sensitive to philosophy and to literature as the essence of the classical culture which was his by inheritance and in whose light he defined his Christian identity. This broad sensitivity helps to account for the diversity of the sources of Stoicism with which he was familiar, whether Greek or Latin, pagan or Christian, no less than for the attitude that he takes toward the Stoic school. As is well known, Augustine felt impelled to take a conscious position on the relationship between Christianity and classical thought, not only in order to repossess his own personal history in the *Confessions* and to achieve his larger apologetic aims in the *City of God*, but also to lay down guidelines for the education of Christian exegetes and preachers in his *De doctrina christiana*. In the latter work the metaphor he evokes for this purpose is the divine counsel given to the Israelites as they moved from slavery in Egypt to the freedom, and the hardships, that would gain for them the promised land: Spoil the Egyptians of their gold and silver.[3] For the Christian Augustine the classical tradition was a treasure which was his by right as a consequence of his labors on its behalf. Its worth was intrinsic. It might justly be carried with him into his new homeland and fitly applied to the new tasks he assumed there. A significant amount of that treasure was Stoic in denomination. Some of it remained legal tender, just as it was, when Augustine crossed the border into Christianity. Some of it, precisely because it retained the value stamped on it by the Stoics, he found to be obsolete currency. Some of this gold and silver he melted down and recast into new forms. But some of it, a hoard that had seemed quite precious to the neophyte Augustine, he found to be fool's gold after subjecting it to long and repeated trials in the crucible of his inner life. Very little of it, for Augustine, was pure decorative tinsel or the flourish of conspicuous intellectual riches used for mere display.

An understanding of these multiple roles of Stoicism in Augustine's thought cannot be detached entirely from an appreciation of his Neoplatonism as well. To be sure, Neoplatonism exerted a more pervasive and formative influence on Augustine than did Stoicism and it often conditions the way he appropriates some of the Stoic doctrines that he finds the most attractive or problematic. At the same time, Augustine

---

[3] *De doctrina christiana* 2.40.60–61, ed. Iosephus Martin and K.-D. Daur, CC, 32 (Turnhout, 1962).

occasionally prefers Stoicism to Neoplatonism or uses it to pose or to analyze issues that he may eventually resolve in more Neoplatonic or Christian terms, a point which has rarely been given the credit it deserves. The burgeoning secondary literature on Augustine and classical philosophy has focused an almost preclusive attention on his debt to Neoplatonism, or to this or that Neoplatonic author, with the most energetic researchers in the field devoting themselves to the question of whether to award the palm to Porphyry or Plotinus.[4] While it reflects the continuing seductiveness of single-source *Quellenforschung* and while it deflects attention away from the other kinds of sources available to Augustine, whether in Greek, in Latin, or in the doxographical tradition,[5] this literature does have two conspicuous merits: It reminds Augustine scholars that the eclectic character of Neoplatonism itself made it one of the many routes by which Augustine's Stoic materials could have reached him. Also, its practitioners, more often than not, are interested in showing how Augustine used the philosophical ideas at issue.

The same can rarely be said for those scholars who have confined themselves to the study of Augustine's Latin sources. Apart from adopting an unrealistically monoglottal conception of Augustine's literacy, these scholars approach their task with a classical bias and a narrow philological methodology. Ignoring Augustine's access to Greek writers, whether pagan or Christian, and to his own Latin Christian forebears, they confine themselves to the hunt for his express *testimonia* to Stoic or Stoicizing classical Latin authors and to the citation of textual parallels. In so doing they reduce Augustine to the level of a passive recipient or neutral conduit of the Latin classics, whose chief importance in intellectual history lies in his role as a stage in the *Nachleben* of the authors or topics involved.[6]

---

[4] Excellent recent reviews of the literature are supplied by Robert J. O'Connell, *Augustine's Early Theory of Man, A.D. 386–391* (Cambridge, Mass., 1968), pp. 26–27; Anton C. Pegis, "The Second Conversion of St. Augustine," *Gesellschaft, Kultur, Literatur: Beiträge Liutpold Wallach gewidmet*, ed. Karl Bosl (Stuttgart, 1975), pp. 73–93; Eugene TeSelle, *Augustine the Theologian* (New York, 1970), pp. 43–55.

[5] The range of Augustine's uses of Greek material both Biblical, patristic, philosophical, and literary, has been established by Berthold Altaner, *Kleine patristische Schriften*, ed. Günther Glockmann, Texte und Untersuchungen zur Geschichte der altchristlichen Literatur, 83 (Berlin, 1967), pp. 129–63, 316–31; Pierre Courcelle, *Late Latin Writers and Their Greek Sources*, trans. Harry E. Wedeck (Cambridge, Mass., 1969), pp. 149–65. For the importance of the doxographical tradition see Aimé Solignac, "Doxographies et manuels dans la formation philosophique de saint Augustin," *REAug*, 1 (1958), 113–48. The most balanced position on Augustine's philosophical sources and the methods most useful for studying them is that of Ragnar Holte, *Béatitude et sagesse: Saint Augustin et le problème de la fin de l'homme dans la philosophie ancienne* (Paris, 1962), p. 112.

[6] This tendency is most pronounced in the work of Harald Hagendahl, *Augustine and the Latin Classics*, Studia graeca et latina Gothoburgensia, 20:1–2 (Göteborg, 1967) and

More specifically, there have been, thus far, three general efforts to assess the place of Stoicism in Augustine's thought, none of which is wholly satisfactory. To their credit, the contributors to this venture have disproved the vestigial and erroneous belief in his indifference or hostility to Stoicism as such[7] and they have taken an important step toward the modification of the exclusively Neoplatonic interpretation of Augustine's philosophy. They have also called attention to some of the passages in Augustine's writings pertinent to a consideration of his place in the Stoic tradition. At the same time, some of these scholars have fallen heir to the shortcomings of other critical approaches. They have by no means uncovered and analyzed all the evidence of Stoicism in Augustine's works. Moreover, they have been inclined to catalogue the ideas they have brought to light rather than to interpret them by showing why and how Augustine appeals to them and how they are related to his concerns as a thinker and to the other intelletual resources on which he drew.

The pioneer essay was published by Gérard Verbeke in a paper listing a number of Stoicizing passages in Augustine, most of them ethical in content and all but one of them located in his earliest works.[8] Implicit in this assortment of *loci* is the idea that Augustine viewed Stoicism primarily as an ethical philosophy and that he was most attracted to it in his youth. On the other hand, when one reads this paper in conjunction with the same author's magisterial study of the Stoic doctrine of *pneuma*, which concludes with Augustine, one can see that Verbeke is well aware of the appeal of other kinds of Stoic material to Augustine across his career and of the linguistic and generic diversity of his Stoic sources.[9] The next survey of Stoicism in Augustine was presented by Charles Baguette in a dissertation whose length gave him ample room to consider Augustine's entire *œuvre*, had he chosen to do so, and to include a broader range

---

is seconded by Charles Baguette, "Le Stoïcisme dans la formation de saint Augustin" (Université de Louvain Ph.D. diss., 1968), pp. 49–132 and Michel Spanneut, "Le Stoïcisme et Saint Augustin," *Forma Futuri: Studi in onore del Cardinale Michele Pellegrino* (Torino, 1975), pp. 897–98. I am grateful to Gérard Verbeke for calling Baguette's dissertation to my attention.

[7] This position, fairly common at the turn of the century and expressed in very influential form by Adolf Harnack, *History of Dogma*, 7 vols., trans. Neil Buchanan and James Millar (London, 1910–12), V, 30, has had several more recent resonances in such works as Fidel Casado, "El repudio de la filosofía antigua en la 'Cuidad de Dios'," *Estudios sobre la Ciudad de Dios*, Numero extraordinario de homenaje a San Agustín en el XVI centenario de su nacimiento (Escorial, 1954), II, 70–75, 85, 90 and Salvador Cuesta, *El equilibrio pasional en la doctrina estoica y en la de San Agustín: Estudio sobre dos concepciones del universo a través de un problema antropológico* (Madrid, 1945).

[8] Gérard Verbeke, "Augustin et le stoïcisme," *RA*, 1 (1958), 67–89.

[9] Gérard Verbeke, *L'Évolution de la doctrine du pneuma du Stoïcisme à S. Augustin* (Paris, 1945).

of topics.[10] Baguette's Augustine is largely disinterested in Stoic physics but his strong attachment to Stoic logic, semantics, and epistemology balances the attention he pays to Stoic ethics. Baguette limits his inquiry to Augustine's earliest works, which restricts the applicability of his conclusions. Another factor that undercuts Baguette's research is his belief that Augustine depended exclusively on classical Latin sources. The most recent overview, published by Michel Spanneut, provides a convenient summary of previous literature and has the distinct merit of considering texts in both the early and the later Augustine that show a clear Stoic influence, whether they are accompanied by express *testimonia* or not. However, Spanneut confines himself to those passages from Augustine's works already brought to light by earlier scholars. He makes no independent scrutiny of the Augustinian corpus himself. His paper thereby suggests that the *loci* in hand constitute the full catalogue of Augustinian material requiring investigation, which is far from the case. Also, like Baguette, Spanneut thinks that all sources of Augustine's Stoicism not found in pagan Latin sources can be safely ignored. He does not seek to account for the Stoicizing themes found even in some of the Augustinian passages he discusses that give broader evidence of Augustine's own learning. Spanneut puts forth a strongly stated developmental thesis. Augustine, he argues, was quite open to Stoicism in his early years as a Christian, but he grew swiftly and increasingly disenchanted with the Stoa after 390, exempting logic alone from that negative judgment. That this impression may be a result of the narrow selection, or preselection, of the Augustinian texts he subjects to scrutiny, as well as to his tendency to study them removed from their literary and theological contexts, is a point to which Spanneut pays insufficient attention.[11]

The appeal of a developmental model for understanding Augustine's relation to Stoicism reflects not only the extremely provisional state of the research into the question to date. It also stems, in part, from the salutary efforts of recent scholars to recover the historical Augustine and to reject the static and overly systematic treatment of his thought that results from the attempt to read him as a proto-scholastic. Yet another inspiration for the developmental approach to Augustine's Stoicism has been his own autobiographical reflections in his *Confessions*. These retrospective assessments of his past states of mind have led some scholars

---

[10] Baguette, "Le Stoïcisme," esp. pp. 1–48, 256–60. Alvin J. Holloway, "The Transformation of Stoic Themes in St. Augustine," (Fordham University Ph.D. diss., 1966) is not a serious addition to the literature of the subject.

[11] Spanneut, "Le Stoïcisme," *Forma Futuri*, pp. 896–914. On a more limited basis the same approach is taken by Eric Osborn, *Ethical Patterns in Early Christian Thought* (Cambridge, 1976), p. 158, 182.

to argue that Augustine underwent a distinct "Stoic stage" in his intellectual life before he became a Christian, and even before he became a Neoplatonist, a stage which he repudiated decisively as his faith matured. This thesis has taken two forms. The first, adumbrated initially by Verbeke,[12] developed most fully by Baguette,[13] and repeated by others,[14] focuses on a passage in *Confessions* 7 where Augustine describes himself as floundering about in the erroneous belief that God is a material being. The state of mind which he ascribes to himself at that point is actually the second phase of his effort to address the same problem. The first phase occurs in *Confessions* 5, at the time when he was attracted briefly to Academic skepticism because of his growing difficulties with Manicheism. Among his current problems with the Manichean distinction between evil and good, equated with matter and spirit, he lists his inability to conceive of God, even of the good God, in any but physical terms, as a being that is a huge extended body. He held that good and evil were also physical and corporeal, although the good had to be thought of as more rarefied in composition than the evil. Augustine's dilemma here, he says, resulted from his incapacity, as yet, to conceive of mind itself *nisi eam subtile corpus esse, quod tamen per loci spatia diffunderetur* ("except as a subtle body diffused through local spaces.")[15] This concept of mind and of the divine nature to which Augustine refers in *Confessions* 5 does indeed have a strongly Stoic filiation, reflecting the Stoic notion that everything which acts is a body. Earlier this Stoic principle had been absorbed and professed positively by Tertullian against Praxeas. At the same time Augustine's adherence to this one Stoic idea, albeit a central one, is evidence too slender to authorize the term "Stoic stage" in connection with his philosophy at this point in his life. Augustine himself, although he is anxious to label and to acknowledge his pre-Christian wanderings in the *Confessions*, does not describe the idea, or himself, as Stoic. He presents himself as attached to a materialistic conception of reality which he ascribes to Manicheism proper, and one which troubled him because it appeared to bespeak a monism radically inconsistent with the metaphysical dualism of that sect.

Matters had changed significantly by the time of Augustine's next report of the state of the question in *Confessions* 7. Now, he says, he no longer conceived of God as corporeal in the sense of a body with a fixed spatial

---

[12] Verbeke, "Augustin et le stoïcisme," pp. 79–81; *L'Évolution*, p. 492.

[13] Baguette, "Le Stoïcisme," pp. 44–46 and at greater length in "Une période stoïcienne dans l'évolution de la pensée de saint Augustin," *REAug*, 16 (1970), 47–77.

[14] Peter Brown, *Augustine of Hippo* (Berkeley, 1967), p. 86; Spanneut, "Le Stoïcisme," pp. 901–04.

[15] *Conf.* 5.10.19–20. The quotation is at 5.10.20, CC, 27, p. 69; trans. Albert C. Outler, Library of Christian Classics, 7 (Philadelphia, 1955), p. 108.

extension. Instead, he held God to be *sive infusum mundo sive etiam extra mundum per infinita diffusum* ("either infused in the world, or infinitely diffused beyond the world.")[16] At the same time, and while he still regarded God as material, he now believed the deity to be incorruptible and unchangeable. This constellation of ideas also failed to cohere, although for reasons different from the inconsistencies mentioned by Augustine in *Confessions* 5. On one level, his problem now was how a material being can exist at all if it lacks distinct and limited physical dimensions, and how anything material can be infinite or immutable. The first of these issues simply did not trouble the Stoics while the second principle, that of an infinite and immutable deity, they rejected. On another level, Augustine worried about how a material yet unchanging deity, and one that permeates the whole universe, can either be, or fail to be, the cause of evil. If evil is matter, then such a God must be identified with evil. But evil, he implies, is associated with corruptibility, which makes it difficult to envision an incorruptible God as in any way its cause.[17] In short, the physics and theology with which Augustine wrestled in *Confessions* 7 reflect a substantial modification of the more strictly Stoic view of the deity, and of being as such, to which he reports his attachment in *Confessions* 5, a modification resulting from the influence of the decidedly unStoic notion of God as immutable. To the extent that these difficulties with Manicheism were inclining Augustine toward a different philosophy, it was clearly not Stoic monism but Neoplatonic transcendentalism. Augustine uses the image of a sponge filled with water to explain his understanding of the mode of God's presence in the world in *Confessions* 7,[18] a simile reminiscent of the image of the honeycomb full of honey used by Tertullian for the same purpose. Tertullian himself had ascribed this idea overtly, if not always correctly, to the Stoics and had invoked it to stress, alternatively, the difference between the divine nature and created matter and the intimate harmony between them.[19] From the advent of his move to Neoplatonism and onward into his writings as a Christian both before and after the *Confessions* Augustine rejects both a corporeal and a more loosely materialistic conception of God. He connects that notion repeatedly with Stoicism and with Tertullian's erroneous theology and anthropology in other works, although he does so only by implication in the *Confessions*. The main thrust of his analysis of his state of mind as reported in *Confessions* 7 is not to relate what he deems to be the onset of a "Stoic stage" in his mental development but rather

---

[16] *Conf.* 7.1.1, CC, 27, p. 92; trans. Outler, p. 135. The whole passage is at 7.1.1–2.
[17] Ibid. 7.3.4.
[18] Ibid. 7.5.7.
[19] See above, ch. 1, pp. 15, 19.

to describe a progressive de-Stoicizing of his theology as a function of the inroads that Neoplatonism was making into his Manicheism.

While the timing and character of the influence of Stoic physics on the pagan Augustine needs refinement, there is no question that an authentic Stoic doctrine is involved, however much Augustine may wish to present it as a feature of the Manicheism with which he was currently struggling. The same cannot be said for the doctrine stressed in the second version of the "Stoic stage" thesis, which places the alleged Stoicism still earlier in Augustine's thinking and which centers it on the aesthetic theory of his De pulchro et apto, which he later destroyed.[20] Three features of the De pulchro et apto, as Augustine describes it in Confessions 4, have been singled out as evidences of his Stoicism at the time: the idea that beauty can be appreciated in material things, the definition of beauty as order or harmony, and the notion that Augustine's distinction between the beautiful and the fitting parallels Cicero's distinction between the honestum and the utile, which in turn is deemed to be an adequate index of the middle Stoic distinction between the good and the preferables. As to these claims, it must be noted that the Stoa held no monopoly on the idea that beauty is sensible. Further, the notion of order or harmony as an attribute of beauty is just as easy to attach to a Pythagorean, a Platonic, or an Aristotelian aesthetic as to a Stoic one. Finally, to the extent that Augustine's pulchro and apto parallel Cicero's honestum and utile they depart, to precisely that extent, from the Stoic position on the good and the preferables, of which Cicero is scarcely an orthodox exponent. To the extent that the Stoics considered beauty in an ethical context, they listed it not as a good but as one of the adiaphora or preferables. On the other hand, Augustine says that in the De pulchro et apto he treated beauty both as that which is beautiful per se and that which is beautiful in relation to something else.[21] In this respect, although he says that he used the word decet to denote fitness in the latter context, he was not invoking the norm of decorum in a specifically Stoic sense. Apart from the foregoing difficulties, the fact that the De pulchro et apto is not available for independent evaluation makes the confident ascription of Stoicism to it a hazardous proposition at best. Augustine himself regards the work as misconceived thanks to his current belief in materialism, which he attributes to Manicheism and not to a mistaken application to aesthetics

---

[20] This position was first advanced by Maurice Testard, Saint Augustin et Cicéron: Cicéron dans la formation et dans l'œuvre de Saint Augustin, 2 vols. (Paris, 1958), I, 53, 60, 68, 172 and is seconded by Robert J. O'Connell, Art and the Christian Intelligence in St. Augustine (Cambridge, Mass., 1978), p. 37; Olivier du Roy, L'Intelligence de la foi en la Trinité selon saint Augustin: Genèse de sa théologie trinitaire jusqu'en 391 (Paris, 1966), pp. 40–42, 51, 54, 274, 414.

[21] Conf. 4.13.20, 4.15.24–26.

of Stoic ethical formulae. The version of the "Stoic stage" thesis as embodied in the pagan Augustine's youthful aesthetic theory has no solid foundation either in its content, so far as that can be ascertained, or in Augustine's understanding of this particular moment in his intellectual life.

It is not only the well-advertised changes in Augustine's own inner states of mind as he moved from paganism to Christianity and then to a less optimistic and more elaborately nuanced position on the dynamics of divine grace and human effort in his later life that have suggested the plausibility of a developmental assessment of his treatment of Stoicism. Another circumstance contributing to this scholarly outlook is a circumspect appreciation of the ways in which Augustine's public life as a prelate and defender of Christian orthodoxy against a shifting and sometimes overlapping series of heresies and schisms urged him to move away from some of the philosophical attitudes of his youth, to appraise them more harshly, or to replace them with different strategies of argument. The details of Augustine's life both before and after his conversion to Christianity are too well known to require extensive recapitulation here. We may briefly recall his north African birth and education for a career as a rhetorician, his teaching at Carthage, Rome, and Milan, the tumultuous quest for wisdom which occasioned the intellectual pilgrimage through Manicheism, Academic skepticism, and Neoplatonism recorded so vividly in the *Confessions*, his baptism as a Christian in 387, his return to north Africa, ordination in 391 and election to the see of Hippo five years later, his onslaughts against Manicheism that continued through the crisis of the Donatist schism, the shift of his attention to the Pelagian heresy in 412, the sack of Rome in 410 with the general defense of Christianity and the review of Greco-Roman culture that it occasioned, and the Vandal invasion of north Africa in the 420s, which brought its own threat of Arian heresy, destruction, and the persecution of the Church up to the gates of Hippo in the year of Augustine's death.

It is certainly true that his pressing need to address Manicheism, Donatism, Pelagianism, and several lesser heresies supplied the occasion for a tremendous number of Augustine's writings and that these imperatives became more acute and more absorbing in his later years. The doctrinal and rhetorical requirements of his polemical works and his need to respond to the ways in which his antagonists had posed the issues go a long way toward explaining the style, form, and focus of Augustine as a controversialist. In his encounters with heresy and schism Augustine argues largely, in most cases almost exclusively, on Scriptural grounds simply because these are the grounds on which his opponents have entered the debate. This tendency is most noticeable in his anti-Donatist works. No Stoicism is here at all, except for a single passing reference to logic in the *Contra Cresconium* that does not touch the substance of the issues joined. While still largely Scriptural, Augustine's anti-Manichean writings contain more extensive applications of Stoicism, both in physics, psychology, and ethics, than is true for any other segment of his polemical *œuvre*. Here, too, he sometimes casts his antagonist as a Stoic philosopher who has been led astray for that reason, in a gambit recalling the rhetorical technique of several earlier apologists. Some of the positive uses of Stoicism which Augustine had exploited in an anti-Manichean connection might have been equally pertinent in his attack on Pelagianism. But some of the Pelagians themselves had written against the Manichees in such a way as to make that strategy inapposite for Augustine, lest he be plunged still deeper into self-contradiction for invoking a different position on the vexed question of the freedom of the will in these two distinct contexts. He tends, therefore, to avoid Stoicism and to rest his case on Scripture in arguing against the Pelagians, with the sole exception of Julianus of Eclanum. Augustine sometimes criticizes Julianus for his alleged espousal of Stoicism while at other times he uses Stoicism as a weapon against Julianus, harking back to still another rhetorical maneuver familiar to readers of the earlier apologists. Many of the moral topics viewed in a Stoicizing light by previous and contemporary theologians, such as sexual ethics and the question of Christian vocations within the Church, are absorbed into one or another of these polemical subdivisions of Augustine's thought and treated accordingly. The contexts in which Stoicism bulks the largest in the work of Augustine the controversialist include some of his earliest writings as a Christian and his *City of God*, where he is measuring Christianity expressly against pagan wisdom more than against heretical aberrations, or is contrasting his present faith with his own past views, or both.

Augustine also calls upon Stoicism in a wide range of connections beyond the overtly polemical, in a number of technical areas, and in ways designed to address the dogmatic, pastoral, exegetical, and educational needs of his congregation and clergy. The immense sweep of his writings, embracing virtually every genre of patristic literature and then some, gave him ample scope in which to explore concerns ranging from catachesis to speculative theology, from semantics to theodicy, from Biblical allegoresis to epistemology. In all these situations he draws on the rich store of classical thought which he brought to his work from his days as a pagan intellectual, coupled with a responsible and continuing expansion, refinement, and reassessment of his knowledge both of Christian and pagan authors over the course of his life. Much of the Stoicism which Augustine applies to these manifold pursuits was assim-

ilated into his thought from his earliest days already tinctured by Neoplatonism, just as his Neoplatonism, for all its force, was colored by Augustine's anti-Manichean need to declare that the material creation is
good and that it has been redeemed by Christ, a position that he often
calls upon Stoicism to reinforce. Some of the Stoic doctrines that appealed to him early in life he later subjects to devastating criticism, on
Christian grounds. However, it must be stressed that there are other Stoic
ideas of which he makes consistent use, whether positively or negatively,
throughout his life. In still other cases, he dramatically adapts Stoic
principles to Christian dogmatic purposes, polemical or not, sometimes
following the paths charted by his Greek or Latin predecessors and
sometimes striking off on his own new directions.

From what has been said already it should be clear that no one analytic scheme, developmental or otherwise, can hope to capture the full
sense of Augustine's place in the Stoic tradition. While neither Stoicism
or any other feature of Augustine's intellectual life can be studied in a
historical or biographical vacuum, it is still true that a purely chronological treatment of Augustine's Stoicism would mask as much as it
makes manifest, highlighting some of his attitudes while obscuring others that are just as pervasive and characteristic of his mentality and just
as influential as models for the Christian appropriation of Stoicism which
Augustine transmitted to his contemporaries and followers. Our own re-
searches indicate that there are three distinct Augustinian orientations
toward Stoicism, all of which can be documented both from his earlier
and his later works and all of which include material from his controversial and his non-controversial writings. The first to be discussed is
the most limited in scope, although it includes some extremely important topics. Here, Augustine uses the Stoic ideas he cites inconsistently
and without any indication that the discrepancies result from a basic rethinking of his views or from any programmatic change in his outlook,
whether internally of externally motivated. The divergences in his handling of Stoicism in this first category, materials that involve physics and
ethics primarily, result entirely from contextual or rhetorical considerations. The second Augustinian orientation toward Stoicism is a consistent one. This category encompasses the largest number of Stoic doctrines found anywhere in Augustine's *œuvre* and includes physics, logic,
epistemology, psychology, rhetoric, and ethics. Here, his treatment of his
Stoic materials remains constant across his career although he may emphasize one aspect of a particular doctrine or another depending on the
situation in which he uses it. Augustine's attitude toward the Stoa in this
second category may be positive, negative, or adaptive. Third, there is
an equally important group of references which clearly reveals a shift in

Augustine's point of view toward the Stoic teachings it involves. His change of mind over time is reflected in a progressive criticism of Stoic ideas or a more restricted or heavily conditioned use of them as he grew older. The number of Stoic themes included in this final category is far smaller than what we find in the second category but they are all central and integrally connected, both to each other and to some of Augustine's most prototypical concerns. The doctrines in the third category focus on ethical questions such as the nature of the good, the virtues, the passions, the sage, and the related physical and psychological issue of free will and providence. Friendship and the nature of the *honestum* and *utile* may be added to this list and are the only topics within it on which he changes in a more Stoic direction. More usually, Augustine abandons his earlier views on the themes in this group and at other times he radically Christianizes them. But in all cases the Stoic material represented by his third orientation is decisively affected by the development of his' doctrinal position as a theologian, both speculative and polemical, and by his mature reflections on the difficulty of living the Christian life, as he experienced it, and on the conditions that he had come to believe that this life requires.

I. Augustine's Inconsistent Uses of Stoicism

There are three assignments that Augustine repeatedly gives to Stoicism in which his portrayal of the Stoa or his use of Stoic ideas is inconsistent, as a function of his argument of the moment. These inconsistencies do not bespeak any substantive reevaluations of Stoicism on his part. His variegated appraisals of the Stoic doctrines at issue, whether he approves of them, disapproves of them, or modifies them, are just as likely to occur in his early, his middle, and his later works. It is also under this heading, and perhaps not surprisingly, that his few strictly *ad hoc* uses of Stoicism as pure rhetorical embellishment can be found. Two of the Stoic topics found in this category, theodicy and natural law, are physical doctrines with significant ethical ramifications. They are both quite important to Augustine. The third, the labeling of Stoics as sages or as anti-sages is, to be sure, ethical, but it serves only to decorate arguments that Augustine constructs on other foundations.

A) *Theodicy*

Augustine's treatments of theodicy, for which he had a number of models in the writings of previous and contemporary Latin Christian authors, share with them and with the Stoics the root idea that the order, beauty, and harmony of the universe attest to its creation and governance by a benevolent and intelligent deity. For the Stoics and for many of their followers the rationality of the cosmos suggested a natural theology argument designed both to identify the world order with the divine *logos* and to assert that the world was, in principle, fully comprehensible to the human mind. The Stoics also used theodicy to claim that there is no evil in the world and that what passes for it is a consequence of a false judgment on man's part which it is fully within his power to correct by adopting a more cosmic and rational outlook. In these critical respects, none of Augustine's uses of Stoic theodicy is entirely Stoic and his major inconsistency resides in the degree to which he treats God, the world, and man, as rational or not. Also, in some contexts he qualifies Stoic theodicy so extensively under the influence of Neoplatonism or Christianity as to compromise many of its basic ingredients.[22]

A good example of an Augustinian application of Stoic theodicy whose apparent conformity with the Stoic position breaks down on a closer inspection of its context and of the non-Stoic doctrines with which it is associated is a passage toward the end of the *City of God* prefacing Augustine's description of the heavenly joys of the holy city in the life to come. Here, he stresses the goodness and providence of God as manifested in the creation. There is a long paragraph expatiating on the wondrous nature of plants, animals, heavenly bodies, and oceans but Augustine's main accent falls on the celebration of man as the crown of creation. He cites not only the beauty and harmony, the utility and aptitude of the human body in all its parts, but also the powers of the human mind, with its talent, its ingenuity, and its creative capacity that give rise to the arts, the sciences, and a host of cultural and technological contributions. The parallels between this passage and Balbus' Stoicizing attack on Epicurean theology in Cicero's *De natura deorum* have been noted, but not their differences. Augustine's concern at this point in the *City of God* is not to refute the idea that the deity takes no heed of men, but rather to praise the Creator in His works.[23] And, having done so, he proceeds to escalate that praise by describing in even more celebratory detail the spiritual gifts, including eternal beatitude, that God showers on mankind as well.

While it is true that some Stoics saw a continuity between the sage's rational behavior in this life and the felicity he might enjoy in a posthumous existence, this was scarcely an orthodox position of their school.

---

[22] TeSelle, *Augustine*, p. 216 notes some of the *loci* to be discussed below although without making any of these discriminations.

[23] *Civ. dei* 22.24. Noted by Maurice Testard, "Note sur le *De Civitate Dei*, XXII, 24: Exemple de réminiscences cicéroniennes de saint Augustin," *Augustinus Magister*: Congrès international augustinien, Paris, 21–24 septembre 1954 (Paris, 1954), I, 193–200, who sees the parallels but not the differences.

Stoic theodicy looked not to the future but to the rationalization of the
evils of the present, evils classified mainly under the headings of natural
catastrophes or the vicissitudes of life. Augustine has occasion to draw
on this aspect of Stoic theodicy as well in the *City of God* in passages
seeking to console Christians who have borne the brunt of a more strictly
man-made historical calamity, the sack of Rome by the Goths. His rationalization of evil in this context associates theodicy with the related
theme of the equanimity of the sage. However, Augustine does not sub-
scribe to the view that, on a cosmic scale, there can be anything good or
reasonable about the miseries which the fortunes of war inflict on innocent people. His argument rests not on an appeal to reason but on the
point that their sufferings are, indeed, real evils which have been permitted to occur by a transcendent and inscrutable God. God's governance of the world, he stresses, is not rationally comprehensible, but mysterious. God's tolerance of real evils, such as the afflictions of war, can
be rationalized and made compatible with the belief in divine benevolence only by seeing them as a means by which God tries and strength-
ens the just man, in a time frame that locates the consummation of the
virtue he acquires thereby not in this world but in an eternal future. The
transitory nature of life on earth is not, for Augustine, a consequence of
a Stoicizing cyclical cosmology but a function of a Neoplatonized Christian appraisal of time and matter that relativizes them in relation to an
eternal world of spirit and truth.[24]

At the same time, there are other contexts in which Augustine calls
on Stoic theodicy in order to stress the point that God and the world are
fully rational and that men can grasp this fact in the present life. He is
particularly likely to use this line of argument in attacking the Manichean equation of evil with matter. He sometimes, but not always, connects this strategy with a Neoplatonic rationale for transcending matter
or with a Christian rationale for revaluing it. A striking example of one
of these approaches is Augustine's account of how the reading of the
Platonists simultaneously enabled him to detach himself from Manicheism, to grasp that evil is not derived from matter, and to overcome the
material world even in its newly perceived goodness. As he relates this
critical stage in his inner history in the *Confessions*, the Platonists taught
him that evil stems not from matter but from the perversion of the human will. This insight leads him into a vision of theodicy that combines
the Psalmist's praise of the beauty, harmony, and wonder of nature as
expressions of the goodness of the Creator with the Neoplatonists' understanding of the same created goods as a ladder of ascent to the pure,

---

[24] *Civ. dei* 1.8–11, 1.15–16, 20.2.

spiritual, uncreated supreme being standing over and above them. In turn, this idea moves Augustine to the realization that the intellectual perception of the Neoplatonic supreme being, seen only momentarily in the trembling glance of the eyes of the soul, was accessible on a more enduring basis in the incarnation of Christ.[25] In this case, while Augustine may pose the question of theodicy in terms that are initially Stoic, the answers he supplies are Neoplatonic and Christian.

In the foregoing example Augustine posits the idea of matter as evil as the error which the theodicy argument corrects. This is only one of his applications of theodicy against the Manichees. His exegesis of the creation story in Genesis provides him with another approach to that question. If God is good, Augustine asks, why did He create harmful animals, such as the vermin that afflict men, their livestock, and their crops, or the creatures that are ugly, nasty, and useless? His response to this objection is quite Stoic. If men took the trouble to consider the place of all created beings in God's universal and rational plan, he observes, they would see that no creatures, however apparently harmful or disgusting, are really evil or superfluous. Some of these creatures may actually be helpful as well as harmful, according to their uses. Even those that are pestiferous to man are, in themselves, wondrously made, and hence beautiful. In that sense they make a positive contribution to the wholeness of the universe (*integritas universitatis*), in which God has disposed all things by measure, number, and weight and in which all things combine to display the sublime reasonableness of the Creator and to sing His praises. This enlightening perspective, he concludes, is one that human reason makes available, and it can be perceived in the humility of the worm just as in the animals that are man's most faithful servitors.[26] Here, Augustine's accent is squarely placed on man's ability to understand the created order and to ascertain within it the hand of a reasonable deity.

Augustine also presents God and the universe as reasonable and knowable in the *De ordine*, his most elaborate exercise in theodicy. In this work he also raises a problem which he adverts to in much more detail elsewhere, and not necessarily in conjunction with theodicy, the perversity of the human will. In the *De ordine* Augustine treats the disordered will as a prime cause of evil and as the only created phenomenon capable of eluding the rational order that God imposes on the rest of the universe. However, while he indicates that order is a moral no less than an intellectual state which man is able to attain through the exercise of his reason and will, he does not analyze the psychological dynamics of

---

[25] *Conf.* 7.12.18–7.18.24.
[26] *De genesi contra Manicheos* 1.16.25–26, *PL*, 34, cols. 185–186.

the perversion of the will here, nor does he explain why God permits this one exception from His own rational design. Rather, the central issues raised by Augustine in this work are God's providence, chance, and causation in the created order and it is to these issues that he applies his arguments from theodicy. As Augustine observes, if we posit that God is not responsible for the evil found in the universe, then His providence is not all-powerful. If the second premise is true, then the order and design of the universe cannot be attributed with confidence to the deity, or to Him alone, but must be the result of chance. On the other hand, if there is indeed a grand cosmic order extending to all creatures, even the most insignificant, how is it that human life is marked by so much restlessness, instability, and waywardness? These questions, says Augustine, would not occur to us at all if we truly understood the nature of the universe and how all its parts cohere; the last question in particular reflects man's lack of self-knowledge as well.[27] Augustine himself bypasses the problem of human waywardness in the De ordine but prescribes theodicy as a cure for man's defective knowledge of the universe in a manner that is quite Stoic, as is his causal and ethical, rather than mathematical or aesthetic, treatment of the theme of order in general. At the same time, after posing the problems that he chooses to resolve in initially Stoic terms, he reformulates them in the light of Neoplatonism and Christianity, although he selects different aspects of these doctrines for this purpose than he does in the theodicy passage of the Confessions.[28]

Augustine's tincturing of Stoic theodicy with Neoplatonism occurs almost immediately in the De ordine and can be seen clearly in his use of the contrast between unity and multiplicity as the metaphysical framework in which he situates his conception of the cosmic order. As he states, there is a single, unitary, coherent plan that somehow gives meaning to the fragmentary, multifarious welter of phenomena that men see around them in the world. Thus, in the De ordine, it is multiplicity in the first instance, not matter, natural catastrophe, or misfortune, that needs to be rationalized. This is an ethical no less than a metaphysical concern,

---

[27] De ordine 1.1.1–3, ed. W. M. Green and K.-D. Daur, CC 29 (Turnhout, 1970).
[28] The best treatment of the De ordine, recognizing these multiple sources, is Josef Rief, Der Ordobegriff des jungen Augustins (Paderborn, 1962), pp. 22–23, 56–76, 80–86, 164–65, 332–34. See also O'Connell, Art and the Christian Intelligence, pp. 22–23, 56; Karl Svoboda, L'Esthétique de saint Augustin et ses sources, Opera facultatis philosophicae Universitatis Masarykianae Brunensis, 35 (Brno, 1933), pp. 53–54, 62, 64–65, 84. On the other hand, Baguette, "Le Stoïcisme," pp. 42–44; Adolf Dyroff, "Über Form und Begriffsgehalt der augustinischen Schrift De ordine," Aurelius Augustinus, Festschrift der Görres-Gesellschaft zum 1500. Todestage des heiligen Augustius, ed. Martin Grabmann and Joseph Mausbach (Köln, 1930), pp. 25–34, 44–46, 56; TeSelle, Augustine, pp. 78–82; Testard, Saint Augustin et Cicéron, I, 172; and Verbeke, "Augustin et le stoïcisme," RA, 1 (1958), 85–87 see only its Stoic dimensions.

for it is the same multiplicity as a feature of the creation that leads man's soul to relax its grip of the unitary order underlying it and to squander its own moral energies.[29] Augustine couples this essentially Neoplatonic conception of disorder with a basically Stoic understanding of the coherent pattern he sees in the cosmos. He explains that all phenomena are caused and that they are connected by an exhaustive and rational chain of events that accounts for everything that happens in the universe. Nothing occurs by irrational chance since nature is governed by a fixed order of causes which the rational deity has established.[30] Augustine's description of the causal nexus is Stoic thus far, but he stops well short of identifying it with the Creator Himself. For the universe, although orderly, is marked by multiplicity, while unity is a radical attribute of the deity.

With the foregoing formulation of the problem of theodicy in place, Augustine proceeds to explain why God is not responsible for evil. One possible answer would be to appeal to the powers God grants to secondary causes, including the human will. Augustine uses this argument elsewhere, but not in the *De ordine*. In the work at hand he deals both with cosmic and with social evils and invokes several other arguments instead. In some cases he tries to define evil out of existence by urging men to lift their minds to a universal perspective which will enable them to see that events or phenomena which appear to be useless, ugly, or harmful are actually good or neutral, in a manner forecasting his approach in the *De genesi contra Manicheos*.[31] In other cases, he agrees that the evils men experience are, indeed, truly evil, but that God deliberately permits them, a point he makes later in the *City of God* although he justifies these evils in the *De ordine* for their punishment of the wicked rather than for their moral education of the innocent.[32] Augustine's most original effort to rationalize evil in the *De ordine* and one that appears only in that work is his claim that some evils are acceptable because they requite or avert still greater evils. Thus, he notes, it is reasonable to tolerate executioners and prostitutes within the human community.[33] But, whichever kind of argument Augustine employs in the *De ordine*, he insists that the exercise of intelligence on the part of man can produce the insight needed to understand that these evils, whether apparent or real, are not inconsistent with the claim that God governs the world both rationally and benevolently.

---

[29] *De ordine* 1.2.3–4.
[30] Ibid. 1.3.6–9, 1.4.11–1.6.16, 1.8.25–26.
[31] Ibid. 2.4.11–12. A similar argument is given in *Contra academicos* 1.1.1, ed. W. M. Green, CC, 29 (Turnhout, 1970).
[32] *De ordine* 2.17.46.
[33] Ibid. 2.4.12.

Once a person has attained this perspective, Augustine adds, he will not be troubled by the vicissitudes of life. He will act at all times according to the principle of order. For order is not merely the rational plan of the universe; it is also a correct ordering of man's intellect and will to that broader reality. The constancy (*mens immobilis*) of the sage, who understands and follows the divine order in all things, will grant him wisdom and happiness, which Augustine illustrates by quoting Vergil on Aeneas' equanimity in *Aeneid* 7.586.[34] Augustine's association of theodicy with the doctrine of the sage and his linking of physics and ethics in this manner are quite Stoic. At the same time, and as early as the *De ordine*, the order of the soul, for Augustine, is not a purely rational notion and it does not refer to the autarchic self-sufficiency of the Stoic sage. It is an *ordo amoris* as much as an *ordo intellectualis*, and one that seeks the highest good in a hierarchical vision of the universe, above which stands a supreme good which the soul yearns to possess in an act of self-transcendence and personal adhesion.[35] This spiritual ascent beyond the world to its Creator is the ultimate means by which the soul may overcome its own multiplicity and disorder, replacing them with the immutability of God Himself. In this way, while Augustine's debt to Stoic theodicy in the *De ordine* is strong indeed, it is heavily conditioned, both in the formulation and in the resolution of the questions it is invoked to answer, by his Christianity and his Neoplatonism.

B) Natural Law

The centrality of reason as the prime or exclusive constituent of God, man, and the universe is the basic Stoic principle attached to the theodicy argument on which Augustine is inconsistent in his handling of that topic. Precisely the same can be said of his treatment of the related constellation of ideas involved in the doctrine of natural law, to which he also adverts both repeatedly and inconsistently. Augustine sometimes equates natural law with reason as a cosmic, an ethical, or a political principle, in a manner evocative of Cicero. At other points he treats natural law as reasonable but as transcendent, not immanent in the world, attaching it to a hierarchical Neoplatonic conception of being and goodness. At other times he identifies natural law with the new covenant of grace revealed by Christ, assimilating it firmly to a divine law that embraces both natural and supernatural phenomena. At still other times

---

[34] Ibid. 1.9.27, 2.4.11, 2.6.18, 2.8.25, 2.19.51; the Vergil quotation is at 2.20.54.
[35] Ibid. 1.9.27, 2.6.18. Rief, *Der Ordobegriff*, pp. 332–34 has a particularly good discussion of this point.

he contrasts the law of nature with the law of God.[36] With one exception the contexts in which Augustine Christianizes the law of nature or subordinates it to the rule of grace are polemical, whether his antagonists are Manichees or Pelagians. The situations in which his treatments of this topic are more closely Stoic or Ciceronian are diverse, ranging from the exegetical to the personal.

Two instances of the non-polemical type occur in Augustine's *De diversis quaestionibus*, an assortment of short essays on various topics written over a span of eight years in his early to middle career. His selectivity in this work sometimes reflects his own personal interests rather than any pressing pastoral or theological imperatives. Such would appear to be the case in *quaestio* 31, where he recapitulates the distinction between the *honestum* and the *utile*, the definition of the cardinal virtues, and the treatment of natural law found in Cicero's *De inventione*. In fact, the most recent edition of this work has shown that Augustine has simply quoted verbatim the apposite passage from Cicero's treatise, in which natural law, custom, and civil law are considered under the heading of the virtue of justice.[37] Cicero's definitions of the virtues, and of natural law itself, are somewhat less Stoic in the *De inventione* than in his later *De republica* and *De legibus* and Augustine's *quaestio* 31 follows suit. Here, too, justice is stated to be a habit of mind, exercised for the common good, which renders to each his own dignity and whose source is nature (*eius initium est a natura profectum*), an innate power ingrained in man that can be distinguished from opinion. Natural law includes the obligations pertaining to religion, reverence, favor, consideration, and truth. Augustine also restates the distinction among natural law (*natura ius*), custom (*consuetudine*), and civil or positive law (*lege ius*) and posits the same rela-

---

[36] An outstanding and fully nuanced treatment of this topic is P. Alois Schubert, *Augustins Lex-aeterna-Lehre nach Inhalt und Quellen*, Beiträge zur Geschichte der Philosophie des Mittelalters, 24:2 (Münster i.W., 1924). On the other hand Robert M. Grant, *Miracle and Natural Law in Graeco-Roman and Early Christian Thought* (Amsterdam, 1952), pp. 27–28 and Johannes Stelzenberger, *Conscientia bei Augustinus: Studie zur Geschichte der Moraltheologie* (Paderborn, 1959), pp. 113–15 note only the Christianizing aspects. R. A. Markus, *Saeculum: History and Society in the Theology of St. Augustine* (Cambridge, 1970), pp. 87–88 notes only its Stoic and Ciceronian aspects; Osborn, *Ethical Patterns*, p. 147, notes only its Stoic and Neoplatonic aspects.

[37] Baguette, "Le Stoïcisme," pp. 26–28 overinterprets the passage by stating that Augustine is here identifying virtue with right reason. P. Beckart, comm. on his ed. and trans. of *De diversis quaestionibus octoginta tribus*, OSA, sér. 1:10 (Paris, 1952), pp. 715–16 sees Augustine as departing from Cicero's distinction between customary and civil law. Testard, *Saint Augustin et Cicéron*, I, 317–31 merely cites the parallels. David L. Mosher, comm. on his trans. of *Eighty-three Different Questions*, FC, 70 (Washington, 1982), p. 58 n. 1 is not aware that the quotation from Cicero is a literal one and fails to note that Cicero has more than one definition of the pertinent terms in his writings. For Cicero on natural law in the *De inventione* and elsewhere see *Stoic Tradition*, I, ch. 2, pp. 88–89, 95–104.

tionship among them that Cicero gives in the *De inventione*. Augustine thus sees custom as derived from natural law to some slight degree and as sanctioned by religion and usage, and civil law as the law written down by statutory legislation and promulgated to facilitate its enforcement.[38] What we have here, in short, is the straightforward repetition of the position Cicero takes on natural law in a rhetorical context, from which Augustine omits only the oratorical uses which Cicero prescribes for this doctrine, as a source for extra-legal arguments that may embellish the case of an advocate who knows perfectly well that they are not the norms that sanction the laws actually administered by the law courts.

Augustine's second reference to natural law in the *De diversis quaestionibus* is at the same time more and less Stoic than the first one. In *quaestio* 53 he mentions the natural law inscribed in the rational soul (*naturalis lex in animam rationalem*), identifying it clearly with reason. However, this point arises in a text dealing with the interpretation of knotty passages in Scripture which, he says, have been placed there by God so that men may exercise their minds in unsnarling them and thereby convert their souls from this world to their own salvation. The natural law of reason to which he refers is both the human intellect as applied to the interpretation of the Bible and the general program of moral education to which the understanding of Holy Scripture leads.[39] Here, then, natural law is a faculty that enables man to move from this world to the next in a specifically Christian manner.

Exegesis also provides another setting in which Augustine considers natural law, in this case one that inclines him to shift his attention from its rationality to its attributes of eternity and ubiquity. In the *Confessions* he shows how this aspect of the doctrine of natural law helped him to resolve a major difficulty he confronted in reading the Old Testament, the fact that different moral standards governed the behavior of the Israelites at different points in their history. Not only did the morés of certain Old Testament worthies contradict those of their descendants, but some of these practices are also inconsistent with Christian ethics. Augustine defuses this exegetical landmine by conflating two Stoic ideas, the notion of a divine law that is the same always and everywhere, which he credits to Cicero, and the casuistic method of Panaetian ethics. Armed with this amalgam, Augustine concludes that God indeed has legislated consistent moral guidelines for men. At all times God's law is designed to curb intemperance, disobedience, self-absorption, and anti-social conduct. But God also makes a casuistic application of these rules to dif-

---

[38] *De div. quaest.* 31.1, ed. Almut Mutzenbecher, CC, 44A (Turnhout, 1975), pp. 41–42.
[39] Ibid. 53.2, CC, 44A, p. 88.

ferent historical ages, according to what He thinks is needful at the time, and, in the case of the shifting customs of the Old Testament era, in the light of the ways He intends His revelation in the Old Testament to foreshadow the New.[40] Here, Augustine makes an original and felicitous combination of two Stoic principles to solve a pressing Christian exegetical problem. And, while the moral guidelines of the eternal law as he describes it are Christian, they are compatible with the Stoic norms of reason, self-control, and social responsibility.

Both the moral and the political dimensions of natural law and the more or less overt equation of natural law with reason that surface in the foregoing examples appear also in Augustine's *De libero arbitrio*, where he uses natural law as an adjunct to theodicy in attacking Manicheism. Augustine's thesis here is that evil derives not from matter but from the sinful exercise of free will. He is thus faced with the task of rationalizing the injuries inflicted by sinners on the innocent, as well as the fact that the malefactors all too often go unpunished. Augustine appeals to the notion of an eternal, just, and rational law equated with God's perfect governance of the world in order to insist on the point that justice will be done in the next life, where both the innocent and the guilty will receive their due. In this connection, while he acknowledges that human laws ought to be enacted, reformed, and enforced in the light of God's eternal law, the very changelessness and rationality of God's law is what enables it to right the wrongs that the civil law may ignore as a function of its human and temporal limitations.[41] In this context, Augustine's handling of natural law as a posthumous remedy for the injustices resulting from man's freedom to sin undermines the Stoic conception of the immutability of natural law as stemming from the nexus of fixed causal relationships that embodies it. He replaces that notion with a Neoplatonic and Christian understanding of eternity as a transcendent metaphysical and moral order that stands above and beyond the natural order.

While the eternal law of the *De libero arbitrio* looks to the future and to the correction of the irrationalities of this life, Augustine, still in his anti-Manichean stance, can also treat the eternal law as embracing and sustaining nature in the here and now, even while he simultaneously redefines the concept of nature itself. This is the line he takes against Faustus in arguing that the Creator and the creation are both reasonable and good. Christianity and Neoplatonism tincture heavily the Stoic aspects of Augustine's position in the *Contra Faustum*, with the Christian

---

[40] *Conf.* 3.7.13–3.8.16.
[41] *De libero arbitrio* 1.6.15, ed. W. M. Green, CC, 29 (Turnhout, 1970). The traditional subdivisions of this work have been followed in preference to Green's.

element predominating. Evil, he asserts, derives from sin, which in turn results from man's rejection of the eternal law in thought, word, or deed. As for the eternal law itself, Augustine's definition makes will as critical a feature of it as reason: *Lex vero aeterna est ratio divina vel voluntas dei ordinem naturalem conservari iubens, perturbari vetens* ("The eternal law is the divine reason or the will of God, which ordains the preservation of the natural order and prohibits its transgression.") In the case of man himself the natural order means that he is composed of body and soul, both of which are natural and good, and also that his soul is superior to his body. This natural superiority of the soul, Augustine continues, enables man to take on immortality and, through the gift of God, to receive faith and to internalize the law of grace. Thus, we men *secundum aeternam legem, qua naturalis ordo servatur, iuste vivimus, si vivamus ex fide non ficta, quae per dilectionem operatur . . . quamdiu per fidem ambulamus, non per speciem* ("live rightly according to the eternal law, which sustains the order of nature, when we live by a faith unfeigned, which works through love, . . . while we walk by faith, not by sight.")[42] Augustine carries this assimilation of natural law to Christian revelation even farther in the *Contra Faustum* when he raises the question of whether Christ's incarnation through a virgin birth was contrary to nature. Here, he seeks to oppose the Manichean idea that Christ's birth and death were illusions, rather than real events, and he stresses that they both occurred naturally. Since nature is part of God's eternal law, Augustine maintains, nothing that God does or ordains is contrary to nature. In this sense His suspension of the usual procedures governing conception in the case of Christ is also natural. The only events that are unnatural are the sins committed by men in defiance of God's law.[43] And so, Augustine radically transforms nature into the will of God and the unnatural into the will to oppose God. He thereby redefines not only moral states made possible by grace but also miracles and extraordinary phenomena as natural events. At the same time, he places them in the control of a causal agent whose operations cannot be fully known or predicted by men.

Human free will is also a point at issue between Augustine and the Pelagians. This is another context in which he thoroughly Christianizes his legal theory but one where he squarely opposes grace to law. Augustine elaborates this view in his commentary on the Epistle to the Romans, a text which he mines heavily for the doctrine of grace which he developed against the Pelagians. His exegesis of Paul outlines four legal categories: before the law, under the law, under grace, and in peace (*ante*

---

[42] *Contra Faustum* 22.27, ed. Iosephus Zycha, CSEL, 25 (Vienna, 1891), pp. 621, 622 for these two quotations. In the same vein see 22.28–29, 22.73.

[43] Ibid. 26.3.

legem, sub lege, sub gratia, in pace). He understands law here in a Pauline sense, as the law of Moses which the covenant of Christ supersedes. However, he treats these categories as progressive moral states, not as phases of legal history or of *Heilsgeschichte*. Before the law, man follows the concupiscence of the flesh. He does not struggle against sin but approves it, not knowing it is wrong. Under the law, man learns what sin is and struggles against it. The law is good because it brings moral enlightenment, teaching what God forbids and enjoining what He requires. Under grace, man neither follows the concupiscence of the flesh nor is drawn to it. Grace washes away his past sins and replaces the inner assent to sin to which he had earlier been liable with the motives of charity and fear of the Lord. In peace, the concupiscence of the flesh no longer exists, for we are in the life to come, where sin and temptation are no longer possible. Augustine concludes that man is endowed with free will so that he can live well in the conditions that precede the state of peace. Man's freedom means not that he can ever be incapable of sin in this life, an error he attributes to the Pelagians, but that he has the capacity to choose not to sin. In this anti-Pelagian setting Augustine sees nature as man's condition prior to the reception of God's revealed law. Nature, so understood, is not so much subordinated to revelation as it is seen as its antithesis. Augustine's anti-Pelagian doctrine of natural law also empties this notion of its rational and physical content. Both God's ways of governing the world and man's ways of perceiving and responding to Him are limited to the moral sphere and reduced to the exercise of will.[44]

At the same time, in another exegetical context and in a moment when the later Augustine sets aside the exigencies of polemic, he posits quite a different relationship between law and grace. In commenting on St. John's statement in his first epistle that charity is the fulfillment of the law, Augustine observes that the love of God and neighbor which grace imparts to the purified soul is not a substitute for the law or a warrant for antinomianism. As he puts it, *Nolite putare consumptionem, sed consummationem* ("Do not think that what is meant is destruction, but rather consummation.")[45] Augustine is referring here to the moral law of the Old Testament which the New Testament confirms, not to those Mosaic regulations which it supersedes. His focus is on the inner intentionality that should irradiate the Christian's observance of this law. To be sure,

---

[44] *Expositio quarumdum propositionum ex Epistola ad Romanos* 13–18, *PL,* 35, cols. 2065–2066. Holte, *Béatitude et sagesse,* p. 240, mistakenly reads this passage as a Stoicizing use of natural law.

[45] *Tractatus in Epistolam Joannis* 10.5, ed. and trans. Paul Agaësse, SC, 75 (Paris, 1961), p. 420. For more on this point see 10.7. Agaësse provides a good commentary in his intro., pp. 79–80.

Augustine is addressing ethics not physics, and the intellectual faculty he seeks to move is not an autarchic human reason but a mind, and above all a heart, informed by divine grace. Nonetheless, his stress on a central intentionality toward the good as the foundation of virtue and his sense of its capacity to transfigure the duties one bears to one's fellow men preserve, despite the radical Christianization of its content, some of the structure and connective tissue of the moral dimension of the original Stoic conception of natural law.

C) The Stoics as Sages and as Anti-Sages

The inconsistencies noted above in Augustine's frequent appeals to arguments from theodicy and natural law are substantial, both in the sense of being extensive and in the sense that these doctrines are important to him, contributing materially to the form or content of the passages in which he includes them. The same cannot be said for Augustine's many positive and negative references to the wisdom and virtue of Stoic philosophers, or of persons traditionally regarded as exponents of Stoic values. These references are entirely *ad hoc*, inspired by the immediate rhetorical requirements faced by Augustine at various points in his writings. He uses them in a strictly decorative manner. Augustine's rhetorical strategies in this connection all have models in the writings of earlier apologists and controversialists, who showed an equal dexterity in using Stoic *exempla* as a way of applying praise or blame. So too, Augustine characterizes Stoics as pagans whose errors have led unwary Christians into heresy and, alternatively, as sages whose ideas or behavior support the truth of Christianity, or his own personal opinion, against paganism or heresy, as well as offering edification for the orthodox. Augustine is fully capable of citing the same Stoic individual as both a good and a bad example, even in the same work, by fastening on different aspects of his history for different purposes. Another traditional ploy that Augustine invokes to relativize the authority of pagan philosophers is to claim that they derived their wisdom from the Bible. But this is a point that he does not belabor and one that he applies only to Plato, not to the Stoics.[46] In a few instances Augustine's decorative references to Stoics speak to their reputation as logicians, with their taste for paradox and their agile and wily dialectics, especially in the case of Chrysippus. He uses this characterization of the Stoics to flay both pagan and heretical antagonists[47] while accepting it without rancor as a

---

[46] *Civ. dei* 8.11; *De doct. christ.* 2.38.43. In the latter reference Augustine cites Ambrose as a source for this idea.

[47] For the pagan see *Epistula* 92, to Nectarius, 409, in *Epistulae*, ed. Al. Goldbacher,

description of himself at the hands of another non-Christian opponent.[48] But his primary use of this kind of rhetorical embellishment is to illustrate and amplify his own ethical views, usually in sharp contrast with inimical opinions.

Augustine has three sets of addressees in mind here: pagans, orthodox Christians, and heretics. His inconsistencies in the use of Stoic moral *exempla* can be found in all of these categories. One strategy he uses to attack pagans is to argue that polytheism is a false religion because of the unedifying conduct of the gods, whom the virtues of some pagans themselves reprove. Figures associated with Stoicism whom he mentions or quotes to show pagan virtue include Seneca, Persius, Cincinnatus, and Cato of Utica, Seneca for his writings if not for his life,[49] Persius for his grasp of the principle of duty,[50] Cincinnatus for his voluntary poverty,[51] and Cato for his chastity.[52] In seeking to console Christians or to exhort them to greater moral fervor Augustine cites some of the same Stoic *exempla virtutem*, extolling Cato for his public spirit,[53] Cincinnatus once more for his detachment from wealth and power,[54] and Regulus for the equanimity he sustained under the horrible tortures inflicted on him by the Carthaginians.[55] However, he joins one of these same figures, Cato, with Lucretia, as detestable examples of a crime absolutely forbidden to Christians, suicide. Augustine himself uses Stoic arguments to attack Lucretia and Cato on this score, invoking the familiar apologetic technique of beating the pagans with their own stick.[56] In Lucretia's case, her suicide disproved her claims to honor rather than substantiating them, since her victimization by a rapist was truly a matter of indifference, not an evil, an argument that echoes the Stoicizing formula *mentem peccare, non corpus*, which Livy puts into the mouths of Lucretia's hus-

---

4 vols., CSEL, 34, 44, 57, 58 (Vienna, 1895–1923). The heretic is Cresconius and is the only Donatist Augustine attacks by appealing to Stoicism. See *Contra Cresconium* 1.14.17, 1.19.24, ed. M. Petchenig, CSEL, 52 (Vienna, 1909). The latter reference has been noted by B. Darrell Jackson, "The Theory of Signs in Augustine's *De Doctrina Christiana*," *Augustine: A Collection of Critical Essays*, ed. R. A. Markus (Garden City, N.Y., 1972), p. 127.

[48] *Ep.* 16, from Maximus, ca. 390; and Augustine's response in *Ep.* 17.
[49] *Civ. dei* 6.10. Noted by Hildegard Cancik, *Untersuchungen zu Senecas Epistulae morales* (Hildesheim, 1967), p. 119.
[50] *Civ. dei* 2.6. Noted by Hagendahl, *Augustine and the Latin Classics*, I, 217.
[51] *Ep.* 92.
[52] *Ep.* 91, to Nectarius, 408.
[53] *Civ. dei* 5.12.
[54] Ibid. 5.18.
[55] Ibid. 1.15, 1.23–24.
[56] On Lucretia, see *Civ. dei* 1.19; on Cato, see ibid. 1.24, 19.4; the quotation is at 1.24. Mary Louise Carlson, "Pagan Examples of Fortitude in the Latin Christian Apologists," *CP* 43 (1948), 101 and Osborn, *Ethical Patterns*, pp. 153–54 note the negative judgment Augustine makes on Cato's suicide but not the moral qualities for which he praises Cato elsewhere.

band and father. For his part, Cato's suicide demonstrated not his fortitude but his cowardice. True fortitude would enable the sage to overcome the evils of this life, not to classify a life beset by hardships as an
evil that he has a right to terminate. Those who praise Cato's suicide,
says Augustine, are opposed to us (*contra nos*). They fail to see that what
Cato was actually doing was evading his orders and responsibilities.

Augustine's controversies with heretics also provoke both positive and
negative citations of Stoic exemplars. Against the Manichee Honoratus,
who, Augustine claims, has erred because he is too proud to accept ecclesiastical authority, he argues that a healthy respect for authority is
basic to the transmission of knowledge in all fields. In the case of philosophical knowledge, the single authority he cites is the Stoic Cornu-
tus,[57] the teacher of Lucan and Persius. Lucan, and the figure of Cato
he delineates in the *Pharsalia* as a man who married and sired children
not for his own venereal pleasure but for the sake of the commonwealth
alone, are also Stoic authorities, albeit purely Musonian ones, whom
Augustine invokes, quoting the apposite lines from Lucan to contest the
sexual ethics of the Pelagian bishop Julianus of Eclanum. Julianus' works,
unfortunately, have not been preserved and our knowledge of what he
taught and how he defended it comes indirectly from Augustine and from
other hostile witnesses. According to Augustine, Julianus held that sexual relations between spouses were a natural good, and one enhanced
by the sacred vows binding a Christian husband and wife. This position
stands in marked contrast to the far more restrictive and grudging attitude toward human sexuality advocated by Augustine in his later years.
Matters were made still more acrimonious between the two prelates by
the fact that Julianus had also written against the Manichees and had
accused Augustine of harboring a crypto-Manichean position in his own
doctrine of marriage. Augustine appears unwilling to address this dis-
turbing challenge in the terms in which Julianus had posed it. Instead,
he offers a lateral counter-attack by citing Lucan's Cato to show that even
the pagans had a worthier, because more ascetic, approach to marriage
than Julianus does.[58] On the other hand, the same Cato serves as an *exemplum vitii* in the *Contra Julianum*, and in the same context of sexual ethics. For Augustine, Cato's role as a model of sexual morality is severely
compromised by the fact that he divorced his wife Marcia. Unlike Lactantius, who sees Cato as a pander in his separation from Marcia so that
she could marry his childless friend Hortensius, Augustine objects to di-

---

[57] *De utilitate credendi* 7.17, ed. and trans. J. Pegon, OSA, sér. 1:8 (Paris, 1951).
[58] *Contra Julianum* 5.9.38, *PL*, 44. Hagendahl, *Augustine and the Latin Classics*, I, 208 has
noted this *locus* but has not analyzed the function of the Lucan reference in Augustine's
argument.

vorce *per se*. He also regards Cato's divorce as a contraceptive strategy
for his own family, which Augustine likewise finds abhorrent, despite
Marcia's subsequent fruitfulness as Hortensius' wife, which he ignores.[59] The twin evils of divorce and contraception are associated in
Augustine's mind with a hedonistic attitude toward sexual behavior,
which he tries in this manner to attach to Julianus' teachings on Christian marriage.

More broadly, Augustine charges Julianus with capitulating to error
on the subjects both of marriage and infant baptism because he followed
the pagan philosophers rather than the venerable Fathers of the Church.
Augustine lists a large number of philosophers in this connection, including the Stoics but going well beyond them, whether or not they had
any known opinions on the points at issue.[60] But it is Julianus on marriage which remains the principal front on which Augustine conducts this
kind of offensive. The most specific accusation he makes concerning Julianus' alleged preference for pagan authorities on sexual ethics is the
charge that he derived his position on the natural good of sexual relations in marriage from the Stoic teaching on animal reproduction found
in the speeches of Balbus and Cotta in Cicero's *De natura deorum*, as if
that subject, or what the Stoics thought about it, had any bearing on the
sexual behavior appropriate for human beings. Here, Augustine's aim is
to show that the Stoic view on animal reproduction is both false and irrelevant to a Christian understanding of marriage. Yet, paradoxically
enough, he is actually more Stoic in this context himself than he stigmatizes Julianus for being. As Augustine points out, for the Stoics, unlike the Aristotelians, there can be no moral community between animals and men because animals are irrational while men are rational.
The Stoics thus did not place animals on a biological continuum that
included men and did not seek to extrapolate ethical rules for men, sexual or otherwise, on the model of animal behavior.[61] Further, and this is
an equally Stoic argument that attacks Julianus from another direction,
Augustine maintains that it is not apposite to invoke the Stoics as authorities on human sexual ethics in any case, because they saw sexual
activity as neither good nor bad but as a matter of indifference, a position that has nothing in common with the range of views taken by Christian theologians on all sides of this issue.[62] In making this point, of course,

---

[59] *Contra Jul.* 5.12.48.

[60] Ibid. 1.4.12, 1.7.35, 2.10.34, 2.10.37, 4.15.75, 5.7.29, 5.14.51 on the subject of marriage and 6.20.64 on the subject of infant baptism. On the first group of *loci* see Testard,
Saint Augustin et Cicéron, I, 244–45.

[61] *Contra Jul.* 4.12.58, 4.14.72. Hagendahl, *Augustine and the Latin Classics*, I, 108 has
noted the first of these *loci* but not the force of Augustine's argument.

[62] *Contra Jul.* 4.12.59, 4.15.75, 5.8.33.

he is trumping the Musonian ace that he plays elsewhere in the *Contra Julianum*. Augustine mentions another heresy, that of Jovinian, who, he claims, used the Stoics to support his erroneous belief in the equality of all sins, the impossibility of post-baptismal sin, and the parity of marriage and celibacy as Christian callings.[63] But the major illustration of his *ad hoc* polemical citations of Stoics as sages and as anti-sages remains his *Contra Julianum*.

II. Augustine's Consistent Uses of Stoicism

In terms of the range of applications that Augustine makes of Stoic doctrines, the largest single subdivision of his thought is unquestionably the one in which he maintains a consistent attitude toward the Stoic ideas he uses. These consistencies stand the test of time, irrespective of the kinds of works in which they are found. In many instances Augustine agrees with the Stoics; in some cases he is partly positive and partly negative; while in still others he is consistently opposed to the Stoa. He occasionally ascribes the teachings at issue specifically to the Stoics and at other times he shows no interest in indicating his sources. The doctrines involved span the three traditional branches of philosophy, logic, physics, and ethics, with the first two being represented more extensively than the third. Augustine applies his consistent uses of Stoicism to a host of different types of works in a wide range of contexts. His handling of some of these Stoic topics is unaffected by the contexts in which they appear, while, with other topics, he may emphasize one aspect or another of the doctrine depending on the needs of his argument in a particular work. Virtually all the Stoic teachings which Augustine treats consistently are important to him. They contribute substantially to the formulation of positions, both philosophical and theological, that are distinctively Augustinian and account for some of his most creative extensions of Stoicism into the realms of Christian exegesis, ethics, and dogma. In some respects, also, his fidelity to Stoic positions is so thorough and is elaborated so repeatedly in this category of his thought as to make him their fullest expositor and transmitter to Latin readers in the later Middle Ages.

A) Epistemology

Epistemology is certainly a field of Stoic philosophy which Augustine knew well and which he delineates with remarkable amplitude and ac-

---

[63] *De haerisibus* 82, ed. R. Vander Plaetse and C. Beukers, CC, 46 (Turnhout, 1969).

curacy. Indeed, one would be hard pressed to find another Latin author of his age, or before it, who conveys more information on this subject. Epistemology is also one of the few Stoic topics which he takes up anywhere in his *œuvre* which he treats philosophically in its own right, as well as citing it in various theological contexts where his emphasis is shaped by pastoral or polemical considerations. Some of Augustine's earliest treatments of epistemological questions are his most detailed, especially those relating to sense perception and the criterion of truth. These were matters on which the neophyte Augustine felt a personal need to clarify his views, particularly regarding doctrines he had held in the past but now rejected. On the other hand, his most elaborate discussion of the transformation of sensory data into ideas held with a firm adhesion occurs in the *City of God*. Augustine's early expositions of sense perception are very well rounded although his applications of this theme in later works are extremely one-sided as a function of the agenda of the passages where he refers to it. His arguments against skepticism and related topics reappear less frequently and are equally affected by contextual considerations but on balance receive a more even-handed treatment.

In David Lindberg's terminology, there were two general approaches to sense perception in antiquity, the intromissive and the extramissive. In the intromissive theory, which may be exemplified by Aristotelianism, sense data are thought to impress themselves on sense organs regarded as passive recipients of that data and neutral conduits of them to the mind. The mind in turn acts on the material supplied to it by the sense organs only at a secondary stage of the process. In the extramissive theory, which may be exemplified by Neoplatonism, the mind takes the initiative, empowering the senses to reach out to their objects and to convey the data extracted from them to the mind. The Stoics took a middle position in this debate. Their own account of sense perception combined intromission with extramission and viewed the entire question in the light of physical and psychological monism and under the heading of their doctrine of *pneuma*.[64] The Stoic universe is a material plenum. Sensation, whether involving sensation at a distance or the perception of objects immediately adjacent to the sense organs, is understood as the impact of one unit of matter upon another. Objects of sensation advertise their presence to the knower by emitting a flow of *pneuma*, or rarefied matter, which interacts with the *pneuma* emitted by the subject's mind through his sense organs. This double flow of *pneuma* provides a material bridge on which the data are brought to the knower's

---

[64] David C. Lindberg, *Theories of Vision from Al-Kindi to Kepler* (Chicago, 1976), pp. 9–11 gives an excellent and concise review of these ancient positions.

mind. Commentators on Stoic epistemology in antiquity, who tended to oppose it, also tended to seize on either the intromissive or the extra-missive side of this theory as problematic, an approach seconded by the classical Latin transmitters of the doctrine whether they criticized or supported it. One of Augustine's most distinctive contributions to the history of the Stoic tradition is his reunification of the two aspects of the Stoic account of sense perception and his reconnection of them with the idea of a rarefied material *pneuma* that relates the subject to the sensory objects he knows in a world conceived as a material plenum. At the same time, it must be noted that Augustine never credits the Stoa expressly with this constellation of ideas. And, notwithstanding his discriminating reconstruction of Stoic epistemology, his own Neoplatonizing tendencies as well as the contexts in which he locates most of his discussions of sense perception lead him to emphasize heavily the extramissive side of the theory.[65]

Augustine gives a thorough, balanced, and authentically Stoic de-scription of sense perception in one of his earliest works, the *De musica*, a fact that may seem surprising given the extensive debts to Platonism, Aristotelianism, and the rhetorical tradition which he also displays in this work.[66] He is, to be sure, concerned primarily with the perception of sound in the *De musica* although he brings in comparisons with some of the other senses. The Stoicizing character of his account of sensation in the final book is by no means compromised by his argument that the

---

[65] The best treatment is by Verbeke, *L'Evolution*, pp. 489–508. Also useful if less fully and vigorously argued is Ulrich Duchrow, *Sprachverständnis und biblisches Hören bei Augus-tin* (Tübingen, 1965), p. 10. Jean Rohmer, "L'Intentionnalité des sensations chez saint Augustin," *Augustinus Magister*, I, 491–98 notes Augustine's Stoic sources but considers only the extramissive dimension. Terry L. Miethe, "St. Augustine and Sense Knowl-edge," *AS*, 8 (1977), 11–19; Margaret Ruth Miles, *Augustine on the Body* (Missoula, 1979), pp. 11, 17; and Ronald Nash, *The Light of the Mind; St. Augustine's Theory of Knowledge* (Lexington, 1969), pp. 43–45, 51 ascribe this theory to Plotinus alone, see only the ex-tramissive side of it, and treat Augustine as a critic of the Stoics. Mary Ann Ida Gannon, "The Active Theory of Sensation in St. Augustine," *NS*, 30 (1956), 162–65 thinks that Augustine is asserting his independence from Plotinus on this point but does not attrib-ute the theory to the Stoics. George Howie, *Educational Theory and Practice in St. Augustine* (New York, 1969), pp. 73–74, 80–81 and Leonardo R. Patanè, *Il pensiero pedagogico di S. Agostino*, 2ª ed. (Bologna, 1969), p. 102 think that he made his own independent confla-tion of Aristotle and Plotinus. Vernon J. Bourke, *Augustine's Quest of Wisdom: Life and Phi-losophy of the Bishop of Hippo* (Milwaukee, 1945), pp. 111–12, 237; F.-J. Thonnard, "Les fonctions sensibles de l'âme humaine selon S. Augustin," *L'Année théologique augustinienne*, 12 (1952), 335–45; and Sofia Vanni Rovighi, "La fenomenologia della sensazione in S. Agostino," *Rivista di filosofia neo-scolastica*, 54 (1962), 18–32 give clear accounts of the doc-trine but do not discuss Augustine's sources.

[66] For the Aristotelian and rhetorical side of the *De musica* see Marcia L. Colish, "St. Augustine's Rhetoric of Silence Revisited," *AS*, 9 (1978), 20–24. To the literature cited there arguing for a purely Platonic or Neoplatonic interpretation of the work may be added O'Connell, *Art and the Christian Intelligence*, ch. 4.

mind should try to rise above corporeal sensations and to understand them in the purer air of reason. On the intromissive side, Augustine defines sounds as impulses impinging on the air, or on the drops of water suspended in the air, which stand between the sources of sound and the ear. He thus sees the objects themselves as emitting data that must transfer themselves to the sense organs across a material medium, *vel in ipso corpore de loco in locum migrat aliquid sive transit* ("as when something runs and crosses from place to place in the body itself.")[67] The extramissive side of sensation is equally Stoic. It is the mind, says Augustine, that initiates the process of sensation, energizing the physical organs in order to acquire the information it wishes to gather through the function of sensation itself. The sense of sight is the paradigm case; even in the *De musica*, Augustine gives the fullest account of extramission in his description of vision. He is particularly interested in the question of how the eye perceives large and multiform objects that are far away. As he explains the process, a visual ray is emitted by the soul through the eye, traversing the space between the eye and its object and enabling the data to travel to the mind. The distention of the eye and mind into space through this visual ray he analogizes with the temporal distention provided by the memory in the perception of musical sounds, whereby the mind can grasp and retain an entire musical phrase although it is made up of individual notes that reverberate in succession and are audible only one at a time:

> Ut igitur nos ad capienda spatia locorum diffusio radiorum juvat, qui ex brevibus pupilis in aperta emicant, et adeo sunt nostri corporis, ut quanquam in procul positis rebus quas videmus, a nostra anima vegetentur; ut ergo eorum effusione adjuvamur ad capienda spatia locorum: ita memoria, quod quasi lumen est temporalium spatiorum, quantum in suo genere quodammodo extrudi potest, tantum eorumdem spatiorum capit.[68]

> Then, as the diffusion of the rays shining out in the open from tiny pupils of the eye, and belonging therefore to our body, in such a way that, although the things we see are placed at a distance, they are yet quickened by the soul, so just as when we are helped by their effusion in comprehending place-spans, the memory too, because it is somehow the light of time-spans, so far comprehends these time-spans as in its own way it too can be projected.

---

[67] *De musica* 6.5.12, ed. Giovanni Marzi (Firenze, 1969), pp. 524–26; trans. Robert Catesby Taliaferro, FC, 4 (New York, 1947), p. 337.
[68] Ibid. 6.8.21, Marzi, p. 550. See also 6.2.2–3, 6.4.7, 6.5.9. For more on memory in a similar vein see *Conf.* 10.10.17; *De genesi ad litteram* 12.16.33, ed. and trans. P. Agaësse and A. Solignac, OSA, sér. 7:48–49 (Paris, 1972).

An equally balanced treatment of sensation which preserves a Stoic combination of both intromission and extramission and which links it with the idea that the mind directs the physical senses can be found in a work of the mature Augustine, the *De trinitate*. In the *De musica* Augustine's even-handed approach to sensation results from the fact that his sole agenda is explaining sensation *per se*. In the passage of the *De trinitate* to be considered next, the same approach results from his precise contextual needs at that point in the work, a fact underscored by his application of the same doctrine much more one-sidedly elsewhere in the same treatise. In the second half of the *De trinitate* Augustine elaborates four analogies of the Trinity in the operations of the human soul, the second of which is the triad of self, love of self, and knowledge of self. In considering self-knowledge, Augustine seeks to explain this experience by contrasting it with man's knowledge of sensory objects. He notes that the mind activates the sense organs, speaking of the visual rays (*radios*) as spiritual forces flowing from the eyes that empower them to see. He also states that images of corporeal objects of sensation flow from those objects into the mind by way of the senses, illustrating the point by referring both to visual and to auditory data.[69] In this context his incorporation of intromission and extramission into his analysis is a direct consequence of the fact that self-knowledge, the phenomenon he wishes to explain by this analogy, is itself a twofold and reciprocal process.

On the other hand, no such exigencies condition most of the contexts in which Augustine repeatedly adverts to the process of sensation. Elsewhere he emphasizes extramission alone and interprets the role of *pneuma* within it as evidence not for a material plenum but for the superiority of the mind over the body, in a manner that preserves a good deal of the Stoic position but which Neoplatonizes it quite appreciably. The contexts in which his theory of sensation contribute to his arguments on other subjects range from polemics against heresy to straightforward expositions of Christian doctrine and to psychology and semantics.

It is in the exegesis of Genesis written by Augustine against the Manichees where he expounds the extramissive side of his theory in the greatest detail and where he reflects a thoroughly Stoic sense of the material character of the pneumatic force that activates the senses. His attack on the idea that matter is evil and that it causes man to sin is based substantially on these twin aspects of the Stoic doctrine. To begin with, he stresses that the perception of material objects is itself an act of the soul:

---

[69] *De trinitate* 9.3.3, 9.6.10, 10.1.1, 10.7.10, ed. W. J. Mountain and Fr. Glorie, CC, 50:1–2 (Turnhout, 1968).

Neque enim corpus sentit, sed anima per corpus, quo velut nuntio utitur ad formandum in se ipsa, quod extrinsecus nuntiatur. Non potest itaque fieri visio corporalis, nisi etiam spiritalis simul fiat.[70]

It is not, therefore, the body that senses but the soul by means of the body, which it sends forth like a messenger to form in the soul itself the external object that it reports. Thus, there can be no corporeal vision without there also being a spiritual vision.

The soul, Augustine makes clear, is not corporeal itself. But, when it decides to take the sensory initiative it does so through a corporeal medium. Augustine describes this medium, *more Stoicorum*, as an airy or fiery impulse, emitted by the sense organs, which acts as a material link with the objects sensed, whether these objects are at a distance from the sense organs or not:

Cum corporea non sit, per subtilis corpus agitat vigorem sentiendi. Inchoat itaque motum in omnibus sensibus a subtilitate ignis, sed non in omnibus ad idem pervenit.[71]

While not corporeal itself, it is by means of the most rarefied body that the soul exercises the power of sensation. The soul, then, initiates the movement in all the senses, using the subtlety of fire, although it does not act in each sense in the same way.

This pneumatic impulse operates in the sense of sight as a visual ray (*acies, radius*) which mixes with the pure air and traverses the distance between eye and object. The ray itself, Augustine acknowledges, is material: *Et certe iste corporeae lucis est radius, emicans ex oculis nostris* ("And certainly this ray emitted from our eyes is a ray of corporeal light.")[72] In the senses of hearing and smell the ray mixes with air that is more or less moist, while in the senses of taste and touch it mixes with the earth.[73] In all cases an immaterial soul works through matter without compromising itself, in opposition to the dualistic Manichean understanding of human nature. At the same time, the order in which Augustine treats and ranks the physical senses activated by *pneuma* reflects a Neoplatonic hierarchization of the physical world, moving downward from their most ethereal to their grossest functions.

There are a number of other contexts, equally polemical and equally restricted to the extramissive dimension of Stoic epistemology, where

---

[70] *De gen. ad litt.* 12.25.51, OSA, sér. 7:49, p. 416. See also 3.5.7.
[71] Ibid. 3.5.7, OSA, sér. 7:48, p. 220. Similarly 3.6.8, 7.20.26–7.21.27.
[72] Ibid. 4.34.54, OSA, sér. 7:48, p. 366. Similarly 12.16.32.
[73] Ibid. 3.5.7, 12.16.32.

Augustine accents different aspects even of that partial perspective on sense perception in the light of his needs at the time. In the *De ordine* the point on which he fastens is the idea that it is not the senses which perceive, but the mind by means of the senses, in supporting the case for a rational understanding of the cosmos, the theodicy argument which he levels against the Manichees in that work.[74] The primacy of the mind over the body also reinforces the anti-Manichean argument for free will as the source of evil in the *De libero arbitrio*, where he stresses that it is either reason (*ratio*) or an inner sense (*sensus interior*) ministering to it that vivifies the senses and evaluates what they report to the mind.[75] The same emphasis on the rule of the mind over the body informs Augustine's treatment of sensation in *De quantitate animae*, where he asserts that the soul empowers the senses in order to refute the view that the soul merely takes note of their activities. He also emphasizes the role of the mind in judging the sense data that it receives, observing that some philosophers, and acute ones too, said that there is no knowledge worthy of the name unless the mind possesses it with such a firm comprehension that nothing can shake it.[76] Here Augustine merely intimates the familiarity with the Stoic analysis of intellectual judgments which he displays in more detail elsewhere. But he does reflect his understanding of the fact that the empirical and intellectual aspects of Stoic epistemology do not contradict each other. There is one further polemical application of the theory of extramission, this time in Augustine's anti-Pelagian invective against Julianus of Eclanum. His point of departure is the ethical implications of the principle that the mind controls the activities of the sense organs. He focuses especially on those sense perceptions that contribute to the sin of lust, as a feature of his charge that Julianus is an advocate of sexual hedonism.[77]

There are also a number of passages in which Augustine adverts to extramission simply to address straightforward questions of semantics, psychology, or Christian doctrine. In his *De magistro* he analyzes the powers of words as signs, developing the theory that their accuracy must be measured by comparing them with what the knower already knows about their significata and that their capacity to produce new knowledge depends on the action of Christ, the Interior Teacher, working in the knower's mind. His assertion that the senses operate under the initiative and guidance of the soul is designed here to support his argument

---

[74] *De ordine* 2.2.6, 2.11.32. Noted by Baguette, "Le Stoïcisme," pp. 8–10.

[75] *De lib. arb.* 2.3.9–2.4.10, 2.5.12–2.16.13.

[76] *De quantitate animae* 23.41–26.51, 30.58–61, ed. and trans. Pierre de Labriolle, OSA, sér. 1:5 (Paris, 1948).

[77] *Contra Jul.* 4.14.66.

for the intrinsic limits and the purely instrumental functions of words as sensory signs.[78] In the *Confessions* Augustine observes that the "words" which created beings "speak" to man as he looks for the Creator in the creation are also sensible signs which the soul interrogates by means of the rays which it emits through the eyes as messengers.[79] In another section of the *De trinitate* analysis of the soul's self-contemplation as an analogy of the Trinity, explicated by comparing it with sense perception, Augustine focuses on extramission in considering the mind's attention as the power that enables it to fix its senses on their objects and thus to overcome the distance and difference between the object and the knowing subject. Here there is a triad involving the sensory object, the sense organ, and the mind's attention that initiates and guides the process.[80]

Two other mysteries of the Christian faith, the incarnation of Christ and the resurrection of the body in the next life, provide difficulties which Augustine elucidates by reference to extramission that are even more novel. The fact that the senses and all their activities arise in the mind, he says, shows that great things can come from small ones and that the spirit can work in the flesh. This thought helps to explain how God could have communicated Himself in the incarnation of Christ through a humble virgin.[81] Equally original are Augustine's applications of the extramissive theory of the function of sight to the resurrection. The swiftness and agility of the resurrected body can be compared to the quickness of the visual ray (*radius, acies, ictus*) even in our present body, which enables the eye to touch its objects almost instantaneously, even across great distances. The heavenly eyes of the resurrected saints, he avers, will enjoy an even more ineffable and marvellous celerity in seeing God.[82] Similarly, the idea that the resurrection, when it comes, will occur in the twinkling of an eye (*ictus oculi*) can be understood by considering the rapidity with which that *ictus* itself operates in the act of physical sight, enabling man to perceive in a flash the heavenly bodies themselves despite their immense distance from the earth.[83] In all these cases, whether Augustine is explicating more narrowly how the senses operate or more broadly how important Christian doctrines can be understood or defended against heresy, the particular questions at issue lead him to emphasize the extramissive side of the theory of sensation he derived from the Stoa. And, he has only to dematerialize the human *pneuma* that ac-

---

[78] *De magistro* 12.39–40, 2nd ed., ed. and trans. F.–J. Thonnard, OSA, sér. 1:6 (Paris, 1952).

[79] *Conf.* 10.6.9, 10.7.11.

[80] *De trin.* 11.2.2–3.

[81] *Ep.* 137, to Volusianus, 412.

[82] *Sermo* 277.10.10–11.11. *PL*, 38–39.

[83] *Sermo* 362.18.20.

tivates and controls the senses, or to treat it as the agent of a purely spiritual human soul, in order to associate this Stoic doctrine with a Neoplatonizing psychology and metaphysics that stands at antipodes to the monism of the Stoics.

Augustine is well aware of the fact that the Stoics placed mind and matter on a continuum, not only in their analysis of sense perception but also in their treatment of the criterion of knowledge and in their conception of common notions. The fact that all men may possess the same common notions, for the Stoics, in no sense means that common notions are innate ideas or pure intellectual intuitions. Rather, common notions, like all other ideas, are grounded in sense data. The same doctrine of *pneuma* that enables the Stoics to view intromission and extramission as complementary aspects of a unitary phenomenon of sensation allows them to locate certitude both in the empirical evidence gathered by the senses and in its rational judgment by the mind. Augustine refers to all of these points and, indeed, attributes them all to the Stoics. Yet, he never presents them as components of one overall theory. His strategy, rather, is to advert to one or another of them, whether positively or negatively, depending on the needs of his argument. He tends to stress the empirical side of the doctrine positively when he attacks Academic skepticism and negatively when he compares Stoic to Platonic epistemology. On the other hand, when he refers to Stoic epistemology in an ethical context, he is inclined to depict the Stoics approvingly as rationalists.

Augustine's most extended discussion of the criterion of truth is found in his early work, the *Contra academicos*. This dialogue is closely modeled on the *Academica* of Cicero but it shows a good deal of independence and discrimination in assessing the history of Platonism as Cicero gives it and it offers a warmer if more constricted appreciation of the Stoic position.[84] Augustine is much more critical of the skepticism of the New Academy than Cicero is. At the same time, he appears to have relied in the first rescension of the *Academica*, where Lucullus presents the Stoic view of

---

[84] The best treatments are Bernard J. Diggs, "St. Augustine against the Academicians," *Traditio*, 7 (1949–51), 72–93; Testard, *Saint Augustin et Cicéron*, I, 172–73, 233; Frederick Van Fleteren, "The Cassiciacum Dialogues and Augustine's Ascents at Milan," *Mediaevalia*, 4 (1978), 62–64. Alven Michael Neiman, "The Arguments of Augustine's *Contra academicos*," *Modern Schoolman*, 59 (1982), 255–79 criticizes Diggs' interpretation as too Cartesian but does not provide a thorough treatment of Augustine's handling of Stoicism or of Cicero in the work. See, more briefly, Baguette, "Le Stoïcisme," pp. 1–4, 15–17 and Verbeke, "Augustin et le stoïcisme," *RA*, 1 (1958), 68–69, 75–76. On the other hand Hagendahl, *Augustine and the Latin Classics*, I, 60–67; II, 498–510 sees this work as a mechanical rehash of Cicero, while John Hammond Taylor, "St. Augustine and the *Hortensius* of Cicero," *Studies in Philology*, 60 (1963), 497 and TeSelle, *Augustine*, pp. 74, 84 see Augustine as preferring the position of the Old Academy and rejecting Stoicism in the *Contra ac*. On Cicero's *Academica* see *Stoic Tradition*, I, ch. 2, pp. 104–09.

the criterion as strictly empirical, rather than on the second version, in which Varro, the parallel speaker, explains that the Stoics held the criterion to be both empirical and rational. Augustine was not the first Latin Christian writer to invoke Stoicism against Academic skepticism. He is preceded by Lactantius in this connection, although Augustine presents the skeptics' position more broadly, as including probabilism as well as the rejection of any sure criterion of truth. Augustine's handling of the latter argument is consistent with Lactantius' attack on absolute skepticism as a self-refuting claim. In opposition to Cicero Augustine adds that probabilism implies a standard against which the more and the less probable can be measured and that it is an inadequate foundation for ethical action. He also sharpens Cicero's critique of the New Academics as false Platonists who have distorted the real nature of the Platonic tradition by asserting that their skepticism is compatible with Plato's epistemology. In Augustine's view, real Platonism, with its doctrine of the direct rational perception of the intelligibles, might indeed supply a powerful weapon against the Stoa, but it is one that the Academics did not wield. Instead, the skeptics have tried to oppose the possibility of certain knowledge by charging, against the Stoics, that the senses are fallible, a case which he thinks they have failed to make. It is under this heading that he introduces most of the Stoic epistemology that he includes in the *Contra academicos*. And, it is because he sets up the dialogue in this manner that he treats the Stoic criterion as a primarily empirical one in this work.

As Augustine observes, Zeno asserted that truth is impressed on the mind so accurately that the *phantasia*, or sensible image, bears the marks of such certitude as to rule out completely the possibility that it is false.[85] Up to this point, the criterion he attributes to the Stoics is one that any other empirical epistemology would share. But Augustine goes on to support the tenability of Zeno's claim that sense data can be known and grasped with certainty, that they provide true knowledge, and that all knowledge, including the knowledge of common notions, derives from them. Here Augustine invokes the traditional empiricist argument that the senses supply the remedies for their own defects and adds the specifically Stoic point that the intellect judges the sense data it receives, a step that is essential to the grasp of the truth of those data with certitude.[86]

While in the *Contra academicos* Augustine clearly implies the more full-blown Stoic analysis of the stages that move the knower from the recep-

---

[85] *Contra academicos* 2.5.11–12, 2.6.14, ed.W. M. Green, CC, 29 (Turnhout, 1970).
[86] Ibid. 3.9.18–3.11.26.

tion of the *phantasia* to the *synkatathesis*, or judgment of what is known, to the *katalepsis*, or formation of a presentation held with certainty, he reserves his most exhaustive exposition of that doctrine to a later work, the *City of God*, where he takes it up in an ethical context. In surveying the schools of ancient philosophy on the good life and related matters, he compares the Peripatetics and Stoics on the passions. Here he cites at length a passage from the *Noctes atticae* where Aulus Gellius relates the behavior of a Stoic philosopher who pales with fear during a storm at sea and is later asked to account for his conduct by one of his ship-mates.[87] The Stoic explains, making reference to Zeno, Chrysippus, and Epictetus, that his school indeed regards the passion of fear as an irra-tional perturbation of the mind and he agrees that death is a matter of indifference. He himself manifested fear during the storm, he says, not because he judged fear to be reasonable or death to be an evil but be-cause of the time lag between his reception of the *phantasia* reporting the storm and his rational assessment of the attitude which that information should, and later did, inspire in him. While, as we shall see below, Au-gustine supports the Stoic theory of the passions on a very selective ba-sis, he agrees wholeheartedly in the passage just noted that intellectual judgment and assent to the data that the senses supply is needed to as-certain the truth and to govern one's moral responses to that truth. Au-gustine is just as capable of using the Stoics' location of the criterion in the mind against the materialism of the Epicureans[88] as he is of classi-fying the Stoic and Epicurean theory of an empirical criterion or the Stoic belief that common notions are based on sense data as a reason for pre-ferring Platonism to both of those schools.[89] In this connection, as in the decision when and whether to reveal his knowledge of the link between intromission and extramission, Augustine's emphasis in describing the Stoic criterion as either empirical or rational, but not as both at the same time, is a function of his agenda of the moment. The main methodolog-ical distinction that can be observed in his handling of these two sets of Stoic epistemological issues is that he never applies the doctrine of the criterion to the explication or defense of Christian teachings.

B) Rhetoric

The rhetorical theory elaborated by Augustine in the last book of his

---

[87] *Civ. dei* 9.4. A. C. Lloyd, "Emotion and Decision in Stoic Psychology," *The Stoics*, ed. John M. Rist (Berkeley, 1978), p. 237; Rohmer, "L'Intentionnalité," *Augustinus Mag-ister*, I, 491; and TeSelle, *Augustine*, p. 84 have noted Augustine's awareness of the Stoic principle of intellectual judgment but have not cited this text.

[88] *Ep.* 118, to Dioscorus, 410/11.

[89] *Civ. dei* 8.7.

De doctrina christiana draws on a number of Stoic points, some of which he could easily have derived from Quintilian or St. Jerome, and combines them with a largely Ciceronian position which he modifies slightly in the interests of Christian homiletics. Augustine heartily endorses Cicero's anti-sophistic call to unite wisdom with eloquence. He agrees that the speaker's task is to delight and to persuade as well as to teach, a triple enterprise in which the Peripatetic appeal to the ethos of the audience as well as to its intelligence replaces the more strictly intellectualistic Stoic principle of addressing the reason of the audience alone.[90] Augustine's few departures from or alterations of Ciceronian rhetoric can be attributed both to Stoicism and to Christianity. He drops Cicero's idea that the style of a discourse should be adapted to its subject. Since the Christian orator will be preaching the Gospel in all cases, he needs only to bear in mind the condition of his audience, the genre of his address, and the need to variegate his diction so as to avoid boredom.[91] The vital importance of communicating the message of salvation means that clarity and plainness of speech should be placed above all other stylistic considerations, a principle which Augustine sums up in a famous comparison:

> Quid enim prodest clavis aurea, si aperire, quod volumus, non potest, aut quid obest lignea, si hoc potest, quando nihil quaerimus nisi patere, quod clausum est?[92]

> Of what use is a gold key if it will not open what we wish? Or what objection is there to a wooden one which will, when we seek nothing except to open what is closed?

This stress on simplicity over embellishment or rhetorical artifice, however, should not be read as an appeal to the Stoic norms of brevity, the plain style, and the use of *verba antiqua*. Augustine's own writing abounds in antitheses, amplifications, neologisms, and syntactical parallelisms and inversions in a style as remote from Cicero's as it is from the rhetorical canons of the Stoics. Further, his deliberate efforts to inspire compunction and unction in his readers and hearers reflects a decidedly non-Stoic emotionalism. At the same time, Augustine shares the Stoic view that the orator's major qualification is his moral character. Eloquence, he

---

[90] *De doct. christ.* 4.4.6, 4.5.7, 4.7.21, 4.12.27–28, 4.7.34. The Ciceronian parallels are summarized by Testard, *Saint Augustin et Cicéron*, I, 235, although he does not note Augustine's modifications of Cicero.

[91] *De doct. christ.* 4.18.35, 4.19.38, 4.20.39–44, 4.22.51–4.26.58.

[92] Ibid. 4.11.26, CC, 32, pp. 134–35; trans. D. W. Robertson (Indianapolis, 1958), p. 136.

agrees, is not merely a function of the speaker's technique but is an expression of his virtue as well. What is involved here goes beyond the speaker's good intention to edify his hearers and to draw them to the good.[93] The preacher also teaches by his own moral example, which, on balance, is his greatest pedagogical asset. And so, reformulating the Stoic principle of the *vir bonus dicendique peritus*, Augustine states: *Habet autem ut obedienter audiamus, quantacumque granditate dictionis maius pondus vita dicentis* ("The life of the speaker has greater weight in determining whether he is obediently heard than any grandness of eloquence.")[94] Finally, and by no means least, the preacher must also acknowledge that it is not either his wisdom, his eloquence, or his virtue that causes his hearers to learn, but the grace of God working through his words.[95] We may say, then, that there are trace elements of Stoic rhetoric that tincture Augustine's Ciceronianism in the *De doctrina christiana* but that there are even more noticeable elements of Christian theology that condition his Ciceronianism and his Stoicism alike.

C) *Language and Logic*

Logic and linguistic theory are branches of the Stoic system whose basic principles were well known to Augustine. He has a firm understanding of the Stoic distinction between words, as corporeal sonic forms and as natural signs of their significata, and *lekta*, as the incorporeal and purely intramental meanings out of which logical propositions are made. He is also well aware of the Stoic treatment of logic as a formal art, in which the validity of propositions derives from their structure and from the internal cogency of the inferences that may be made on that basis. Augustine is also familiar with the Stoic hypothetical syllogisms and appreciates the fact that their form expresses this particular approach to logic, since they are structurally designed to display logical relationships rather than what may be possible or actual in the world outside the mind. Not only does Augustine know these principles, he assents to them consistently after having expounded most of them in his early work, the *De dialectica*, where he indicates their Stoic origins.[96] He also explores and

---

[93] Ibid. 2.7.9–11.
[94] Ibid. 4.27.59, CC, 32, p. 163; trans. Robertson, p. 164. For more on this topic see 4.27.60–4.29.62.
[95] Ibid. 4.16.33.
[96] On the *De dialectica* see *Stoic Tradition*, I, ch. 5, pp. 329–30. To the literature cited there may be added Robert H. Ayers, *Language, Logic, and Reason in the Church Fathers: A Study of Tertullian, Augustine, and Aquinas* (Hildesheim, 1979), pp. 69–74; Baguette, "Le Stoïcisme," pp. 22–24; Karl Barwick, "Elementos estoicos en san Agustín: Huellas varronianas en el *De dialectica* de Agustín," *Augustinus*, 18 (1973), 101–30; "Probleme der

applies Stoic logic and linguistic theory frequently throughout his career, with both fidelity and originality, in a wide range of contexts that
run all the way from logic and semantics proper to exegesis, to polemics,
and to ethical and dogmatic theology. To the extent that he sees any
problems in the teachings of the Stoa on logic and linguistics he resolves
them by appealing to some other aspect of that same theory.

The fundamental distinction between the word as sonic form and natural sign and the *lekton* as an intramental intention, to which Augustine
attaches the respective terms *verbum* and *dicibile* in the *De dialectica*, he
repeats with great clarity in the *De quantitate animae*:

> Cum ergo nomen ipsum sono et significatio constet, sonus autem ad aures,
> significatio ad mentem pertineat.[97]

> Now a noun is made up of its sound and its meaning. The sound pertains
> to the ears and the meaning to the mind.

He expands on the implications of both the linguistic and logical sides
of this distinction, his emphasis conditioned by the agenda before him
in a given work. In the *De quantitate animae* itself Augustine makes this
point as a way of exploring the distinction between the body and the soul
and the superiority of the latter to the former. A similar concern inspires
some of his other applications of Stoic semantics. He restates the Stoic
definition of articulate human speech as contrasted with the inarticulate
cries of animals and men, regarding speech as a physical phenomenon,
the impulses of sound that strike the air between the source of sound and
the ear, in the Varronian formula transmitted more or less faithfully by
the Latin grammarians. He may alter the vocabulary he uses to express
the terms involved depending on the context. In a sermon on the birth
of St. John the Baptist Augustine notes that while both an inarticulate
cry (*vox*) and a word (*verbum*) are composed of sounds that strike the air,
verba alone are signs that convey an intelligible message. The reason for
the terminology he chooses here is his wish to analogize John to the *vox*
and to reserve for Christ the *verbum* as God's incarnate revelation.[98]

There are other kinds of messages that are spiritual or inaudible but

---

stoischen Sprachlehre und Rhetorik," *Abhandlungen der sächsischen Akademie der Wissenschaft
zu Leipzig*, philologisch-historische Klasse, 49:3 (Berlin, 1957), pp. 8–28; Jean Collart,
"Saint Augustin grammarien dans le *De magistro*," *REAug*, 17 (1971), 290; Duchrow,
Sprachverständnis, pp. 42–62; Alain LeBoulluec, "L'allégorie chez les Stoïciens," *Poétique*,
23 (1975), 302; Jean Pépin, *Saint Augustin et le dialectique* (Villanova, 1976), pp. 21–60,
72–98; Raffaele Simone, "Semiologia agostiniana," *La Cultura*, 7 (1969), 89, 95–96, 99;
Svoboda, *L'Esthétique*, pp. 57–59.

[97] *De quant. an.* 32.66, OSA, sér. 1:5, p. 366.
[98] *Sermo* 288.3–4.

which are described metaphorically as "speech" and analyzed in a similar way. Augustine does so more than once in an exegetical context. In comparing the cry of the soul mentioned by the Psalmist with ordinary human speech, he notes that *id est, non corporis voce, quae cum strepitu verberati aëris promitur, sed voce cordis* ("it is not the corporeal voice, which goes forth as a sound reverberating in the air, but the voice of the heart.")[99] Much more difficult to explain in terms of the Stoic conception of language is the literal sense in which God can be said to speak in Holy Scripture. Problems of this sort occur particularly in the expositions of Genesis in which Augustine tries to explain the literal meaning of the imperative sentences through which God is shown creating the world. He assents to the view that language consisting of sonic forms striking the air sequentially between a speaker's vocal cords and a hearer's ear cannot apply literally to God, Who is neither a physical nor a temporal being. Augustine is forced to admit that the Scriptural reports of God's creative commands must be understood in a spiritual sense. Trying to salvage what he can in this retreat from a literal exegesis, he adds that the creation account in Genesis has been given in this form to show the temporal and corporeal character, not of God, but of the created order and of the human beings to whom the Biblical revelation is addressed.[100]

Both the exegetical imperative and the ascendancy of the spirit over the body visible in some of the foregoing examples contribute to the more elaborate semantic theory developed by Augustine in his *De magistro* and *De doctrina christiana*, whose debts to Stoicism are no less clear. Although Augustine stresses the purely instrumental role of verbal signs as conveying knowledge to a learner in the first instance in relation to the action of the Interior Teacher in the learner's mind, he nonetheless outlines a linguistic theory in the *De magistro* which reflects the Stoic view of words as material, sensible reverberations of the air that are natural signs of their objects, whether those objects are physical phenomena, abstract ideas, or other words.[101] Nouns and verbs are easy to account

[99] *Enarrationes in Psalmos* 3.4, ed. D. Eligius Dekkers and Ioannes Fraipont, CC, 38–40 (Turnhout, 1956), 38, p. 8.

[100] *De gen. ad litt.* 1.9.16–17, 1.9.19–20, 2.6.12–14.

[101] *De mag.* 1.2–2.3, 4.7–5.16. Scholars who have noted the influence of Stoic semantics in the *De mag.* include G. Bardy, in the notes to the trans. by F.-J. Thonnard, OSA, sér. 1:6 (Paris, 1952), pp. 482–83; Collart, "Saint Augustin grammarien," *REAug*, 17 (1971), 290–91; Duchrow, *Sprachverständnis*, pp. 71–73; Louis G. Kelly, "Saint Augustine and Saussurean Linguistics," *AS*, 6 (1975), 50; Cornelius Petrus Mayer, *Die Zeichen in der geistigen Entwicklung und in der Theologie des jungen Augustins* (Würzburg, 1969), pp. 234–47; *Die Zeichen in der geistigen Entwicklung und in der Theologie Augustins: Die antimanichäische Epoche* (Würzburg, 1974), pp. 234–35, although his interpretation is overly Platonic; Alfred Schindler, *Wort und Analogie in Augustins Trinitätslehre* (Tübingen, 1965), pp. 77–81; Michael Schmaus, *Die psychologosche Trinitätslehre des hl. Augustinus* (Münster i. W.,

for here, but Augustine faces greater difficulties in explaining how parts of speech such as prepositions and conjunctions can signify, given the fact that they have no objective referents and no meanings outside of the syntactical relationships which they designate in particular propositions. In dealing with this problem he notes that such words have a significance that is grammatically cogent and understood by all in connection with the rules of that discipline. Further, even words such as *si*, *ex* or *de* can be treated as nouns when they function as the subjects of sentences.[102] A much tougher nut to crack is the question of how and what the word *nihil* signifies. *Nihil* is, to be sure, a noun, but the significatum it names is non-existent as such. Augustine makes and happy, the influential, choice of invoking the doctrine of *lekta*, or words that have a purely intramental meaning, in resolving the difficulty posed by words like *nihil* within the framework of a Stoic linguistics which regards words as natural signs.[103] Words, he concludes, may signify both real things and inner intentionalities that have no objective correspondences, a double possibility which Stoic semantics makes available.

In the *De doctrina christiana* Augustine continues to view verbal signs as playing an instrumental role in the acquisition of religious knowledge although the exegetical and homiletic burden of this work inclines him to emphasize their powers more strongly than he does in the *De magistro*. He develops further the sign theory of the *De magistro*, departing terminologically if not materially from the views on this subject articulated by the Stoics and by Augustine in some of his earlier works.[104] All signs, he states, point to something else. They may be subdivided into natural signs (*signa naturalia*) and conventional signs (*signa data*). In understanding Augustine's vocabulary here it is important to note that he regards both classes of signs as natural in the original Stoic sense. The Stoics had entered the ancient debates on whether words are natural or conventional

---

1927), p. 339 n. 4; Simone, "Semiologia agostiniana," *La Cultura*, 7 (1969), 89, 95 n. 10, 106–09. Recent summaries of this work which do not discuss Augustine's sources include Luigi Alici, *Il linguaggio come segno e come testimonianza: Una rilettura di Agostino* (Roma, 1976), ch. 1; Goulven Madec, "Analyse du *De magistro*," *REAug*, 21 (1975), 63–71; Nash, *The Light of the Mind*, pp. 84–93.

[102] *De mag.* 2.3–4. Mary Sirridge, "Augustine: Every Word Is a Name," *NS*, 50 (1976), 183–92 argues that Augustine here is forecasting a definition of syncategorematic terms. But Simone, "Semiologia agostiniana," pp. 108–09 rightly notes that he is discussing parts of speech here in a functional, not a metalinguistic sense.

[103] *De mag.* 2.3–4, 7.19.

[104] *De doct. christ.* 1.2.2, 2.1.1–2.3.4–5. The Stoic influence in this work has been noted by Duchrow, *Sprachverständnis*, pp. 153–59; Jackson, "Theory of Signs," *Augustine*, pp. 92–147; Mayer, *Die Zeichen*, II, 95–104, 302–34, again reading the material Platonically; Schindler, *Wort und Analogie*, pp. 81–86; Simone "Semiologia agostiniana," pp. 99–102. Summaries without discussions of the Stoic sources include Alici, *Il linguaggio*, ch. 1 and R. A. Markus, "St. Augustine on Signs," *Phronesis*, 2 (1957), 60–83.

signs and had come down squarely on the side of natural signification. However, like the other ancient philosophers who had contested this point, they focused on the way that words acquire their denotations. On the other hand, Augustine draws his distinction between *signa naturalia* and *signa data* in the light of their intentional or unintentional character as signs. As he describes them, natural signs are automatic or unintentional, in the way that smoke signifies fire or a man's facial expression signifies his feelings. These signs, like the Stoics' verbal signs, are sensible in themselves and they refer to physical or psychological realities. But they do so involuntarily. For Augustine, conventional signs are also physical and they likewise correspond truly with the things they signify. But, unlike automatic natural signs, conventional signs are used deliberately by animate or intelligent beings to express their ideas, intentions, and feelings to other beings. Like natural signs, Augustine's conventional signs may be non-verbal. But he concentrates on verbal signs because his goal in the *De doctrina christiana* is to teach hermeneutics and preaching. Both the authors of the Bible and the pastor in the pulpit convey their messages through words. In the context of the more general semantic theory developed in the *De doctrina christiana*, the words in the Biblical text or the preacher's sermon are conventional signs, in Augustine's sense, in that they are deliberate human statements designed to impart religious knowledge to men. Whether these statements are literal or metaphorical, they are natural, in the strict Stoic sense that they are physical phenomena which accurately represent the realities they signify.

There are a number of logical and linguistic issues touched on briefly in the *De magistro* or *De doctrina christiana* which Augustine discusses in much greater detail elsewhere. One is the vexing question of how negative or privative term signify within a semantic theory that treats words as natural signs of real significata. Already noted with regard to *nihil* in the *De magistro*, this problem is one he addresses most typically in contexts that are exegetical, or anti-Manichean, or both. In his frequent anti-Manichean analyses of the creation story in Genesis Augustine attacks the claim that there is a metaphysical power responsible for the creation of evil, whose activities are denoted by the void (*inanitas*) over which the spirit of the deity hovered, by the creation of negative entities such as darkness (*tenebrae*), or by the very existence of the nothingness (*nihil*) out of which all sub-divine beings were created. In tackling this assignment Augustine repeatedly insists that negative terms such as *tenebrae*, *nihil*, or *inanitas* do not signify actual species of any kind, created by God or by any other power. The Creator creates species, not their absence. The terms at issue denote the absence of species, not the presence of some kind of negative species. Nor can such absences be regarded, necessarily, as evils. Here Augustine compares the terms denoting physical and metaphysical privation in Genesis with musical rests and with the shadows or blank spaces in pictorial art, which contribute to the overall composition, which are necessary to the aesthetic comprehension of music and painting, and which thus add to the beauty and order of the whole. Aside from this aesthetic argument, which parallels Augustine's strategy for rationalizing the existence of ugly or harmful creatures in the theodicy arguments against the Manichees which he places in the same works, he accuses the Manichees themselves of playing word games that ignore the capacity of words to signify intentions as well as natural phenomena. When Scripture speaks of *inanitas* or *nihil*, or when it mentions *tenebrae* in the same breath as *lux*, he concludes, *nihil, inanitas,* and *tenebrae* do not denote real things but are used as perfectly comprehensible grammatical negatives of their opposites.[105] In this context, then, Augustine employs the doctrine of *lekta* as a weapon against both the metaphysics and the alleged lexicographical reductionism of the Manichees.

The idea that words, and especially logical propositions, may have a purely intentional and intramental significance is a point on which Augustine enlarges in his repeated applications of the Stoic hypothetical syllogisms to epistemological and theological issues. He uses both the conditional ("if-then") and the disjunctive ("either-or") forms for these purposes. Augustine is well aware of the rhetorical capacities of this type of argument as well as its more strictly logical force. One of his most interesting hypothetical arguments, involving both the conditional and the disjunctive, is found in his *Contra academicos*, where it serves to undermine the skeptics' claim that truth can never be known with certainty. At two points in the dialogue Augustine shifts the debate from the certitude man may have of events *in rerum natura* to truth as a condition attaching to logical propositions in the light of their structure. If the antecedent of the syllogism "If the senses are deceptive, then they still convey a knowledge that the world exists" is true, then the consequent is logically tenable and enables us to state a positive fact that we know. Similarly, we can confirm with certitude one part of an "either-or" syl-

---

[105] Augustine's fullest treatments are in *De genesi ad litteram imperfectus liber* 5.25–6.26, *PL*, 34, cols. 229–231 and *De gen. contra Man.* 1.4.7, 1.9.15, *PL*, 34, cols. 176–177, 180. See also *Conf.* 10.12.19, 12.3.3; *De natura boni* 25.25, 2nd ed., ed. and trans. B. Roland-Gosselin, OSA, sér. 1:1 (Paris, 1949), pp. 464–66. For more on Augustine's analysis of negative, privative, and relative terms see Marcia L. Colish, "Carolingian Debates over *Nihil* and *Tenebrae*: A Study in Theological Method," *Speculum*, 59 (1984), 769–76. For more on Augustine's analysis of musical rests, in a non-polemical context, see *De musica* 3.7.16–3.8.19, 4.1.1–4.2.3, 4.7.8, 4.10.11–4.15.29 and Colish, "St. Augustine's Rhetoric of Silence," *AS*, 9 (1978), 21–24.

logism when the other part is negated.[106] In these examples Augustine shows his awareness of the principle that the verification of the propositions making up these syllogisms inheres in the formal structure of the syllogisms rather than in their content. He makes the argument that he makes here in order to wrest from the skeptics the assent to the notion that, at least on the level of logical inference, there exists such a thing as certitude or truth. His strategy, indeed, is diametrically opposed to that of the Old Academic interlocutor in Cicero's *Academica* who advances arguments based on Stoic hypotheticals in order to show their defects as indices of any necessary truths about the extra-mental world, as if to say that nothing can be proved, not even in the field of logic. For his part, on the other hand, Augustine draws the conclusion that the hypotheticals demonstrate the capacity of the mind to verify logical propositions, a position that bolsters the arguments he makes elsewhere in the *Contra academicos* for the certitude about the natural world available through sense data, according to Zeno.

Augustine gives several other examples of how hypothetical syllogisms can be used in debates on theological matters. Passages of this sort are found both in the *De diversis quaestionibus* and the *De doctrina christiana*, which illustrate both the utility of this technique as a rhetorical strategy and Augustine's understanding of its limitations as a means of establishing objective theological truth. The two selections from the *De diversis quaestionibus* have a vaguely anti-Manichean coloration. Augustine applies the conditional syllogism to the proof that Christ's body was not an illusion and to the disproof of the power of chance, by means of the following formulae: "If Christ's body was an illusion, then He was a deceiver. If He was a deceiver, then He was not the Truth;"[107] and "If anything happens by chance, then providence does not govern the whole world."[108] In these passages Augustine does not comment on the relationship between the logical verifiability of the consequences of the syllogisms and the metaphysical or theological truth of the statements that comprise them, but he does address that question specifically in the *De doctrina christiana*. He takes it up in the section of the work where he discusses the utility of logic as a discipline of the liberal arts in the work of the exegete. Here he states clearly that the force of a conditional syllogism lies in its structure, not in the content of its propositions. When the consequent is true or false, so is the antecedent true or false, truth and

---

[106] *Contra ac.* 3.11.24, 3.13.29. Noted by Baguette, "Le Stoïcisme," pp. 4–5; Jackson, "Theory of Signs," *Augustine*, pp. 121–22; TeSelle, *Augustine*, p. 86; Verbeke, "Augustin et le stoïcisme," *RA*, 1 (1958), 77–78.

[107] *De div. quaest.* 14.

[108] Ibid. 24.

falsity being formal attributes of the propositions. Augustine acknowledges quite plainly that it is possible to formulate a conditional syllogism with premises that are factually incorrect which will nonetheless lead to a logically valid conclusion. He sums up this point by observing: *Quapropter aliud est nosse regulas conexionum, aliud sententiarum veritatem* ("In this way it is one thing to know the rules of valid inference, another to know the truth of propositions,")[109] *veritas* in this passage referring to the objective truth. He concludes that the art of logic is neutral in itself and that it should be employed in the service of truth.

Another weapon from the armory of Stoic logic and one that Augustine always wields polemically is the principle that a proposition will be negated more exhaustively when a negative term, such as *non*, is placed before the entire proposition than when it is placed before the verb. Like Jerome, he uses this idea mainly to attack the claim that man can attain sinlessness in this life, which he attributes to the Pelagians. Augustine takes this Stoic notion farther than Jerome does but not as far as some later theologians took it. Jerome had contrasted the *posse peccare* that man retains in this life with the *posse non peccare* of God, a formula which, in terms of Stoic logic, would attribute to God a capacity to sin as well as not to sin which Jerome actually holds that the deity does not have. Augustine agrees that man in this life retains both the *posse peccare* and the *posse non peccare*. One contrast he draws is between men, who possess free will, and the subhuman creatures that lack it. The formula *non posse peccare* can be attached to subhuman beings because they, by nature, having no free will, are incapable both of vice and virtue. A second contrast he draws is between the *posse peccare* and *posse non peccare* of men in this life and the *non posse peccare* of the blessed in heaven. Men in both states possess free will, Augustine notes, but the saints possess a free will renewed by grace and a consequent freedom from temptation; they now desire only the good.[110] While Augustine's handling of this topic enlarges it substantially in comparison with Jerome's, neither thinker is alert to the supreme appositeness of the *non posse peccare* formula to the supreme being, Whose eternal incapacity to sin is itself one of His perfections. Augustine instead treats this formula as an index of an infrarational nature or of a human nature that at one time did possess the capacity to sin but which has lost that defect thanks to the final victory over sin by grace.

Another polemical context in which the logical force of negative terms is given extended play is in connection with Augustine's critique of Ar-

[109] *De doct. christ.* 2.34.52, CC, 32, p. 68; trans. Robertson, p. 70. For the whole passage see 2.32.50–2.34.54. Noted by Jackson, "Theory of Signs," pp. 125–26.

[110] *Contra Faustum* 22.28, CSEL, 25, p. 632; *Civ. dei* 22.30.3, CC, 48, pp. 863–64.

ian Christology and of the arguments which current Arians were evidently using to defend their position. Among other things, Augustine's rebuttal is suggestive of the adaptability of the Arians as debaters and the flexibility with which they had shifted their strategy since the Nicene era and the days of Marius Victorinus. According to Augustine, the Arians claim that the terms *pater* and *filius*, which signify a relationship, do apply properly to God, while the terms *genitus* and *ingenitus*, which signify absolute states, do not. They have also attempted to substitute the term *non genitus* for *ingenitus* in order to underscore the idea that the whole conception of begottenness or begetting, as absolute states, is inappropriate to the deity. Augustine attacks this position on two levels, using the principle that words can signify intramental intentions as well as the Stoic understanding of the force of different kinds of negative words. He argues that it is ridiculous to say that *pater* and *filius* denote something different from *ingenitus* and *genitus* notwithstanding their differences in grammatical form. Begottenness means the same thing as sonship whether or not these terms are grammatically parallel. In developing this point Augustine notes that there may be terms, such as *invicinus*, which are not in use, but which are grammatically isomorphic with other terms, such as *inimicus*, which are in use. The relations signified by these terms are directly analogous and perfectly comprehensible despite the accident of usage which makes one of them grammatically acceptable and the other a barbarism. Next, he tackles the Arians' substitution of *non genitus* for *ingenitus*, which, he charges, is a ploy invoking the superior negating power of *non* designed to distract attention from the fact that the two terms denote exactly the same thing. Whether we use the term *ingenitus* or *non genitus* or *pater* to describe God the Father, it means the same thing as fatherhood as a relationship. In no sense do the terms *ingenitus* and *non genitus* deny the possibility or propriety of attributing begottenness to a divine Person; they merely indicate that this concept does not apply to God the Father. In this way, Augustine stresses the idea that theological truths cannot be circumscribed by logical or grammatical conventions, under the heading of the distinction between words as natural signs and words as *lekta* expressing meanings. The agenda of the moment explains the primacy he gives to the second element in this Stoic doctrine as a means of undermining the Arians' logical and grammatical reductionism.[111]

The clear sense of the Stoic distinction between speech as a corporeal natural sign and *lekta* as immaterial intramental intentions that undergirds the foregoing applications of verbal and logical arguments in Au-

---

[111] *De trin.* 5.7.8, CC, 50, pp. 214–15. Colish, "Carolingian Debates," pp. 769–76.

gustine's *œuvre* also provides the foundation for two more substantive and sustained positions which he developed across his career, his analysis of lying as both a semantic and an ethical phenomenon and his use of the theme of the inner and outer word as a means of conceptualizing the relations between the Father and the Son. The first of these topics shows considerable originality on Augustine's part. It is true that a number of classical Latin writers from Nigidius Figulus onward had raised the question of how it was possible to tell lies and falsehoods in a semantic system that regarded words as natural and accurate signs of their significata. Some classical authors also observed that the doctrine of *lekta* made it possible to explain how two different speakers could mean different things by the same words.[112] But it was Augustine who first pulled these Stoic themes together to produce a theory of lies and false statements that is, at the same time, a creative extension of Stoic linguistics and an instrument flexible enough to be useful to him for a number of different purposes.

Augustine's first essay on lying appears in his early work, the *De magistro*, where he distinguishes between a lie and a falsehood on the basis of the capacity of words to signify both real things and inner intentions. In this case it is the intentionality of the speaker which he accents. A lie is a lie because of the speaker's evil intention to mislead or deceive. Telling the truth requires a correct ethical intention. The truthful speaker must be in a state of good conscience.[113] But, Augustine notes, one may be in a state of good conscience and still be in a state of error or ignorance. In this situation one tells a falsehood but not a lie. Lying statements, he says, may or may not be objectively false, for it is the speaker's intention that is the criterion of the lie. A speaker who makes a mistake in good conscience tells a falsehood. A speaker who intends to tell a lie is in fact a liar even when what he says is objectively accurate. If the statements of liars are objectively untrue as well, then the speakers are *mentientes atque fallentes*.

In addition to reducing lies entirely to bad faith in the *De magistro*, Augustine raises and answers a series of related questions. Do people who do not say what they mean invariably tell lies? He mentions four cases of this sort which he does not think can be called lying. First, there is the familiar pedagogical situation in which a teacher expounds a particular doctrine to his students, a doctrine which he personally does not espouse. His discourse signifies its referent truly insofar as he reports the doctrine at issue correctly, even though it does not express his own con-

---

[112] See *Stoic Tradition*, I, ch. 5, pp. 324–25, 328, 339.
[113] *De mag.* 12.39 and 13.41–43 for this whole topic.

victions. Also, if the doctrine happens to be erroneous as well, his words do not correspond with objective reality either. Still, Augustine points out, one can say that the speaker's words express his intentions, since his intention as a teacher is to convey the views he reports to his students. In the other three cases the statements of the speaker may be wrong but the error is unintentional, since the speakers are not seeking to deceive their hearers. Thus, their statements cannot be called lies, whether or not they signify external reality. One may, for instance, repeat something by rote that one has previously memorized, mouthing the words without paying attention to them. One may inadvertantly commit a *lapsus linguae.* Or, one may commit a barbarism or a solecism. In these three cases absence of mind, sheer accident, or ignorance are involved. But no lie has been told although a falsehood may have been uttered if the statement is objectively untrue. The most original feature of Augustine's theory of lying in the *De magistro,* which well accords with his desire in that work to emphasize the semantic limits of speech, is his preclusive focus on ethical intentionality as the essence of the lie. In so doing he can retain the Stoic belief in the natural significance of words while stressing more heavily the intentionalities of speakers within the same Stoic outlook.

Augustine develops an alternative solution to the same problem in the *De doctrina christiana* which, while clearly dependent on the *De magistro* and other works where he treats logic and semantics, provides a different definition of lying. As we have already seen, the exegetical and homiletic focus of this work leads Augustine to place greater weight on the communicative power of words here than in the *De magistro* and inclines him to expatiate on the formal character of logical predications, whose truth claims lie in their logical verifiability whether or not their terms refer to extramental realities that are objectively possible or true. The fact that he is dealing with the understanding and expression of the truth revealed in Scripture in the *De doctrina christiana* also affects Augustine's reformulation of the question of lying. As before, he now defines falsehood as objective error in the absence of bad faith, familiar examples of which are the pagan myths told in poetic fictions. However, he now attaches three conditions to lying statements: they must combine objective untruth, the intention to deceive, and a misguided sense of what is to be loved and hoped for.[114] Lying, here, involves much more than the speaker's wrong moral attitude toward the hearer. It also involves his wrong moral attitude toward the truth. In particular, Augustine invokes this theory to show that Biblical authors neither lie nor contradict them-

---

[114] *De doct. christ.* 1.36.40, 1.40.44, 2.35.53.

selves or each other. Texts in which such things appear to happen can be understood aright by reading them in their literary and theological contexts or by applying typological analysis to them.[115] Augustine also wants to show that the misconstruction of a Biblical text on the part of an exegete may be a mistake but that it is not a lie so long as the error is an unwitting one. The exegete, he stresses, must recognize that words signify the saving message only partially. But, the association of human words with Christ's incarnation endows them with a God-given power to signify the supreme truth and goodness and to move mankind toward them. The failure of an exegete and preacher to conceive of words in this way and to use them for this purpose, or lying, reflects a defective love of self and neighbor, which impels the liar to denature the significative capacities of language so that it is deprived of the role that God has assigned it in the economy of His redemption.

Augustine also devotes two entire treatises to the topic of lying, his *De mendacio* of 395 and *Contra mendacium* of ca. 420. Aside from sharing the same express agenda and the same semantic assumptions derived from Stoicism they share a concern with the interpretation of Scripture, although in a polemical vein. The particular concerns of each of these works incline Augustine to draw more heavily on the *De magistro* definition of lying in the *De mendacio* and on the *De doctrina christiana* definition in the *Contra mendacium*. The *De mendacio* arose from a debate between Augustine and Jerome over the interpretation of the Epistle to the Galatians. Augustine also states his position on that subject in his own treatise on Galatians and in an exchange of letters with Jerome not entirely free from asperity on both sides. In Augustine's view, if Jerome's interpretation prevailed, it would be necessary to admit that Sts. Peter and Paul had told lies or practiced deception, a possibility which he flatly dismisses for a Biblical author both here and in the *De doctrina christiana*, which he was composing at about the same time. In elaborating his opposition to the idea that a Biblical author would lie, Augustine broadens his analysis of lying to include a rejection of the well-intentioned lie in particular and of lying as such in general. He thus returns to the definition of a lie as residing exclusively in the speaker's deceptive intention, eliminating the criterion of objective untruth:

> Ex animi enim sui sententia, non ex rerum ipsarum veritate vel falsitate mentiens aut non mentiens iudicandus est . . . Culpa vero mentientis est in enuntiendo animo suo fallendi cupiditas.[116]

---

[115] Ibid. 3 passim.

[116] *De mendacio* 3.3, ed. Iosephus Zycha, CSEL, 41 (Vienna, 1900), p. 415; trans. Mary Sarah Muldowney, FC, 16 (New York, 1952), p. 55. See also 2.2. For literature on the *De mendac.* see Colish, "St. Augustine's Rhetoric of Silence," *AS*, 9 (1978), 16–20, to which may be added Duchrow, *Sprachverständnis*, pp. 129–34.

For a person is to be judged as lying or as not lying according to the intention of his own mind, not according to the truth or falsity of the matter itself. . . . In reality, the fault of the person who tells a lie consists in his desire to deceive in expressing his thoughts.

Having reasserted this principle, Augustine then sets two tasks for himself in the *De mendacio*: first, the distinction of lies from falsehoods and second, the classification and criticism of every kind of lie that can be told.

Properly speaking, he begins, to lie (*mentire*) is distinguishable from telling a jocose lie (*iocis mendacia*),[117] from a mixture of fact and fiction,[118] and from falsehood (*falsum dicere*).[119] A speaker uses a jocose lie or a mixture of fact and fiction to amuse others. Both he and his audience are aware of this fact; hence, no deception occurs. In addition to adding this category of statements to his analysis, Augustine also changes his definition of falsehood. Elsewhere he regards a falsehood as a statement that is objectively false but voiced without a deceptive intention. But in the *De mendacio* he seeks to eliminate the criterion of objective untruth from the falsehood, just as he does from the lie. In a falsehood, says Augustine, the speaker believes that his statement is true. It may in fact be true or not. But, even if it is objectively false, he speaks in good faith. The liar's statement may also be objectively true or not. But, even if it is objectively true, he lies because he says the opposite of what he thinks, with the intent to deceive. If a true statement can be a lie, given the speaker's evil intention, an untrue statement can be a lie even if it springs from the speaker's wish to do good to the hearer, insofar as the speaker seeks to promote the hearer's well-being through deceit. A lie, as a deliberate deception, remains a lie regardless of the reason why the liar tells it, reasons which may be good or bad, and regardless of whether the lie expresses the objective truth or not.[120]

Having defined lying as a deceitful intention, irrespective of the ends that lies may serve and their correspondence with objective reality, Augustine now proceeds to specify eight kinds of lies and to grade them in order of their ethical seriousness. Their gravity is assessed in terms of the provocations which inspire them. Although Augustine clearly sees some provocations, and some lies, as more or less weighty, he insists throughout this analysis that there are no circumstances under which a lie is ever morally permissible.[121] The most reprehensible kind of lie is

---

[117] *De mendac.* 2.2.
[118] Ibid. 11.18.
[119] Ibid. 3.3.
[120] Ibid. 4.4.
[121] Ibid. 5.5–21.42. For the schema of the eight types of lies see the summaries at 14.25 and 21.42.

the lie uttered in the teaching of religion. Such a lie is inconceivable in the case of Biblical authorities—the brunt of his controversy with Jerome over Galatians. Next come lies that injure someone unjustly and that benefit one person at the expense of another. The fourth kind of lie, while not the worst kind, is nonetheless a quintessential expression of this sin, for it is the lie told as an end in itself, out of the sheer joy of lying, which is vicious *per se*. Then comes the lie told to please others. The sixth type of lie, which harms no one and benefits someone, has its own special interest in the history of the Stoic tradition because it evokes a Stoicizing passage in Horace. A needy man who steals but one measure of grain from the countless thousands belonging to a rich man is still guilty of theft, says Augustine, for his guilt is a function of his evil intention regardless of how much he actually injures his victim.[122] Seventh comes the lie which harms no one and which saves someone from harm. Last is the lie which harms no one and which wards off a violent sexual attack. While this provocation is the most acute one that Augustine can imagine, he concludes by restating the point that the ends never justify the means. With this elaborate analysis of lying he brings to a close a treatise that expands considerably on a question stemming from a narrow exegetical debate and one that presupposes both the Stoic theory of *lekta* and of natural verbal signification and coordinates with them the theme of the primacy of ethical intentionality.

The polemical issue that inspired Augustine to write the *Contra mendacium* was the Priscillianist heresy, a matter far more serious than the interpretation of Galatians. This heresy had arisen in Spain in the 370s and was still flourishing in the second decade of the fifth century despite its condemnation by the Council of Toledo in 400. Heresy in general was Augustine's *bête noire* and the Priscillianists were particularly alarming because they appeared to be perpetuating or reviving Manichean views against which he had battled earlier in his career and which he earnestly hoped he had vanquished.[123] The particular feature of the Priscillianist controversy which Augustine attacks in the *Contra mendacium* is not any of the substantive doctrines of the sect but the heretics' defense of lying in order to conceal their views from strangers, as well as the practice of certain Spanish Catholics who dissembled their own faith in the effort to penetrate the Priscillianists' cell groups and win them back to orthodoxy. In dealing with both kinds of lying Augustine repeats many of the points he had already made in the *De mendacio* and elsewhere, distinguishing between falsehoods and lies on the grounds of the speaker's in-

---

[122] Ibid. 12.19. Cf. Horace, *Epistula* 1.16.55–66.
[123] The fullest background on this movement is provided by Henry Chadwick, *Priscillian of Avila: The Occult and the Charismatic in the Early Church* (Oxford, 1976).

tention. In this connection he notes that a heretic is not a liar insofar as he believes that his faith is true and he does not seek to conceal it. It is thus not Priscillianist beliefs that make the Priscillianists liars but the fact that they dissimulate their real convictions.[124] He also condemns lies of all kinds after arranging them in a hierarchy that places lies falsifying the faith at the top of the list.[125] He adds to his theoretical reasons for objecting to lying a practical one, observing that, if a Priscillianist discovers that a Catholic has been lying to him, his trust will be shattered and he will flee from the truths of faith toward which the Catholic seeks to lead him.[126]

Augustine devotes considerable attention in the *Contra mendacium* to Scriptural exegesis, owing to the fact that the Priscillianists sought a Biblical warrant for their justification of lying. But his main shift in emphasis, which inspires him to revert to the definition of lying in the *De doctrina christiana*, stems from the fact that the truths of the faith and the conversion of heretics are at stake. In defining a lie, he therefore places more stress on its objective untruth and on its effects on its audience than he does in the *De mendacio* or the *De magistro*. For Augustine, the Catholic who lies about his faith is a worse sinner than the heretic. The heretic sins unknowingly (*contra scientiam*), the Catholic knowingly (*contra conscientiam*); despite the Catholic's good intention of saving the heretic's soul his words are false both objectively and subjectively. Further, in sinking to the Priscillianists' own level by lying, the Catholic loses any moral advantage he otherwise might have had. The Priscillianist's beliefs are falsehoods and in masking them he lies; the Catholic's beliefs are true and in denying them he lies three times over, sinning against what is, against what he believes, and against the heretic whom he tries to deceive. Lying, Augustine thus concludes, is intrinsically immoral, particularly the lying of the Catholic in this case.[127] The most original feature of the *Contra mendacium* is Augustine's attachment of a functional analysis of the inexpediency of lying as a pious fraud to the theoretical analysis of lying that derives both from his own ethical outlook and from his absorption of Stoic semantics and logic. And, as with the *De doctrina christiana* before it, his agenda in the *Contra mendacium* inclines him to balance the emphasis he gives to truth as a natural characteristic of verbal signs and as a subjective state manifesting a speaker's inner intention.

While Augustine's major expositions of lying are found in the four works just discussed, he makes references to this topic that call upon the

---

[124] *Contra mendacium* 3.4, 5.8, ed. Iosephus Zycha, CSEL, 41 (Vienna, 1900).
[125] Ibid. 3.4, 7.18–9.22.
[126] Ibid. 4.7.
[127] Ibid. 3.4–7.17, 10.23.

same Stoic assumptions in other settings, some addressed to exegetical issues, some to dogmatic questions, and some to ethical concerns. The context in each case helps to explain why he applies the *De magistro* and *De mendacio* definitions of lying in some quarters and the *De doctrina christiana* and *Contra mendacium* definitions in others. His stress on a combination of objective error with self-deception and the wrong moral intention is strong in the *Confessions*, where Augustine describes as lies the false ideas and values that he held in his pre-Christian days.[128] In explaining a passage in the Psalms warning that God will punish liars, he also gives equal weight to objective error and a deceptive intention in defining the lie, as well as summarizing the types of lies as he does in *De mendacio* and exempting the jocose lie from his strictures for the same reasons as he gives there.[129] On the other hand, in his *Enchiridion*, a moral handbook deeply influenced by the position on free will and predestination he had taken against the Pelagians in his later years, Augustine stresses the importance of evil intention over objective truth in defining a lie and in distinguishing it from a falsehood. The bad will that leads to lying, in a person who lacks the guidance of grace, may indeed promote evil, he notes, but those predestined to salvation who are injured thereby may yet use the circumstance, with God's help, to manifest their perseverance and to strengthen their virtue.[130]

The final example of Augustine's treatment of lying occurs in his *De trinitate*, where it is organically connected to the last topic to be considered under the heading of his uses of Stoic logic and linguistic theory, the distinction between the *logos endiathetos* and *logos prophorikos* as a means of exploring the relationship between the Father and the Son. The idea that the eternal generation of the Son by the Father could be analogized to the Stoic *logos endiathetos*, or the incorporeal intramental *lekton*, while the incarnate Christ could be analogized to the sensible spoken *logos prophorikos*, was scarcely a new idea in Augustine's day. It had a long history already in the writings of the Greek Christian theologians of the Nicene and immediately post-Nicene period, although it had been dropped in favor of other kinds of Stoicizing arguments by more recent Trinitarian controversialists such as Marius Victorinus.[131] Augustine himself had appropriated this idea as an adjunct to Trinitarian theology well before the composition of his masterpiece on that subject. He uses it consistently for that purpose throughout his career both in summaries of the

---

[128] *Conf.* 5.3.5, 10.41.66–10.42.67.
[129] *Enar. in Ps.* 5.7.
[130] *Enchiridion ad Laurentium* 5.17–6.19, 7.22, ed. E. Evans, CC, 46 (Turnhout, 1969).
[131] For the literature on this topic see above, ch. 3, p. 135 n. 107.

creed,[132] statements of semantic theory,[133] extended discussions of the Gospel account of the relations between Father and Son,[134] and briefer homiletic exegeses of similar passages of Scripture,[135] as well as in sermons delivered in the Christmas season and on related feast days.[136] In all these cases the same analogy between the Father and Son and the inner and outer word (*verba cogitata atque prolata*)[137] involves the Stoic contrast between incorporeal *lekta* and external physical speech. The *De trinitate*, however, is the place where Augustine expounds this principle in the greatest detail as well as qualifying the force of the analogy as applied to the Trinity by combining it with the analysis of lying found in his other works.

As is the case with the other Augustinian works where these themes appear, the *De trinitate* assumes the Stoic distinction between words and *lekta* which undergirds both the contrast between the inner and outer word and the simultaneously subjective and objective conception of lying. Augustine is just as concerned with delineating the limits of human language as an analogy of the Trinity as he is with developing it on the positive side. He draws on the amalgam of Stoic ideas just noted both to build up this analogy and to break it down.[138] Within the purely intramental realm, Augustine notes, the word begotten is coessential with and equal to the begetter and none of the knowledge possessed by the begetter is lost in the act of generating the inner word. In these respects man's generation of his own inner word in the act of thinking is analogous to the Father's eternal generation of the Son. Secondly, while man may express his inner word outwardly in transient, corporeal speech, his inner word continues to remain fully present to him within his intellect and memory. In a similar way, God the Son remains consubstantial and coeternal with God the Father and fully present within the timeless and transcendent Trinitarian family even when He enters the world of time and matter as the incarnate Savior.[139]

---

[132] *De fide et symbolo* 3.3–4, ed. Iosephus Zycha, CSEL, 41 (Vienna, 1900). Noted by Baguette, "Le Stoïcisme," pp. 17–20; Roy, *L'Intelligence de la foi*, pp. 428–30.

[133] *De doct. christ.* 1.13.12.

[134] *In Ioannis Evangelium Tractatus CXXIV* 20.10, ed. D. Radbodus Willems, CC, 36 (Turnhout, 1954).

[135] *Sermo* 52.20.

[136] *Sermo* 188.1.1, 288.3–4.

[137] *Sermo* 188.1.1.

[138] *De trin.* 10.1.2–3, 15.28.51. The best study of Augustine's argument in the *De trin.* in relation to his own uses of the inner word-outer word distinction in his earlier works is Schindler, *Wort und Analogie*, pp. 86–118. See also Georges Bavaud, "Un thème augustinien: Le mystère de l'Incarnation, à la lumière de la distinction entre le verbe intérieure et le verbe proféré," *REAug*, 9 (1963), 95–101; Duchrow, *Sprachverständnis*, pp. 122–27, 137–48; Kelly, "St. Augustine," *AS*, 6 (1975), 51–52; Simone, "Semiologia agostiniana," *La Cultura*, 7 (1969), 89, 95 n. 10, 99, 110; TeSelle, *Augustine*, p. 225.

[139] *De trin.* 7.1.1, 9.7.12–9.8.13, 9.10.15–9.12.17.

At the same time Augustine does not fail to show how this Trinitarian analogy in the mind of man falls short of its divine significatum. He notes that man requires corporeal signs with which to express his ideas while God has the power to communicate Himself in a direct and unmediated way. He adds that human thought and speech involve a sequential process, for they, like the human condition itself, are part of the temporal order. By contrast, God's articulation of His Word, both internally and externally, is not a temporal process but an instantaneous event. Augustine also observes that man's words, although they are naturally accurate signs, are, in their very capacity as signs, not identical with the ideas or things they signify. But Christ, the incarnate Word, is consubstantial with and equal to God the Father; the fullness of divinity dwells within Him.[140] There is a final reason why human thought and language have limits as analogies of the Trinity. Men are capable of lying, but God cannot lie.[141] In the *De trinitate* Augustine considers the problem of lying on three levels: lies of thought, lies of speech, and lies of action. All of them presuppose the capacity of words to signify their referents naturally and all of them entail both a departure from objective truth and a defective moral orientation on the part of the subject. Since Augustine defines thought as interior speech, he holds that thoughts may be lies when a man's ideas are false and when he deliberately compasses evil within his mind. A man's external statements can be lies when these false mental and moral attitudes are expressed in utterance. Actions may also be lies. As sensible signs they are a species of verbal signs, says Augustine, recalling his discussion of *signa data* in the *De doctrina christiana*. Actions are lying statements when they are deliberately misleading and hypocritical. This analysis of lying in the *De trinitate* simultaneously extends Augustine's other applications of Stoic semantics and logic to that subject in two directions, pushing it backward into the realm of thought and forward into the realm of action, even as he yokes it with the more traditional use of the Stoic contrast between the inner and outer word as a way of probing the similarities and differences between the mind of man and the Trinity.

D) Physics

The *De trinitate* also provides a link between Augustine's consistent uses of Stoic logic and linguistic theory and his consistent uses of Stoic physics. While his approach to Stoic logic and semantics is quite positive and

---

[140] Ibid. 15.13.22–15.16.26, 15.27.50.
[141] Ibid. 15.10.17–15.11.20.

creative, his attitude toward Stoic physics is mixed. Some physical doctrines of the school he accepts warmly and applies extensively while others he consistently rejects. In the *De trinitate* Augustine makes positive
use of Stoic physics in a manner recalling the Trinitarian theology of
Marius Victorinus. He simultaneously enlarges on the same theme and
connects it with the arguments from Stoic logic and linguistics which he
develops in the same work. Both Victorinus and Candidus, his Arian
antagonist, had grounded one of their major Trinitarian analogies on a
triadic conception of the deity derived from Neoplatonism which they
had linked with the Stoic principle that God is an active force. Victorinus had Stoicized this conception still further by purging it of its hierarchical aspect and by viewing the three divine attributes of action, motion, and intelligence as equal manifestations of the same divine essence
and as functional correlatives of each other. He had also compared this
notion of the Trinity as *tridynamos* with the human faculties which the
divine Persons parallel.[142] Augustine adumbrates a similar position in
the *Confessions* and develops it fully in the *De trinitate*, where he stresses
that God is the supremely active being Whose operations flow from a
common substratum of essence that is metaphysically coextensive with
them.[143] He also orchestrates Victorinus' idea of drawing analogies between the Trinity and human psychology, calling on mental faculties that
are distinct but that operate in and through each other.

Augustine imposes three changes on Victorinus' theology, both in
substance and in emphasis. First, he begins by considering man's psychology and then moves to its prime analogate in the Trinity, reversing
the directionality of Victorinus' argument. Second, Augustine substitutes for Victorinus' triad of motion, action, and intelligence a series of
psychological triads of his own. He begins with the lover, the beloved,
and the love that unites them.[144] He then moves on to man's self, his love
of self, and his knowledge of self.[145] His next example of a Trinitarian
analogy in the mind of man is man's memory, intellect, and will.[146] He
enlarges finally on this third analogy in man's *memoria dei, intellectus dei,*

---

[142] See above, ch. 3, pp. 136–41.

[143] This point has been brought out well by Harry Austryn Wolfson, *The Philosophy
of the Church Fathers*, 3rd rev. ed. (Cambridge, Mass., 1970), I, 353. The same idea is
related, unconvincingly, to the Stoic doctrine of *oikeiosis* by Pierre Hadot, "L'Image de
la Trinité dans l'âme chez Victorinus et chez saint Augustin," *Studia Patristica*, 6, ed. F.
L. Cross, Texte und Untersuchungen zur Geschichte der altchristlichen Literatur, 81
(Berlin, 1962), pp. 437–40; John Burnaby, *Amor Dei: A Study of the Religion of St. Augustine*
(London, 1938), p. 118; and Oliver O'Donovan, *The Problem of Self-Love in St. Augustine*
(New Haven, 1980), pp. 48–56.

[144] *De trin.* 8.10.14.

[145] Ibid. 9.3.3–9.5.8.

[146] Ibid. 10.10.13, 10.11.17–10.12.19, 11.3.6; *Conf.* 3.11.12, 13.16.19.

and *amor dei*, which he then rephrases into a triad of *meminit, intellegit*, and *digilit* to emphasize, by the shift from a nominal to a verbal formula, the dynamic character of the deity and man's mental faculties alike.[147] Augustine's third departure from Victorinus lies in the fact that he is concerned not only with building up the positive side of these analogies but also with displaying their limitations. God's vitality, he stresses, is unconditioned and constant. His faculties of memory, intellect, and will are not subject to interruptions and His knowledge is not dependent on corporeal senses or sequential processes, since it is entirely spiritual, eternal, and instantaneous. God's mind embraces not just Himself and passing objects but everything that is. And, in God there is no gap whatever between His essence and His activity.[148] For all these reasons the human mind cannot serve as a perfect mirror of the Trinity. This conclusion accents the transcendence of God in an argument which parallels the Augustinian analysis of the difference between God and man as moral beings and as users of signs in the same work. Another contribution of Augustine's analogizing of God to man's mental faculties and his underlining of the limits of that same analogy is his ability to extend Victorinus' comparison between the divine and human natures on a functional, not a substantial, basis, avoiding both the divinization of the human soul, on the one hand, and the attribution to it of a material nature, on the other.

Augustine's Trinitarian theology is unquestionably his most important application of Stoic physics to the doctrine of God. At the same time there are two other Stoic theological ideas to which he refers and on which he takes a consistently negative position. One is the allegorization of the pagan gods as forces of nature and as manifestations of a single omnipotent deity. The other is the principle that God is material or corporeal. Previous Latin apologists such as Minucius Felix and Lactantius had indicated their familiarity with the Stoics' defense of polytheism and their effort to enhance its intellectual respectability by the allegoresis of the gods. Minucius had approved the Stoic practice as paving the way to Christian monotheism. Augustine joins Lactantius in attacking it. While he agrees that allegorization spiritualizes the gods and that the resultant theology is preferable to the grosser versions of pagan religion, he thinks that this practice reinforces the basic untruth of polytheism

---

[147] *De trin.* 13.8.11, 13.16.20, 14.12.15–14.19.25. The shift from a nominal to a verbal formula and its significance here have been brought out well by Walter H. Principe, "The Dynamism of Augustine's Terms for Describing the Highest Trinitarian Image in the Human Soul," unpublished. I am greatly indebted to Father Principe for permission to see the text in proof.

[148] *De trin.* 15.3.5–15.6.9; *Conf.* 1.4.4, 1.6.10.

rather than eliminating it. Further, it glamorizes forces of nature that are forces of nature *tout court*. And, insofar as it leads to the idea of monotheism, the deity in question is by no means the true God.[149]

A second principle of Stoic theology which Augustine consistently rejects is the notion of God as material or corporeal or identifiable with the physical element of fire. Augustine expressly ascribes this doctrine to the Stoics both individually and as a group. He sometimes uses it to show that the authority of the Stoics in one field is conditioned by their errors in another, as when he praises Zeno's epistemology in one breath while condemning his view of God as fire and his conception that everything which acts is a body in the next, a mistake, he notes, which was disseminated widely by Chrysippus.[150] More typically this criticism arises in the context of Augustine's comparisons among the schools of ancient philosophy, designed both to attack their plausibility *en bloc* because of their mutual disagreements on God or the *arche* and to argue that the Platonists, with their non-corporeal conception of the deity, came closest to the Christian truth.[151] Augustine also attributes the idea that God is corporeal to Tertullian.[152] Although he does not state that Tertullian was a dévoté of Stoic physics, he implies that it was the Stoa which led him astray.

Augustine's rejection of the corporality of God is closely linked in his mind to the twofold conviction that the human soul is neither material nor in any way consubstantial with the divine nature. He associates the idea of the corporality of the soul with Tertullian as well but he is much more likely to bring it up as an argument against the materialism of the Manichees, against the Donatists, or, more specifically, against the Stoics themselves.[153] The most interesting change he rings on the Stoa in this

---

[149] The fullest treatment is in *Civ. dei* 7.27, 7.30, 19.17. Scholars who have noted these *loci* include Hagendahl, *Augustine and the Latin Classics*, I, 247–48, 273–97; II, 520; R. A. Markus, "St. Augustine and *theologia naturalis*," *Studia Patristica*, 6, ed. F. L. Cross, Texte und Untersuchungen zur Geschichte der altchristlichen Literatur, 81 (Berlin, 1962), pp. 476–79; and TeSelle, *Augustine*, pp. 248–49. Augustine makes similar points, although more concisely, in *Sermo* 197.1, 197.6, as noted by O'Connell, *Augustine's Early Theory of Man*, pp. 96–99; and in *De consensu evangelistarum* 1.29.45, ed. Franciscus Weirich, CSEL, 43 (Vienna, 1904).

[150] *Contra ac.* 3.17.38–39.

[151] *Civ. dei* 8.5–6; *De cons. evang.* 1.23.30.

[152] *De haer.* 86.

[153] Against Tertullian see *De haer.* 86; *De gen. ad litt.* 10.25.41, 10.26.45; against the Manichees see *De gen. ad litt.* 7.12.19–7.15.21, 10.5.8; *De gen. contra Man.* 2.8.11; *De quant. an.* 4.5–6, 13.22–14.23, 17.30; *De trin.* 10.7.9–10, 10.10.13–10.15.16; against Vincentius Victor, leader of a Donatist splinter group, see *De natura et origine animae* 1.5.5, 1.7.7, 2.2.4–2.5.9, 3.3.3, 3.4.4, 4.12.17–4.13.19, ed. and trans. F.-J. Thonnard, OSA, sér. 3:22 (Paris, 1975); against the Stoics implicitly see *Ep.* 1, to Hermogenianus, 386, the man to whom he also sent a copy of the *Contra ac.*, where the doctrine that everything which acts is a body is clearly stated. The *loci* in *De quant. an.* and *De gen. ad litt.* have been noted

connection is his explanation that the *magnitudo animi* of Hercules, venerated as a Stoic saint, refers to his moral character and not to the physical distention of his soul as a measurable corporeal entity.[154]

Augustine refers consistently to a few other physical doctrines of the Stoa although they play a less important role in his thought than the ones already mentioned. Some of them he approves and others he criticizes. They all merit notice because he serves as virtually the only Latin Christian transmitter of them. In three cases, to be sure, it is impossible to classify his attitude as either consistent or inconsistent given the fact that he makes only one reference to the topic in his entire *oeuvre*. The only idea in this group for which Augustine had a possible Latin Christian forerunner is the doctrine of *krasis*, or the capacity of two physical elements to occupy the same space at the same time while retaining their own properties and not joining to form a compound or a new *tertium quid*. Tertullian had used this principle to explain the union of the divine and human natures in Christ, an application of Stoic *krasis* that is less surprising in his case, given his belief in the corporality of God and the human soul, than it is in Augustine's. Despite Augustine's repeated objections to Tertullian's theology and anthropology he nonetheless seconds the idea of *krasis* as a way of describing the hypostatic union, although he hastens to add that this is an analogy with distinct limits for that purpose, since Christ combines in His person an immaterial divine nature with an immaterial human soul and a material human body.[155] Another Stoic doctrine concerning the behavior of physical elements, with which Augustine shows a familiarity unique among the Latin Christian writers of the apologetic and patristic age, is the idea that the elements are all capable of changing into each other (*omnia in omnia posse mutari atque converti*). In the *De genesi ad litteram* he notes that some people advance this theory and that he hopes to discuss it in detail at some other time.[156] In fact he never returned to this theme and he is openminded if non-committal about it in this single reference. Augustine is similarly vague in naming his source for the idea of a cyclical cosmology. But he is unequivocal in rejecting it, on both psychological and theological grounds. If the world decomposed and reconstituted itself in an endless cycle, he says, a person who had attained wisdom and beatitude through protracted effort and suffering would have to start all over again in every age. He could never enjoy true blessedness, which requires the posses-

---

by Guido Mancini, *La psicologia di S. Agostino e i suoi elementi neoplatonici* (Napoli, 1938), pp. 39, 41 and the *locus* in the *De trin.* has been noted by Verbeke, *L'Évolution*, pp. 498–99.

[154] *De quant. an.* 17.30.
[155] *Ep.* 137, to Volusianus, 412.
[156] *De gen. ad litt.* 3.3.4.

sion of an unchanging good. Further, the belief that Christ was born, was crucified, and was resurrected once and for all time makes the notion of the cyclical repetition of history fundamentally untenable.[157]

Another theme from Stoic physics which Augustine is unique among his compeers in putting to use, a use that is primarily polemical, is the idea of time. The Stoics defined time as the interval of movement. Time is a medium in which real events take place but it is an entity that has no substance or content of its own. The Stoics thus classified time, along with space, the void, and *lekta*, as incorporeals, which do not exist but merely subsist. From this standpoint, only present time subsists because time itself is definable only in terms of movements that are actually taking place.[158] Augustine's own conception of time picks up the idea that time can be reduced to the present. The past, he notes, no longer exists; the future does not yet exist; only the present is actual. He applies this principle to explain the timelessness of God, Who dwells in an eternal present in which everything that may be past and future to men is simultaneously present in the divine mind. One of the major uses to which Augustine puts this idea, which will be treated below, is in his analysis of God's foreknowledge. Another is in his reply to the question, posed by the Manichees, as to what God was doing before He created the universe. Augustine's answer is that the question is meaningless because time itself did not exist before God created it. The creation, both before it emerged in time and after God produced it in visible form, remains in His eternally present Word. The psychological argument that time present is the only time really experienced by man is an adjunct to this polemic. As Augustine notes, even for men, the past is the soul's present memory; the present is the soul's present attention; and the future is the soul's present expectation. If this phenomenon is comprehensible in the experience of men, then the notion of the eternal present as applied to God should not be so difficult to grasp.[159]

The two remaining applications of Stoic physics found in Augustine, seminal reasons and the mind as the *hegemonikon* of man, are not unique to him among the Latin Christian writers of his age. But they are doctrines which he embraces enthusiastically and uses repeatedly in contexts that are very important to him. Augustine expands in particular on the subject of seminal reasons. He gives this doctrine the multiple assignment of accounting for the development of natural phenomena, both

---

[157] *Civ. dei* 12.13, 12.20.
[158] See *Stoic Tradition*, I, ch. 1, pp. 25–26.
[159] This theme is developed most fully in *Conf.* 11.10.12–11.14.17. In an anti-Manichean vein see also *De gen. contra Man.* 1.2.3–4 and in a non-controversial vein see *De div. quaest.* 17.

normal and abnormal, according to their own implanted laws, of explaining the maturation of man's spiritual capacities, of resolving vexed exegetical questions in the creation story in Genesis, of refuting metaphysical ideas to which he objects, and of explicating miracles or events that occur through the direct intervention of divine grace.[160] Augustine uses a number of terms to denote seminal reasons, including *semina, primordia semina, germina*, and *rationes insita*. As an explanation for natural phenomena that develop over a span of time, of latent causes implanted earlier that enable organisms to move through their natural life cycles, this notion is fully Stoic, as is Augustine's use of it to account for apparently uncaused phenomena, such as spontaneous generation. In all these cases the effects are natural, resulting from causes that are preprogrammed (*praeseminata*) in the creatures in question.[161] This principle is particularly useful to Augustine in accounting for the discrepancies in the creation story in Genesis, a problem especially pressing in the light of the Manichean reading of the text that he seeks to refute. Augustine wrestles with the question of how plants could have been created on the third day when the sun itself, necessary in demarcating day from night and a precondition for the existence of plant life, was not created until the fourth day. There is also the problem of unformed matter, which appears to precede the creation of specific creatures but which itself must

---

[160] The fullest and best studies are by F.-J. Thonnard, "Les raisons séminales selon Saint Augustin," *Proceedings of the XIth International Congress of Philosophy*, Brussels, August 20–26, 1953 (Amsterdam, 1953), XII, 146–52; "Razones seminales y formas substanciales: Agustinismo y tomismo," *Sapientia*, 6 (1951), 262–72; and Jules M. Brady, "St. Augustine's Theory of Seminal Reasons," *NS*, 38 (1964), 141–58, although the author limits his analysis to the *De gen. ad litt.* Other good if briefer treatments include Baguette, "Le Stoïcisme," pp. 24–25; Bourke, *Augustine's Quest of Wisdom*, pp. 225–27, 231–34; Howie, *Educational Theory*, p. 111 n. 2; Osborn, *Ethical Patterns*, p. 151; Verbeke, "Augustin et le stoïcisme," *RA*, 1 (1958), 82–85. Charles Boyer, "La théorie augustinienne de raisons séminales," *Miscellanea agostiniana*, Testi e studi pubblicati a cura dell'Ordine eremitano di S. Agostino nel XV centenario della morte del santo dottore (Roma, 1931), II, 795–819 tends to overemphasize the exegetical applications of the doctrine; Hans Meyer, *Geschichte der Lehre von dem Keimkräften von der Stoa bis zum Ausgang der Patristik nach den Quellen dargestellt* (Bonn, 1914), pp. 123–84, 212–24 sees the doctrine as applying only to organic life; Michael J. McKeough, *The Meaning of the Rationes Seminales in St. Augustine* (Washington, 1926) sees them only in the context of divine providence. Rita Marie Bushman, "St. Augustine's Metaphysics and Stoic Doctrine," *NS*, 26 (1952), 283–304; Grant, *Miracle and Natural Law*, p. 28; and TeSelle, *Augustine*, p. 227 tend to read this doctrine in Augustine too Neoplatonically. Svoboda, *L'Esthétique*, pp. 88–89, 112–13 finds it in the *De quant. an.*, where it does not occur. William A. Christian, "Augustine on the Creation of the World," *Harvard Theological Review*, 46 (1953), 16–17 notes the doctrine in Augustine but not its Stoic source. For a good bibliography of the earlier efforts to relate Augustine on seminal reasons to transformism and evolutionism see the intro. to the trans. of *De gen. ad litt.* by Agaësse and Solignac, OSA, sér. 7:48, pp. 667–68.

[161] *De gen. ad litt.* 2.15.30, 3.12.19–20, 3.14.22–23, 4.33.51, 5.6.18–19, 5.7.20; *De gen. ad litt. imp.* 14.50.

be understood as subject to creation *ex nihilo*. These and related difficulties are resolved by Augustine by an appeal to the principle of seminal reasons, through which God created everything instantaneously, on
whichever day of creation the text of Genesis says they emerged.[162]

Seminal reasons also enable Augustine to dispense with two Platonic
metaphysical doctrines to which he takes exception. One is the theory
of exemplars or ideal forms standing between God and the world. He
objects to exemplars understood as distinct entities and creative intermediaries because they would dilute God's monopoly on the power to
create. He also rejects the view of exemplars as entities which have always existed, which would infringe on God's exclusive claim to the attribute of eternity.[163] The second problematic Platonic doctrine is the idea
that human souls pre-exist before individual persons come into being.[164]
This notion would interfere with the principle that God creates everything *ex nihilo*. In response, Augustine can say that God creates everything atemporally and by Himself, in seminal form, whenever He intends His creatures to take on their phenomenal existence.

Seminal reasons likewise assist Augustine in dealing with matters of
a more strictly theological nature. They explain the alternations in nature that stem from flux and reflux, the systolic and diastolic character
of some natural phenomena that may be controlled externally or that
may result from contingencies or freedoms that inhere in the given nature of certain creatures. The changes and contingencies that are involved in these natural processes or choices may have periodic effects
that are or that seem to be harmful, at least to an observer not conversant with the system of the universe implanted seminally by God, of
which they are manifestations or effects. Seminal reasons can thus be
correlated with the idea of divine providence and theodicy, specifying
the manner in which God governs the universe and assisting in an understanding of how apparent evils can be rationalized and how a universal causal order, freedom, and contingency can be reconciled.[165]

Even more striking as Christianizations of the idea of seminal reasons
are Augustine's uses of this doctrine to account for miracles and for the
special actions of God's grace. In explaining a long list of miracles reported in the Bible, including the flowering of Aaron's staff and the conversion of Moses' staff into a brazen serpent, Augustine yokes them with
the spiritual possibilities occasioned by grace, such as the gift and ma-
turing of faith in the mind of the believer and the resurrection of the body

---

[162] *De gen. ad litt.* 5.4.9–11, 5.13.29–5.17.36, 6.15.26; *De gen. contra Man.* 1.7.11–12.
[163] *De trin.* 4.16.21–4.17.23.
[164] *De gen. ad litt.* 7.22.32–7.24.35.
[165] Ibid. 5.20.41–5.33.45.

in the life to come. In all cases these supernatural phenomena are placed on a continuum with the capacity of natural phenomena to move through their life cycles and are explained in terms of seminal reasons implanted by God in His original creation. In this way God guides the world which He redeems even as He rules the world He first created, whether His action is direct or indirect, whether it supports or alters the normal course of events, whether it is responsible for unique occurrences which do not permanently change the creatures in which they take place, whether it is a progressive and general revelation of His truth or a gratuitous personal intervention into the lives of individual men, renewing their natures in the pilgrimage of faith and sanctifying them eternally in the life to come.[166] These recurrent and multiple applications of the principle of seminal reasons in the wide range of contexts where Augustine calls upon them to deal with physical, metaphysical, and theological problems reflects his own capacity to make both faithful and innovative use of his Stoic material. They also make Augustine himself the richest source for the Stoic idea of seminal reasons in the age of the Latin apologists and Church Fathers.

A final case of a Stoic physical doctrine which Augustine invokes consistently, repeatedly, and approvingly is the idea that the human soul is the ruling principle of the human constitution. This idea is central to Augustine's psychology. It has been noted above as the foundation of the extramissive side of his theory of sense perception, in which the mind takes the initiative in causing a rarefied pneumatic force to issue from the sense organs. Augustine stresses that the mind, as the preeminent faculty in man's nature, governs all of man's activities as well. With the Stoics, he is non-committal on whether this *hegemonikon* is located in the brain or the heart. But, more importantly, he sees the mind as controlling everything man does. It is the force empowering the parts of the body to cohere, it initiates the functions of nutrition, growth, reproduction, sensation, and locomotion, as well as ruling memory, intellection, the exercise of the arts and sciences, the perception of the good, the acquisition of moral discipline, and the purification of man's soul. This program organizes the manifold activities of the mind under the headings of the vegetative, animate, and rational soul as put forth by the Peripatetic school and it also accents Augustine's Neoplatonic sense of the priority of the spiritual over the physical side of human nature. He adds to this Neoplatonized and Aristotelianized conception of the Stoic *hegemonikon* the Christian goal of spiritual renewal and communion with a

---

[166] The fullest treatment of this theme is in *De trin.* 3.8.13–14. See also *Civ. dei* 22.14; *De gen. contra Man.* 1.7.11–12.

personal God as the ultimate human possibilities energized by the mind.[167]

E) Ethics

This stress on the mind as the ruling power in man appeals to Augustine not only because it confirms his own psychological proclivities. It is also of central importance to him because of its ethical corollaries. As with the Stoics themselves, he locates virtue within the soul; he sees moral acts as defined by the inner intentionalities of the subject; and he agrees wholeheartedly that the passions arise in the mind and not in the body or in any infrarational faculties of man. These ethical principles are as organically related to each other and to the doctrine of the *hegemonikon* for Augustine as they are for the Stoics. Apart from the consonance of some of these ideas with the ethics of the Bible, another reason for the firm and consistent support which Augustine gives to them is their utility as a weapon against the Manichean idea that matter is the cause of evil. Aside from the requirements of external polemic, Augustine's insistent opposition to the Manichean position suggests that it was one that he felt a personal need to keep refuting throughout his life as a Christian.

Augustine consistently defines the passions as the standard Stoic quartet of pleasure, pain, desire, and fear (*laetitia, tristitia, cupiditas* or *amor, metus* or *timor*) and he insists over and over again that they originate not in the body but in the mind. With the Stoics he sees the passions as false judgments, perturbations of the mind that are contrary to reason (*perturbationes animi, inrationabiles animi motus, motus animi contra rationem*). Augustine may make some or all of these points in passing;[168] he may subject the particular passions to their end in view,[169] he may offer his definition as a prelude to some other aspect of the Stoic theory of the passions which he wants to criticize;[170] or he may stress the point in or-

---

[167] The fullest account is in *De quant. an.* 33.70–78. See also *De nat. et orig. an.* 4.6.6; *De trin.* 6.9.10.

[168] *Ep.* 9, to Nebridius, 389; *De sermone Domine in monte* 1.9.24, ed. Almut Mutzenbecher, CC, 35 (Turnhout, 1967). In *De immortalitate animae* 5.7, ed. and trans. Pierre de Labriolle, OSA, sér. 1:5 (Paris, 1948) Augustine combines these passions arising in the mind with several passions derived from the body, his unique reference to that idea. A good commentary is C.W. Wolfskeel, *De immortalitate animae of Augustine: Text, Translation and Commentary* (Amsterdam, 1977), p. 76.

[169] *De lib. arb.* 1.3.8–1.4.10, 1.8.18. This point has been handled extremely well by Robert J. O'Connell, "*De libero arbitrio* I: Stoicism Revisited," *AS*, 1 (1970), 58.

[170] *Quaestiones in Genesis* 30, in *Quaestiones in Heptateuchum*, ed. I. Fraipont, CC, 33 (Turnhout, 1968). Here Augustine cites the same passage from Aulus Gellius to which he refers in *Civ. dei* 9.4 although he uses it for a different purpose.

der to underscore the basic changeableness of the human mind.[171] His most detailed analysis of the question of the passions is in the *City of God*, where he is concerned with comparing the Stoic position expressly with the views of other ancient schools on this subject and with assessing the accuracy of various classical authors as transmitters of the doctrine, as well as with assessing it from a Christian perspective.

Augustine first adverts to the passions in the section of the *City of God* where he criticizes paganism under the heading of the mythic religion, following Varro's subdivision of ancient paganism into civic, mythic, and philosophical theology. He argues against the practice of worshipping demons, as decribed by Apuleius. These demons, he observes, are understood by their dévotés to be subject to the passions, even as men are; and he concludes that it is pointless to worship beings that are no better than men.[172] In his consideration of the respective merits of the ancient philosophers on theology, the good life, and related matters, Augustine gives a lengthy and circumstantial account of the Stoic theory of the passions, ascribed expressly to them, in the forms presented by Cicero and Aulus Gellius. As Augustine reads Cicero's comparison between the Aristotelian and Stoic positions, Cicero has conflated the Peripatetic view of the origin of the passions with the purely intellectualistic conception of their genesis taught by the ancient Stoics. Augustine reinforces his understanding of the Stoic view by referring to Gellius' description of the Stoic on board a ship during a storm at sea who explains his manifestation of the passion of fear in terms of the time lag required to form a correct intellectual judgment of the sense data he has received about the storm. This passage, which, as already noted, is also a good source for Augustine's grasp of Stoic epistemology, is one he discusses here in order to underscore the fact that the Stoics located the passions in the mind. Cicero, for his part, had assimilated the Stoics to the Peripatetics by claiming that the Stoic preferables were, in practice, the same as the bodily goods admitted by the Aristotelians. Augustine, while agreeing with Cicero that the debate between these schools is terminological, not real, holds that position because he sees all the schools reviewed in this passage as elevating the mind over the body. They differ, he claims, mainly in their prescriptions for allaying the passions, although they all say that the wise man can subject the passions to reason, a point he makes by concluding this argument with his famous reference to Aeneas as a Stoic sage.[173]

---

[171] *Conf.* 4.15.25, 10.25.36; noted by Hagendahl, *Augustine and the Latin Classics*, I, 148–49, 150–52; II, 511–16 and Howie, *Educational Theory*, p. 84, who is not aware of their Stoic origin; *De trin.* 6.6.8.

[172] *Civ. dei* 8.17, 9.3.

[173] Ibid. 9.4, summarized at 14.5. A number of scholars have noted the parallels be-

Of considerable value for the information on the Stoic theory of the passions which it conveys, this report and Augustine's summary of it later in the *City of God* are also of interest as an index of his independence in handling his Ciceronian sources and for the implicit criticism he makes of Cicero's own ability to grasp correctly the philosophical material that he presents in his own works. If Augustine feels free to dissent from Cicero's interpretation of the Stoic doctrine of the passions, he is no less discriminating in handling Vergil as a source for that same position. While, as noted, he can praise Vergil's presentation of Aeneas as a man with Stoic equanimity, he can also quote the poet's description of the tormented souls in the underworld in *Aeneid* 6 (*hinc metuunt, cupiuntque, dolent gaudentque*) while observing quite correctly that Vergil, unlike the Stoics, locates the origins of the passions in the body, not the soul, and that he views the body as the prison of the soul. This is an idea, Augustine notes, which Vergil derived from Plato, not from the Stoa, and it is a point on which he thinks that Plato was in error and that the Stoics were in greater accord with Christianity. As he himself states flatly, regarding the position of Plato and Vergil, *tamen aliter se habet fides nostra* ("but our faith holds quite otherwise.")[174]

The view that the passions, no less than correct moral judgments, arise in the mind has a number of ethical corollaries for the Stoics of which Augustine is well aware. Some of them he accepts, some he rejects, and still others he subjects to progressive revision or reformulation. The themes apposite to this topic that fall into the third of these categories will be discussed below in the final subdivision of this chapter. Augustine's willingness to dismember this constellation of ideas, to agree with some of them and to disagree with others, reflects the freedom with which he evaluates the individual components of Stoic ethics. His endorsement of the idea that moral acts are primarily intellectual acts, not consequences of infrarational functions or material aspects of the human personality, informs his assent to the Stoic principle that virtue lies within, in the good conscience of the individual who possesses a correct moral intention. This is an idea which Augustine applies gladly to the rational assent and the consistent orientation of the conscience that underlie virtuous and vicious choices whether the context involves the cardinal virtues and their opposites or ethical standards derived from Christian rev-

---

tween Augustine and Cicero here but not the Augustinian nuances. See Hagendahl, *Augustine and the Latin Classics*, I, 148–49, 179–84, 341–44; II, 511–16; Howie, *Educational Theory*, p. 84, although without noting the Stoic source; Testard, *Saint Augustin et Cicéron*, I, 243; Verbeke, "Augustin et le stoïcisme," *RA*, 1 (1958), 73.

[174] *Civ. dei* 14.13, CC, 48, p. 417. The same quotation from and objection to *Aeneid* 6.730–32 occurs at 21.3, 21.13. Noted, along with Augustine's critique of Vergil, by Hagendahl, *Augustine and the Latin Classics*, I, 346–47.

elation. The same conviction enables him to accept the Stoic paradoxes surrounding the sage or the just man as a person who possesses all things because he possesses virtue.[175] On the other hand, Augustine consistently rejects the idea that all sins are equal, despite the fact that it is a logical corollary of the principle that vice flows from a fixed intentionality to do evil. As in his analysis of lying noted above, he goes to great lengths to grade sins in a hierarchical order. He takes this position quite deliberately in opposition to the Stoic teaching on the equality of sins.[176]

There remain two other Stoic or Stoicizing ethical topics on which Augustine takes a consistent position, whether hostile or neutral, which are related, if more tenuously, to the Stoic intellectualization of ethics. One is the question of the *adiaphora*, or things indifferent. The Stoics had treated the virtuous as the rational, the vicious as the irrational, and the *adiaphora* as neither rational nor irrational and as hence ethically neutral. While some Stoics graded the *adiaphora* as more or less preferable and regarded them as not inconsistent with virtue, the school as a whole held the *adiaphora* to be morally irrelevant and expendable as such if they came into any conflict with virtue. Augustine has two kinds of reasons for rejecting this doctrine, one exegetical and the other ethical. In seeking to understand the ritual prescriptions of the Mosaic law that were subsequently annulled by the Gospel, he stresses that it is not proper to say either that these rituals were superseded because they were evil at the time, or that they are good and deserve to be followed by Christians, or that they are neither good nor bad. He ascribes to "some philosophers" whom he does not name the view that any moral questions exist at all that can be relegated to such an ethical twilight zone. Instead, he proposes that the ceremonies of the Old Testament were good and that they foreshadowed the Christian revelation to come; thus, in the Christian era, they are no longer needed, resolving the difficulty with the aid of typological exegesis.[177] On an ethical level Augustine dismisses the idea of *adiaphora* because he sees the vicissitudes of life which the Stoics included in that category either as created goods or as real evils, neither of which is ethically neutral. In the case of the created goods, man must

---

[175] This idea is a dominant theme running throughout the entire *Conf.* See also *De gen. contra Man.* 2.14.21; *Sermo* 21.8, 72.2, 74.3. Excellent treatments of this topic are provided by Pierre Courcelle, *Connais-toi toi-même de Socrate à Saint Bernard*, 3 vols. (Paris, 1974–75), I, 142–44; "L'Immanence dans les 'Confessions' augustiniennes," *Hommages à Jean Bayet*, ed. Marcel Renard and Robert Schilling (Bruxelles, 1964), pp. 167–71.

[176] Augustine's most detailed and express references to this idea as a Stoic principle he rejects are in *Ep.* 92, *Ep.* 104, and *Ep.* 167.4–17, to Jerome, 415. See also *De haer.* 82, where he attributes it to the heretic Jovinian, and *De serm. Dom. in monte* 1.9.24. Commentators who have noted some of these *loci* include Hagendahl, *Augustine and the Latin Classics*, I, 68–69; Testard, *Saint Augustin et Cicéron*, I, 247.

[177] *Ep.* 82, to Jerome, 405.

learn to grade them and to order his ethical response to them so that he does not endow them with a greater or lesser value than they truly possess. In the case of the earthly ills, man must learn to appraise them as tokens of the transient nature of life on earth and as obstacles which he can overcome and through which he can grow in virtue with God's help.[178]

The final topic in Stoic ethics which Augustine treats consistently, if in a decidedly unStoic way, is cosmetic theology. This theme had been and was to be elaborated in a Christian vein by a considerable number of Augustine's Latin Christian predecessors, contemporaries, and successors. These cosmetic theologians sometimes handle the topic in a manner quite compatible with the Stoic norm of virtue as life in accordance with reason and with the principle that the sage's presentation of self should witness his wisdom and virtue to society. Some of them confine their application of cosmetic theology to women and to persons living in celibate vocations and others use it as a means of exhorting men and married couples as well. It must be said that cosmetic theology is definitely an afterthought for Augustine, a topic lying at the outer margins of his ethical and pastoral outlook. His chief, and only, contribution to the history of this *topos* is that he is the first Latin Christian writer to Christianize it entirely and to empty it completely of its Stoic content. While he refers expressly to Cyprian and Ambrose on this subject he does so only to compare their techniques as Christian rhetoricians, devoting no attention to the substance or rationale of their arguments.[179] His own most extended foray into cosmetic theology is found in a handbook of instructions written for an extremely unruly community of monks in his diocese, in which he criticizes them for wearing their hair long. He accuses the monks of hypocritically masking their vices by imitating the tonsorial practice of the Old Testament priesthood and enjoins them to look to their souls instead, to reform their disorderly way of life, and to cut their hair as a sign of humility. Augustine offers no non-Scriptural reasons for his prescriptions.[180] In a similar vein, in a letter to a fellow bishop outlining the comportment appropriate for married women, he reduces the question to the norm of what Scripture permits or forbids. On this basis, he says, there is no need to legislate on jewelry or clothing but that women should cover their heads in public, as St. Paul requires. Augustine remarks in passing that good character is the best adornment for both men and women before moving on to the main burden of the

---

[178] A particularly rich analysis is in *Civ. dei* 19.4 and a good commentary on this theme is Rief, *Der Ordobegriff*, pp. 276–82.

[179] *De doct. christ.* 4.21.47–50.

[180] *De opere monachorum* 31–33, ed. Iosephus Zycha, CSEL, 41 (Vienna, 1900).

letter, the problem of the wearing of amulets as a pagan survival.[181] Augustine ignores the assistance that a Stoicizing line of argument could have offered to his case. His handling of this originally Stoic *topos* suggests that his consistent applications, and rejections, of Stoic ethics extend to the trivial and the superficial as well as to subjects of profound importance and great centrality to his thought.

III. Uses of Stoicism in Augustine Indicating the Development of His Thought

We come at length to the third and last major Augustinian orientation toward Stoicism, in which he subjects the Stoic ideas he uses to successive waves of reevaluation, abandoning positions that had appealed to him early in life, rejecting some of them outright, altering some of them, and radically Christianizing others. Largely ethical in character, this body of Stoic material also involves some important and closely related features of psychology and physics. At issue are the definition of the *summum bonum*, the idea of the sage, the nature of virtue and man's capacity to attain it by an autarchic exercise of reason and will, and the associated question of free will in relation to God's governance of the universe. In handling all these doctrines Augustine moves progressively away from the uncompromising rationalism of Stoic ethics, anthropology, and theology and replaces it decisively with a Christian vision of reality in which human nature, vitiated by sin, is dependent on God in the practice of virtue. The emphasis he places on this principle is more than Christian; it is specifically Augustinian. This development of his thought was occasioned both by the crystallization of his own dogmatic position on grace, predestination, the Church, and the sacraments in his debates with the Donatists and Pelagians and by his own inner experience of the difficulties of living the Christian life and the conditions which he came to believe that it required.[182] As a consequence of this two-fold motivation, the criticism to which he subjects the Stoic ideas that he programmatically reformulates or dismisses is grounded partly on the rule of faith as he interprets it and partly on his own personal analysis of the psychological inadequacy of Stoic doctrine. The counter-Stoic views which Augustine develops are elaborated most fully in the works of his maturity. But some of his misgivings concerning the Stoic conception of the good life begin to appear even in his earliest works. In all cases, Augustine's rationale for casting off those Stoic principles that he came

---

[181] *Ep.* 245, to Possidius, n.d.

[182] This double aspect in the development of Augustine's thought is brought out beautifully by Brown, *Augustine of Hippo*, esp. parts 3–5.

to regard as unsatisfactory will be visible most clearly through a chronological presentation of his emerging disaffection from them.

A) The Summum Bonum, Virtue, the Sage

The definition of the *summum bonum* as virtue alone, as an end in itself, as attainable by correct intellectual judgments and the exercise of a rationally instructed will, as the sole and sufficient possession of the sage, and as a good within man's power that can never be lost, is a constellation of Stoic ideas which Augustine expressly attributes to that school and toward which he shows a marked partiality in his earliest works. His sympathy with this ethical position continues, on the whole, into the mid-390s. When he modifies any of these themes up to that point he is more likely to do so under the influence of Neoplatonism or, to a far lesser extent, Aristotelianism, rather than by Christianizing them. When he reviews the schools of philosophy on the nature of the *summum bonum* for the first time in his *Contra academicos* Augustine clearly prefers the views of Zeno and Chrysippus, who define it as virtue, over those of the Epicureans, who define it as pleasure. He adds that, in contrast with the skeptics, the Stoics rightly insist that man's capacity to know the truth with certainty is necessary for his understanding of the nature of the good life and of how to attain it.[183] In the *De beata vita* he adds that the Stoic conception of the good life appeals to him because it centers on the possession of a value that can be acquired with security and always retained. Only such a good can lead to happiness, he asserts, because happiness consists in obtaining what one wants and possessing it permanently. At the same time, Augustine connects this Stoic argument for virtue as the *summum bonum* with a Neoplatonic conception of the good as transcendent and eternal, which, he notes, is the only kind of good that can never be lost. Thus, the psychological conditions attaching to happiness, which he derives from the Stoa, are met for him only in a Neoplatonic kind of deity Whose eternity and detachment from the transient world provides the only sure haven for the soul.[184] Virtue, he

---

[183] *Contra ac.* 1.2.5, 1.5.15, 1.8.22–23, 3.7.16–3.8.18. See also *De beata vita* 2.4, ed. W. M. Green, CC, 29 (Turnhout, 1970).

[184] *De beata vita* 2.10.12. This combination of Stoicism and Neoplatonism has been discussed extremely well by Burnaby, *Amor Dei*, p. 47; Gösta Hök, "Augustin und die antike Tugendlehre," *Kerygma und Dogma*, 6 (1960), 106–14; O'Connell, *Augustine's Early Theory of Man*, pp. 16–17, 26–27, 193–96, 203–05; Martin Sicherl, "Platonismus und Stoizismus in den Frühschriften Augustins," *Acta Philologica Aenipontana*, ed. Robert Muth, 2 (1967), 63–65; TeSelle, *Augustine*, pp. 67–68; Van Fleteren, "The Cassiciacum Dialogues," *Mediaevalia*, 4 (1978), 68, although he treats Cicero's ethics as equivalent to Stoicism. On the other hand, Pierre Courcelle, "Deux grands courants de pensée dans

concludes, is the only thing in the flux of the temporal order that shares the divine attribute of permanence: *Est autem aliquid, si manet, si constat, si semper tale est, ut est virtus* ("But a thing really has being when it remains, stands firmly, and is always the same, as is the case with virtue.")[185]

Virtue, moreover, can be acquired by the sage through the autonomous exercise of his reason and will. As Augustine avers repeatedly in his early works, all men are either sages or fools: *omnem non stultum manifestum est esse sapientem* ("manifestly, every man who is not foolish is wise.")[186] Fools act irrationally while sages follow right reason; sages enjoy the exclusive possession of wealth, self-sufficiency, and happiness, Stoic paradoxes which Augustine illustrates by citing with approval the Horatian and Ciceronian description of the sage's perfection in the image of a sphere.[187] His most pointed contrast between the sage and the fool, *more Stoicorum*, is found in his *De ultilitate credendi*, in an argument designed to show that Catholic authorities are true sages who should therefore be believed:

> Nam omne factum, si recte factum non est, peccatum est: nec recte factum esse ullo modo potest, quod non a recta ratione profisciscitur. Porro recta ratio est ipsa virtus. . . . Solus igitur sapiens non peccat. Stultus ergo omnis peccat, nisi in iis factis in quibus sapienti obtemperavit.[188]

> For every deed, if it is not rightly done, is a sin; nor can one in any way do rightly what does not proceed from right reason. Moreover, right reason is virtue itself. . . . The wise man alone, therefore, does not sin. And every fool, then, sins save in those acts in which he obeys the wise man.

With the Stoics Augustine also unites free will and reason as the faculties jointly employed by the sage in making correct moral judgments and

---

la littérature latine tardive: Stoïcisme et néo-platonisme," *REL*, 42 (1965), 125–26 and José Oroz Reta, "Séneca en San Agustín," *Estudios sobre Séneca: Ponencias y comunicaciones*, Octava semana española de filosofía (Madrid, 1966), pp. 331–51 accent only Augustine's Stoic borrowings.

[185] *De beata vita* 2.8, CC, 29, p. 70; trans. Ludwig Schopp, FC, 5 (New York, 1948), p. 54.
[186] Ibid. 3.28, CC, 29, p. 80; trans. Schopp, p. 76.
[187] The sphere image is in *De quant. an.* 16.27 and is noted by Hagendahl, *Augustine and the Latin Classics*, I, 188. Cf. Horace, *Sat.* 2.3.87–88; Cicero, *De nat. deor.* 2.10.45 ff. On the other features of this *topos* see *De beata vita* 3.27–33; *Contra ac.* 1.9.24; *Ep.* 3, to Nebridius, 387; *De lib. arb.* 1.3.28–29, 1.13.27; *Soliloquiorum* 1.11.19, *PL*, 32. On the theme of wisdom and folly more broadly see Baguette, "Le Stoïcisme," pp. 29–31, 34–37; Hagendahl, *Augustine and the Latin Classics*, I, 152; Verbeke, "Augustine et le stoïcisme," *RA*, 1 (1958), 74.
[188] *De util. cred.* 12.27, OSA, sér. 1:8, p. 274, trans. Luanne Meagher, FC, 4 (New York, 1947), p. 428. This interconnection of the virtues has been noted by Baguette, "Le Stoïcisme," pp. 26–28; Verbeke, "Augustin et le stoïcisme," pp. 71–72.

choices. In the *De libero arbitrio*, and not surprisingly in the light of the anti-Manichean focus of that work, he stresses the point that the exercise of free will lies within man's power. Man alone is thus responsible for vice and virtue, for good and evil. However, the Stoicism of this argument, although strong, is tinctured here, as in several of Augustine's other early works, by his Neoplatonic tendency to regard good and evil as the eternal and the transient.[189]

Regardless of this fact, Augustine sees the virtues arising from the function of free will as permanent acquisitions, which cannot be lost or taken from the sage against his will and which he defines in a specifically Stoic manner in the *De libero arbitrio*. Prudence, he says, is *appetendarum et vitandarum rerum scientia* ("the knowledge of what we should seek and avoid,") which accents the practical ethical directionality of that virtue. Fortitude is *animae adfectio, qua omnia incommoda et damna rerum non in nostra potestate constitutarum contemnimus* ("a disposition of the soul by which we shun all inappropriate and miserable things that are not in our power,") a definition stressing the Stoic idea that the things in our power are the only things that are ethically relevant. Temperance is *adfectio coercens et cohibens appetitum ab his rebus quae turpitur appetuntur* ("the disposition that constrains or impedes our desire for those things which are wrongfully desired,") while justice is the virtue *qua sua cuique tribuuntur* ("which renders to each his own,") formulae suggesting the capacity of reason to judge what is fitting for the individual and society and to educate man's responses accordingly.[190] There are other passages in Augustine's early works where he gives different, and less thoroughly Stoic definitions of the cardinal virtues. One is his quotation of Cicero's *De inventione* formulae in the *De diversis quaestionibus*, which recapitulates Cicero's own combination of Stoicism with Aristotelianism and Roman values.[191] Another is in the *De genesi contra Manicheos*, where he treats the four rivers of Paradise as symbolizing the cardinal virtues in a set of definitions that blends Platonism with Aristotelianism and leaves only temperance to the Stoics.[192] Here he views prudence as the contemplation of transcendent and ineffable truth, fortitude as an almost infrarational heat that catalyzes courageous action, temperance as the control of desires that conflict with reason, and justice as the primary virtue that coordinates and integrates the other three. But, whatever the particulars of the defini-

---

[189] *De lib. arb.* 1.15.31–32, 1.16.34, 2.1.1–33, 2.20.54. Noted by Roy, *L'Intelligence de la foi*, p. 240; Svoboda, *L'Esthétique*, p. 91; TeSelle, *Augustine*, pp. 111–12.
[190] *De lib. arb.* 1.13.27, CC, 29, p. 228. There is a similar definition of wisdom in *Contra ac.* 1.6.16.
[191] *De div. quaest.* 31.1–3.
[192] *De gen. contra Man.* 2.10.14.

tions Augustine gives to the cardinal virtues in his early works, he treats them, typically, as goods which are ends in themselves, which comprise the *summum bonum*, which are the sole requirements for the happy life, and which can be attained by man on his own intellectual and volitional initiative.

Yet, it is in some of these same early works that Augustine begins to question the adequacy of this Stoic ethical orientation and to reformulate it, not only under the influence of Neoplatonism and other philosophical alternatives but in the light of basic Christian premises, a process which he continues to deepen in his later works. Starting with the *De beata vita* and the *De libero arbitrio*, Augustine observes that the true good is more than the gratification of an autarchic Stoic rationality in a transcendent Neoplatonic *summum bonum*. Rather, the supreme good is the personal Christian God, Who alone can satisfy our yearning for spiritual security. Further, this deity is Christ, the saving Truth Who first seeks us out and Who perfects us in the theological virtues of faith, hope, and charity.[193] These virtues, like all virtues, are goods, he notes, but they cannot be identified with the *summum bonum* itself. For all goods, greater and lesser, spring from God and must be ordered to God, Who alone is the supreme good. Virtues, thus, are only intermediary goods (*media bona sunt*) and are means to the end of man's possession of perfect wisdom and truth in God Himself.[194] Free will, moreover, for all its force, is an instrumentality, enabling man to reach that end. It is not an end in itself, an observation which pointedly criticizes the autarchy of the Stoic sage as a form of idolatry and as an absolutizing of man's own power of self-determination.[195]

Augustine's first thoroughgoing reformulation of the topic of virtue in his early works occurs in the treatise he composed between 388 and 390 contrasting the morals of the Catholic Church with those of the Manichees. As a framework for this comparison, he begins by posing the question of the happy life and how to seek it, repeating the idea that the happy life is the possession of what one wants, which must be the supreme good, a good more excellent than man and one that cannot be lost. The *summum bonum*, he states, can thus be found neither in man's body nor in his soul but must be something greater than both. The soul is not a satisfactory end for, if this were the case, men would foolishly seek what they already have. But, even more potent as a critique of the autarchy and constancy of the Stoic sage is the point that the good must

---

[193] *De beata vita* 3.18–22, 3.34–36.
[194] *De lib. arb.* 2.19.50, CC, 29, p. 271. Noted by O'Connell, *Art and the Christian Intelligence*, pp. 52–53.
[195] *De lib. arb.* 2.19.51.

be free from loss or change, an exemption, he observes, which the soul
does not enjoy. Thus one must look to the transcendent eternal God as
the *summum bonum*.[196] This God, further, is not merely an object of intellectual contemplation. He is a person Who is also an object of love, a
love which man expresses by believing in the authority of God's revelation and by obeying His moral law.[197]

The love of God also serves as the foundation for Augustine's redefinition of the cardinal virtues, a move that accomplishes two simultaneous objectives. First, in arguing against the Manichees as he does in
this treatise, it enables him to show the basic continuities between the
ethics of the Old and New Testaments despite the changes in specific
moral injunctions imposed on God's people over time. Second, and quite
apart from the exegetical and polemical utility of this idea, it allows him
to retain the Stoic principle that the virtues are united by their common
source while substituting for a purely human intentionality as that source
a well-spring that combines the divine initiative with the human response. All the virtues, Augustine thus agrees, are one, and virtue leads
to the happy life. But virtue is now defined as the perfect love of God,
under the fourfold dispositions of love itself:

> Itaque illas quatuor virtutes . . . sic etiam definire non dubitem, ut tem-
> perantia sit amor integrum se praebens ei quod amatur; fortitudo, amor
> facile tolerans omnia propter quod amatur; justitia, amor soli amato ser-
> viens, et propterea recte dominans; prudentia, amor ea quibus adjuvatur
> ab eis quibus impeditur, sagaciter seligens. Sed hunc amorem non cujus-
> libet, sed Dei esse diximus, id est summi boni . . . Quare definire etiam sic
> licet, ut temperantiam dicamus esse, amore Deo sese integrum incorrupt-
> umque servantem; fortitudinem, amorem omnia propter Deum facile per-
> ferentem; justitiam, amorem Deo tantum servientem, et ob hoc bene im-
> perantem ceteris, quae homini subjecta sunt; prudentiam, amorem bene
> discernentem ea quibus impedire potest.[198]

> Therefore, these four virtues . . . I would not hesitate to define as follows:
> temperance is love giving itself wholeheartedly to that which is loved, for-

---

[196] *De moribus ecclesiae catholicae et de moribus manicheorum* 1.3.3–1.6.10, 1.8.13, 1.14.24,
2nd ed., ed. and trans. B. Roland–Gosselin, OSA, sér. 1:1 (Paris, 1949). Noted by Burnaby, *Amor Dei*, pp. 47–48.

[197] *De moribus* 1.8.13–1.11.19.

[198] Ibid. 1.15.25, OSA, sér. 1:1, pp. 174–76, trans. Donald A. Gallagher and Idella
J. Gallagher, FC, 56 (Washington, 1966), pp. 22–23. Scholars who have rightly stressed
the centrality of Augustine's shift from reason to love as the locus of moral intentionality
and who have located it first in this work include Burnaby, *Amor Dei*, pp. 47–137; Hök,
"Augustin und die antike Tugendlehre," *Kerygma und Dogma*, 6 (1960), 125–28; Holte,
Béatitude et sagesse, pp. 201–04, 263; Anton Maxsein, *Philosophia cordis: Das Wesen der Personalität bei Augustinus* (Salzburg, 1966), passim and esp. pp. 52–54, 95–108; Rief, *Der Ordobegriff*, pp. 332–34.

titude is love enduring all things willingly for the sake of that which is loved, justice is love serving alone that which is loved and thus ruling rightly and prudence is love choosing wisely between that which helps it and that which hinders it. Now since this love, as I have said, is not love of things in general, but rather love of God, that is, of the supreme good, . . . we can define the virtues thus: temperance is love preserving itself whole and unblemished for God, fortitude is love enduring all things willingly for the sake of God, justice is love serving God alone and, therefore, ruling well those things subject to man, and prudence is love discriminating rightly between those things which aid in reaching God and those things which might injure it.

Having redefined the virtues in this way and having shifted their source from rational judgment to love, Augustine continues to discuss them as ways of quelling the irrational passions that deflect man from God, under the general heading of the Neoplatonic contrast between the transient and the eternal.[199]

Augustine goes on to develop this notion of virtue as an expression of the love of God and as a means to the *summum bonum* rather than as an end in itself in his middle and later works, insisting that the good must be an eternal and personal God Who can never be lost and Who can be loved as well as known.[200] His fullest elaboration of this theme is found in the criticism of the Stoic doctrine of the good in his *De trinitate* and *City of God*. Here he once more recapitulates the teachings of the various philosophers on this subject. Neither the Stoics nor any of the other schools produced an acceptable theory of the good, he observes, for virtue requires the knowledge of God supplied by faith and the recognition that the acquisition of the supreme good does not lie entirely within our power. It is, hence, both the limited truth of the Stoic definition of the good and the inner failure of autarchy as a psychic possibility on which Augustine rests his case.[201] He charges the Stoics, along with many other philosophers, with mistakenly adopting a purely rational and purely human reference point, which, by that very fact, is incapable of satisfying the yearning for ethical value and psychological security that fuels the sage's quest.

Augustine is by no means the first of the Latin Christian writers of his age to reject the Stoic claim that virtue is an end in itself. But his reasons for doing so are quintessentially Augustinian ones. Lactantius had argued that it is impossible to persevere in virtue without the hope of a posthumous reward. He had also noted that we cannot say that virtue has always been within our power since we acquire it at some particular

---

[199] *De moribus* 1.19.35–1.25.46. Noted by Osborn, *Ethical Patterns*, p. 159.
[200] *De div. quaest.* 35.1–2; *Conf.* 10.29. Noted by Burnaby, *Amor Dei*, pp. 48–49.
[201] *De trin.* 13.5.8–13.7.10. Noted by Burnaby, *Amor Dei*, pp. 50–51, 192.

point in life and we will cease to need it when we die. Ambrose's analysis had emphasized instead the limits of the virtues on a psychological level. With Augustine he treats them as means, not as ends, and sees them as capable of operating fully only when grace makes up for their deficiencies. Augustine's approach includes this Ambrosian perspective but links it to a more acute perception of man's drive for the possession of a good that can never be lost as the dynamic element in the original Stoic position. He retains that central insight as well as the Stoic idea of the interconnection of the virtues, while replacing the Stoic content supported by this framework with a Christian one, both in his redefinition of the virtues as the love of God and in his relocation of the entire problem in an *ordo amoris* that is, at the same time, a structure of values and a statement about man's dependence on God's grace. What all men seek in the moral life, he concludes, is peace, and *pax omnium rerum tranquillitas ordinis* ("the peace of all things is the tranquillity of order.") The right order is the order of love, supplied by God, which provides both the only adequate program for the happy life and the only possible means to attain it.²⁰² It is no accident, according to Augustine, that the only philosophers mentioned in Scripture are the Epicureans and Stoics who are depicted disputing with St. Paul in Acts 17:18. Both of these schools, he has come to think by the end of his life, advocate equally pernicious distortions of the *summum bonum*. In their own diverse ways they are equally guilty of placing their hope in man himself. But the hope of a Christian, for Augustine, must rest in God. For it is God Who grants to man the power to will the good and it is God Who inspires man to transform a good will into good deeds. For the Christian, in short, not only must one say that virtue is a means, not an end. One must also acknowledge that virtue is not an achievement, but a gift.²⁰³

The theme of the *ordo amoris* and the transformation of a purely rational intentionality into the God-given motivation of charity, which bulks so large in the later Augustine's criticism of Stoic ethics, also serves as the basis for the positive doctrine of love which he elaborates in his mature works. Here, too, however, there is already an inkling of that later development in one of his earliest treatises, the *De musica*, where he speaks of the *conversionem amoris in Deum* ("conversion of love in God")²⁰⁴ which marks the Christian life on earth and which will be consummated when that love is enjoyed eternally in Heaven. Augustine sometimes uses his redefinition of the virtues as the love of God to resolve exegetical and

---

²⁰² *Civ. dei* 19.13. See also 5.20, 8.8, 10.18, 14.2–3, 14.5, 19.1, 19.4.

²⁰³ *Sermo* 150.3–5, 150.8–10, 156.7 for the references to Acts; also *Ep.* 118; noted by Burnaby, *Amor Dei*, p. 71; Testard, *Saint Augustin et Cicéron*, I, 247–48.

²⁰⁴ *De musica* 6.16.51–55. The quotation is at 6.6.51, Marzi, p. 624.

dogmatic problems in his later works, although he rejects the pendant doctrine of the equality of the vices. This position leads him to redefine sin itself as the absence of charity in his exegesis of James 2:10, where the apostle states that those who offend in any way against the law are guilty of disobeying all of it. Augustine interprets this passage by arguing that all virtues are forms of charity and that a person may lack charity to a greater or lesser degree and in different particulars. Thus, sins, as expressions of defective charity, can be graded, while still adhering in some sense to the apostle's position.[205] The equality and mutual coinherence of the virtues is also useful as an analogy of the relations among the Persons of the Trinity. And, since the virtues have been recast as modes of the love of God, they are features of man's life *in via* which will pass away in the next life as faith is replaced by sight, except for their traces in the memory.[206]

But Augustine's most profound and extensive application of his reformulation of the Stoic doctrine of virtue occurs in contexts where he expatiates on the moral state of the Christian who already has been progressively purified by grace in this life. In such persons, the capacity to love God and their fellow man has been ingrafted and strengthened in them by God. They resemble St. Paul, who was so rooted by God in charity that he brought forth good fruit. So, too, the Christian whose mind and heart have been renewed by grace will be able to discriminate between the loving or selfish intentionalities that may inspire the selfsame outward acts. He will do whatever he does out of love alone and he will have the discernment to translate his loving intentions into appropriate actions. This doctrine may be regarded as Augustine's most radical Christianization of Stoic ethics. It is in this sense that he can counsel his own saintly version of the Stoic sage, *Dilige et quod vis fac* or *Dilige et dic quod voles* ("Love and do what you will;" "Love and say what you wish") in the confidence that this kind of hearer will understand that he speaks not of the obliteration of man's moral duties but of their total transvaluation and irradiation by charity.[207]

---

[205] *Ep.* 167.4–17; noted by John P. Langan, "Augustine on the Unity and the Interconnection of the Virtues," *Harvard Theological Review*, 72 (1979), 84–95; Hök, "Augustin," *Kerygma und Dogma*, 6 (1960), 119–20; Osborn, *Ethical Patterns*, p. 168; Verbeke, "Augustin et le stoïcisme," *RA* 1 (1958), 71–72.

[206] *De trin.* 6.4.6, 14.19.12. Noted by Hans-Jürgen Horn, "Antakoluthie der Tugenden und Einheit Gottes," *Jahrbuch für Antike und Christentum*, 13 (1970), 26–28.

[207] *In Ep. Joan.* 7.8; for the whole argument see 6.6, 7.6–8, 8.1. This point, if not its Stoic source, has been noted by Agaësse, intro. to his trans., SC, 75, pp. 79–80; Johannes B. Bauer, "'Dilige et quod vis fac'," *Wissenschaft und Weisheit*, 20 (1957), 64–65; Jacques Gallay, "Dilige et quod vis fac: Notes d'exégèse augustinienne," *RechSR*, 43 (1955), 545–55. For the second quotation see *Expositio Epistolae ad Galatas* 57, *PL*, 35.

B) Apatheia and Eupatheia

Another theme in Stoic ethics, closely related to the teaching on the virtues and the powers of the sage, which Augustine rethinks and revises over the course of the years, is the doctrine of *apatheia* as a condition of the sage's exercise of virtue. While Augustine adheres consistently to the Stoic view of the passions as irrational intellectual judgments he does not support the idea of *apatheia* consistently. He defends the possibility and desirability of *apatheia* in his earliest works but subsequently modifies or rejects this position on both theological and psychological grounds. This process of revision had begun by the late 380s and early 390s. It is connected both with his growing disenchantment with the notion that man possesses moral autarchy and with the need to address the problem of God's anger, inherited from previous theologians, which he faced in his first essays in exegesis from the pulpit. His reassessment of *apatheia* then deepened as he moved to the development of his doctrine of grace against the Pelagians and to his positive stress on love as the key to virtue in his later life.

At the beginning of his life as a Christian Augustine regarded the imperturbability of the sage and his freedom from the passions as fully possible for man to attain by himself and as imparting to the mind of the wise man the very immutability which he sought in God as the supreme good. Thus, the *mens immobilis* of the sage could be achieved simply by his own ordering of his mind and will and by his fixing his attention on God. Having done so, the wise man would be strong (*fortis*), liberated from all fear, whether of destitution, pain, or death.[208] Indeed, the sage would be free from all wayward desires. He would enjoy a profound tranquillity of mind (*magna mentis tranquillitate*) and he would live in harmony with the part of the mind that is divine (*secundum divinam illam partem animi*).[209] Freedom from fear, especially, is the particular feature of *apatheia* to which Augustine returns in his last fully positive reference to the *tranquillitas animi* marking the sage.[210]

But, in the course of composing his sermons on the Psalms, which he began in 392, Augustine came up against the problem of explaining the passion of anger which the Psalmists attribute to God, as well as the righteous indignation that they deem acceptable for men. Apart from the utility of some of the arguments made by earlier apologists on this ques-

---

[208] *De ordine* 2.6.8, 3.8.25. Baguette, "Le Stoïcisme," pp. 37–39 has noted several but by no means all of the *loci* pertinent to Augustine on *apatheia* here and elsewhere. A good discussion of this point in *De ordine* is provided by O'Connell, "*De libero arbitrio* I," AS, 1 (1970), 58.

[209] *Contra ac.* 1.4.11. Noted by Duchrow, *Sprachverständnis*, pp. 23–24.

[210] *De div. quaest.* 34.

tion in opposing their own pagan or heretical antagonists, Augustine had a stake in defending his definition of the passions as irrational intellectual judgments in the context of his anti-Manichean brief. He too seeks to present God's anger and man's righteous indignation as acceptable. He resolves the dilemma by arguing that, in such cases, the state of mind described by the Psalmists is not a passion but an expression of power or virtue: *Iram autem et furorem Domine Dei non perturbationem mentis intellegi* ("For the anger and fury of the Lord God should not be understood as a perturbation of the mind.")[211] A similar exegetical imperative informs his discussion of the Epistle to the Romans, where he repeats the point that God suffers no passions (*perturbationes*). God's *ira* is thus not a passion but should be seen, rather, as *vindicatio* or requital for man's sin.[212] Augustine also invokes the doctrine of *eupatheia* as a companion piece and as a modification of the doctrine of *apatheia* provided by the Stoics themselves to support the idea that God is compassionate, in polemics with heretics and pagans alike. Against the Manichee Faustus, he uses a eupathetic conception of God as a Stoic weapon in attacking his opponent's theology while, on the other hand, he criticizes the Stoics, and by extension his pagan antagonist Nectarius, for granting to God and seeking in Him the quality of mercy which they impute to man as a moral weakness, here holding men to a strict *apatheia* which is relaxed in the case of the deity.[213]

Much more central to Augustine is the question of whether *apatheia*, associated or not with *eupatheia*, can appropriately define the moral state of the virtuous Christian. He begins to explore the positive answer to this question, recasting it in Christian terms, as early as his *De moribus*, in a series of observations paralleling Ambrose's view that *apatheia* is desirable and possible for the Christian, but only with the help of God's grace. The love of God, Augustine notes, enables the Christian to remain untroubled by misfortune and inspires him with the charitable desire to perform corporal works of mercy for his neighbor, however personally distasteful they may be. The serene tranquillity of mind (*mente tranquilla, rationis tranquillitate serenatur*) imparted by grace thus permits the Christian to overcome both fear, grief, and fastidiousness and to combine detachment in these respects with the feeling of mercy which God's love empowers him to shed upon his fellow man.[214] In his subsequent refer-

---

[211] *Enar. in Ps.* 2.4

[212] *Ad Romanos* 9. Similarly, *Civ. dei* 15.25; noted by Pierre de Labriolle, "Apatheia," *Mélanges de philologie, de littérature et de histoire anciennes offerts à Alfred Ernout* (Paris, 1940), p. 218.

[213] *Contra Faustum* 22.18; noted by Holte, *Béatitude et sagesse*, pp. 256–60; *Ep.* 92.

[214] *De moribus* 1.8.3–1.11.19, 1.26.48–1.28.58. The terms denoting Christian *apatheia* are at 1.27.53–54, OSA, sér. 1:1, p. 214. This point has been noted by Roland-Gosselin, in the comm. on his trans., p. 520 and by Osborn, *Ethical Patterns*, pp. 164–65.

ences to this topic Augustine treats the triumph over the passions as a process in which the Christian comes to recognize the transience of this life and his own moral infirmity, a realization inspiring him to look to God for the strength and patience to overcome tribulation. While this argument preserves and Christianizes Stoic *apatheia* it is used to attack the idea of Stoic autarchy and to replace it with the principle of man's dependence on God.[215] By associating both the passions and the humility before God needed to quell them with the conditions of the Christian's life *in via*, Augustine can also criticize the Stoics for claiming that *apatheia* is possible in this life on man's initiative, while reserving to the saints in the resurrection to come, of whom the Stoics knew nothing, the sole access to the state of *apatheia*.[216]

Concurrent with some of these attempts to Christianize *apatheia* or to salvage it in modified form, Augustine comes to similar conclusions by making a frontal attack on the Stoic doctrine of the passions and redefining them as moral states that are intrinsically good. Love, he asserts, is the desire to have what one wants, and joy is its possession. Fleeing from what one hates is fear, while feeling its presence is pain. All four affective states are good, he says, when the object of love is good and when the will is upright in seeking what it seeks, and evil if the reverse is the case.[217] This insight reflects the premise that moral attitudes are conditioned by their objective goals and subjective intentionalities. It also stems, for Augustine as for Lactantius and for other Christian writers, from the need to explain the goodness inhering in passions manifested by Biblical exemplars of virtue. After citing the same passage from Aulus Gellius describing the Stoic philosopher's account of his pallor during a storm at sea that he employs in the *City of God* to explore Stoic epistemology and ethics, Augustine uses it to reject expressly the Stoic view of the passions as unacceptable in commenting on the fear of the Lord expressed by Abraham, which he sees as a profoundly praiseworthy moral state.[218] But Augustine reserves his fullest fire for his exegesis of the Gospel of John, in exploring the unique and exemplary merits of the passion of Christ. Christ Himself truly suffered in mind and body. This fact, says Augustine, makes vain the wisdom of the world, here typified as the Stoics: *Pereant argumenta philosophorum qui negant in sapientem cadere perturbationes animorum* ("Down with the arguments of the philosophers who deny that the wise man can suffer perturbations of the soul.") Rather, like Christ the Lord the Christian should properly feel fear at

---

[215] *Civ. dei* 1.15, 9.3; *Ep.* 155, to Macedonius, ca. 414.
[216] *Sermo* 348.3.
[217] *Civ. dei* 14.7.2.
[218] *Quaest. in Gen.* 30.

the thought that a human soul may be lost, sorrow when one actually is
lost, desire to win salvation for his fellow men, and joy when this actually takes place:

> Istae sunt certe quatuor quas perturbationes vocant, timor et tristitia, amor
> et laetitia. Habeant eas iustis de causis animi christiani, nec philosopho-
> rum stoicorum, vel quorumcumque similium consentiatur errori; qui pro-
> fecto quemadmodum vanitatem existimant veritatem, sic stuporem depu-
> tant sanitatem, ignorantes sic hominis animum, quemadmodum corporis
> membrum, desperatius aegrotare, quando et doloris amiserit sensum.[219]

> These are certainly four of what they call passions: fear and sorrow, love
> and joy. And the minds of Christians have just cause for feeling them, if
> not the Stoic philosophers and whoever else like them agrees with this er-
> ror. For they indeed enlarge their vanity to the extent that they deem it a
> verity, thus regarding insensibility as soundness, ignoring that the soul of
> man, just as the members of his body, is the more gravely ill when it has
> lost even the capacity to feel pain.

This crushing judgment against Stoic *apatheia* cannot, ultimately, be
mitigated for Augustine by the admission of the *eupatheia*. In some contexts he criticizes *apatheia* by the debater's strategy of omitting the doctrine of *eupatheia* entirely, drawing for this purpose on the Ciceronian objection to Stoic ethics as impossibly harsh.[220] But in the passage in which
he subjects both *apatheia* and *eupatheia* to his most searching analysis, he
recognizes the fact that the Stoics deem the *eupatheia* of will, satisfaction,
and caution to be acceptable alternatives to desire, pleasure, and fear,
although they do not substitute any *eupatheia* for pain. The sage, they
teach, rightly exercises will in seeking the good. Satisfaction is the appropriate concomitant of possessing that good, which is the sage's own
condition. Caution assists him in avoiding evil. Since pain or sorrow arise
from an evil that has befallen and since the Stoics think that no wise man
succumbs to evil, *ipso facto*, they advocate no eupathetic passion corresponding to it. While Augustine does give the Stoics credit for acknowl-
edging that some passions can be good, he thinks that their doctrine is
seriously deficient. For one thing, fools and wicked men no less than sages
may manifest will, satisfaction, and caution, although, to be sure, in
pursuit of the false goods which they seek. Even more important, the
Christian can rightly manifest the four original Stoic passions as well as
the *eupatheia* which the Stoics approve when these passions are ordered
to the love of God and neighbor.

---

[219] *Tract. in Ioan.* 60.3, CC, 36, p. 479.
[220] *Civ. dei* 9.5. Noted by Hagendahl, *Augustine and the Latin Classics*, I, 76–77, 155–156;
Testard, *Saint Augustin et Cicéron*, I, 243.

This norm, Augustine adds, permits the Christian to attach still other emotions and affections to the list, which can be approved for the same reasons. Insofar as they spring from charity, the supreme virtue, and insofar as they are expressed and exercised in a fitting way, they are good. The behavior of God the Father and the incarnate Christ, Who display compassion, love, and sorrow, demonstrates the truth of this claim. For men to lack such affections in the present life would be an index of *inmanitas in animo, stuporis in corpore* ("blunted sensibilities both of mind and body.")[221] The goal of *apatheia* or *impassibilitas*, even when it means a freedom from those passions that are contrary to reason, is unattainable in this life, for the simple reason that man, as a sinner, is always capable of capitulating to them. Not even Adam and Eve before the Fall possessed *apatheia*, Augustine maintains, otherwise they could not have felt the desire for the forbidden fruit.[222] It is only in the next life, in which the saints will be free from the capacity to sin, that *apatheia* will be possible for man. But, going still farther, Augustine adds that, even in the state of blessedness, some of the passions, such as love and joy, will not only be retained but will also be consummated, enjoyed and possessed eternally in a perfect and perpetual security. And, it is those men who display these feelings during their pilgrimage on earth who witness their membership in the City of God, intimating thereby the manner of citizenship they will bear immortally within it.[223] Here, although Augustine credits Cicero with the essentials of the Stoic doctrine which he examines and demolishes, he provides a critique of far greater psychological penetration than Cicero does, based squarely on the theological centrality of love as a divine attribute and as a human virtue and on his temperamental inclination to locate man's humanity not so much in his mind as in his heart.

C) Free Will and Providence

Parallel with the development of Augustine's attitude toward *apatheia* and affected by the same circumstances are the programmatic changes that he makes in his doctrine of free will. In his earliest works Augustine links the freedom of the will with the act of making the intellectual judgments out of which the passions and their corresponding virtues arise. Particularly in connection with his anti-Manichean dossier of the time, he insists that the freedom of the will places virtue and vice within our

---

[221] *Civ. dei* 14.8-9. The quotation is at 14.9, CC, 48, p. 428; trans. Marcus Dods (New York, 1950), p. 454.
[222] Ibid. 14.10.
[223] Ibid. 14.9. Noted by Burnaby, *Amor Dei*, p. 95.

power, and that moral decisions involve volitional choices and not merely knowledge or ignorance.[224] In his later returns to the anti-Manichean stance in the *City of God* he repeats the same position in order to insist on the point that evil stems not from created material things but from a misdirected will that freely desires them in an inordinate manner.[225] But, by the time he had come to review his own past life in the *Confessions* in the effort to understand his own current state after more than a decade as a Christian, Augustine had grown far less confident both of the freedom of the will and of its unaided power to find and to adhere to the good. The chief characteristic of the human will which the story of his conversion had made clear to him by the late 390s was its mutability, its inconstancy, and the competing drives within it, a phenomenon as self-evident in the process of his conversion itself as it was in the fact of his own and others' generic capacity for both moral growth and back-sliding. The theme of the divided will, which finds its *locus classicus* in Augustine's account of his personal history on the eve of his conversion in *Confessions* 8 and which he makes the architectonic principle of the history of mankind which he elaborates in the *City of God*, becomes a definition of human nature itself for the late Augustine, underscoring the fallibility of man in comparison with God. The best statement of this idea is found in his sermons on the Gospel of John. While God is always the same, Augustine says, the human soul is changeable:

> Animae vero vita, valde aliter atque aliter: vivebat stulta, vivit sapiens; vivebat iniqua, vivit iusta; nunc meminit, nunc obliviscitur; nunc discit, nunc discere non potest; nunc perdit quod didicerat, nunc percipit quod amiserat; mutabilis vita animae.[226]

> The life of the soul, to be sure, is extremely variable. It used to live foolishly, now it lives wisely; it used to live sinfully, now it lives righteously; now it remembers, now forgets; now it learns, now it is incapable of learning; now it loses what it formerly learned, now it understands what it had lost. The life of the soul is mutable.

Similarly, the soul is beset by competing desires and it cannot always do what it wants. Even when the will settles on a goal, human weaknesses and inner conflicts may immobilize or frustrate man's good intentions.[227] Given these psychological realities, the mature Augustine finds the Stoic belief in the constancy and autarchy of the sage a profoundly

---

[224] *De lib. arb.* 1.12.25–26, 3.24.71–73. A good analysis is provided by O'Connell, "*De libero arbitrio* I," *AS*, 1 (1970), 49–68.

[225] *Civ. dei* 12.6, 12.8, 14.6–7.

[226] *Tract. in Ioan.* 19.11, CC, 36, p. 194. Similarly, 20.12.

[227] Ibid. 20.4.

naive one. Coupled with his pressing need to refute Pelagianism at the close of his career, this insight moved him to espouse the view that man's will is free only to sin and is capable of virtue only when freed by grace. Augustine specifically taxes the Pelagian Julianus of Eclanum with advocating the position, on Stoic grounds, that virtue is a natural possibility.[228] He makes essentially the same point about the necessity of grace for man's exercise of a good will in his heavily anti-Pelagian *Enchiridion*.[229] And, his nomination of obedience as the mother of the virtues in the *City of God*,[230] rather than Stoic prudence, Aristotelian justice, or Ambrosian temperance, reflects the deep misgivings of the later Augustine about man's ability to function as a moral agent *sui iuris*.

This replacement of the confidence he had felt, in the bright new dawn of his conversion, by his growing pessimism about man's powers inspired yet another revision of an earlier position in which Augustine had been heavily influenced by Stoicism, the relation between man's free will and God's providence. In this connection, while the development of his mature doctrine of grace and predestination inclined him toward a progressive depreciation of free will, Augustine does more than merely to reject or to Christianize the Stoic teaching. Rather than abandoning Stoicism, what he does is to accent different aspects of the Stoic view of fate and contingency at different points in his career, depending on whether he wants to stress free will or predestination and on whether he is measuring himself primarily against the Manichees or the Pelagians. His growing conviction of the psychological and theological truth of his anti-Pelagian arguments in his later life also inspires Augustine to review and to criticize his classical sources for the Stoic doctrine as well. Indeed, the Pelagians' own strategy of quoting the anti-Manichean Augustine against the anti-Pelagian Augustine leads him to refrain from citing the Stoics directly in his anti-Pelagian treatises and to apply the aspect of their position on free will which he seeks to use against the Pelagians in a somewhat more oblique manner.

Augustine's fullest evocation of the Stoics on fate and free will in defense of free will against the Manichees in his early career is found in his *De libero arbitrio*. Here, Augustine's principal aim is to show that the sole cause of evil in the world is a disordered will and that the capacity to will rightly as well as wrongly lies fully within man's power. No superhuman force is hence responsible for evil.[231] This claim leads to the problem of whether free will itself is necessary. In undercutting the

---

[228] *Contra secundam Juliani Responsionum imperfectus opus* 1.35, *PL*, 45.
[229] *Enchirid.* 4.15–15.17, 8.23–25, 9.30–32.
[230] *Civ. dei* 14.12.
[231] *De lib. arb.* 2.19.52–53, 2.20.54, 3.17.48–3.18.53.

Manichean view that some souls are innately capable of virtue and others are not, Augustine argues that all men have the same volitional capacity as a feature of the human nature common to all. He uses an analogy to explain this point which is reminiscent of the example of the cylinder used by Chrysippus to draw the same conclusions. A stone, says Augustine, being heavy by nature, tends to fall downward if it is unimpeded. But it may or may not be impeded, or set in motion, at a particular time. Similarly, free will is a natural endowment of man. To be sure, the possession of free will is a determined aspect of human nature as God has created it. But the choices men make in exercising their free will are thereby free, not necessary or determined.[232]

However, Augustine goes on, if this is the case, how can the world be governed by divine providence, a claim on which he also relies heavily in his anti-Manichean polemics. Augustine makes two important modifications of this topic as he had inherited it from classical philosophy. First, he eliminates completely the category of fortune or fate, whether as a synonym for God's ordering of the world or as an agency through which God operates. Second, he redefines providence as God's foreknowledge and argues for its compatibility with free will through an analysis of the divine psychology which, in turn, calls upon the theory of time as reducible to the present which Augustine also applies to a number of other problems. According to this view, God's providence resides in the fact that He knows what will happen before it takes place, whether it occurs as a necessary consequence of a cause or as the deliberately chosen act of a free moral agent. Although men, for instance, grow old and die of necessity, they do not make moral choices under any necessity. Man's free will is in no sense reduced merely because God knows how he will use it. Similarly, the fact that God knows ahead of time that a man will sin and that He will punish the man for his sin does not constrain the sinner to sin of necessity. Foreknowledge, Augustine stresses, is not the same thing as causation. God, in any event, lives in the eternal present. Everything He knows is known by Him in an utterly instantaneous manner, notwithstanding the fact that the events He knows will occur in the temporal sequence that governs the existence of created beings. God knows that some events will happen necessarily and others freely and His knowledge does not reduce the latter kind of event to the former. God's providence, to be sure, is responsible for an orderly nexus of causes in the universe and also for the creation of man with free will. As Augustine sums up his argument in the *De libero arbitrio, quia neque ipsos ideo coegit peccare quia fecit quibus potestatem utrum vellent dedit* ("the fact

---

[232] Ibid. 3.1.2–3.2.5.

that God has created men does not force them to sin just because He has given them the power to do so if they choose.")[233]

The emphasis on God's foreknowledge, not on His causal agency in the *De libero arbitrio*, is designed precisely to undermine the Manichean claim that God is responsible for the evils men do, whether by endowing some men with evil souls or by locating evil in matter. These themes reappear in several other anti-Manichean polemics or contexts. Augustine reiterates the point about man's freedom to choose the good or the evil in opposing dualism or psychic determinism as the cause of evil in his *De duabus animabus*,[234] although without relating the point to divine providence. He does make that connection in his *Contra Fortunatum*, where he observes that God's foreknowledge (*praescientia*) of man's sins does not cause those sins and that men cannot have merit or be responsible for their actions unless they can do the good voluntarily.[235] Augustine returns to the theme of man's moral responsibility in a sermon stressing that neither fortune nor fate, the devil, God, or any other metaphysical principle necessitates human choices, in an *ad hominem* argument reminiscent of both Juvenal and of Sallust and the other Roman historians who delineate fatalists as defeatists who refuse to take personal responsibility for what they achieve or fail to achieve.[236] In all these anti-Manichean connections Augustine's accent falls squarely on the defense of free will and this is the aspect of the Chrysippean position which he emphasizes the most strongly.

On the other hand, the later Augustine, while continuing to draw on the same Chrisippean argument and while retaining his redefinition of providence as divine foreknowledge, places much greater weight on the idea of God's universal causation. This argument is found at length, with the express citation of some of the classical sources from which he derived it coupled with an evaluation of them, in Book 5 of the *City of God*. This passage can be read as a covert criticism of Pelagianism as well as an overt assessment of pagan thought on fate and free will.[237] Augustine

---

[233] Ibid. 3.3.6–3.6.18. The quotation is at 3.5.14, CC, 29, p. 283; trans. Robert P. Russell, FC, 59 (Washington, 1968), p. 178.

[234] *De duabus animabus* 10.15, ed. and trans. Régis Jolivet, OSA, sér. 2:17 (Paris, 1961).

[235] *Contra Fortunatum* 15–16, ed. and trans. Régis Jolivet, OSA, sér. 2:17 (Paris, 1961).

[236] *Enar. in Ps.* 7.9.

[237] The best overall analysis is provided by W. Rordorf, "Saint Augustin et la tradition philosophique antifataliste: A propos de De Civ. dei 5, 1–11," *VC*, 28 (1974), 190–202. The anti-Pelagian dimension is brought out well by Harry A. Wolfson, "Philosophical Implications of the Pelagian Controversy," *Proceedings of the American Philosophical Society*, 103 (1959), 561–62. Augustine's criticism of his Ciceronian sources is treated well by Testard, *Saint Augustin et Cicéron*, I, 239–42. Hagendahl, *Augustine and the Latin Classics*, I, 70–75, 248–49; II, 527–29, 533–35 notes Augustine's Ciceronian and Senecan references but not his handling of them. Richard Sorabji, *Necessity, Cause, and*

begins by considering the case for astral determinism, which he rejects on principle and in practice. On principle, he refuses to let created beings, such as the heavenly bodies, share in God's unique causal power or control of the universe. In practice, too, the astrologers are unable to explain satisfactorily how twins born under the same stars can have differing personalities or fortunes. The claim that the heavenly bodies move so swiftly that they can assume a new configuration between the birth of one twin and another he dismisses as specious. Augustine also observes that the influence of diet and exercise, as the medical writers argue, undermines the force of the stars on human life. Augustine notes that there are some pagan thinkers who argue not that the stars themselves produce effects but rather that they are signs or portents of events ascribable to other causes. This point of view he prefers to the astral determinist position, although he notes that it still fails to account for the differing circumstances of twins born under the same signs. Now the Stoics had taught that the stars signify the events linked by the causal nexus which they identified with the divine *logos*, a theory they used to rationalize the practice of divination. It is not the Stoics' own position that Augustine ascribes to them here but astral fatalism, which he attributes to Posidonius. He ignores the environmental approach of Posidonius in this connection. He adds that the mathematician Nigidius Figulus also endorsed astral fatalism and that he tried, unsuccessfully in Augustine's opinion, to reply to the objection leveled against it concerning the fates of twins. As an astrologer, Posidonius' main contribution to the Stoic tradition was to elaborate on the mental states that made a seer receptive to the understanding of astral portents. The idea that Posidonius was an astral determinist is one Augustine derived from Cicero's *De divinatione* and *De natura deorum*, which depict the Stoics as the most virulent proponents of fatalism and determinism and which reflect what the Stoics' ancient critics said about them on this subject rather than what they actually taught.[238]

However, in the next section of Book 5, where he moves to consider the views of the pagans who locate fate not in the arrangement of the stars but in the whole chain of universal causes which they equate with

---

Blame: Perspectives on Aristotle's Theory (Ithaca, 1980), p. 80 adds Aulus Gellius to the list of Augustine's sources. Christian Parma, *Pronoia und Providentia: Der Vorsehungsbegriff Plotins und Augustins* (Leiden, 1971) sees Neoplatonism as Augustine's chief source and omits Stoicism. Eleuterio Elorduy, "La metafísica agustiniana," *Pensamiento*, 11 (1955), 142–45 sees Augustine as deriving his Stoicism via Neoplatonism but does not trace his position on fate and free will to any authors in particular.

[238] *Civ. dei* 5.1–6. Augustine draws a similar connection between mathematicians and astral determinists in *De doct. christ.* 2.21.32–2.22.34 and criticizes them there for the same reasons.

the power and will of God, Augustine indicates his knowledge of the fact that this, indeed, is the Stoics' position. He also shows his awareness of the compatibility of this doctrine with free will, and of Cicero's error in depicting the Stoics as unvarnished determinists. He does so by adverting to the Chrysippean theory which Cicero himself had cited, with approval, in his *De fato*.[239] Augustine quotes Seneca's *Ducunt volentem fata, nolentem trahunt* to underline the Stoics' belief in a universal law called fate, to which the sage must order his understanding and will. He adds that Cicero objected to this belief because it entails or supports divination, to which Cicero took exception. Cicero, he also notes, conflated fatalism as such with the astral determinism which he ascribed to the Stoa. While praising Cicero's attack on astrology and divination, Augustine recognizes that astral determinism is not the same thing as the equation of fate, as an orderly series of causes, with God, a Stoic position whose adherants he himself thinks are *multo . . . tolerabiliores* ("far more tolerable") than the astrologers,[240] because they provide greater scope for the doctrine of God's providence and foreknowledge. For, says Augustine, if God exists, He must govern the world and know the future, an idea that Cicero failed to grasp because he thought that it would make free will impossible. On this point, Augustine observes, the Stoics were more correct than Cicero because they knew that, although God destines all things, this does not make all events occur necessarily. In contrast, Cicero mistakenly held that divine foreknowledge meant necessitarianism.

In presenting his own counter-argument to that claim, Augustine repeats the Chrysippean coordination of free will and universal causation, making the same essential points that he had made in the *De libero arbitrio*. Here, too, he argues that God's providence can be defined as a foreknowledge that does not alter the intrinsic necessity or contingency of the various kinds of events that God foreknows. Augustine confines himself less preclusively to man's free will in this connection in the *City of God* than he had in the *De libero arbitrio* and other early works. He is, rather, concerned more generally with the God-given capacities of a wide range of creatures acting as secondary causes that may have necessary or contingent effects. Among the contingent effects he considers he includes the free choices of other animate beings besides men. While he thinks the Stoic's application of the term "fate" to the causal order is regrettable, he recognizes that they are not unmitigated necessitarians.

---

[239] *Civ. dei* 5.8–11 for this whole argument. Augustine also notes the Stoics' position on divine providence at 17.41 but in a setting where he contrasts their view with that of the Epicureans and uses the disagreements of the philosophers as a reason for rejecting all of them.

[240] Ibid. 5.9, CC, 47, p. 136.

With respect to God the term "necessity" can be attributed to His eternity, His infallibility, and His omnipotence without circumscribing Him in any way, for in His case these traits are not limitations but perfections. One can say that men necessarily have free will, as a consequence of the nature that God has given them, but this is a necessity that creates liberty rather than constraining it and that in no sense conflicts either with the power of the Creator Who chose to endow men with freedom or with His foreknowledge of how man will choose to exercise it.

While Augustine is certainly interested in showing that divine foreknowledge does not limit human free will in the *City of God*, he is just as concerned with showing that free will does not limit God's omnipotence and omniscience. And, although he observes that man must possess free will in order to live a meaningful moral life, he omits the theme of ethical merit which he had earlier seen man as capable of acquiring through the exercise of free will. Instead, he views the importance of the relationship between man's free will and his responsibility for his actions from the standpoint of God's justice in rewarding and punishing men in the next life. Augustine thus sides with the Stoics' emphasis on the divinely ordained governance of the world through a chain of interconnected causes, purged of its fatalistic or astral determinist associations, as a way of underscoring God's control of the world despite the existence of freedom and contingency in some of His creatures. And, although Augustine translates providence into foreknowledge in this section of the *City of God* as he had earlier, he clearly associates this notion with a deity conceived much more causally than the God of the *De libero arbitrio*, a point visible not only by his posing of the question initially in terms of determinism and necessitarianism but also by the examples he provides in the latter part of Book 5 to amplify and illustrate this theme. They are all cases in which God ordains the prosperity or adversity of rulers, both pagan and Christian.[241] The God with Whom Augustine is treating in this part of the *City of God*, then, is the God Who is the Lord of history and the anti-Pelagian predestinarian God Who has chosen and guided the members of the heavenly city from all eternity.

D) Friendship, the Honestum and the Utile

There are two final ethical topics, friendship and the nature of the *honestum* and the *utile*, on which Augustine's thought undergoes a programmatic change. These themes can be related to the problem of free will and fate in that, in each case, he derived his initial position from Cicero

---

[241] Ibid. 5.21–26.

and his move away from it involves an implicit criticism of Cicero and the emergence of a view that is not only Christianized, and sometimes Neoplatonized, but which is also more Stoic than Cicero's in certain respects. Augustine takes up both of these subjects for the first time in his *De diversis quaestionibus*. His original definitions of the *honestum* and the *utile* and of friendship are found in *quaestio* 31, where he quotes Cicero's *De inventione* verbatim. He thus reiterates Cicero's idea that the *honestum* comprises the four cardinal virtues, which are to be sought for their own sake but which allow considerable room for private rights, interests, and dignities under the heading of the virtue of justice. Similarly, Augustine lists friendship under the rubric of the *utile*, along with glory, rank, and grandeur, which are sought for the advantages they confer and not as ends in themselves. All these definitions involve a Ciceronian and Peripatetic value structure, however initially Stoic the terminology may be.[242]

In the very same work and in an adjacent *quaestio* comes Augustine's first modification of his view of the *honestum* and the *utile*, one that rejects not only the *De inventione* formulae but also the more substantial revision of Cicero's position in his *De officiis*. The influence of Ambrose has been seen here, and it is likely,[243] although Augustine takes another tack. Augustine begins by dismissing the conflation of the *honestum* with the *utile*. To say that everything good is useful, or that everything useful is good, he states, blurs one's moral point of view and confuses the relations between means and ends. He himself parallels the distinction between the *honestum* and the *utile* with his own distinction between *frui* and *uti*. The things to be enjoyed remain ends in themselves, but they are no longer defined as the virtues. They are now seen as objects of intellectual contemplation and aesthetic delectation, aspects of the *intelligibilem pulchritudinem, quam spiritualem nos proprie dicimus* ("intelligible beauty, which we properly call spiritual.") The *utile*, on the other hand, now refers to divine providence, which governs the created world. It is in the light of a well-ordered use and enjoyment of created goods, says Augustine, that we should seek our spiritual ends, the chief of which is the knowledge and love of God. Here Augustine divests worldly goods of any kind of moral finality while Neoplatonizing and Christianizing his conception of the supreme good. In his last reformulation of this theme in the *De doctrina christiana* Augustine asserts that the eternal God is not only the supreme good but the only good Whom it is proper to enjoy. The *fruitio dei* becomes the reference point against which everything else is measured. But in this case the *utilia* are the liberal arts, considered from the per-

---

[242] *De div. quaest.* 31.1–3.
[243] Ibid. 30. Noted by Beckaert in his comm., OSA, sér. 1:10, pp. 714–15.

spective of how they help or hinder the exegete and preacher in understanding and communicating the saving truth of Holy Scripture.[244] However Neoplatonic his hierarchical moral schema is in general, Augustine's final handling of this question serves to reStoicize it in union with a specifically Christian program, in that he treats the liberal arts not as Ciceronian *utilia* or *officia* but as Stoic preferables. They may be graded as better, or worse, or as neutral in their contribution to the moral end they serve, but they are different in kind from it.

As for friendship, Augustine drops entirely, and much more abruptly, the wholly or partly utilitarian conception of this *topos* found both in the *De inventione* and in Cicero's later works, replacing it with a definition of friendship as a freely chosen relationship between wise men unconditioned by worldly advantages, *more Stoicorum*. At the same time, he Christianizes this doctrine by locating the source of true friendship in the friends' common possession of the virtue of charity and in their common yearning for eternal beatitude.[245] Augustine is actually more Stoic in his handling of Christian friendship than contemporaries such as Ambrose and John Cassian, who are more sensitive to the need to view the Christian friends as men *in via*, eager to correct each other's faults, rather than seeing themselves or each other as perfected sages. On the other hand, Augustine is less Stoic than Jerome on friendship, in that it never occurs to him to extend the possibility of this kind of relationship to persons who are not members of his own sex. The two Stoic themes of friendship and the preferables, in any event, are the only cases in which the development of Augustine's ideas over time leads him to adopt a more Stoic rather than a less Stoic position in the course of his career. Within the category of his thought which we have labelled a programmatic change of attitude toward Stoicism, they are the exceptions that prove the rule.

Conclusion

From the extended consideration of Stoicism in St. Augustine which we have just completed it should be clear that his knowledge of the philosophy of the Stoa is as accurate, as extensive, and as discerning as his applications of it are complex and multiform. In the numerous contexts

---

[244] *De doct. christ.* 1.3.3–1.22.21. Burnaby, *Amor Dei*, pp. 104–07 sees this shift as an exclusively Platonizing one. Baguette, "Le Stoïcisme," pp. 31–34 does not include this topic in his discussion of the theme of *officium* in Augustine.

[245] *Ep.* 155, to Macedonius, ca. 414; *In Ep. Joan.* 8.5. The latter reference is noted by Luigi Franco Pizzolato, "L'amicizia in S. Agostino e il 'Laelius' di Cicerone," *VC*, 28 (1974), 208–15.

in which he locates his appropriations of Stoic doctrine Augustine has ample and repeated occasion to draw on it both positively and negatively, whether *ad hoc*, in a consistent manner, or with an increasingly critical and adaptive outlook. All of these orientations toward Stoicism are strongly represented in his thought and all of them are equally Augustinian. The bishop of Hippo was recognized at once by his contemporaries and immediate successors as the premier theological mind of his time. His writings had already begun to be rifled and anthologized by excerpters within a decade or so after his death. This tendency had the effect of grouping together, for use as proof texts, Augustinian *loci* on the same subjects irrespective of their original contexts, however much those contexts contribute to a grasp of his attitude toward the Stoic material which these passages contain. The same procedure also had the effect of promoting an uncontextual reading even of works such as the *Confessions* and the *City of God*, despite the importance of their structure and organization for an understanding of their message. With these circumstances in mind, it may be useful to close this chapter by recalling that later Latin students of Augustine could find in his works a tremendous amount of information about the teachings of the Stoics, whether attested, approved, or disapproved by Augustine himself. Having already devoted our attention to the personal and contextual considerations inspiring his own multiple approaches to this material, it may be most convenient to summarize it here topically, under the traditional subdivisions of logic, physics, and ethics.

The first two of these branches of Stoic philosophy are heavily represented in Augustine's thought. There are the areas in which his support for the Stoa is the most extensive and where he makes his own most creative applications of its teachings both to philosophical and to theological problems. Except for the fact that he omits a full-scale discussion of the hypothetical syllogisms, his knowledge of Stoic logic and of Stoic semantics is extremely acute and wide-ranging, both in its general spirit and in its specific details and implications. He is aware of the Stoics' differentiation between words as natural signs, articulate sonic forms distinguishable both from the inarticulate cries of animals and men and from the incorporeal intramental *lekta*, or intellectual intentions which make up logical propositions. He has a firm grasp of the essentially propositional character of Stoic logic and of the force of various ways of expressing negation. This understanding of Stoic logic and semantics is clearly visible in Augustine's early works devoted expressly to logic and epistemology. He also applies these doctrines with adroitness, appositeness, and originality to the solution of a host of semantic, logical, and theological problems ranging from sign theory *per se* to exegesis, from the analysis of lies and falsehoods to the powers and limits of theological statements, and to the analogies and dis-analogies between human mental operations and the nature of the Trinity.

Augustine's response to Stoic physics is less accepting and the range of physical doctrines on which he draws is more selective. The chief issues on which he invokes Stoic physics, whether positively or negatively, are the nature of God and the nature of man. He forcefully rejects both Stoic monism and the idea that everything which acts is a body, in favor of a spiritual conception of God and of the human soul and a hierarchization both of the created universe and of man's faculties that owes much to Neoplatonism. He provides a good deal of information on Stoic theodicy, providence, and natural law, conceived as an orderly nexus of causes associated with a rational and benevolent deity, although he sometimes resituates these themes in a setting of revealed law and predestinarian theology which substitutes the divine will for the divine reason and which limits the natural intelligibility of God's governance of the world. Augustine appreciates the utility of the Stoic notion of time as a way of recasting the *topos* of God's providence into divine foreknowledge and as a way of describing the mental operations of the deity, both in resolving exegetical problems concerning God's activities before the creation of the world and in asserting the compatibility of divine providence and human free will. He reports, and maintains an open mind on, the Stoic doctrine of *krasis* and on the idea that all the elements are capable of changing into each other. On the other hand, he opposes strongly the cyclical cosmology with which the Stoics connected these two principles, as he does any identification of God with the created world. The Stoic physical theme that Augustine orchestrates the most exhaustively is the idea of seminal reasons, which he uses to explain the foresight of God in ordaining natural phenomena whether ordinary or extraordinary as well as His activity in the workings of grace and in the performance of miracles.

The central psychological themes which Augustine borrows from the physics of the Stoics are their notion of the mind as the *hegemonikon* of man and their epistemology. He agrees with the doctrine of the *hegemonikon* although he situates this idea within a hierarchical anthropology which views the body as different from and as inferior to the mind. Although he departs from the Stoics' psychological monism, Augustine endorses their insistence that the passions arise from false intellectual judgments, similarly locating the passions in man's mind and will, not in his body. Augustine also retains the Stoic understanding of sense perception as both an extramissive and an intromissive process, in which the mind is active and not merely passive and in which sensation is catalyzed by a pneumatic force operating in a world seen as a material plenum. He is nonetheless reluctant to equate this material *pneuma* with the mind itself, preferring to treat it as a subordinate mental faculty through which the mind energizes the senses. While Augustine clearly presents both the intromissive as well as the extramissive sides of the phenomenon of sense perception, the assignments which he gives to this doctrine, ranging from exegesis to sexual ethics to the description of the resurrected body in the life to come, incline him to refer to the extramissive aspect much more frequently. Augustine also replicates the Stoic conviction of the possibility of attaining certain knowledge and he is aware of the fact that the Stoics located the criterion both in sensation and in the intellectual judgment of sense data. He outlines both the empirical side of this doctrine, which includes the sensory foundation of common notions, as well as the stages through which the sensory *phantasia* is converted into a *synkatathesis* or intellectual judgment and a *katalepsis* held with certainty.

Although the psychology of the Stoics is organically related to their ethics, Augustine feels quite free to unshackle ethical ideas that he approves or discards from these connecting links. Of all the subdivisions of the philosophy of the Stoa, ethics is unquestionably the one that he handles with the most selectivity and independence and with the most discrimination concerning the intermediary sources by which it reached him. While Augustine agrees that the mind of man is the *hegemonikon* and that the passions as well as correct moral judgments arise in the intellect, he rejects the corollary notion of the equality of all sins stemming from a consistent orientation toward evil. At the same time, he accepts the complementary principle of the equality and co-inherence of the virtues while progressively redefining the central intentionality that animates them as the love of God. Augustine rejects the third ethical category of the Stoics, the *adiaphora*, arguing that nothing is really ethically neutral. He retains the view, on the other hand, that, since men are rational and animals are not, ethical norms for men cannot be extrapolated from animal behavior. He also preserves the principle of Panaetian casuistry although he applies it only to God's enforcement of His own law, rather than to man's exercise of moral choice. Augustine has a thorough and circumspect understanding of the Stoic conception of the sage. He admires some of the sage's attributes, such as his resolute adherance to a *summum bonum* that can never be lost and his imperturbability in the face of misfortune. But Augustine casts off the idea that the sage, his virtue, and the *summum bonum* he seeks can be viewed in purely human terms. He is particularly critical of the doctrine of *apatheia* as a moral state that is either possible or desirable. His agreement with the principle that virtue lies within man's autarchic power to attain and retain is sharply circumscribed by his experience of the divided will and severely limited by his mature position on grace and predestination and his conception of the *ordo amoris*, developments of his own theological outlook that eventually lead him to dismiss Stoic autarchy as an exercise in illusion and self-deification. The same principle that no created good can be an end in itself informs Augustine's Christianization of the themes of friendship and the preferables. In the latter case he combines this ethical idea with the semantic theory he derived from the Stoa to undergird his subordination of learning, teaching, and preaching to the ethical attitude of the speaker and his audience and to the instrumentality of human language, and of men themselves, as signs and channels of divine illumination.

Augustine is most likely to ascribe his Stoic ideas to members of that school, or to Stoicism more generally, in cases where he criticizes Stoic doctrines or uses them *ad hoc* than in cases where he approves them or uses them as constructive principles in his own thought. This tendency stems less from his lack of familiarity with the ultimate provenance of his Stoic ideas or from his awareness of how they had been transmitted as it does from the rhetorical exigencies of the contexts in which he makes his Stoic references. Whether or not he gives the Stoics their due, he provided later medieval readers with a remarkably deep, broad, and accurate trove of information about Stoic philosophy. He also laid before his readers a number of models, some complementary and some competing, of how a Christian scholar might apply Stoicism to philosophical and theological questions, both as an inheritance from the classical world that he could use with confidence or as a pagan alternative against which to measure himself as a Christian. Augustine's sixth-century successors were not slow to mine that vein. But, for all his towering authority, Augustine shared with his Latin predecessors, both pagan and Christian, the occasional misreadings, the preference for selected aspects of Stoicism, and the creative adaptations of Stoicism that were to mark the approaches to that tradition in the last century of the Latin patristic age.

CHAPTER FIVE

THE SIXTH CENTURY:
LOOKING BACKWARD AND AHEAD

The authors treated in this chapter span the entire sixth century chronologically and represent the chief centers in north Africa, Italy, southern France, and Spain where classical learning and Christian culture survived in the age of the Germanic successor states. In eminence they are a decidedly mixed lot, ranging from figures as major as Gregory the Great and Boethius to those as minor as Licinianus of Cartagena and Julianus Pomerius. Two of them, Boethius and Cassiodorus, were laymen who could best be classified as entrepreneurs in their intellectual endeavors. All but one of the rest were bishops, some of whom had been monks enroute to the prelacy, whose works reflect the exegetical, homiletic, pastoral, or polemic responsibilities of their office. Despite their heterogeneity, these sixth-century authors display certain characteristics as a group that earmark them inescapably as men of their times and that set them off from most of their counterparts in the fourth and fifth centuries. They all lived in an age marking the conclusive replacement of the Roman Empire throughout western Europe and north Africa by the regimes of a series of Germanic conquerers. On one level this situation created a new threat to the orthodox faith, since, except for the Merovingian Franks, the Germans were Arians to the extent that they were Christianized at all. The efforts of the eastern emperor Justinian to recover the western Empire and to subject the Church there to caesaropapism contributed still another source of political disruption and religious jeopardy to the already turbulent picture. Aside from the challenges to the Catholic faith entailed by these political changes, the Germanic conquests had a significant, and negative, effect on classical learning, hitherto supported by the Roman state. Christian thinkers, both clerics and laymen, were keenly aware of the educational problems posed by the collapse of the state-run educational system and several of those to be discussed below deliberately took on the task of preserving the classical tradition, with a clear-eyed understanding of the fact that no one else would assume this duty if they failed in it.

A third result of the Germanic conquests was the breakdown of literary community among the Latin Christian writers themselves, a function of the political separation of the former provinces of the Roman Empire from each other under their several Germanic rulers. Aside from

Gregory the Great, whose status as pope and whose broad conception of his office made him the eyes and ears of his world, the vast majority of the Latin writers of the sixth century worked in virtual isolation from each other. Even when they were interested in the same questions, which is frequently the case, they often remained quite unaware of what their coevals or older contemporaries had said about them. They were far more likely to respond to the ideas of the authors who had lived a century or more before their time. Despite these problems of communication, it is also true that the Latin Christian thinkers of the sixth century display some striking similarities in their intellectual interests and methods, visible in their treatment of the Stoic tradition no less than in their approach in general. With a few exceptions—and the exceptions are important—they focus narrowly on ethics of the most practical sort. There is a general decline in speculation as the interest in the derivation, interconnection, and inner dynamics of the Stoic doctrines involved gives way before the need to resolve immediate personal or pastoral dilemmas. Few of these thinkers appear to have had the time or resources to make independent investigations into the questions that concerned them. They typically seize on the philosophical ideas they want to use, from whatever indirect source is readily available, without stopping to document them. The incidence of named *testimonia* to Stoics and to specific Stoic doctrines declines precipitously in comparison with the preceding century or so. Even more exiguous is a sense of the context in which these Stoic ideas had been put, whether by the Stoics themselves, by Stoicizing classical authors, or by Latin Christian intermediaries. The result, not surprising, is a tendency toward dilution, both of the Stoic force of the ideas and of the sense of the intellectual configurations within which previous thinkers had situated them. It is only in rare cases that the sixth-century writers seek to adjust Stoicism to competing philosophical views, whether positively or negatively. When this occurs, the honors go to Neoplatonism and, to a lesser extent, to Aristotelianism. They are far more likely to absorb what Stoicism they absorb into a Christian mentality that is lightly burdened by philosophy of any kind. To the extent that later medieval readers could gain any notion of how Stoic thought could accord with Christianity from a perusal of the writers of the sixth century it was not as a technical philosophy, not as a world view, and not even as a full-scale ethics, but as a handful of ethical ideas, abstracted from their contexts and gleaned largely from the earlier Church Fathers, some to be criticized but most to be accepted as compatible with Christianity, that could be pressed into service to meet the exigent practical educational and pastoral needs of an embattled and fragmented Christian society whose theology and whose classical culture were now equally on the defensive. For most of the authors of the day the task was not innovation but preservation, and their predecessors of the earlier patristic age were the great models for the integration—or separation—of Stoicism and Christianity that they envisaged in their own works.

I. Looking Backward: The Minor Figures

This backward-looking stance is the dominant attitude in the sixth century and its exponents populate the largest subdivision of our cast of characters, cutting across the categories of major and minor figures. However extensively these authors may have written, their Stoic references are limited to a restricted range of topics—the passions, the nature of the soul, natural law, and cosmetic theology. In virtually all cases, the sixth-century writers recapitulate the Christian applications of Stoicism to these questions that had been in circulation since the fourth century if not earlier. Cosmetic theology is the only one of these topics to which they can remotely be said to have made fresh contributions. Such few innovations, when they occur, are a response to new social conditions. But, even so, like the more traditional contemporary applications of this *topos*, they are framed in imagery drawn from earlier Latin Christian models.

A) Julianus Pomerius

One may well begin with Julianus Pomerius, if only for the reason that his unique reference to Stoicism is, at the same time, one of the century's few express citations of the Stoa and the one that is easily the most dependent on a previous patristic authority, in this case Augustine. Like his mentor, Julianus (late fifth century-early sixth century) was born in north Africa and emigrated northward to enhance his fortunes as a professional rhetorician, although in Arles rather than Italy. He was later ordained to the priesthood and bore the title of abbot, but nothing definite is known about his ecclesiastical career. Julianus wrote four treatises, on the soul, on the contempt of the world, a rule for nuns, and *De vita contemplativa*. Only the last named work has survived. In it Julianus criticizes the Stoic theory of the passions in a passage lifted bodily from Augustine's *City of God*.[1] The context, however, is quite different from Augustine's. Where Augustine treats this subject in the course of a broad survey of the inadequacies of the various schools of pagan philosophy on the good life, Julianus includes the Stoic passions merely as an appendix

---

[1] Julianus Pomerius, *De vita contemplativa* 3.31.1–5, *PL*, 59.

to his positive discussion of the Christian virtues and what promotes them.

Following Augustine, Julianus notes that the Stoics teach that there are four passions (*affectiones*) which they foolishly regard as vices: fear, sorrow, desire, and pleasure (*timere, dolere, cupere, laetari*). The idea that these passions are vices he rejects outright on Biblical grounds; since they were manifested by many Old and New Testament worthies, including Christ Himself, they must be pleasing to God. Vice, rather, is the absence of affections rightly ordered to their proper ends. In themselves, says Julianus, the passions are morally neutral. They may bear virtuous or vicious fruit depending on how they are directed. Thus, he adds, we should disdain the Stoics, who say that the passions should be utterly extinguished to the point where the sage has no feelings at all. Having thus erroneously ascribed *anaesthesia* to the Stoics in place of their doctrine of *apatheia*, Julianus goes on to note that their admission of the *eupatheia* is hence a contradiction. He reports the same eupathetic qualifications of the Stoic passions as Augustine: *cautionem pro timore, pro laetitia gaudium, et voluntate pro cupiditate* ("caution instead of fear, joy for pleasure, and willing for desiring.")[2] He also observes that the Stoics supply no eupathetic substitute for grief, since this passion would only arise as a consequence of sorrow for sin and the sage, according to the Stoics, is incapable of sin, a claim which Julianus, like Augustine, regards as false and presumptious. A series of arguments from Scripture follow to combat this position, coupled with the Ciceronian view, by way of Augustine, that some emotions are good. Julianus also states that Vergil is opposed to the Stoics here because he disparaged happiness as an attainable goal. On this note Julianus concludes that the passions are conditioned by the ends they serve *sine aliqua Stoicorum distinctione superflua* ("without any unnecessary Stoic distinction.")[3]

Close as he is to Augustine on the Stoic passions, there is still a noticeable dimming of Augustine's account in Julianus' handling of this theme. Aside from his somewhat garbled interpretation of Vergil and his confusion of *apatheia* with *anaesthesia*, which are not found in Augustine, he omits the analysis of the origin of the passions in false judgments, which Augustine includes. Further, while Augustine also rejects the idea that anyone can be incapable of sin in this life, his own attack on that claim is based on its psychological implausibility, while Julianus rests his case on a barrage of Scriptural proof texts. Thus, Julianus is content to repeat the externals of the Stoic doctrine reported by Augustine with-

---

[2] Ibid. 3.31.2, *PL*, 59, col. 515B.
[3] Ibid. 3.31.5, *PL*, 59, col. 516C.

out absorbing the spirit of Augustine's own inquiry into the inner logic
and psychological dynamics of that position.

B) Caesarius of Arles

Caesarius (ca. 470–543) studied rhetoric under Julianus at Arles and
went on to a far better documented career as a churchman. After several
years as a monk at Lérins he was ordained a priest and in 499 became
abbot of another monastery near Arles. He was elected bishop of Arles
in 503. Caesarius' episcopal administration stressed ecclesiastical reform, preaching, and pastoral work more than dogmatic or speculative
theology, although his works touch on most of the genres of patristic literature. They include letters dealing with political matters, Trinitarian
polemics aimed at the Arians, a compendium of Christian doctrine directed against assorted heretics, a treatise on grace, a rule for nuns, a
commentary on Apocalypse, and a substantial collection of *sermones ad
populum*. There has been an exaggerated claim that the theme of examination of conscience in Caesarius' sermons derives from Stoicism.[4] His
chief contribution to the history of the Stoic tradition lies, rather, in the
field of cosmetic theology, in his application of Paulinus of Nola's imagery for the defense of the monastic tonsure to an allegorical exegesis
of the story of Samson and Delilah designed to offer moral guidance to
the male sex in general.[5] Caesarius sets this message in an ideological
framework combining natural law, as he understands it, with the law of
God, and in a social context in which the Romano-Germanic conventions with which Paulinus wrestled have been replaced by the Merovingian mystique of the long-haired kings.

It is a fact that the male members of all the Germanic tribes now in-
stalled in the former Roman Empire wore their hair long. But, the Merovingian Franks who held sway in Gaul appear to have gone farther than
any of their cognates in associating long hair not only with masculinity
but also with the awesome power attached to the kingship. Much contemporary evidence survives to illustrate this notion, from the depiction
of Merovingian kings with long hair on their seals and coins to the belief, recorded by Gregory of Tours somewhat later in the century, that
a male member of the royal family would lose the magic aura and the
eligibility to rule thought to inhere in the line of Clovis if his hair were

---

[4] Pierre Courcelle, *Connais-toi toi-même de Socrate à Saint Bernard*, 3 vols. (Paris, 1974–75),
I, 195-98.
[5] Caesarius' literary dependence on Paulinus has been demonstrated by Antonio Salvatore, *Due omelie su Sansone di Caesario di Arles e l'Epistola 23 di Paolino da Nola* (Napoli,
1969), pp. 32–37.

ever cut. Gregory cites a particularly graphic instance in his report of an internecine cabal in which two sons of Clovis sought to disqualify two of their nephews who were in the queen mother's protection. Having secured the persons of the young princes, they sent an emissary to the queen bearing a naked sword in one hand and a pair of scissors in the other, asking her to decide on the fate of her grandsons. She chose the sword, replying that she would rather see them dead than with their hair cut short. And so it was done.[6] Princes bested in such fratricidal struggles were sometimes forced into monasteries as a way of disposing of them as political rivals. But is was not the fact of monastic vows but his tonsure, whether monastic or not, that prevented a male member of the ruling house from aspiring to the throne. The masculine haircut, in sixth-century Gaul, was the equivalent of political castration. While kings, to be sure, were men set apart, the mysterious power associated with their uncut hair could not fail to convey a more general belief in the connection between uncut hair and masculinity as such. This pagan survival remained pervasive despite the fact that the Merovingians had been titular Catholics since Clovis' dramatic conversion at the beginning of the century.

Such being the case, Caesarius faced a delicate task in seeking to explicate the meaning of Samson's haircut. The easy way out would have been to follow the traditional line, citing Samson as a sinner befuddled by lust who received his due punishment. But this strategy would have involved an encomium on the long-haired Samson before his lapse which might imply that Caesarius was putting his episcopal stamp of approval on the still-pagan tonsorial ideology of the Frankish kings. At the same time, it was clearly necessary to condemn Delilah for cutting Samson's hair and Samson for failing to withstand her blandishments. Caesarius arrives at a felicitous solution which draws on Paulinus of Nola's image of the *Christus novacula*, with the razor wielded in two directions:

> Est autem novacula nunc salutiferae, nunc pestiferae sectionis. Remedii et decoris novacula nobis Christus dominus est, qui de corde nostro cogitationes malignas et noxias circumcidit, vitia radit animae. . . Novacula ergo salutifera Christus est, et novacula mostifera diabolus est.[7]

---

[6] Gregory of Tours, *Historia francorum* 3.18, ed. Wilhelmus Arndt, *MGH*, Scriptorum rerum Merovingicarum (Hannover, 1885), I, 861. On this theme more generally see J. M. Wallace-Hadrill, *The Long-Haired Kings and Other Studies in Frankish History* (New York, 1962), pp. 245–47.

[7] Caesarius of Arles, *Sermo* 120.2, ed. D. Germani Morin, CC, 103 (Turnhout, 1953), p. 501; trans. Mary Magdalene Mueller, FC, 47 (Washington, 1964), II, 194–95. I have altered the translation slightly.

Now there is one razor which cuts in a wholesome manner, another which does so in a harmful way. For us, the razor of healing and beauty is Christ our Lord, who cuts wicked and hurtful thoughts from our heart and shaves vice from our soul . . . Thus, the salutary razor is Christ, while the deadly one is the devil.

Here, the cutting of hair is allegorized to represent the cutting off either of virtues or vices, depending on who plies the razor and for what purposes. Delilah, in Caesarius' exposition, clearly represents the temptress, the devil's minion. But Samson's capitulation to her allure means much more than man's yielding to sexual temptation. It also signifies, for Caesarius, a surrender to an incorrect ordering of natural and supernatural priorities in which man is subordinated to woman, the spirit to the flesh, and the Church to the Synagogue, which Samson and Delilah signify respectively.[8] Caesarius' remarkable balancing act unites a subtle criticism of Merovingian values with an elaborate allegorical reading of Scripture and with an echo, faint but still discernible, of the Stoic association between natural law and ethics, although in this case he sternly reverses the Stoic position on the moral equality of the sexes.

C) Leander of Seville

With Leander of Seville, elder brother of the more famous Isidore and his predecessor as bishop of that see from 579 to 600, we move across the Pyrenees but remain with the topic of cosmetic theology. Leander's only surviving work is his *De institutione virginum et contemptu mundi*, written for his sister Florentina, a nun. In genre and directionality it looks backward to the advice offered by Cyprian to the uncloistered female celibates of an earlier day. To the extent that Leander invokes nature as a norm he shares Caesarius' view that, in the natural order, women are inferior to men, an idea he interprets in a strictly biological sense.[9] This point appears only in the introduction to Leander's rule for nuns. In the natural order, he states, women who wear cosmetics, perfume, jewelry, and elaborate clothes practice deception for unchaste reasons, even if they do so to please the husbands to whom they are subjected. Since this is so, he concludes, how much the worse are these adornments in the case of nuns, whose supernatural calling frees them from the rule of husbands.[10] Here, the original Stoic elements in the *topos* are all but invisi-

---

[8] Caesarius elaborates these themes in the passage following the one cited, *Sermo* 120.2–4.

[9] Leander of Seville, *De institutione virginum et contemptu mundi*, proemium, *PL*, 72, col. 880A.

[10] Ibid., cols. 879A–880A, 881A–C.

ble. Leander's treatise suggests that, by the end of the sixth century, Latin Christian writers had exhausted the applications of Stoic cosmetic theology to women and that they now invoked it as a set of thoroughly Christian, and thoroughly banal, commonplaces.

D) Fulgentius of Ruspe

Yet, the same *topos* that receives such jejune treatment in Leander's hands had undergone some slight development earlier in the century, a fact that can be documented from the work of Fulgentius of Ruspe. Cosmetic theology for women is one of the points of contact between Fulgentius and the Stoic traditon, although not the only one. The scion of a senatorial family from Carthage, Fulgentius (ca. 462–527) entered the civil service after completing his education and rose to the rank of procurator of his native city. He was attracted to the ascetic life, entered a monastery, and became its co-abbot. But political convulsions caused by the incursions of the Berbers and religious oppression at the hands of the reigning Arian Vandals forced his community to flee. Fulgentius was about to join the desert monks in the Thebaid in ca. 499 when he was prevailed upon to enter the pastoral ministry instead. He did so after a pilgrimage to Rome and some further years as a monk, being elected bishop of Ruspe in ca. 502. His tenure was interrupted by exile on two occasions owing to the Vandals' persecution of Catholic churchmen. Fulgentius' writings are more variegated than those of many of his contemporaries. They fall into three categories: a series of Trinitarian polemics addressed to the Vandal king Trasimund and other prominent Arian leaders; a series of works defending Augustine's doctrine of predestination, grace, and free will against the Pelagians; and a series of short treatises on episcopal administration and individual moral problems, and his letters. Throughout his *œuvre* Fulgentius sees the vindication of Augustinian orthodoxy as his mission. His references of Stoicism, none of which are express, are largely unrelated to this goal, and they rarely replicate either the emphasis or the profundity of his esteemed model.

Aside from the cosmetic theology found in two of his letters to female correspondents, Fulgentius makes two other allusions to Stoic doctrines, both playing a marginal role in the arguments in which they are placed. He devotes a brief section of his *De veritate praedestinationis et gratiae dei* to a rehearsal of the errors rampant on the divine and human natures, including and criticizing Tertullian's view that both God and the human soul are material.[11] Unlike Augustine, it does not occur to Fulgentius to

---

[11] Fulgentius of Ruspe, *De veritate praedestinationis et gratiae dei* 3.33, ed. J. Fraipont in

draw on Stoicism in dealing with the larger question of providence and free will, the central theme of the book. However, he is somewhat more successful in making the relevant connections in an anti-Pelagian letter addressed to several fellow bishops. Here, he contrasts the natural law and the written, or Old Testament, law with the law of grace. His cursory definition of the natural law as the bond of human society (*societatis humanae vinculum*) might conceivably be Stoic, at least if Fulgentius had given any indication of what he thought that bond actually was. In any event, his main point is to associate both the natural and the written law with free will and to insist that they are superseded by the Christian law of grace.[12] His polemical agenda thus encourages Fulgentius to draw a sharp distinction between nature and God, in contrast with earlier patristic and apologetic authors who had assimilated natural law as right reason to the law of God.

Fulgentius' cosmetic theology has a stronger Stoic coloration, despite the fact that it is mediated through earlier writers such as Cyprian and Jerome. His chief contribution in this context is to spiritualize the advice these authorities had given to widows and consecrated virgins by applying to these vocational groups within the Church the insights that Paulinus of Nola had developed for Christian spouses. The "virtue unadorned" motif that internalizes the mutual appeal of husband and wife in Paulinus' epithalamium is extended by Fulgentius to the celibate callings as well. In so doing, he preserves Paulinus' respect for the moral value of whatever path a Christian may follow even though the rhetorical necessities of the letters in which he outlines his cosmetic theology require him to emphasize the superiority of the celibate life. In his letter to the widow Galla, Fulgentius recapitulates the arguments made by Jerome against the remarriage of widows, but without disparaging the merits of the Chritian wife:

> Si ergo sanctae mulieres, etiam coniugatae, non sunt monilibus commodandae, sed moribus, et eo magis humilitate debent ornari quam veste, qualis debet esse viduae habitus et incessus, quae non homini viro cupit placere, sed Christo?[13]

> If, then, holy women, even though married, are fitly adorned not with their jewels but with their morals, and should be beautified more by their humility than by their finery, what ought to be the dress and comportment of a widow, who seeks to please not a human husband but Christ?

Opera, CC, 91–91A (Turnhout, 1968). All citations to Fulgentius will refer to this edition.

[12] *Epistula* 17.54.

[13] *Ep.* 2.25, CC, 91, p. 205.

While Fulgentius does not refer to the Stoic norm of *naturam sequere* in this connection he does reflect an authentic sense of the Stoic principle that different styles of life may be equally good provided that their duties are undertaken unselfishly and with a proper moral intention. He writes in a markedly similar vein to Proba, a nun who was sister to the widow Galla. He does not go into detail on how nuns should dress. Instead, he emphasizes the splendor of the virtues which should adorn them, above all a true spirit of inner chastity. Mere outward chastity is not enough, he stresses. It is the cultivation of purity of spirit alone that is the *raison d'être* of the monastic life. The nun can serve neither God nor the community that supports the convent without this virtue.[14] In sharp contrast to Leander of Seville, who speaks only of the negative and external disciplines attached to monastic life, Fulgentius subordinates asceticism to the positive spiritual values which the nun should embody and the sincerity and conviction that should irradiate her outward expression of them, a note that harmonizes the Stoics' moral emphasis on inner intentionality with a sensitive appreciation of the Christian monastic calling.

E) Licinianus of Cartagena

While there will still be more to be said on the subject of cosmetic theology below, it is the first point mentioned in our discussion of Fulgentius, the materiality of the soul, that connects him with the next two figures to be considered, Licinianus of Cartagena and Cassiodorus. Licinianus, bishop of Cartagena (d. 581), wrote a letter, one of his few extant works, to the deacon Epiphanus, combating the teachings of an unnamed contemporary bishop who denied the spirituality of the human soul. Licinianus harks back to Gennadius of Marseilles for the form of his argument, despite the fact that Gennadius maintained the opposite position, while he models his positive case on that of Claudianus Mamertus, whom he quotes in support of it along with the Bible, Jerome, and Augustine. Souls, he concludes, while they are created and exist in time, do not therefore exist in space or have the attributes of corporality, materiality, or physical extension.[15]

---

[14] *Ep.* 3.22.

[15] Licinianus of Cartagena, *Epistula* 1.1–14, ed. P. A. C. Vega, Scriptores ecclesiastici hispano-latini veteris et medii aevi, 3 (Escorial, 1935). On Licinianus' use of previous arguments see the intro. to Vega's ed., pp. 7–8 and José Madoz, "Un caso de materialismo en España en el siglo VI," *Revista española de theología*, 8 (1948), 210–27.

F) Cassiodorus

The continuing interest in the idea that the soul is material and the continuing belief that the positive side of this debate was also tenable in the sixth century are both well illustrated by Cassiodorus. Despite his unimpugnable credentials as an educator and as one of the most encyclopedic transmitters of the classical culture of his age, Cassiodorus ranks as a less than major figure in the history of the Stoic tradition. Aside from the valuable report on the Stoic hypothetical syllogisms which he gives in his *Institutes*,[16] his only other point of contact with Stoicism is the psychology and related ethics found in his *De anima*, the first work that Cassiodorus wrote after his retirement from the service of the Ostrogothic court and before he founded his model school at Vivarium. The *De anima* supports the Stoics' position on the materiality of the soul and provides information, in part, about their theory of sense perception and their doctrine of the *hegemonikon*. These views are mingled with the teachings of competing schools, sometimes in such a way as to undermine them without the author's apparent realization of the lack of coherence that results. He also includes an accurate picture of the Stoic sage, although he is confused on the eligibility of women for that honor. Cassiodorus' *Institutes* and translations reflect his thorough familiarity with most of the pagan and Christian Latin literature of his time, as well as his knowledge of Greek. The fact that Augustine is the only authority he mentions by name in the *De anima* does not therefore exhaust the possible range of sources on which he could have drawn for his psychology.[17] The real problem with this work is not its putative sources but the clangor of the opposing views that Cassiodorus juxtaposes in it with such evident unconcern for the resulting inconsistencies.

Cassiodorus' conception of the composition of the soul is an initial case in point. His attempts to blend Stoic materialism with Neoplatonic spiritualism are not a great success. On the one hand, he says that the soul is composed of an etherial type of matter. The very term soul in Latin (*anima*) derives, he notes, from the Greek word for wind (*anema*). As wind is made up of air, so the soul is made up of a similarly rarefied substance (*substantiam tenuem*), a trait it shares with angels and the powers of the air (*potestatibus aeriis*). This etherial substance is created, invisible, and immortal and is spread throughout the body of man, although it is also

---

[16] See M. L. Colish, *Stoic Tradition*, I, ch. 5, pp. 333–34.

[17] Cf. James J. O'Donnell, *Cassiodorus* (Berkeley, 1979), pp. 118–19, who reviews the literature on this point but treats Augustine as the only possible source. He provides a summary of *De anima*, pp. 121–30 which shows little interest in the philosophical issues raised by the work.

capable of surviving without the body.[18] Already we see Cassiodorus conflating a Neoplatonic soul with a Stoic one. Moving farther from the Stoa, he says that the substance of the soul is distinct both from God and from the four elements of earth, air, fire, and water that make up the human body and the physical world. Yet, the soul can be understood as fiery in nature. At least, this is an opinion that Cassiodorus mentions which he does not reject. So, the soul's substance is air-like and fire-like although it has nothing in common with the ordinary elements of air and fire. Its composition is unique. It is material though not corporeal, since it lacks the physical attributes of bodies, such as extension in space. At the same time, the soul can be affected by the body with its passions and the body is its prison (*carcer suus*).[19] A certain Stoic element does inhere in this psychology but it must be said that Cassiodorus' account is a mélange of competing theories whose opposition he neither notices nor resolves.

In any event, he regards the soul as the ruling principle in each man, accounting for what he wills[20] and governing all his sensory, physical, and intellectual faculties. In this connection Cassiodorus refers to the soul as the principal part, the ruling part, or the vital heat of the mind (*principale, imperativa, vitalis calor animi*) in its manifold role in directing man's five senses, his capacity to move at will from place to place, and his intellectual judgments of the true and the good.[21] The sequence in which Cassiodorus presents this doctrine recapitulates the Peripatetic subdivision of the faculties of the soul into vegetative, animate, and rational, although the idea that the soul is directly responsible for all of these activities is decidedly Stoic.

If the Stoic notion of the *hegemonikon* inspires Cassiodorus to think that all acts of sensation arise in the intellect and are the result of conscious states, his analysis of how moral judgments are made and his sense of the capacity of women as well as men to attain virtue are only partly Stoic. For Cassiodorus, as for other ancient psychologists, the senses of sight and hearing are the most difficult to explain since they can perceive objects that are not immediately adjacent to the sense organs. Cassiodorus shares with Augustine and others an active theory of sensation which incorporates implicitly the Stoic doctrine of *pneuma* as an expla-

---

[18] Cassiodorus Senator, *De anima* 3, ed. J. W. Halporn in *Opera*, I, CC, 96 (Turnhout, 1973).

[19] Ibid. 4–5. The inconsistencies in this doctrine are addressed manfully by James W. Halporn, "Magni Aurelii Cassiodori Senatoris liber De anima," *Traditio*, 16 (1960), 43, 46 and Artur Schneider, "Die Erkenntnislehre bei Beginn der Scholastik," *Philosophisches Jahrbuch der Görres-Gesellschaft*, 34 (1921), 228–29.

[20] *De an.* 3.

[21] *De an.* 8. Also noted by Halporn, "De anima," pp. 45–47.

nation of sense perception. According to this view, a power within the soul (*vis animae spiritalis*) is emitted through the sense organs, creating a material bridge between them and their objects on which sense data can travel to the brain.[22] However, Cassiodorus omits the complementary half of the Stoic account of sense perception in which the objects sensed also emit a flow of *pneuma* which interacts with the *pneuma* flowing from the brain through the sense organs.

Still, he shares with other exponents of this aspect of the Stoic theory the wish to intellectualize or spiritualize the sensory functions by putting the soul actively in charge of them. At the same time, however, he does not share the ancient Stoic and Augustinian intellectualizing of the passions. He agrees with the Platonists, Aristotelians, and middle Stoics in locating the origin of the passions in man's infrarational faculties or in the body. But, he also states that the origin of vice is not the passions but original sin, which inclines man to abuse his free will.[23] Even as the doctrine of free will shifts the motive force away from man's sub-rational nature and toward the intellect, which re-Stoicizes the analysis of moral choice to some extent, Cassiodorus' Christianizing of this question removes from the subject the intellectual autonomy in moral decision-making which the Stoa ascribed to him. Cassiodorus does not take a clear stand on whether vice and the passions promoting it stem primarily from the body or from the will. Nor does he find it necessary to make a preemptive decision on this question, apparently because he thinks that the moral discipline needed to repress vice and encourage virtue would be much the same in either case.

Another point on which Cassiodorus hesitates in the *De anima* is how and why women can possess the psychological traits earmarking the sage. He is quite forthright and authentically Stoic in his description of the sage, whose inner tranquillity will be equal even to the terrifying cosmic commotion ushering in the Apocalypse:

Fixa mens non nutat, non fluctuat, non movetur, et in tanta pacis stabilitate defigitur ut nihil aliud praeter illam contemplationem vel quaerere vel cogitare patiatur.[24]

His resolute mind does not falter, does not waver, and is not distressed; it remains fixed in such steadfastness of peace that it is moved by nothing else except that contemplation, either in inquiring or in reflecting.

---

[22] *De an.* 11. Also noted by Halporn, "De anima," p. 47; Schneider, "Erkenntnislehre," pp. 232–36.

[23] *De an.* 12.

[24] *De an.* 15, CC, 96, p. 567.

In discussing these fully Stoic attributes of the sage Cassiodorus acknowledges that sex is no bar to virtue, basing this moral egalitarianism on the same foundation as the Stoics do, the idea that the soul has the same composition in all members of the human race. He embellishes this point by citing a string of Christian widows and virgins as female *exempla virtutis*. However, despite this psychological analysis, for which he gets full Stoic marks, and despite the evidence which he himself adduces to support it, Cassiodorus is still hard pressed to explain how women can attain virtue just as well as men, given their lack of membership in the stronger sex (*sexus valentior*).[25] Here, as throughout his consideration of the human soul in his *De anima*, Cassiodorus finds himself in the grip of an unresolved contradiction, although this is one he admits he is aware of. At the same time, and notwithstanding his maddening inconsistencies, he is one of the few writers of his century to indicate much knowledge of the Stoic doctrine of the soul and the only one with extant works who supports the notion of the soul's material nature. The success of his *Institutes*, in comparison with his *De anima*, suggests that he was far more gifted as a compiler and doxographer than as an analytic or synthetic thinker. But, by the same token, the fame earned by the *Institutes* assured for Cassiodorus' other works, including the *De anima*, the respectful attention of later medieval readers.

II. St. Gregory the Great

Gregory the Great (ca. 540–604) is, by any accounting, a commanding presence in the history of western Europe in the second half of the sixth century. His title as the last of the Latin Church Fathers is as fully merited as his reputation as the first of the major medieval popes. Born in Rome of a wealthy and distinguished senatorial family, Gregory received the best education available in his day and followed the *cursus honorum*, reaching the rank of prefect of Rome in 573. Soon afterwards he became a monk and founded six abbeys out of his own personal fortune. He entered the diaconate in 578 but secular politics reclaimed him, and he served as ambassador to Constantinople between 579 and ca. 586. On his return to Rome Gregory once more sought monastic seclusion, becoming the head of the abbey of St. Andrew in 586. It was during his period as abbot that he wrote his major treatise on the spiritual life, the *Moralia in Job*. Gregory was called from the cloister yet again in 590, this time to become pope.

To his new duties Gregory brought his skills and experience as a sec-

---

[25] *De an.* 13.

ular politician and an exalted sense of his pontifical responsibilities toward the world no less than to the Church. His voluminous letters which, read as a whole, are the best source extant for Gregory and his times, show his unremitting labors as an ecclesiastical statesman seeking to promote peace and the liberty of the Church in an age when Italy was prostrated by the power struggle raging among the Ostrogoths, Lombards, and Byzantines. Gregory was just as concerned with ensuring the health of local churches throughout the Roman communion in his insistence on the appointment of qualified men to clerical office and in the swift retribution he meted out to simoniacs and those unfit to serve. He was energetic in the organization of missions to the Germanic north, in his patronage of Benedictine monasticism, in his dissemination of a unified and dignified liturgy, and in his encouragement of his brother bishops in their efforts to evangelize their Germanic overlords or at least to mitigate their persecution of orthodox Christians. Gregory confronted no less manfully the most massive and intractable problems of his age, which had fallen on the shoulders of the Church by default—food supply, the allocation of agrarian resources, water supply, public works, poor relief, care of the sick, the orphaned, and the aged—with his characteristic mixture of vision, efficiency, and compassion. Equally typical of his style of leadership was his keen sense of the value of the object lesson and his judicious weighing of priorities in the light of their comparative urgency.

Despite the enormous press of his pontifical obligations, Gregory found time to do a good deal of writing. While he produced no dogmatic or controversial theology, his works span most of the genres of patristic literature. Biblical commentary, on Ezekiel, the first book of Kings, the penitential Psalms, the Song of Songs, the Gospels, and the concord of Scriptural testimonies, comprises the largest segment of his *œuvre*. Gregory's essay in monastic spirituality, the *Moralia*; his saints' lives in dialogue form; his liturgical sacramentary; and his *Regula pastoralis*, a handbook for pastoral ministers, were his most popular and influential works. Many of the interests reflected in Gregory's writings can also be found in those of his patristic predecessors. With Jerome he shares a deep involvement in Biblical exegesis and a concern with the production of Christian *exempla virtutis*. With Augustine he shares much of his spiritual doctrine and his commitment to Christian education from the pulpit. With Ambrose Gregory shares an activist conception of the role of prelates in church-state relations, an emphasis on ethics, and a genius for administration. Yet, for all his parallelism with and dependence on the earlier Fathers, Gregory's writings and policies alike reflect a unique personality and the need to address a situation of political and ecclesiastical turmoil so acute that it would have beggared the imaginations of a Jerome, an Ambrose, and an Augustine. While Gregory does indeed look backward toward the giants of the patristic age which he brought to a close, his gaze is firmly fixed on his own present world, a world on which he left his own distinctively Gregorian impression.

Gregory does not possess a speculative mind and there are no express references to the Stoics or to any other school of philosophy anywhere in his writings. At the same time, and despite his tendency to equate the classical tradition with literature, he draws on a certain amount of Stoicism, above all in his analysis of virtue. While Gregory's applications of Stoicism are not numerous they are thoughtful and consistent. They are also thoroughly assimilated into an outlook marked as strongly by its profound Christian spirituality as by its Roman practicality. Gregory has been well described as "a contemplative condemned to action."[26] It would be even better to describe him as a papal Cincinnatus with no hope of ever regaining his plow, who gave unstintingly of his richest gifts of mind and heart to his public responsibilities, while retaining within himself a state of recollection so firmly grafted into his being that it could never be dislodged.

The apparent polarities between the active and the contemplative life suggested by this image have strongly colored the ways in which commentators have formulated the question of Gregory's relation to the classical tradition in general and to Stoicism in particular. The older view saw as the principal key to Gregory's attitude his remarks about classical literature in letters he wrote to two contemporary bishops, Desiderius of Vienne and Leander of Seville. Gregory criticizes Desiderius for teaching grammar, *quia in uno se ore cum Iovis laudibus Christi laudes non capiunt* ("for the same mouth cannot sound the praises of Jupiter and Christ.")[27] He goes on to outline the host of other duties urgently awaiting Desiderius' attention which he is neglecting in order to indulge his literary tastes. Gregory's letter to Leander serves as the dedicatory preface to his *Regula pastoralis*. Invoking the rhetorical *topos* of the modest author, he apologizes for a literary style that Leander may find rough (*incultus*) or mediocre (*tepidus*), pleading the excuse of ill health. While accepting the blame for any graceless features that his prose may have, he adds, he has not refrained from publishing the *Regula*, for it would be shortsighted to subject the divine message to the rules of Donatus (*ut verba*

---

[26] Jean Leclercq, *The Love of Learning and the Desire for God: A Study of Monastic Culture*, trans. Catherine Misrahi (New York, 1961), p. 36.

[27] Gregory the Great, *Epistola* 11.34 in *Registrum epistolarum*, 2 vols., ed. Paulus Ewald and Ludovicus M. Hartman, *MGH*, Epistolarum, 1-2 (Berlin, 1891–99), II, 303.

caelestis oraculi restringam sub reguli Donati).[28] There is also a third letter
apposite to the point, written to a hermit, Secundinus, whom Gregory
thanks for certain writings Secundinus has sent him, which, he says, merit
praise for their truth, charity, and love for the celestial homeland rather
than for a recherché eloquence or elaborate figures of speech.[29] This
letter to Secundinus has passed unnoticed and it is the first two cited that
have provided the point of departure for scholarly assessments of Gregory's classicism.

Despite the obvious contextual qualifications and rhetorical conventions attached to the letters to Desiderius and Leander, late nineteenth
and early twentieth-century critics agreed, on this basis, to dismiss
Gregory as an obscurantist, an old-style Tertullian *redivivus* with an un-
qualified hostility to the classics, a position that has now been given the
decent burial it deserves.[30] The initial strategy for reversing the older view
was the countercitation of Gregory's positive references to classical authors, from his Ciceronian *O tempora, o mores,*[31] to his reminiscence of Seneca's view of the freedom of speech between friends under the rubric of
aliquid saeculare auctoris ("from some secular author,")[32] to his less specific
allusions to the *Dream of Scipio,*[33] to Juvenal,[34] and to Persius.[35] An analogous line of argument, from the same perspective, has been to note the
correctness, the clarity, and even the rhetorical cultivation apparent in
Gregory's own literary style.[36]

More thoroughgoing than this rather narrow philological revisionism,
although it still focuses on a literary conception of the classical tradition,

---

[28] *Ep.* 5.53a, *MGH*, I, 357. Remigio Sabbadini, "Gregorio Magno e la grammatica,"
Bolletino di filologia classica, 8 (1902), 205–06 argues that this letter indicates that Gregory
thought that there was a special grammar applying to sacred texts that was different
from Donatus but does not demonstrate that such a "sacred grammar" can actually be
found in Gregory's exegesis or theology.

[29] *Ep.* 19.147, *MGH*, II, 142.

[30] The most exhaustive recent review of the literature on this issue can be found in
Claude Dagens, *Saint Grégoire le Grand: Culture et expérience chrétiennes* (Paris, 1977), pp.
18–24, 31–34. See also Nino Scivioletti, "I limiti dell' 'ars grammatica' in Gregorio
Magno," *Giornale italiano di filologia,* 17 (1964), 210–27.

[31] *Ep.* 5.37, *MGH*, I, 322. Noted by Pierre Courcelle, "Grégoire le Grand à l'école de
Juvenal," *Studi e materiali di storia della religione,* 38 (1967), 170; Leonhard Weber, *Hauptfragen der Moraltheologie Gregors des Grossen: Ein Bild altchristlicher Lebensführung* (Freiburg
in der Schweitz, 1947), p. 66.

[32] *Ep.* 1.33, *MGH*, I, 47. Noted by Robert Gillet in the intro. to his ed. of *Moralia in
Job,* Bks. I and II, 2nd ed., SC, 32 bis (Paris, 1975), p. 103.

[33] Pierre Courcelle, "Saint Benoît, le merle, et le buisson d'épines," *Journal des savants,*
152 (1967), 154–61.

[34] Courcelle, "Grégoire le Grand," pp. 170–74.

[35] Pierre Courcelle, "'Habitare secum' selon Perse et selon Grégoire le Grand," *REA,*
69 (1967), 266–79.

[36] E. K. Rand, *Founders of the Middle Ages* (New York, 1957), pp. 25–28.

has been the tendency to treat Gregory as a man who was on familiar terms with the classics but who subordinated them to his broader concerns. Some scholars see these concerns as essentially practical and administrative, even as legalistic and disciplinary. They depict Gregory as a Roman of the old school, neither a theorist nor an aesthete but a public-spirited ruler interested in doing his job effectively and using whatever instruments came to hand for that purpose. This interpretation has appealed more to biographers of Gregory than to students of his thought.[37] A second approach has been to assess Gregory's classicism in the light of his Christianity, from which perspective it has not received very high marks. Scholars in this camp see Gregory's faith not merely as relativizing his classical culture but even as rupturing his connection with it, whether from the standpoint of the doctrine of learned ignorance, the primacy of spiritual experience, or the ascetic's temperamental aversion from secular learning.[38] There is also a third interpretation, in which the businesslike administrator and the master of the inner life merge in Gregory the educator. This middle position moves away from the letters to Desiderius and Leander to the attitudes Gregory reflects in his *Dialogues* and *Regula pastoralis*, situating him firmly in the tradition of Augustine's *De doctrina christiana*.[39]

Such a view has much to recommend it, but it still needs refinement. Gregory certainly shares Augustine's utilitarian conception of the applicability of the classics to Christian instruction and he is even more willing than Augustine to substitute a wooden for a golden key in unlocking his store of knowledge in that endeavor. He is quite ready to bow to popular literary tastes, as is amply evident in his saints' lives, where he freely employs the stock formulae, the well-worn clichés, and the awe-struck respect for the saint as miracle worker that had become conventions of that genre. Gregory also develops a rhetoric even farther removed from Cicero's than that of Augustine, which he deploys in contexts as diverse as his sermons *ad populum*, his rules for priests, and his spiritual teachings for monks, a rhetoric reflecting an awareness of the fact that he cannot take for granted the intellectual rigor of his audience. While Gregory's primary goal, like Augustine's, is to communicate with his readers

---

[37] F. Homes Dudden, *Gregory the Great: His Place in History and Thought*, 2 vols. (London, 1905), II, 285–95; Jeffrey Richards, *Consul of God: The Life and Times of Gregory the Great* (London, 1980), pp. 50, 263–65.

[38] Dagens, *Saint Grégoire* is the most elaborate and recent proponent of this view. He is much in the debt of Leclercq, *Love of Learning*, pp. 34–44. Other leading examples are Henri-Irénée Marrou, "Saint Grégoire le Grand (v. 540–604)," *La Vie spirituelle*, 69 (1943), 450 and Scivioletti, "I limiti dell' 'ars grammatica'," pp. 227–37.

[39] Claude Dagens, "Grégoire le Grand et la culture: De la 'sapientia huius mundi' à la 'docta ignorantia'," *REAug*, 14 (1968), 17–26; Richards, *Consul of God*, pp. 27–29, 261.

and hearers and while his pedagogical requirements are the criterion of how extensively he spoils the Egyptians, we should not look to Gregory to find a Christian humanist: it is impossible to imagine him either weeping for Dido or praising Aeneas as a model of Stoic equanimity and self-mastery.

The most innovative approach to the study of Gregory and the classics has shifted attention away from Latin literature and has focused instead on Greek philosophy. In this connection, scholars have acknowledged that it is possible to detect the presence and influence of philosophical ideas despite the absence of express *testimonia* or overt reference to them on the part of the author at issue. The critics have also recognized that Stoicism is the philosophy that exerted the greatest attractive force on Gregory. As is often the case in the first flush of a new insight, they have occasionally overinterpreted Gregory's Stoicism on this account. His description of God as the cause of causes, the life of the living, and the reason of rational creatures (*causa causarum, vita viventium, ratio rationabilem creaturem*) and his statement that God is ubiquitous have led some scholars erroneously to ascribe to him a Stoic or Stoicizing immanentalism.[40] Several commentators have been too ready to read the Stoic *hegemonikon* into Gregory's use of the term *mens*, or even the term *caput*, when these terms do not bear out such an interpretation.[41] Gregory's view that, as a consequence of sin, man is reduced to a mode of knowing through the palpable touch of the physical eye, as it were, has been treated as a reflection of Stoic epistemology,[42] although he makes no reference to the doctrine of *pneuma* and does not explain whether the soul or the sensed object, or both, take an active role in the process of sensation. In two cases, the attribution of a Stoic sensibility to Gregory's position on predestination and grace[43] and his putative criticism of the doctrine of *apatheia*,[44] the texts cited by the commentators do not actually mention the points in question.

While in the above respects Gregory has been Stoicized a bit too enthusiastically, he does indeed make use of a thoroughly Christianized

---

[40] *Moralia in Job* 30.4.17, *PL*, 76, col. 533C; also 16.31.38, ed. and trans. Aristide Bocognano, SC, 212 and 221 (Paris, 1974–75), 221, p. 196. This view is supported by Michael Frickel, *Deus totus ubique simul: Untersuchungen zur allgemeinen Gottengegenwart im Rahmen der Gotteslehre Gregors des Grossen* (Freiburg, 1956), pp. 58–61, 59 n. 234 and Bocognano, intro. to his ed., SC, 212, p. 24; 221, pp. 196–97 n. 4.

[41] Courcelle, *Connais-toi toi-même*, I, 213–24, with a list of all the *loci*, Bocognano, intro. to his ed. of *Moralia*, SC, 212, p. 17; Gillet, comm. on his ed. of *Moralia* at 1.5.55, SC, 32 bis, p. 69 n. 3.

[42] *Moralia* 5.61, SC, 32 bis and Gillet's comm. on this text, p. 24.

[43] Dagens, *Saint Grégoire*, p. 272.

[44] Pierre Riché, *Education and Culture in the Barbarian West: Sixth through Eighth Centuries*, trans. John J. Contreni (Columbia, S.C., 1978), p. 151.

Stoicism in three distinct ethical contexts. In order of their increasing importance to Gregory, they are cosmetic theology, the classification of moral types and the means of inculcating virtue in them, and the inter-relation of the virtues. In the first two cases the requirements of pastoral ministers are uppermost in his mind while in the third he directs his analysis primarily to monastic and lay audiences.

Gregory rings the final change to be noted in this book on the *topos* of cosmetic theology and thereby indicates both the durability of its appeal and its plasticity in the hands of Christian Latin authors since the time of Tertullian. Gregory's treatment of this theme either arises from, or is referred to, an interpretation of the Old Testament in which he shows a balanced appreciation of the historical significance of the tonsorial customs of the ancient Israelites and the possibility of edifying contemporary priests through a tropological reading of the Old Testament text. That this type of counseling struck a responsive chord in Gregory's own mind can be seen clearly in a letter written to Cyriacus, his counterpart in the see of Constantinople, composed six years after his elevation to the papacy. It was Cyriacus who initiated this correspondence because he, like Gregory, had been forced to renounce a life of monastic seclusion in accepting the call to the patriarch's throne. He thus appealed to Gregory for advice on how to cope with the tension he felt between his monastic inclinations and his pastoral responsibilities. Gregory takes Cyriacus' dilemma straight to his heart and finds insight into it in Ezekiel 44:20, where the prophet lays down guidelines for Old Testament priests: "They shall not shave their heads or let their locks grow long; they shall only trim the hair of their heads." The hair mentioned by Ezekiel, says Gregory, signifies the cares of this life. As with the growth of hair, so the administrative burdens of high ecclesiastical office grow insensibly and involuntarily. They must be dealt with somehow. Applying Ezekiel's rule tropologically, he concludes that, just as the Israelite priest had to wear his hair at moderate length, so the Christian prelate should devote his attention with moderation to the temporal needs of his flock, without either neglecting his people nor allowing their secular requirements to distract him from their spiritual ends, or his own.[45] Gregory makes exactly the same point, using the same passage from Ezekiel as his warrant, in the advice to priests working at the level of the local parish which he had included a year earlier in his *Regula pastoralis*.[46]

Gregory is well aware of the fact that there is no one monolithic position on hair in the Old Testament and that masculine tonsorial con-

---

[45] *Ep.* 7.5, *MGH*, I, 447.
[46] *Regulae pastoralis* 2.7, *PL*, 77.

ventions could bear a number of different meanings at different points in Old Testament history. While Ezekiel instructs priests to wear their hair at moderate length, hair that had never been cut could also be an appropriate Levitical style or a sign of dedication to God's service. So it was in the case of the prophet Samuel, whose mother, in praying for the birth of a son, pledged him to the Lord and vowed that no razor would ever touch his head. In his exegesis of this passage from the first book of Kings, Gregory interprets hair as an abundance of material goods. Like crops that are cut in order to be harvested, hair is cut so that its owner can enjoy his wealth. Preachers, therefore, should imitate Samuel in shunning the razor, so as to manifest their detachment from the goods of this world. For the clergy, he concludes, the razor signifies greed for those material goods that are evils for pastors (malorum pastorum cupiditas).[47] On the other hand, Gregory observes that in Numbers 8:7 Levites are required to shave. The meaning he finds in this text is perfectly compatible with his interpretation of Samuel's tonsorial style, even though the two sets of original prescriptions contradict each other. But customs may well have changed by Samuel's day. In the context of Numbers, Gregory reads hair as signifying the fleshly imagination, the superfluities and corruptions that pertain to the worldly life that the priest has left behind, which he should therefore set aside. And, he adds, the priest should shave rather than plucking out his unwanted hair as an act of moral discipline, to remind him of the daily vigilance he must exercise against thoughts inimical to his ministry and to the life of contemplation.[48] Gregory draws precisely the same conclusion from a Scriptural text in which shaving refers to something quite different from the hairstyles of Levites or prophets. Job, he notes, shaved his head when his children died, since this practice was a sign of mourning among the ancients. For the moderns what it means is the drawing of the soul away from superfluous thoughts and presumptuous attitudes.[49]

What is striking throughout this array of examples of Gregorian cosmetic theology, apart from the fact that the moral drawn in each case is directed to men who are pastors at one rank or another in the ecclesiastical hierarchy, is the consistency of the ethical message that Gregory extrapolates from the Biblical texts he interprets despite their original diversity. Gregory has an impressive sense of context that enables him to read different Old Testament precepts as applying to different Old Testament situations. While he is sensitive to Biblical history Gregory is scarcely a literalist. The discrepancies embedded in the literal level of

---

[47] In librum I Regum 1.28, ed. Patricius Verbraken, CC, 144 (Turnhout, 1973), p. 69.
[48] Moralia 5.59, SC, 32 bis.
[49] Ibid. 2.16.29, 2.52.82, SC, 32 bis.

the text are swiftly dissolved in the alembic of tropological exegesis. Gregory's cosmetic theology, then, is of genuine interest from the standpoint of the history of Biblical hermeneutics. It also holds a unique place in the history of Christian transformations of this theme in the age of the Latin apologists and Church Fathers. Gregory, to be sure, shares with Caesarius of Arles the idea that the razor can cut both ways and he has a parallel interest in the allegoresis of the Old Testament in the explication of that idea. But, in contrast to all previous cosmetic theologians, Gregory does not lay down any prescriptions of his own for the physical appearance of the people for whom he writes. Taking the principle of the primacy of inner intentionality in ethics one step farther even than the Stoics, Gregory concerns himself only with the moral attitude which various tonsorial styles may signify. How Christian priests in the here and now actually choose to barber themselves is a matter of no earthly importance to him.

If a priest's tonsorial presentation of self is inconsequential, the way he carries out his obligation to teach his people through his preaching office is a vital concern. Gregory devotes the whole third book of his *Regula pastoralis* to this subject. In so doing he brings together the moral classification of the types of people whom the preacher must edify with an analysis of the moral no less than the rhetorical qualifications he brings to the pulpit. This Gregorian guide to homiletics is, to be sure, indebted to Augustine's *De doctrina christiana*. At the same time, Gregory seeks to combine the Stoic casuist with the Stoic sage who is a *vir bonus dicendique peritus*. And, he exemplifies his recommendations for the rhetoric of preaching in his own prose style, a style that departs noticeably both from Ciceronian and from Augustinian rhetoric, although by no means in the direction of Stoic brevity and simplicity.

The chief difficulty faced by the preacher of sermons *ad populum* is the heterogeneity of his congregation, made up as it is of many individuals with a wide range of mental, moral, and situational characteristics. He is charged with conveying what each of these individuals needs most for his own moral education without thereby neglecting the requirements of the rest of his audience. Gregory's first step in coming to grips with this formidable assignment is to catalogue the various kinds of people likely to be found in any congregation, so that the preacher will not ignore any of them in planning his homiletic strategy. Gregory thus opens Book 3 with an elaborate moral typology that could be described as a way-station between Panaetian casuistry and the *sermones ad status* of the later Middle Ages. With both of these approaches he acknowledges that all kinds of people can come to be sages, or saints, and that the precise application of general moral principles to particular cases is conditioned by the individual's nature and circumstances. There are also a number of important differences between Gregory and the Stoic casuists. Gregory writes for the instruction of the teacher, who will then go on to apply his analysis in the guidance of the people he serves; he does not offer his advice directly to the individuals whose task it is to make the specific ethical decisions that will affect their own lives. Secondly, the norm of moderation and balance which Gregory invokes for the preacher is a norm based on common sense and practicality, not on any kind of abstract theory or ideal. Gregory is concerned with what is fair, what is responsible, and what will work in the real world. His approach is as remote from the Aristotelian criterion of the golden mean as it is from the intellectualistic Stoic conception of prudence. Finally, Gregory lists a sizable number of types, fully three dozen. He takes into account much more than age, sex, and status. He also includes, and indeed pays far more attention to, such matters as an individual's besetting sin or paramount virtue, his depth of understanding or lack of perception, and his personal history and experience. Gregory thereby creates a moral typology based primarily on temperament, intellectual endowment, and character traits rather than on the givens of a person's biological condition or social circumstances. In the specific advice that follows Gregory's listing of types, furthermore, his classification by character traits tends to cut across the other kinds of categories in which a person may find himself involuntarily, thus effectively recasting in psychological terms the traditional Panaetian schema.[50]

In turning from Gregory's moral typology to its application by the preacher in his sermons it will be useful to quote a rather lengthy passage from Book 3 of the *Regula pastoralis*, partly because it illustrates so clearly both the typology in practice and the norm of homiletic moderation and partly because it expresses so well the rhetoric that Gregory advocates by example as well as by precept:

> Haec sunt quae praesul animarum in praedicationis diversitate custodiat, ut sollicitus congrua singulorum vulneribus medicamina opponat. Sed cum magni sit studii ut exhortandis singulis serviatur ad singula, cum valde laboriosum sit unumquemque de propriis sub dispensatione debitae considerationis instruere, longe tamen laboriosius est auditores innumeros ac diversis passionibus laborantes, uno eodemque tempore voce unius et tanta arte vox temperanda est, ut cum diversa sint auditorium vitia, et singulis inveniatur congrua, et tamen sibimetipsi non sit diversa; ut inter passiones medias uno quidem ductu transeat, sed more biceptis gladii tumores cog-

---

[50] For the list of character types see *Reg. past.* 3.1. Dagens, *Saint Grégoire*, pp. 125–26 has noted the sources for Gregory's schema in Stoic casuistry and also sees the codification of sins in contemporary penitentials as a source. The latter claim cannot be substantiated.

itationum carnalium ex diverso latere incidat, quatenus sic superbis praedicetur humilitas, ut tamen timidis non augeatur metus, sic timidis infun-
datur auctoritas, ut tamen superbis non crescat effrenatio. Sic otiosis ac
torpentibus praedicetur sollicitudo boni operis, ut tamen inquietis immod-
eratae licentia non augeatur actionis. Sic inquietis ponatur modus, ut tam-
en otiosis non fiat torpor securus. Sic ab impatientibus extinguatur ira, ut
tamen remissis ac lenibus non crescit negligentia. Sic lenes accendatur ad
zelum, ut tamen iracundis non addatur incendium. Sic tenacibus infun-
datur tribuendi largitas, ut tamen prodigis effusionis frena minime laxen-
tur. Sic prodigis praedicetur parcitas, ut tamen tenacibus periturum rerum
custodia non augeatur. Sic incontinentibus laudetur conjugium, ut tamen
jam continentes non revocentur ad luxum. Sic continentibus laudetur vir-
ginitas corporis, ut tamen in conjugibus despecta non fiat fecunditas car-
nis. Sic praedicanda sunt bona, ne ex latere juventer et mala. Sic laudanda
sunt bona summa, ne desperentur ultima. Sic nutrienda sunt ultima, ne dum
sufficere creduntur, nequaquam tendatur ad summa.[51]

These are the things that a director of souls should observe in the various
phases of his preaching, so that he may carefully propose the remedies indicated by the wound in each given case. But whereas it is very laborious
to instruct each one in what applies to him in particular by urging appropriate considerations, the task is a far more laborious one when on one and
the same occasion one has to deal with a numerous audience subject to different passions. In this case the address must be formulated with such skill
that, notwithstanding the diversity of failings in the audience as a whole,
it carries a proper message to each individual, without involving itself in
self-contradictions. Thus, in one direct stroke, it should pass straight
through the passions. Yet, this should be as with a double-edged sword, so
as to lance the tumours of carnal thoughts on both sides: humility is to be
preached to the proud in a way not to increase fear in the timorous, and
confidence infused in the timorous, as not to encourage the unbridled im-
petuosity in the proud. The idle and the remiss are to be exhorted to zeal
for good deeds, but in a way not to increase the unrestraint of intemperate
action in the impetuous. Moderation is to be imposed on the impetuous
without producing a sense of listless security in the idle. Anger is to be banished from the impatient, but so as not to add to the carelessness of the
remiss and easy-going. The remiss should be fired with zeal in such a manner as not to set the wrathful ablaze. Bountiful almsgiving should be urged
on the niggardly without slackening the rein on prodigality. Frugality is to
be indoctrinated in the prodigal, but not so as to intensify in the niggardly
their tenacity of things doomed to perish. Wedlock is to be preached to the
incontinent, but not so as to recall to lust those who have become continent. Physical virginity is to be commended to the continent, yet so as not
to make the married despise the fecundity of the body. Good things are so
to be preached as not to give incidental help to what is bad. The highest
good is to be so praised, that the good in little things is not discarded. Attention should be called to the little things, but not in such a way that they
are deemed sufficient and there is no striving for the highest.

---

[51] *Reg. past.* 3.36, *PL*, 77, cols. 121C–122B; trans. Henry Davis, ACW, 11 (Westminster, Md., 1950), pp. 226–27.

In this passage longwindedness is not an end in itself but serves a particular pedagogical function. Gregory's rhetorical amplification of his central idea by means of a catalogue of specific examples is designed to emphasize and clarify the principle at issue for readers he regards as perhaps incapable of grasping it if it were stated theoretically or aphoristically, or of working out its implications by themselves. Gregory underscores his main point in a series of sentences constructed isomorphically, both syntactically and in terms of diction, that reinforce the intellectual content he wants to convey. At the same time, he uses two or three alternative forms of his parallel sentences, substituting synonymous verbs in analogous grammatical contexts. He sometimes denotes the vices and virtues by means of abstract nouns used as the subjects of their sentences while at other times these traits are denoted by means of adjectives used as nouns that function grammatically as indirect objects. Gregory thus preserves enough variety in the literary texture of this long reduplicative passage to avoid stultification even though his basic rhetorical strategy is to hammer in his message through repetition. Like the Stoic rhetoricians, Gregory appeals to the intellect of his audience and to their sense of duty, not to their emotions. But his stylistic technique is the antithesis of theirs. And, while he shares their view that the speaker's moral excellence is one of the qualities that enables him to communicate effectively, he modifies it by allying it with the Ciceronian and Augustinian principle that the speaker's efficacy is also conditioned by the moral state of his hearers.[52]

In the passage just quoted, Gregory does not present the vices and virtues in any kind of hierarchical order. He treats them all as of equal importance. The ultimate goal of the moral life is to triumph over all the vices and to acquire all the virtues, although, since a pastor is ministering to individual souls as they are, he must make their particular temperaments his starting point. When Gregory examines the moral life from the perspective of the virtues themselves rather than from the standpoint of ethical education, he expresses quite clearly the Stoic doctrine of the interrelation of the virtues and their origin in a single intentional attitude on the part of the moral subject.[53] In this connection he applies a parallel analysis to the cardinal virtues, to the Christian virtues, and to the two sets of virtues working together. Aside from his extension of the Stoic coordination of the virtues to the moral powers that Christians may possess through the grace of God, his chief modification of the Stoic position lies in his understanding of the common origin of the virtues and

---

[52] Ibid. 3.40; see also *Moralia* 30.82.
[53] This point has been noted by Gillet in his ed. of *Moralia*, SC, 32 bis, pp. 106–08 although he ascribes to Gregory's ethics more Neoplatonism than it contains.

his placement of the whole question of virtue in the context of his distinction between the inner and the outer man.

Gregory discusses the topic of the mutual implication of the virtues at length in several places, both in his *Moralia* and in his exegetical sermons on Ezekiel. Although the former is a treatise directed to monks and the latter a group of addresses to a lay congregation, Gregory's teaching and his rhetorical strategy are the same in both works. One of the reasons why Gregory chose Job as the basis for his analysis of the spiritual life, he tells us, is that Job was a sage who possessed all the virtues at once. In Job's case, the same inner dynamic that binds together the cardinal virtues in his soul connects the Christian virtues as well. Gregory treats the cardinal virtues first, as propaedeutic to the Christian virtues. They then serve as ethical categories that can be assimilated to and transfomed by the Christian virtues. But the essential relationships among the virtues can be established initially in the case of the cardinal virtues:

> Ita itaque virtus sine aliis, aut omnino nulla est, aut imperfecta. Ut enim sicut quibusdam visum est, de primis quattuor virtutibus loquar, prudentia, temperantia, fortitudine, atque justitia; tanto perfectae sunt singulae, quanto vicissim sibimet conjunctae. Disjunctae autem perfectae esse nequaquam possunt, quia nec prudentia vera est quae justa, temperans et fortis non est, nec perfecta temperantia quae fortis, justa et prudens non est, nec fortitudo integra quae prudens, temperans et justa non est, nec vera justitia quae prudens, fortis, et temperans non est.[54]

> And so one virtue without another is either none at all or but imperfect. For that (as it has seemed to some persons) I may speak of the four first virtues, viz. prudence, temperance, fortitude, and justice; they are severally so far perfect, in proportion as they are mutually joined to one another. But separated they can never be perfect. For neither is it real prudence which has not justice, temperance, and fortitude, nor perfect temperance which has not fortitude, justice, and prudence, nor complete fortitude which is not prudent, temperate, and just, nor genuine justice which has not prudence, fortitude, and temperance.

Gregory makes essentially the same point about the equality and mutuality of the cardinal virtues in his explanation of the four feathers held in the hand of the man who is one of the four symbols of the evangelists in Ezekiel's vision. These feathers represent as well the four cardinal virtues, which are equally dependent on each other.[55] It will be noted here

---

[54] *Moralia* 22.2, *PL*, 76, col. 212C–D; trans. J. Bliss, Library of the Fathers, 4 vols. (Oxford, 1844–50), I, 546–47. I have altered the translator's punctuation slightly. The same point is made, with greater economy, at 1.54 and 21.6.

[55] *Homeliae in Hiezechihelem prophetam* 1.3.8, ed. Marcus Andriaen, CC, 142 (Turn-

that Gregory does not single out any one of the cardinal virtues as paramount or as prior to the others. Nor does he provide a definition of the cardinal virtues. He simply takes them as read and proceeds to discuss their functional interrelations.

With this foundation laid, Gregory goes on to associate the cardinal virtues with the Christian virtues, applying a directly analogous line of argument to the resulting amalgam. There is, he notes, no true chastity without humility, no true humility without pity, no mercy without justice, no righteousness without trust in God. Moreover, wisdom (*sapientia*) is of less value if it lacks understanding, while understanding is useless if it is not based on the wisdom that probes the higher truths. Counsel (*concilium*) is of no account if it lacks fortitude, which empowers it to translate what it compasses into appropriate actions, while fortitude needs counsel lest it rush headlong into unreasonable heroics. Knowledge (*scientia*) is vain if it is not applied to piety, neglecting to put into practice the good it knows, while piety without knowledge is useless. For, if it is not illuminated by discernment, piety will not know the best way to show mercy. Holy fear (*timor*) would deter us from good deeds unless the other virtues mentioned allayed its trepidation and armed it for action. So, Gregory concludes, just as the cardinal virtues and the gifts of the Holy Spirit nourish each other in their own particular configurations, so also these two types of virtue combine in ministering to each other as well.[56] Like the zeal for righteousness, the gentleness of spirit, the guarding of humility, and the fervor of charity represented by the four evangelists symbolized by the four beasts of Ezekiel's vision, all the virtues spring from one common source:

> Ab ipso fonte misericordiae, ab ipsa radice mansuetudinis, ab ipsa virtute justitiae, id est a Mediatore Dei et hominum Deo Dominus traxerunt.[57]

> They are drawn forth from the same fount of mercy, the same root of meekness, the same power of justice, that is, the Lord God, mediator between God and man.

Thus Gregory Christianizes the Stoic principle of the interconnection of the virtues. While retaining the pagan virtues, he unites them with the Christian virtues both in their functional interrelations and in their common source. As Gregory recasts the Stoic idea of the virtues deriving

---

hout, 1971), p. 37. An almost identical passage, listing prudence first, can be found at 2.10.8. Weber, *Hauptfragen*, pp. 211–12 argues that Gregory follows Ambrose in placing moderation above the other virtues but this is not borne out by the evidence.

[56] *Moralia* 1.45, 22.2.

[57] *In Hiezech.* 1.2.19, CC, 142, p. 28.

from a single origin he sees them arising not merely from the sage's fixed ethical intentionality toward the good but from the deity, Who provides the norms of the ethical life and the grace that empowers man to internalize these values and to manifest them in action. In this life, for Gregory, the consequences of sin will prevent man from combating vice and acquiring virtue either autonomously or once and for all. Man's moral struggle is constant and he can never be assured that the conquest of one vice will free him from attack by another.[58] This Christian sense of the dynamics of sin and grace prevents Gregory from accepting the full correlatives of the Stoic doctrine of the sage who possesses all the virtues. Further, his own interpretation of the Christian life tinctures his appropriation of the Stoic contest between vice and virtue by subordinating it to the tension between the inner and the outer man.[59] In Gregory's ethics this distinction reflects neither the Stoic opposition between reason and the irrational nor the Neoplatonic warfare between soul and body. Nor, despite his debts to Augustine, does he posit this distinction as a means of emphasizing the difference between the transient and the eternal. Rather, drawing on the teaching of St. Paul, Gregory associates the outer man with the false sense of self and the false goods, whether physical or spiritual, that draw man away from his true self and from God. Man's true self and God converge in the inner man, in which are integrated the powers and affections enabling man to put his knowledge into operation in this life, gaining his heavenly home through the best service of his fellow man. This unification of human and divine in the inner man, for Gregory, is not the Stoic identification of the human *logos* with the divine *logos*. Rather, it is a theandric collaboration made possible by grace. It is in the light of this Gregorian *idée maîtresse* and in the perspective of his conscientious striving to harmonize thought and deed, prayer and action, that Gregory understands and transvalues the Stoic conception of virtue.

III. Boethius

When Gregory the Great and his episcopal colleagues looked backward they fixed their gaze on the theological learning and pastoral guidance to be found in their apologetic and patristic forebears, much of which they rephrased more or less uncritically although in some cases

---

[58] *Moralia* 7.35, 9.55.

[59] An excellent account of this basic theme in Gregory's ethics is provided by Paul Aubin, "Intériorité et extériorité dans les Moralia in Job de saint Grégoire le Grand," *RechSR*, 62 (1974), 117–66. Some judicious remarks on its relation to Stoicism can be found in Dagens, *Saint Grégoire*, pp. 76–77, 171–73, 178–79.

they succeeded in making a distinctly personal application of it to their own needs. Boethius, too, may be said to look backward in response to the pressing problems of the day, both educational, ecclesiastical, and personal. But his chief distinction in the history of the Stoic tradition, as it is in the intellectual history of his century more broadly, is Boethius' position as the last Christian Latin thinker of his age to address philosophical questions as such, and with an integrally philosophical outlook. The authorities to whom he appealed were the commentators and continuators of the Peripatetic and Neoplatonic schools, both recent and current. It was in the context of the highly eclectic approach of these two schools, which had borrowed heavily from each other and from the Stoa in late antiquity, that Boethius conceived the life work of translating and reconciling the thought of Plato and Aristotle cut short by his untimely death. Much of the Stoicism known to Boethius arrived by way of intermediary Greek, and to a lesser extent Latin, contributors to the interpretation of these two philosophical traditions. By the same token, Boethius tends to appropriate and to apply the Stoic doctrines that interest him in the light of Aristotelian and Neoplatonic teachings.[60] At the same time, and while this practice is often unacknowledged by Boethius it is a critical feature of his importance as a transmitter, he occasionally Stoicizes in significant ways his treatment of the philosophies to which he gives his primary allegiance.

Boethius (ca. 480–525/6) was the scion of a senatorial family with a longstanding tradition of participation in public affairs, allied by blood or marriage to the leading aristocratic dynasties of Imperial and post-Imperial Italy. After an elaborate education in Rome and Athens[61] he married the daughter of Symmachus, a descendant of the same Symmachus who had debated with Ambrose of Milan in the Altar of Victory episode more than a century earlier, and entered the service of Theodoric the Ostrogoth. Boethius rose to the rank of consul in 510 and be-

---

[60] Boethius' relation both to Christianity and to these two schools of ancient philosophy has undergone considerable revision since the late nineteenth century. That a consensus, reflected in our own account, has now been reached is visible in the recent and outstanding review of the historiography found in C. J. de Vogel, "Boethiana I;" "Boethiana II," *Vivarium*, 9 (1971), 44–66; 10 (1972), 1–40; "The Problem of Philosophy and Christian Faith in Boethius' Consolatio," *Romanitas et Christianitas: Studia Iano Henrico Waszink*, ed. W. den Boer et al. (Amsterdam, 1973), pp. 357–70; and above all in Luca Obertello, *Severino Boezio*, 2 vols. (Genova, 1974), I, 409 and the entire second volume, which is an exhaustive annotated bibliography with entries in chronological order, documenting the changes in scholarly views on all aspects of Boethian studies.

[61] Pierre Courcelle, "Boèce et l'école d'Alexandrie," *Mélanges de l'école française de Rome*, 52 (1935), 185–223 argues that Boethius' Hellenic education took place in Alexandria rather than Athens, a view that has not won the support of other biographers. Since Boethius was conversant with the works of authors from both centers the matter is probably one of marginal importance.

came master of the offices in 522. He remained a leading member of Theodoric's court until he was charged with involvement in an Italo-Byzantine plot against the king, was imprisoned, and summarily executed in 525 or 526. This death brought to a halt an extraordinary program of translations and commentaries, undertaken out of Boethius' sober awareness of the fact that the erstwhile Roman school system was incapable of functioning under Ostrogothic rule. While the Ostrogoths were more conciliatory toward their Roman and Catholic subjects than were most of the other Germanic conquerers, their tolerance no less than their commitment to cultural patronage had distinct elastic limits. Even before he assumed major political office Boethius had undertaken the task of preserving in Latin the classical quadrivium as well as the translations and commentaries on the logic of Aristotle with which he initiated his vast scheme of Platonic and Aristotelian interpretation and synthesis. He continued these endeavors notwithstanding the press of curial business and the need to engage in a philosophical defense of Chalcedonian orthodoxy in the face of an upsurge of Monophysite and Nestorian heresy that was impeding negotiations between the eastern and western Churches.[62] Boethius' most famous work is his last one, the *Consolation of Philosophy*, written in prison while he awaited execution. From the standpoint of the Stoic tradition his theological treatises and his translations of the Greek authorities on arithmetic, geometry, astronomy, and music can be disregarded. None of these works shows any trace of Stoicism. It is, rather, to Boethius' logical commentaries and his *Consolation* that we must look for his understanding and use of Stoicism.

As a logician Boethius draws on a number of sources, some of which he expressly credits and some not.[63] He usually treats Latin commen-

---

[62] On the chronology of Boethius' works see Obertello, *Severino Boezio*, I, part 2, ch. 8 with a discussion of all the relevant literature; and Joachim Gruber, *Kommentar zu Boethius De consolatione philosophiae* (Berlin, 1978), pp. 1–13. On the background and chronology of Boethius' theological works in particular see Viktor Schurr, *Die Trinitätslehre des Boethius im Lichte der "skythischen Kontroversen"* (Paderborn, 1935); summarized more recently by Henry Chadwick, *Boethius: The Consolations of Music, Logic, Philosophy, and Theology* (Oxford, 1981), pp. 22–46, ch. 4 and H. Liebeschütz, "Boethius and the Legacy of Antiquity," *The Cambridge History of Later Greek and Early Medieval Philosophy*, ed. A. H. Armstrong (Cambridge, 1967), p. 544. The ascription of the *De fide catholica* to Boethius has been established convincingly by H. Chadwick, "The Authorship of Boethius' Fourth Tractate, *De fide catholica,*" *JTS*, n.s. 31 (1980), 551–56; *Boethius*, pp. 175–80.

[63] Single-source *Quellenforschung* has had its enthusiasts in this connection. Ammonius and his disciple Porphyry receive support from Pierre Courcelle, *Late Latin Writers and Their Greek Sources*, trans. Harry E. Wedeck (Cambridge, Mass., 1969), pp. 282–84, 289–95. Authors favoring Apuleius are cited by Chadwick, *Boethius*, p. 297 n. 9. James Shiel, "Boethius' Commentaries on Aristotle," *Mediaeval and Renaissance Studies*, 4 (1958), 217–44 argues for a different late Neoplatonic mentor in the case of each of Boethius' commentaries. Peripatetic sources, especially Themistius, at least for the commentaries

tators, to the extent that he consults them, as inadequate, including
Marius Victorinus and Cicero, who were in some respects more faithful
transmitters of Stoicism than were the Peripatetics and Neoplatonists on
whom Boethius relies. Despite the fact that his principal sources either
attacked Stoicism or assimilated it to their own school doctrine, Boethius manages to absorb from them an appreciation of the essentially
formal and propositional nature of Stoic logic as well as some important
features of Stoic semantics.[64] Boethius' commitment to logic as a formal
art is strong, but it is not entirely consistent. And, on the few occasions
when he refers to Stoic ideas on physics or ethics in his logical works, he
forces them to bow before the prevailing winds of Aristotelianism.

The one exception to that rule is Boethius' commentary on Porphyry's *Isagoge*, where it is Neoplatonism instead that holds sway. Boethius
wrote two successive commentaries on the *Isagoge* based on two translations, the first derived from the Latin version of Marius Victorinus and
the second made by Boethius himself out of his irritation with Victorinus' alleged mistakes. Since the original translation of Victorinus is not
extant it is impossible to assess the merits of this claim. However, it has
been established that the commentaries adhere to Porphyry closely,
without significant departures.[65] Following Porphyry's lead, Boethius
Neoplatonizes the concept of being, treating prime natures as incorporeal and seeing as his major task the explanation of their relation to gen-
era and species understood as corporeal. He regards the Porphyrian account of substance and accidents from this perspective as an accurate

---

on the *Topics*, receive support from James J. Murphy, *Rhetoric in the Middle Ages: A History
of Rhetorical Theory from Saint Augustine to the Renaissance* (Berkeley, 1974), pp. 68–71 and
Eleonore Stump, "Boethius's Works on the Topics," *Vivarium*, 12 (1974), 77–79, who also
gives a detailed critique of contrasting views. Much more plausible is the position accepting Boethius' eclectic use of multiple sources put forth by Chadwick, *Boethius*, ch. 3;
Richard McKeon, "The Hellenistic and Roman Foundations of the Tradition of Aristotle in the West," *Review of Metaphysics*, 32 (1979), 710–15; Obertello, *Severino Boezio*, I,
421–24, 446–47; Rand, *Founders*, p. 149.
    [64] This point has been brought out clearly by Karel Berka, "Die Semantik des Boe-
thius," *Helikon*, 8 (1968), 454–59; Obertello, *Severino Boezio*, I, 412–24, 594, 599, 603. See
also Chadwick, *Boethius*, pp. 126, 151; Michael Elsässer, *Das Person-Verständnis des Boethius* (Münster, 1973), pp. 13–14. Jonathan Barnes, "Boethius and the Study of Logic,"
in Margaret Gibson, ed., *Boethius: His Life, Thought and Influence* (Oxford, 1981), p. 83,
argues unpersuasively that Boethius was completely dismissive of Stoic logic.
    [65] Paul Monceaux, "L'Isagoge latin de Marius Victorinus," *Philologie et linguistique:
Mélanges offerts à Louis Havet par ses anciens élèves et ses amis* (Paris, 1909), pp. 291–310 argues that Boethius' first version can be used to reconstruct Victorinus' lost translation,
even in the absence of an independent witness, a position rejected by Lorenzo Minio-
Paluello in the intro. to his ed. of *Porphyrii Isagoge*, trans. Boethius, *AL*, 1:6–7 (Bruges-
Paris, 1966), p. xxxviii n. 1. See also Minio-Paluello, "Boezio," *Dizionario biografico degli
italiani* (Roma, 1969), XI, 152. These problems in comparing Victorinus and Boethius
are also ignored by Luigi Adamo, "Boezio e Mario Vittorino tradattori e interpreti
dell'Isagoge di Porifiro," *Rivista critica di storia della filosofia*, 22 (1967), 141–64.

report of Aristotle's. In this work Boethius refers to the Stoics only to disparage their teaching on the categories because it disagrees with Aristotle's, a remark indicating both his awareness of the fact that the two schools differed on the categories and that he expects his readers to know what that difference is without his assistance.[66]

In his own direct commentaries on Aristotle's *Categories* Boethius does not return to that theme, and mentions Stoic dialectic only in his discussion of the logic of opposition. Here, he observes that the Peripatetics and Stoics disagree. Despite their proverbial longiloquence as logicians, he says, the Stoics neglected this question. He himself outlines four types of opposition: by contrariety, by partial difference, by disposition and privation, and by affirmation and negation.[67] Boethius' own schema admits of opposites that are not mutually exclusive, an idea he illustrates with the example of vice and virtue. This point leads him to reject expressly the ancient Stoic principle that virtue and vice are absolute and antithetical states with only the *indifferentia* between them.[68] In his first two sets of logical commentaries, then, Boethius adduces the Stoics only to criticize them, and on points not always pertinent to Stoic logic. The most telling note, which connects his rather cursory commentary on the *Categories* with his far more substantial commentaries on Aristotle's *De interpretatione*, is his attack on the Stoic understanding of vice and virtue, not on the grounds of its psychological implausibility but because of its failure to square with the logical relations he posits between affirmation and negation.

This latter point is one that Boethius explores in detail in the *De interpretatione* commentaries, especially in his extended discussion of future contingents. There is also an important section at the beginning of this work dealing with sign theory and epistemology in which we can see Boethius' first attempt to Stoicize Aristotelian logic. Boethius' translation of the *De interpretatione* is, on the whole, quite accurate, although he relocates some passages in the text under the influence of other commentators. He also emphasizes some themes more than Aristotle does and changes some examples.[69] Boethius takes sharp exception to the Stoic epistemology in favor of the Aristotelian, whereby data are impressed on the senses, which then impress a sensible image on the intellect, which then extracts the intelligible components from the sensible image and forms them into concepts. While the Stoics, he notes, use the metaphors

---

[66] Anicius Manlius Severinus Boethius, *In Isagogen Porphyrii commenta*, editio I, 1.11, ed. Samuel Brandt, CSEL 48 (Vienna, 1906).

[67] *In Categorias Aristotelis* 4, *PL*, 64.

[68] Ibid. 4.

[69] Minio-Paluello, "Boezio," p. 151.

of wax impressed by a seal, or marble incised by a chisel, or paper written on by ink to describe the moment when the senses receive their data, the Stoic doctrine omits the stage in which material data are transformed into immaterial ideas in the mind. Boethius does not note that the reason why the Stoics did not account for this transformation is because, in rejecting the idea of a mind-body split, they also rejected the notion that any such transformation indeed takes place. None the less, Boethius sides with the major philosophers, from Plato to Aristotle to Speusippus to Xenocrates, in asserting that the Stoic position is defective, and mainly because it fails to describe the formation of concepts (*significationes intellectum*), the chief signs of the things man knows.[70]

Boethius' acceptance of the idea that concepts are the primary kinds of signs is also borne out in his treatment of signification itself. In his translation he follows Aristotle closely, agreeing that we can distinguish things (*res*), the affections of the soul (*passiones animae*) that are their signs (*similitudines*), and speech (*oratio*), which enables men to express those signs whether orally (*in voce*) or in written form (*litterae*). All *orationes*, in turn, are verbal signs (*voces significativae*) that acquire their denotations conventionally (*secundum placitum*).[71] In the first version of his commentary Boethius repeats but tightens up the language in his translation, calling the elements in Aristotle's threefold distinction *res*, *intellectus*, and *voces* and defining *intellectus* more precisely as the signs through which things themselves are known. *Intellectus* is a less ambiguous term than the Aristotelian *passiones animae* but it retains the original Aristotelian sense that the mind is passive in the reception of sensory information. While continuing to agree that words are signs of things only in a secondary, derivative, and conventional manner in comparison with concepts, which are natural products, Boethius goes on to modify Aristotle's linguistic theory by importing into it some salient Stoic elements. Although he uses the term *secundum placitum* to explain how words acquire their denotations in his translation, he substitutes the term *secundum positionem* in his commentary. *Positio*, on one level, refers to the imposition of meanings on words. Men, Boethius observes, may conceptualize the same things in the same ways but they do not always impose the same names on them, both because they speak different lan-

---

[70] *Commentarii in librum Aristotelis De interpretatione*, editio II, 1.1, ed. Carolus Meiser, 2 vols. (Leipzig, 1878–80), II. Konrad Bruder, *Die philosophischen Elemente in den Opuscula sacra des Boethius: Ein Beitrag zur Quellengeschichte der Philosophie der Scholastik* (Leipzig, 1928), p. 23 and ch. 2 in general sees Boethius advocating as well the active theory of sensation taught by the Neoplatonists, but that theory is treated in the *Consolation of Philosophy* and not in the *De interp.* commentaries.

[71] Boethius, trans., *De interpretatione vel Periermenias* 1, 2, 4, ed. Lorenzo Mino-Paluello, *AL*, 2:1-2 (Bruges-Paris, 1965), pp. 5–6.

guages and use different alphabets—a multilingual perspective alien to Aristotle—and because they use synonymous names for the same things even when they speak a common tongue. *Positio*, on another level, refers to the fact that words acquire different meanings according to their grammatical functions and syntactical positions in the propositions in which speakers use them and hearers hear them.[72] Some parts of speech, like prepositions and conjunctions, are meaningful only thanks to their syntactical position, while other parts of speech, like nouns and verbs, may signify naturally (*naturaliter*) or according to their syntactical position (*secundum positionem*). *Orationes* that signify both *naturaliter* and *secundum positionem* may be classified as perfect *orationes* while those that signify only *secundum positionem* are imperfect, for the statements in which they appear can be parsed in more than one way and hence can bear more than one interpretation. Boethius amplifies this point in the second version of his commentary, where he attributes specifically to the Stoics, by way of Porphyry, the idea that nouns and verbs signify their referents naturally, observing that Plato's *Cratylus* gives a thorough discussion of the whole question.[73] Even though he uses the Stoicizing formula inherited from the Roman grammarians, which sees articulate human words as sonic reverberations produced naturally, as the air is struck by the tongue,[74] he continues to insist that concepts are the truly natural and prior signs in comparison with words.

Boethius' conflation of Stoic and Aristotelian semantics Stoicizes his Aristotelianism in a number of ways. First, he draws on Stoic linguistics in defining words as material, sonic forms distinguished from the inarticulate cries of animals, signs that are produced naturally and that, in the case of nouns and verbs, also signify their referents naturally. Even though he still regards concepts as the primary signs of things and relegates words, or some words, to a mode of signification *secundum positionem*, he draws here on the Stoic principle that propositions are the context in which language acquires its logical cogency and that propositions are significant not in terms of their correspondence with extramental reality but in terms of their syntactical construction. From this standpoint, the prime criterion of the tenability of a proposition is its conformity to the rules of formal logic, not its relation to facts and events *in rerum natura*.

---

[72] *Comm. in De interp.*, editio I, 1.1.

[73] Ibid., editio I, 1.1–2; editio II, 1.2–3, 2.4. See on this point the excellent accounts by Berka, "Die Semantik des Boethius," pp. 454–56; Obertello, *Severino Boezio*, I, 594, 599, 603, 606–14. Less useful is Alvin Plantinga, "The Boethian Compromise," *American Philosophical Quarterly*, 15 (1978), 129–38.

[74] *Comm. in De interp.*, editio II, 1, praefatio.

This principle is one that Bothius applies inconsistently, not only in his analysis of semantics but also in his repeated discussions of the syllogism, both in his *De interpretatione* commentaries and elsewhere. As we will see below, he sometimes Stoicizes his treatment of the syllogism and at other times he Aristotelianizes those forms of the Stoic hypothetical syllogism to which he refers. Boethius signalizes both features of his approach to the syllogism briefly in his *De interpretatione* commentary.[75] His most elaborate modification of Aristotelianism under the impact of Stoic propositional logic in this work, however, is his analysis of future contingents.

As with his handling of sign theory, Boethius recapitulates Aristotle's position on future contingents faithfully in his translation of the *De interpretatione* but alters it in his commentary. Aristotle himself judges the affirmation or negation of statements about contingencies according to the truth of the things to which they refer.[76] He gives several examples, the first being a sea battle that may or may be fought tomorrow but which does not have to be fought at all. If it does take place, it occurs as chance would have it. The sea battle can be contrasted with the whiteness of a white thing that has been and currently is white, of which we can say with confidence that it will continue to be white in the future, of necessity. Another example, analogous to the sea battle, is the case of a cloak that may either be worn out or cut into pieces. Before a choice is made regarding the disposition of the cloak, either alternative is possible, not actual, and the option to choose one outcome over the other remains open. The human decision that determines the disposition of the cloak occurs by chance, not by necessity, both in the sense that the person making the decision is just as capable of choosing one alternative as the other and in the sense that the cloak is equally susceptible of either treatment. For Aristotle, and for Boethius in his translation, the statements we may make about the sea battle, the cloak, and the continuing whiteness of the white object are true according to how these things actually are and what is of their essence. The same rule applies to attributes predicated with qualifications or without them. One may say that a particular man has two feet and that the same man is a skillful cobbler. The first attribute applies to him without qualification, of necessity, while the second may well be true of him but it is not true necessarily; it describes his aptitudes and circumstances accurately, but it does not describe a necessity of his nature.[77] In all these cases, as J. L. Ackrill has well observed, "Aristotle does not . . . draw a sharp distinction be-

[75] Ibid., editio I, 1.4.
[76] Boethius, trans., *De interp.* 9.
[77] Ibid. 11.

tween logical and causal necessity; he treats laws of logic and laws of nature as on a par."[78] It is precisely this parity that Boethius breaks down in treating the laws of logic as paramount throughout his analysis of contingency.

Boethius' account comes closest to Aristotle's in his discussion of present contingencies. Here, he repeats Aristotle's example of a man's capacity to be two-footed and a skilled cobbler, merely substituting a man's capacity to be three-eyed or immortal in relation to his capacity to sit down or not at a particular moment. He emphasizes, as Aristotle does, that free moral agents have options which they may choose to exercise or not. While the powers and limitations that a being has *in rerum natura* are reference points for both thinkers, Boethius stresses the importance of the structure of the propositions in which these references to contingency are expressed, interpreting necessity and contingency, possibility and impossibility, according to the laws of identity and contradiction.[79] He exploits this approach much more systematically in his handling of future contingencies. Future events cannot be confirmed or denied, he notes, since the future itself is changeable (*variable et instabile*). Thus, it is impossible to verify some particular state of affairs in the future from the standpoint of nature. Rather, what one can do and what Boethius proceeds to do is to consider the logical necessity of certain propositions as corollaries or inferences of other propositions. On this basis he distinguishes four kinds of future contingents: propositions that will be capable of confirmation or denial as such (a trait that not all propositions formally enjoy), propositions that will be capable of confirmation or denial *in toto*, propositions that will be verifiable in some respect but negatable in another, and propositions whose truth is definite in one sense but whose falsity is indefinite in another sense. All four types of propositions are susceptible of an analysis whose truth claims inhere in their logical cogency in the here and now, although none of them can be confirmed or denied in the present since they are all contingent *per se*, referring to a future in which some things occur by chance (*casu*).[80]

The idea of chance itself provides Boethius with a platform from which to criticize the Stoic position on fate and free will as he understands it. Even though he has absorbed the Stoics' propositional approach to logic, without being forthright concerning his debts in this connection, he expressly attacks the Stoic doctrine of fate as a strict causal necessitarianism that rules out all chance and free will. It is certainly possible to

[78] A. J. Ackrill, comm. on his trans. of Aristotle, *Categories and De Interpretatione* (Oxford, 1963), p. 133.
[79] *Comm. in De interp.*, editio I, 1.9 and Bk. 2 passim.
[80] Ibid., 1.9, pp. 106–08, 110–17.

accomodate chance within a causal system while retaining freedom and contingency. Boethius follows Aristotle in illustrating this claim with the example of a farmer who accidentally finds a treasure buried in a field he is plowing, although its discovery was not the intention of the person who buried the treasure or of the farmer himself. While the acts leading to the burial and the discovery of the treasure are perfectly explicable in causal terms, the outcome was not planned by anyone and could not have been predicted. The Stoics, Boethius argues, maintain such a rigid necessitarianism as to make them incapable of giving a comprehensible explanation of this kind of event. Likewise, their limitation of possibility, impossibility, and necessity to events that are not impeded externally, to events that will never occur because they are impeded externally, and to events that are what they are under all circumstances, respectively, is far too narrow. It clutters up the form of simple propositions; it annihilates the very idea of logical impossibility; and it denies the fact that alternative outcomes may be equally admissible in some cases or that a chain of events may be ruptured by some unforeseen calamity. Furthermore, Boethius says, fate itself is not omnipotent. It is not the cause of all but the agent of still greater causes. Fate can do only what is possible and it cannot do what is impossible. Thus, not even fate can destroy those future contingencies that lie within the realm of logical possibility. It is for this reason, Boethius concludes, that he has discussed the subject of contingency as well as the Stoics' misconstruction of it in logical terms, *ad artem logicam disputationem transtulit, cum de propositionibus loqueretur* ("so as to transfer it to the art of logical disputation, which deals with propositions.")[81]

In the foregoing line of argument Boethius follows the opinion, repeated often in antiquity by critics of the Stoics and perpetuated at some points by Augustine and by the more recent Neoplatonists, that the Stoics advocated an unredeemed fatalism, an interpretation that fails to do them full justice. While Boethius misconstrues the Stoics on this point, he seizes accurately on the fact that they treated the entire question of fate and future contingents in a causal context much more unrelieved than the

---

[81] Ibid., 3.9. The quotation is at p. 198. Richard Sorabji, *Necessity, Cause, and Blame: Perspectives on Aristotle's Theory* (Ithaca, 1980), pp. 93, 122 n. 7 gives a clear account of Boethius' defense of Aristotle and attack on Stoicism by means of a strategy that replaces Aristotle's approach with a propositional analysis, derived from Ammonius, although he does not trace it back to Stoic logic itself. I am indebted to Christopher Gill for this reference. Chadwick, *Boethius* pp. 160–62 traces Boethius' critique of the Stoics to Porphyry. See also William Kneale and Martha Kneale, *The Development of Logic* (Oxford, 1962), p. 190; Claudio Leonardi, "I commenti altomedievali ai classici pagani, da Severino Boezio a Remigio d'Auxerre," *La cultura antica nel'occidente latino dal VII all'XI secolo*, Settimane di Studio del Centro Italiano di Studi sull' alto medioevo, 22, 18–24 aprile 1974 (Spoleto, 1975), I, 468.

setting in which Aristotle discusses it in the *De interpretatione*. In effect, Boethius challenges one Stoic teaching, which he refers to overtly, by judging it in the light of the formal approach to logic which he inherited from the Stoa without being entirely aware of it. And, although he defends the Aristotelian position on contingency against the Stoic, he is just as likely to apply the same logical criteria against Aristotle. It is true that he finds some details of the Stoic analysis of propositions unwieldly. Their division of propositions (*enuntiationes*) into possible and impossible, their treatment of possible propositions as either necessary or not necessary, and their treatment of the propositions that are not necessary as either possible or impossible he regards as foolish and tautological because it views the possible both as a genus and as a species of the not necessary.[82] Still, in his own exposition of future contingents he departs from Aristotle's technique of analyzing the significance of propositions whose verb is in the future tense and substitutes an analysis that depends on a conception of possibility and necessity viewed strictly in terms of the logical principles of identity and contradiction. He holds his own approach as preferable to Aristotle's because its criteria are the formal rules of logic that transcend temporal categories altogether.[83] A similar outlook informs his elaborate discussion of the affirmation and negation of definite and indefinite propositions, which also reflects clearly his recognition of the Stoic idea that the placement of a negative particle before the verb carries a lesser negative force than its placement before the entire proposition, to perfect the negation (*perficere negationem*), even though he mistakenly attributes to the Stoics the wish to compound ambiguities in so doing.[84] Indeed, throughout his commentaries on the *De interpretatione* Boethius tends to read the Stoics through Aristotelian and, to a lesser extent, through Neoplatonic spectacles, and to judge them harshly and not quite fairly on that account, even though he freely applies to the Aristotelians, as well as to the Stoics, a reformulation of the issue of contingency based on a systematic application to it of some of the Stoics' most distinctive contributions to ancient logic.

Boethius' repeated considerations of the syllogism, which he takes up briefly in his *De interpretatione* commentaries and expands on in several other works, also show an analogous conflation of Stoic and Aristotelian logic, but one in which the Aristotelian accent is more pronounced. Par-

---

[82] *Comm. in De interp.*, editio II, 5.12, p. 393. On this point see Chadwick, *Boethius*, pp. 160–62; Margaret E. Reesor, "*Poion* and *poiotes* in Stoic Philosophy," *Phronesis*, 17 (1972), 279–85.

[83] *Comm. in De interp.*, editio II, 3.9.

[84] Ibid. 4.10–5.10. The quotation is at 4.10, p. 258. Boethius expressly attributes to the Stoics and to Theophrastus an elaborate consideration of this topic, ibid. 1, praefatio; 2.4, 2.5. Chadwick *Boethius*, pp. 166–67, sees Porphyry as Boethius' source.

ticularly to the point here are his frequent disquisitions on the Stoic conditional syllogism ("if it is light, it is day"), of which his knowledge and appreciation are limited and which he Aristotelianizes as much as he can. Given the semantic doctrine he develops in his *De interpretatione* commentaries it is not surprising to find Boethius looking askance at hypothetical syllogisms as defective forms, for two reasons. First, their key words are prepositions and conjunctions that can never be natural signs of things since they can signify only in terms of their syntactical position in propositions. Second, propositions dependent on conditional formulations can never bear a demonstrable correlation with external reality, since their truth criteria inhere in their logical form alone.[85] While Boethius is perfectly willing to apply the norms attaching to formal propositional logic to the subject of contingency, he is far less willing to do so in discussing syllogisms. The very features that made hypothetical syllogisms attractive to the Stoics make them imperfect forms for Boethius. His method for correcting their perceived defects is to Aristotelianize them, so far as their structure permits, by reformulating them as categorical or causal syllogisms whose terms denote fixed essences or facts that are empirically verifiable. The classic Stoic formula ("if it is light, it is day") is framed deliberately in terms of phenomena that are shifting circumstances, in order to underscore the point that one cannot leap from logical to ontological conclusions. Boethius substitutes for it either the form "if he is a man, he is an animal" or the form "if she has given birth, she has slept with a man" or both, syllogisms whose terms refer to natural events that are either always the case or connected causally in a naturally verifiable manner. He acknowledges that his understanding of this whole subject has been influenced by Porphyry. Were it not for Porphyry, he states, the doctrine of the Stoic hypothetical syllogisms would be unknown in Latin,[86] an observation reflecting Boethius' ignorance of, or unwillingness to credit, the Latin treatments of the Stoic hypotheticals from Cicero to Marius Victorinus, which present a fuller and more accurate account of them than Boethius does.[87]

The narrowness of Boethius' perspective can be seen most clearly in his treatise on the hypothetical syllogisms and his commentary on Cicero's *Topica*, one of the most influential Latin sources for them. Boethius

---

[85] *Comm. in De interp.*, editio II, 5.10. This point is discussed in detail for all the works in which Boethius treats the hypothetical syllogism by Berka, "Die Semantik des Boethius," *Helikon*, 8 (1968), 456–59.

[86] *Comm. in De interp.*, editio II, 3.9.

[87] On this point see M. L. Colish, "The Stoic Hypothetical Syllogisms and Their Transmission in the Latin West through the Early Middle Ages," *Res Publica Litterarum*, 2 (1979), 19–26; *Stoic Tradition*, I, 84, 331–32, 334, 339; see also Chadwick, *Boethius*, pp. 115, 117–18, 173.

neither replicates the Stoics nor imitates Cicero; nor does he merely repeat the general ancient opinion.[88] On the one hand, he systematically
converts the Stoic hypotheticals he treats into Aristotelian categorical or
causal forms, so far as possible. On the other hand, he converts the treatises in which he discusses them *in extenso* into essays in propositional
logic.[89] He does not appear to notice the tension between the conflicting
sets of criteria he invokes in this dual process. Boethius' *De hypotheticis
syllogismis* is his most exhaustive work on this subject. Claiming that he
has found nothing on the hypothetical syllogism in Latin and that he has
relied on Theophrastus and Eudemus,[90] he confines himself to two of the
five Stoic hypothetical forms, the conditional ("if it is light, it is day")
and the disjunctive ("it is either light, or it is night"). Boethius dismisses
the disjunctive after the most perfunctory consideration, stating that it
cannot prove anything with necessity,[91] and concentrates on the conditional. He recasts it sometimes as a categorical and sometimes as a causal
syllogism depending on whether he wants to weigh its probative force
with reference to simultaneous phenomena or with reference to phenomena that have a temporal cause-effect relationship. In either case he is
interested in validating the first half of the hypothetical with a predi-
cative conclusion that can be tested in the light of natural entailment and
not merely in terms of the relations between the elements in the proposition.[92]

Boethius' main concern, expressed by the space it occupies in the body
of the treatise, is to develop a series of variations on the conditional syllogism, both the syllogism with two terms in its Stoic or Aristotelianized
form ("If A, then B; but A, therefore B") or with three terms ("If A, then
B; if B, then C; but if A, therefore C"). He subjects these schemata in
detail to various modes of affirmation, negation, and double negation and
to further subdivision into necessary and contingent forms, emerging with
some forty variants on the originals which effectively situate the issue of
their analysis within the realm of propositions and their structure, rather
than their content. As an essay in Stoic logic, the *De hypotethicis syllogis-*

---

[88] See on the contrary René van den Driessche, "Sur le 'De syllogismo hypothetico'
de Boèce," *Methodos*, 1 (1949), 294; Kneale and Kneale, *Development of Logic*, p. 191; Luca
Obertello, intro. to his ed. and trans. of Boethius, *De hypotheticis syllogismis* (Brescia, 1969),
pp. 9, 25, 50; Eleonore Stump, comm. on her trans. of Boethius, *De topicis differentiis* (Ithaca, 1978), p. 208. Henry Chadwick, "Introduction," in Gibson, ed., *Boethius*, p. 4, repeats this skewed consensus and omits the other Latin intermediaries of the Stoic hypothetical syllogisms.

[89] Driessche, "Sur le 'De syllogismo hypothetico'," p. 298; Karl Dürr, *The Propositional Logic of Boethius* (Amsterdam, 1951), ch. 4–5.

[90] *De hyp. syll.* 1.1.3, ed. Obertello.

[91] Ibid. 3.11.1–7.

[92] Ibid. 1.3.6–7, 1.2.1, 1.2.4.

mis reveals Boethius' ignorance of the full range of hypothetical syllogisms and his willingness to take seriously only the conditional form; in this connection he may be described as infra-Stoic. On the other hand, the multiplicity of the changes he rings on the conditional syllogism and his use of its original form merely as a launching pad into realms of variation uncharted by the Stoics entitles him to be called a post-Stoic.[93] At the same time, his propositional emphasis is entirely Stoic and his recasting of the Stoic conditionals by the substitution of categorical and causal terms is quite Aristotelian.

Much more restricted in scope, but essentially in the same vein, is Boethius' handling of hypothetical syllogisms in his commentary on Cicero's *Topica* and in his own *De differentiis topicis*. In the first treatise he notes that Victorinus had written a book on topics and disparages it as lacking in pertinence to Cicero's work. He agrees with Cicero that the Stoics said little of value on *topoi* and he shares Cicero's definition of common notions (*ennoia, prolepsis*) as Platonic innate ideas.[94] Yet, his own commentary is scarcely congruous with Cicero's. Cicero had outlined four of the five Stoic hypotheticals and had assimilated them to the Aristotelian enthymeme, or rhetorical syllogism.[95] Although he cites many illustrations from legal cases in the effort to persuade readers that logic is pertinent to oratory, Boethius places the whole question in a logical, not a rhetorical, context and confines himself to the conditional and disjunctive syllogisms, once more dismissing the disjunctive peremptorily and reformulating the conditional in categorical and causal terms, which, here as elsewhere, he prefers because the terms can be universalized or verified empirically. He then subjects the conditional syllogism to a much more elaborate series of affirmations and negations than Cicero does in his own *Topica*.[96] The only doctrinal allusion to the Stoa that Boethius makes in his commentary on Cicero's *Topica* refers not to logic but to physics, in a marginal remark repeating his criticism of Stoic necessitarianism but this time in comparison with the Aristotelian theory of causation.[97] Still more limited is Boethius' reference to the conditional syllogism in *De differentiis topicis* where, mentioning only "the Greeks" as his source, he rephrases the conditional once more into categorical and

---

[93] Ibid. 2.4.4–3.9.7. A useful summary and analysis of the post-Stoic aspects of this procedure is provided by I. M. Bocheński, *A History of Formal Logic*, trans. and ed. Ivo Thomas (Notre Dame, 1961), pp. 138–39. See also Chadwick, *Boethius*, pp. 168–73; A. N. Prior, "The Logic of Negative Terms in Boethius," *Franciscan Studies*, 13 (1953), 1–6; Obertello, comm. on his ed., p. 463.

[94] *In Topica Ciceronis commentaria* 1, 3, *PL*, 64.

[95] See Colish, *Stoic Tradition*, I, 84–85.

[96] *In Top. Cic.* 4–5.

[97] Ibid. 5.

causal forms. Observing that the conditional syllogism so recast refers both to natural and to logical entailment, he treats it as having less probative force than syllogisms which move from universal first premises to particular conclusions.[98] Boethius' handling of this whole subject in his *De differentiis topicis* and in his commentary on Cicero's *Topica* is clearly dependent on his lengthier exposition of it in the *De hypotheticis syllogismis*. Still, and although they do so in a more restricted manner, these two later treatises carry forth the basic, if decidedly ambiguous, relationship between Aristotelian and Stoic logic found in his earlier and more elaborate logical works.

While Boethius' logical treatises reflect a syncretism in which an explicit Aristotelianism and a largely implicit Stoicism struggle for supremacy, with each school winning part of the honors, his *Consolation of Philosophy* places Neoplatonism in the foreground, but with far less doxography or overt comparison. The author of the *Consolation* was a man exploiting the resources of memory and sensibility in order to assuage a profound personal sorrow. He assimilates Stoic, Aristotelian, and Christian elements into his prevailingly Neoplatonic outlook in a manner that goes beyond the question of the *Consolation*'s detectable analogies and antecedents.[99] The combination of ingredients flowing into Boethius' argument eludes the kind of analysis that would content itself with the mechanical weighing of his sources or his attitude toward the relationship between paganism and Christianity. The *Consolation* reflects Boethius' belief that classical philosophy contains an authentic wisdom fully compatible with patristic theology and his own Christian faith. The elements involved are combined so thoroughly in Boethius' mind that the specification of their similarities and differences is no longer important for him. What is of critical concern to him is the intellectual guidance and moral strength that philosophy could supply, which he imbibes and reexpresses with a freedom, a freshness, and an immediacy that guar-

---

[98] *De differentiis topicis* 2, PL, 64.

[99] The history of the interpretation of the *Consolation*, from its treatment as a purely pagan work to the agonizings over its pagan content once Boethius' Christianity was established to its over-Christianization to its treatment as a patchwork quilt to its subjection to the single-source *Quellenforscher* to the present state of scholarly consensus, which our own assessment reflects for the most part, is presented exhaustively in the section of Obertello, *Severino Boezio*, II, devoted to this work. For some excellent recent and post-Obertello statements of the current view, see Chadwick, *Boethius*, ch. 5; Pierre Courcelle, *La Consolation de Philosophie dans la tradition littéraire: Antécédents et postérité de Boèce* (Paris, 1967), passim and esp. pp. 8–9, 18–28, 333–35; Raffaello Del Re, intro. to his ed. and trans. of Boethius, *Philosophiae consolatio* (Roma, 1968), pp. 16–21; Gruber, *Kommentar*, pp. 36–40, although he cites as Stoic some ideas that are commonplaces, pp. 145, 148–49; Helga Scheible, *Die Gedichte in der Consolatio Philosophiae des Boethius* (Heidelberg, 1972), p. 4; Vogel, "Philosophy and Christian Faith," *Romanitas et Christianitas*, pp. 357–70.

anteed for the *Consolation* the classic status it enjoyed in medieval literature and beyond.

Both as a theodicy and as an explanation of the sufferings of the just the *Consolation* far outstrips Lactantius' *De opificio dei*, Salvian's *De gubernatione dei*, Augustine's *De ordine*, Gregory's *Moralia*, or Dracontius' *De laudibus dei*, its most obvious model.[100] The formal structure and the substance of Boethius' book make it a much more sophisticated exercise in self-consolation than Dracontius' poem, despite the close situational parallels between the two authors. At the same time, the *Consolation* is both less Stoic and less Christian than any of these previous or later works, even though the chief points of contact between Boethius and the Stoic tradition here are similar—the doctrine of the sage marked by an *apatheia* and autarchy heavily dependent on his free will, and the rationalization of bad fortune as a moral problem which the sage can master with the right inner attitude and with a perspective focusing on God's providential governance of the world. Boethius Neoplatonizes this argument mainly by equating the deity with a timeless, spiritual *summum bonum*, which he contrasts sharply with the mutable world with its material goods and evils. For Boethius, as for Augustine, the infinite duration of the supreme good gives it the power to grant a unique psychological security to its possessor. With Augustine, also, Boethius sees this same eternity of the deity as a way to reconcile providence with free will. However, Boethius' approach to the tension between matter and spirit, time and eternity, is less Biblical and more dualistic than Augustine's and his conception of the nature of evil is as much metaphysical as moral. Boethius unquestionably brings a number of important Stoic ethical doctrines into play in the *Consolation*. In all cases, their value to him lies in their ability to sustain Boethius in a non-Stoic universe. While he preserves some of the central attributes of the Stoic sage and the Stoic theodicy, Boethius extracts from the rationalism and the moral autonomy embedded in these clusters of ideas a psychology of escape from the world of time, matter, and history.

Boethius begins by posing the problems he wants to address in initially Stoic terms, which he then reshapes by endowing them with an increasingly non-Stoic content and by placing them in an increasingly non-Stoic context as the *Consolation* progresses. This procedure requires a certain amount of repetition, a technique of composition consistent with the pedagogical presentation of ideas in a dialogue where the *magistra*, Lady Philosophy, summarizes and reviews the points established at each major stage of the argument. Philosophical schools and their represent-

---

[100] The only previous author to note the parallel with Dracontius is Rand, *Founders*, p. 160. On Dracontius see above, ch. 3, pp. 108–09.

atives are mentioned in her first speech, as a means of indicating her identity and her credentials for enjoining Boethius to remember the true self as a sage he has forgotten in his grief. He has, she reminds him, been educated in the school of the Eleatics and Academics.[101] In describing her own history and the depredations which her mantle has suffered she names Socrates and Plato as her prime mentors, whose heritage was torn to shreds by the Epicureans and Stoics. Yet even the schools unfaithful to Platonism produced wise men who bravely endured affliction for their views. Here she mentions Anaxagoras, Zeno of Elea, Canius, Seneca, and Soranus. Their bond is scarcely a doctrinal one. Rather, it is the situational similarity they share with Boethius, the victimization by tyrants or intolerant governments.[102] The note on which Philosophy opens her discourse suggests clearly that the philosopher's highest claim to authority lies in the moral consolation provided by his teaching and example, and that the chief misfortune which philosophy can temper is not a cosmic or natural calamity but the unjust political treatment of the wise and virtuous man.

Philosophy's insistence on the point that Boethius is a sage, albeit a forgetful one, leads to a definition of the wise man that is quite Stoic, although it also lays the foundation for Boethius' deStoicizing of the concept later in the work. The sage is always calm (*serenus*) because he has ordered his life well. He is unconquered (*invictus*) whatever misfortunes befall him, be they storms, volcanic eruptions, thunderbolts—or the power and rage of tyrants. Without pausing to explore the sage's response to the natural disasters mentioned first, Boethius concentrates on the avoidance of both hope and fear as the way to disarm unjust rulers. In a Senecan vein he remarks that the man who remains tied to those passions *nectit qua valeat trahi catenam* ("fastens the chain by which he will be drawn.")[103] Capitulation to the passions is a matter of voluntary choice. As with the decision to avoid the passions, it lies within our own power. The sage who exercises his autarchy to acquire *apatheia* will truly govern himself however unfairly his prince or his fellow citizens may requite him.[104] The very same freedom of choice that enables a misguided innocent to fall prey to the passions is what empowers his persecutors

---

[101] *Philosophiae consolatio* 1. pr. 1.10, ed. Ludovicus Bieler, CC, 94 (Turnhout, 1957). Bieler's edition will be used throughout.

[102] Ibid. 1. pr. 6–7, 9. The otherwise judicious assessment of Obertello, *Severino Boezio*, I, 735–45 does not emphasize the political dimension sufficiently.

[103] *Phil. cons.* 1. met. 4. The quotation is at line 18; trans. Richard Green (Indianapolis, 1962), p. 9.

[104] Ibid. 1. pr. 5. The Stoic features of Boethius' treatment of the sage and the passions have been noted by Gruber, *Kommentar*, pp. 109–110, 112, 158, 208, 259, 260, 295, 361, 371, although he errs in connecting with it the idea of seminal reasons, pp. 117–118; Scheible, *Die Gedichte*, pp. 44–45, 56, 57, 77–78, 80, 83, 99–100, 135.

and accusers to afflict him. This thought leads Boethius to observe that, in some respects, human free will is regrettable. If the benevolent God Who rules the universe had not endowed men with freedom, the wicked would not be able to do so much damage. Yet, Boethius and Lady Philosophy agree, God and His ordering of the universe are reasonable and good.[105] So ends the first book of the *Consolation*. Both the dilemma as it is posed and the ingredients provided for its solution at the beginning of the work are fully Stoic, except at one salient point. Boethius is a sage. Yet, he has been able to lose sight of his true nature. If this is the case, the constancy of the sage is not a permanent state, *more Stoicorum*, but is erratic and subject to change, a thought that provides a transition between the statement of the issues in Book I and Boethius' subsequent reformulation of them.

That the virtue of the sage is not enduring, an end in itself, or the *summum bonum* emerges in the second and third books of the *Consolation*. In an argument showing that alleged evils are not evil and that alleged goods are not good, Boethius moves to the conclusion that nothing in the changing material world can be the true good. He first disposes of bad fortune, not as a misinterpretation of the cosmic order but as a real evil, although one that may be redeemed if the sage accepts it as a means of moral education.[106] While still partly Stoic, the moral terrain is clearly beginning to shift. Boethius' relativizing of the alleged goods moves him still further away from the Stoa. Worldly goods, he asserts, are not truly good for we cannot possess them fully. They are given to us for our use but we do not own them. We are only their stewards. Hence, the fact that they may be withdrawn from us abruptly and unpredictably gives us no cause to plead injustice. In any event, he asks, what is a just reward? What do men really deserve? Greedy and insatiable as they are, can they themselves be fit judges of their own deserts?[107] This line of argument has a distinctly Christian coloration, suggesting that men are not their own masters but fallible creatures dependent on a higher power whose decisions are beyond man's capacity to comprehend or to judge. Lady Philosophy next observes that, despite Boethius' unjust punishment, he can still take pleasure in the goods that remain to him, such as his distinguished background and nurture, the virtue of his wife, and the achievements of his sons, goods which a Stoic would dismiss as *adiaphora*. When Boethius complains that, even so, he suffers from the memory of lost joys, Philosophy repeats that his satisfaction in the goods he retains should allay that sorrow.[108]

---

[105] *Phil. cons.* 1. pr. 4-pr. 6.
[106] Ibid. 2. pr. 1, 2. pr. 8.
[107] Ibid. 2. pr. 2-met. 2.
[108] Ibid. 2. pr. 4.

Boethius the author presents Boethius the speaker in the dialogue as a man undergoing progressive enlightenment under Philosophy's tutelage. The arguments concerning good and evil which she has presented thus far are all propaedeutic. They have been measured according to Boethius' perceived capacity to learn and they are all designed to lead up to the main point which she is now confident of his ability to grasp: all earthly goods are intrinsically limited and transient. Even in the very act of enjoying an earthly good one's happiness is shadowed by the fear of losing it. The *summum bonum* must be a good engendering a happiness that can be possessed completely, retained permanently, and therefore enjoyed securely. Hence, no earthly good, not even the autarchy of the sage, can be the supreme good. Just as no one can possess perfectly a changing material good, so the sage cannot possess himself absolutely. Autarchy can be lost, as Boethius' experience itself testifies, since men are subject to moral backsliding and the reappropriation of wisdom. The true security, stability, and tranquillity of mind that liberates the sage from man's inhumanity to man can only be attained if he sets his sights on a goal that transcends man and nature alike, a good that is exempt from change.[109]

Boethius first intimates what such a good might be in adverting to the love that binds the universe and human society together, observing that true happiness would be the rule of that love in each man's soul. This bond of love has been viewed as Stoic but we are already at a considerable remove from the rational divine *logos* or *tonos* which is consubstantial with the *hegemonikon* of the sage.[110] By definition, the supreme good for Boethius cannot be one that is identical with or immanent in the mutable physical world. Rather, it is a good he equates with a transcendent, spiritual, immutable God. Boethius' deity combines the freedom, the fatherhood, and the omnipotence of the Christian God and the perfect state of rest enjoyed by the Aristotelian unmoved mover with the uncaused self-sufficiency and superabundance of the Neoplatonic One. Such a good, once obtained, stills all further desires and grants the only

---

[109] Ibid. 2. pr. 4.12-met. 7.
[110] Ibid. 2. pr. 8. The Stoicism of this idea has been stressed in too unmodified a way by Chadwick, *Boethius*, p. 232; William Thomas Fontaine, *Fortune, Matter and Providence: A Study of Anicius Severinus Boethius and Giordane Bruno* (Scotlandville, La., 1939), p. 10: Gruber, *Kommentar*, pp. 227–28, 243; Michael Lapidge, "A Stoic Metaphor in Late Latin Poetry: The Binding of the Cosmos," *Latomus*, 39 (1980), 833–37; Scheible, *Die Gedichte*, pp. 92–93, 149–50, 262–63; C. J. de Vogel, "Amor quo caelum regitur," *Vivarium*, 1 (1963), 4–6, 35. More recently De Vogel, "Amor quo caelum regitur: Quel amour et quel dieu?" *Atti del Congresso internazionale di studi Boeziani*, ed. Luca Obertello (Roma, 1981), 193–200 has modified her view and now accents the Pythagorean-Neoplatonic dimensions of Boethius' use of the idea.

true liberation from affliction.[111] In describing God Boethius invokes the Stoic image of the helmsman keeping the ship of the universe sailing on an even keel.[112] Yet, his God lacks the direct hand on the rudder which the Stoics' deity maintains. He may be watchful and unsleeping, but there is a significant metaphysical distance between Him and His creation, a distance wide enough to require natural and supernatural intermediaries. Man cannot find this God by looking to nature or by scrutinizing the depths of his own soul. The only way for man to reach Him is to break the chains of earth (*terrae solvere vincula*).[113] Boethius' stress on the psychic security gained by the possession of the eternal *summum bonum* is Augustinian. But the metaphysics and psychology associated with that moral state are decidedly Neoplatonic.

It is within the framework of this strongly Neoplatonic opposition between matter and spirit, change and immutability, that Boethius now reintroduces and redefines the principles that virtue requires *apatheia*, that virtue lies within, and that the sufferings of this life are a test of character. The autarchy that enables man to meet these tests successfully depends on a freedom of the will that wins him detachment from the body, now signalized as the source from which the passions arise.[114] Boethius' idea that good and evil are mixed in each man's lot[115] reflects a conception of human nature in which the soul is seen to be entrapped by the body. Man's possession of a body thus replaces both Augustine's disordered will and the Stoics' false judgments as the explanation of moral evil. Nor does Boethius hesitate to define evil as non-being or the privation of the good, thus firmly attaching it to the negative Neoplatonic valuation of the metaphysical status of matter as such.[116] The sage, for Boethius, continues to undergo trials, but these trials are designed to help him detach his soul from his body. In this connection Boethius recasts

---

[111] *Phil. cons.* 3. met. 1-pr. 11.

[112] Ibid. 3. pr. 12.14. Scheible, *Die Gedichte*, pp. 174, 184–87 treats this point judiciously although Paul G. Chappuis, "La théologie de Boèce," *Jubilé Alfred Loisy: Congrès d'histoire du christianisme*, 3, ed. P. L. Couchoud (Paris, 1928), pp. 22–24, 26–27, 29–30 errs in depicting Boethius as an immanentalist.

[113] *Phil. cons.* 3. met. 12.3–4. Good discussions of this point are provided by Gaetano Capone Braga, "La soluzione cristiana del problema del 'summum bonum' in 'Philosophiae consolationis libri quinque' di Boezio," *Archivo di storia della filosofia italiana*, 3 (1934), 101–16; Chadwick, *Boethius*, pp. 222, 228–34, 241, 249; James Collins, "Progress and Problems in the Reassessment of Boethius," *The Modern Schoolman*, 33 (1945), 22; Courcelle, *La Consolation de Philosophie*, pp. 161–76; Volker Schmidt-Kohl, *Die neuplatonische Seelenlehre in der Consolatio Philosophiae des Boethius* (Meisenheim am Glan, 1965).

[114] *Phil. cons.* 4. met. 2–met. 4, pr. 7.

[115] Ibid. 4. pr. 5, pr. 6.40–50.

[116] Ibid. 4. pr. 2. An excellent treatment of this point is found in Ernst Gegenschatz, "Die Freiheit der Entscheidung in der 'consolatio philosophiae' des Boethius," *Museum Helveticum*, 15 (1958), 110–29.

Hercules as a Neoplatonic saint, whose ordeals all signify the triumph of mind over matter. Hercules' final labor, his self-immolation, is the supreme example of his willingness to abandon his body and the earthly life itself, and it was for this ultimate act of moral heroism that he merited heaven.[117]

Just as Boethius substitutes a Neoplatonic for a Stoic Hercules, so he redefines the human and divine natures in terms of which the sage struggles for wisdom and virtue. The sage must apply his free will to the liberation of his soul, seen as his true moral ego, from imprisonment in a physical body. The body's materiality makes it changeable; but the soul, too, is subject to change, even though it is spiritual. The soul must thus move beyond itself in quest of the divine *summum bonum* which alone possesses unity, immutability, simplicity, and eternity and which transcends the world. God governs the mutable and multifarious world with an unchanging providential order, bridging the metaphysical distance between Himself and the world, without involving Himself directly in the affairs of lower beings, through the agency of fate, which in turn may use tertiary agents such as natural phenomena, angels and devils, and men, in applying the decree of providence to particular events.[118] While God Himself is able to keep His entire providential plan in mind, the same cannot be said for men. Their ignorance of the cosmic sweep of providence cannot be removed entirely by education or by a more rational understanding. God's ways are not completely knowable. Failure to predict the fated outcome of events is a sign of the limits of the human condition, exemplified for Boethius by Lucan's Cato.[119] The task of philosophy is not to give man unfounded hopes but to teach him how to exercise what freedom he has in a world whose final comprehension will always elude him. Boethius does not seek to resolve the tensions which he builds into the human condition by appealing either to the suprarational contemplation of the Neoplatonic mystic or to the Christian conviction of the accessibility of the unknown God through the incarnate Christ. The metaphysical and moral landscape that he depicts is rather more stark than that proposed by either of these two alternatives. Put another way, Boethius outlines a philosophy that teaches man how to die more than it teaches him how to live well. Yet, it is within this framework that he situates the extended discussion of providence, fate, and free will with which he ends the *Consolation*.

There are a number of important differences between Boethius' handling of this subject in the *Consolation* and in his earlier *De interpretatione*

---

[117] *Phil. cons.* 4. met. 7.
[118] Ibid. 4. met. 5–pr. 6.
[119] Ibid. 4. pr. 6.32–33.

commentary. A comparison of these twin treatments of the same theme will provide a useful insight into the continuities and discontinuities in Boethius' approach to Stoicism that are visible more broadly as one moves from his logical works to his *Consolation*. In both settings he lays an Aristotelian foundation for his defense of chance, contingency, and free will and for his distinction between absolute and conditional necessity. He also uses the same, or directly analogous, examples to establish the claim that chance and contingency can be explained within the framework of a causal system and that the characteristics necessarily inhering in intelligent beings include free choice. In the *Consolation*, as in the *De interpretatione* commentary, the express or understood thesis which these examples are designed to counter is Stoic necessitarianism, as Boethius understands it.[120] However, in the *Consolation*, the chief objective of his refutation of fatalism is not to make way for contingency in general but to establish the reality of free will, which, Boethius stresses, is mandatory if man is to lead a meaningful moral life.[121] Ethics, therefore, holds the center of the stage, rather than logic. The consideration of free will that follows in the *Consolation*, moreover, is dependent on Boethius' Neoplatonizing of metaphysics and psychology earlier in the work. We may grade free will, he notes, depending on the link in the chain of being occupied by its possessor. While free will is an attribute of all rational beings, only God and the other celestial beings, having no connection with material bodies, can exercise it perfectly. They experience no hiatus between knowing and willing and accomplishing what they want. On the other hand, human beings do experience a disjunction between their knowledge, their will, and their power, one that they can increase or decrease by the way they use their freedom. Human free will is greatest when a man has been detached from his body in the life to come and when he applies his freedom to the contemplation of God. Man is less free when his soul is joined to his body. He is still less free when his body chains him to earth; and he is totally enslaved when he allows his body to govern his reason. Here Boethius regards the body not as part of man's natural endowment but as sub-natural, a component of his constitution that cannot be redeemed by his freedom of will but whose rejection is both an index of his moral liberty and a means to it.[122]

---

[120] Ibid. 5. pr. 1–met. 1, pr. 6. Cf. Vincent Cioffari, *Fortune and Fate from Democritus to St. Thomas Aquinas* (New York, 1935), pp. 82–91; Ernst Gegenschatz, "Die Gefährdung des Möglichen durch das Vorauswissen Gottes in der Sicht des Boethius," *Wiener Studien*, 79 (1966), 517–30; and Gregor Maurach, "Boethiusinterpretationen," *Römische Philosophie*, ed. Gregor Maurach, Wege der Forschung, 193 (Darmstadt, 1976), pp. 388–89 who see Boethius as more of a supporter than as a critic of the Stoics here.

[121] *Phil. cons.* 5. pr. 3.

[122] Ibid. 5. pr. 2. There is a good account of this point in Neal W. Gilbert, "The Concept of Will in Early Latin Philosophy," *Journal of the History of Philosophy*, 1 (1963), 33–34.

This thorough Neoplatonizing of the purpose of free will and of the human condition in which it labors still leaves open its relationship to fate and providence. In his *De interpretatione* commentary, Boethius had attacked Stoic fatalism and had reoriented the Aristotelian approach to future contingents by taking the question out of the realm of causation and natural priority and posteriority. Instead he had analyzed it from the timeless standpoint of propositional logic and its formal rules of inference and entailment. In this way Boethius had used the Stoic conception of logic to reformulate the Aristotelian doctrine of chance and contingency. In the *Consolation*, he applies propositional logic once more to the problem of fate and freedom, with the same results.[123] But this is by no means his only or his major way of placing events in time under the judgment of timeless criteria. His appeal to propositional logic serves as a tributary to his main line of argument in Book 5 of the *Consolation*, which rests on his redefinition of providence as divine foreknowledge. By viewing God's governance of the world in terms of His foreknowledge rather than in terms of His causation of all events, Boethius deals necessitarianism a blow from another direction, preserving free will and contingency metaphysically as well as logically. His claim that God's foreknowledge precludes His causation of everything He knows will happen, whether it happens by necessity or by contingency, is based on an analysis of God's nature and mode of knowing. Since God is pure intellect and since He is eternal, His thought processes are utterly instantaneous and totally exempt from the sequential, temporal mode of knowledge that applies to men. Past, present, and future simply have no meaning with reference to the divine epistemology. The notion that God's knowledge is atemporal had been developed by the Neoplatonists; it is fully consistent with their view of the deity as simple, unchanging, and transcendent. However, the Neoplatonists had not associated this doctrine with causality, future contingents, and free will. Although Boethius refers to Cicero in this connection he does not advert to the Chrysippean image of the cylinder, which Cicero had reported in transmitting the Stoic position on fate and free will in his *De fato*. Boethius' chief model is Augustine. Not only had Augustine supplied an exhaustive critique of necessitarianism, which he sometimes attributes tendentiously to the Stoics, he had also been the first thinker to equate the God Who lives in the eternal present with a divine omniscience that does not annul the contingencies and freedoms inhering in His creatures, however, broadly or narrowly Augustine chooses to view those freedoms in different con-

---

[123] *Phil. cons.* 5. pr. 3–met. 3. Courcelle, *La Consolation de Philosophie*, pp. 210–21 places too preclusive an emphasis on this line of argument in Book 5; Obertello, *Severino Boezio*, I, 721, 724–25 gives a more judicious account.

texts.[124] Boethius' principal departure from Augustine, in this connection, is his retention of fate as a cosmic intermediary between God and nature, a metaphysical agent which Augustine firmly banishes from the scene.

Boethius' only specific reference to the Stoics in the last book of the *Consolation* touches neither on the formal approach to logic which he borrows from them without acknowledgment nor on the unrelieved fatalism which he mistakenly ascribes to them. It occurs, rather, in the section of the book where he contrasts the human and divine ways of knowing. Here, he criticizes the Stoics for advocating the same kind of intromissive epistemology which he praises the Aristotelians for espousing in his *De interpretatione* commentary. The Stoics' failure to preserve the Aristotelian epistemology, in Boethius' logical works, is evaluated from the perspective of semantics. He approves the Aristotelian view for its capacity to render a better account of how and why concepts, not words, are the primary signs of things. In the *Consolation*, on the other hand, the epistemology that Boethius attaches to the Stoa is compared unfavorably with the extramissive theory taught by the Neoplatonists. In neither context does Boethius show any awareness of the fact that the Stoic position combined intromission with extramission. His argument in the *Consolation* reflects his wish to show that the human intellect takes the initiative in cognition, activating the senses, even in a human mode of knowing in which the mind is tied to the body, subject to error, and forced to operate in a temporal sequence. If the mind of man can take the initiative and can play an active role in human cognition, how much the freer and more powerful, how much the more absolute and universal is the knowledge of God, Who is pure intellect untrammeled by matter and time.[125] Here Boethius uses a fragmented view of the Stoic epistemology to criticize the Stoics in favor of the Neoplatonists, even as he uses a fragmented view of Stoic logic both to criticize the Stoics and to revamp

---

[124] *Phil. cons.* 5. met. 2, pr. 4, pr. 5, pr. 6. The Augustinian dimension in this Neoplatonic strategy as used by Boethius has been treated sensitively by Dorothea Frede, *Aristoteles und die "Seeschlacht": Das Problem der Contingentia Futura in De interpretatione 9* (Göttingen, 1970), pp. 122–24; Obertello, *Severino Boezio,* I, 732; and Nelson Pike, "Divine Omniscience and Voluntary Action," *Philosophical Review,* 74 (1965), 24–46. On the other hand, Chadwick, *Boethius,* pp. 241–47; Courcelle, *Late Latin Writers,* p. 305; Peter Huber, *Die Vereinbarkeit von göttlicher Vorsehung und menschlicher Freiheit in der Consolatio Philosophiae des Boethius* (Zürich, 1976); and Sorabji, *Necessity, Cause, and Blame,* p. 125 see only the Neoplatonic aspect. On Augustine see above, pp. 228–32.

[125] *Phil. cons.* 5. met. 4–pr. 5. Gruber, *Kommentar,* p. 104 states that Boethius criticizes the Stoic epistemology while on pp. 377–78, 399, 401–03 he ascribes to the Stoa the active theory of sensation which Boethius credits to the Platonists, as does Scheible, *Die Gedichte,* pp. 164–65, 166. Neither commentator notes that the Stoic epistemology combines intromission with extramission.

the Aristotelians in his logical works. But, while Aristotle and the Stoa are strong enough to impose conditions on each other in the hands of Boethius the logician, neither can resist the assimilative force of his Neoplatonism in the *Consolation*. In both segments of his *œuvre*, and with these differences in focus and directionality, Stoicism is important to Boethius for its help in defining the issues he seeks to address and the approaches that he takes to them, however much that Stoicism, whether logical or ethical, is revalued in the perspective of Boethius' more pervasive philosophical affinities.

IV. The Anonymous *Contra philosophos*

The intellectual discontinuities and the literary isolation which so many sixth-century Latin Christian authors experienced are strikingly evident as we move from Boethius to the *Contra philosophos*. Although the anonymous author of this work lived in Ostrogothic Italy in the generation after Boethius and was interested in some of the same problems, he was all but unaware of Boethius' writings and considerably at odds with his point of view. For the Anonymous, Aristotelianism might never have existed and the Neoplatonists were enemies rather than trusted guides. And, while he uses a few Greek words and cites several Greek authors, his chief sources are Latin, above all Augustine's *City of God*. Far from contributing to what has been called the Hellenic renaissance of sixth-century Italy,[126] the *Contra philosophos* is quite simply oblivious of it. Indeed, this work points to the need to revise substantially the idea that Christian writers in that milieu turned mainly to the Greeks to buttress their faith, whether against heresy or against paganism. In his reverence for Augustine and in his dependence on the *City of God*, from which he derives the majority of his information, the Anonymous is certainly in tune with the backward-looking tendencies of his age. But his work is no mere summary, *catena*, or *florilegium* of Augustine, however much it may appear to have in common with those genres. The author also makes independent use of a wide range of literary, philosophical, theological, and legal texts quite apart from Augustine. He manages to combine a certain fidelity to his sources with a more up-to-date perspective that reflects his own contemporary knowledge and concerns. Moreover, even in those quarters where his reliance on patristic authority is the heaviest, he strikes a distinctively forward-looking note in the way he uses it. He treats Augustine not merely as a model for the critique of ancient

---

[126] Courcelle, *Late Latin Writers*, p. 273; Arnaldo Momigliano, "Cassiodorus and Italian Culture of His Time," *Proceedings of the British Academy*, 41 (1955), 208–14.

philosophy or for its absorption into Christian thought but also as a source for the teachings of the philosophers themselves. And, in contrast to Augustine and Boethius alike, he sees the Neoplatonists as the greatest organized challenge to the Christian faith, with the Stoics functioning partly as a threat and partly as a positive resource.

The status of the author of the *Contra philosophos* as an unknown quantity applies just as much to his intellectual outlook as to his personal identity. While the *Contra philosophos* has been in print since 1949 it has thus far attracted the attention only of textual critics and editors seeking to establish its provenance, to date it, and to describe the paleographical features of the two fifteenth-century manuscripts in which it is preserved. These matters having now been settled,[127] we may turn with confidence to the substance of the work itself and its place in the thought of its century. Since the *Contra philosophos* has not hitherto been studied by an intellectual historian it may be useful, before considering its contribution to the Stoic tradition, to describe it more generally and to give a brief indication of its form, structure, and content.

The *Contra philosophos* is a dialogue in five books, containing thirty-one two-party debates between a Christian interlocutor, Augustinus, and a series of fifteen representatives of pagan religion and philosophy. The cast of pagan characters includes Apuleius, Cicero, Hermes, Iamblichus, "Mathematicus," Plato, Plotinus, Porphyry, "Romanus," Sallust, Scaevola, Scipio, Seneca, "Stoicus," and Varro. The speeches of all parties are drawn primarily from the *City of God* although the author also refers to seven other Augustinian works, to six other Christian writers from Tertullian to Quodvultdeus, to twenty-two pagan authors from Homer to Porphyry, and to the unclassifiable *Corpus iuris civilis*, Martianus Capella, and pseudo-Boethius. After Augustine, Apuleius, Cicero, Plotinus, Porphyry, Varro, and Vergil are used the most frequently.[128] The interlocutors, whether represented in this list or not, do not always mention their sources and do not always advocate the positions with which their names are historically associated. Two of them, Plato and Varro, serve more as doxographers than as proponents of their own philosophies. The debates in the first three books recapitulate the Varronian subdivision of pagan theologies into natural, civic, and mythological. The last two books focus on Neoplatonism, treated as a religion more than as a philosophy. The only two philosophical schools which the Anonymous presents as serious alternatives to Christianity, both in their con-

---

[127] Diethard Aschoff, in the intro. to his ed. of Anonymous, *Contra philosophos*, CC, 58A (Turnhout, 1975), pp. v–xli gives a thorough review of the previous literature on the text as well as his own detailed editorial description.

[128] See Aschoff's *index autorum*, pp. 361–71.

tent and in the fact that their spokesmen are the only pagans who attack
Augustinus as well as trying to repel his own onslaughts, are the Neoplatonists and the Stoics. The Neoplatonists enjoy much more recognition as a school than the Stoics. Neoplatonic interlocutors generally pro-
fess Neoplatonic doctrines, which are identified as such. On the other
hand, Stoicism, while it crops up repeatedly in the *Contra philosophos*, is
often put forth by speakers earmarked as representing other traditions
and is by no means exhausted by the interlocutor denominated as Stoic.
Moreover, Stoicism is sometimes criticized, sometimes accepted without
comment, and sometimes used as a weapon against other pagan positions.

The Anonymous dismisses civic religion on the grounds that the pagan gods, so given over to unedifying behavior themselves, could not in-
still true virtue in the Romans. Here Scipio and Cicero defend the traditional Roman values while Augustinus counters with the Augustinian
point that these virtues are intrinsically limited and that they were pow-
erless to save Rome from civil war and external conquest, a critique
drawing heavily on Cicero's own *De natura deorum* as it had been used by
the earlier apologists as well as by the *City of God*. The author invokes
the same Ciceronian arguments against the mythic theology, which he
castigates for its fictitiousness and for the vulgar superstition it promotes, while Varro makes the essentially Stoic case in favor of allego-
rizing the gods as forces of nature.[129] Although neither he nor Varro
mentions the Stoics expressly, Seneca too supports this position, citing
the arguments he had made in his *De superstitione*, now lost, for purifying
the myths of their anthropomorphisms and rendering popular religion
more intellectually respectable.[130] Augustinus' counterclaim stresses that
this strategy has exactly the reverse effect of the one intended, since the
rationalizing of myths makes it easier for people to believe them and
harder for them to recognize the lies which the veil of allegoresis seeks
to hide.[131]

A much more substantial consideration of Stoicism is found in the
section of the work devoted to natural theology. However, its thrust is
blunted by the fact that the author sometimes misrepresents the Stoic
position or turns the Stoics into critics of teachings which they actually
espoused. The central question at issue in this context is fatalism and
free will. Astral determinism is professed by the interlocutor named
Mathematicus, who cites Posidonius and the medical writers in support
of his case. Augustinus asserts that Mathematicus has misunderstood the

---

[129] *Contra phil.* 3.125.
[130] Ibid. 3.130–31.
[131] Ibid. 3.125, 3.131–32.

medical writers, who stressed factors such as diet and exercise rather than the influence of the stars on human events. As for Posidonius and the other true proponents of astral determinism, Augustinus repeats the argument of the *City of God*, noting that they can neither demonstrate their claims nor account for the differing fortunes of twins conceived under the same planets.[132] Mathematicus cannot refute this objection and retires from the field after repeating that Posidonius was a distinguished member of his school who defended astrology.[133] While the *Contra philosophos*, like the *City of God*, gives a correct report of Posidonius' views here, neither Mathematicus nor Augustinus recognizes that he was a Stoic and that his teaching on sidereal influences is a specific application of that school's general theory of causation which refers to the signs of causes, not to causation itself.

This blind spot is evident also in the speech of Stoicus, who next takes the floor as an opponent of astral determinism, which, he asserts, was rejected by his own school. The Stoics, he says, replaced it with a more rational and all-embracing conception of causation, that of universal fatalism: *Sed omnium conexionem seriemque causarum, quae fit omne quod fit, fati nomine appellamus* ("But we call fate the connection between all things by a series of causes, which effects everything that happens.")[134] When Augustinus replies that the supreme cause is the will of God, which transcends, directs, and is unbound by the nexus of natural causes, Stoicus counters with the idea that fate is actually the same thing as the supreme will of Augustinus' God, citing in support of that point Seneca, a famous member of his school. Augustinus resists this attempt to assimilate his own position to Stoic fatalism, arguing that, if there were only one cause of all things, God would be responsible for evil as well as good and creatures would be deprived of free will.[135] This objection inspires an attack, if not an entirely apposite one, on the Christian conception of God. As Stoicus notes, a God Who does not will the salvation of all men is a God who cannot will the good consistently. A deity with a defective will cannot be regarded as the supreme being. If this line of argument is not entirely responsive to the prior point made by Augustinus, neither is Augustinus' own effort to defend Augustine's doctrine of predestination, election, reprobation and the damnation of unbaptized infants, for which he falls back on a Scriptural defense that would in no way convince a pagan opponent.[136]

---

[132] Ibid. 2.81–82.
[133] Ibid. 2.85.
[134] Ibid. 2.88, CC, 58A, p. 100.
[135] Ibid. 2.89–90.
[136] Ibid. 2.90.

A way out of the logical and rhetorical impasse in which Stoicus and
Augustinus have trapped themselves is now offered by Cicero. It is Cicero who presents the most accurate version of the Stoic position on fate
and freedom in the *Contra philosophos*. But, far from attributing it expressly to the Stoics, as the historical Cicero and Augustine had done,
he states it as his own personal view and as a better way to refute the
claims of astral determinism than is the universal fatalism espoused by
Stoicus. The solution Cicero offers is the one from the *De fato*, the Chrysippean reconcilation of necessity and contingency, whereby beings must
act in accordance with the necessities of their own natures but whether
they act or are acted upon in those ways at particular times is a contingent matter. Having stated this case, Cicero indicates his own difficulties with the Augustinian doctrine of predestination. Since the Stoic deity is identified with the natural order and is hence not an atemporal
being, except in the sense that the cyclical order of the cosmos is itself
eternal, Cicero can see no reason to attribute foreknowledge to him or
to regard him as living in an eternal present. In any event, he points out,
since contingency is compatible with the causal order of nature, according to the Chrysippean explanation he has just given, we do not have to
worry about trying to save contingency by substituting divine foreknowledge for divine causation.[137] This is, indeed, a powerful argument
against the Augustinian reformulation of the question. But, Augustinus
is basically unwilling to address it. He wants to retain his hold on the
doctrine of foreknowledge whether he needs it or not for the present purposes, despite his namesake's approval of the position given by Cicero
in the *De fato*. Augustinus attempts to counter Cicero by criticizing him
as if he had been defending the fatalism of Stoicus rather than by coming to grips with the alternative argument that Cicero has in fact put
forth. At this decidedly low point in Augustinus' handling of the debate,
Cicero throws away his advantage by asserting that divine foreknowledge is equivalent to complete divine necessitarianism. Divine necessitarianism, in turn, would obviate all contingency and free will; and this,
he says, is the reason why he rejects the idea of God's foreknowledge.[138]
The Anonymous has shifted the grounds in this argument so as to enable Augustinus to retrieve his own position. Augustinus now recapitulates the reasons why foreknowledge and causation are not the same
thing and why foreknowledge does not impede free will and contingency, in terms familiar to readers of the *City of God* or, for that matter,
the *Consolation of Philosophy*. He even adds a new wrinkle to this conclu-

---

[137] Ibid. 2.94.
[138] Ibid. 2.95.

sion by referring to the experience of the divided self as an argument against divine necessitarianism. The impulses that drive men toward their fluctuating goals cannot be ascribed to an eternal universal cause.[139] While the divided self was certainly high on the list of psychological phenomena to which Augustine repeatedly adverted, he does not himself invoke it in this particular connection.

The overall treatment of the theme of fatalism and freedom in the *Contra philosophos* illustrates well the author's handling of Stoic physics. He is not always very clear about the teachings of the Stoics despite the accuracy of the accounts given by the sources he uses. He feels free to misconstrue or to manipulate the doctrine in question so as to lead to conclusions he prefers, however maladroit the logic or rhetoric in aid of his argument may be. He is less willing than Augustine himself to support the Chrysippean position on necessity and contingency expounded by Cicero in his *De fato* and is more insistent than Augustine on the need to convert causation into foreknowledge under all circumstances. The Anonymous is also quite free in his attribution of Stoic doctrine to his various pagan interlocutors in this part of the work. The fullest account is given by Cicero, not by Stoicus. The deterministic view which Stoicus shares with Mathematicus suggests both the Anonymous' tendency to conflate the Stoics on fate and free will with pagan natural theology as such and to regard it as less compatible with Christian theology than Augustine does.

In the section of the *Contra philosophos* devoted to Neoplatonism the Anonymous is at the same time closer to Augustine and farther away from him. It is true that the *City of God* notes the religious qualities of Neoplatonism as well as its metaphysics and anthropology. But the Anonymous places his primary emphasis on the Hermetic and esoteric side of late Neoplatonism, more of which was now in evidence than in Augustine's day, as its chief threat to Christianity. Theurgy, the transmigration of souls, the hierarchy of spiritual beings or *daimones* between God and the sublunary world—these are the main teachings he uses to typify the school. In the portion of the last two books where Stoicism comes into play, the Anonymous uses it to attack the Neoplatonic conception of the body as evil. His main weapon here is a modified acceptance of the Stoic theory of the passions. Enroute to that theme, however, he does make two dismissive references to Stoicism, one physical and the other ethical, which are presented in the speeches of Plato and Varro acting as doxographers. Plato alludes to an unnamed group of philosophers who taught that God and the human soul are corporeal, a view

---

[139] Ibid. 2.96–100.

that both he and Augustinus reject without ado and without connecting it very closely to the argument occupying them at that point.[140] Varro, recapitulating the section of the *City of God* where Augustine had cited him on the differing pagan definitions of the *summum bonum*, notes that the Epicureans located it in the body while the Stoics located it in the soul, adding that the Stoics would not regard physical torture as an evil, an idea that Augustinus derides on grounds of common sense.[141]

Augustinus does not regard the body as incidental, but, by the same token, he repudiates the Neoplatonic view of the body as the prison of the soul and as the source of all human miseries. It is in the context of objecting to Iamblichus' advocacy of this position that Augustinus states, citing the Stoics, Cicero, and Vergil as his authorities, that the passions, far from arising from the body, are mental in origin (*perturbationes in animo*). Here he follows his namesake, although Augustine himself shows greater discernment in using Vergil as a source for the Stoic theory of the passions. While Augustinus agrees that some passions promote vice, there are others, which the Stoics call *eupatheia* (*constantias*) which are reasonable and conducive to virtue. We may eupathetically rejoice in the good or experience sorrow for sin. The meritorious nature of these feelings, he adds, is supported by Holy Scripture.[142] Iamblichus charges Augustinus with misunderstanding the Stoics on this issue, and with considerable plausibility. It would be impossible, he notes, himself echoing the *City of God* here, for a Stoic sage to experience the eupathetic sorrow for sin mentioned by Augustinus since the sage, by definition, is incapable of sin. Augustinus concedes this point but maintains that the rest of the Stoic doctrine on the passions is correct and in accord with Christianity.[143] Iamblichus then raises a further objection, arguing that *apatheia* (*impassibilitas*), while it may be possible for the soul, is impossible for the body. Augustinus concedes this point as well, agreeing that *apatheia* cannot be attained fully in this life. But, the reason why it is not attainable is not, as Iamblichus thinks, because the soul is mired in a material body but because man is beset by the experience of the divided will. Once his internal struggles have been stilled in the next life, he may, if he is in the ranks of the blessed, enjoy the imperturbability of the Stoic sage.[144]

In this debate Iamblichus often represents the Augustinian position on the Stoic doctrine of the passions more accurately than Augustinus

---

[140] Ibid. 2.243–44.
[141] Ibid. 5.259, 5.261.
[142] Ibid. 2.283–85.
[143] Ibid. 2.285–86.
[144] Ibid. 5.287–88.

does. With the *City of God*, Iamblichus invokes the idea of *eupatheia* to undermine the idea of *apatheia* and to criticize the Stoic conception of the moral perfection of the sage. On the other hand, by transferring the problem of the passions from the body to the will, Augustinus can emerge with a conclusion that is both more Augustinian and more Stoic than Iamblichus' position. This exchange of views on the Stoic passions, side by side with the debates on fate and free will earlier in the *Contra philosophos*, reflect both the boundaries of the Anonymous' concern with Stoicism and the measure of his dependence on and independence from his Augustinian model. In both contexts the *City of God* provides a fuller and more accurate report of the Stoics' teachings than is given by any of the interlocutors in the *Contra philosophos*, whether they are supporting or attacking the Stoic view. Unlike Augustine, the Anonymous opposes all versions of Stoicism on fate and free will. When he misrepresents that position he leaves it to his pagan speakers to do so. He tries to reduce Stoicism to a rigid fatalism which he equates with pagan natural theology and which he finds useless in supporting the Christian doctrine of providence. However, when he turns to the Stoic theory of the passions, his Christian interlocutor shares the exposition of the doctrine with his pagan antagonist. Both the pagan and the Christian speakers are well versed both in the Stoic view and in Augustine's reasons for supporting most of it and modifying some of it. The Anonymous retains much of the Stoic teaching and assimilates it to Christian ethics, as a means of refuting the metaphysical dualism which he sees as the Neoplatonists' greatest philosophical challenge to Christianity. Conspicuous for its absence is the Manicheism against which Augustine had used the weapon of the Stoic theory of the passions himself. The differences in the ways that the Anonymous approaches the major Stoic themes that he addresses in the *Contra philosophos* and the flexibility with which he handles his sources for them suggest why this work merits attention, not only for its use and abuse of Augustine as a philosophical transmitter but also for its own individual contribution to the history of the Stoic tradition.

V. Martin of Braga

The belief that Stoic ethics provided the most solidly engineered bridge between the classical past and the Christian present was the central assurance animating Martin of Braga (510/20–579), with whom our story comes to a close. So fully convinced was Martin of the complete parity between Stoic and Christian ethics that he confidently produced a treatise on the cardinal virtues, the *Formula vitae honestae*, whose content he lifted bodily from Seneca, most probably from a lost Senecan *De officiis*.

Martin passed off this pseudo-Senecan larcency as his own work and dedicated it to Miro, king of the Suevians, who ruled his corner of north-western Spain. Martin went immediately to his classical source, making few if any detours through the thickets of apologetic or patristic inter-pretation. In so doing he displays a calm certitude in his ability to grasp Seneca by himself no less than an astute awareness that no one in his own milieu, least of all Miro, was likely to detect an act of intellectual homage so total and so unacknowledged that a less tolerant age would have called it a bare-faced plagiarism. Medieval men, however, did not hold Martin's kind of literary fidelity in such despite. The *Formula vitae honestae* is his most famous and influential work, reproduced, sometimes with other titles, and commented on repeatedly during the Middle Ages. It became one of the period's most popular means of access to Stoic eth-ics and to the member of the Roman Stoa who was to surface later as the widely recognized and warmly respected *Seneca morale.*[145] As the com-piler of the first pseudo-Senecan handbook of the Middle Ages, Martin created a new literary genre and a new method of philosophical trans-mission, through which Stoicism under Christian auspices could look ahead with optimism, despite the clouded prospect that lay between the sixth century and the Carolingian renaissance to come.

Martin was a native of the region of Tours who crossed the Pyrenees in ca. 550 with the goal of converting the Suevians from Arianism to the orthodox faith. This mission was a success. After founding a monastery at Dumium Martin became its abbot and then bishop of Dumium in 556, followed by his elevation to the archbishopric of Braga in or before 570. There are a few contemporary references to Martin's scholarship. Greg-ory of Tours describes him as the most learned man of his day and says that he acquired some of his education in the east.[146] Martin's philo-sophical knowledge is celebrated by Venantius Fortunatus (ca. 530–ca. 600), a bishop of Poitiers with whom Martin corresponded, although only Venantius' side of the exchange has survived. In a tone strongly remi-niscent of the decorative and complimentary attributions of Stoicism found in Sidonius Apollinaris, Venantius lists the Stoics, Chrysippus, and

---

[145] The best descriptions and assessments of this work are found in Claude W. Bar-low, intro. to his trans. of Martin of Braga, *Formula vitae honestae*, FC, 62 (Washington, 1969), pp. 3–13; Ernst Bickel, "Die Schrift des Martinus von Bracara formula vitae hon-estae," *Rheinisches Museum für Philologie*, n.F. 6 (1905), 505–51; A. Liefooghe, "Les idées morales de Saint Martin de Braga," *Mélanges de science religieuse*, 11 (1954), 113–46; G. M. Ross, "Seneca's Philosophical Influence," *Seneca*, ed. C. D. N. Costa (London, 1974), p. 130. For the later medieval influence of the *Formula* see Claude W. Barlow, intro. to his ed. of Martin of Braga, *Opera omnia*, Papers and Monographs of the American Acad-emy in Rome, 12 (New Haven, 1950), pp. 7, 204–05, 208–33; Ross, "Seneca's Philo-sophical Influence," pp. 130–31.

[146] Gregory of Tours, *Hist. franc.* 5.37.

Cleanthes along with Plato, Aristotle, the Peripatetics, Hilary, Gregory, Ambrose, and Augustine as authors at whose wells Martin has drunk deeply, in contrast to his own superficial learning.[147] This letter serves as a surer guide to Venantius' rhetoric than to Martin's reading. His own works reflect a Greco-Latin culture that, while narrow, was both thorough and appositely applied to Martin's tasks as an abbot and bishop. Martin's translation of the Greek *Apophthegmata patrum* and his treatises on humility, pride, and vanity are closely dependent on John Cassian and were probably written for his monks. His catechetical guide *De correctione rusticorum*, his works on the baptismal rite and the dating of Easter, and his compilation of the canons of the councils of Braga document Martin's activities as a prelate. Outside of the *Formula* he produced one other pseudo-Senecan pastiche as an essay in individual pastoral counsel, the *De ira* dedicated to Vitimer, bishop of Auria. Martin's *De ira* is an epitome of the Senecan treatise with the same title.[148] Only the opening and closing lines are Martin's own. The rest is nearly identical with Seneca's text, given some changes in phraseology, word order, and the location of passages. Martin's technique of composition in the *De ira* shows his familiarity with Seneca's work and his ability to make a clear and readable abridgement of it. Although it is Senecan, however, Martin's *De ira* cannot be called Stoic. The most he says about the origins of the vice of anger and the way to allay it is to make the commonplace and commonsensical observation that anger is opposed to reason and that the way to avoid it is to think before you act.[149] Martin's *Formula* reveals a similar method in his approach to his Senecan source but, in contrast to the *De ira*, it breathes the authentic air of Roman Stoic ethics.

The *Formula* is little more than a definition and a brief description of the cardinal virtues, which Martin names as *prudentia, magnanimitas, continentia*, and *justitia* and which he discusses in that order. Both his placement of wisdom at the head of the list, his treatment of it as practical wisdom, and his appeal to nature as its criterion are completely Stoic. The essence of prudence, he says, lies in its judgment of things according to reason and nature:

> Quisquis ergo prudentiam sequi desideras, tunc per rationem recte vives, si omni prius aestimes et perpenses et dignitatem rebus non ex opinione multorum sed earum natura constituas.[150]

---

[147] Venantius Fortunatus, *Carminum libri* 5.1, in Martin's *Opera omnia*, ed. Barlow, pp. 294–96.

[148] The best discussion of the *De ira* is by Claude W. Barlow, "A Sixth-Century Epitome of Seneca, *De ira*," *TAPA*, 68 (1937), 26–42 and the intro. to his ed. in *Opera omnia*, pp. 145–48.

[149] Martin of Braga, *De ira*, 3.26, 6.9–14, ed. Barlow.

[150] *Formula* 2, ed. Barlow, trans. Barlow, FC, 62, p. 88.

> You will live rightly and with reason if you first judge and weigh every-
> thing in advance and place a value upon things from their own natural
> worth rather than from what most people think of them.

Prudence being practical, it involves not only a judgment based on truth
but one that considers the likely consequences of various courses of action and the differing circumstances conditioning the application of ethical principles to cases. Martin's accent is squarely on goals that are attainable: *Id quaere quod potest inveniri, id disce quod potest sciri, id opta quod
optari coram omnibus potest* ("Look for something that can be found, learn
something that can be known, hope for something that can be hoped for
in public.")[151]

In describing fortitude as magnanimity Martin preserves the Stoic
tendency to internalize this virtue, which he sees as applying not so much
to physical courage and endurance as to inner confidence and freedom
from fear, inner joy and openness.[152] His denomination of temperance
as *continentia* reflects no wish on his part to redefine this virtue in terms
of Christian sexual asceticism. Martin's approach to temperance remains entirely Stoic. *Naturam sequere* is the norm of temperance, which
demands what nature requires, not what one's desire seeks. Further, this
virtue reflects the sage's state of inner security:

> Si continens fueris, usque eo pervenies ut te ipso contentus sis. Nam qui
> sibi ipse satis est cum divitiis natus est.[153]

> If you would be continent, you must reach the point of being satisfied with
> yourself, for he who is sufficient to himself was born with riches.

Precisely the same condition attaches to intellectual pleasures, to food,
possessions, demeanor, speech, leisure, and work. The guardian of temperance, for Martin as for the Roman Stoics, is decorum, which shows
the wise man how to be courteous without sycophancy, vanity, or inconstancy and which guides him in balancing mercy and generosity with
severity.

Justice is the one virtue of the four which reveals signs of rethinking
on Martin's part. He receives some assistance here from Aristotle, Cicero, and Ambrose as well as from Seneca. Martin roots justice firmly in
the Stoic foundation of natural law:

---

[151] Ibid., trans. Barlow, p. 90.
[152] Ibid. 3.
[153] Ibid. 4, trans. Barlow, p. 91.

Quid est autem justitia nisi naturae tacita conventio in adiutorium mul-
torum inventa? Et quid est justitia nisi nostra constitutio, sed divina lex, et
vinculum societas humanae?[154]

What is justice but a silent agreement of nature invented for the aid of many?
And what is justice but our own constitution, a divine law and the bond of
human society?

In describing the nature of this law and bond Martin follows Ambrose
in viewing it as the love and fear of God and the imitation of Him as the
model of universal benevolence. And, in raising with Cicero and Ambrose the question of the relations between justice and expediency, he
answers, with Ambrose, that there is nothing useful except what justice
commands.[155] This point strikes the only specifically Christian note in
the *Formula*, and it is associated with the Aristotelian norm of the golden
mean in putting the principles of justice into practice. More strictly Ciceronian is the attention Martin devotes to the leader who bears broad
social responsibilities. All men should seek justice, but the ruler must
also prevent and punish crime and rectify the injustices of others. The
examples given by Martin stress the comportment of the head of state
who is especially obliged to be a paragon of justice because of the influence he has over his people,[156] an emphasis reminding the reader that
the *Formula*, like some of Seneca's moral essays, was also written as a
mirror of princes.

Whether Martin was any more successful in ministering to Miro than
Seneca was in turning Nero into a philosopher king, his *Formula* is an
eloquent witness to the multiplicity of the paths by which the Stoic tradition made its way from antiquity into the Latin west up to the end of
the sixth century. Martin's *Formula* was one of many possible itineraries
offering diverse routes to similar goals, whose travellers sometimes shared
their provisions on the journey and sometimes followed idiosyncratic
tracks or took side trips of their own. The historian can observe the range
of these alternatives not only in the flood tide of the apologetic and patristic age but also within the more restricted compass of the sixth century, despite the hardships under which Martin and his contemporaries
labored. Martin himself strikes off in a decidedly new direction as the
initiator of a burgeoning tradition of pseudonymous Stoic literature in
the Middle Ages. Although his approach is his own, he reflects as thoroughly as do many of the other Latin Christian writers of his century

---

[154] Ibid. 5, trans. Barlow, p. 94. I have altered the translation slightly.
[155] Ibid.
[156] Ibid. 5, 10.

how the experience of limitations could fuel a commitment to an enterprise of culture in which the Stoic inheritance could continue to stimulate, to inform, and to enrich the thought of Christian intellectuals in their own efforts to forge a meaningful connection between their past, their present, and their future.

BIBLIOGRAPHY

Primary Sources

Ambrose. *Opera*. Ed. Carolus Schenkl, M. Petschenig, and Otto Faller. 7 vols. in 9. Corpus scriptorum ecclesiasticorum latinorum, 32:1–2, 73. Vienna, Hoelder-Pichler-Tempsky, 1897–1968.

—. *Epistolae. Patrologia latina cursus completus*, 16. Ed. J. P. Migne. Paris, 1880.

—. *De officiis ministrorum*. Trans. H. de Romestin. *A Select Library of the Nicene and Post-Nicene Fathers of the Christian Church*. Ser. 2:10. Ed. Philip Schaff and Henry Wace. New York, The Christian Literature Company, 1896.

—. *De officiis ministrorum libri tres. Patrologia latina cursus completus*, 16. Ed. J. P. Migne. Paris, 1880.

—. *La pénitence*. Trans. Roger Gryson. Sources chrétiennes, 179. Paris, Éditions du Cerf, 1971.

Anonymous. *Contra philosophos*. Ed. Diethard Aschoff. Corpus christianorum, series latina, 58A. Turnhout, Brepols, 1975.

Arator. *De actibus apostolorum*. Ed. Arthur Patch McKinlay. Corpus scriptorum ecclesiasticorum latinorum, 72. Vienna, Hoelder-Pichler-Tempsky, 1951.

Aristotle. *Categories and De interpretatione*. Transl. J. L. Ackrill. Oxford, Clarendon Press, 1963.

Arnobius Afer. *Adversus nationes libri VII*. 2ª ed. Ed. C. Marchesi. Torino, I. B. Paraviae, 1953.

—. *The Case against the Pagans*. Trans. George E. McCracken. Ancient Christian Writers, 7–8. Westminister, Md., Newman Press, 1949.

Augustine. *The Advantage of Believing*. Trans. Luanne Meagher. Fathers of the Church, 4. New York, Cima Publishing Co., Inc., 1947.

—. *Answer to Skeptics*. Trans. Denis J. Kavanagh. Fathers of the Church, 5. New York, Cima Publishing Co., Inc., 1948.

—. *The Catholic and Manichean Ways of Life*. Trans. Donald A. Gallagher and Idella J. Gallagher. Fathers of the Church, 56. Washington, Catholic University of America Press, 1966.

—. *On Christian Doctrine*. Trans. D. W. Robertson. Library of Liberal Arts. Indianapolis, Bobbs-Merrill Company, Inc., 1958.

—. *The City of God*. Trans. Marcus Dods. New York, Random House, 1950.

—. *De civitate dei*. Ed. Bernardus Dombart and Alphonsus Kalb. Corpus christianorum, series latina, 47–48. Turnhout, Brepols, 1965.

—. *Commentaire de la première épître de S. Jean*. Ed. and trans. Paul Agaësse. Sources chrétiennes, 75. Paris, Éditions du Cerf, 1961.

—. *Confessions*. Trans. Albert C. Outler. Library of Christian Classics, 7. Philadelphia, Westminster Press, 1955.

—. *Confessionum*. Ed. Lucas Verheijen. Corpus christianorum, series latina, 27. Turnhout, Brepols, 1981.

—. *De consensu evangelistarum*. Ed. Franciscus Weihrich. Corpus scriptorum ecclesiasticorum latinorum, 43. Vienna, F. Tempsky, 1904.

—. *Contra academicos. De beata vita. De ordine. De magistro. De libero arbitrio*. Ed. W. M. Green and K.–D. Daur. Corpus christianorum, series latina, 29. Turnhout, Brepols, 1970.

—. *Contra Cresconium*. Ed. M. Petschenig. Corpus scriptorum ecclesiasticorum latinorum, 52. Vienna, F. Tempsky, 1909.

—. *Contra Faustum*. Ed. Iosephus Zycha. Corpus scriptorum ecclesiasticorum latinorum, 25. Vienna, F. Tempsky, 1891.

—. *Contra Faustum*. Trans. Richard Stothert. *A Select Library of the Nicene and Post-Nicene*

Fathers of the Christian Church. Ser. 1:4. Ed. Philip Schaff. Buffalo, The Christian Literature Company, 1887.

—. *Contra Fortunatum.* Ed. and trans. Régis Jolivet. Œuvres de Saint Augustin. Sér. 2:17. Paris, Desclée de Brouwer, 1961.

—. *Contra Julianum. Patrologia latina cursus completus,* 44. Ed. J. P. Migne. Paris, 1865.

—. *Contra secundam Juliani Responsionum imperfectum opus. Patrologia latina cursus completus,* 45. Ed. J. P. Migne. Paris, 1865.

—. *De diversis quaestionibus octoginta tribus.* Ed. Almut Mutzenbecher. Corpus christianorum, series latina, 44A. Turnhout, Brepols, 1975.

—. *De diversis quaestionibus 83.* Ed. and trans. P. Beckaert. Œuvres de Saint Augustin. Sér. 1:10. Paris, Desclée de Brouwer, 1952.

—. *De doctrina christiana.* Ed. Iosephus Martin and K.–D. Daur. Corpus christianorum, series latina, 32. Turnhout, Brepols, 1962.

—. *De duabus animabus.* Ed. and trans. Régis Jolivet. Œuvres de Saint Augustin. Sér. 2:17. Paris, Desclée de Brouwer, 1961.

—. *Eighty-three Different Questions.* Trans. David L. Mosher. Fathers of the Church, 70. Washington, Catholic University of America Press, 1982.

—. *Enarrationes in Psalmos.* Ed. D. Eligius Dekkers and Ioannes Fraipont. Corpus christianorum, series latina, 38–40. Turnhout, Brepols, 1956.

—. *Enchiridion ad Laurentium.* Ed. E. Evans. *De haerisibus.* Ed. R. Vander Plaetse and C. Beukers. Corpus christianorum, series latina, 46. Turnhout, Brepols, 1969.

—. *Epistulae.* Ed. Al. Goldbacher. Corpus scriptorum ecclesiasticorum latinorum, 24, 44, 57, 58. Vienna, Hölder-Pichler-Tempsky, 1895–1923.

—. *Expositio Epistolae ad Galatas. Patrologia latina cursus completus,* 35. Ed. J. P. Migne. Paris, 1902.

—. *Expositio quarundum propositionum ex Epistola ad Romanos. Patrologia latina cursus completus,* 35. Ed. J. P. Migne. Paris, 1902.

—. *The Free Choice of the Will.* Trans. Robert P. Russell. Fathers of the Church, 59. Washington, Catholic University of America Press, 1968.

—. *De genesi ad litteram.* Ed. and trans. P. Agaësse and A. Solignac. Œuvres de Saint Augustin. Sér. 7:48–49. Paris, Desclée de Brouwer, 1972.

—. *De genesi ad litteram imperfectus liber. Patrologia latina cursus completus,* 34. Ed. J. P. Migne. Paris, 1887.

—. *De genesi contra Manichaeos. Patrologia latina cursus completus,* 34. Ed. J. P. Migne. Paris, 1887.

—. *The Happy Life.* Trans. Ludwig Schopp. Fathers of the Church, 5. New York, Cima Publishing Co., Inc., 1948.

—. *Homilies on the Gospel of John.* Trans. John Gibb and James Innes. *A Select Library of the Nicene and Post-Nicene Fathers of the Christian Church.* Ser. 1:7. Ed. Philip Schaff. New York, The Christian Literature Company, 1888.

—. *De immortalitate animae.* Ed. and trans. Pierre de Labriolle. Œuvres de Saint Augustin. Sér. 1:5. Paris, Desclée de Brouwer, 1948.

—. *In Ioannis Evangelium Tractatus CXXIV.* Ed. D. Radbodus Willems. Corpus christianorum, series latina, 36. Turnhout, Brepols, 1954.

—. *On Lying.* Trans. Mary Sarah Muldowney. Fathers of the Church, 16. New York, Fathers of the Church, Inc., 1952.

—. *De magistro.* 2nd ed. Ed. and trans. F.–J. Thonnard. Notes by G. Bardy. Œuvres de Saint Augustin. Sér. 1:6. Paris, Desclée de Brouwer, 1952.

—. *De mendacio. Contra mendacium. De opere monachorum. De fide et symbolo.* Ed. Iosephus Zycha. Corpus scriptorum ecclesiasticorum latinorum, 41. Vienna, F. Tempsky, 1900.

—. *De moribus ecclesiae catholicae et de moribus manichaeorum.* 2nd ed. Ed. and trans. B. Roland-Gosselin. Œuvres de Saint Augustin. Sér. 1:1. Paris, Desclée de Brouwer, 1949.

—. *On Music.* Trans. Robert Catesby Taliaferro. Fathers of the Church, 4. New York, Cima Publishing Co., Inc., 1947.

—. *De musica.* Ed. Giovanni Marzi. Collana di classici della filosofia cristiana, 1. Firenze, Sansoni, 1969.

—. *De natura boni.* 2nd ed. Ed. and trans. B. Roland-Gosselin. Œuvres de Saint Augustin. Sér. 1:1. Paris, Desclée de Brouwer, 1949.

—. *De natura et origine animae.* Ed. and trans. F.-J. Thonnard. Œuvres de Saint Augustin. Sér. 3:22. Paris, Desclée de Brouwer, 1975.

—. *Quaestiones in Heptateuchum.* Ed. I. Fraipont. Corpus christianorum, series latina, 33. Turnhout, Brepols, 1968.

—. *De quantitate animae.* Ed. and trans. Pierre de Labriolle. Œuvres de Saint Augustin. Sér. 1:5. Paris, Desclée de Brouwer, 1948.

—. *De sermone Domine in monte.* Ed. Almut Mutzenbecher. Corpus christianorum, series latina, 35. Turnhout, Brepols, 1967.

—. *Sermones. Patrologia latina cursus completus,* 38–39. Ed. J. P. Migne. Paris, 1865.

—. *Soliloquiorum. Patrologia latina cursus completus,* 32. Ed. J. P. Migne. Paris, 1877.

—. *De trinitate.* Ed. W. J. Mountain and Fr. Glorie. Corpus christianorum, series latina, 50:1–2. Turnhout, Brepols, 1968.

—. *The Trinity.* Trans. Stephen McKenna. Fathers of the Church, 45. Washington, Catholic University of America Press, 1963.

—. *De utilitate credendi.* Ed. and trans. J. Pegon. Œuvres de Saint Augustin. Sér. 1:8. Paris, Desclée de Brouwer, 1951.

Ausonius. *Opuscula.* Ed. Sextus Prete. Leipzig, B. G. Teubner, 1978.

—. *Works.* 2 vols. Trans. Hugh G. Evelyn White. Loeb Classical Library. London, William Heinemann, 1919–21.

Benedict of Nursia. *Regula.* Ed. Jean Neufville. Trans. Adalbert de Vogüé. Sources chrétiennes, 181–182. Paris, Éditions du Cerf, 1972.

Boethius, Anicius Manlius Severinus. *In Categorias Aristotelis. Patrologia latina cursus completus,* 64. Ed. J. P. Migne. Paris, 1891.

—. *Commentarii in librum Aristoteles Perihermenias.* 2 vols. Ed. Carolus Meiser. Leipzig, B. G. Teubner, 1876–80.

—. *The Consolation of Philosophy.* Trans. Richard Green. Library of Liberal Arts. Indianapolis, Bobbs-Merrill Company, Inc., 1962.

—. *De differentiis topicis. Patrologia latina cursus completus,* 64. Ed. J. P. Migne. Paris, 1891.

—. *De hypotheticis syllogismis.* Ed. and trans. Luca Obertello. Brescia, Paideia Editrice, 1969.

—. *In Isagogen Porphyrii commenta.* Ed. Samuel Brandt. Corpus scriptorum ecclesiasticorum latinorum, 48. Vienna, F. Tempsky, 1906.

—. *Philosophiae consolatio.* Ed. Ludovicus Bieler. Corpus christianorum, series latina, 94. Turnhout, Brepols, 1957.

—. *Philosophiae consolatio.* Ed. and trans. Raffaello Del Re. Roma, Edizioni dell'Ateneo, 1968.

—. *In Topica Ciceronis commentaria. Patrologia latina cursus completus,* 64. Ed. J. P. Migne. Paris, 1891.

—. *De topicis differentiis.* Trans. and comm. Eleonore Stump. Ithaca, Cornell University Press, 1978.

—, trans. *De interpretatione vel Periermenias.* Ed. Laurentius Minio-Paluello. *Aristoteles latinus,* 2:1–2. Bruges-Paris, Desclée de Brouwer, 1965.

—, trans. *Porphyrii Isagoge.* Ed. Laurentius Minio-Paluello. *Aristoteles latinus,* 1:6–7. Bruges-Paris, Desclée de Brouwer, 1966.

Caesarius of Arles. *Sermones.* Ed. D. Germani Morin. Corpus christianorum, series latina, 103–104. Turnhout, Brepols, 1953.

—. *Sermons.* Vol. 2. Trans. Mary Magdeleine Mueller. Fathers of the Church, 47. Washington, Catholic University of America Press, 1964.

Cassian, John. *Conférences.* Ed. and trans. E. Pichery. Sources chrétiennes, 42, 54, 64. Paris, Éditions du Cerf, 1955–59.

—. *Institutions cénobitiques.* Ed. and trans. Jean-Claude Guy. Sources chrétiennes, 109. Paris, Éditions du Cerf, 1965.

—. *The Works of John Cassian.* Trans. Edgar C. S. Gibson. *A Select Library of the Nicene and Post-Nicene Fathers of the Christian Church.* Ser. 2:11. Ed. Philip Schaff and Henry Wace. Grand Rapids, Wm. B. Eerdmans Publishing Company, 1955.

Cassiodorus Senator. *De anima*. Ed. J. W. Halporn. Corpus christianorum, series latina, 96. Turnhout, Brepols, 1973.

Claudianus Mamertus. *Opera*. Ed. Augustus Engelbrecht. Corpus scriptorum ecclesiasticorum latinorum, 11. Vienna, C. Geroldi Filium, 1885.

Commodianus. *Instructiones*. Libro secondo. Ed. Antonio Salvatore. Collana di studi latini, 17. Napoli, Libreria Scientifica Editrice, 1968.

—. *Instructionum*. Ed. Joseph Martin. Corpus christianorum, series latina, 128. Turnhout, Brepols, 1960.

Cyprian. *Correspondance*. 2 vols. 2nd ed. Ed. Le Chanoine L. Bayard. Collection des Universités de France, publiée sous le patronage de l'Association Guillaume Budé. Paris, Les Belles Lettres, 1945–61.

—. *Letters*. Trans. Rose Bernard Donna. Fathers of the Church, 51. Washington, Catholic University of America Press, 1964.

—. *Opera*. Ed. R. Weber, M. Bévenot, M. Simonetti, and C. Moreschini. Corpus christianorum, series latina, 3–3A. Turnhout, Brepols, 1972–76.

—. *Opera omnia*. 3 vols. in 1. Ed. G. Hartel. Corpus scriptorum ecclesiasticorum latinorum, 3:1–3. Vienna, C. Geroldi, 1868–71.

—. *Treatises*. Trans. Roy J. Deferrari et al. Fathers of the Church, 36. New York, Fathers of the Church, Inc., 1958.

Dracontius. *De laudibus dei*. Liber I. Ed. and trans. James F. Irwin. Philadelphia, University of Pennsylvania Press, 1942.

Faustus of Riez. *Opera*. Ed. Augustus Engelbrecht. Corpus scriptorum ecclesiasticorum latinorum, 21. Vienna, F. Tempsky, 1891.

Filastrius of Brescia. *Diversarum hereseon liber*. Ed. F. Heylen. Corpus christianorum, series latina, 9. Turnhout, Brepols, 1957.

Firmicus Maternus, Julius. *The Error of the Pagan Religions*. Trans. Clarence A. Forbes. Ancient Christian Writers, 37. New York, Newman Press, 1970.

—. *De erroris profanarum religionum*. 2nd ed. Ed. Agostino Pastorino. Firenze, La Nuova Italia, 1969.

Fulgentius of Ruspe. *Opera*. Ed. J. Fraipont. Corpus christianorum, series latina, 91–91A. Turnhout, Brepols, 1968.

Gaudentius of Brescia. *Tractatus*. Ed. Ambrosius Glueck. Corpus scriptorum ecclesiasticorum latinorum, 68. Vienna, Hoelder-Pichler-Tempsky, 1936.

Gregory the Great. *In expositionem Beati Job Moralia*. Patrologia latina cursus completus, 75–76. Ed. J. P. Migne. Paris, 1849.

—. *Homeliae in Hiezechihelem prophetam*. Ed. Marcus Andriaen. Corpus christianorum, series latina, 142. Turnhout, Brepols, 1971.

—. *In librum I Regum*. Ed. Patricius Verbraken. Corpus christianorum, series latina, 144. Turnhout, Brepols, 1973.

—. *Moralia in Job*. Books I and II. 2nd ed. Ed. Robert Gillet. Trans. André de Gaudemaris. Sources chrétiennes, 32 bis. Paris, Éditions du Cerf, 1975.

—. *Moralia in Job*. Books XI–XVI. Ed. and trans. Aristide Bocognano. Sources chrétiennes, 212, 221. Paris, Éditions du Cerf, 1974–75.

—. *Morals on the Book of Job*. 4 vols. Trans. J. Bliss. Library of the Fathers. Oxford, John Henry Parker, 1844–50.

—. *Pastoral Care*. Trans. Henry Davis. Ancient Christian Writers, 11. Westminster, Md., Newman Press, 1950.

—. *Regulae pastoralis*. Patrologia latina cursus completus, 77. Ed. J. P. Migne. Paris, 1849.

—. *Registrum epistolarum*. 2 vols. Ed. Paulus Ewald and Ludovicus M. Hartman. Monumenta germaniae historica, Epistolarum, 1–2. Berlin, Weidmann, 1891–99.

Gregory of Tours. *De cursu stellarum ratio*. Ed. Br. Krusch. Monumenta germaniae historica, Scriptores rerum Merovingicarum, 1. Hannover, Hahn, 1885.

—. *Historia francorum*. Ed. Wilhelmus Arndt. Monumenta germaniae historica, Scriptores rerum Merovingicarum, 1. Hannover, Hahn, 1885.

—. *The History of the Franks*. Trans. Lewis Thorpe. Harmondsworth, Penguin Books, 1974.

Hilary of Poitiers, *In Matthaeum*. Ed. and trans. Jean Doignon. Sources chrétiennes, 254, 258. Paris, Éditions du Cerf, 1978–79.

—. *Tractatus super Psalmos*. Ed. Antonius Zingerle. Corpus scriptorum ecclesiasticorum latinorum, 22, Vienna, F. Tempsky, 1891.

Jerome. *Commentaire sur Saint Matthieu*. Vol. I. Trans. Émile Bonnard. Sources chrétiennes, 242. Paris, Édition du Cerf, 1977.

—. *Commentarii in prophetas minores*. Ed. M. Andriaen. Corpus christianorum, series latina, 76. Turnhout, Brepols, 1969.

—. *Commentariorum in Danielem libri III (IV)*. Ed. Franciscus Glorie. Corpus christianorum, series latina, 75A. Turnhout, Brepols, 1964.

—. *Commentariorum in Esaiam*. Ed. Marc Andriaen, Corpus christianorum, series latina, 73–73A. Turnhout, Brepols, 1963.

—. *Commentariorum in Mattheum*. Ed. D. Hurst and M. Andriaen. Corpus christianorum, series latina, 77. Turnhout, Brepols, 1959.

—. *Epistulae*. 3 vols. Ed. Isidorus Hilberg. Corpus scriptorum ecclesiasticorum latinorum, 54–56. Vienna, F. Tempsky, 1910–18.

—. *Hebraice quaestiones in libro Geneseos. Liber interpretationis Hebraicorum nominum. Commentarioli in Psalmos. Commentarius in Ecclesiasticen*. Ed. Paul de Lagarde, Germanus Morin, and Marc Andriaen. Corpus christianorum, series latina, 72. Turnhout, Brepols, 1959.

—. *In Hieremiam libri VI*. Ed. Siegfried Reiter. Corpus christianorum, series latina, 74. Turnhout, Brepols, 1960.

—. *The Letters*. Vol. I. Trans. Charles Christopher Mierow. Ancient Christian Writers, 33. Westminister, Md., Newman Press, 1963.

—. *Letters and Select Works*. Trans. W. H. Freemantle. *A Select Library of the Nicene and Post-Nicene Fathers of the Christian Church*. Ser. 2:6. Ed. Philip Schaff and Henry Wace. New York, The Christian Literature Company, 1893.

—. *Lettres*, 8 vols. Ed. and trans. Jérôme Labourt. Collection des Universités de France, publiée sous le patronage de l'Association Guillaume Budé. Paris, Les Belles Lettres, 1949–63.

—. *Lives of Famous Men*. Trans. Ernest Cushing Richardson. *A Select Library of the Nicene and Post-Nicene Fathers of the Christian Church*. Ser. 2:3. Ed. Henry Wace and Philip Shaff. New York, The Christian Literature Company, 1906.

—. *Opera omnia. Patrologia latina cursus completus*, 23, 26. Ed. J. P. Migne. Paris, 1883, 1884.

—. *Tractatus sive homeliae in Psalmos, in Marci evangelium aliaque varia argumenta*. New ed. Ed. Germanus Morin. Corpus christianorum, series latina, 78. Turnhout, Brepols, 1958.

—. *De viris inlustribus*. Ed. Carl Albrecht Bernoulli. Sammlung ausgewählter kirchen- und dogmengeschichtlicher Quellenschriften, 11. Freiburg i. B., J. C. B. Mohr, 1895 [repr. Frankfurt, Minerva G.M.B.H., 1968].

Julianus Pomerius. *The Contemplative Life*. Trans. Mary Josephine Suelzer. Ancient Christian Writers, 4. Westminster. Md., Newman Bookshop, 1947.

—. *De vita contemplativa. Patrologia latina cursus completus*, 59. Ed. J. P. Migne. Paris, 1847.

Lactantius, Lucius Caecilius Firmianus. *The Divine Institutes*. Trans. Mary Francis McDonald. Fathers of the Church, 49. Washington, Catholic University of America Press, 1964.

—. *The Minor Works*. Trans. Mary Francis McDonald. Fathers of the Church, 54. Washington, Catholic University of America Press, 1965.

—. *Opera omnia*. Ed. Samuel Brandt and George Laubmann. Corpus scriptorum ecclesiasticorum latinorum, 19, 27. Vienna, F. Tempsky, 1890–97.

Leander of Seville, *De institutione virginum et de contemptu mundi*. Trans. Claude W. Barlow. Fathers of the Church, 62. Washington, Catholic University of America Press, 1969.

—. *Regula, sive liber de institutione virginum et contemptu mundi, ad Florentinam sororem. Patrologia latina cursus completus*, 72. Ed. J. P. Migne. Paris, 1849.

Licinianus of Cartagena. *Epistulae*. Ed. P. A. C. Vega. Scriptores ecclesiastici hispano-latini veteris et medii aevi, 3. Escorial, Typis Augustinianis Monasterii, 1935.

Martin of Braga. *Formula vitae honestae*. Trans. Claude W. Barlow. Fathers of the Church, 62. Washington, Catholic University of America Press, 1969.

—. *Opera omnia*. Ed. Claude W. Barlow, Papers and Monographs of the American Academy in Rome, 12. New Haven, Yale University Press, 1950.

Minucius Felix, Marcus. *Octavius*. Trans. Rudolph Arbesmann. Fathers of the Church, 10. New York, Fathers of the Church, Inc., 1950.

—. *Octavius*. Ed. and trans. Jean Beaujeu. Collection des Universités de France, publiée sous le patronage de l'Association Guillaume Budé. Paris, Les Belles Lettres, 1964.

—. *The Octavius*. Trans. G. W. Clarke. Ancient Christian Writers, 39. New York, Newman Press, 1974.

Novatian. *Opera*. Ed. G. F. Diercks. Corpus christianorum, series latina, 4. Turnhout, Brepols, 1972.

—. *The Trinity. The Spectacles. Jewish Foods. In Praise of Purity. Letters*. Trans. Russell J. DeSimone. Fathers of the Church, 67. Washington, Catholic University of America Press, 1972.

Palermo, Giovanni, trans. "Cassiodoro, l'Anima," *Orpheus*, 23 (1976), 41–143.

Paulinus of Nola. *Carmina*. Ed. Guilelmus de Hartel. Corpus scriptorum ecclesiasticorum latinorum, 30. Vienna, F. Tempsky, 1894.

—. *Epistulae*. Ed. Guilelmus de Hartel. Corpus scriptorum ecclesiasticorum latinorum, 29. Vienna, F. Tempsky, 1894.

—. *The Poems*. Trans. P. G. Walshe. Ancient Christian Writers, 40. New York, Newman Press, 1975.

Prudentius. *Carmina*. Ed. Mauricii P. Cunningham. Corpus christianorum, series latina, 126. Turnhout, Brepols, 1966.

—. *The Poems*. Vol. 2. Trans. M. Clement Eagan. Fathers of the Church, 52. Washington, Catholic University of America Press, 1965.

Querolus. Trans. G. E. Duckworth. *The Complete Roman Drama*. Vol. 2. Ed. George E. Duckworth. New York, Random House, 1942.

Querolus sive Aulularia. Ed. Gunnar Randstrand. Göteborgs Högskolas Årsskrift, 57:1. Göteborg, Wettergren & Förlag, 1951.

Regula magistri. Ed. and trans. Adalbert de Vogüé. Sources chrétiennes, 105. Paris, Éditions du Cerf, 1964.

Salvian. *Œuvres*. Vol. 2. Ed. and trans. Georges Lagarrigue. Sources chrétiennes, 220. Paris, Éditions du Cerf, 1975.

—. *On the Governance of God*. Trans. Eva M. Sanford. Records of Civilization. New York, Columbia University Press, 1930.

—. *Opera omnia*. Ed. Franciscus Pauly. Corpus scriptorum ecclesiasticorum latinorum, 8. Vienna, C. Geroldi, 1883.

—. *The Writings of Salvian the Presbyter*. Trans. Jeremiah O'Sullivan. Fathers of the Church, 3. New York, Cima Publishing Co., Inc., 1947.

Sidonius Apollinaris. *Poems and Letters*. 2 vols. Ed. and trans. W. B. Anderson. Loeb Classical Library. Cambridge, Mass., Harvard University Press, 1936–65.

Tertullian, Quintus Septimus Florens. *Adversus Marcionem*. 2 vols. Ed. and trans. Ernest Evans. Oxford, Clarendon Press, 1972.

—. *Adversus Praxean liber*. Ed. and trans. Ernest Evans. London, SPCK, 1948.

—. *De anima*. Ed. J. H. Waszink. Amsterdam, J. M. Meulenhoff, 1947.

—. *Apologetical Works*. Trans. Rudolph Arbesmann, Emily Joseph Daly, and Edwin A. Quain. Fathers of the Church, 10. New York, Fathers of the Church, Inc., 1950.

—. *De carne Christi*. Ed. and trans. Ernest Evans. London, SPCK, 1956.

—. *Le chair de Christ*. Ed. and trans. Jean-Pierre Mahé. Sources chrétiennes, 216. Paris, Éditions du Cerf, 1975.

—. *Disciplinary, Moral and Ascetical Works*. Trans. Rudolph Arbesmann, Emily Joseph Daly, and Edwin A. Quain. Fathers of the Church, 40. New York, Fathers of the Church, Inc., 1959.

—. *Opera*. Ed. E. Dekkers et al. Corpus christianorum, series latina, 1–2. Turnhout, Brepols, 1954.

—. *De pallio*. Ed. S. Costanza. Collana di studi classici, 3. Napoli, Libreria Scientifica Editrice, 1968.

—. *The Treatise against Hermogenes*. Trans. J. H. Waszink. Ancient Christian Writers, 24. Westminster, Md., Newman Press, 1956.

—. *Treatises on Marriage and Remarriage*. Trans. William P. Le Saint. Ancient Christian Writers, 13. Westminster, Md., Newman Press, 1951.

—. *Treatises on Penance*. Trans. William P. Le Saint. Ancient Christian Writers, 28. Westminster, Md., Newman Press, 1959.

Turner, C. H., ed. "The *Liber ecclesiasticorum dogmatum* Attributed to Gennadius." *Journal of Theological Studies*, 7 (1906–07), 78–99.

Victor, Claudius Marius. *Alethia*. Ed. P. F. Hovingh. Corpus christianorum, series latina, 128. Turnhout, Brepols, 1960.

Victorinus, Laurentius i.e. Marius. *Explanationum in Rhetoricam M. Tullii Ciceronis*. *Rhetores latini minores*. Ed. Carolus Halm. Leipzig, B. G. Teubner, 1863.

Victorinus, Marius. *In Epistulam Pauli ad Galatas*. Ed. Albrecht Locher. Leipzig, B. G. Teubner, 1972.

—. *Opera theologica*. Ed. A. Locher. Leipzig, B. G. Teubner, 1976.

—. *Theological Treatises on the Trinity*. Trans. Mary T. Clark. Fathers of the Church, 69. Washington, Catholic University of America Press, 1981.

—. *Traités théologiques sur la Trinité*. Ed. Paul Henry. Trans. Pierre Hadot. Sources chrétiennes, 68–69. Paris, Éditions du Cerf, 1960.

Vollmer, Frederick, ed. *Poetae latini minores*. Vol. 5. Leipzig, B. G. Teubner, 1914.

Wolfskeel, C. W., ed. and trans. *De immortalitate animae of Augustine: Text, Translation and Commentary*. Amsterdam, B. R. Grüner Publishing Co., 1977.

Secondary Sources

Aall, Anathon. *Der Logos: Geschichte seiner Entwicklung in der griechischen Philosophie und der christlichen Literatur*. 2 vols. Leipzig, O. R. Reisland, 1869–99.

Adamo, Luigi. "Boezio e Mario Vittorino traduttori e interpreti dell'Isagoge di Porfiro." *Rivista critica di storia della filosofia*, 22 (1967), 141–64.

Alès, Adhémar d'. *Novatien: Étude sur la théologie romaine au milieu du III⁴ siècle*. Paris, Gabriel Beauchesne, 1924.

—. *La théologie de Saint Cyprien*. Paris, Gabriel Beauchesne, 1922.

—. *La théologie de Tertullien*. 3ᵐᵉ éd. Paris, Gabriel Beauchesne, 1905.

Alfonsi, Luigi. "Boezio nella tradizione culturale della letteratura latina." *Orpheus*, 2 (1955), 10–16.

—. "Cultura classica e cristianesimo: L'impostazione del problema nel proemio delle *Divinae institutiones* di Lattanzio e nell'*Ep.* XVI di Paolino da Nola." *Le Parole e le Idee*, 8 (1966), 163–76.

—. "Problemi filosofici della Consolatio boeziana." *Rivista di filosofia neo-scolastica*, 35 (1943), 323–28.

—. "Romanità e barbarie nell'Apologia di Boezio," *Studi Romani*, 1 (1953), 605–16.

—. "Storia interiore e storia cosmica nelle 'Consolatio' boeziana," *Convivium*, n.s. 23 (1955), 513–21.

—. "Studi boeziani I." *Aevum*, 19 (1945), 142–57.

—. "Studi boeziani II." *Aevum*, 25 (1951), 132–46, 210–29.

Alici, Luigi. *Il linguaggio come segno e come testimonianza: Una rilettura di Agostino*. Roma, Edizioni Studium, 1976.

Altaner, Berthold. *Kleine patristische Schriften*. Ed. Günther Glockmann. Texte und Untersuchungen zur Geschichte der altchristlichen Literatur, 83. Berlin, Akademie-Verlag, 1967.

—. *Patrology*. Trans. Hilda C. Graef. New York, Herder and Herder, 1960.

Antin, Paul. *Recueil sur saint Jérôme*. Collection Latomus, 95. Bruxelles, Latomus, 1968.

Armstrong, A. H., ed. *The Cambridge History of Later Greek and Early Medieval Philosophy*. Cambridge, The University Press, 1967.

Armstrong, A. H. and Markus, R. A. *Christian Faith and Greek Philosophy*. London, Darton, Longman & Todd, 1960.

Association Guillaume Budé. *Actes du VIIe congrès*, Aix-en-Provence, 1–6 avril 1963. Paris, Les Belles Lettres, 1964.

Aubin, Paul. "Intériorité et extériorité dans les Moralia in Job de saint Grégoire le Grand." *Recherches de science religieuse*, 62 (1974), 117–66.

Ayers, Robert H. *Language, Logic, and Reason in the Church Fathers: A Study of Tertullian, Augustine, and Aquinas*. Hildesheim, Georg Ohms Verlag, 1979.

Bärthlein, Karl. "Zur Lehre von der 'recta ratio' in der Geschichte der Ethik von der Stoa bis Christian Wolff." *Kant-Studien*, 56:1 (1965), 125–55.

Baguette, Charles. "Le Stoïcisme dans la formation de saint Augustin." Université de Louvain Ph.D. diss., 1968.

—. "Une période stoïcienne dans l'évolution de la pensée de saint Augustin." *Revue des études augustiniennes*, 16 (1970), 47–77.

Baltes, Matthias. "Gott, Welt, Mensch in der consolatio philosophiae des Boethius: Die Consolatio philosophiae als ein Dokument platonischer und neuplatonischer Philosophie." *Vigiliae Christianae*, 34 (1980), 313–40.

Barbero, Giorgio. "Seneca e la conversione di San Cipriano." *Rivista di studi classici*, 10 (1962), 16–23.

Bardy, Gustave. "Saint Jérôme et la pensée grecque." *Irénikon*, 26 (1953), 337–62.

Barlow, Claude W. "A Sixth-Century Epitome of Seneca, De ira." *Transactions and Proceedings of the American Philological Association*, 68 (1937), 26–42.

Barnes, Timothy David. *Tertullian: A Historical and Literary Study*. Oxford, Clarendon Press, 1971.

Barrett, Helen M. *Boethius: Some Aspects of His Times and Work*. New York, Russell & Russell, 1965 [repr. of Cambridge, 1940 ed.].

Barthel, Bernhard. *Über die Benutzung der philosophischen Schriften Ciceros durch Laktanz*. Teil I. Beilage zum Programm des königl. Gymnasiums in Strehlen, 244. Strehlen, 1903.

Barwick, Karl. "Elementos estoicos en san Agustín: Huellas varronianas en el De dialectica de Agustín." *Augustinus*, 18 (1973), 101–30.

—. "Probleme der stoischen Sprachlehre und Rhetorik." *Abhandlungen der sächsischen Akademie der Wissenschaft zu Leipzig*, philologisch-historische Klasse, 49:3. Berlin, Akademie-Verlag, 1957.

Basabe, Enrique. "San Jerónimo y los clásicos." *Helmantica*, 2 (1951), 161–92.

Bauer, Johannes B. "'Credo, quia absurdum' (Tertullian, De carne Christi 5)." *Festschrift Franz Loidl zum 65. Geburtstag*. Ed. Viktor Flieder. Wien, Verlag Brüder Hollinek, 1970, I, 9–12.

—. "'Dilige et quod vis fac'." *Wissenschaft und Weisheit*, 20 (1957), 64–65.

Bavaud, Georges. "Un thème augustinien: Le mystère de l'Incarnation, à la lumière de la distinction entre le verbe intérieure et le verbe proféré." *Revue des études augustiniennes*, 9 (1963), 95–101.

Baylis, Harry James. *Minucius Felix and His Place among the Early Fathers of the Latin Church*. London, SPCK, 1928.

Beckaert, A. "L'étude de la philosophie chez les Pères: Sens et méthode." *Studia Patristica*, 5. Ed. F. L. Cross. Texte und Untersuchungen zur Geschichte der altchristlichen Literatur, 80. Berlin, Akademie-Verlag, 1962, pp. 430–45.

Becker, Carl. "Der 'Octavius' des Minucius Felix: Heidnische Philosophie und frühchristliche Apologetik." *Sitzungsberichte der bayerische Akademie der Wissenschaften*, philosophisch-historische Klasse, 2. München, 1967.

Behr, Ernst. *Der Octavius des M. Minucius Felix in seinem Verhältnisse zu Cicero's Büchern de natura deorum*. Gera, 1870.

Benson, Edward White. *Cyprian: His Life, His Times, His Work*. New York, D. Appleton and Company, 1897.

Benz, Ernst. *Marius Victorinus und die Entwicklung der abendländischen Willensmetaphysik*. Forschungen zur Kirchen- und Geistesgeschichte, 1. Stuttgart, W. Kohlhammer, 1932.

Berka, Karel. "Die Semantik des Boethius." *Helikon*, 8 (1968), 454–59.

Beutler, Rudolf. *Philosophie und Apologetik bei Minucius Felix*. Weida i. Thür., Thomas & Hubert, 1936.

Beyenka, Mary Melchior. *Consolation in Saint Augustine*. Catholic University of America Patristic Studies, 83. Washington, Catholic University of America, 1950.

Bickel, Ernst. *Das asketische Ideal bei Ambrosius, Hieronymus und Augustin: Eine kulturgeschichtliche Studie*. Leipzig, B. G. Teubner, 1916.

—. "Die Schrift des Martinus von Bracara formula vitae honestae." *Rheinisches Museum für Philologie*, n.F. 6 (1905), 505–51.

Blum, Wilhelm. "Das Wesen Gottes und das Wesen des Menschen nach Salvian von Marseille." *Münchener theologische Zeitschrift*, 21 (1970), 327–41.

Bocheński, I. M. *A History of Formal Logic*. Ed. and trans. Ivo Thomas. Notre Dame, University of Notre Dame Press, 1961.

Boehrer, Stephen L. *Gaudentius of Brescia: Sermons and Letters*. Catholic University of America Studies in Sacred Theology, ser. 2:165. Washington, Catholic University of America, 1965.

Boissier, Gaston. *La fin de paganisme: Étude sur les dernières luttes religieuses en occident au quatrième siècle*. 4me éd. 2 vols. Paris, Hachette, 1903.

Borchardt, C. F. A. *Hilary of Poitiers' Role in the Arian Struggle*. Kerkhistorische Studiën, 12. The Hague, Martinus Nijhoff, 1966.

Bourke, Vernon J. *Augustine's Quest of Wisdom: Life and Philosophy of the Bishop of Hippo*. Milwaukee, Bruce Publishing Company, 1945.

Boyer, Charles "La théorie augustinienne des raisons séminales." *Miscellanea agostiniana*. Testi e studi pubblicati a cura dell'Ordine eremitano di S. Agostino nel XV centenario della morte del santo dottore. Roma, Tipografia Poliglotta Vaticana, 1931, II, 795–819.

Brady, Jules M. "St. Augustine's Theory of Seminal Reasons." *New Scholasticism*, 38 (1964), 141–58.

Braga, Gaetano Capone. "La soluzione cristiana del problema del 'summum bonum' in 'Philosophiae consolationis libri quinque' di Boezio." *Archivo di storia della filosofia italiana*, 3 (1934), 101–16.

Brandt, Samuel. "Uber die Quellen von Laktanz' Schrift De opificio dei." *Wiener Studien*, 13 (1891), 255–92.

Brandt, Theodor. *Tertullians Ethik: Zur Erfassung der systematischen Grundanschauung*. Gütersloh, C. Bertelsmann, 1928.

Braun, René. *"Deus christianorum": Recherches sur le vocabulaire doctrinal de Tertullien*. Publications de la Faculté des lettres et sciences humaines d'Alger, 41. Paris, PUF, 1962.

—. "Tertullien et la philosophie païenne: Essai de mise au point." *Bulletin de l'Association Guillaume Budé*, ser. 4:2 (1971), 231–51.

Bray, Gerald Lewis. *Holiness and the Will of God: Perspectives on the Theology of Tertullian*. Atlanta, John Knox Press, 1979.

Brown, Peter. *Augustine of Hippo*. Berkeley, University of California Press, 1967.

Brox, Norbert. "Anima naturaliter non christiana." *Zeitschrift für katholische Theologie*, 91 (1969), 70–75.

Bruder, Konrad. *Die philosophischen Elemente in den Opuscula sacra des Boethius: Ein Beitrag zur Quellengeschichte der Philosophie der Scholastik*. Leipzig, Felix Meiner, 1928.

Brunner, Johannes N. *Der hl. Hieronymus und die Mädchenerziehung auf Grund seiner Briefe an Laeta und Gaudentius: Eine patristisch-pädagogische Studie*. Veröffentlichungen aus dem kirchenhistorischen Seminar München, 3:10. Ed. Alois Knöpfler. München, J. J. Lentnerschen Buchhandlung, 1910.

Burger, Franz Xaver. *Minucius Felix und Seneca*, München, C. H. Beck'sche Verlagsbuchhandlung, 1904.

Burnaby, John. *Amor Dei: A Study of the Religion of St. Augustine*. London, Hodder & Stoughton, 1938.

Bushman, Rita Marie. "St. Augustine's Metaphysics and Stoic Doctrine." *New Scholasticism*, 26 (1952), 283–304.

Calabi, Ida. "Le fonti della storia romana nel De civitate dei di Sant'Agostino." *La parola del passato*, 10 (1955), 274–94.

Campenhausen, Hans von. *The Fathers of the Latin Church*. Trans. Manfred Hoffmann. London, Adam & Charles Black, 1964.

Cancik, Hildegarde. *Untersuchungen zu Senecas Epistulae morales.* Spudasmata, 18. Hildesheim, Georg Olms Verlagsbuchhandlung, 1967.

Cantalamessa, Raniero. *La cristologia di Tertulliano.* Paradosis, 18. Friburgo, Edizioni Universitarie Friburgo Svizzera, 1962.

Cardman, Francine Jo. "Tertullian on the Resurrection." Yale University Ph.D. diss., 1974.

Carlier, V. "Minucius Félix et Sénèque," *Le Musée Belge,* 1 (1897), 258–93.

Carlson, Mary Louise. "Pagan Examples of Fortitude in the Latin Christian Apologists." *Classical Philology,* 43 (1948), 93–104.

Carton, Raoul. *Le christianisme et l'augustinianisme de Boèce.* Paris, Marcel Rivière, [1930?].

Casado, Fidel. "El repudio de la filosofía antigua en la 'Ciudad de Dios'." *Estudios sobre la Ciudad de Dios.* Numero extraordinario de homenaje a San Agustín en el XVI centenario de su nacimiento. Escorial, Real Monasterio de San Lorenzo, 1954, II, 67–93.

Cavallera, Ferdinand. *Saint Jérôme: Sa vie et son œuvre.* Spicilegium Sacrum Lovaniense, 1–2. Louvain, Spicilegium Sacrum Lovaniense; Paris, Champion, 1922.

Chadwick, Henry. "The Authenticity of Boethius' Fourth Tractate, *De fide catholica.*" *Journal of Theological Studies,* n.s. 31 (1980), 551–56.

—. *Boethius: The Consolations of Music, Logic, Theology, and Philosophy.* Oxford, Clarendon Press, 1981.

—. *Priscillian of Avila: The Occult and the Charismatic in the Early Church.* Oxford, Clarendon Press, 1976.

Chadwick, Nora K. *Poetry and Letters in Early Christian Gaul.* London, Bowes & Bowes, 1955.

Chadwick, Owen. *John Cassian: A Study in Primitive Monasticism.* Cambridge, The University Press, 1950.

—. *John Cassian.* 2nd ed. Cambridge, The University Press, 1968.

Chappuis, Paul. "La théologie de Boèce." *Jubilé Alfred Loisy: Congrès d'histoire du christianisme,* 3. Ed. P.-L. Couchoud. Paris, Éditions Rieder, 1928, pp. 15–40.

Christian, William A. "Augustine on the Creation of the World." *Harvard Theological Review,* 46 (1953), 1–25.

Christophe, Paul. *Cassien et Césaire: Prédicateurs de la morale monastique.* Gembloux, J. Duculot, 1969.

Chroust, Anton-Hermann. "The Function of Law and Justice in the Ancient World and the Middle Ages." *Journal of the History of Ideas,* 7 (1946), 298–320.

Cilento, Vincenzo. *Medio evo monastico e scolastico.* Milano, Riccardo Ricciardi Editore, 1961.

Cioffari, Vincenzo. *Fortune and Fate from Democritus to St. Thomas Aquinas.* New York, 1935.

Circis, Peter. *Ennoblement of Pagan Virtues: A Comparative Treatise on Virtues in Cicero's Book De officiis and in St. Ambrose's Book De officiis ministrorum.* Rome, Typis Pontificiae Universitatis Gregorianae, 1955.

Clark, Mary T. "The Earliest Philosophy of the Living God: Marius Victorinus." *Proceedings of the American Catholic Philosophical Association,* 41 (1967), 87–93.

—. "The Psychology of Marius Victorinus." *Augustinian Studies,* 5 (1974), 149–66.

Codina, Victor. *El aspecto cristológico en la espiritualidad de Juan Casiano.* Orientalia Christiana Analecta, 175. Roma, Pont. Institutum Orientalium Studiorum, 1966.

Colish, Marcia L. "Carolingian Debates over *Nihil* and *Tenebrae*: A Study in Theological Method," *Speculum,* 59 (1984), 757–95.

—. "Cosmetic Theology: The Transformation of a Stoic Theme." *Assays: Critical Approaches to Medieval and Renaissance Texts,* ed. Peggy A. Knapp and Michael A. Stugrin, 1 (1981), 3–14.

—. "Pauline Theology and Stoic Philosophy: An Historical Study." *Journal of the American Academy of Religion,* 47, Supplement (March 1979), B 1–21.

—. "St. Augustine's Rhetoric of Silence Revisited." *Augustinian Studies,* 9 (1978), 15–24.

—. "The Stoic Hypothetical Syllogisms and Their Transmission in the Latin West through the Early Middle Ages." *Res Publica Litterarum,* 2 (1979), 19–26.

—. "The Stoic Theory of Verbal Signification and the Problem of Lies and False Statements from Antiquity to St. Anselm." *Archéologie du signe.* Ed. Lucie Brind'Amour and Eugene Vance. Papers in Mediaeval Studies, 3. Toronto, Pontifical Institute of Mediaeval Studies, 1983, pp. 17–43.

—. *The Stoic Tradition from Antiquity to the Early Middle Ages.* Vol. I: *Stoicism in Classical Latin Literature.* Studies in the History of Christian Thought, 34. Ed. Heiko A. O-berman. Leiden, E. J. Brill, 1985.

Collart, Jean. "Saint Augustin grammarien dans le *De magistro.*" *Revue des études augustiniennes,* 17 (1971), 279–92.

Collins, James. "Progress and Problems in the Reassessment of Boethius." *The Modern Schoolman,* 33 (1945), 1–23.

Colombo, Sisto. "Osservazioni sulla composizione letteraria e sulle fonti di M. Minucio Felice." *Didaskaleion,* 3 (1914), 79–121.

Corsaro, Francesco. "Garbata polemica anticristiana nella anonima commedia tardo-imperiale *Querolus sive Aulularia.*" *Miscellanea di studi di letteratura cristiana antica,* 13 (1963), 11–21.

—. *Querolus: Studio introduttivo e commentario.* Bologna, Riccardo Patròn, 1965.

Courcelle, Pierre. "Boèce et l'école d'Alexandrie." *Mélanges de l'école française de Rome,* 52 (1935), 185–223.

—. *Connais-toi toi-même de Socrate à Saint Bernard.* 3 vols. Paris, Études Augustiniennes, 1974–75.

—. *La Consolation de Philosophie dans la tradition littéraire: Antécédents et postérité de Boèce.* Paris, Études Augustiniennes, 1967.

—. "Deux grands courants de pensée dans la littérature latine tardive: Stoïcisme et néo-platonisme." *Revue des études latines,* 42 (1965), 122–40.

—. "Grégoire le Grand à l'école de Juvenal." *Studi e materiali di storia della religione,* 38 (1967), 170–74.

—. "'Habitare secum' selon Perse et selon Grégoire le Grand." *Revue des études anciennes,* 69 (1967), 266–79.

—. "L'humanisme chrétien de Saint Ambroise." *Orpheus,* 9 (1962), 21–34.

—. "L'Immanence dans les 'Confessions' augustiniennes." *Hommages à Jean Bayet.* Ed. Marcel Renard and Robert Schilling. Collection Latomus, 70. Bruxelles, Latomus, 1964, pp. 161–71.

—. *Late Latin Writers and Their Greek Sources.* Trans. Harry E. Wedeck. Cambridge, Mass., Harvard University Press, 1969.

—. "Parietes faciunt christianos?" *Mélanges d'archéologie, d'épigraphie et d'histoire offerts à Jérôme Carcopino.* Paris, Hachette, 1966, pp. 241–48.

—. *Recherches sur Saint Ambroise: "Vies" anciennes, culture, iconographie.* Paris, Études Augustiniennes, 1973.

—. "Saint Benoît, le merle, et le buisson d'épines." *Journal des savants,* 152 (1967), 154–61.

—. "Virgile et l'immanence divine chez Minucius Felix." *Mullus: Festschrift Theodor Klauser, Jahrbuch für Antike und Christentum,* Ergänzungsband, 1. Münster i. W., As-chendorffsche Verlagsbuchhandlung, 1964, pp. 34–42.

Coyle, Alcuin F. "Cicero's *De officiis* and the *De officiis ministrorum* of St. Ambrose." *Franciscan Studies,* 15 (1955), 224–56.

Cuesta, Salvador. *El equilibrio pasional en la doctrina estoica y en la de San Agustín: Estudio sobre dos concepciones del universo a través de un problema antropológico.* Madrid, Consejo Superior de Investigaciones Científicas, Instituto Filosofico "Luis Vives", 1945.

Dagens, Claude. "Grégoire le Grand et la culture: De la 'sapientia huius mundi' à la 'docta ignorantia'." *Revue des études augustiniennes,* 14 (1968), 17–26.

—. *Saint Grégoire le Grand: Culture et expérience chrétiennes.* Paris, Études Augustiniennes, 1977.

Daly, C. B. "Novatian and Tertullian: A Chapter in the History of Puritanism." *Irish Theological Quarterly,* 19 (1952), 33–43.

Daniélou, Jean. *A History of Early Christian Doctrine before the Council of Nicaea.* Vol. III: *The Origins of Latin Christianity.* Trans. David Smith and John Austin Baker. London, Darton, Longman & Todd, 1977.

—. "Novatien et le De mundo d'Apulée." *Romanitas et Christianitas: Studia Iano Henrico Waszink*. Ed. E. den Boer et al. Amsterdam, North-Holland Publishing Company, 1973, pp. 71–80.

Dassmann, Ernst. *Die Frömmigkeit des Kirchenvaters Ambrosius von Mailand: Quellen und Entfaltung*. Münsterische Beiträge zur Theologie, 29. Münster i. W., Aschendorffsche Verlagsbuchhandlung, 1965.

Day, Archibald A. *The Origins of Latin Love-Elegy*. Oxford, Basil Blackwell, 1938.

Décarie, Vianney. "Le paradoxe de Tertullien." *Vigiliae Christianae*, 15 (1961), 23–31.

Delhaye, Philippe. "Le dossier anti-matrimonial de l'*Adversus Jovinianum* et son influence sur quelques écrits latins du XIIᵉ siècle." *Mediaeval Studies*, 13 (1951), 65–86.

Deman, Th. "Le 'De officiis' de saint Ambroise dans l'histoire de la théologie morale." *Revue des sciences philosophiques et théologiques*, 37 (1953), 409–24.

DeSimone, Russell J. *The Treatise of Novatian the Roman Presbyter on the Trinity: A Study of the Text and the Doctrine*. Studia Ephemerides "Augustinianum", 4. Roma, Institutum Patristicum "Augustinianum", 1970.

Diggs, Bernard J. "St. Augustine against the Academicians." *Traditio*, 7 (1949–51), 72–93.

Dill, Samuel. *Roman Society in the Last Century of the Western Empire*. 2nd rev. ed. London, Macmillan and Co., 1921.

Doignon, Jean. *Hilaire de Poitiers avant l'exil: Recherches sur la naissance, l'enseignement et l'épreuve d'une foi épiscopale en Gaule au milieu du IVᵉ siècle*. Paris, Études Augustiniennes, 1971.

—. "Le *Placitum* eschatologique attribué aux stoïciens par Lactance (*Institutions divines* VII, 20): Un exemple de contamination de modèles littéraires." *Revue de philologie*, 51 (1977), 43–55.

Domínguez del Val, Ursicino. "El senequismo de Lactance." *Helmantica*, 23 (1972), 289–323.

Dooley, William Joseph. *Marriage according to St. Ambrose*. Catholic University of America Studies in Christian Antiquity, 11. Washington, Catholic University of America Press, 1948.

Draeseke, Joannes. "M. Tulli Ciceronis et Ambrosii episcopi Mediolanensis de officiis libri tres inter se comparantur." *Rivista di filologia e d'istruzione classica*, 5 (1876), 121–64.

Driessche, René van den. "Sur le 'De syllogismo hypothetico' de Boèce." *Methodos*, 1 (1949), 293–307.

Duchrow, Ulrich. *Sprachverständnis und biblishes Hören bei Augustin*. Tübingen, J. C. B. Mohr (Paul Siebeck), 1965.

Dudden, F. Homes. *Gregory the Great: His Place in History and Thought*. 2 vols. London, Longmans, Green, and Co., 1905.

—. *The Life and Times of St. Ambrose*. 2 vols. Oxford, Clarendon Press, 1935.

Dürr, Karl. *The Propositional Logic of Boethius*. Amsterdam, North-Holland Publishing Company, 1951.

Duval, Yves-Marie. *Le Livre de Jonas dans la littérature chrétienne grecque et latine: Sources et influence du Commentaire sur Jonas de saint Jérôme*. 2 vols. Paris, Études Augustiniennes, 1973.

Dyroff, Adolf. "Über Form und Begriffsgehalt der augustinischen Schrift De ordine." *Aurelius Augustinus*. Festschrift der Görres-Gesellschaft zum 1500. Todestage des heiligen Augustinus. Ed. Martin Grabmann and Joseph Mausbach. Köln, J. P. Bachem, 1930, pp. 15–62.

Carl Martin Edsman, *Ignis Divinus: Le feu comme moyen de rajeunissement et d'immortalité. Contes, legendes, mythes et rites*. Skrifter utgivna ar Vetenskaps-Societeten i Lund. Lund, C.W.K. Gleerup, 1949.

Eiswirth, Rudolf. *Hieronymus' Stellung zur Literatur und Kunst*. Klassische-philologische Studien, 16. Ed. Hans Herter and Wolfgang Schmid. Wiesbaden, Otto Harrassowitz, 1955.

Elorduy, Eleuterio. "La metafisica agustiniana." *Pensamiento*, 11 (1955), 130–69.

Elsässer, Michael. *Das Person–Verständnis des Boethius*. Inaugural-Dissertation, Julius-Maximilians-Universität zu Würzburg. Münster, 1973.

Emeneau, M. B. "Ambrose and Cicero." *Classical Weekly*, 24 (1930), 49–53.

Ewald, Paul. *Der Einfluss der stoisch-ciceronianischen Moral auf die Darstellung der Ethik bei Ambrosius.* Leipzig, Ernst Bredt, 1881.

Faggi, Adolfo. "Il 'somatismo' o 'corporatismo' degli Stoici." *Atti della Reale Accademia delle scienze di Torino*, classe di scienze morali, storiche e filologiche, 67 (1931–32), 59–70.

Faider, Paul, *Études sur Sénèque.* Gand, Van Rysselberghe & Rombout, 1921.

Favez, Charles. *La consolation latine chrétienne.* Paris, J. Vrin, 1937.

—. "L'Inspiration chrétienne dans les consolations de saint Ambroise." *Revue des études latines*, 8 (1930), 82–91.

—. "Saint Jérôme pédagogue." *Mélanges de philologie, de littérature et d'histoire anciennes offerts à J. Marouzeau.* Paris, Les Belles Lettres, 1948, pp. 173–81.

Fessler, Franz. *Benutzung der philosophischen Schriften Ciceros durch Laktanz: Ein Beitrag zur klassischen Philologie.* Leipzig, B. G. Teubner, 1913.

Festugière, A.–J. "La composition et l'esprit du *De anima* de Tertullien." *Revue des sciences philosophiques et théologiques*, 33 (1949), 129–61.

Fichter, Joseph H. *Saint Cecil Cyprian: Early Defender of the Faith.* St. Louis, B. Herder Book Co., 1942.

Fiske, Adele M. "Hieronymus Ciceronianus." *Transactions of the American Philological Association*, 96 (1965), 119–38.

Folliet, Georges. "'Deificare in otio': Augustin, *Epistula* 10, 2." *Recherches augustiniennes*, 2 (1962), 225–36.

Fontaine, William Thomas. *Fortune, Matter and Providence: A Study of Anicius Severinus Boethius and Giordano Bruno.* Scotlandville, La., University of Pennsylvania, 1939.

Fortin, Ernest L. *Christianisme et culture philosophique au cinquième siècle: La querelle de l'âme humaine en Occident.* Paris, Études Augustiniennes, 1959.

—. "The *Viri Novi* of Arnobius and the Conflict between Faith and Reason in the Early Christian Centuries." *The Heritage of the Early Church: Essays in Honor of the Very Reverend Georges Vasilievich Florovsky.* Ed. David Neiman and Margaret Schatkin. Orientalia Christiana Analecta, 195. Roma, Pont. Institutum Studiorum Orientalium, 1973, pp. 197–226.

Francœur, Mary Petronilla. "The Relationship in Thought and Language between Lucius Annaeus Seneca and Martin of Braga," University of Michigan Ph.D. diss., 1944.

Frassinetti, Paolo. "Gli scritti matrimoniali di Seneca e Tertulliano." *Istituto lombardo di scienze e lettere, Rendiconti*, classe di lettere e scienze morali e storiche, 88, ser. 3:19 (1955), 151–88.

Frede, Dorothea. *Aristoteles und die "Seeschlacht": Das Problem der Contingentia Futura in De interpretatione 9.* Hypomnemata, 27. Göttingen, Vandenhoeck & Ruprecht, 1970.

Fredouille, Jean-Claude. *Tertullien et la conversion de la culture antique.* Paris, Études Augustiniennes, 1972.

Frickel, Michael. *Deus totus ubique simul: Untersuchungen zur allgemeinen Gottgegenwart im Rahmen der Gotteslehre Gregors des Grossen.* Freiburger theologische Studien, 69. Freiburg, Herder, 1956.

Frotscher, Paul Gotthold. *Des Apologeten Lactantius Verhältnis zur griechischen Philosophie.* Leipzig, Oswald Mutze, 1895.

Fuetscher, Lorenz. "Die natürliche Gotteserkenntnis bei Tertullian." *Zeitschrift für katholische Theologie*, 51 (1927), 1–34, 217–51.

Galdi, M. "De Tertulliani 'De cultu feminarum' et Cypriani 'ad virgines' libellis commentatio." *Raccolta di scritti in onore di Felice Ramorino.* Pubblicazioni della Università cattolica del Sacro Cuore, ser. 4:7. Milano, Vita e Pensiero, 1927, pp. 539–67.

Gallay, Jacques. "Dilige et quod vis fac: Notes d'exégèse augustinienne." *Recherches de science religieuse*, 43 (1955), 545–55.

Gannon, Mary Ann Ida. "The Active Theory of Sensation in St. Augustine." *New Scholasticism*, 30 (1956), 154–80.

Geffken, Johannes. *Kynika und Verwandtes.* Heidelberg, Carl Winter, 1909.

Gegenschatz, Ernst. "Die Freiheit der Entscheidung in der 'consolatio philosophiae' des Boethius." *Museum Helveticum*, 15 (1958), 110–29.

—. "Die Gefährdung des Möglichen durch das Vorauswissen Gottes in der Sichte des Boethius." *Wiener Studien*, 79 (1966), 517–30.

Gennaro, Salvatore. "Il classicismo di Lattanzio nel 'de ave phoenice'." *Miscellanea di studi di letteratura cristiana antica*, 9 (1959), 1–18.

Ghellinck, Joseph de. "Quelques mentions de la dialectique stoïcienne dans les conflits doctrinaux du IVe siècle." *Philosophia perennis: Festgabe Josef Geyer zum 60. Geburtstag*. Ed. Fritz-Joachim von Rintelin. Regensburg, Josef Habbel, 1930, I, 57–67.

Gibson, Margaret, ed. *Boethius: His Life, Thought and Influence*. Oxford, Basil Blackwell, 1981.

Gigon, Olof. "Lactantius und die Philosophie." *Kerygma und Logos: Festschrift für Carl Andresen zum 70. Geburtstag*. Ed. Adolf Martin Ritter. Göttingen, Vandenhoeck & Ruprecht, 1979, pp. 196–213.

Gilbert, Neal. "The Concept of Will in Early Latin Philosophy." *Journal of the History of Philosophy*, 1 (1963), 17–35.

Gilson, Étienne. *History of Christian Philosophy in the Middle Ages*. New York, Random House, 1955.

Giorgianni, Virgilio. *Il concetto del diritto e dello stato in S. Agostino*. Il pensiero medioevale, collana di storia della filosofia, diretta da Carmelo Ottaviano, ser. 1:2. Padova, CEDAM, 1951.

Gossel, Guilelmus. *Quibus ex fontibus Ambrosius in describendo corpore humano hauserit (Ambros. Exaem. VI 54–74)*. Leipzig, Dr. Seele & Co., 1908.

Grant, Robert M. *Miracle and Natural Law in Graeco-Roman and Early Christian Thought*. Amsterdam, North-Holland Publishing Company, 1952.

Gronau, Karl. *Poseidonios und die jüdisch-christliche Genesisexegese*. Berlin, B. G. Teubner, 1914.

Gruber, Joachim. *Kommentar zu Boethius De Consolatione philosophiae*. Texte und Kommentare: Eine altertumswissenschaftliche Reihe, 9. Berlin, Walter de Gruyter, 1978.

—. "Salvianus 'De gubernatione dei'." *Der altsprachliche Unterricht*, 21 (1978), 60–66.

Grützmacher, Georg. *Hieronymus: Eine biographische Studie zur alten Kirchengeschichte*. 3 vols. in 2. Studien zur Geschichte der Theologie und der Kirche, 6:3, 10:1–2. Leipzig, Dieterich'sche Verlags-Buchhandlung, 1901–08.

Guy, Jean-Claude. *Jean Cassien: Vie et doctrine spirituelle*. Collection théologie pastorale et spiritualité, recherches et synthèses, 9. Paris, P. Lethielleux, 1961.

Hadot, Pierre. "L'Image de la Trinité dans l'âme chez Victorinus et chez saint Augustin." *Studia Patristica*, 6. Ed. F. L. Cross. Texte und Untersuchungen zur Geschichte der altchristlichen Literatur, 81. Berlin, Akademie-Verlag, 1962, pp. 409–42.

—. *Marius Victorinus: Recherches sur sa vie et ses œuvres*. Paris, Études Augustiniennes, 1971.

—. *Porphyre et Victorinus*. 2 vols. Paris, Études Augustiniennes, 1968.

—. "Typus: Stoïcisme et monarchianisme au IVe siècle d'après Candide l'Arien et Marius Victorinus." *Recherches de théologie ancienne et médiévale*, 18 (1951), 177–87.

Hagendahl, Harald. *Augustine and the Latin Classics*. Studia graeca et latina Gothoburgensia, 20:1–2. Göteborg, Almquist & Wiksell, 1967.

—. "Jerome and the Latin Classics." *Vigiliae Christianae*, 28 (1974), 216–27.

—. *Latin Fathers and the Classics: A Study of the Apologists, Jerome and Other Christian Writers*. Studia graeca et latina Gothoburgensia, 6. Göteborg, Almquist & Wiksell, 1958.

Hager, Fritz–Peter. "Zur Bedeutung der griechischen Philosophie für die christliche Wahrheit und Bildung bei Tertullian und bei Augustin." *Antike und Abendlande*, 24 (1978), 76–84.

Halporn, James W. "Magni Aurelii Cassiodori Senatoris liber De anima." *Traditio*, 16 (1960), 39–109.

Hammer, Hans. "Johannes Cassian: Christliche und heidnische Bildung." *Pharus*, 21 (1930), 241–55.

Harnack, Adolf. *History of Dogma*. 7 vols. Trans. Neil Buchanan and James Millar. London, Williams & Norgate, 1910–12.

Hasler, F. *Ueber das Verhältniss der heidnischen und christlichen Ethik auf Grund einer Vergleich-ung des ciceronianischen Buches "De officiis" mit dem gleichnamigen des heiligen Ambrosius.* München, Georg Franz, 1866.

Hatch, Edwin. *The Influence of Greek Ideas and Usages upon the Christian Church.* Hibbert Lectures, 1888. London, Williams & Norgate, 1898.

Hatinguais, Jacqueline. "Vertus universitaires selon Ausone." *Revue des études anciennes,* 55 (1953), 379–87.

Heim, François. "L'influence exercée par Constantin sur Lactance: La théologie de la victoire." *Lactance et son temps: Recherches actuelles.* Actes du IVe colloque d'études historiques et patristiques, Chantilly, 21–23 septembre 1976. Ed. J. Fontaine and M. Perrin. Paris, Éditions Beauchesne, 1978, pp. 55–70.

Heinze, Richard. "Tertullians Apologeticum." *Bericht über die Verhandlungen der königlich sächsiche Gesellschaft der Wissenschaft zu Leipzig,* philologisch-historische Klasse, 62 (1910), pp. 281–488.

Henry, Paul. "The *Adversus Arium* of Marius Victorinus, the First Systematic Exposition of the Doctrine of the Trinity." *Journal of Theological Studies,* n.s. 1 (1950), 42–55.

Hiltbrunner, Otto. "Die Schrift 'De officiis ministrorum' des hl. Ambrosius und ihr ciceronianische Vorbild." *Gymnasium,* 71 (1964), 174–89.

Hinchliff, Peter. *Cyprian of Carthage and the Unity of the Christian Church.* London, Geoffrey Chapman, 1974.

Hök, Gösta. "Augustin und die antike Tugendlehre." *Kerygma und Dogma,* 6 (1960), 104–30.

Holloway, Alvin J. "The Transformation of Stoic Themes in St. Augustine," Fordham University Ph.D. diss., 1966.

Holte, Ragnar. *Béatitude et sagesse: Saint Augustin et le problème de la fin de l'homme dans la philosophie ancienne.* Paris, Études Augustiniennes, 1962.

Horn, Hans-Jürgen. "Antakoluthie der Tugenden und Einheit Gottes." *Jahrbuch für Antike und Christentum,* 13 (1970), 5–28.

Howie, George. *Educational Theory and Practice in St. Augustine.* New York, Columbia University Teachers College Press, 1969.

Huber, Peter. *Die Vereinbarkeit von göttlicher Vorsehung und menschlicher Freiheit in der Consolatio Philosophiae des Boethius.* Zürich, Juris Druck & Verlag, 1976.

Isaac, J. *Le Peri hermeneias en occident de Boèce à saint Thomas: Histoire littéraire d'une traité d'Aristote.* Bibliothèque thomiste, 29. Paris, J. Vrin, 1953.

Ivánka, Endre von. "Die stoische Anthropologie in der lateinischen Literatur." *Anzeiger der österreichische Akademie der Wissenschaften,* philosophisch-historische Klasse, 87 (1950), 178–92.

Jackson, B. Darrell. "The Theory of Signs in St. Augustine's *De Doctrina Christiana.*" *Augustine: A Collection of Critical Essays.* Ed. R. A. Markus. Garden City, N.Y., Doubleday & Company, Inc., 1972, pp. 92–147.

Jagielski, Hubertus. *De Firmiani Lactantii fontibus quaestiones selectae.* Königsberg, Ex Officina Kuemmeliana, 1912.

Jannaccone, Silvia. "S. Girolamo e Seneca." *Giornale italiano di filologia,* 16 (1963), 326–38.

—. "Sull'uso degli scritti filosofici di Cicero da parte di S. Girolamo." *Giornale italiano di filologia,* 17 (1964), 329–41.

Karpp, Heinrich. *Probleme altchristlicher Anthropologie: Biblische Anthropologie und philosophische Psychologie bei den Kirchenvätern des dritten Jahrhunderts.* Beiträge zur Förderung christlicher Theologie, 44:3. Gütersloh, C. Bertelsmann Verlag, 1950.

Kelly, J. N. D. *Jerome, His Life, Writings, and Controversies.* London, Duckworth, 1975.

Kelly, Louis G. "Saint Augustine und Saussurean Linguistics." *Augustinian Studies,* 6 (1975), 45–64.

Klingner, Fridericus. *De Boethii Consolatione philosophiae.* Philologische Untersuchungen, 27. Ed. A. Kiessling and U. von Wilamowitz-Moellendorff. Berlin, Weidmannsche Buchhandlung, 1921.

Kneale, William and Kneale, Martha. *The Development of Logic.* Oxford, Clarendon Press, 1962.

Koch, Hugo. *Cyprianische Untersuchungen.* Arbeiten zur Kirchengeschichte, 4. Bonn, A. Marcus und E. Weber, 1926.
—. "Zur novatianischen Schrifttum." *Zeitschrift für Kirchengeschichte,* 38 (1920), 86–95.
Koster, Severin. "Vir bonus et sapiens (Ausonius 363 p. 90 P.)." *Hermes,* 102 (1974), 590–619.
Kotek, Ferdinand. "Anklänge an Ciceros 'De natura deorum' bei Minucius Felix und Tertullian." *Jahres-Bericht des kais. kön. Ober-Gymnasiums zu den Schotten in Wien,* 1900–01. Wien, Verlag des k.k. Ober-Gymnasium zu den Schotten, 1901, pp. 3–51.
Krafft, Peter. *Beiträge zur Wirkungsgeschichte des älteren Arnobius.* Klassisch-philologische Studien, 32. Wiesbaden, Otto Harrassowitz, 1966.
Krause, Wilhelm. *Die Stellung der frühchristlichen Autoren zur heidnischen Literatur.* Wien, Verlag Herder, 1958.
Küppers, Jochen. "Zum Querolus (p. 17.7–22R*) und seiner Datierung." *Philologus,* 123 (1979), 303–23.
Kunst, Carolus. *De S. Hieronymi studiis Ciceronianis.* Dissertationes philologiae Vindobonenses, 12:2. Wien, F. Deuticke, 1918.
Labhardt, André. "Tertullien et la philosophie ou la recherche d'une 'position pure'." *Museum Helveticum,* 7 (1950), 159–80.
Labriolle, Pierre de. "Apatheia." *Mélanges de philologie, de littérature et d'histoire anciennes offerts à Alfred Ernout.* Paris, C. Klincksieck, 1940, pp. 215–23.
—. "Le 'De Officiis ministrorum' de saint Ambroise et le 'De Officiis' de Cicéron." *Revue des cours et conférences,* 16:2 (1907–08), 177–86.
—. *The Life and Times of St. Ambrose.* Trans. Herbert Wilson. St. Louis, B. Herder Book Co., 1928.
—. "Saint Augustin et Sénèque." *Revue de philologie, de littérature et d'histoire anciennes,* sér. 3:2 (1928), 47–49.
Langan, John P. "Augustine on the Unity and the Interconnection of the Virtues." *Harvard Theological Review,* 72 (1979), 81–95.
Lapidge, Michael. "A Stoic Metaphor in Late Latin Poetry: The Binding of the Universe." *Latomus,* 39 (1980), 817–37.
Laurin, Joseph-Rhéal. *Orientations maîtresses des apologistes chrétiens de 270 à 361.* Analecta Gregoriana, 61, Series facultatis historiae ecclesiasticae, B 10. Roma, Universitas Gregorianae, 1954.
Lausberg, Marion. "Christliche Nächstenliebe und heidnische Ethik bei Laktanz." *Studia Patristica,* 13:2. Ed. Elizabeth A. Livingstone. Texte und Untersuchungen zur Geschichte der altchristlichen Literatur, 116. Berlin, Akademie-Verlag, 1975, pp. 29–34.
Lazzati, Giuseppi. "Il 'De natura deorum' fonte del 'De testimonio animae' di Tertulliano?" *Atene e Roma,* ser. 3:7 (1939), 153–66.
LeBonniec, Henri. "Tradition de la culture classique: Arnobe, témoin et juge des cultes païens." *Bulletin de l'Association Guillaume Budé,* sér. 4:2 (1974), 201–22.
LeBoulluec, Alain. "L'allégorie chez les Stoïciens." *Poétique,* 23 (1975), 301–21.
Leclercq, Jean. *The Love of Learning and the Desire for God: A Study of Monastic Culture.* Trans. Catherine Misrahi. New York, Fordham University Press, 1961.
Leonardi, Claudio. "I commenti altomedievali ai classici pagani, da Severino Boezio a Remigio d'Auxerre." *La cultura antica nell'occidente latino dal VII all'XI secolo.* Settimane di studio del Centro Italiano di Studi sull'alto medioevo, 22, 18–24 aprile 1974. Spoleto, Presso la Sede del Centro, 1975, I, 459–504.
Leonardi, C., Minio-Paluello, L., Pizzani, U., and Courcelle, P. "Boezio." *Dizionario biografico degli italiani.* Roma, Istituto della Enciclopedia Italiana, 1969, XI, 142–65.
Liefooghe, A. "Les idées morales de saint Martin de Braga." *Mélanges de science religieuse,* 11 (1954), 133–46.
Lindberg, David C. *Theories of Vision from Al-Kindi to Kepler.* Chicago, University of Chicago Press, 1976.
Lloyd, A. C. "Emotion and Decision in Stoic Psychology." *The Stoics.* Ed. John M. Rist. Berkeley, University of California Press, 1978, pp. 233–46.

—. "Nosce teipsum and Conscientia." *Archiv für Geschichte der Philosophie*, 46 (1964), 188–200.

Löpfe, Dominikus. *Die Tugendlehre des heiligen Ambrosius*. Sarnen, Louis Ehrli & Cie, 1951.

Loi, Vincenzo. "Il concetto di 'iustitia' e i fattori culturali dell'etica di Lattanzio." *Salesianum*, 28 (1966), 583–625.

—. "Cristologia e soteriologia nella dottrina di Lattanzio." *Rivista di storia e letteratura religiosa*, 4 (1968), 237–87.

—. *Lattanzio nella storia del linguaggio e del pensiero teologico pre-niceno*. Bibliotheca Theologica Salesiana, 1:5. Zürich, Pas-Verlag, 1970.

—. "Problema del male e dualismo negli scritti di Lattanzio." *Annali della Facoltà di lettere, filosofia e magistero dell'Università di Cagliari*, 29 (1961–65), 37–96.

Lorenz, Rudolf. "Die Herkunft des augustinischen Frui Deo." *Zeitschrift für Kirchengeschichte*, 64 (1952–53), 34–60.

Lortz, Joseph. *Tertullian als Apologet*. 2 vols. Münsterische Beiträge zur Theologie, 9–10. Münster i. W., Aschendorffsche Verlagsbuchhandlung, 1927–28.

—. "Vernunft und Offenbarung bei Tertullian." *Der Katholik*, 4:11 (1913), 124–40.

McDonald, H. D. "The Doctrine of God in Arnobius, *Adversus Gentes*," *Studia Patristica*, 9:3. Ed. F. L. Cross. Texte und Untersuchungen zur Geschichte der altchristlichen Literatur, 94. Berlin, Akademie-Verlag, 1966, pp. 75–81.

McKeon, Richard. "The Hellenistic and Roman Foundations of the Tradition of Aristotle in the West." *Review of Metaphysics*, 32 (1979), 677–715.

McKeough, Michael J. *The Meaning of the Rationes Seminales in St. Augustine*. Catholic University of America Philosophical Studies, 15. Washington, Catholic University of America, 1926.

Madec, Goulven. "Analyse du *De magistro*." *Revue des études augustiniennes*, 21 (1975), 63–71.

—. *Saint Ambroise et la philosophie*. Paris, Études Augustiniennes, 1974.

Madoz, José. "Un caso de materialismo en España en el siglo VI." *Revista española de teología*, 8 (1948), 203–30.

Maes, Baziel. *La loi naturelle selon Ambroise de Milan*. Analecta Gregoriana, 162, Facultatis theologicae, B 52. Roma, Presses de l'Université Grégorienne, 1967.

Mancini, Guido. *La psicologia di S. Agostino e i suoi elementi neoplatonici*. Napoli, Casa Editrice Rondinella Alfredo, 1938.

Markus, R. A. *Saeculum: History and Society in the Theology of St. Augustine*. Cambridge, The University Press, 1970.

—. "St. Augustine and *theologia naturalis*." *Studia Patristica*, 6. Ed. F. L. Cross. Texte und Untersuchungen zur Geschichte der altchristlichen Literatur, 81. Berlin, Akademie-Verlag, 1962, pp. 476–79.

—. "St. Augustine on Signs." *Phronesis*, 2 (1957), 60–83.

Marrou, Henri-Irénée. "Le fondateur de Saint-Victor de Marseille: Jean Cassien." *Provence Historique*, 16 (1966), 297–308.

—. "Saint Grégoire le Grand (v. 540–604)." *La Vie Spirituelle*, 69 (1943), 442–55.

Marsili, Salvatore. *Giovanni Cassiano ed Evagrio Pontico: Dottrina sulla carità e contemplazione*. Studia Anselmiana, 5. Roma, Herder, 1936.

Maschi, Carlo Alberto. "Un problema generale del diritto in Sant'Ambrogio e nelle fonti romano-classico." *Sant'Ambrogio nel XVI centenario della nascita*. Pubblicazioni dell'Università cattolica del S. Cuore, ser. 5, scienze storiche, 18. Milano, Vita e Pensiero, 1940, pp. 423–30.

Maurach, Gregor. "Boethiusinterpretationen." *Römische Philosophie*. Ed. Gregor Maurach. Wege der Forschung, 193. Darmstadt, Wissenschaftliche Buchgesellschaft, 1976, pp. 385–410.

Mayer, Cornelius Petrus. *Die Zeichen in der geistigen Entwicklung und in der Theologie Augustins: Die antimanichäische Epoche*. Würzburg, Augustinus-Verlag, 1974.

—. *Die Zeichen in der geistigen Entwicklung und in der Theologie des jungen Augustins*. Würzburg, Augustinus-Verlag, 1969.

Maxsein, Anton. *Philosophia cordis: Das Wesen der Personalität bei Augustinus*. Salzburg, Otto Müller Verlag, 1966.

Meijering, E. P. *Tertullian contra Marcion: Gotteslehre in der Polemik Adversus Marcionem I-II*. Philosophia Patrum, 3. Leiden, E. J. Brill, 1977.

Meslin, Michel. *Les Ariens d'occident, 335-430*. Paris, Éditions du Seuil, 1967.

Meyer, Hans. *Geschichte der Lehre von dem Keimkräften von der Stoa bis zum Ausgang der Patristik nach den Quellen dargestellt*. Bonn, Peter Hansteins Verlagsbuchhandlung, 1914.

Micaeli, Claudio. "L'influsso di Tertulliano su Girolamo: Le opere sul matrimonio e le seconde nozze." *Augustinianum*, 19 (1979), 415–29.

Micka, Ermin F. *The Problem of Divine Anger in Arnobius and Lactantius*. Catholic University of America Studies in Christian Antiquity, 4. Washington, Catholic University of America, 1943.

Miethe, Terry L. "St. Augustine and Sense Knowledge." *Augustinian Studies*, 8 (1977), 11–19.

Miles, Margaret Ruth. *Augustine on the Body*. American Academy of Religion Dissertation Series, 31. Missoula, Scholars Press, 1979.

Moingt, Joseph. *Théologie trinitaire de Tertullien*. Théologie: Études publiées sous la direction de la Faculté de théologie S. J. de Lyon-Fourvière, 68–70. Paris, Aubier, 1966.

Momigliano, Arnaldo. "Cassiodorus and Italian Culture of His Time." *Proceedings of the British Academy*, 41 (1955), 207–45.

Monceaux, Paul. *Histoire littéraire de l'Afrique chrétienne depuis les origines jusqu'à l'invasion arabe*. Vols. I–II. Paris, Ernest Leroux, 1901–02.

—. "L'Isagoge latin de Marius Victorinus." *Philologie et linguistique: Mélanges offerts à Louis Havet par ses anciens élèves et ses amis*. Paris, Hachette, 1909, pp. 291–310.

Moreschini, Claudio. "Tertulliano tra stoicismo e platonismo." *Kerygma und Logos: Festschrift für Carl Andresen zum 70. Geburtstag*. Ed. Adolf Martin Ritter. Göttingen, Vandenhoeck & Ruprecht, 1979, pp. 367–79.

Morgan, James. *The Importance of Tertullian in the Development of Christian Dogma*. London, Kegan Paul, Trench, Trubner & Co., Ltd., 1928.

Muckle, J. T. "The De Officiis Ministrorum of Saint Ambrose." *Mediaeval Studies*, 1 (1939), 63–80.

Müller, Gregor Anton. *Die Trostschrift des Boethius: Beitrag zu einer literarhistorischen Quellenuntersuchungen*. Berlin, Emil Ebering, 1912.

Munz, Peter. "John Cassian." *Journal of Ecclesiastical History*, 11 (1960), 1–22.

Murphy, James J. *Rhetoric in the Middle Ages: A History of Rhetorical Theory from Saint Augustine to the Renaissance*. Berkeley, University of California Press, 1974.

Nash, Ronald H. *The Light of the Mind: St. Augustine's Theory of Knowledge*. Lexington, University Press of Kentucky, 1969.

Neiman, Alven Michael, "The Arguments of Augustine's *Contra academicos*." *Modern Schoolman*, 59 (1982), 255–79.

Neuhausen, Karl August. "Zu Cassians Traktat De amicitia (Coll. 16)." *Studien zur Literatur der Spätantike*. Ed. Christian Gnilka and Willy Schetter. Antiquitas, 1:26. Bonn, Rudolf Habelt Verlag GmbH, 1975, pp. 181–218.

Newlands, G. M. *Hilary of Poitiers: A Study in Theological Method*. European University Studies, ser. 23. Bern, Peter Lang, 1978.

Nitzsch, Friedrich. *Das System des Boethius und die ihm zugeschriebenen theologischen Schriften*. Berlin, Wiegandt und Grieben, 1860.

Nodet, Charles-Henri. "Position de Saint Jérôme en face des problèmes sexuels." *Mystique et continence: Travaux scientifiques du VII᷈ᵉ congrès international d'Avon*. Paris, Les Études Carmélitaines chez Desclée de Brouwer, 1952, pp. 308–56.

Nonnoi, Dario. "Saint'Agostino e il diritto romano." *Rivista italiana per le scienze giuridiche*, n.s. 9:3–4 (1934), 3–94.

Norris, R. A. *God and World in Early Christian Theology*. New York, Seabury Press, 1965.

Obertello, Luca. *Severino Boezio*. 2 vols. Genova, Accademia Ligure di Scienze e Lettere, 1974.

O'Connell, Robert J. *Art and the Christian Intelligence in St. Augustine* Cambridge, Mass., Harvard University Press, 1978.

—. *Augustine's Early Theory of Man, A.D. 386-391*. Cambridge, Mass., Harvard University Press, 1968.

—. "*De libero arbitrio* I: Stoicism Revisited." *Augustinian Studies*, 1 (1970), 49–68.

O'Donnell, James J. *Cassiodorus*. Berkeley, University of California Press, 1979.

O'Donovan, Oliver. *The Problem of Self-Love in St. Augustine*. New Haven, Yale University Press, 1980.

Oehler, Klaus. "Der Consensus omnium als Kriterium der Wahrheit in der antiken Philosophie und der Patristik." *Antike und Abendlande*, 10 (1961), 103–29.

Ogilvie, R. M. *The Library of Lactantius*. Oxford, Clarendon Press, 1978.

Olphe-Galliard, M. "La pureté de cœur d'après Cassian." *Revue d'ascétique et de mystique*, 17 (1936), 26–60.

Opelt, Ilona. "Ein Senecazitat bei Hieronymus," *Jahrbuch für Antike und Christentum*, 6 (1963), 175–76.

—. *Hieronymus' Streitschriften*. Bibliothek der klassischen Altertumswissenschaften, n.F. 2:44. Heidelberg, Carl Winter, 1973.

Oroz Reta, José. "Séneca en San Agustín." *Estudios sobre Séneca: Ponencias y communicaciones*. Octava semana española de filosofía. Madrid, Consejo Superior de Investigaciones Científicas, Instituto Luis Vives de Filosofía, 1966, pp. 331–57.

—. "Séneca y San Agustín." *Augustinus*, 10 (1965), 295–326.

Osborn, Eric. *Ethical Patterns in Early Christian Thought*. Cambridge, The University Press, 1976.

Oświecimski, Stephanus. *De scriptorum romanorum vestigiis apud Tertullianum obviis quaestiones selectae*. Polska Akademia Umiejetności, Archiwum Filologiczne, 24. Kraków, Nakładem Polskiej Akademii Umiejeetności, 1954.

Otten, Robert T. "*Amor, caritas* and *dilectio*: Some Observations on the Vocabulary of Love in the Exegetical Works of St. Ambrose." *Mélanges offerts à Mlle. Christine Mohrmann*. Utrecht, Spectrum, 1963, pp. 73–83.

Otto, Stephan. "Der Mensch als Bild Gottes bei Tertullian." *Münchener theologische Zeitschrift*, 10 (1959), 276–82.

—. *"Natura" und "Dispositio": Untersuchung zum Naturbegriff und zur Denkform Tertullians*. Münchener theologische Studien, 2, systematische Abteilung, 19. München, Max Hueber Verlag, 1960.

Paredi, Angelo. *Saint Ambrose: His Life and Times*. Trans. M. Joseph Costelloe. Notre Dame, University of Notre Dame Press, 1964.

Parma, Christian. *Pronoia und Providentia: Der Vorsehungsbegriff Plotins und Augustins*. Studien zur Problemgeschichte der antiken and mittelalterlichen Philosophie, 6. Leiden, E. J. Brill, 1971.

Pascal, Carlo. *Letteratura latina medievale: Nuovi saggi e note critiche*. Catania, Francesco Battiata, 1909.

Pastorino, Agostino. "La filosofia antica in Sant'Ambrogio." *Bolletino di studi latini*, 7 (1977), 88–104.

Patanè, Leonardo R. *Il pensiero pedagogico di S. Agostino*. 2ª ed. Bologna, Riccardo Patròn, 1969.

Patch, Howard Rollin. "Fate in Boethius and the Neoplatonists." *Speculum*, 4 (1929), 62–72.

—. "Necessity in Boethius and the Neoplatonists." *Speculum*, 10 (1935), 393–404.

—. *The Tradition of Boethius: A Study of His Importance in Medieval Culture*. New York, Oxford University Press, 1935.

Pease, Arthur Stanley. "The Attitude of Jerome towards Pagan Literature." *Transactions of the American Philological Association*, 50 (1919), 150–67.

—. "Caeli enarrant." *Harvard Theological Review*, 34 (1941), 163–200.

Pegis, Anton C. "The Second Conversion of St. Augustine." *Gesellschaft, Kultur, Literatur: Beiträge Liutpold Wallach gewidmet*. Ed. Karl Bosl. Stuttgart, Anton Hiersemann, 1975, pp. 73–93.

Pellegrino, Michele. *Salviano di Marsiglia*. Lateranum, nova series 6:1–2. Roma, Facultas Theologica Pontificii Athenaei Lateranensis, 1940.

Penco, Gregorio. "La vita ascetica come 'filosofia' nell'antica tradizione monastica." *Studia monastica*, 2 (1960), 79–93.

Pépin, Jean. *Saint Augustin et la dialectique*. Villanova, Villanova University Press, 1976.
—. *Théologie cosmique et théologie chrétienne (Ambroise, Exam. I.1.1–4)*. Paris, PUF, 1964.
Pérez del Valle, Luis M. "Providencia, destino y libertad en el 'De fato' de Tertulliano." *Helmantica*, 21 (1970), 79–113.
Pfligersdorffer, Georg. "Zu Boethius De Interpr. Ed. Sec. I p. 4, 4 sqq. Meiser, nebst Beobachtungen zur Geschichte der Dialektik bei den Römern." *Wiener Studien*, 66 (1953), 131–54.
Pichery, E. "Les idées morales de Jean Cassien." *Mélanges de science religieuse*, 14 (1957), 5–20.
Pichon, René. *Les derniers écrivains profanes*. Paris, Ernest Leroux, 1906.
—. *Lactance: Étude sur le mouvement philosophique et religieux sous le règne de Constantin*. Paris, Hachette et Cie, 1901.
Pietrusiński, Dionysius. "Quid Lactantius de ethnicorum philosophia, litteris, eloquentia iudicaverit et quomodo iis usus sit." *Latinitas*, 12 (1964), 274–79.
Pike, Nelson. "Divine Omniscience and Voluntary Action." *Philosophical Review*, 74 (1965), 27–46.
Pizzolato, Luigi Franco. "L'amicizia in S. Agostino e il 'Laelius' di Cicerone." *Vigiliae Christianae*, 28 (1974), 203–15.
Plantinga, Alvin. "The Boethian Compromise." *American Philosophical Quarterly*, 15 (1978), 129–38.
Plinval, Georges de. *Pélage: Ses écrits, sa vie et sa réforme*. Paris, Librairie Payot, 1943.
Pohlenz, Max. *Vom Zorne Gottes: Eine Studie über den Einfluss der griechischen Philosophie auf das alte Christentum*. Forschungen zur Religion und Literatur des Alten und Neuen Testaments, 12. Göttingen, Vandenhoeck & Ruprecht, 1909.
Poirier, Michel. "'Consors naturae' chez saint Ambroise: Copropriété de la nature ou communauté de nature?" *Ambrosius Episcopus*. Atti del Congresso internazionale di studi ambrosiani nel XVI centenario della elevazione di sant'Ambrogio alla cattedra episcopale, Milano, 2–7 dicembre 1974. Ed. Giuseppi Lazzati. Milano, Vita e Pensiero, 1976, II, 325–35.
Pons, Amilda A. *L'œuvre de raison chez Marc-Aurèle et Saint Augustin*. Torre Pellice, Imprimerie Alpine, 1908.
Préaux, Jean. "Les quatre vertus païennes et chrétiennes: Apothéose et ascension." *Hommages à Marcel Renard*. Ed. Jacqueline Bibauw. Collection Latomus, 101. Bruxelles, Revue des Études Latines, 1969, I, 639–57.
Principe, Walter H. "The Dynamism of Augustine's Terms for Describing the Highest Trinitarian Image in the Human Person." Unpublished.
Prior, A. N. "The Logic of Negative Terms in Boethius." *Franciscan Studies*, 13 (1953), 1–6.
Quain, Edwin A. "St. Jerome as a Humanist." *A Monument to Saint Jerome: Essays on Some Aspects of His Life, Works and Influence*. Ed. Francis X. Murphy. New York, Sheed & Ward, 1952, pp. 203–32.
Quasten, Johannes. *Patrology*. Vol. II. Westminster, Md., Newman Press, 1953.
Quispel, G. "Anima naturaliter christiana." *Latomus*, 10 (1951), 163–69.
Rambaux, Claude. "La composition du *De patientia* de Tertullian." *Revue de philologie*, 53 (1979), 80–91.
—. *Tertullien face aux morales des trois premiers siècles*. Collection d'études anciennes. Paris, Les Belles Lettres, 1979.
Rand, Edward Kennard. *Founders of the Middle Ages*. 2nd ed. Cambridge, Mass., Harvard University Press, 1929 [repr. New York, Dover Books, 1957].
—. "On the Composition of Boethius' Consolatio philosophiae." *Harvard Studies in Classical Philology*, 15 (1904), 1–28.
Rapisarda, Emanuele. *La crisi spirituale di Boezio*. Catania, Centro di Studi di letteratura cristiana antica, 1947.
Rauch, Gotthard. *Der Einfluss der stoischen Philosophie auf die Lehrbildung Tertullians*. Halle, Buchdruckerei des Waisenhauses, 1890.
Reeb, Jakob. *Ueber die Grundlagen des Sittlichen nach Cicero und Ambrosius: Vergleich ihrer*

Schriften de officiis. Programm der kgl. Studien-Anhalt Zweibrücken zum Schlusse des Studienjahres 1875–76. Zweibrücken, August Kranzbühler, 1876.

Reesor, Margaret E. *"Poion* and *poiotes* in Stoic Philosophy." *Phronesis,* 17 (1972), 279–85.

Refoulé, François. "Tertullien et la philosophie." *Revue des sciences religieuses,* 30 (1965), 42–45.

Rendall, Gerald H. "Minucius Felix." *Church Quarterly Review,* 128 (1939), 128–33.

Ricci, Maria Lisa. "Definizione della *prudentia* in Sant'Ambrogio (a proposito di *De Excessu fratris* 44–48)." *Studi italiani di filologia classica,* 41 (1969), 247–62.

—. "Fortuna di una formula ciceroniana presso Sant'Ambrogio (a proposito di *iustitia).*" *Studi italiani di filologia classica,* n.s. 43 (1971), 222–45.

Richards, Jeffrey. *Consul of God: The Life and Times of Gregory the Great.* London, Routledge & Kegan Paul, 1980.

Riché, Pierre. *Education and Culture in the Barbarian West: Sixth through Eighth Centuries.* Trans. John J. Contreni. Columbia, University of South Carolina Press, 1978.

Rief, Josef. *Der Ordobegriff des jungen Augustinus.* Abhandlungen zur Moraltheologie, 2. Paderborn, Ferdinand Schöningh, 1962.

Ring, Thomas Gerhard. *Auctoritas bei Tertullian, Cyprian und Ambrosius.* Cassiciacum, 29. Würzburg, Augustinus-Verlag, 1975.

Roberts, Robert E. *The Theology of Tertullian.* London, Epworth Press, 1924.

Roger, M. *L'Enseignement des lettres classiques d'Ausone à Alcuin: Introduction à l'histoire des écoles carolingiennes.* Paris, Alphonse Picard et Fils, 1905.

Rohmer, Jean. "L'Intentionnalité des sensations chez saint Augustin." *Augustinus Magister.* Congrès international augustinien, Paris, 21–24 septembre 1954. Paris, Études Augustiniennes, 1954, I, 491–98.

Rordorf, W. "Saint Augustin et la tradition philosophique antifataliste: A propos de De Civ. dei 5, 1–11." *Vigiliae Christianae,* 28 (1974), 190–202.

Ross, G. M. "Seneca's Philosophical Influence." *Seneca.* Ed. C. D. N. Costa. London, Routledge & Kegan Paul, 1974, pp. 116–42.

Rossetti, Luigi. "Il 'De Opificio Dei' di Lattanzio e le sue fonti." *Didaskaleion,* 6:3 (1928), 115–200.

Rousseau, Philip. "Cassian, Contemplation and the Coenobitic Life." *Journal of Ecclesiastical History,* 26 (1975), 113–26.

Roy, Olivier du. *L'Intelligence de la foi en la Trinité selon saint Augustin: Genèse de sa théologie trinitaire jusqu'en 391.* Paris, Études Augustiniennes, 1966.

Sabbadini, Remigio. "Gregorio Magno e la grammatica." *Bolletino di filologia classica,* 8 (1902), 204–06, 259–60.

Saffrey, H. D. "Saint Hilaire et la philosophie." *Hilaire et son temps.* Actes du colloque de Poitiers, 29 septembre–3 octobre 1968 à l'occasion du XVI⁰ centenaire de la mort de Saint Hilaire. Paris, Études Augustiniennes, 1969, pp. 247–65.

Sage, Michael M. *Cyprian.* Patristic Monograph Series, 1. Cambridge, Mass., Philadelphia Patristic Foundation, Inc., 1975.

Salvatore, Antonio. *Due omelie su Sansone di Cesario di Arles e l'Epistola 23 di Paulino da Nola.* Napoli, Loffredo, 1969.

Saumagne, Charles. *Saint Cyprien Evêque de Carthage, "Pape" d'Afrique (248–258).* Études d'antiquités africaines. Paris, Éditions du CNRS, 1975.

Scaglioni, Carlo. "'Sapientia mundi' e 'dei sapientia': L'Esegesi di I Cor. 1,18–2,5 in Tertulliano." *Aevum,* 46 (1972), 183–215.

Scheible, Helga. *Die Gedichte in der Consolatio Philosophiae des Boethius.* Heidelberg, Carl Winter, 1972.

Scheid, N. "Die Weltanschauung des Boëthius und sein 'Trostbuch'." *Stimmen aus Maria-Laach,* 39 (1890), 374–92.

Schelowsky, Georg. *Der Apologet Tertullianus in seinem Verhältnis zu der griechisch-römischen Philosophie.* Leipzig, Oswald Mutze, 1901.

Schilling, Otto. *Naturrecht und Staat nach der Lehre der alten Kirche.* Görres-Gesellschaft zur Pflege der Wissenschaft im katholischen Deutschland, Veröffentlichungen der Sektion für Rechts- und Sozialwissenschaft, 24. Paderborn, Ferdinand Schöningh, 1914.

Schindler, Alfred. *Wort und Analogie in Augustins Trinitätslehre*. Hermeneutische Untersuchungen zur Theologie, 4. Tübingen, J. C. B. Mohr, 1965.

Schmaus, Michael. *Die psychologische Trinitätslehre des hl. Augustinus*. Münsterische Beiträge zur Theologie, 11. Münster i. W., Aschendorffsche Verlagsbuchhandlung, 1927.

Schmid, W. "Boethius and the Claims of Philosophy." *Studia Patristica*, 2:2. Ed. Kurt Aland and F. L. Cross. Texte und Untersuchungen zur Geschichte der altchristlichen Literatur, 64. Berlin, Akademie-Verlag, 1957, pp. 368–75.

Schmidt, Theodor. *Ambrosius, sein Werk de officiis libri III und die Stoa*. Augsburg, J. P. Himmer, 1897.

Schmidt-Kohl, Volker. *Die neuplatonische Seelenlehre in der Consolatio Philosophiae des Boethius*. Beiträge zur klassischen Philologie, 16. Meisenheim am Glan, Verlag Anton Hain, 1965.

Schneider, Artur. "Die Erkenntnislehre bei Beginn der Scholastik." *Philosophisches Jahrbuch der Görres-Gesellschaft*, 34 (1921), 225–64.

Schubert, P. Alois. *Augustins Lex-aeterna-Lehre nach Inhalt und Quellen*. Beiträge zur Geschichte der Philosophie des Mittelalters, 24:2. Münster i. W., Aschendorffschen Verlagsbuchhandlung, 1924.

Schultzen, F. "Die Benutzung der Schrift Tertullians 'de monogamia' und 'de ieiunio' bei Hieronymus adv. Iovinianum." *Neue Jahrbücher für deutsche Theologie*, 3 (1894), 485–502.

Schulze, Martin. *Die Schrift des Claudianus Mamertus, Presbyters zu Vienne, über das Wesen der Seele (De statu animi)*. Dresden, Rammingsche Buchdruckerei, 1883.

Schurr, Viktor. *Die Trinitätslehre des Boethius in Lichte der "skythischen Kontroversen"*. Forschungen zur christlichen Literatur- und Dogmengeschichte, 18:1. Paderborn, Ferdinand Schöningh, 1935.

Schuster, Mauriz. "Minucius Felix und die christlichen Popularphilosophen." *Wiener Studien*, 52 (1934), 163–67.

Scivioletto, Nino. "I limiti dell''ars grammatica' in Gregorio Magno." *Giornale italiano di filologia*, 17 (1964), 210–38.

Seibel, Wolfgang. *Fleisch und Geist beim heiligen Ambrosius*. Münchener theologische Studien, 2, systematische Abteilung, 14. München, Kommissions-Verlag Karl Zink, 1958.

Seliga, Stanislaus. "Tertullianus et Cyprianus de feminarum moribus pravis." *Munera philologica Ludovico Ćwikliński bis sena lustra professoria claudenti ab amicis collegis discipulis oblata*. Poznan, Societatis Philologiae Polonorum, 1936, pp. 262–69.

Sepulcri, Alessandro. "Gregorio Magno e la scienza profana." *Atti della R. Accademia delle scienze di Torino*, 39 (1903–04), 962–76.

Seyr, Franz. "Die Seelen- und Erkenntnislehre Tertullians und die Stoa." *Commentationes Vindobonenses*, 3 (1937), 51–74.

Shiel, James. "Boethius' Commentaries on Aristotle." *Mediaeval and Renaissance Studies*, 4 (1958), 217–44.

Shortt, C. DeLisle. *The Influence of Philosophy on the Mind of Tertullian*. London, Elliot Stock, 1933.

Sicherl, Martin. "Platonismus und Stoizismus in den Frühschriften Augustins." *Acta Philologica Aenipontana*, 2. Ed. Robert Muth (1967), 63–65.

Siegert, Julia. *Die Theologie des Apologeten Lactantius in ihrem Verhältnis zur Stoa*. Bonn, Rhenania-Druckerei, 1921.

Silk, Edmund T. "Boethius's Consolatio philosophiae as a Sequel to Augustine's Dialogues and Soliloquia." *Harvard Theological Review*, 32 (1939), 19–39.

Simone, Raffaele. "Semiologia agostiniana." *La Cultura*, 7 (1969), 88–117.

Siniscalco, Paolo. *Ricerche sul "De resurrectione" di Tertulliano*. Verba Seniorum, n.s. 6. Roma, Editrice Studium, 1966.

Sirridge, Mary. "Augustine: Every Word Is a Name," *New Scholasticism*, 50 (1976), 183–92.

Sixt, G. "Des Prudentius Abhängigkeit von Seneca und Lucan." *Philologus* 51, n.F. 5 (1892), 501–06.

Smith, Macklin. *Prudentius' Psychomachia: A Reexamination.* Princeton, Princeton University Press, 1976.

Solignac, Aimé. "Doxographies et manuels dans la formation philosophique de saint Augustin." *Recherches augustiniennes,* 1 (1958), 113–48.

Sorabji, Richard. *Necessity, Cause, and Blame: Perspectives on Aristotle's Theory.* Ithaca, Cornell University Press, 1980.

Spanneut, Michel. "La notion de nature des Stoïciens aux Pères de l'Église." *Recherches de théologie ancienne et médiévale,* 37 (1970), 165–73.

——. *Permanence du Stoïcisme de Zénon à Malraux.* Gembloux, J. Duculot, 1973.

——. *Le Stoïcisme des pères de l'Église de Clément de Rome à Clément d'Alexandrie.* 2ᵐᵉ éd. Paris, Éditions du Seuil, 1969.

——. "Le Stoïcisme et saint Augustin." *Forma Futuri: Studi in onore del Cardinale Michele Pellegrino.* Torino, Bottega d'Erasmo, 1975, pp. 896–914.

——. *Tertullien et les premiers moralistes africains.* Gembloux, J. Duculot, 1969.

Stead, G. C. "Divine Substance in Tertullian." *Journal of Theological Studies,* n.s. 14 (1963), 46–66.

Stelzenberger, Johannes. *Die Beziehungen der frühchristlichen Sittenlehre zur Ethik der Stoa.* München, Max Hueber, 1933.

——. *Conscientia bei Augustinus: Studie zur Geschichte der Moraltheologie.* Paderborn, Ferdinand Schöningh, 1959.

Stevenson, J. "Aspects of the Relations between Lactantius and the Classics." *Studia Patristica,* 4:2. Ed. F. L. Cross. Texte und Untersuchungen zur Geschichte der altchristlichen Literatur, 79. Berlin, Akademie-Verlag, 1961, pp. 497–503.

——. "The Life and Literary Activity of Lactantius." *Studia Patristica,* 1:1. Ed. Kurt Aland and F. L. Cross. Texte und Untersuchungen zur Geschichte der altchristlichen Literatur, 63. Berlin, Akademie-Verlag, 1957, pp. 661–77.

Stewart, Hugh Fraser. *Boethius: An Essay.* Edinburgh, William Blackwood and Sons, 1891.

Stier, Johannes. *Der specielle Gottesbegriff Tertullians.* Göttingen, E. U. Huth, 1899.

——. *Die Gottes- und Logos-Lehre Tertullians.* Göttingen, Vandenhoeck & Ruprecht, 1899.

Stock, Brian. "Cosmology and Rhetoric in *The Phoenix* of Lactantius." *Classica et mediaevalia,* 26 (1965), 246–57.

Stramondo, Giuseppina. "Echi e riflessi classici nel *De mortalitate* de Cipriano." *Orpheus,* 10 (1963), 159–85.

Stump, Eleonore. "Boethius's Works on the Topics." *Vivarium,* 12 (1974), 77–93.

Süss, Wilhelm. "Über das Drama 'Querolus sive Aulularia'." *Rheinisches Museum für Philologie,* n.F. 91 (1942), 59–122.

Sulowski, Jan. "The Sources of Boethius' 'De consolatione philosophiae'." *Sophia,* 29 (1961), 67–94.

Svoboda, Karl. *L'Esthétique de saint Augustin et ses sources.* Opera facultatis philosophicae Universitatis Masarykianae Brunensis, 35. Brno, 1933.

Swift, Louis J. "*Iustitia* and *ius privatum*: Ambrose on Private Property." *American Journal of Philology,* 100 (1979), 176–87.

Taylor, John Hammond. "St. Augustine and the *Hortensius* of Cicero." *Studies in Philology,* 60 (1963), 487–98.

Tescari, Onorato. "Echi di Seneca nel pensiero cristiano e vice versa." *Unitas,* 2 (1947), 171–81.

TeSelle, Eugene. *Augustine the Theologian.* New York, Herder and Herder, 1970.

Testard, Maurice, "Étude sur la composition dans le *De officiis ministrorum* de saint Ambroise." *Ambroise de Milan: XVIᵉ centenaire de son élection épiscopale.* Ed. Yves-Marie Duval. Paris, Études Augustiniennes, 1974, pp. 155–97.

——. "Note sur le *De Civitate Dei*, XXII, 24: Exemple de réminiscences ciceroniennes de saint Augustin." *Augustinus Magister.* Congrès international augustinien, Paris, 21–24 septembre 1954. Paris, Études Augustiniennes, 1954, I, 193–200.

——. "Observations sur le thème de la *conscientia* dans le *De officiis ministrorum* de saint Ambroise." *Revue des études latines,* 51 (1973), 219–61.

——. *Saint Augustin et Cicéron: Cicéron dans la formation et dans l'œuvre de Saint Augustin.* 2 vols. Paris, Études Augustiniennes, 1958.

—. *Saint Jérôme: L'Apôtre savant et pauvre du patriciat romain.* Collection d'études anciennes, publiée sous le patronage de l'Association Guillaume Budé. Paris, Les Belles Lettres, 1969.

Thamin, Raymond. *Saint Ambroise et la morale chrétienne au IV* siècle: Étude comparée des traités "Des devoirs" de Cicéron et de saint Ambroise.* Annales de l'Université de Lyon, 8. Paris, G. Masson, 1895.

Thiaucourt, C. "Les Académiques de Cicéron et le *Contra Academicos* de saint Augustine." *Mélanges Boissier: Recueil de mémoires concernant la littérature et les antiquités romaines dédié à Gaston Boissier.* Paris, Albert Fontemoing, 1903, pp. 425–30.

Thomas, Leonhard. *Die Sapientia als Schlüsselbegriff zu den Divinae Institutiones des Laktanz mit besonderer Berücksichtigung seiner Ethik.* Freiburg in der Schwietz, Paulusdruckerei, 1959.

Thonnard, F.-J. "Les fonctions sensibles de l'âme humaine selon S. Augustin." *L'Année théologique augustinienne,* 12 (1952), 335–45.

—. "Les raisons séminales selon Saint Augustin." *Proceedings of the XIth International Congress of Philosophy.* Brussels, August 20–26, 1953. Amsterdam, North-Holland Publishing Company, 1953, XII, 146–52.

—. "Razones seminales y formas substanciales: Agustinismo y tomismo." *Sapientia,* 6 (1951), 262–72.

Tibiletti, Carlo. "Cultura classica e cristiana in S. Girolamo." *Salesianum,* 11 (1949), 97–117.

—. "Filosofia e cristianesimo in Tertulliano." *Annali della Facoltà di lettere e filosofia, Università di Macerata,* 3–4 (1970–71), 97–133.

—. "Giovanni Cassiano: Formazione e dottrina." *Augustinianum,* 17 (1977), 355–80.

—. "Un opuscolo perduto di Tertulliano: Ad amicum philosophum." *Atti dell'Accademia delle scienze di Torino,* classe di scienze morali, storiche e filologiche, 95 (1960–61), 122–66.

—. "Seneca e la fonte di un passo di Tertulliano." *Rivista di filologia e di istruzione classica,* n.s. 35 (1957), 256–60.

—. "Stoicismo nell'Ad martyras di Tertulliano." *Augustinianum,* 15 (1975), 309–23.

Timothy, H. B. *The Early Christian Apologists and Greek Philosophy Exemplified by Irenaeus, Tertullian and Clement of Alexandria.* Philosophical Texts and Studies, 21. Assen, Van Gorcum & Comp. B.V., 1973.

Tixeront, J. "Des concepts de 'nature' et de 'personne' dans les pères et les écrivains ecclésiastiques des V° et VI° siècles." *Revue d'histoire et de littérature religieuses,* 8 (1903), 582–92.

Tourscher, Francis E. "Studies in St. Jerome and St. Augustine: The Classics and Christian Culture." *American Ecclesiastical Review,* 61 (1919), 648–63.

Trillitzsch, Winfried. "Hieronymus und Seneca." *Mittellateinisches Jahrbuch,* 2 (1965), 42–54.

—. *Seneca im literarische Urteil der Antike: Darstellung und Sammlung der Zeugnisse.* 2 vols. Amsterdam, Adolf M. Hakkert, 1971.

Turcan, M. "Saint Jérôme et les femmes." *Bulletin de l'Association Guillaume Budé* (1968), pp. 259–72.

Van Fleteren, Frederick. "The Cassiciacum Dialogues and Augustine's Ascents at Milan." *Mediaevalia,* 4 (1978), 59–82.

Vanni Rovighi, Sofia. "La fenomenologia della sensazione in S. Agostino." *Rivista di filosofia neo-scolastica,* 54 (1962), 18–32.

—. "Le idee filosofiche di Sant'Ambrogio," *Sant'Ambrogio nel XVI centenario della nascita.* Pubblicazioni dell'Università cattolica del S. Cuore, ser. 5, scienze storiche, 18. Milano, Vita e Pensiero, 1940, pp. 237–58.

Vasey, Vincent R. "Proverbs 17.6b (LXX) and St. Ambrose's Man of Faith." *Augustinianum,* 14 (1974), 259–76.

Vechiotti, Icilio. *La filosofia di Tertulliano: Un colpa di sonda nella storia del cristianesimo primitivo.* Pubblicazioni dell'Università di Urbino. Urbino, Argalià, 1970.

—. *La filosofia politica di Minucio Felice: Un altro colpa di sonda nella storia del cristianesimo primitivo*. Pubblicazioni dell'Università di Urbino. Urbino, Argalià, 1973.

Verbeke, Gérard. "Augustin et le stoïcisme." *Recherches augustiniennes*, 1 (1958), 67–89.

—. *L'Évolution de la doctrine du pneuma du Stoïcisme à S. Augustin*. Bibliothèque de l'Institut Supérieur de Philosophie, Université de Louvain. Paris, Desclée de Brouwer; Louvain, Éditions de l'Institut Supérieur, 1945.

—. *The Presence of Stoicism in Medieval Thought*. Washington, Catholic University of America Press, 1983.

Vermander, Jean-Marie. "Un arien d'occident méconnu: Firmicus Maternus." *Bulletin de littérature théologique*, 81 (1980), 3–16.

Violardo, Giacomo. *Il pensiero giuridico di San Girolamo*. Pubblicazioni della Università cattolica del Sacro Cuore, ser. 2, scienze giuridiche, 55. Milano, Vita e Pensiero, 1937.

Vogel, C. J. de. "Amor quo caelum regitur." *Vivarium*, 1 (1963), 2–34.

—. "Amor quo caelum regitur: Quel amour et quel dieu?" *Atti del Congresso internazionale di studi Boeziani*. Ed. Luca Obertello. Roma, Herder, 1981, pp. 193–200.

—. "Boethiana I;" "Boethiana II." *Vivarium*, 9 (1971), 49–66; 10 (1972), 1–40.

—. "The Problem of Philosophy and Christian Faith in Boethius' Consolatio." *Romanitas et Christianitas: Studia Iano Henrico Waszink*. Ed. W. den Boer et al. Amsterdam, North-Holland Publishing Company, 1973, pp. 357–70.

Vogt, Hermann Josef. *Coetus sanctorum: Der Kirchenbegriff des Novatian und die Geschichte seiner Sonderkirche*. Theophaneia: Beiträge zur Religions- und Kirchengeschichte des Altertums, 20. Bonn, Peter Hanstein Verlag GMBH, 1968.

Walla, Marialuisa. "Der Vogel Phönix in der antiken Literatur und die Dichtung des Laktanz." Universität Wien Ph.D. diss., 1965.

Wallace-Hadrill, J. M. *The Long-Haired Kings and Other Studies in Frankish History*. New York, Barnes & Noble, Inc., 1962.

Warkotsch, Albert, trans. *Antike Philosophie im Urteil der Kirchenväter: Christlicher Glaube im Widerstreit der Philosophie*. München, Ferdinand Schöningh, 1973.

Waszink, J. H. "Observations on Tertullian's Treatise against Hermogenes." *Vigiliae Christianae*, 9 (1955), 129–47.

Weber, Leonhard. *Hauptfragen der Moraltheologie Gregors des Grossen: Ein Bild altchristlicher Lebensführung*. Paradosis: Beiträge zur Geschichte der altchristlichen Literatur und Theologie, 1. Freiburg in der Schweitz, Paulusdruckerei, 1947.

Wehrli, Fritz. "L. Caelius Firmianus Lactantius über die Geschichte des wahren Gottesglaubens." *Philomathes: Studies and Essays in the Humanities in Memory of Philip Merlan*. Ed. Robert B. Palmer and Robert Hamerton-Kelly. The Hague, Martinus Nijhoff, 1971, pp. 251–63.

Weiss, Bardo. "Die 'anima naturaliter christiana' in Verständnis Tertullians." *Mitteilungen und Forschungsbeiträge der Cusanus-Gesellschaft*, 13 (1978), 293–304.

Weyman, Carl. "Seneca und Prudentius." *Commentationes Woelfflinianae*. Leipzig, B. G. Teubner, 1891, pp. 281–87.

Wickert, Ulrich. "Glauben und Denken bei Tertullian und Origenes." *Zeitschrift für Theologie und Kirche*, 62 (1965), 153–77.

—. *Sacramentum unitatis: Ein Beitrag zum Verständnis der Kirche bei Cyprian*. Beiheft zur Zeitschrift für die neutestamentliche Wissenschaft und die Kunde der älteren Kirche, 41. Berlin, Walter de Gruyter & Co., 1971.

Wiesen, David. *St. Jerome as a Satirist: A Study in Christian Latin Thought and Letters*. Cornell Studies in Classical Philology, 34. Ithaca, Cornell Univerity Press, 1964.

Williams, Bernard. "Tertullian's Paradox." *New Essays in Philosophical Theology*. Ed. Antony Flew and Alasdair MacIntyre. London, SCM Press Ltd., 1961, pp. 187–211.

Witke, Charles. *Numen litterarum: The Old and the New in Latin Poetry from Constantine to Gregory the Great*. Mittellateinische Studien und Texte, 5. Leiden, E. J. Brill, 1971.

Wlosok, Antonie. *Laktanz und die philosophische Gnosis: Untersuchungen zu Geschichte und Terminologie der gnostischen Erlösungsvorstellung*. Abhandlungen der heidelberger Akademie der Wissenschaften, philosophisch-historische Klasse, 2. Heidelberg, Carl Winter, 1960.

Wojtczak, Georgius. *De Lactantio Ciceronis aemulo et sectatore.* Polskiej Akademii Nauk, Archiwum Filologiczne, 22. Wrocław, Zakład Narodowy im. Ossolińskich, 1969.

Wolfson, Harry Austryn. "Philosophical Implications of the Pelagian Controversy." *Proceedings of the American Philosophical Society,* 103 (1959), 544–62.

—. *The Philosophy of the Church Fathers.* Vol. I: *Faith, Trinity, Incarnation.* 3rd rev. ed. Cambridge, Mass., Harvard University Press, 1970.

Wrozł, Ludwig. "Die Psychologie des Johannes Cassianus." *Divus Thomas,* ser. 2:5 (1918), 181–213, 425–56; 7 (1920), 70–96; 9 (1922), 269–94.

Ziegenaus, Anton. *Die trinitarische Ausprägung der göttlichen Seinsfülle nach Marius Victorinus.* Münchener theologische Studien, systematische Abteilung, 41. München, Max Hueber Verlag, 1972.

Ziwsa, Carl. "Entstehung und Zweck der Schrift Cyprians 'de bono patientia'." *Festschrift Johannes Vahlen zum siebenzigsten Geburtstag gewidmet von seinen Schülern.* Berlin, Georg Reimer, 1900, pp. 543–49.

Zschimmer, Wilhelm. *Salvianus, der Presbyter von Massilia, und seine Schriften: Ein Beitrag zur Geschichte der christlich-lateinischen Literatur des fünften Jahrhunderts.* Halle, Lippertsche Buchhandlung, 1875.

INDEX OF NAMES

INDEX OF SUBJECTS

Studies in the History
of Christian Thought

EDITED BY HEIKO A. OBERMAN